Quest
FOR
Adventure

CHRIS BONINGTON

Quest
FOR
Adventure

BOOK CLUB ASSOCIATES

LONDON

Frontispiece] the world from space

*Type set in Great Britain by
Rowland Phototypesetting Ltd., Bury St. Edmunds.
Colour origination by Adroit Photo Litho Ltd., Birmingham.
Printed by Hazell, Watson & Viney, Aylesbury.
Bound by Dorstel Press, Harlow.*

Contents

The Poles

Air

Space

Beneath the Earth

Maps and Drawings

To my fellow venturers

Author's Note

The writing of this book has resembled an expedition or voyage in many ways. For me certainly it has been an adventure of the mind. But as on an expedition I am indebted to a huge number of people for their help, encouragement and advice in putting together this book.

Firstly to my fellow venturers who have talked to me, replied to my letters and in many instances gave me their hospitality, I owe an immense debt. I feel I have made many new friendships and have been able to gain both an understanding and very real respect for venturers in different fields from my own.

But the production of the book also has needed a great deal of help. If I, the writer, resemble the climber who is out in front making the summit push, I could not possibly do this without the backing of my support team. In this respect I should like to extend my thanks to my literary agent, George Greenfield, who has become over the years a close friend and adviser helping to mastermind many of my own expeditions as well as literary efforts; to Margaret Body, my patient and very understanding editor in Hodders; Betty Prentice, who not only typed my manuscript but did a lot of first line editing, including the correction of my appalling spelling; to Louise Wilson who typed all the transcripts of my taped interviews, often against a background noise of music and clinking glasses; to Audrey Salkeld who compiled my Chronology of Adventure and provided a mine of background information, particularly in the climbing field; to Anne-Marie Ehrlich, my picture researcher, who showed the ingenuity of a super detective in collecting all the pictures; to Brian and Constance Deare for taking so much trouble to perfect the maps and drawings; and to Trevor Vincent for his skill and sensitivity in designing the book.

I should also like to thank the staff of the Carlisle Public Library who have chased up so many of the reference books I have needed.

But most of all I should like to thank my wife, Wendy, who has been my first line adviser, reading my manuscript, criticising, encouraging and discussing it as the book has evolved.

C.B. 1981

Introduction

The what and the why of adventure is the reason for this book. I should like to go back to my own beginnings, since I suspect that it is only through one's own experience that one can analyse motives and feelings. For me it started with a picture book of the Scottish hills, picked up at the age of sixteen. The pictures were in monochrome, showing rolling hills, rocky crags and shimmering waters. I was captivated in a way that I had never been before, longed to be amongst them, to reach their tops, to see beyond the confines of the page.

And then came a trip to stay with my grandfather in Ireland. He lived to the south of Dublin, and from his garden I could see the Wicklow Hills. I caught a bus and set out on my first mountaineering expedition to climb one of the outlying hills but fled, frightened, when a great cloud of cumulus threatened to engulf me. I had no compass and anyway did not know how to read one.

But this was adventure. Tentatively, I was stepping into the unknown, had an awareness of danger – admittedly more imagined than real – and a love of the wild emptiness of the hills around me. The following winter a school friend and I hitch-hiked up to Wales. It was the long hard winter of 1951, and the whole country was clad in snow. Viewed from Capel Curig the Snowdon massif had for us all the scale and majesty of a Himalayan peak. Clad in school macs and wearing Army boots, we tried our Everest by the Crib Goch Ridge, but were avalanched off a long way from the top. My school friend had had enough and hitched home, but I stayed on and made a solitary attempt on Glyder Fach the next day. It was a brilliant blue, sparkling day with great galleons of cloud sweeping over the tops. Once again I fled, afraid of getting lost, but on the way down stopped to watch some climbers on the Milestone Buttress, just above the road. They were roped together, moving slowly up the sheer rock, one at a time, tiny coloured blobs against the grey of the rock and the white of the snow that covered every ledge. I knew then that that was what I wanted to do. I can't define why or how, had never read a book about rock climbing, didn't even know that the game existed.

I found a friend of the family who did a little climbing and he took me to Harrison Rocks, a small outcrop of sandstone just south of London. It wasn't ten metres high. You climbed with the protection of a rope hitched round one of the many trees at the top of the crag. At the end of the day, I knew that I had found something I was good at and loved doing. The basic satisfaction of climbing is both physical and mental – a matter of co-ordination similar to any other athletic attachment. But in climbing there is the extra ingredient of risk. It is a hot, heady spice, a piquance that adds an addictive flavour to the game. It is accentuated by the fascination of pitting one's ability against a personal unknown and winning through. Being master of one's destiny, with one's life literally in one's hands, is what gives climbing its fascination.

It also gives a heightened awareness of everything around. The pattern of lichen on rock, a few blades of grass, the dark, still shape of a lake below, the form of the hills and cloud mountains above might be the same view seen by the passenger on a mountain railway, but transported to his viewpoint amongst a crowd, he cannot see what I, the climber, can. This is not an elitist ethic, but rather the deeper sensuous involvement that the climber has with the mountains around him, a feeling heightened by the stimulus of risk.

These are the elements of adventure that I have discovered in climbing – the physical satisfaction of having complete command over one's body, a sense of risk in the process, an awareness of beauty and the exploration of the unknown. At its most satisfying this would mean one of the rapidly dwindling unknown parts of the world, but almost equally satisfying is a personal unknown, even if others have trodden that path before.

The romantic adventurer has always had strong links with science and intellectual curiosity; the very act of trying the unknown, whether it be a stretch of unclimbed rock, a sheet of polar pack ice or an attempt to be the first to sail alone around the world, holds a challenge of the mind as well as the body.

But there is one more ingredient that appears in almost every adventure, as it does in everyday life – the spirit of competition, gratification of ego, call it what you will. In theory, climbing is a non-competitive sport. In practice, however, there is a very high level of competition. At its simplest level, a group of climbers bouldering almost inevitably start to compete, trying to outdo each other, to solve a climbing problem that has beaten the others. On bigger crags or mountains, it is reflected in the sense of urgency to be the first to complete a new route, be it on Scafell, the North Wall of the Eiger or Everest itself. In any activity competition is a spur to progress. Although there are undoubtedly exceptions, I am sure that most of us respond to the stimulus of competition and, having won, enjoy the fruits of success, be it the approval of one's peers or acclaim from a much wider field.

History has offered plenty of opportunities for the adventurously inclined to sail the seas in search of merchandise or plunder, to trek overland to distant Cathay, but adventure as we know it today is a very recent phenomenon. The concept of climbing mountains or sailing small boats just for the fun of it could only come to those with sufficient wealth and time to indulge their whims. It came on the back of the Industrial Revolution, which brought a certain amount of leisure and money, at least to a privileged minority and, at the same time, the growing safety and blandness of urban life sparked the desire to escape and seek the stimulus of the unknown, the thrill of defying danger and enjoying the physical beauty of nature entirely for its own sake. During the first half of the twentieth century, adventure games remained the prerogative of a small, middle-class minority. If you were working a six day week, with only a week's holiday each year, even if you were able to afford to buy a small boat, you would not have had time to sail it. It was cheaper to go climbing, but, without a full weekend, there was not enough time to get started. In addition, two destructive world wars consumed the energies and, in many cases, the lives of two generations.

It has only been since the Second World War that the field has been laid open to almost anyone in the developed world who craves such a release. This is the reason why people in their thousands tramp the hills, sail their boats, fly their gliders. The ordinary person has been given both the time and the money to do it. It is also why comparatively few people from the Third World play the adventure game – they have not yet reached this level of affluence or leisure. The Sherpa in Nepal is happy to be a high-altitude porter, frequently enters into the spirit of an expedition, is keen to reach the summit, but he is still doing this entirely professionally. It would not occur to him to organise his own expedition to his own mountains. The more successful ones could undoubtedly afford it, for they are well off, even by Western standards, but I suspect they are too busy consolidating their new-found positions. They are members of a society in a state of fast transition and it is their children or grand-children who will, perhaps, feel the restless urge towards adventure for its own sake.

In this book I want to look at a wide spectrum of adventurous activities, to see what they have in common, not so much in motive – the why of it – but rather the 'how'. In studying what took place in an adventure, be it an attempt to row the Atlantic, cross one of the Poles, or climb a mountain, the reasons for doing it emerge on their own. But the field of adventure is so wide I have given myself a few ground rules in deciding which ventures to study.

To me, adventure involves a journey, or a sustained endeavour, in which there are the elements of risk and of the unknown, which have to be overcome by the physical skills of the individual. Furthermore, an adventure is something that an individual chooses to do and, where the risk involved is self-imposed and threatens no one but himself. It could be argued that the man who volunteers to join the Army, or becomes a mercenary or perhaps a member of the security services, is also an adventurer answering the tempting call to play the danger game. I am aware that this is what attracted me to the Army when I became a professional soldier for a few years. It is something the recruiting posters play upon, but in the end one cannot escape from the fact that the soldier's adventures and thrills are at the expense of others, and that part of the thrill of adventure can become the thrill of the hunt. This goes outside my own ground rules.

There are different levels of adventure which one can separate in the same way as the athlete distinguishes between a hundred yards sprint or a marathon. The hundred yards dashes of adventure are activities that are very intense but of short duration. Take the solo rock climber making a new route in North Wales or the English Lake District. His is undoubtedly the ultimate in adventure, for his life is literally in his hands and, if he makes a mistake and is a couple of hundred metres above the ground he will almost certainly die. He is faced with the challenge of the unknown and the extreme limits of muscular control. It needs an intense level of commitment, but the period involved is comparatively short. At the top of the crag the tension is over and the climber can return to a pint at the pub, home, family, friends. The same can be said of other extreme-risk sports – steep gully skiing, white water canoeing, hang gliding or dinghy sailing on a stormy day; in all there is an immense concentrated commitment.

The marathons of adventure are to Himalayan peaks, to the Poles and across the oceans. The biggest difference is the obvious one of scale, where the element of time is perhaps as important as size. The immediate risk and skill level might not be so concentrated, but the expedition requires both physical and mental stamina, the capacity to live with others for a long period of time or, perhaps even harder, to be alone and self-sufficient.

From my own point of view I have worked my way through the various levels of the game; first as a necky young rock climber, tackling the most difficult rock climbs in Britain, next to the middle-distance of the Alps, with climbs like the Central Pillar of Frêney and North Wall of the Eiger and then, in more recent years, to the great peaks of the Himalaya, with all the complexities of logistics, human relations and the sheer scale of everything involved.

In this book I want to look at my fellow marathon-runners, to see what we have in common, where we are different. I am not unduly concerned by the level of mechanical aid used in the adventures I have selected, since in almost every case some kind of tool or mechanical assistance is needed. My own personal ethic in planning an expedition has always been to use the minimum force that I have felt would give the enterprise concerned a chance of success. Thus, on the South-West Face of Everest, we had a team of very nearly a hundred, using oxygen, specially-designed tents that were like miniature fortresses, and the best equipment available at the time. Since five expeditions that had been similarly equipped had failed, this seemed a reasonable scale of effort at that particular time. Having achieved success, I would never want to launch a similar expedition, since the challenge is forever to reduce the size and force of each enterprise to its most fundamental simplicity. Reinhold Messner succeeded in climbing Everest from the north side on his own, without the help of oxygen. One day, no doubt, someone will do the same on the much steeper South-West Face.

The same principle permits me to include man's venture to the moon. Although this was a supreme achievement of modern technology, nothing less could have possibly succeeded. Before starting this book, I was not at all sure what – if anything – I, a climber, had in common with one of the astronauts. Writing this book has helped me to find out.

In my selection of adventures I have only been able to deal with a limited number of subjects in the detail that is essential to convey the story of what happened. So I have chosen the ventures which have been important, innovative 'firsts' – the first ascent of Everest, the first crossings of both Poles, the first crossing of the Atlantic by balloon, the first non-stop solo voyage round the world. I am uncomfortably aware that I will inevitably have left out many ventures that readers will feel are either more representative or more outstanding than those I have included; my answer can only be that the ones I have chosen are examples which, I hope, will illustrate a broad spectrum of post-war adventure.

I am fascinated by what seems at first glance to be impossible. To me, the ultimate in adventure is to convert this impossible to the feasible, and this is what all the adventures I have chosen have in common. Together they represent a complex mosaic, the component pieces of which differ enormously in so many ways, but which contribute to a fascinating overall pattern.

Kon-Tiki

The world was still recovering from war; the rubble of ruined European cities had not yet been cleared, there were food shortages and everywhere people were trying to pick up the threads of their lives where they had been left five or six years earlier. Thor Heyerdahl was one of those millions. Like so many others, his life and career had been interrupted at a crucial point; he had made the best of frustrating, uncomfortable and sometimes dangerous years through the war and now, in 1946 at the age of thirty-two, was returning to the intellectual quest that was the driving force of his life.

Heyerdahl never considered himself to be an adventurer. 'I don't think I'd call myself a real adventurer, although I suppose I've become one. I don't look for adventure for the sake of adventure. The closest I can say that I go to it is that I love nature. I love the wilderness and to be in touch with the wilderness.'

As a boy and young man this took him on long walks and ski treks in the Norwegian mountains. His clear, analytical and intensely inquisitive mind led him into science and his passion for nature channelled him to biology, which he studied at university. It was during his university course that he conceived his scheme to renounce present-day material benefits by going to live for at least a year on a Pacific island without a single product of modern technology. He even set about finding himself a mate to share this return to Paradise, and together they sailed to Tahiti in 1937 and were landed by a copra schooner on the shores of the beautiful and incredibly remote Fatu Hiva, an island in the Marquesas group. Originally, Heyerdahl had intended to deny himself all modern implements, but the South Sea Island chief who had befriended them in Tahiti persuaded him to take along a machete and a metal cooking pot. These were the only concessions they made; they took no drugs, medicines or even matches.

At first it seemed a paradise, a Garden of Eden where bananas and coconuts grew in abundance, where it was always warm and lush and beautiful; but the hand of Western man had already affected the balance of its society. Originally, the island had had a population of several thousand but they had been decimated by white man's diseases and only a handful of ragged, rather suspicious natives were left. The idyll quickly began to wear thin; the natives did their best to part them from their money and possessions; they were caught in the middle of a feud between a Catholic missionary and a native Protestant pastor whose flock had shrunk to one – his sexton. The natives became increasingly hostile, slipping poisonous centipedes and scorpions into the dried grass of their bedding; soon, they were covered in sores that would not heal; in the rainy season they were permanently soaked to the skin and began to suffer from malnutrition in this island paradise. The bananas were out of season and all the coconuts had been harvested. They ended up hiding in a remote sea cave, afraid for their lives, while they waited for the copra schooner to make its annual visit to the island and carry them away.

But there had been many idyllic moments and it was on Fatu Hiva that the seeds of an idea which was to dominate his life to the present day were sown. Sitting on the beach one moonlit evening, admiring the waves, his wife said, 'It's queer, but there are never breakers like this on the other side of the island.' They were sitting on the windward, eastern shore, and the mighty waves, driven before the prevailing trade wind, had surged all the way across 4,300 sea miles of empty ocean from South America. How Heyerdahl came to use this simple observation as one more link in his theory connecting the old Polynesian god, Tiki, with the legendary Peruvian sun god, Kon-Tiki, is now well known. A world war intervened, however, before he was given his chance to prove that the people with white skins and long beards who had built the monuments in the Andes before the arrival of the Incas and who were said to have fled from them across the Pacific on their balsa-wood rafts could have been the ancestors of the Polynesian islanders.

His research all seemed to be fitting together, but he was unable to persuade any of the academics to take it seriously. They resented the intrusion of this unknown young Norwegian whose only qualification was an honours degree in biology. The main stumbling block was the question of how the South American Indians could possibly have crossed 4,000 miles of ocean to the nearest South Pacific Island, Easter Island, with its silent guard of huge stone figures. Neither the South American Indians nor the Polynesians had discovered how to make a planked boat with a keel, but the Indians had used big sea-going rafts, driven by sails, for their coastal trade. The wood they used was balsa, very light and buoyant, but it also absorbed water and the experts declared that there was no way a balsa-wood raft could stay afloat for more than a few hundred miles without becoming waterlogged and sinking. Therefore, quite obviously, there was no way that the South American Indians could possibly have crossed the Pacific Ocean.

Faced with this impasse, there seemed only one way to prove that at least the journey could have been made. In desperation Heyerdahl decided to build a balsa-wood raft and sail it from Peru to the Pacific Islands. His purpose was to prove his theory possible, but the spirit that drove him on was the same restless, adventurous curiosity that had taken him to Fatu Hiva before the war. He knew practically nothing about the sea or boats, was even frightened of water, but once he had made up his mind he plunged into the planning with a thoroughness that eventually was to ensure his success.

He met a young engineer called Herman Watzinger at the seaman's hostel in New York where he was living while he tried to win acceptance for his theory. They began talking and Watzinger, having expressed an interest in Heyerdahl's plans, was promptly invited to join him. Apart from anything else, Heyerdahl probably needed someone close at hand to confide in and share both the work and the rebuffs that inevitably accompany any expedition in its early stages. Slowly, he managed to raise the money, much of it from personal loans which somehow he would have to repay at the conclusion of an expedition which all the pundits guaranteed would fail. He also got together all the food and equipment he reckoned they would need. Here, he was faced with a fundamental decision of whether he should try to reproduce in full the experience of the pre-Incas, carrying only the food he assumed they would probably have used in ancient times. In this instance, influenced perhaps by his experience on Fatu Hiva, he decided against it, feeling that the challenge of sailing a balsa-wood raft across the Pacific was quite enough. They planned, therefore, on using Army processed rations, cooked on a kerosene stove. Initially Heyerdahl did

*A remarkably homogeneous
and well balanced crew:
from left to right
Knut Haugland, Bengt Danielsson,
Thor Heyerdahl, Erik Hesselberg,
Torstein Raaby and
Herman Watzinger.*

baulk when Watzinger suggested they needed wireless communications, not so much to call for help which, anyway, would not be available in the empty reaches of the Pacific, but to send out reports on their progress and weather information which could be useful for meteorological research. Eventually Heyerdahl agreed to this.

He had decided on a crew of six and therefore needed to find four more for the team. On this, his first venture, he wanted people he knew well and immediately invited three old friends, Erik Hesselberg, an easy-going giant of a man who had been to navigation school and had sailed several times round the world in merchant ships before settling down as an artist. He would be the only crew member with any experience of the sea. The other two were old friends of Heyerdahl's wartime days in the Norwegian Resistance, Knut Haugland and Torstein Raaby, both of whom were skilled wireless operators. The sixth place was to be filled only when they reached Peru, by Bengt Danielsson, a Swedish ethnologist who was interested in Heyerdahl's migration theory and attracted by the romance of the adventure. The team was formed, as in the case of so many ventures, through a combination of personal friendship and chance meetings, and yet it all worked out, mainly through Heyerdahl's instinctive judgement of personality. He was attracted by people with a sense of humour who were easy-going and would fit into a small group, and yet who had the drive and determination to carry a venture through.

At last, in March 1947, Watzinger and Heyerdahl flew down to Lima to start building their raft. They were armed with a host of introductions to important people, ranging all the way up to the President of Peru. Heyerdahl understood the art of personal and public relations. These introductions and his confident but easy manner were to prove invaluable in getting the help he needed to get the project under way. But first he had to get the balsa logs for the raft. The Incas had cut them in the coastal jungle of Ecuador, floating them down the rivers to make up their sea-going rafts on the coast. It seemed simple enough, but Heyerdahl was quickly told that he had arrived at the wrong time of the year. They were now in the rainy season and it would be impossible to reach the jungle where the big tree trunks they would need could be found. They would have to wait another six months for the dry season. He certainly could not afford to do this and so resolved to get into the jungle from the landward side, the Ecuadorian highlands. Eventually, after several misadventures, he managed to reach the jungle and find someone who could guide him to some suitable trees. At last he could feel that the venture was under way.

They cut twelve large balsa logs near the banks of the Palenque river, tied them together in a rough raft and floated down to the sea where they were loaded onto a coastal steamer and carried to Callao, the sea port of Lima. By going to the President of Peru, Heyerdahl had managed to get permission to build the raft in the Naval Base. The rest of his team had now assembled in Lima and the next few weeks were spent building their reproduction of a pre-Inca raft.

Sea-going rafts had been in use well into the nineteenth century and so there were plenty of pictures from which to copy the basic design. Since the Incas had not discovered the use of iron, no nails or wire hawsers were used. They chose nine of the thickest logs for the raft, floating them side by side to see how they fitted naturally into each other, with the longest log of about thirteen metres in the middle and the remaining ones ranked symmetrically at either side to give the effect of a bluntly tapered bow. Deep grooves were then cut in the wood to give both protection to the ropes binding the logs together and also to stop them slipping. At various places where there were gaps between the logs, five solid fir planks were squeezed between them to protrude a metre and a half down into the water to act as a kind of centreboard or keel, to limit sideways drift. This had been a feature of the old Inca rafts. Herman Watzinger, the engineer, supervised the construction of the raft, helped by Bengt Danielsson, who was the only member of the crew who could speak fluent Spanish and thus transmit Watzinger's instructions to the Peruvian workers.

Heyerdahl put a great deal of thought not just into the seaworthiness of his craft, but also into the little details of day-to-day living on what was to be their tiny world for the months ahead:

Building a sea-going raft. Nine of the thickest balsa wood logs cut in the Ecuador jungle were floated side by side in Callao harbour to see how they fitted naturally against each other, with the longest, about thirteen metres, set in the middle.

We gave the little deck as much variation as possible. The bamboo strips did not deck in the whole raft, but formed a floor forward of the bamboo cabin and along the starboard side of it where the wall was open. The port side of the cabin was a kind of back-yard full of boxes and gear made fast, with a narrow edge to walk along. Forward in the bows, and in the stern as far as the after wall of the cabin, the nine gigantic logs were not decked in at all. So when we moved round the bamboo cabin we stepped from yellow bamboos and wicker-work down on to the round grey logs astern, and up again on to piles of cargo on the other side. It was not many steps, but the psychological effect of the irregularity gave us variation and compensated us for our limited freedom of movement. Right up at the masthead we placed a wooden platform, not so much in order to have a look-out post when at last we came to land, as to be able to clamber up while en route and look at the sea from another angle.

They were immensely proud of their raft as it took shape in the Naval Dockyard, surrounded by submarines and destroyers, the modern weapons of war. Their many visitors were less impressed, however. They were assured the balsa would absorb water and they would sink like a stone before they were half way. Or the ropes would wear through and the whole thing disintegrate. The dimensions were all wrong. The raft was so small it would founder in a big sea and yet was just long enough to be lifted on the crests of two waves at the same time. So it would break in half and that would be the end of them.

'Are your parents still living?' one well-wisher asked Heyerdahl. When he replied that they were, the man commented: 'Your mother and father will be very grieved when they hear of your death.'

No-one gave them any chance of success and the amazing thing is that their morale remained so high. Knut Haugland told me that this was largely the result of the confidence which they all had in Heyerdahl's planning, judgement and attitude to risk. He did not believe in taking risks – he was convinced that the raft would carry them across the Pacific. Of the team the most seriously worried was Bengt Danielsson, partly perhaps because he had known Heyerdahl for the shortest time but also because he had lost his heart to a local girl. He was tempted to withdraw and it is a tribute to his own courage and Heyerdahl's personality that he stayed on with the expedition in spite of his doubts.

At last, on the 28th April, everything was ready. A huge crowd had assembled around the harbour to watch the send-off; dignitaries from the Government and embassies had also joined the throng. The decks of *Kon-Tiki* were piled high with a chaos of bananas, fruit and sacks of fresh food, purchased at the last minute. There was a babble of excited talk, well-wishers thronging the boat, whilst all the crew, with the exception of the leader who was weighed down with a sense of responsibility, had gone off for a last drink with friends and sweethearts. The noise on the quay rose to a crescendo; the tug which was going to tow them out to sea had arrived, nosing its way up to the throng of small boats crowded around *Kon-Tiki*. A motor launch carrying the tow rope sidled up to the raft as Heyerdahl, with a nightmare vision of being towed out into the Pacific without a crew, tried to explain with his few available words of Spanish they would have to wait.

But nobody understood. The officers only smiled politely, and the knot at our bows was made fast in more than exemplary manner. I cast off the rope and flung it overboard with all manner of signs and gesticulations. The parrot utilised the opportunity afforded by all the confusion to stick its beak out of the cage and turn the knob of the door, and when I turned round it was strutting cheerfully about the bamboo deck. I tried to catch it but it shrieked rudely in Spanish and fluttered away over the banana clusters. With one eye on the sailors who were trying to cast a rope over the bows, I started a wild chase after the parrot. It fled shrieking into the bamboo cabin, where I got it into a corner and caught it by one leg as it

The radio equipment behind the cardboard partition was primarily for transmitting useful meteorological information. Calling for help in an emergency would have been a fruitless exercise on a small raft in the empty reaches of the Pacific.

The voyage of Kon-Tiki.

tried to flutter over me. When I came out again and stuffed my flapping trophy into its cage, the sailors on land had cast off the raft's moorings and we were dancing helplessly in and out with the backwash of the long swell that came rolling in over the mole. In despair I seized a paddle and vainly tried to parry a violent bump as the raft was flung against the wooden piles of the quay. Then the motor-boat started, and with one jerk the *Kon-Tiki* began her long voyage. My only companion was a Spanish-speaking parrot which sat glaring sulkily in a cage. People on shore cheered and waved, and the swarthy cinema photographers in the motor-boat almost jumped into the sea in their eagerness to catch every detail of the expedition's dramatic start from Peru. Despairing and alone I stood on the raft looking out for my lost companions, but no-one came. So we came out to the *Guardian Ries*, which was lying with steam up ready to lift anchor and start. I was up the rope-ladder in a twinkling and made so much row on board that the start was postponed and a boat sent back to the quay. It was away a good while, and then it came back full of pretty *señoritas*, but without a single one of the *Kon-Tiki*'s missing men. This was all very well, but it did not solve my problems and while the raft swarmed with charming *señoritas*, the boat went back on a fresh search for *los expedicionarios noruegos*.

An hour went by and the other five members of the crew trickled back to the wharf to be ferried out to *Kon-Tiki*. It was a delightfully haphazard, slightly chaotic departure that underlined the relaxed control Heyerdahl exerted on his team and the free, essentially happy, spirit of the entire enterprise.

Accompanied by a fleet of small boats, the tug towed them out into the bay. Soon they were bucking up and down in the Pacific swell, as the tug hauled them fifty miles out, beyond the coastal winds and currents, into the open sea. The tug cast off and the six men were left alone in the empty ocean on a vessel of a design that had last sailed off the coast of South America two hundred years before, but had only

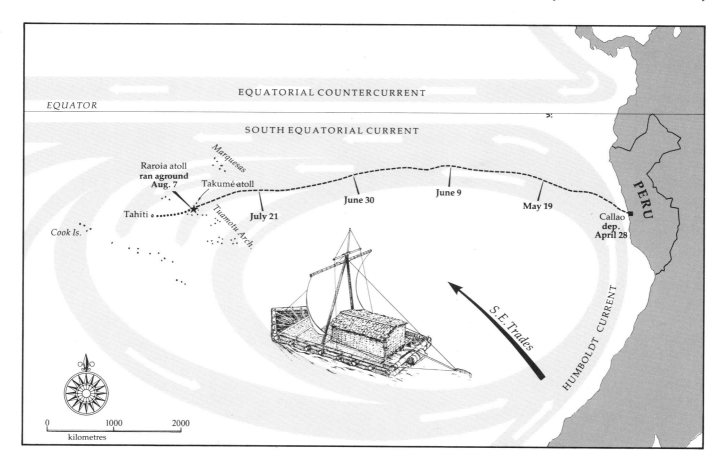

ventured out into the Humboldt Current on the morning offshore wind and had always returned to land on the evening shore winds. It was, perhaps, a thousand years since a pre-Inca fleet had carried the god-king Tiki and his tall, fair-skinned people in their desperate flight towards the setting sun across the great empty ocean. What did Tiki think he was going to find? How could he know there was going to be land at the end of the voyage, or was he content to entrust the lives of his people to the sun god whom they were following?

The crew of the modern-day *Kon-Tiki* raised the mainsail, with its stylised picture of the head of Tiki, and waited for the wind to drive them ever westward. At first hesitantly, and then with a steadily growing strength, the South-East Trades drove them remorselessly into the empty ocean of the South Pacific. That night they saw the lights of two steamers; they signalled with their kerosene lamps but the lookouts were not alert, not expecting to see anyone, let alone a pre-Inca raft heading out into the Pacific. These were to be the last two boats they saw all the way across. They were now totally committed. There was no way they could sail against the wind; all they could do was to sail before it, relying on the constant direction of the South-East Trades to take them to their 4,000-mile-distant destination.

That night the seas rose steadily, piled high by the growing wind; great rollers of dark water swept down, so much faster than the raft, curling above the stern, breaking over it and smashing down onto the deck. The two helmsmen, always on duty on the great six-metre steering oar, were learning from scratch how to control this prehistoric boat. They quickly discovered that the best way was to lash a cross-piece onto the handle of the oar so that they had a kind of lever to turn against the immense force of the seas but, as the waves increased, they found that they had

The mainsail bore the stylised head of Tiki, pre-Inca sun god of Peru, whose legendary migration west towards Polynesia inspired Thor Heyerdahl's voyage.

to lash the steering oar loosely in position to prevent it being torn from their hands. When the great combers came rolling in from behind, the helmsmen had to leap up and hang on to a bamboo pole that projected from the cabin roof, while the waves surged across the deck beneath their dangling feet, before running away between the numerous gaps and chinks between the logs. Already, quite a few of the prophesies of doom had been laid low. The raft rose and fell easily between the crests and troughs of the waves with the buoyancy of a cork. They could not be swamped because the water simply flowed away through the logs and over the side. The worst that could happen was that the cabin could be swept by a breaker, particularly if they let themselves get abeam to the waves, but provided they kept the stern into the sea, the waves rarely reached the cabin before dissipating.

After three days of battering by heavy seas the wind eased and the waves became more even. The team were able to settle into a steady rhythm of living, though there were still some serious worries. Would the balsa wood become waterlogged? After a week, Heyerdahl surreptitiously broke off a small chunk of wood and dropped it into the sea; it sank like a stone. The prophets of doom might have been right after all. Then he dug his knife into the wood and found that only the outer inch or so had absorbed water and most of the log was still dry. With luck the sap further in would act as an impregnation and check the absorption.

Each man took a two-hour turn at the great six-metre steering oar, learning prehistoric steering from scratch. Lashing a cross-piece onto the handle of the oar provided a lever to turn against the immense forces of the sea.

They were now totally committed and the worst prophesies of doom confounded. Kon-Tiki rose and fell between wave crests and troughs as buoyantly as a cork, and could not be swamped because the water simply flowed away between the logs or over the sides.

Another cause for concern was that the ropes holding the raft together might be worn through by abrasion. There was a constant movement and flexing as the raft responded to the contours of the waves, shifting, creaking, water gurgling between the logs. Lying in the little shelter at night it was easy to imagine the constant friction and stress on the cordage, and the consequences if it started to come apart. Each day they examined the ropes, but there was no sign of wear; the balsa wood was so soft that the ropes had cut deep into it, getting their own protection and, at the same time, lubrication from the salt water in the smooth channels they had worn.

Day followed day, with blue skies, the constant wind of the South-East Trades, a blazing sun that dropped over the western horizon each evening, just as it always had done, just as it had led the original Kon-Tiki and his fleet of rafts to their unknown destination.

The modern-day sailors were already beginning to tire of their processed foods, but the sea provided plenty of alternatives. Travelling only a few inches above the sea's surface, and little faster than the current, weed and barnacles on the under-surface of the raft gave small fish an attractive shelter and it soon became a moving home for fish as well as humans. The variety was incredible. It ranged from clouds of tiny, multishaped and coloured plankton to the huge whales which harvested the plankton. They were accompanied by shoals of sardine, dorado (dolphin), schools of porpoise, flying fish, which provided breakfast each morning, and a huge variety they had never seen or heard of before. Some of them were new discoveries. One night, Torstein Raaby, who was sleeping by the entrance of the shelter, was awakened when the lamp by his head was knocked over. He thought it was a flying fish, grabbed for it in the dark and felt something long and slimy that wriggled out of his hand and landed on Herman Watzinger's sleeping bag. Eventually, when they managed to light the lamp, they saw an extraordinary snake-like fish with dull black eyes, long snout and a fierce jaw, filled with long sharp teeth. Watzinger grabbed it and under his grip a large-eyed white fish was suddenly thrown up from the stomach out of the mouth of the snake-like fish; this was quickly followed by another. These were obviously deep-water fish and, later on, the team were to discover that they were the first people ever to see alive the *Gempylus,* a deep-water mackerel, though its skeleton had been seen in the Galapagos Islands and on the coast of South America.

A few days later Knut Haugland saw the biggest and ugliest shark he had ever seen. At least fifteen metres long, as it swam round the raft and then started ducking underneath it, its head was near the surface on one side and the tail lashing the water on the other. The head was broad and flat, like a frog, with two small eyes at the side and jaws over a metre wide. If angered, it could undoubtedly have smashed the raft to pieces with its massive tail. It was the very rare whale shark, the biggest of the species, and it circled the craft for over an hour, the crew watching it, apprehensive yet fascinated. At last, as it cruised under the raft and came up the other side, just beneath Erik Hesselberg, he drove a harpoon into its head with all the force he could muster. The shark erupted into fury, lashed the water with its huge tail and plunged into the depths. The strong rope attached to the harpoon parted as if it were cotton and a few moments later a broken-off harpoon shaft came to the surface.

They devised games to lure sharks onto hooks baited with dorado, or they would simply allow the shark to bite through the dorado, which it could do with a single snap of its powerful jaws; as it turned to swim away one of the crew would seize the shark by the tail and heave the tail up onto the stern logs, where it would thrash around until it either managed to heave itself off and regain its freedom, or until they managed to drop a noose over the tail and so caught it until it thrashed away its life.

And the days slipped by with the routine of daily sun shots, the recording of windspeed and weather, the daily radio call, the round of fishing and the turns at the steering. Heyerdahl, as skipper, kept a gentle, unobtrusive but positive control over his little crew, his natural air of authority leavened by a rich sense of humour. They had agreed to various rules which they all enforced: that the helmsmen should always be attached by a rope to the raft and that no-one should swim away from the raft for fear of being swept away – they could not possibly sail back against the wind to pick anyone up. Losing someone overboard was a nightmare risk of the voyage and it happened on the 21st July, when they were getting close to the Pacific Islands. A gust of wind caught one of the sleeping bags which were hanging out to air; Watzinger dived to catch it, toppled on the edge of the deck, was unable to regain his balance and flopped into the sea:

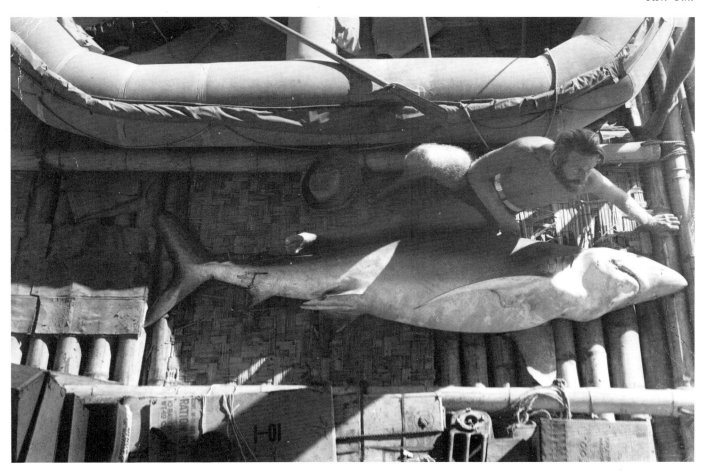

The crew devised games to lure sharks onto hooks baited with dolphin. They even had some sharks begging like dogs for dinner scraps, but they never lost their respect for the five or six rows of razor-sharp teeth.

We heard a faint cry for help amid the noise of the waves, and saw Herman's head and waving arm, as well as some vague green object twirling about in the water near him. He was struggling for life to get back to the raft through the high seas which had lifted him out from the port side. Torstein, who was at the steering oar aft, and I myself, up in the bows, were the first to perceive him, and we went cold with fear. We bellowed 'man overboard!' at the pitch of our lungs as we rushed to the nearest life-saving gear. The others had not heard Herman's cry at all because of the noise of the sea, but in a trice there was life and bustle on deck. Herman was an excellent swimmer, and though we realised at once that his life was at stake, we had a fair hope that he would manage to crawl back to the edge of the raft before it was too late.

Torstein, who was nearest, seized the bamboo drum round which was the line we used for the lifeboat, for this was within his reach. It was the only time on the whole voyage that this line got caught up. The whole thing happened in a few seconds. Herman was now level with the stern of the raft, but a few yards away, and his last hope was to crawl to the blade of the steering oar and hang on to it. As he missed the end of the logs, he reached out for the oar-blade, but it slipped away from him. And there he lay, just where experience had shown we could get nothing back. While Bengt and I launched the dinghy, Knut and Erik threw out the lifebelt. Carrying a long line, it hung ready for use on the corner of the cabin roof, but today the wind was so strong that when they threw the lifebelt it was simply blown back to the raft. After a few unsuccessful throws Herman was already far astern of the steering oar, swimming desperately to keep up with the raft, while the distance increased with each gust of wind. He realised that henceforth the gap would simply go on increasing, but he set a faint hope on the dinghy, which we had now got into the water. Without the line which acted as a brake, it would perhaps have been practicable to drive the rubber raft to meet the swimming man, but whether the rubber raft would ever get back to the *Kon-Tiki* was another matter. Nevertheless, three men in a rubber dinghy had some chance, one man in the sea had none.

Then we suddenly saw Knut take off and plunge head first into the sea. He had the lifebelt in one hand and was heaving himself along. Every time Herman's head appeared on a wave-back Knut was gone, and every time Knut came up Herman was not there. But then .we saw both heads at once; they had swum to meet each other and both were hanging on to the lifebelt. Knut waved his arm, and as the rubber raft had meanwhile been hauled on board, all four of us took hold of the line of the lifebelt and hauled for dear life, with our eyes fixed on the great dark object which was visible just behind the two men. This mysterious beast in the water was pushing a big greenish-black triangle up above the wave-crests; it almost gave Knut a shock when he was on his way over to Herman. Only Herman knew then that the triangle did not belong to a shark or any other sea monster. It was an inflated corner of Torstein's water-tight sleeping bag. But the sleeping bag did not remain floating for long after we had hauled the two men safe and sound on board. Whatever dragged the sleeping bag down into the depths had just missed a better prey.

It had been a narrow escape and everyone was badly shaken, but there was no time to reflect before another storm was upon them. They were hammered by winds and sea for another five days. At the end of it the steering oar was broken, the sail rent and the centreboards below the raft hung loose and almost useless, the ropes that held them tight having parted or lost their tension with the violent motion of the waves. The gaps between the logs were now very much wider and everyone had to be on their guard to avoid catching an ankle in between the constantly flexing logs; but the raft was still sound, the cargo dry and the crew were fit. On the 17th July they had their first visit by land-based birds, two large boobies; the flying fish, also, were of a different species, similar to those that Heyerdahl could remember catching off the coast of Fatu Hiva which was now only 300 miles to the north.

They began to worry about their landing – probably the most dangerous part of the entire voyage. Heyerdahl had vivid memories of the huge surf smashing against the jagged cliffs of Fatu Hiva. The coral atolls to the south could be even more dangerous, with their widespread reefs like hidden minefields lying just below the surface. If caught on one of these, *Kon-Tiki* and its crew could be smashed to pieces by the breaking surf while still far out from any island haven. Swept before the wind, their ability to manoeuvre was slight; it was unlikely that they would be able to creep round an island or reef into its sheltered lee.

For a couple of days they headed towards Fatu Hiva, but then a north-easterly wind blew them down towards the Tuamotu atolls. They were now accompanied by the constant scream of sea birds, as they wheeled and dived upon the raft. Land was undoubtedly close by. At last, at dawn on the 30th July, they sighted a low silhouette, little more than a faint shadow against the red-gold blaze of the rising sun, on the far horizon. They had passed it during the night; there was no chance of back-tracking against the wind; they would have to wait until they were swept onto another island. They were subdued rather than jubilant:

No extravagant outbursts were to be heard on board. After the sail had been trimmed and the oar laid over, we all formed a silent group at the mast head or stood on deck staring towards the land which had suddenly cropped up, out in the middle of the endless all dominating sea. At last we had visible proof that we had been moving in all these months; we had not just been lying tumbling about in the centre of the same eternal circular horizon. To us it seemed as if the island were mobile and had suddenly entered the circle of blue empty sea in the centre of which we had our permanent abode, as if the island were drifting slowly across our own domain, heading for the eastern horizon. We were all filled with a warm quiet satisfaction at having actually reached Polynesia, mingled with a faint momentary disappointment at having to submit helplessly to seeing the island lie there like a mirage while we continued our eternal drift across the sea westward.

Later that day they sighted another island; having seen early enough this time they were able to head for it. Soon they could pick out the dense palm trees that grew down·to the shore, could see the still waters of the lagoon inside the reef, but between them and the end of their voyage was the reef itself, a confusion of white, thundering spray that occasionally cleared to show the jagged brown teeth of coral. If thrown onto this their chances of survival would be slight. Edging in as close as they dared, they could actually see the separate trunks of the trees, the texture of the sand on the beach, so very close to them and yet still unattainable. As they coasted down, parallel to the reef, there was a mixed feeling of holiday excitement tinged with underlying fear. Erik Hesselberg, a big Peruvian sun-hat on his head, played the guitar and sang sentimental South Sea songs; Bengt Danielsson prepared an elaborate dinner, which they ate sitting on the bamboo deck under the cloudless blue sky. Somehow, all this emphasised the incongruous menace of the tumbling, crashing surf between them and safety.

It was beginning to get dark and they were very nearly at the end of the island when they spotted some figures amongst the trees; two canoes came streaking out through the surf and in a few minutes, for the first time in three months, they spoke to strangers – the descendants, perhaps, of Kon-Tiki and the original voyagers. With a mixture of sign language and the few words of Polynesian that Heyerdahl could remember, they indicated that they wanted to find a way in through the reef. The islanders replied by saying 'Brrrrrr', indicating that the white men should switch on their engine. They could not conceive that there was none and Heyerdahl had to make them feel underneath the stern to prove that this was the case.

Then they joined in trying to paddle the raft in towards land. Two more canoes came out but, as dusk fell, an offshore easterly built up, slowly pushing them away from the reef. It was now pitch dark; they gathered from the islanders that there were only the four sea-going canoes on the island, although there were plenty of men on shore who could help paddle them in, if only they could get out to the raft. Knut Haugland volunteered to take the rubber dinghy in to collect some more helpers and disappeared into the dark.

But the wind steadily increased in strength as they were blown out from the shelter of the island and they began to wonder if Haugland would ever manage to return. They paddled desperately, but were growing increasingly exhausted. At last, out of the dark came a shout. He had managed to return with some of the islanders, but now it was too late; quite obviously, they would never get to the island. The Polynesians leapt back into their canoes and paddled home into the dark toward the invisible island. It hardly seemed to matter any more, so glad were the crew to be reunited. They had become such a tight-knit little group over the months, that this seemed the most important thing of all. After all, there were more islands for them to land on.

They sailed on, drifting ever closer to the dangerous reefs of the Takume and Raroia atolls; then the wind veered to the north, bringing a hope of creeping round to the south of them. They were tense, worrying days, the memory of the breakers smashing down onto the coral reef all too vivid. Now so close to success, they could very easily lose their lives within easy sight of their goal. On the morning of the 7th August they sighted some low-lying coral islands in their path; they were being swept inexorably towards them and soon they could see the white chain of breaking surf that barred their way to safety.

The previous days had been spent in preparation for their seemingly inevitable shipwreck, as they packed all their documents and films into waterproof bags, securing them in the cabin which they lashed with a tarpaulin. Also, with great difficulty, they pulled up the centreboards, now encrusted with sea weed and barnacles, through the gaps between the logs to reduce their draft to the minimum. As they worked they drifted ever closer to the crashing breakers. Heyerdahl kept the log almost to the last moment:

> 9.45: The wind is taking us straight towards the last island but one, we can see behind the reef. We can now see the whole coral reef clearly; here it is built up like a white and red speckled wall which just sticks up out of the water in a belt in front of all the islands. All along the reef white foaming surf is flung up towards the sky. Bengt is just serving up a good hot meal, the last before the great action! It is a wreck lying in there on the reef. We are so close now that we can see right across the shining lagoon behind the reef, and see the outlines of other islands on the other side of the lagoon.
>
> 9.50: Very close now. Drifting along the reef. Only a hundred or so yards away. Torstein is talking to the man on Rarotonga. All clear. Must pack up log now. All in good spirits; it looks bad, but *we shall make it*!

Now very nearly amongst the wild upsurge of breaking waves, to give themselves a few more moments to tap out their position on the morse key of the radio, they dropped the heavy anchor, attached to their thickest length of rope. It held just long enough to swing *Kon-Tiki* round, so that the stern was facing the reef, then started dragging along the bottom as the raft was swept inexorably towards the thundering, boiling spray of the great Pacific waves smashing onto the reef.

> When we realised that the sea had got hold of us, the anchor rope was cut, and we were off. A sea rose straight up under us and we felt the *Kon-Tiki* being lifted up in the air. The great moment had come; we were riding on the wave-back at breathless speed, our ramshackle craft creaking and groaning as she quivered under us. The excitement made one's blood boil. I remember that, having no other inspiration, I waved my arm and bellowed 'hurrah!' at the pitch of my lungs; it afforded a certain relief and could do no harm anyway. The others certainly thought I had gone mad, but they all beamed and grinned enthusiastically. On we ran with the seas rushing in behind us; this was the *Kon-Tiki*'s baptism of fire; all must and would go well.
>
> But our elation was soon damped. A new sea rose high astern of us like a glittering green glass wall; as we sank down it came rolling after us, and in the same second in which I saw it high above me I felt a violent blow and was submerged under floods of water. I felt the suction through my whole body, with such great strength that I had to strain every single muscle in my frame and think of one thing only – hold on, hold on! I think that in such a desperate situation the arms will be torn off before the brain consents to let go, evident as the outcome is. Then I felt that the mountain of water was passing on and relaxing its devilish grip of me. When the whole mountain had rushed on, with an earsplitting roaring and crashing, I saw Knut again hanging on beside me, doubled up into a ball. Seen from behind the great sea was almost flat and grey; as it rushed on it swept just over the ridge of the cabin roof which projected from the water, and there hung the three others, pressed against the cabin roof as the water passed over them.

The raft was still afloat, lying in the trough of the breakers just short of the reef. Another wall of water came rolling in, towered above the raft, toppled and smashed down upon it, engulfing the raft, tearing at the men, so tiny and puny, who clung to it. Another and then another wave swept across them and each time they were edged closer to the sharp jaws of the reef, then the biggest wave of all, a sheer green wall curling above them, smashed over the raft, lifting it onto the reef itself, so that the raft was now held immobile against the savage force of the sea. They clung on to their bits of rope, lungs bursting as the sea boiled around them, and then it fell away leaving a momentary lull when they could glimpse the appalling havoc. The cabin was smashed flat, the mast broken like a matchstick but, worst of all, Heyerdahl could see only one other member of his crew:

The supreme test for Kon-Tiki *as she is hurled by the breakers onto the Raroia coral atoll. The crew clung on, lungs bursting.*

I felt cold fear run through my whole body. What was the good of my holding on? If I had lost one single man here, in the run in, the whole thing would be ruined, and for the moment there was only one human figure to be seen after the last buffet. In that second Torstein's hunched up form appeared outside the raft. He was hanging like a monkey in the ropes from the masthead, and managed to get onto the logs again, where he crawled up on the debris forward of the cabin. Herman too now turned his head and gave me a forced grin of encouragement, but did not move. I bellowed in the faint hope of locating the others, and heard Bengt's calm voice call out that all hands were aboard. They were lying holding onto the ropes behind the tangled barricade which the tough plating from the bamboo deck had built up.

The cabin was smashed flat and the mast broken like a matchstick, but the logs still held together in their bonds. Kon-Tiki *was a wreck, but an honourable wreck.*

Wave followed wave. Each time they were pulled a little further over the reef; each time the undertow tore at them, trying to draw them back into the maelstrom of breakers. But the force of the waves began to diminish and soon were just foaming around the stranded raft. They were able to let go their holds, take stock of the damage, and found that the raft was still remarkably intact, with the cabin flattened rather than destroyed, the logs still held together by their bonds.

Exhausted but jubilant, they salvaged vital items of gear and then waded through the still waters behind the reef to a low-lying palm-covered island. Their voyage was over; they had proved that a balsa wood raft could cross the Pacific Ocean.

Heyerdahl wrote: 'I was completely overwhelmed. I sank down on my knees and thrust my fingers down into the dry warm sand.'

The voyage of *Kon-Tiki* was the first great romantic venture after the Second World War and it caught the imagination of the entire world, particularly once Heyerdahl had published his book telling the story. There was an element of lighthearted schoolboy adventure of near escapes with sharks and storm, of desert islands and palm trees, combined with the fascination of Heyerdahl's determination to prove how a legend could actually have been fact. This venture provided the general public with exactly the relief from the drab violence and ugliness of war that everyone wanted.

But Heyerdahl had less success with his fellow scientists, who dismissed his voyage as an adventurous stunt with little relevance to serious scientific proof or study. Part of the reason was because Heyerdahl wrote his popular account first, so that he could pay off the huge debts incurred in making the voyage. His serious study, *American Indians in the Pacific*, was not finished until 1952. But when confronted by hostile academics, he showed the same implacable but good-humoured determination that he had shown through the frustrations of preparing for and making his voyage. Slowly, he won over the academic world to his view. Final victory did not come, however, until after he had mounted another expedition, this time one that was purely scientific, to Easter Island, 'the navel of the world', whose strange giants of stone had mystified all the scientists who gazed upon them.

Heyerdahl chartered a trawler and took a team of archaeologists to the island, to complete the first comprehensive dig that had ever been made there. Once again he used his breadth of view and intense curiosity combined with a deep humanity to gain a completely original view of what had happened on the island. The story of his discoveries on Easter Island is, intellectually, as exciting an adventure as anything on board *Kon-Tiki*. As before, he wrote a popular book that deservedly became a huge best-seller and then followed it by a serious study, *Easter Island and the East Pacific*. The academic world was at last convinced that his theory of migration must be correct, giving him their unanimous endorsement at the Tenth Pacific Science Conference in Hawaii in 1961.

But for Heyerdahl the mystery was not completely solved. There was the intriguing similarity between the pyramids and other archaeological remains of Mexico and Peru and those of ancient Egypt and Mesopotamia. There was no evidence of any such civilisations further north on the American continent, the acknowledged route of countless migratory waves of people who had crossed the Bering Straits from Asia. Was it possible that ancient man had crossed the Atlantic from the Mediterranean? In the case of the Pacific migrationary theory, Heyerdahl had been on his own, but on the Atlantic there were two schools of thought already, the Diffusionists who believed that there must have been some kind of migration direct from Europe to Mexico, and the Isolationists who considered that this was impossible and that the Aztec and Inca civilisations had evolved on their own amongst the Indians who had originated from Asia. Their strongest argument was that the American Indian had not discovered the use of the ribbed and planked wooden hull which, of course, both the Phoenicians and Vikings had. On the other hand, both reed boats and balsa rafts were in use in America and had been used on the Nile and in Mesopotamia at the dawn of civilisation.

Heyerdahl was immediately fascinated by the prospect of the practical experiment, of re-creating a reed boat and sailing it across the Atlantic. Once again, it was the spirit of science and adventure. On the first attempt they were baulked just short of success, when their boat, *Ra I*, disintegrated. He returned the following year with a boat whose design they had improved in the light of experience, and this time managed to complete the crossing, reaching the island of Barbados. Also, on *Ra II*, they took only food which would have been available in ancient times – grain, dried nuts, fruit, olive oil and wine. They ate better than any of them had ever done on previous expeditions!

But still he was not content. *Ra II*, like *Kon-Tiki*, had only been able to sail before the wind. It had therefore been at the mercy of the wind and currents and could only have made a one-way voyage. Heyerdahl wanted to discover whether these reed boats could have manoeuvred against the wind, whether they could have sailed the high seas, through the Persian Gulf, the Indian Ocean and the Red Sea, carrying merchandise and passengers between the ports of the ancient world. And so *Tigris* was born, his latest and probably final venture.

Tigris was a reed boat built on the banks of the River Tigris, using the reeds of the Marsh Arabs under the direction of a group of Bolivian Indians from Lake Titicaca, the only men who still build and sail boats made from reeds. The boat was a success; she could carry a good load, could sail the seas with and against the wind, but to Heyerdahl's eyes the real problems derived from the world around them, not from wind and sea, but from what man has done to the land and ocean. They had innumerable narrow escapes when nearly run down by giant tankers, saw hideous slicks of oil and chemicals polluting the Persian Gulf and Indian Ocean and were barred from landing anywhere on the shores of the Red Sea because of the conflicts in the area. Finally, in protest against unrestricted armament delivery from industrialised nations to a corner of the world where civilisation began, Heyerdahl and his crew decided to burn *Tigris*, in a dramatic gesture of disillusionment at what man is doing to his planet.

There are so many levels to Heyerdahl's adventures, the pure, thrilling romantic adventure, the fascinating and practical work of historical detection and, on yet another level, that of social experiment, for on both *Ra* and *Tigris*, Heyerdahl sought to affirm his belief that people of different countries and backgrounds can work and live together by selecting an international crew, many of whom he did not even know personally before hand.

For a man who does not consider himself to be an adventurer, Heyerdahl has throughout his life tackled some extraordinarily challenging and potentially dangerous schemes, but has done so, not for the sake of playing a risk game, but rather because he was prepared to accept the risks and then neutralise them as far as he could to attain his end. As an outstandingly bold and innovative man of science and of action, Heyerdahl emerges as one of the great adventurers of the post-war period.

Rowing the Atlantic

John Ridgway has the look of a retired prize-fighter who, after a lifetime spent in the ring, has come through heavily scarred. A squashed nose, a wry, slightly crooked grin, limbs that are hung awkwardly upon his body, all contribute to the impression. He knew little of the warmth of love during childhood. Adopted as a baby, his adoptive mother died when he was still a child and he felt he had little in common with his adoptive father, a successful businessman. He was sent to the Nautical College, Pangbourne, but was not gifted academically; nor was he a natural games-player. He fought his way into the first rugby XV through sheer tenacity and courage on the field. This was to be the pattern over the next few years.

With no hope of passing the entrance exam into the Royal Naval College, Dartmouth, Ridgway opted for the Merchant Navy but after one voyage as a cadet in a cargo ship decided that this was no life for him. He found life on board ship both cramped and drab, missed the physical exercise he had enjoyed at school and made no real friends. He therefore left to do his National Service, applied for a regular commission and managed to get into the Royal Military Academy, Sandhurst where, once again, his guts and determination helped him through. He did badly at all the academic subjects but threw himself into physical activities, distinguishing himself at boxing, not so much through skill as sheer dogged perseverance, getting more commendations as a good loser than actually winning bouts. As a result of this he became captain of boxing and a junior under-officer in his last term; it also helped get him one of the two available places in the much sought after Parachute Regiment.

His military career seemed to be off to a good start but he became discontented with the round of exercises and administration that make up so much of peacetime soldiering. He enjoyed stretching himself to the limit, yearned for adventure; it was this that took him into long distance canoe racing and led him to buy a sixty-foot ketch named *English Rose II*, with plans of sailing it to Cyprus.

But perhaps the most important development in his life was the start of a love affair, that was to prove long-lasting, with a corner of North-West Scotland. Ridgway first became aware of it while flying north from Inverness, on his way to an Army exercise. He returned when on leave and fell in love with this windswept land of peat hags and tiny lochans, of bare glaciated rocks and heather and grass, of peninsulas thrusting gnarled fingers into the Atlantic Ocean, guarding the sheltered sea lochs. This was to become the focus of his life. The other focal point was the girl he was to marry.

Ridgway met Marie Christine d'Albiac in 1962. With long blonde hair, fine bone structure and classic good looks, she was the daughter of an Air Marshal and had enjoyed a happy and secure childhood. They married in 1964 and Ridgway resigned his commission, hoping to find a broader and freer life in the North-West of Scotland. But reality was far from the romantic idyll; he could find no way to make a real living and was reduced to unloading fish lorries at thirty bob a night. At least, though, he found Ardmore, the place that was to become his home – a group of crofts lying in the shelter of Scotland's most northerly woodland, on the sheltered side of the Ardmore peninsula. He applied for crofting rights and over the next year, once again through sheer tenacity, obtained them on one of the houses. But he lost the struggle to make a living in the free, open spaces of the far north, being forced back to London where, unable to get a job, he went on the dole before finally admitting defeat and returning to the Parachute Regiment. He longed to return to Ardmore, however, and was looking desperately for the means of doing so.

He spent as much time as he could up at Ardmore, using his free rail passes to go there for weekends. One morning he was listening to the radio over breakfast and heard Jack de Manio interview a journalist called David Johnstone about his plans to row the Atlantic the following year. Ridgway was intrigued and spent the rest of the day wandering over the peat hags, thinking about the project and of the possibilities of his own involvement. The immediate inspiration for the row seems to have stemmed from the single-handed trans-Atlantic crossing by American journalist, Robert Manry, in the thirteen and a half-foot *Tinkerbelle*. (*Tinkerbelle* remained the smallest boat to make the crossing until 1979, when another American, Gerry Spiess, did it in the ten-foot *Yankee Girl*.) When Ridgway got in touch with him Johnstone had already selected his companion, John Hoare, a fellow-journalist who had answered an advertisement in *The Times*, so there was never any real prospect of Ridgway's inclusion in the project. Moreover when they met Ridgway and Johnstone found little in common and it is unlikely that they would have been able to work together anyway.

In the following months Ridgway merely thought about the project and was only spurred into positive action in February 1966, when he read in the *People* newspaper that Johnstone's plans were well advanced and that he aimed to set out from Boston at the beginning of June that year in *Puffin*, a rowing boat specially designed for the venture.

In his autobiography, *Journey to Ardmore*, Ridgway wrote: 'I still saw the venture as the opportunity I had waited for; it was a golden chance after the disappointment and dole of 1964. If I failed to grasp this chance, then I did not deserve another one and must resign myself to a life of dull compromise and mediocrity.'

Ridgway now sat down with a fellow officer in the Parachute Regiment to make a detailed military appreciation of the problem. They concluded that it was possible to row the Atlantic but, to compete with Johnstone – and Ridgway was undoubtedly fired by the thought of competition – there were only ninety-two days in which to find a suitable boat, a companion and all the necessary supplies and provisions. At the time Ridgway was £120 overdrawn at the bank, which showed no enthusiasm for extending his overdraft. An application for extension on the mortgage of his house was turned down and when he approached several newspapers for sponsorship they said firmly that they did not feel like backing potential disasters. But he did not give up. Initially he had wanted the same type of boat as Johnstone had bought. This was designed for the job. It also cost £2,000, which Ridgway did not have.

There were sixty-seven days to go when he received a letter from one of his friends in Ardmore, enclosing a brochure with a picture of a Yorkshire dory. Not only did it look suitable, it was only £185 and Ridgway 'phoned in the order without even seeing it. Now he had a boat, but still had not found a partner. Several friends, fellow officers in the Regiment, had declined the invitation or been forced to withdraw.

It was on the 15th April, only six weeks before Johnstone and Hoare were due to set out, that Ridgway found his partner. Chay Blyth, a sergeant in the Regiment, had heard about the venture and decided to volunteer. They had known each other ever since Ridgway had joined the Paras. Blyth, a lance-corporal in his platoon, had canoed with him in the Parachute Regiment long-distance race from Devizes to Westminster. His background was very different from that of Ridgway. He came from Hawick, a small border town in southern Scotland; his father had worked on the railway and he was the youngest of seven children. There had never been much money around, but there was a great deal of love. As a result, he was a more secure, relaxed person than Ridgway but, at the same time, had a tremendous competitive drive to break out of the inevitably narrow confines into which he had been born. Stockily but strongly-built with a slight tendency to fat whenever he lets himself get out of condition, his is very much a swimmer's build and it was at this that he distinguished himself as a boy, swimming at county level and for the Scottish schools. He left school at sixteen, taking the only job available at the local factory, but he wanted to broaden his horizons, had a streak of adventure, and therefore joined the Army and opted for the Parachute Regiment.

He was very conscious of the limits imposed by his background, that he was non-commissioned and that, however successful he was in the Army, he could never rise above a comparatively junior rank. He wanted to break out of this rut but did not quite see how. He just knew that he had to fight hard to do it. He told me: 'I think I'm basically an opportunist. If there had been an expedition going to Baghdad, I'd certainly have put my name down for it. It wasn't the challenge of the thing itself, because it didn't really matter what it was, I was keen to have a go.' Chay Blyth's experience of water was limited to the canoe race on the Thames. He had been to sea only once, on the cross-Channel ferry, and had only rowed once, on the Serpentine in Hyde Park.

Ridgway and Blyth had two things in common: a drive for adventure that was strongly motivated by a discontent with their present circumstances, and the fact that they were both married to girls who were prepared to go to the very limit to support them in their ambitions. In all other ways they could not have been more different and yet their very difference was to give them a mutually supporting compatibility. Ridgway was not practical. As an officer he had never really had to look after himself; there was always the batman to do it. Blyth remembers when Ridgway, fresh from Sandhurst, was brewing his own tea over a solid fuel tablet and solemnly took out a tea bag, carefully opened it up and poured the tea leaves into the cup. Blyth, on the other hand, was very practical, used to putting into practice the orders of his officers.

Ridgway knew the rudiments of navigation, had at least been in a boat before and was used to planning out an enterprise. Blyth was used to taking orders and bringing plans to their fruition and so this dissimilar pair fitted together like a jigsaw, Ridgway rushing around ordering gear, fixing up free flights to Canada, signing contracts, while Blyth sorted out the supplies Ridgway had ordered, made sure they were waterproofed and concentrated on the small detail.

Back in 1896, George Harbo and Frank Samuelson, two American oyster fishermen of Norwegian extraction, set out from New York to row the Atlantic, were capsized in mid-ocean, managed to right their boat and reached the Scilly Isles in an incredible fifty-five days. What was even more extraordinary was that they set out again after a few days' rest to row on to Le Havre, to reach the true shores of Europe. Their boat was put on exhibition in Paris and they lectured about their achievement. Comparatively little is now known about them, though their motives were perhaps very similar to those of their mid-twentieth-century counterparts. Their feat, however, was so long ago that they were all but forgotten in the excitement of modern sponsorship and what had become a race between Johnstone and Hoare and Ridgway and Blyth to be the first across the Atlantic. At this stage Johnstone and Hoare were the favourites; they were ahead of their competitors in planning the venture, had a specially-designed boat and were fully covered by newspaper sponsorship. They took their boat out to the United States by sea in early May and it was during the voyage that Johnstone made a vital change of plan. One of the ship's officers persuaded him that he would be better off putting the boat into the sea at Cape Hatteras, on the coast of North Carolina, since they would then be rowing straight into the waters of the Gulf Stream which they hoped would carry them across the Atlantic. This meant, however, that they would be adding 500 miles on to their journey.

May 21st was a bad day for Ridgway; they had flown out to Canada four days earlier and had travelled to Boston, but he was now struck down with blood-poisoning. This, combined with nervous exhaustion caused by weeks of worry and hard work, put him into hospital. That day one of the nurses plunged him into depression when she told him that Johnstone and Hoare had set out from Virgina Beach, between Chesapeake Bay and Cape Hatteras. He was out of hospital on the 24th, and plunged immediately into the final preparations, his spirits raised by the news that Johnstone and Hoare were having a desperate struggle to break away from coastal tide-rips.

Ridgway's boat, *English Rose III*, was of a similar design to the dories traditionally used by the Cape Cod fishermen, and a few of them were still alive. They took Ridgway and Blyth under their wing, advised them on improvements to the boat and gave them tips on rowing. In the frantic rush to get organised, Ridgway and Blyth had not had time to practise rowing or, for that matter, to give the dory any sea trials. Johnstone and Hoare were in the same state. To ensure beating the challenge imposed by Ridgway, Johnstone had pushed forward his departure date, but in doing so had abandoned his sea rowing trials and had even set out without vital items of equipment which included the external buoyancy which would have helped *Puffin*'s self-righting qualities. The decision to start at Virginia Beach, also, was beginning to seem a mistake. Although a fortnight ahead of Ridgway and Blyth, they were squandering this lead in their struggle to row against adverse winds, which more than cancelled the benefit of the Gulf Stream.

On the advice of the fishermen, Ridgway had raised the sides of his boat by twenty-three centimetres. This probably saved their lives in the storms that were to hit them later on. Even so, when they pushed off from the jetty at 5.30 on the afternoon of the 4th June, their boat seemed terribly puny against the gigantic scale of the Atlantic. Unlike *Puffin*, which had a little covered shelter built into the bow, *English Rose III* was completely open. Bow and stern were covered for a metre at each end to act as some kind of brake against the waves, but the body of the boat was just like any ordinary rowing boat. They had a U-frame over which they could fit a canvas canopy, but this would give only partial shelter at best. One hundred and twenty gallons of water in polythene containers was stowed under the floor and round the well of the boat and they had food for eighty days, most of it pre-cooked rice and dehydrated curry. They also had a radio, navigation instruments and a cine camera. Spare clothes were down to a minimum; they did not have sleeping bags, just a space blanket each, planning to sleep in their clothes and waterproofs. The boat was so full of fresh food and last-minute additions to their supplies that they could hardly stretch their legs; even rowing was awkward.

They were deafened and exhilarated by the cheers of the huge crowd that had gathered on the shore at the little Cape Cod fishing town of Orleans; a small fleet of boats accompanied them out of harbour, as they rowed steadily out to sea, towards that rounded, grey, featureless horizon that would stretch before them for over 3,000 miles. The escort flotilla began to thin out until, at last, they were on their own. As they rowed into the dusk, the boat moving with an almost imperceptible speed, the low coastline of Cape Cod dropped below the horizon and they were in the middle of a circle of empty sea that would shift and change from glassy-smooth to mountainous waves, from brilliant blue to angry foam-flecked green. Their muscles, unaccustomed to the work, soon began to ache; their buttocks were sore, but they kept on through the night until midnight, fearful of the ridicule they would receive if they were swept back to shore. Throughout the voyage, both expressed a greater horror of calling off the voyage and returning to Britain as failures than of death itself. It was this that kept them going.

To Ridgway the journey seemed to fall into three parts. First they had to row 300 miles of coastal waters. This would bring them to the Gulf Stream, which he hoped would help them all the way across the Atlantic towards Ireland. About half-way across the Atlantic they would come within range of the British Coastal Command

Rowing the Atlantic

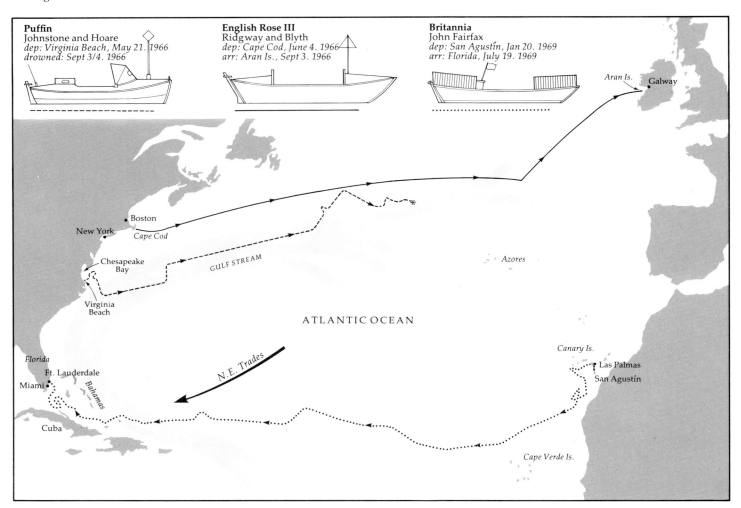

Puffin
Johnstone and Hoare
dep: Virginia Beach, May 21. 1966
drowned: Sept 3/4. 1966

English Rose III
Ridgway and Blyth
dep: Cape Cod, June 4. 1966
arr: Aran Is., Sept 3. 1966

Britannia
John Fairfax
dep: San Agustín, Jan 20. 1969
arr: Florida, July 19. 1969

Shackleton air patrols and, with a bit of luck, they would be able to make contact with their Saab radios. This was an important goal to Ridgway and he made this their third stage. For the first stage, Ridgway planned that they should row together for twelve hours through the day and then hold up on the sea anchor and sleep for eight, the remaining four hours being used for cooking and any other chores that had to be done. Once they reached the Gulf Stream, he hoped that they would have built up to an even greater degree of fitness and so could row for twelve hours non-stop, rowing together during the day but one at a time at night, two hours on and two hours off.

This was the plan, but for the first week of their voyage they were faced with daunting disappointment. It was so foggy for much of the time they could not even see the tips of their oars. They were in a sea lane and so were in constant fear of being run down but, worst of all, the wind blew from the east threatening to drive them ignominiously back to America. For Ridgway the first twenty-four hours were hell; he was sea-sick, while Blyth, who had never been to sea before, was completely unaffected. And yet, in spite of all their troubles, they kept doggedly on as day stretched into repetitive, grinding day of endless toil. After a week the weather cleared sufficiently for Ridgway to take a sun sight, to gain an accurate position. He placed them in the middle of Vermont; a second sight put them in a slightly more credible position but showed they had made painfully little progress; they were still short of the Gulf Stream and at this rate it would be full five months before they got to the other side. Apart from the problems of fatigue and running out of food, this would take them into the savage cold of the autumn and the violence of wintry storms. They were both worried, but hid their fears from each other, jollying each other on when either was slightly down.

A rhythm of living and a pattern of relationship now began to emerge. Although Ridgway consulted Blyth as equal partner on the voyage, Blyth was happy to refer to Ridgway as skipper, both on the grounds of their relative ranks as captain and sergeant and, of course, because Ridgway had some experience of the sea and Blyth none. A logical division of jobs was that Blyth, forever practical, did most of the cooking, while Ridgway looked after the navigation. But the relationship was a subtle one, in which a combination of friendly one-upmanship and a growing dependence on each other played. Ridgway was more prone to ups and downs in mood, was less certain of himself than Blyth. This came out in small things. In the early stages they had not worked out a way of taking rests; Ridgway would not admit to being tired nor ask for a rest and therefore went about it obliquely, suggesting it might be an idea to have something to eat, perhaps stow the gear more tidily or lanoline their hands, which were by now becoming sore and blistered from the continuous rowing. Blyth would stonewall each suggestion, knowing full well that this was Ridgway's way of suggesting they had a rest until, at last, he forced Ridgway to admit that it was a rest he wanted – which of course Blyth wanted just as much.

I have played similar games in the mountains, plodding up towards a high camp with a climbing partner, longing for a rest but determined not to be the first to suggest it. In the hills a camera provides a useful excuse for a rest with honour – must stop to get a picture!

In those first twelve days they ran the full gamut of experience, which was to be repeated over and over again before they finally reached the other side. On the twelfth day they heard over the radio that Hurricane Alma was on its way up the Eastern seaboard; it was most unusual to have a hurricane so early in the season, but it was on its way. They battened everything down, so that if they were capsized they

Overleaf]
English Rose III *was similar in design to the traditional dories used by Cape Cod fishermen. In America the fishermen advised John Ridgway to raise the sides of his boat, which is probably what saved their lives in the hurricane that hit them later.*

would not lose all their provisions. They had handles on the bottom of the boat, which gave a chance of righting it in the event of it going over. They had practised the drill in the Solent before leaving England, but had no illusions about what it might be like in the open sea in a storm. Already they had seen how swiftly an oar that Ridgway had let go was swept away in the waves. Their fate would probably be the same if they were thrown out of the boat.

The hurricane hit at dawn. They were awakened brutally by a torrent of water smashing down upon them, soaking them, filling the boat, cold grey thundering water, and the scream of the wind in the black-grey of the dawn. They bailed for their lives; if the boat had filled completely, so that the thwarts were under water, they would have been doomed, for the water would have poured in as fast as they were able to bail. It was a terrifying situation; the fury of the waves, coming from every direction, was so great they both found themselves praying for survival. For six hours they kept it up until, at last, the seas began to subside and they were able to take it in turns. They were soaked to the skin, shivering with cold, exhausted. Late that afternoon Blyth got the stove going and they had some curry. That night they huddled together in their soaking clothes but finally dropped off into a sleep of complete exhaustion. The following morning was clear enough to take a sight and they discovered they had been swept back yet again to only 120 miles from their start.

Later that morning a trawler came past, heading for Boston. The skipper offered them a lift. 'Give up, Mac. Use your heads; you'll never make it.'

Ridgway knew a second of temptation. Warm baths, good food, a return to Marie Christine, safety and an end to this endless effort, but he thrust it away. The thought of failure was worse than anything that could possibly happen to them on the Atlantic. They declined the offer politely and heaved on the oars. Day slipped into day; there were more storms, ships passed them, quite often not even noticing the tiny boat, in spite of their efforts to gain attention. There was drudgery but there was also contentment and a wealth of experience and observation that the sailor on a bustling merchant ship, or even the yachtsman, is divorced from. Birds took shelter both in the lee of the boat and actually on it; porpoises gambolled around it, whales cruised up to have a look and sharks provided a potentially deadly escort. They had one or two frightening escapes.

Shortly after the hurricane they had a tranquil, calm day and decided to sort out their chaotically piled stores. Ridgway finished his end before Blyth, who suggested he went in for a swim. Instinctively Ridgway rejected the idea and, instead, took up the oars and started to row. As he took the first stroke a dark shadow came into sight from below the craft. A huge shark had been sheltering from the sun immediately under their keel. On another occasion a shark started to play with the boat, rubbing up against it with his back, butting the rudder, until they deterred it by pouring a bottle of shark-repellent into the sea. Even though the water in the Gulf Stream was pleasantly warm and it was often oppressively hot in the boat, they went in for a swim only once, when Ridgway was anxious to inspect the rudder for possible damage. They were always afraid of sharks and, perhaps, regarded the sea as a constant threat.

Each day they took the water temperature, as the way to tell if they had reached the Gulf Stream. The coastal waters were around 10°C, while the Gulf Stream would be around 20°. After nearly three weeks they were at last in it and it was time to launch into phase two, to row continuously, twenty-four hours a day, resting only for five minutes each hour or when it became too rough to row, rowing together through the day, two hours on, two hours rest at night. As the voyage went on they

Ridgway and Blyth only went swimming once each in the entire crossing. They were constantly wary of sharks and played no games with their potentially deadly escorts. One curious shark nosed around the rudder and used the keel as a rubbing post.

John Ridgway a month out. The voyage was taking its physical toll. Both suffered from boils and swollen blistered hands.

became more bold, finding that they dared use their oars in increasingly stormy conditions. Even so, progress was frighteningly slow. Then Blyth discovered that about a third of their rations had been contaminated by sea-water and were inedible. This meant they had to reduce their daily intake.

The days crept by in unrelenting toil, but there were moments of real elation, especially when the wind was coming from the west and they were riding on the high waves like a roller coaster, feeling with every stroke of the oar that they were getting closer to home. On days like this they sang at their oars. But then at night, one of them huddled under the canopy plunged into the sleep of exhaustion and the other alone with his thoughts in the pitch dark, the great waves seemed black, evil and threatening as they smashed down out of the dark. This was the time when each wondered about their chances of survival and prayed they would be spared to get back to their wives.

The voyage was also taking its toll on them physically; both of them had painful boils and blistered hands, made more painful by the salt water. The sheer repetitiveness of their days, the continuous labour of rowing and their reduced diet, was undoubtedly dulling their wits. They sank into a mental torpor. 'Physically we were becoming automatons and mentally, cabbages,' observed Ridgway. He was acutely aware of the dangers presented by their state of mind. In an emergency, when fast reactions were needed, this could have been fatal.

While in this state they had the only angry words of the entire voyage. It was Ridgway's rest period and he had dropped off into a doze. Blyth saw that they were swinging off course and thought the rudder needed adjusting, so asked Ridgway to do it. He was so tired and deadened in his mind he just muttered, 'It can wait until morning.' At which Blyth, in a rage, shouted, 'Blast you. If you can't fix the rudder properly, I'll do it myself.'

In fact it just meant a couple of seconds' pause to stop rowing and readjust the rudder lines. Both thought over the outburst for a few moments and almost simultaneously apologised. What is remarkable is just how little friction there was between these two men. The stress, discomfort and constant threat of danger drew them together. There were long periods when they talked very little, others, when the seas were easy, when they talked of the future, of their homes and ambitions, of their religious convictions, which were conveniently casual on dry land but increasingly strong as they rowed their way towards the middle of the Atlantic, and a hundred other topics. They had brought no books with them, feeling that they would have no time or place for reading; they certainly never had time to get bored. They were either rowing, sleeping or, if the weather was too rough to row, they were busy bailing out the boat as the waves slopped on board.

Slowly, they were creeping across the Atlantic. They reached the half-way mark – another thousand miles to go. Although now they were convinced they could do it, lack of food was becoming an increasingly serious problem. Several ships had seen their signal, an anorak tied to an oar, and stopped to talk to them. Their wireless had proved ineffective, particularly after it had been soaked in one of their regular duckings. They had not been able to get any response from the Coastal Command 'planes and were dependent upon contacts with shipping to let the outside world and their wives know of their progress. They had refused several offers of supplies, wanting to be completely self-sufficient but now, eight weeks out, with a thousand miles to go, they realised they had to get some more rations if they were to survive, let alone finish the row. But as so often happens, the moment you want something – be it a policeman on a dark night in the city or a ship in the middle of the Atlantic – there was nothing at all and then, even worse, a ship did sail past, just a thousand metres away. It was a big cargo boat. They waved their oar with the anorak tied to it; they fired one of their three remaining flares, but the ship drove inexorably on, no-one on deck, just the blank, opaque windows of the bridge, behind which a watch officer and look-out were perhaps reading a book or having a mug of cocoa in the warm, insulated comfort of the giant ship.

During the next few days they saw several more ships, but they just ploughed on past. One foggy night they were nearly run down. Ridgway wrote:

> We heard its engines softly at first. Then they grew steadily louder. We could hear plainly the thump-thump-thump of the diesels. As the ship drew closer, we could hear the great rush of it through the water. But we could not tell which direction it was coming from – there were no lights and the sound enveloped us in the fog. I blew our pitifully small fog-horn a couple of times and then gave up. We just sat there staring wildly around us and waiting to be destroyed. Then the thing roared past us, still without showing any lights, and the thump-thump-thump receded. We slumped back in relief as the swells from the wake began to lift our boat.

In some ways these reminders of man's presence emphasised their isolation. The vapour trails of jet aircraft were even more remote as they cleaved the sky, carrying their passengers across in a few hours a journey which was already into its sixtieth day for them.

Ridgway wrote in his diary: 'Depression seems to tie my empty stomach in knots. We are both filled with remorse over the worry we are causing our wives . . .' Later on he wrote: 'the cumulative effect of spending night after night in an open boat in the middle of the Atlantic, with the Plough, the North Star, Sirius and Mars always in the same position gives you a feeling that you have made no progress at all during the day, that you are rowing your guts out and getting nowhere.'

They were now on half-rations and the following week, if they still could not stop a ship, they resolved to reduce it to quarter-rations. And yet they kept going, drawing on each other and the very strong feeling of the presence of God. Ridgway

English Rose III *had started with provisions for eighty days, but a third became contaminated by sea water. At first Ridgway and Blyth reduced rations rather than take on supplies from passing ships until, eight weeks out, they realised they must get more provisions to survive. They were on quarter rations before the British cargo ship* Haustellum *saw them and stopped. John Ridgway going aboard.*

wrote in his log: 'So impressive is the night that it is so hard not to believe there is some Almighty presence which orders these things. We both feel that we will finish alright and that, if we were to die, it would have happened already. We will walk off this boat humbler and more appreciative men, and possibly even a little wiser.'

And then at last, on the 13th August, a ship did stop. It was *Haustellum*, a British cargo ship. They were invited on board, were stood a princely meal and took on plenty of rations. Now they had enough food to complete the journey and, even more important, their morale had been raised even though their voyage was by no means over. But only ten days later once again they faced despair. To reach the coast of Ireland, they had to work their way north; the nights were getting longer, the sea colder and the winds seemed to be playing with them, coming from the south, driving them even further to the north. John Ridgway wrote:

> If only I could express the misery of it all. For seven hours, and every one of them as black as the inside of a coal bunker, we hung on to life grimly. We were wet through. Chay's rubber suit was frayed right through and water soaked onto his bottom and his back and around tears in the arms. My suit was torn across the chest and water just poured onto my stomach – I had never felt so cold in the whole of my life, despite the hard work I did through the night hours.
>
> I wondered why we went on. Why did we not just sit down and call it a day. Death would be peace, all peace from this agony. We went on though for, as Chay is always saying, we have a taste for pain. I wondered how true this was and whether we were not sick, social misfits.

The winds verged over to the east, as if to drive them back into the centre of the Atlantic. By rowing twenty-four hours a day they could do little more than maintain their position. It must have been like one of the circles of Dante's Hell. There was none of the taut excitement that a climber knows in his struggle against adverse conditions on a mountain; it was an implacable struggle of attrition which, had they given up completely, would have ended up at best with failure, at worst in death. They even discussed whether or not to pack it in – to pull the red handle of the Saab radio which would automatically send out a distress signal. In his log of the 26th August, Ridgway wrote: 'At 9.30 I gave Blyth the opportunity to call it a day if he wished. I pointed out the hazards of a landfall on the cliffs of South-West Ireland. He is enormously strong and said "Go on" without hesitation. If he wants to go on, then I shall go on – why I can't tell you, but I just will go on and on and on.'

And they did, slowly creeping eastwards, getting ever closer to Ireland. They met another ship, the *Finnalpino* from Finland, and got some more food. They had come through their own most serious crisis which was as much mental as physical, and were once again convinced they would succeed. Blyth had summed it up earlier when he wrote: 'It was that day, June 25th, that I began to realise that the success or failure of the row would depend on our mental state, not the physical.'

At last, on Saturday, 3rd September, a grim grey day with low dark clouds and a gale-force wind, Ridgway sighted land, a dark indistinct line against the grey horizon. Neither showed much emotion, but Chay confessed, 'Inside, my stomach was turning over and over and I had to make a tremendous effort to go on rowing.' But as they drew closer to the land the gale built up steadily, dashing great waves halfway up the cliffs that barred their way. They made their landfall off the coast of Galway in the Aran Islands. First they had to get into the sheltered lee of the islands without being dashed against the cliffs, but there was no time to feel fear, just the elation of nearing the end of their journey. They were singing together as they rowed through the wild seas, slipping through a gap in the islands and then rowing towards the lighthouse. But they could see the lighthouse man waving at them frantically to keep away, so turned towards the main island.

It was at this point that Ridgway reached for the latrine bucket; he had been longing to use it for several hours but there had been no time. The lighthouseman, watching them through a telescope, thought they must be using it to bail out the boat and were therefore in difficulties; he called out the Aran lifeboat. When it arrived Ridgway and Blyth debated briefly the ethics of accepting help but finally decided that it would be ungallant to reject it and allowed themselves to be towed into the little fishing village of Kilronan. They had rowed about 3,500 miles in ninety-two days, a really extraordinary feat of sheer dogged determination.

Only a few weeks later, *Puffin* was found capsized in the middle of the Atlantic with no sign of Johnstone or Hoare, but in the boat was Johnstone's very full and detailed log that took them, presumably, up to the day some catastrophe had finally capsized them. A hurricane is reported to have swept that portion of the Atlantic

Journey's end.
Chay Blyth walks up the sandy beach at Kilronan harbour in the Isles of Aran on Sunday, 4th September 1966.

around that date. Blyth and Ridgway had had their share of narrow escapes, had undoubtedly at times been lucky to be alive, but their success and the failure and death of the others cannot be ascribed to luck alone. For a start Johnstone and Hoare were much slower than the other pair, therefore spending a longer period exposed to danger and creeping into the violent autumnal weather. The reason for this was partly the design of their boat which, in the event, proved difficult to row and manoeuvre. But much more important, perhaps, was the attitude that emerged from Johnstone's log. Johnstone and Hoare worked well together as a team, but both hated the rowing. A revealing passage reads: 'There is a strange angle to this effort of rowing which we both seem to notice. When things are very discouraging it is hard to find the energy – say when it is important to row against the wind in the first week of the voyage; and when we are swinging along – a hundred miles a day – why bother to add one's puny fifteen or twenty miles.'

This was very different from the attitude of Blyth and Ridgway, who were used to years of discipline, of hauling logs pointlessly over assault courses, of long gruelling military exercises, of the Devizes to Westminster canoe race. They even enjoyed it, as expressed by Ridgway: 'I had always experienced the greatest exaltation from testing myself to the limit. Climbing hills with a fifty pound pack, canoeing for twenty hours on end, and driving myself to a state of exhaustion gives me a kind of pride that my body could stand so much and I suppose that was one of the underlying motives of rowing the Atlantic.'

This was reflected on their row by their constant self-discipline at the treadmill of the oars. While Johnstone and Hoare rather hoped to be carried across the Atlantic on what turned out to be the illusory escalator of the Gulf Stream, Ridgway and Blyth had never had any illusions and just kept rowing.

Their success also gave them the reward that they both needed – a position in the world, a sense of identity, of opportunity to break out of the rut that each felt he was in. Ridgway was able to use the money he made from the book and other promotional activities to set up an adventure school at Ardmore; at last he was able to go and live and work in the place that meant so much to him. Blyth also left the Army but it was to take him a little longer to find the life he wanted. His own greatest triumph was still to come when, in the early 'seventies, he sailed the ketch *British Steel* single-handed non-stop round the world – the wrong way, from east to west against the prevailing winds.

Ridgway and Blyth had been a wonderfully close team on *English Rose III* and had talked of further ventures together, but on getting back to England the publicity, the pressures of money and ego took their toll in a way that so often happens when the spot light goes on the world of shared adventure. Relations were not helped by their difference in Army rank, even a difference in awards. Ridgway was made a Member of the British Empire (MBE), while Blyth received the BEM (British Empire Medal) which is one subtle step lower. There was never any outward split, but they began to see less of each other and then, three years later, found themselves in direct competition.

Across two oceans

John Fairfax has been an adventurer since the age of nine, when he read a children's adventure book and announced to his mother that that was what he wanted to be. She gave the standard grown-up's reply, 'You can't make a living doing that,' and, no doubt, dismissed it as childish fantasy – but in Fairfax's case it wasn't. He was born in Italy in 1937; his mother was Bulgarian, his father an English BBC correspondent. The marriage broke up shortly after he was born and he has only once seen his father since. He was ten when his mother took him to the Argentine and settled in Buenos Aires. Fairfax told me: 'I was a little foreign boy who had just arrived. The first year I was too busy fighting off my mates. As soon as I'd settled that problem, I was then one of those that started the fights. I don't go by Queensberry Rules. I'd just go in and kick them in the balls.'

He was not particularly handsome, nor at first glance well-built, but this last impression is deceptive, for it conceals an exceptional physique. John Fairfax is extremely quick and very strong. Throughout adolescence he sought adventure, running away from home, going hunting in the Mato Grosso, chasing girls and eventually knocking about the Caribbean, fishing, scuba-diving and doing a little wheeling and dealing. It was an exotic life. He very nearly married the daughter of a Jamaican fishing boat owner, but took off a fortnight before the wedding. Fairfax was not yet ready to settle down to a comfortable career running his in-laws' fishing fleet. Eventually the Caribbean grew too hot for him and he had no choice but to get out.

In 1966 he returned to Buenos Aires, where he read of Ridgway's and Blyth's achievement. Although he had seldom rowed a boat, he did understand the sea, was an experienced skipper and a superb skin-diver. If they could row the Atlantic, so could he – and do it alone, something that had never been done before.

John Fairfax arrived in London towards the end of 1966. He was twenty-nine, knew no-one and, in spite of his name and British passport, could speak only a smattering of English. He had £300, and needed to find another £5,000 to buy a suitable rowing boat and finance his scheme. It had been difficult enough for John Ridgway; for Fairfax, it seemed almost impossible. The media, frightened by the fate of Johnstone and Hoare in *Puffin*, did not want to sponsor an unknown, inexperienced foreigner who thought he could row the Atlantic on his own.

He had always fancied himself a lucky gambler and, in desperation, tried to win the necessary funds in the casinos. His £300 soon went. He did not even have enough money to pay the rent on a tiny furnished room. His English was so poor, it seemed impossible to get a proper job. He washed dishes in a little restaurant by night and chased sponsorship by day. But as almost always seems to happen, perseverance paid off. On one of the stands at the Boat Show, he took his courage in both hands and managed to waylay Uffa Fox. The famous yacht designer's initial reaction was the inevitable: '"Row the Atlantic single-handed, eh? And what on earth makes you think you can do it, my boy?" Gripping the edge of the table so hard it hurt, I leaned forward and told him, "Mr. Fox, I don't need the earth to tell me what I can do. I *know*."'

Whatever it was about the determined young man that persuaded Uffa Fox, a few weeks later, some blueprints arrived through the post. Fairfax had the design of his boat and, even more important, the encouragement of a man respected in all nautical circles. But still he had no money with which to pay for the boat to be built.

In desperation he put an advertisement in the Personal column of *The Times*, hoping to find a rich benefactor. He received just six replies – three from cranks, one from a student offering to help build the boat, one with a cheque for a pound from a family in North London and, finally, one from a girl offering to help with his secretarial work. She happened to live close to where Fairfax had his furnished room, so he arranged to call round to see her. Sylvia Cook, in her late twenties, was a keen oarswoman who worked as a secretary at a London art gallery. She had just ended a disastrous eighteen-month marriage, was restless, discontented with life in London, yet not sure what she wanted to do. John Fairfax's venture had caught her imagination.

When he first arrived, she was not at all sure whether it was truly John Fairfax, or perhaps his agent. 'I couldn't believe that the real thing would come and see little old me.' He told her tale after incredible tale of his adventures and left after a couple of hours, saying he would be in touch. There had been no mention of secretarial work and very little of the Atlantic row. She didn't hear anything for a fortnight, and then one day he arrived at the gallery where she worked. 'As soon as I was told that there was someone to see me, I knew it was him. My heart gave a little flutter.'

She started doing his secretarial work and, at the same time, their friendship grew – almost to John's surprise. He had always been attracted to sexy, very glamorous girls. Sylvia was the same height as he, pleasant-looking without being super-glamorous. She had an easy-going, warm personality and John found himself dropping his other girl friends as he grew steadily closer to Sylvia. After a while, it seemed a good idea for him to move into her flat which she shared with three other girls; apart from anything else, it would save money which was still desperately short. Slowly, his preparations came together. He went rowing on the Serpentine in Hyde Park; Sylvia typed letters; John changed agents; the *Daily Sketch* put up some money for exclusive rights to the story and he was able to start building the boat which Uffa Fox had designed. It was both bigger and more complex than the craft that Ridgway and Blyth had rowed across the North Atlantic. It also had more safety features, with self-bailing vents, so that it would empty itself whenever broached by waves, and a self-righting buoyancy chamber that really did seem to work. The boat also had two small chambers, fore and aft, where he would be able to get some shelter from the elements. Fairfax named her *Britannia*; although he had spent so little time in Britain, he was intensely patriotic and very proud of his British blood and passport.

He was planning to cross the Atlantic Ocean from the Canary Islands to Miami. Considerably longer than the route chosen by Ridgway and Blyth, it did have the advantage of kinder, more tropical, temperatures which would suit someone who had spent most of his life in relatively warm climes.

One problem presented by the longer distance was the extra food and water he would need. Fairfax examined this very carefully. Dr. Alain Bombard, a French scientist, had made the same crossing in a rubber dinghy with a small sail in 1952.

Uffa Fox designed Britannia *for John Fairfax and attended her launching at Clare Lallow's yard, Cowes, Isle of Wight.*

Bombard had wanted to prove that castaways could live off the sea and therefore took with him neither provisions nor water, depending entirely on fish and plankton. It took him sixty-five days to sail from the Canaries to Barbados, but he was in a terrible state by the end of his voyage. For liquid he had depended on a combination of salt water and the juices from the fish he caught. With insufficient fresh water to flush his system, he suffered from a surfeit of fish protein, and was little more than a skeleton covered in appalling sores.

Fairfax could not afford to get into such a state, for he would need all his strength to keep rowing on to Miami. Although convinced that he could, at least in part, live off the sea, he was determined to have fresh water for the entire journey and sufficient emergency rations to keep him going, just in case he could not catch enough fish. It would not have been possible to carry water for over a hundred days without hopelessly overloading the boat, so he had a simple water distillation plant installed, based on a pressure cooker, which could distil half a gallon of sea water in five hours.

At last, in January 1969, he was ready to set out on his voyage. *Britannia* had been shipped down to Las Palmas and Fairfax flew there with Sylvia and an entourage of media men and sponsors. His mother flew from the Argentine to wave him off. Once in the Canaries, he put them all to work, collecting all the odd items that every expedition inevitably leaves to the last minute.

On the 20th January he pushed off from the beach at San Agustín and started his long row. It was a tranquil day with a light, south-westerly breeze, and the sun blazed down from a cloudless sky. Steadily, he pulled away from shore, heaving on the oars till he was out of sight of land, and then lay out in the sun, swilling a bottle of beer. But the honeymoon did not last long. That evening the wind built up, the waves buffeted the boat and, although the self-bailing system worked superbly and the boat felt very stable, he was unable to row her in a north-westerly direction, which he needed to take him clear of the Canary Islands. Although he rowed through the night, the following morning the cliffs of Gran Canaria were still little more than fifteen miles away.

> I felt hungry, damp, sore, thirsty, sleepy – and no Sylvia to look after my needs.
> Most silly, this, going to sea without a girl. My first resolution of the day, first day a bare twenty-odd hours after leaving the beach of San Augustin, was that next time I would make sure to correct the situation by having a soft, plump passenger.

It did not get any easier. There were no signs either of the fish that he was relying on to supplement his diet, or of the North-East Trades which he needed to help him across the Atlantic. Slowly, remorselessly, he was being blown back towards the coast of Africa. The single-handed yachtsman can, at least, relax for short periods, confident that his sails, directed by automatic steering, are driving him in the right direction. Ridgway and Blyth had kept up their momentum by rowing twenty-four hours a day, taking turns at resting. But when the solitary oarsman takes some rest, the boat becomes a piece of flotsam, blown by the wind, carried by the currents. With the wind against him, he was trying to row eighteen or nineteen hours a day, merely to reduce his drift, painfully aware of the hours of rowing it would take him to regain each precious mile. And then, on the fifth day out, he pulled a muscle in his back.

To admit impotence, real or imaginary, is a soul-destroying attitude, the beginning of the end. With what felt like hot irons burning deep into my back, I could not row, but I did. For brief periods of five or maybe ten minutes, I forced myself to grab the oars and row – sometimes biting on a piece of wood, at others screaming my head off into the wind.

San Agustín in the Canary Islands was John Fairfax's starting point for the long row to Miami, a considerably longer route across the Atlantic than that chosen by Ridgway and Blyth, but in kinder temperatures.

Slowly, the muscle mended, but Fairfax was still being swept inexorably to the east.

All this time he was living on dehydrated rations. It does not matter how they are described on the packet, after a few days they all taste exactly the same. It was sixteen days before he was able to harpoon a sea turtle. Turtle stew was a wonderful respite from processed foods. Then he spotted a ship lying hove-to on his course. Like Ridgway and Blyth, Fairfax was happy to take advantage of any ship he might meet; he went on board and was regaled with a hot bath, bacon and eggs, cold beer and strong coffee. *Skauberg* was on her way to Buenos Aires and the skipper offered Fairfax free passage for himself and his boat. He was sorely tempted. After almost a month, he had hardly made any progress in the right direction, but he turned down the offer and returned to *Britannia*.

At last, on the twenty-third day, the wind turned to the north-east. Now he was being swept in the right direction, but even this brought its problems. *Britannia*'s one fault was her inability to run in a straight course before the wind. She would not surf on the crests of the waves, but had a tendency to yaw away and turn sideways on to the waves, wallowing helpless in the troughs. This meant that he had to pull much harder on one oar than on the other, which was not only tiring but also broke the rhythm of his rowing.

The fair winds did not last long; all too soon another storm blew up from the south-west, tossing *Britannia* from one wave to the next, but the boat was like a cork, bobbing unsinkable in the wild seas. Soaked, chilled and exhausted, John Fairfax struggled with the sea and, somehow, maintained an almost improbable cockiness in his log – sounding a little like a comic-strip Odysseus in his allusions to the gods.

> Since leaving we have had eighty-five per cent south-westerly winds – this is an area where there is supposed to be nothing else but north-easterlies; so much for our luck! Have the gods abandoned me? Where are you Venus? You, the most brilliant, beautiful body in the sky, have you forgotten me? I haven't made any sacrifices to you for a month now, but what do you expect? I am in the middle of the Atlantic, on my own, in case you haven't noticed; what can I do? Just give me a hand and I promise you the most beautiful orgy I can think of at the other side. You are my star; you have never failed me yet. Why now? Come on, old girl, give me a hand and I will beat the sea. All I need is a break to get out of here, that's all.

At least there were now some fish around and he was accompanied for most of the time by a speedy shoal of dorado which he harpooned primarily for food, but also out of boredom, and as a release from frustration at his slow progress.

A few days after his escort of dorado arrived, he had his first brush with a shark. Having just made himself a cup of tea, he was standing, easily balanced against the sway of the waves, when a huge bump against the boat sent him sprawling on the deck. He looked over the side and saw a dark shape sweeping underneath the boat. It returned to the attack, seemingly bent on battering the boat to bits. Quickly, Fairfax pulled up the rudder; he could not afford to lose this. But his natural reaction to the onslaught was one of counter-aggression. The fish was much too big to be taken by his harpoon gun; he contemplated tying a knife to the end of an oar, but this, also, would probably be ineffective. He'd trap the brute. He tied some dorado meat on a piece of string and started baiting the shark, enticing it close to the boat and then jerking the tasty morsel out of reach. He kept this up for some time, teasing the shark to a near frenzy, until he was ready for the final play. As it lunged forward to seize the bait, Fairfax passed a lasso of half-inch nylon rope over its snout and around the gills, pulling it tight just short of the dorsal fin. He had taken the precaution of attaching the end of the lasso to one of the cleats in the bow. As soon as the shark sensed what had happened it went berserk, towing the boat behind it in its

Taking advantage of a calm to spruce up – for his goddess, Venus, perhaps.

desperate bid to escape. But the rope held and the shark soon lost its strength, so Fairfax was able to haul it back towards the boat. Soon he had it hauled half-way out of the water, lying along the full length of the gunwale. Out of curiosity, he slit open the stomach to find two dozen baby sharks, just ready for birth. That night he made a cryptic note in his log: '. . . killed them all and dedicated my victory to Venus. I suppose that is what she wanted; women are all the same.' During the voyage he caught other sharks in a similar manner. His vendetta was very similar to that of Thor Heyerdahl's crew on *Kon-Tiki*.

Completely at home in the sea, John Fairfax went swimming almost every day. Meeting a shark in the water, however, was an altogether more serious matter than ensnaring one from the comparative safety of the boat. On his thirty-second day he was scraping barnacles off the hull. It was a still day with hardly a wave and yet within the sea there was the sense of its vast depth, the threat of the unknown emphasised by the way the barnacles and cirripedes slowly sank, like fluttering snowflakes, down the shafts of light into the blue gloom below. Suddenly, with that instinctive feeling of lurking danger, he glanced down and behind. Hardly twenty metres away, steadily rising from the gloom, was one of the biggest sharks he had ever seen. He could see it very clearly; its symmetrical tail, streamlined body and unusually long snout showed that it was a mako, a breed with a reputation for aggression.

His first reaction was the natural one – to get out of the water just as fast as he could, but he restrained it. The shark was too close, would be upon him before he had time to get his legs into the boat. They might prove too tempting a target. He knew that sharks rarely attack a human unless provoked, but the dark shape was sweeping steadily, confidently straight at him. Bracing himself against the boat, Fairfax waited, knife held ready. Huge and menacing, the shark was upon him, as if bent on scraping him along the length of the hull. As it swept up to him, Fairfax slashed with the knife, hoping to cut its nose and thus frighten it off. But the shark swerved at the last moment; the knife caught the underbelly, plunged in, while the shark swerved to explode with a sudden burst of energy, lunging away and, in doing so, ripped itself from mouth to tail. Although struck a tremendous blow on the shoulder, Fairfax was able to heave himself back on board.

There was no sign of the shark; the sea was translucent, calm, as if the incident had never happened. Within the hour Fairfax was back overboard, finishing off scraping the hull. Was it courage? Lack of imagination? Or was it just complete affinity with the sea, its dangers and occupants?

There were more brushes with sharks, more storms, the occasional ship, but progress remained desperately slow. He had been going for two months and was still only level with the Cape Verde Islands. Because of the distance he had been swept south, he was no nearer to his objective than when he had started. He did not want just to cross the Atlantic and reach the Caribbean; he had set his heart on getting to Florida. He did not want to be a piece of flotsam at the mercy of the waves; he had to be the navigator, who chose a course and then followed it. He worked all the harder to adjust his course, but the boat was too heavy and so he took an even more committing decision. He decided to dump overboard all but a month's food and rely on the fish that followed the boat and the chance of meeting up with a ship. Also, he resolved to increase the daily stint at the oars from ten hours to twelve. This left all too little time to rest, sleep, fish, cook and carry out the daily routine of mending, maintenance and housekeeping that is necessary on even the smallest and simplest boat, with no leeway at all for sickness or injury. The almost inevitable friction sores, caused by long hours on the sliding rowing seat, became an increasing problem; every rowing session was one of excruciating torture, even though he did his best to improve the padding on the seat, and to dry out the sores with surgical alcohol. Eventually they healed, but then came a more serious injury.

It was his birthday, a wild, stormy day with waves three metres high buffeting the boat. He was standing, legs braced to the familiar bucking motion, about to drink a toast from a bottle of brandy, when he suddenly noticed a huge, freak wave tumbling down towards him. Before he could dive for the cover of the bow shelter, the wave was upon him with tons of foaming, tumbling water crashing down onto the deck. Like a piece of flotsam, Fairfax was swept away, smashed over the deck and then overboard into the maelstrom of waves. He was still clutching his bottle of brandy, his thumb protectively over the bottle neck, though it must have seemed fairly unlikely he would ever have a chance of finishing it. But his luck held, for the boat was swept on to him and he was able to grab the gunwale and pull himself back aboard, thumb still firmly over bottle. Alas, the sea water had got into the brandy but, more seriously, he had hit his leg badly against the rowing seat and cut open the sole of his right foot. He commented in his log:

> A chunk of flesh the size of a very large bean has burst out and looks like a sausage when the skin is split and the meat comes out. Wonder what is going to happen to it? Never had a wound like this before. Will it rot, dry up or be reabsorbed? Wounds don't heal well at sea, and I can hardly keep my foot dry. If it starts to rot, I will have to cut it away, I guess.

The wound healed slowly, but because he could only put weight on one foot while rowing, his progress slowed to a crawl. There were days when he was sick, lying in the covered 'rathole' shelter, sweating out a fever and hoping that the boat would not be swept back any of those hard-earned miles of ocean.

> In order to survive, I was returning to the primeval, shedding the veneer with which civilisation had coated my animal instincts. I became a naked savage, a beast of prey, that to feel alive was compelled to search for means of escaping the tediousness that threatened the urge to go on fighting. Because I was almost always desperately tired, every now and then I had to find release from my self-imposed slavery. Somehow I could still laugh at myself – that, and bloody reckless sorties against the fish that *Britannia* lured to her, were my best outlets.

And Fairfax kept going, knowing despair and fatigue, yet bouncing back each time, sometimes with an almost lunatic aggression, as he described in his log on 31st May:

> Been very ill, with high temperature, and feeling weak as a baby. Have not rowed at all and, at one time yesterday, nearly went off my head. In fact, I did. As I was vomiting over the side, a shark came by and started swimming around *Britannia* in lazy circles. A tiger shark, looking very mean, and as I stared at it, an overpowering hate slowly began to boil up inside me and suddenly, screaming like a madman, I pulled out my knife and dived at it. Luckily, the shark did not seem interested and slowly swam away, with me in hot pursuit. I don't know for how long this went on, but finally the shark sounded and disappeared – and as I came to my senses and looked around, for a while I could not see *Britannia*. Finally, I was on top of a swell and saw her about five hundred yards from me, drifting away. It was my great fortune that at the time there was barely a whisper of wind; otherwise I would never have been able to catch up with her. Venus really must have been looking after me.
> When I made it back and climbed over the side, little lights seemed to twinkle all around me. I was still swimming and there was fog and I could not see anything and *Britannia* was drifting away and then the white belly of the shark appeared and stood between me and *Britannia* and I plunged and slashed at it, cursing and yelling as I felt the blade go through, tearing, ripping again and again. Then I regained my senses and saw I had been slashing at the white canvas of my rain catcher, and I just stared at it – then crawled into my rathole

and lay down pounding the deck with my fists, until finally I cried myself to sleep. I can't remember ever before in my life breaking down like that, and I hope it does not happen again. It is most unpleasant.

Today I still feel bad, but not quite so much as yesterday. There is no wind whatsoever; the sea is like a mirror, and it is very hot.

Did not row at all.

On the 29th June, his hundred and sixtieth day at sea, Fairfax sighted land at last. It was a tiny island, little more than a grassy mound jutting out of the sea between the Bahamas to the north and Cuba to the south. Landing on the deserted island, he revelled in being able to run over the hot sands, went spear-fishing offshore to catch a lobster, and then pushed off to complete his voyage. He had rowed the Atlantic, done it by himself, and rowed further than anyone had ever done before. Already he had gone considerably further than John Ridgway and Chay Blyth. He could so easily have rowed a few miles to the north, to land on one of the Bahamas, but that was not enough. He was determined to reach the point he had chosen, even if it meant another month of exhausting drudgery and a heightened level of danger. For he was now in the hurricane belt and knew from his Caribbean days that, if he were caught in the path of one, his chances of survival were thin. But he had had so many other narrow escapes that this hypothetical risk was of small account. It was the monotonous, lonesome drudgery of rowing that was pushing him to the limit. Even close to the coast of Florida, he was still being swept back southwards towards Cuba. But he rowed on, until at last, on the 19th July after 180 days at sea, he completed the last half mile, surrounded by a fleet of motor cruisers and yachts, onto a beach about half-way between Miami and Fort Lauderdale.

That same day Neil Armstrong, Buzz Aldrin and Michael Collins were orbiting the moon in preparation for their historic landing. They had taken off only a few days earlier, perched in their space craft on top of the gigantic Saturn V rocket. You could not have two greater extremes in styles of adventure – or indeed of propulsion – than the contrast between the simplicity and self-reliance of the solitary rower and the technological complexity and massive back-up of flight in space.

On reaching land, like Chay Blyth, Fairfax swore that never again would he set foot in a rowing boat, but the bad memories slide away surprisingly quickly, and he had always been intrigued by the thought of the greatest row of all – the Pacific Ocean. The distance between the coasts of America and Australia is twice that of the Atlantic, but at least there would be some exotic islands on the way and this time John Fairfax had no intention of making this voyage alone. He was determined to have company, and who better than his loyal girl friend, Sylvia Cook?

Once again Uffa Fox designed a boat, this time a thirty-three footer, the length of an ocean-going yacht, and Clare Lallow, who built *Britannia*, built *Britannia II* as well. Fairfax thought up various schemes to finance his trip, the most bizarre being a £10,000-challenge to the *Miami Herald*, one of whose writers had questioned his claim to have slit open the belly of a shark on his Atlantic row on the grounds that a shark's belly would be much too tough. John offered to fight any shark other than the great white, which is particularly large and vicious, in exactly the same circumstances. The paper did not take up the challenge, so Fairfax decided to have the fight filmed and sell the resulting documentary. He found a large hammerhead, took it on and managed to kill it, but unfortunately the film, while proving that he had been successful, was not of sufficiently good quality to make a documentary. At least Fairfax had the satisfaction of towing the carcase back to Miami and dumping it on the steps of the *Miami Herald*. But still he had no money.

After some initial indecision, Sylvia Cook agreed to join John Fairfax on his bid to row 8000 miles across the Pacific.

Sylvia could barely manage the length of a swimming pool, but she adapted to life on board with amazing resilience.

Eventually, he managed to gain the support of the Sunday *People* and raised enough to get the boat built, though barely enough for their stores for the crossing.

Sylvia, meanwhile, was having doubts, caught between powerful urges:

> Of course I had reasons, other than simply that Johnny had asked me, for wanting to undergo the trip. I felt that my life had been far too easy so far; I had never endured any serious hardship or discomforts, nor even faced a real crisis. I wanted to find out my own reactions, would I be thrown into a panic at the critical moment of an emergency, or had I been deceiving myself through my life in assuming I would stay calm and capable no matter what?

But an equally strong urge was her desire to have children. All along John had told her never to think of either marriage or children. They were living together but it was a very open relationship, something that Sylvia totally accepted, though as she told John:

> I'm thirty now, and I want my own children. This thing is going to make me thirty-four before I can even start looking for the prospective father, then a couple of years to get to know him and get married, then another couple before the baby arrives. That makes me thirty-eight before I've even started a family.

John took her resignation from the venture with his customary calm and told her that he would advertise for a girl replacement. He guessed, perhaps, that Sylvia could never bring herself to allow someone else to make the trip and, sure enough, in a couple of days she announced that she had changed her mind.

A few months later, in April 1971, they were battling with the unpredictable currents of San Francisco Bay; they had already made three attempts to clear the Golden Gate Bridge but had been driven back by head winds each time. Now, starting on a still, windless night, they had managed to clear the bridge but had then been caught in a series of unpredictable cross-currents that were sweeping them mercilessly towards the rocky coastline and the ultimate humiliation of shipwreck at the very start. Although the boat handled well, she was so big and long, so heavily laden for the 8,000-mile voyage, that she was at the mercy of the waves and currents no matter how hard Sylvia and John worked at the oars. Fortunately, they escaped the current just short of the rocks and were able, slowly, laboriously, to row out to sea.

It was very different from the Atlantic, for the Eastern Pacific seaboard is swept by a cold current from the Arctic and, as a result, although they were only slightly further north than the Canaries – from where Fairfax had started his Atlantic row – the temperature of the water was very much colder. Quickly they settled into some kind of routine but life was, at best, uncomfortable. With the increased size of the boat there was a tapered bow shelter three metres long. They could both just cram into this rathole to shelter from the rain and spray, but whenever a wave broke over the boat the bitterly cold waters swept the deck, sluicing the rathole and soaking them, their clothing and their sleeping bags. The stern shelter was smaller and acted as the galley.

One serious problem quickly emerged. Their radio transmitter, which Fairfax had used successfully on the Atlantic, and which had then been reconditioned by the manufacturers, would not work. It was of limited value in an emergency since, if they were to founder in a storm, they would drown long before any help could arrive, but they were worried about the impact on their parents if there were no news from them for the months it would take to reach their first Pacific island. There was also the question of the reports they were contracted to send to the Sunday *People*.

In the aftermath of the worst storm Fairfax had ever experienced there was no question of rowing. The storm lasted for three days.

Voyage of **Britannia II**

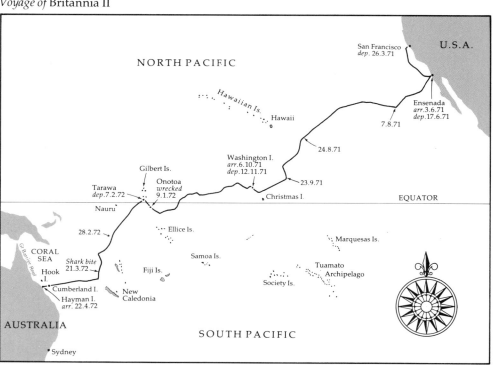

NORTH PACIFIC

San Francisco
dep. 26.3.71

U.S.A.

Hawaiian Is.

Hawaii

Ensenada
arr. 3.6.71
dep. 17.6.71

7.8.71

24.8.71

Washington I.
arr. 6.10.71
dep. 12.11.71

23.9.71

Gilbert Is.

Tarawa
dep. 7.2.72

Onotoa
wrecked
9.1.72

Christmas I.

EQUATOR

Nauru

28.2.72

Ellice Is.

Marquesas Is.

CORAL
SEA

Samoa Is.

Shark bite
21.3.72

Fiji Is.

Tuamato
Archipelago

Hook
I.

Society Is.

Gt Barrier Reef

Cumberland I.

Hayman I.
arr. 22.4.72

New
Caledonia

AUSTRALIA

SOUTH PACIFIC

Sydney

Fairfax decided, therefore, to return to land to get the radio repaired. This was no easy matter, for the prevailing winds and currents were taking them south and, somehow, they had to edge their way back in, across wind and current.

At this point they were hit by a series of violent storms, the worst that Fairfax had ever experienced. The boat was so well designed that there was little danger of her sinking or capsizing, but they were awash in the raging seas for days on end. There was no question of rowing – it was a matter of passive survival, or putting out a drogue anchor to keep their bow facing into the waves and to try to slow their drift with the wind, and then just sitting it out, soaked to the skin with the cold waters of the Pacific. It was almost impossible to cook and they went for several days at a time without any hot food. John, who could not stand the constriction of a safety line, was washed overboard almost every day, but because he was such a strong swimmer, he was always able to regain the boat. Sylvia, on the other hand, could barely swim – she could just about manage a length in a swimming pool – a fact which was hardly reassuring in a raging sea. In addition she was appallingly sea-sick.

The climax came when a huge wave smashed over the boat while Sylvia was struggling to heat enough water to give them their first hot meal in several days. John saw it coming, yelled a warning, and then it was upon them, a great boiling mass of foaming water that engulfed the boat, swept John with it, and slammed Sylvia headfirst into the cubbyhole of the galley towards the burning gas stove which was only extinguished within an inch of her face. And then the water was around her, over her, the boat seemed to be lying on its side, the floor near-vertical, bags of clothing and stores piled on top of her. Sylvia fought her way out of the cubbyhole but there was no sign of John, just tumbling waves on every side of the steeply listing, bucking boat. And then an arm appeared out of the water as he pulled himself on board, and got the boat back on an even keel before reassuring a tearful Sylvia. But Sylvia was amazingly resilient:

> As I sat weeping on the deck, I looked up and there within a hundred yards of us was a ship. She was quite small, painted a dull mid-green with white, and some of her crew were on deck waving to us and signalling if we wanted anything. Really a very ordinary little ship, but to see how horribly she wallowed in those ghastly seas, to see her cheerful crew, and to realise she had turned off course in such horrible conditions just to come and see how we were, was a real tonic. The way she yawed and rolled made me feel almost sea-sick to watch, and I felt so sorry for those aboard her that I forgot how frightened I had been ten minutes before, and stood up to wave back and signal that we were OK and that we didn't need a thing! She'll never know it, but she was the most important ship of our whole crossing, and left the fondest memories.

The storm raged on for another three days. They lost their rudder and Sylvia was sea-sick for most of the time. Even when the wind dropped at last, it was still bitterly cold with the sun glaring down from an empty blue sky. Everything was soaking wet and both of them were covered in sea-water boils; Sylvia was particularly badly affected, her backside a huge red, itching, stinging sore. The only respite they could get was by covering themselves with a coat of Vaseline jelly, but this was soon rubbed off by their soaked, salt-stiffened garments.

What was worse, they had not even started their voyage, were still trying to fight their way back to land and even this was a desperate struggle. After a month at sea, at last they saw the lights of a town on the eastern horizon, though they were not sure whether it was Los Angeles or San Diego. It was neither; they had been blown even further to the south, but it was another ten days before they were able to struggle those last few miles to land.

John Fairfax was a confident and strong swimmer. He had even tried to raise money for his Pacific row by offering to wrestle with sharks.

They made their landfall a few miles south of the Mexican sea port of Ensenada. The toll of damage was serious; half the waterproof hatchways had failed under the severe hammering, and the bulk of their supplies were ruined. The boat had taken a severe battering and they were now penniless, having spent everything on the initial kitting out. But both John and Sylvia are remarkably good at making friends, partly because of the romantic appeal of their adventure and partly the easy-going warmth yet determination of their personalities. They secured free accommodation at one of the motels, got the people of the boatyard working on repairs and cabled home for more money. They spent two weeks in Ensenada, working on the boat, replenishing their supplies and finding time for some happy, boozy parties. John could not help being amazed at Sylvia's determination to continue the trip after their appalling start. He told me:

When we put in at Ensenada, I was sure one hundred per cent that she'd say 'No further! There's no way you're going to get me back into that.' Not only that, but she had no way of knowing that it was not going to be like that all the way and yet she set out again. And that to me is fantastic for a girl to do. I don't know many men who would have done it, never mind a girl. For me this kind of life is natural, so there is no great achievement in my doing it, since I've been doing this sort of thing since I was a little boy. Not only that, I actually like it, but she didn't even enjoy it. What woman would? She couldn't even swim properly, only went over the side twice and that was a comedy. I even had to make a little ladder for her to get back in.

After a fortnight in Ensenada they set out, refitted, their radio transmitter repaired, the town band playing and the Mayor waving them off. They were back again a few days later. Whoever had fitted their new rudder had forgotten to fix an essential locking pin and they had lost it. A few more days and they were ready, this time with a spare. They accepted a tow out of the harbour – they had already rowed it once – and this time they really were on their way.

The following months slipped by in a monotonous routine of rowing and fishing and cooking and living, sometimes in storm, but mostly in fair, increasingly hot weather. Both took turns at the oars; John was the undisputed captain, making the decisions, doing the navigation and most of the odd jobs around the boat, while Sylvia took charge of the galley and did all the cooking. Their role allotment was certainly on rigorously traditional male–female lines, with John the hunter, leader and provider, Sylvia the follower and cook. It worked because both of them were happy with their roles, probably forming an easier partnership than that of two men, where rivalry and ego can all too easily creep in. This aspect of the relationship worked really well, but some of John's dreams while alone on the Atlantic worked out differently. Getting back from the Atlantic row he had written:

> The way I felt for most of the time, I could have ravaged all of King Solomon's harem twice over and still gone back for more. When I think of all those magnificent burning sunsets, those beautiful warm, starry nights – and all I had to rest my hands on was a bleeding pair of oars.

But now, on the Pacific, reality was a little different:

> She was there all the time and anyway you were too tired to want to make love. I don't think we made love more than five times in the whole year.

After four months at sea they had crossed the equivalent of the Atlantic and were still barely half-way. They had seen the occasional ship, but had had no sight of land. It was time for a rest, for fresh food and new faces. They headed for the Line Islands, a tiny group of atolls in the vastness of the Pacific. Narrowly missing their first targets of Christmas Island and Fanning Island, due to the vaguaries of the wind, they finally reached Washington Island on the 6th October. It was a green jewel with white sandy beaches hammered by creamy surf, straight out of a tourist brochure. They stayed for six weeks. Washington Island was owned by a private company which harvested the copra, had a population of 480, and was governed by the Australian manager of the company. It was a wonderfully relaxed, happy period, with Sylvia observing and sharing in the island life and John speargun fishing in the reefs. Leaving the island was hard for both of them, Sylvia writing in her log: 'Once more my only reality is the sea and this little boat with all it contains. How I long for the day when this, too, will become a dream.'

There was a desperate sense of anticlimax, of an adventure that had gone on too long. They were getting on each other's nerves. Syvlia commented: 'He drives me

Their roles were along rigorously traditional male-female lines, John the hunter and navigator, Sylvia the cook.

mad by not answering, or mumbling unintelligibly through his pipe. I drive him mad by talking, not that I find much to say, but he's so damned miserable I feel I have to cheer him up – it never seems to sink into my thick head that I always have the reverse effect.'

Christmas arrived on a windy, choppy day, which only their escort of seagulls, dorado and sharks seemed to enjoy. Sylvia and John spent most of the day bickering, but by New Year's Day the weather had improved; it was a glassy calm and the mood was more suited to celebration. They had crossed the Equator the night before. They had a feast of tinned ham, asparagus and potato salad, fresh onions, chutney and mustard, all washed down with a bottle of champagne. The climax was a Christmas cake baked on Washington Island. They even had some presents to open. Tipsy, happy and relaxed, they finally collapsed into their cubbyhole and slept. Life wasn't so bad after all.

A Christmas drink, but on a windy, choppy day that only their escort of seagulls, dorado and sharks seemed to enjoy.

At sea, so long as they had the fuel to distil fresh water, they could come to comparatively little harm, for *Britannia II* had already proved she could weather almost any storm and they were accompanied by plenty of fish. It was the landfalls that were the most dangerous parts of the voyage, but they had now been rowing for nearly ten months and needed the occasional rest on an island to maintain morale as much as anything else.

Now approaching the Gilbert Islands, Fairfax resolved to head for the tiny atoll of Onotoa. They sighted the island on the morning of 9th January and were being driven down towards it by a ten-knot wind. The safest approach would have been to aim for one end of the island and then to row round onto the leeward side, thus eliminating the risk of being driven onto the coral reef which would inevitably ring the atoll, but this also carried the possibility of their being swept past the island, unable to row back against the wind. Gambling on finding a gap in the coral reef, Fairfax headed straight for the island. They were so low in the water that they were only two miles away when the line of breaking surf appeared, stretching, white and menacing, as far as the eye could see in either direction. There was no gap and they were being driven inexorably towards it.

Desperately, they rowed through the morning, trying to clear the reef, but now they were too close – and getting ever closer. Watching each breaking wave, they could even see the brown heads of coral jutting through the seething foam. But it was the roar of thousands of tons of water smashing down onto the reef that was most frightening. Fairfax dropped the anchor, even though the water was still much too deep for it to reach the bottom; at least it would be there, ready as soon as the bottom began rising towards the reef. It held when they were only twenty metres from the breaking waves. He knew that it couldn't be for long. Fairfax recalled in his log:

> I can't remember what Sy was doing during this time, and other than yelling at her to stay with the boat whatever happened, I completely forgot her. *Britt* was unlikely to capsize, but even if she did she would be safer on board, especially as she didn't know how to swim. I had barely finished unshipping the rudder when, with a lurch, the anchor line snapped and *Britt* started drifting again. There remained only one thing for me to do. I had seen a little gap between two upthrusting coral heads, wide enough for *Britt* to squeeze through. Beyond that it was very shallow, but the coral was flat all the way to the beach. *Britt* was lying broadside to it but, miraculously, just then there was a lull. However, the next breaker would smash her right against it, unless I managed to point her head to the gap.
>
> There was only one way I could do this in time. Without any thought beyond the safety of my boat, I dived into the churning water and, grabbing the eyebolt of the bow, I pushed, attempting with the mad strength of desperation to swing her round. If I failed it would be curtains for me, as I would undoubtedly be squashed against the coral by *Britt*, but this at the time I did not even consider. Somehow, I managed to get her round. How far I shall never know, for suddenly all went dark and with a tremendous lurch *Britt* jumped forward, sweeping me aside and under with such force that I lost my grip on her. It all happened in a second. One moment I was hanging onto her, pushing like mad, the next I was in a swirling maelstrom of foam and felt her go right over me like an express train on one side of my body, while the other touched the coral bed.

John's action had saved not only the boat, but perhaps their lives as well. *Britannia* was now lying almost up-ended in shallow waters, still buffeted by breakers but these had lost the worst of their power. They now had a large audience of islanders who had raced into the shallows, to help pull them out of danger. They had survived, but the boat's hull had been stove in and they had not yet reached their objective. Wasting no time John returned to the reef to dive for the lost rudder and anchor.

Landfall in the Gilbert Islands. After the hazards of clearing the reefs of Onotoa, islanders help pull Britannia *out of the shallows.*

There were insufficient facilities on Onotoa to repair *Britannia*, but they managed to get a tow to the island of Tarawa, where there was a boatyard. They stayed here for a month, while the boat was being repaired, but this time they were glad to be away, partly because the end of the voyage was at last in sight and partly because, although they had been hospitably entertained, Tarawa was a crowded, urban little island run by the British. They felt that they were in a kind of tropical suburbia that bore little resemblance to the romantic image of a South Sea island. They left Tarawa on the 9th February. They had been rowing for too long, driven on only by the ambition to complete a long, and now tedious voyage, for which they had sacrificed so much.

Onotoa had lacked the facilities for reparing the damaged hull and sheared rudder, so Britannia was towed to neighbouring Tarawa.

Tarawa was a tropical suburbia, bearing little resemblance to the romantic image of a South Sea Island, and John and Sylvia were anxious to be off to complete their voyage.

Seaworthy again, John and Sylvia leave Tarawa.

But the boredom was not to last long, and soon they were faced with a series of crises which they were very lucky to survive. It started with just another session of fishing. There were only a few small fish around, but they would not respond to the fishing line, so John went after them with his harpoon gun. A small white tip shark, just over a metre long, was hovering around, but it wasn't big enough to offer any real threat and John ignored it until it darted in on his catch.

John wrote: 'That did it. No shark, big or small, has ever taken anything away from me without paying for it and that cheeky beggar wasn't going to be an exception.'

He speared the shark through the head, but didn't kill it and then, when he came to try to pull out the spear, found it was stuck, with the shark struggling to break free. Fairfax was determined not to lose the spear, a point of pride as much as anything else:

> I closed in, grabbed the little bastard by the gills with my left hand, the tail with my right and kept him immobilised as I swam back to the boat. Once alongside, I pulled the spear free and passed the gun to Sy. By then the white tip was struggling very feebly, and I should have let it go at that. Problem is, I hate sharks so much I just couldn't resist the temptation of doing a real job on that one. So I asked Sy to pass me a very sharp buck knife we keep for skinning fish, and proceeded to rip its belly all the way from mouth to tail!

The shark exploded into life, twisting, writhing, snapping in the blood-clouded water, while Fairfax hung on to the gills and tail to keep the savage teeth out of reach of his own limbs. He had drifted away from the boat, could feel the shark beginning to lose its strength and so relaxed his own grip. Suddenly, with a convulsive wrench, the shark slipped from his grasp, whipped behind him and sank its teeth into his upper arm. He felt a searing pain, but managed to seize the shark once again and tore it away from his arm. The dying shark escaped, slowly sinking out of sight into the blue below.

Blood was welling from John's wound, staining the sea around him. He was a good forty yards from the boat and losing strength fast. Somehow, he managed to swim the intervening distance and Sylvia hauled him on board. In her words: 'The wound was ghastly, looked like a joint of veal, pulsating and bleeding profusely. It was about six inches long, more than an inch wide and over an inch deep, a great chunk of meat missing from the middle.'

It hadn't been a particularly big shark, but when John Fairfax went at it with a buck knife it exacted its revenge.

With a tourniquet Sylvia managed to stop the flow of blood, but the greatest fear was infection, always a high risk with a shark bite. Fairfax swigged down some tetracyline tablets, a gulp of whisky and some hot, sweet tea. Soon, he had recovered sufficiently to tell Sylvia to take some photographs to record the event. But he was desperately worried by the wound, more afraid of gangrene, which could mean amputation, than death, which was a much more likely consequence if they could not get him to a hospital. Their radio transmitter had packed up long ago, their only hope was a passing ship, they were still far from land, John was unable to row and Sylvia could only manage stretches of eight hours at a time. In the following days of grinding worry, two ships did pass, one barely half a mile away.

And then the barometer plummeted; it could mean only one thing – a cyclone and they were right in its path. There was nothing they could do. John was still helpless and, even if he had not been, it would have been impossible to row in heavy seas. All they could do was to huddle in their tiny shelter and wait for it to pass over them. It was a tribute to Uffa Fox's design that the boat withstood the appalling hammering of the huge seas and ferocious winds. Like a cork, they bobbed on the waves, just safe as long as they weren't tossed onto a reef – and there were plenty around them. But their luck was in and, at last, the cyclone left them exhausted, soaked and battered, but still alive. John's wound still showed no signs of infection and, even though it was cruelly painful, he began to row.

They heard a call on their little transistor radio for shipping to look out for them. They also learned that their cyclone had been named Emily, that it had hit the Australian coast and claimed the lives of six sailors. Shortly afterwards another cargo ship steamed past, little more than 500 metres away, again without noticing their frantic efforts to gain attention.

They had no choice, they would have to make it to Australia on their own. But the dangers were not finished. They still had to find a way through the Great Barrier Reef which guards the Queensland coast some ninety miles offshore. At high tide, you could see nothing except the line of surf from the huge, crashing breakers which could smash *Britannia* to pieces. At low tide, the coral heads protruded from the sea all around them like a thousand expectant teeth. They had to wait for a dead calm before they dared try to get through the Barrier, and therefore dropped anchor and tried patiently to wait it out. Unable to swim, unable to do anything but think of the consequences should the anchor cable part, it was a nerve-wracking, painful vigil. And then, on the third night, John woke from a doze to sense that something was desperately wrong. They had come adrift from the anchor. With no spare, they were now drifting, helpless, towards the reef. There was nothing they could do. There was no point in rowing because they could not see where to go. John recalled:

We lashed the rudder at what I thought was the best angle of drift for *Britannia* to head towards the gap we had seen during the day, put on life-jackets and life-lines and cuddled against each other in front of the rathole. Two hours went by, and although we did not actually make love, that was perhaps after a whole year in that lousy, stinking, lovely little boat, the most tender, romantic time we ever had . . .

It was an unbelievable, fantastic ride. Every so often we could hear the tumultuous roar of breakers all around us, sometimes near, sometimes far and *Britt* would be in the grip of some vicious current or other, spin around like a toy boat, while the water around us seemed to boil in a frenzy of bubbles and foam as eddies met counter eddies, but always she would break free and go drifting on, blindly, presumably following the line of least resistance, like a piece of flotsam.

They were in shallow waters, a maze of reefs and uncharted rocks. It was as if they were approaching an uninhabited continent. Only once did they see a light which they thought was probably an illegal fishing boat, since the light was doused and vanished like a will-o'-the-wisp the minute they shouted and flashed an SOS with their torch.

At last they sighted land on the 20th April. There were still no signs of human habitation, though an hotel was marked on their map of the island they were approaching. They rowed throughout the day, working their way around to the lee side and, in the dark, stumbled upon an anchored boat. Their voyage was over.

In the postscript of his book John Fairfax wrote: 'To the great surprise of all and sundry we are still speaking to each other. Not only that, but we are better friends than ever, with a new, hard-earned respect for one another.'

This was undoubtedly so, but Sylvia had no intention of being involved in John's next project – a schooner with a mainly female crew, to wander the oceans of the world, filming, adventuring and, no doubt, boosting John's male fantasies. The project fell through for lack of financial support, and John became involved in an attempt to salvage a load of lead from a wreck off Washington Island. Sylvia went along as cook, but unfortunately their ship drifted onto a reef, to join the wreck they had come to salvage.

Their relationship had always been one of easy-going companionship and then John met an American girl, fell in love and they are now living together in Florida. John Fairfax's ambition is to make ten million dollars. At the time of writing he has a long way to go, but Sylvia Cook has realised one ambition. She has a son called Martin.

The man who raced himself

Just a week before Ridgway and Blyth reached the coast of Ireland, Francis Chichester set out to circumnavigate the world in his yacht, *Gipsy Moth IV*. About the only thing these two ventures had in common was the fact that they were both ocean voyages. In each case the voyage had been pioneered by someone else. The Atlantic had been rowed by Harbo and Samuelson. The world had been circumnavigated by Joshua Slocum, sailing single-handed from 1895 to 1898. This had been a magnificent achievement, for he had none of the self-steering equipment and strong, lightweight gear and winches used by the modern yachtsman. Slocum's voyage, however, had been a fairly leisurely though very adventurous cruise, with plenty of stops on the way. He had avoided the empty, storm-ridden expanses of the Southern Ocean and got round the tip of South America by going through the Magellan Straits.

Francis Chichester was very different from either John Ridgway or Chay Blyth, both in age and the approach he took to his adventure. When Chichester set sail from Plymouth on the 27th August 1966 he had already established his individuality and success several times over, not just in the field of sailing but also as a pioneer of long-distance solo flying. Not only did he aim to sail round the world single-handed, he meant to go faster, with fewer stops, than anyone had ever done before. With his great sense of history, he wanted to follow the old clipper route but, characteristically, was not content merely to follow the clippers; he sought to beat their time from England to Sydney and then back home to England round Cape Horn. His plan was to make only the one stop at Sydney, and achieve the longest continuous voyage ever attempted by any small craft, let alone one that was single-handed. Only nine small boats had been round the Horn and, of these, six had been capsized or pitchpoled. No single-handed boat had ever been round. The fact that Chichester was sixty-five when he set out on his attempt made it even more remarkable.

He had always had an intensely competitive urge, combined with an adventurous, technically-minded curiosity. The son of an English parson, he had a lonely childhood with little love or understanding at home. He was sent off to prep school and then to Marlborough, a public school that has produced several outstanding venturers, including John Hunt. Like many of his fellow-adventurers', his school career was undistinguished and, at the age of eighteen, without consulting his father, he decided to abandon all ideas of going to university and the career in the Indian Civil Service which had been planned for him and, instead, emigrated to New Zealand, travelling steerage with £10 in his pocket. It sounds like the classic schoolboy adventure story, and Chichester certainly lived up to this conception. He was determined to make his fortune and took on a variety of jobs, ending up in property development. At the age of twenty-seven he was making £10,000 a year – in those days a great deal of money. He returned to England in 1929, having achieved his aim of making £20,000 before going back home.

There was nothing particularly original about a wealthy young businessman taking up flying, but now, after twenty-four flying hours of instructions, he decided to buy a 'plane and fly it back to Australia, hoping to beat the time taken by Hinkler, the only other man to do it. Chichester did not get the record, but he did manage to fly his 'plane back to Sydney. He also flew back into the depression, which took away the greater part of the fortune he had built, but he did not let this deter him and threw most of his energy into further flying projects. In those days flying was adventurous in a way that it has long ceased to be. There were no radio beacons or flight control paths. The Gipsy Moth had an open cockpit, a range of under a thousand miles and a top speed of just over a hundred miles an hour.

No-one had ever flown across the Tasman Sea from New Zealand to Australia. Chichester now dreamt up a plan of flying all the way from New Zealand to England over the Pacific, thus circumnavigating the globe, flying solo, something that had not yet been done. For a start, though, flying the Tasman Sea offered a huge challenge. It was 1,200 miles wide, two-thirds the distance across the Atlantic, with weather which is even more unpredictable. Even if he stripped everything out of the Gipsy Moth and carried extra petrol tanks, his 'plane could not have made that distance in a single hop. Looking at a map, he noticed there were two inhabited islands on the way, Norfolk and Lord Howe, but neither had airfields. Then he got the idea of fitting floats to the aircraft so that he could land on the sea, but still he had to find the islands – Norfolk Island, 481 miles out into the featureless ocean, and Lord Howe another 561 miles on. There were no radio aids and so he would have to do it by a combination of dead reckoning and taking shots of the sun, no easy matter while flying a juddering, bucking 'plane. He only had to be a half-degree out in his reckoning and he could miss the island altogether; he would not have enough fuel to get back to New Zealand, had no radio to call for help and would have had little chance of being picked up by a ship. He hit upon the technique of aiming off – of intentionally missing the island to one side, so that he knew which way to turn when he had calculated he had gone far enough. It is a technique used by orienteers aiming for a checkpoint in the middle of a featureless country, but for them the penalty for a mistake is dropping a few places in a race, for Chichester it could well have been his life.

An Australian, Menzies, beat him to the first solo flight across the Tasman Sea, flying it in a single hop with a 'plane that had sufficient fuel capacity. This did not deter Chichester, who was fascinated by the navigational challenge of trying to make a landfall on a tiny island. He was busy learning astro-navigation, adapting a sextant to his own specialist use as a solo pilot.

Ready at last, on the 28th March 1931, he took off from the far north tip of New Zealand, full of apprehension about what he was trying to do:

At noon I flew over the edge of New Zealand; it was Spirit's Bay, where the Maoris believed there was a vast cavern through which all the spirits of the dead passed. I flew from under the cloud into the clear sky. All my miserable anxieties and worries dropped away, and I was thrilled through and through. Over my left shoulder, the last of New Zealand receded rapidly. Ahead stretched the ocean, sparkling under the eye of the sun; no sport could touch this, it was worth almost any price. I seemed to expand with vitality and power and zest.

He was putting into practice a whole series of techniques he had developed for calculating drift and position as a solo flyer:

I had to try a sextant shot to find out how far I was from the turn-off point, and at the same time to check my dead reckoning. I trimmed the tail as delicately as I could to balance the 'plane, but she would not stabilise and I had to use the control-stick the whole time while adjusting the sextant . . . I had just got the sun and horizon together in the sextant, when terrific acceleration pressing my back made me drop the sextant. I grabbed the stick and eased the seaplane from its vertical nose dive into a normal dive and then flattened it out.

He managed to get a sun sight, took some more shots and, at last, came to the point where, according to his dead reckoning and after working out his sun sight, he should make his right-angled turn. He was now going to put his theory into practice:

The moment I settled on this course, nearly at right-angles to the track from New Zealand, I had a feeling of despair. After flying in one direction for hour after hour over a markless, signless sea, my instinct revolted at suddenly changing direction in mid-ocean. My navigational system seemed only a flimsy brain fancy: I had been so long on the same heading that the island must lie ahead, not to the right. I was attacked by panic. Part of me urged, for God's sake, don't make this crazy turn! My muscles wanted to bring the seaplane back onto its old course. 'Steady, steady steady,' I told myself aloud. I had to trust my system, for I could not try anything else now, even if I wanted to.

He made his landfall at both Norfolk and Lord Howe Island before disaster struck. A squall during the night sank the seaplane at its anchorage in the harbour. It seemed a complete write-off, but Chichester would not accept defeat and resolved to rebuild the 'plane and its engine, sending for what parts he needed, even though he had very little experience of the necessary practical mechanics. The wings alone had about 4,000 separate wooden struts, some of them no thicker than a pencil. He had to take them to pieces, repair or remake the damaged parts and put them together again. He also had to strip and clean the engine – ironically, the only part to give serious trouble was the brand-new replacement magneto. With the help of the islanders, he took just ten weeks to do it and complete his crossing of the Tasman Sea, staking his life on his makeshift repairs.

But this, of course, was only the start of his Odyssey. He was determined to fly to Britain across the Pacific and might have if his journey – and very nearly his life – had not been terminated when his plane hit some unmarked electricity cables across the mouth of a Japanese harbour.

Back in England he met Sheila. His first marriage had been unhappy and short-lived. His marriage to Sheila, however, was to be the bedrock of all his further achievements. But these were still far away. In 1939 the war intervened, putting a stop to any ideas he, or anyone else, had of adventure. Chichester volunteered for the Royal Air Force but was told that his eyesight was not good enough and he was too old. He refused to be rejected and finally managed to find himself a niche, teaching navigation to flyers.

At the end of the war he started a map publishing business which commanded all his energies until 1953, when he became restless for adventure. He abandoned the idea of flying as being too expensive and now lacking in adventure. He liked the idea of sailing, however, particularly as it was something he could share with his wife and son, Giles. But he had not the temperament of the casual weekend yachtsman. Almost immediately he started racing, first crewing for experienced skippers, but as soon as possible entering his own boat, which he had named *Gipsy Moth II*. At first he had little success but he learnt fast, using his skill and knowledge as a navigator as well as his inventive ingenuity to improve his boat's chances. He was leading a similar life to that of many active, successful businessmen, working hard through

Gipsy Moth IV.

the week, then stretching himself at weekends and holidays on the yachting circuit.

But this regime took its toll. Chichester was a worrier over business matters; whilst decisive, with superb split-second judgement at the controls of a 'plane or helm of his yacht, he could be indecisive when it came to decisions over money or long-term planning. I can sympathise with this seeming contradiction, being very similar in temperament. The world of the sea, air or mountain is wonderfully simple, a place of black and white, of life or death, but the world of commerce, or even every-day life, is so much more complex.

He became very run down and, in 1957, he faced the greatest crisis of his life. A massive cancerous growth was discovered in his lung. His chances of survival seemed slight. The surgeons wanted to operate but Sheila Chichester stood out against it, feeling that it would almost certainly kill him and sensing, perhaps, that even if it did not, it would leave him an invalid. With the help of his family he fought through the illness, going to the very brink of death before the cancerous cells became inactive and he was on his way back on the road to recovery. He commented: 'When I was a boy at home, I used to hear my father pray every Sunday, "From sudden death, good Lord deliver us." This had always puzzled me; sudden death seemed a fine way to go out. Now the meaning seemed clear; the prayer should read, "From death before we are ready to die, good Lord deliver us."'

As soon as he finished a short convalescence he started crewing for fellow yachtsmen as navigator, but during his illness he had seen a notice on the board of the Royal Ocean Racing Club, proposing a single-handed race across the Atlantic. This immediately appealed to him as having all the right ingredients, the huge scale of the challenge, the need for innovation and the fact that it was for an individual solo effort. He instinctively knew from his flying days that he functioned best working by himself. Later, in *Alone Across the Atlantic*, he wrote: 'Somehow I never seemed to enjoy so much doing things with other people. I know now I don't do a thing nearly as well when with someone. It makes me think I was cut out for solo jobs and any attempt to diverge from that lot only makes me half a person. It looks as if the only way to be happy is to do fully what you are destined for.'

Already, he had on the stocks a new boat, *Gipsy Moth III*, which was bigger and faster than his previous one, and just thirty-two months after being taken ill, only fifteen from a shaky convalescence, he was on the start line with three other boats. At the age of fifty-eight, when most other men have long before slowed up, he was about to enter the most exacting race that had ever been devised. Pushing himself and his boat to the limit, using his cunning as a navigator and his ingenuity in designing solo sailing devices, particularly his self-steering gear, Miranda, he won the race in forty and a half days.

Most men would have been content with such a record, but not Chichester; convinced that he could improve on it, he did not want to wait for the next trans-Atlantic race and, in 1962, set out on his own to try to beat his own record, cutting it down to thirty-three days fifteen hours. He was already looking for other challenges and it was at this stage that he started thinking of circumnavigating the globe on the old clipper trail. In 1964 he entered the trans-Atlantic race once again but, although he broke his own record by coming in a few minutes short of thirty days, he was beaten by the outstanding French sailor, Eric Tabarly. *Gipsy Moth III* was now four years old, whilst Tabarly's boat was very much lighter and had been specially designed for the race, but more than this, Tabarly – besides being a superb sailor – was a very much younger man and single-handed racing is a ferociously strenuous game, demanding not only skill but also tremendous stamina. After this race Chichester saw, perhaps, that he could no longer compete with a rising generation of experienced sailors in this particular field, but he was already one step in front of it with his plans to circumnavigate the globe, thus confirming not just his ability but also his position as a great innovator and pioneer.

Chichester's aim was almost unbelievably ambitious; in wanting to race the clippers round the world, he was taking on three or four masted boats of up to ninety metres in length with crews of over forty. A fast time for a clipper was around a hundred days. To equal this Chichester would have to sail around 137.5 miles a day, averaging six knots, day and night throughout the voyage to Sydney. To do this, he wanted an even bigger and faster boat than *Gipsy Moth III*; she would have to be robust enough to face the ferocious seas of the Southern Ocean and yet be a craft which he, now aged sixty-five, could handle on his own.

Speed in a yacht is determined by the length of the boat on the waterline, combined of course with the design of the hull and its sail area. *Gipsy Moth III* had been built while he was ill, practically without supervision, and, but for a few almost inevitable teething problems, she had proved an excellent boat of which Chichester had been very fond. His new boat, *Gipsy Moth IV*, suffered perhaps from over-supervision, with the ideas of the designer, John Illingworth, and those of Chichester at times coming into conflict.

The whole project was obviously going to cost a great deal of money – more than Chichester could afford to pay out of his own pocket. He was grateful, therefore, when his cousin, Lord Dulverton, offered to pay for the boat. There were changes and modifications throughout, and as a result it took longer to build, cost considerably more than had been planned and even when it was launched finally, in the spring of 1966, only a few months before he was due to sail, there still seemed to be some serious faults. At the launch, several things went wrong; the bottle of champagne, swung by his wife Sheila, did not break on first impact, the boat stuck on the launching ramp and Chichester had to leap down to give it a push to make sure it slid down the greased way and then, when it hit the water, in Chichester's words, 'There, the hull floated high on the surface; she didn't look right. Then, two or three tiny ripples from a ferry steamer made folds in the glassy surface, and *Gipsy Moth IV* rocked fore and aft. "My God," Sheila and I said to each other, "she's a rocker!"'

To help finance the voyage Chichester agreed to send back radio reports to the Sunday Times *and* The Guardian.

An intensely competitive man, Francis Chichester was sixty-five and already had a reputation as a 'thirties solo long-distance flyer, when he followed up winning the first Observer *single-handed Atlantic race with the idea of racing the clipper ships round the world.*

They barely had time enough left to correct her tendency to rock and heel or to sort out all the other problems, some of which appeared to have been fundamental to the design of the boat. Chichester described all these troubles at length in his book *Gipsy Moth Circles the World* and grumbled about them at the time, earning a fair amount of criticism from both friends and the press for what, at times, sounded like peevish recrimination. On the other hand, one needs to understand how he must have felt, trying to combat these faults on his own over a long period, across thousands of miles of storm-wracked ocean.

He was ready to sail from Plymouth on the 27th August 1966. Sheila, his son Giles and a close friend had crewed the boat with him from London to Plymouth; they sailed with him out into the harbour, were taken off by boat and he was left on his own, tacking up and down behind the start line, competitive as always, determined to cross the line the very moment the start-gun fired, even though he was racing against no-one but himself and the voyage ahead was over 14,000 miles.

At sixty-five, despite age and his struggle against illness, he was extraordinarily fit and trim. He had become a vegetarian, mainly to combat arthritis, and regularly undertook yoga-based exercises, becoming a great believer in the benefits of standing on his head. Chichester was only around five foot nine and yet, because he was lithe and wiry and through the sheer vibrant energy of his personality, he gave the impression of being a much taller man, with his strong face, firm jaw, thin lips that almost vanished when he smiled and prominent nose, framed by glasses. A laconic, dry sense of humour made him good company. I only met him once, when he took me out to lunch in 1972; he wanted to learn as much as possible about the climber's use of jumar clamps in climbing a rope. He thought he might be able to use them to climb his mast, if he had to do any work on it. He was a delightful host but it was easy to see the single-minded determination below the surface. It was that of someone

Francis Chichester's circumnavigation

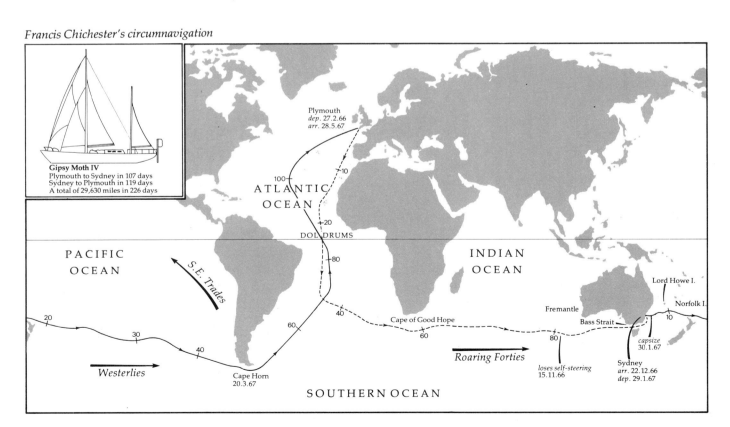

who would use anyone and anything to the full to achieve his objectives and, of course, without this drive he would not have achieved a fraction of what he had done in a uniquely full life.

As he set sail from Plymouth there were no regrets and few doubts. He was used to being alone – indeed he welcomed it. Very matter-of-factly he got down to the business of solitary sailing. The key challenge of the voyage was the empty wind-swept seas of the Southern Ocean and, in a way, the run down the Atlantic was a time to shake down, to sort out problems, work out systems, even to get one's sea legs. During the first few days Chichester suffered from sea-sickness; at the same time, being in the shipping lanes, he had the constant worry of being run down by an unobservant merchant ship, one of the greatest hazards of any yachtsman, particularly a solitary one. In a normal race *Gipsy Moth IV* would have had a crew of six, taking turns to sleep, change the sails, run watches, cook the meals and take care of the endless round of minor repairs and maintenance that beset any yacht being driven hard.

Time for ablutions.

Francis Chichester kept himself and his boat neat and shipshape whenever possible.

Chichester was racing himself on the longest race that anyone had ever undertaken, intensely aware of each day's progress, setting himself targets that he was determined to attain. Fifty-one days out, he reached the latitude of the Roaring Forties, the great Southern Ocean where the winds, uninterrupted by land, are spun by the revolution of the earth in a westerly direction and the seas are driven up by the winds into fifteen metre waves. It is a watery wilderness of chill winds and rain, of successive depressions that carry violent storms, where there is very little let-up for a solitary yachtsman. This is where the stress to man and boat is at its most acute. With day after day of high seas everything becomes damp; there is no opportunity for drying out sleeping bags and the only way to dry out one's clothes is to go to bed wearing them, still damp, and dry them by one's own body heat. On wild nights the solo sailor usually goes to bed fully clad in oilskins, to avoid the delay of getting dressed each time some emergency summons him on deck through the night. The boat itself is permanently heeled, when it isn't being tossed all over the place by squall or storm. There is little or no relaxation, rarely an uninterrupted sleep of more than a few hours, the agony of time and time again forcing oneself out of the comparative warmth of a damp sleeping bag, into the savage wind, spray and rain of a pitch-black night to adjust sails, to put the boat back on course. This means stumbling across a bucking deck in the dark, waves smashing in from all sides, struggling with ropes and winches, clearing fouled yards with numbed fingers.

Chichester wrote:

I was fagged out and I grew worried by fits of intense depression. Often I could not stand up without hanging on to some support and I wondered if I had something wrong with my balancing nerves. I felt weak, thin and somehow wasted, and I had a sense of immense space empty of any spiritual – what? I didn't know. I knew only that it made for intense loneliness and a feeling of hopelessness, as if faced with imminent doom. On November 5 I held a serious conference with myself about my weakness. When I got up that morning I found that I could not stand on my legs without support, just as if I had emerged from hospital after three months in bed. I was exhausted after a long struggle with the radio on the previous evening, and a long-drawn battle with the mainsail during the night finished me off. Then I thought, 'Husky young men on fully-crewed yachts during an ocean race of a few days have been known to collapse from sheer exhaustion. I have been doing this single-handed for more than two months. Is it any wonder that I feel exhausted?' That cheered me up a bit, and I made two resolutions: firstly to try to relax and take some time off during the day; secondly to eat more nourishing food.

He managed to keep going through a combination of determination and self-discipline, but the boat's gear was now beginning to fall apart. One of the most important pieces of equipment, and certainly the most fragile, is the self-steering. This is a small vane or even sail, usually at the stern, which is either linked to the rudder itself or sometimes to a small, extra rudder, which reacts to any change of course the boat takes to bring it back onto its original heading in relation to the wind; it enables the solitary yachtsman to get some sleep at night, to work on maintenance jobs during the day and even to relax occasionally to read a book. It is not the complete panacea, however, and to get the best from the boat the sailor must constantly check the trim of the sails and make minor adjustments to the course, even in a steady wind.

Chichester's self-steering gear was slightly damaged in the first storm to hit him in the Roaring Forties and, some days later, completely destroyed – an experience shared by almost all single-handed circumnavigators. It was a grim moment for Chichester:

> The sight of the self-steering gear broken beyond repair acted like a catalyst. At first I turned cold inside and my feelings, my spirit, seemed to freeze and sink inside me. I had a strange feeling that my personality was split and I was watching myself drop the sails efficiently and lift out the broken gear coolly. My project was killed. Not only was my plan to race a hundred days to Sydney shattered, but to make a non-stop passage there was impossible too. Then I found that I was not really crestfallen; it was a relief. I realised that I had been waiting for this to happen for a long time.

He altered course to head for Fremantle, Western Australia, and started to adjust his tackle to try to make the boat sail on its own without the self-steering. On the 17th November his resolve returned. His habitual ingenuity had, at least partly, solved the problem. He swung the boat back on course for Sydney. He realised that now he had little hope of reaching his target of a hundred days, but he came extraordinarily close to it, pulling into Sydney harbour on the 12th December to find a hero's welcome on his 107th day.

The first part of his journey was over. He had made both the longest and fastest ever non-stop single-handed voyage. But it had taken a severe toll; he was undoubtedly weakened and tired, both physically and mentally. He was very sensitive about two pictures taken on his arrival in Sydney, one of him embracing his son, Giles, who towered over him, making him look like a frail old man in tears, and another of him seeming to be helped by a policeman off the boat. As a result of these there was a strong outcry both in the press and from close friends. Lord Dulverton, the principal owner of the *Gypsy Moth IV*, sent a telegram urging him to abandon his

An experiment in self-photography reveals the lighter side of a keen competitor.

Sea trials in Sydney Harbour where Gipsy Moth IV *was completely overhauled before the second half of the voyage.*

circumnavigation, newspaper columnists and prominent members of the yachting world foretold doom but Chichester, although needled by the constant sniping, was determined to go on. To this end he had the boat completely overhauled, altered the shape of the keel, increasing its weight and changing the stowage.

After seven weeks he set out from Sydney on the 29th January with a boat that was not only completely overhauled but whose sailing characteristics had also been improved. Both he and his boat were put to the test all too soon. A tropical storm was forecast in the Tasman Sea, but this had not deterred him. He was buffeted throughout the day by violent winds and mounting seas, and was feeling queasy from what, at the time, he thought was sea-sickness, though later decided was the after-effects of Australian champagne. As a result he could not bring himself to secure with a rope the net carrying his two big genoa sails, which were stowed amidships. He fled below from the bucking deck, took off his oilskins and lay down on the bunk, the only way of withstanding the violent rocking of the boat. Switching off the light he dropped off into the fitful sleep of the sailor who, rather like a wild animal, probably

78

always has some level of consciousness to detect any change in the state of the boat. He did not hear the huge wave which must have hit the boat, but was conscious of her rolling over. It just did not stop.

'I said to myself, "Over she goes!" I was not frightened, but intensely alert and curious.'

This is the sensation shared, I think, by most people in the actual moment of disaster; I have had the same feeling in a climbing fall, with a flash of curiosity wondering what it will be like when I hit the ground. Most of us feel fear, but this is usually in anticipation of danger rather than at the time of disaster. Then, there is no time for it; there is even an excitement in getting out of the situation. Chichester describes his own response:

> Then a lot of crashing and banging started, and my head and shoulders were being bombarded by crockery and cutlery and bottles. I had an oppressive feeling of the boat being on top of me. I wondered if she would roll over completely and what the damage would be; but she came up quietly the same side that she had gone down. I reached up and put my bunk light on. It worked, giving me a curious feeling of something normal in a world of utter chaos. I have only a confused idea of what I did for the next hour or so. I had an absolutely hopeless feeling when I looked at the pile of jumbled up food and gear all along the cabin. Anything that was in my way when I wanted to move I think I put back in its right place, though feeling as I did so that it was a waste of time as she would probably go over again. The cabin was two foot deep all along with a jumbled-up pile of hundreds of tins, bottles, tools, shackles, blocks, two sextants and oddments. Every settee locker, the whole starboard bunk, and the three starboard drop lockers had all emptied out when she was upside down. Water was swishing about on the cabin sole beside the chart table, but not much. I looked into the bilge which is five feet deep, but it was not quite full, for which I thought, 'Thank God.'

I am sure Chichester's approach to the shambles to which his boat had been reduced and the danger of another capsize, was as matter-of-fact as his description. On deck, most important of all, he found that his mast was still standing with the rigging undamaged, mainly because he had taken down all the sails before turning in that night. A mono hull boat, when rolled over by waves or wind, will always right itself because of the weight of ballast and that of the keel; the real danger, though, is that the mast might break, particularly if there is any sail set. There is also the danger that the dog house, coach roof or hatches might be smashed, laying the boat open to the waves. Fortunately, in Chichester's case, there was no damage and his only loss was one of the genoa sails and some lengths of rope he had failed to tie down the night before.

The wind was still howling through the rigging, the seas mountainous, but he was desperately tired and realised he needed to conserve his energies. He decided, therefore, 'To Hell with everything', went down below, cleared the mess of cutlery, plates and bottles from his bunk, snuggled down into the soaking wet bedding, fully dressed in his oilskins, and fell into a deep sleep, not waking until it was broad daylight.

When he awoke the wind was still gusting at between forty and fifty-five knots but he set to, first checking the boat for serious structural damage and then starting the appalling task of clearing up the mess. Although only two days out, it never occurred to him to return to Sydney or call in at a New Zealand port. Damage to the boat was superficial and, remarkably, the self-steering gear had survived the capsize, though the socket for the vane shaft was very nearly off. He fixed this, however, without too much trouble and sailed on, north of New Zealand, heading for Cape Horn.

There were more crises, falls and minor injuries, the constant wear and tear to his own sixty-five-year-old frame and that of his boat. There were more storms, but none as dangerous as that of the Tasman Sea and when, at last, he reached the Horn – the most notorious place for storms anywhere in the world – it was almost an anticlimax. The seas were big and the wind strong, but they were nothing to some of the seas that Chichester had had to face. It was also positively crowded compared to the Southern Ocean. The Royal Naval Ice Patrol ship HMS *Protector* had come there to greet him, a tiny Piper Apache chartered by the *Sunday Times* and BBC flew from Tierra del Fuego to film him from the air as his boat, under the storm jib, raced through the white-capped seas of the Horn. In some ways it was a natural focal point of the voyage, a kind of oceanic summit but, like reaching the summit of a mountain, the adventure was by no means over; having got up, you have got to get back down again. In Chichester's case he had a long haul, a good 9,000 miles. There were more storms, more wear and tear, but he was now heading into kinder climes.

Yet he never stopped competing with himself, never ceased trying to get the very best out of his boat, making runs of up to 188 miles a day, driven on by the winds of the North-East Trades, doing 1,215 miles in a week. These were records for single-handed sailing, something of which he was intensely aware.

And then, at last, towards the end of May he entered the English Channel and came in to a welcome that is certainly unique in post-war adventure – even greater, perhaps, than that for John Hunt and his party after Everest. It had been announced on his arrival at Sydney that Chichester would receive a knighthood. This honour no more than reflected the huge popular acclaim he had already achieved. He was met by a fleet of boats outside Plymouth; a quarter of a million people watched him sail into the harbour and many millions more saw his arrival on television.

One man who was not there was Donald Crowhurst, a businessman and amateur sailor who had followed Chichester's voyage avidly, had been inspired, as had others, to wonder if he could perhaps cap this achievement by sailing single-handed non-stop round the world. That day Crowhurst chose to go off sailing with a friend in the Bristol Channel. They listened to the commentary of Chichester's arrival on the yacht radio and, perhaps out of envy, chose to belittle and joke about the adulation Chichester was receiving. But the yachting world joined the vast majority of the British public in recognising not just Chichester's achievement but the enormous stature of the man himself. The whole voyage of 29,630 miles had taken just nine months and one day, from Plymouth to Plymouth, of which the sailing time was 226 days.

Chichester was an innovator, one of the greatest ever in the adventure field. It is in no way belittling to the achievement of Ed Hillary and Tenzing to say they achieved what they did on Everest as part of a team, using traditional methods and following practically all the way in the steps of the Swiss team that so nearly reached the summit in 1952; (indeed, it was the Swiss team that broke some of the greatest physical and psychological barriers).

Chichester, on the other hand, brought a completely new concept to small boat sailing, both in terms of distance and speed; he set his own rules, conceived his own challenges and had done so throughout his life, from the days he set up flying records in the 'thirties until this, his crowning glory. His achievement in going round the world on his own with only one stop, faster than any small boat had done so previously, would have been an extraordinary feat for a man of any age; the fact that he was sixty-five made it all the more incredible and certainly increased its public appeal still further.

Chichester undoubtedly enjoyed both the acclaim and the money he was able to

After the Tasman Sea the Horn was almost an anticlimax. Chichester races round it under a storm jib in what was only a Force 7 gale.

make by exploiting his achievement. Several of his friends have mentioned, sometimes wryly, that he was a good self-publicist. Perhaps he was, but I am quite sure that the real drive that spurred him on was not the need to establish himself, which Ridgway and Blyth felt. In Chichester the most important motive seems to have been his intense competitiveness, combined with an adventurous curiosity that was undoubtedly technically orientated. He was not interested in the direct physical effort required to climb a mountain or row the Atlantic; he enjoyed working through machines that were still sufficiently simple to have a close and direct contact with the elements, firstly in the open cockpit of the Gipsy Moth and then behind the helm of his yachts.

The competitiveness and curiosity never left him; having circumnavigated the globe he sought other challenges that he, an ageing but indomitable and realistic man, felt he could meet. Once again he created the competition, wrote his own rules and then tried like hell to win. He had a new boat built, *Gipsy Moth V*, which was even bigger than *Gipsy Moth IV* and very much easier to sail. He set himself the challenge of sailing 4,000 miles in twenty days, to average 200 miles a day – this in his seventieth year. He didn't quite make it, taking twenty-two and three-tenths days for the run. On the way back across the Atlantic he was hit by a storm as ferocious as any he had encountered in the Southern Ocean; his boat capsized but recovered, and he was able to sail her back to port.

But by now his health was beginning to fail; he was a sick man but, still refusing to give up, he entered for the 1972 trans-Atlantic single-handed race. His agent, George Greenfield, described how at the start he was so weak he could barely climb down a ten-foot ladder from the wharf to his boat. He set sail all the same, in considerable pain, heavily dosed with pain-killing drugs. A short way out into the Atlantic he was involved in a collision with a French weather ship that had come in too close. It is not clear what their intentions had been, whether to give him help or whether just out of curiosity, but the collision broke *Gipsy Moth*'s mast and damaged the hull. There was no question of being able to continue the race. His son, Giles, and friend and editor of many of his books, John Anderson, were flown out by Royal Naval helicopter to help him and Giles, with a Royal Naval crew, sailed the boat back to Plymouth.

Chichester went straight into hospital and died shortly afterwards from cancer. His prayer – at least in part – had been answered: 'From death before we are ready to die, good Lord deliver us.'

Few people can have led such a full life.

Blue sky but not much wind.

Bowling home in the North-East Trades.

Golden Globe

Robin Knox-Johnston, first officer of the passenger liner *Kenya* berthed at London, watched the arrival of Francis Chichester on television and immediately began to wonder whether it would be possible to sail round the world without a single stop.

He analysed his motives for me.

In a way, it's relatively simple. One: I think there are so few things to do in this world and so many people, that it is rather nice to turn round and say you're the first to do something. Two: I was happy in the Merchant Navy but in some ways frustrated by the fact that while in South Africa I had very briefly commanded a ship and I realised that this would be my future for the next thirty-five years; I also wondered whether it offered enough. I thought I'd get terribly bored. Just looking at my peers, I could see that they were fat and getting fatter, that the job didn't require an awful lot of them and I thought that life should offer more. And thirdly, I heard that Tabarly was building a new trimaran, *Pen Duick IV*, which I thought he must be planning to use to beat Chichester's time round the world. At the time the French were being very arrogant, trying to keep us out of the Common Market, and then when Tabarly had just won the single-handed trans-Atlantic race *Paris Match* had screamed that the Anglo-Saxon Ocean had been dominated by the French and that we weren't even a second-rate power – we were third-rate.

That annoyed me intensely and I felt that if anyone was going to do it, it should be one of us because we wouldn't make the fuss that they would about it.

And so, with a desire to make his mark and get out of a career which was not entirely satisfactory – motives very similar to those expressed by Ridgway – combined with a strong, even aggressive sense of patriotism, Knox-Johnston resolved to sail single-handed around the world.

He had always loved the sea, building his first boat, a raft made from orange boxes, at the age of seven. This sank the moment he climbed onto it. He was the eldest of a family of four boys and one girl; his father worked in a shipping office before the war and took an active part in local government, becoming mayor of Beckenham. They were a typical well-to-do suburban family with all the boys going to public school.

Knox-Johnston, almost from the very beginning, wanted to go to sea. The Royal Navy was his first choice but he failed the physics paper in the entrance exam for Dartmouth, could not bring himself to sit again and therefore opted for the Merchant Navy, joining the British India Steam Navigation Company's cadet ship *Chindwara* as an officer cadet. The cadets worked the ship as seamen and, at the same time, received the theoretical and technical training they were going to need as Merchant Navy officers. It gave Knox-Johnston the basic grounding that was going to be so useful to him as a lone sailor. Whereas Ridgway had found the life of a cadet on a merchant ship both lonely and frustrating, Knox-Johnston loved it. He was also a boxer, very fast and probably more aggressive than Ridgway; he was a winner, rather than a good loser. A vast fund of restless, exuberant energy led him into running races up Table Mountain, scuba diving and playing in a ship-board group which was very popular at all the ports of call, particularly in South Africa.

He met Sue in England and they married on completion of his cadetship before going out to Bombay where he was to be based for the next four years, running pilgrims and cargo to the Persian Gulf. He thoroughly enjoyed his work as third officer and filled his leisure time swimming and scuba diving in the clear seas of the Gulf. He even thought of building a dhow, but was dissuaded because it would have been very difficult to sell; finally he decided to go in with a fellow-officer to build an ocean-going family cruiser that they could use both as a base for skin diving and to sail back to England. They wrote off to a firm in Poole, Dorset, for a set of plans and, though the design was old-fashioned, Knox-Johnston liked the look of it; it was obviously very robust. He also had good materials to work with, for Indian teak, one of the finest boat materials known, was readily available. Rigging plans had not been included; these were an extra, so Knox-Johnston, with characteristic ingenuity, designed his own. The boat was built by Indian craftsmen using the traditional tools and methods with which the old eighteenth-century ships of the line had been built. Knox-Johnston named her *Suhaili*, the name given by Arab seamen in the Persian Gulf to the south-east wind.

She was not a modern-looking, streamlined boat; her jib boom, broad beam and the square cut raised cabin gave her a homely, old-fashioned but very durable appearance. She was not finished until September, 1965, too late for the North-East Monsoon which would have driven her across the Indian Ocean to the coast of Africa. Knox-Johnston had to return to Britain anyway, to sit the examination for his Master's Ticket and fulfil his Royal Naval Reserve service. In addition, his personal life was a mess; his marriage had broken up and his wife had returned to Britain. It was not until the following year that he, his brother and a friend returned to Bombay and sailed *Suhaili* back, with a long stop in South Africa where they all took on jobs to replenish funds. He sailed non-stop from Cape Town to Gravesend, thus confirming *Suhaili*'s seaworthiness and also the excellence of her balance. *Suhaili* could be sailed for long periods close hauled with very little attention.

Knox-Johnston was not a yachting man, had done practically no racing and comparatively little messing about in small boats, but he was a professional seaman who, through his down-to-earth apprenticeship, knew every aspect of the job at sea in a way that he would not have had he gone to Dartmouth and risen up through the ranks of the Royal Navy. His long-distance sail from Bombay to London had also given him the kind of practical experience that he was going to need to get round the world. Even so, having decided to try a non-stop single-handed circumnavigation, he found it difficult, as a completely unknown Merchant Navy officer, to convince potential sponsors.

Ideally he wanted a new and bigger boat made from steel, but to pay for it he needed £5,000. He tried to sell *Suhaili* but there were no buyers; she was, perhaps, too old-fashioned in appearance. He wrote over fifty letters to various firms asking for sponsorship but without success. He even applied to his own company for support but, although they had a warm respect for his ability and sympathy for the project, the board refused, telling him that times were hard. Knox-Johnston would not give in, however, and resolved to attempt his circumnavigation in *Suhaili*. At least he knew all her foibles and she had even touched the Roaring Forties around the Cape of Good Hope.

Suhaili was not a modern streamlined boat but she was eminently seaworthy and well balanced, and after sailing her home from the Indian Ocean Robin Knox-Johnston knew all her foibles. This photograph is remarkable in that he took it himself in mid-ocean during the Golden Globe circumnavigation.

Commander Bill King had Galway Blazer II *specially designed and built for the race and was one of the favourites at the start.*

Knox-Johnston was not the only person to be inspired by Chichester's achievement. By the end of 1967 at least five sailors were planning the voyage. The most advanced in his plans was Commander Bill King, an ex-submarine skipper with plenty of good contacts in the ocean-racing world. He already had sponsorship from the *Daily* and *Sunday Express* and in close consultation with Blondie Hasler, the Daddy of the trans-Atlantic solo races and pioneer of self-steering gear, was having built a specially-designed boat with a streamlined deck surface and revolutionary junk rig. The two masts were self-supporting without any stays, with a single big square sail to each. This makes it easier to sail single-handed, but imposes a great deal of strain on the mast. At this stage King undoubtedly seemed to be one of the favourites.

But the most serious contender was Bernard Moitessier, a lean almost frail looking man of forty-three, with the gaunt features of an ascetic which were lightened by a warm smile betraying an impish sense of humour. Born in Saigon, he had spent all his early years in the Far East, most of them at sea in small sailing boats, at first traditional cargo-carrying junks and later in boats he had built himself, wandering, a vagabond of the sea, across the Pacific and Indian Oceans. Having sailed with his wife from Tahiti to the coast of Portugal, a voyage of 14,212 miles, he already held the long distance record for small boats. He was not obsessively competitive in the way that Chichester was. Moitessier was a romantic adventurer who loved the sea with an intense, almost mystical passion. It was the thought of committing himself and his boat to this gigantic voyage of over 30,000 miles, to be alone in the oceans with the wind and the restless sea, that attracted him more than the idea of establishing a record. Publicity was a painful means of getting the money he needed for the voyage. Like Knox-Johnston, he was planning to use his own, well-tried boat, but *Joshua*, named after Joshua Slocum, was eminently better suited to the voyage than *Suhaili*; she was bigger, had a welded steel hull, which Knox-Johnston had wanted, and was built for both speed and strength.

John Ridgway had no trouble in getting sponsorship. Now he was a celebrity, a name that the press could recognise, that manufacturers could use to promote their products. Originally he had intended to enter the 1968 Atlantic single-handed race and had been promised a boat for this; with Chichester's successful circumnavigation, he changed his mind, but for a time used the single-handed race as a cover to keep his own plans secret. He did confide in Chay Blyth, however, never thinking that his one-time partner might become a competitor. Blyth's spirit of competition was immediately kindled when he heard that Ridgway was entering the Atlantic single-handed race. He told me: 'For Christ's sake, knowing John as I did then, if he could do this thing, there was absolutely no way in the world that I could not.' This sense of competition was probably kindled by the stress that had already entered their relationship with Ridgway getting the lion's share of attention after their rowing the Atlantic. At this stage Blyth did not have a boat, had never sailed before and knew nothing of navigation, but with the same dogged but practical determination that he had rowed the Atlantic, he started preparing for the voyage, getting the loan of a production model thirty-foot family cruiser *Dytiscus III* and then, when he learned that Ridgway had changed his objective to a solo circumnavigation, he did so as well. Ridgway felt a great sense of betrayal, partly because he thought Blyth should have told him earlier, but also there seems to have been a feeling that Blyth had broken a partnership – even though Ridgway was doing this equally on his own account.

Donald Crowhurst, who had been so scathing about Chichester's reception, had also entered the lists. He was a keen weekend sailor and had his own boat, certainly

If he had been a competitor rather than a romantic adventurer, Bernard Moitessier could have surely won the race for the fastest time. But for him the purity of solitude in the vast oceans was more important than breaking records.

was more experienced than Chay Blyth, but he had never exposed himself to the
levels of risk and hardship that Blyth had known both on the Atlantic and in the
course of his work in the Parachute Regiment. Crowhurst was thirty-five, happily
married and the father of four young children. He was born in India where his father
had worked on the railways, but they returned to Britain at the time of Independence, when the family went through the painful process of transition faced by so
many ex-colonial families. Donald Crowhurst was doing moderately well at Loughborough College when he was forced to leave after getting his school certificate, his
father having died of a heart attack and his mother being desperately hard-up. He
joined the RAF and continued his studies in electrical engineering at Farnborough
Technical College, eventually learning to fly and getting a commission. The story
could have been the same as that of Ridgway – or, for that matter, myself – but in
Crowhurst there was always a need to be the centre of attention, to seem to be the
daring leader of practical jokes, of wild pranks, racing round in souped-up cars (he
owned a Lagonda for a time, until he smashed it). The adventure was superficial, of
the bar-room variety. One of his pranks led to him being asked to leave the RAF, so
he went into the Army, was commissioned, but continued to lead the same sort of
life, lost his licence for a variety of driving offences and was finally caught trying to
borrow someone's car without their permission. This led to the resignation of his
commission.

Shortly after this he met Clare, an attractive dark-haired Irish girl who was
captivated by his whirlwind courtship and mercurial personality. They got married
and, after a number of unsatisfactory jobs in electronics, settled in Bridgwater,
Somerset, where he set up in business manufacturing electronic aids for yachts on
the South Devon coast. He had excellent ideas, but was less adept at putting them

*John Ridgway had intended
entering for the 1968 Atlantic
single-handed race, but changed
his mind after Francis Chichester's
successful circumnavigation
had thrown down the gauntlet,
even though* English Rose IV
*was not entirely suited to
the longer voyage.*

through and by 1967 his small company, Electron Utilisation, was very nearly bankrupt. The challenge of sailing round the world, therefore, was immensely attractive on several levels. He enjoyed pottering about in his boat; still more, he loved the grand gesture, the boast of out-sailing Chichester round the world; also, it seemed to present a wonderful solution to the vexing and dreary problems besetting him in his business. Once he had been round the world there would be plenty of acclaim and money; people really would sit up and take notice. At the time it appeared to be an attractive way out of all his tribulations.

But at the moment he was unknown and had a packet of debts. His first idea was to approach the Cutty Sark Trust, who were planning to put *Gipsy Moth IV* on permanent display alongside the famous clipper *Cutty Sark* at Greenwich. Crowhurst suggested that it was a waste of a good boat to mount it in concrete, when she could be immortalised still further by a non-stop circumnavigation of the world, and he offered to charter her for a fee of £5,000. He bombarded the Trust with letters, approached Lord Dulverton, the owner, and when he proved unresponsive lobbied through the yachting press, getting a great deal of support for his request; but the Trust remained adamant and he did not get the boat. Chichester was consulted at this stage and made some enquiries about Crowhurst's sailing background, quickly discovering that he had no real ocean-sailing experience and was little more than a competent off-shore yachtsman. Crowhurst was undeterred, however, and continued to seek a boat and sponsorship.

Donald Crowhurst – winning would solve everything.

The idea of sailing around the world non-stop had been a natural evolution inspired by Chichester's voyage, but perhaps it was inevitable that, once it became obvious that several sailors wanted to make the voyage, someone should try to turn it into a race. Robin Knox-Johnston, through his agent, George Greenfield, who also represented Francis Chichester, had approached the *Sunday Times* for sponsorship for the voyage. The editor, Harold Evans, stalled in giving a reply, having already heard that Knox-Johnston was not the only one planning to make the attempt. Murray Sayle, a swashbuckling Australian journalist who had handled the Chichester story for the *Sunday Times*, was told to have a look at the field and report back on who was most likely to succeed. He came up with 'Tahiti Bill' Howell, Australian dentist with a good ocean-racing record who was planning to enter the *Observer* single-handed Atlantic race and then continue round the world. In the event, he abandoned the round-the-world project. Of all the contestants Sayle dismissed Knox-Johnston with his slow old boat, his down-to-earth modest manner and lack of sailing experience as the least likely to win.

It was at this stage that the *Sunday Times* decided to declare it a race, thus ensuring that, as race organisers, they would automatically get good coverage of all the contestants whether or not they had bought their exclusive stories. Their main worry was that the sailors who had already made their plans, and in some cases were sponsored by rival newspapers, might not want to play the *Sunday Times'* game. Features editor, Ron Hall, and Murray Sayle found an ingenious solution to the problem. For a start they did not require a formal entry into the race, merely laying down that departure and return should be recorded – as it inevitably would be – by a national newspaper or magazine. Boats could, therefore, set out from where and when they liked. But because it was felt dangerous to encourage anyone to arrive in the Southern Ocean before the end of the Southern winter, or not to be past Cape Horn before the beginning of the following winter, starting dates were restricted to between the 1st June and 31st October 1968. Obviously, the boats which set out earliest would have the best chance of getting round first, even though they might not make it in the fastest time. It was decided, therefore, to have two prizes – a trophy which was to be the Golden Globe, for the first round, and a cash prize of £5,000 for the fastest time. This would also have the attraction of extending interest in the race even after the first entrant had got home.

In the event, all the sailors tacitly accepted the race, though some were more influenced than others by the rules imposed by the race organisers. It raises the question of where adventure ends and organised competition takes over, of whether the quality of the experience was enhanced by the introduction of a formal race, admittedly with a very loose set of rules. There had been an element of a race already, since each person setting out to sail round the world non-stop wanted to be the first to do it. The situation is similar, in mountaineering terms, to the desire of climbers to be the first to achieve a particularly difficult climb. The media delighted in describing the race as 'the Mount Everest of sailing'. In the field of mountaineering, however, a direct race for the summit is barely practicable and, anyway, in expedition terms the Himalayan countries do not allow more than one expedition on any one route up a mountain at the same time. The situation can arise, however. In 1963 I was a member of a team that made the first ascent of the Central Tower of Paine, a granite tower in South Patagonia. After we had been there for about two months, having made very little progress, an Italian team who had the same objective arrived at the foot of the mountain. What evolved was undeniably a race to get to the top first which I am glad to say we won.

There is, however, a long tradition of ocean racing, and there was certainly every

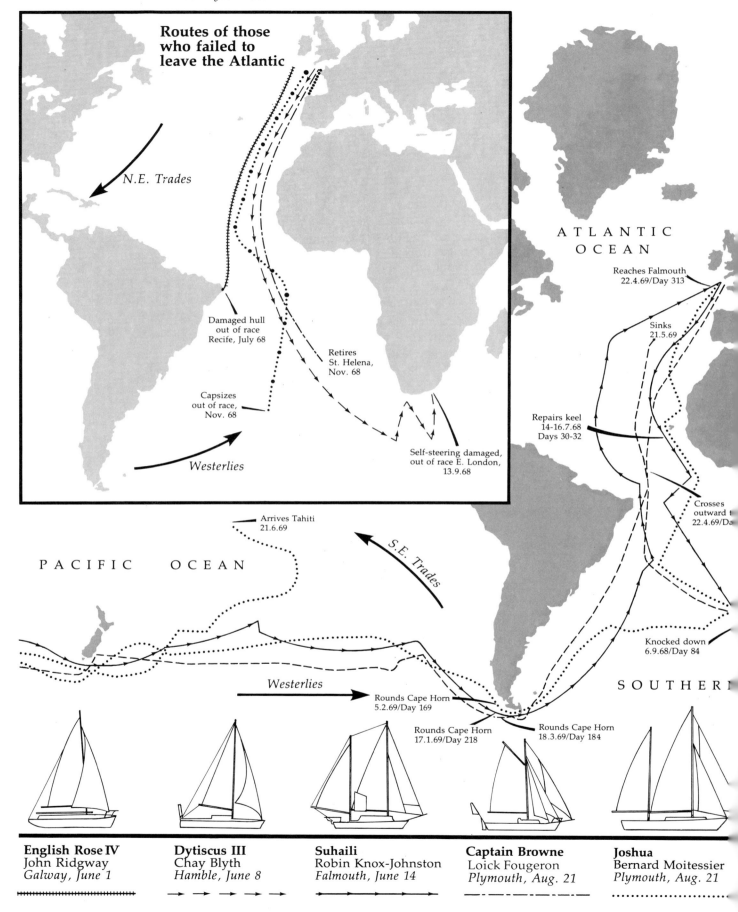

Routes of those who failed to leave the Atlantic

N.E. Trades

ATLANTIC OCEAN

Reaches Falmouth
22.4.69/Day 313

Sinks
21.5.69

Repairs keel
14-16.7.68
Days 30-32

Crosses
outward t
22.4.69/Da

Damaged hull
out of race
Recife, July 68

Retires
St. Helena,
Nov. 68

Capsizes
out of race,
Nov. 68

Self-steering damaged,
out of race E. London,
13.9.68

Westerlies

Arrives Tahiti
21.6.69

S.E. Trades

PACIFIC   OCEAN

Knocked down
6.9.68/Day 84

Westerlies

Rounds Cape Horn
5.2.69/Day 169

Rounds Cape Horn
17.1.69/Day 218

Rounds Cape Horn
18.3.69/Day 184

SOUTHER

English Rose IV	**Dytiscus III**	**Suhaili**	**Captain Browne**	**Joshua**
John Ridgway	Chay Blyth	Robin Knox-Johnston	Loick Fougeron	Bernard Moitessier
Galway, June 1	*Hamble, June 8*	*Falmouth, June 14*	*Plymouth, Aug. 21*	*Plymouth, Aug. 21*

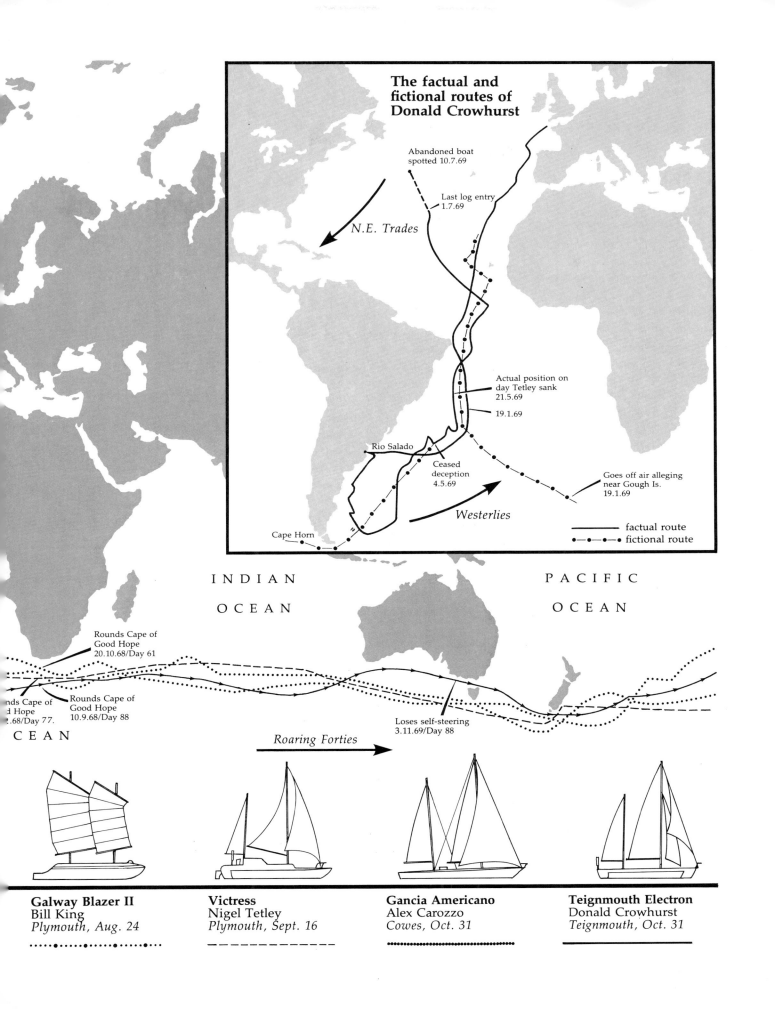

The factual and fictional routes of Donald Crowhurst

Abandoned boat spotted 10.7.69

Last log entry 1.7.69

N.E. Trades

Actual position on day Tetley sank 21.5.69

19.1.69

Rio Salado

Ceased deception 4.5.69

Goes off air alleging near Gough Is. 19.1.69

Cape Horn

Westerlies

⸺⸺⸺ factual route
•—•—• fictional route

INDIAN OCEAN

PACIFIC OCEAN

Rounds Cape of Good Hope 20.10.68/Day 61

Rounds Cape of Good Hope 10.9.68/Day 88

nds Cape of d Hope .68/Day 77.

OCEAN

Loses self-steering 3.11.69/Day 88

Roaring Forties

Galway Blazer II
Bill King
Plymouth, Aug. 24

Victress
Nigel Tetley
Plymouth, Sept. 16

Gancia Americano
Alex Carozzo
Cowes, Oct. 31

Teignmouth Electron
Donald Crowhurst
Teignmouth, Oct. 31

ingredient of adventure in an attempt to sail single-handed non-stop round the world. The element of racing would add still further stress, for each man would need to push his boat to the utmost, yet if he pushed too hard the boat might not last the course. The test was to prove a harsh one.

First off the mark was John Ridgway, in *English Rose IV*. For sentimental reasons he wanted to start from the Aran Islands, his landfall when he rowed the Atlantic. He set out on the earliest date possible, the 1st June, acutely aware that his thirty-foot sloop would need all the time he could get to beat the bigger boats which were to set out later on in the summer. Things went wrong right from the start. Both the BBC and ITN had sent out camera crews to film his departure. The BBC launch very nearly crashed into his stern, threatening the vital self-steering gear. Ridgway, nerves stretched anyway, screamed abuse at them and they veered off, but then the trawler carrying the ITN crew swung in close to get a final telling shot, misjudged it and smashed into the starboard side, splintering the wooden rubbing strip that protected the hull itself. It was impossible to see if there was any structural damage, but Ridgway had a terrible feeling of ill-omen waving for the last time to his wife, Marie Christine, as the trawler swung away.

Chay Blyth had sent Ridgway a telegram 'LAST ONE HOME'S A CISSY. WHO CARES WHO WINS?' It was a conciliatory gesture, but both knew that they cared very much who got home first. Blyth set sail a week later on *Dytiscus III*. He had tried for sponsorship but his lack of sailing experience stood against him.

'They always brought in some retired naval officer,' he told me, 'and then asked very intricate questions about navigation and, of course, I had no idea at all. They'd then ask intricate questions about sailing and I wouldn't know the answers to those either. The interviews always came to an abrupt halt.'

But he had persevered, using most of the profits from his row across the Atlantic to finance the voyage. He learnt navigation at night and had a fortnight's sailing instruction, though he reckoned that in the end it amounted to little more than four days' actual practical experience. His replies to the queries of reporters about his motives and attitudes were down-to-earth:

'Out there it's all black and white. I'm not particularly fond of the sea, it's just a question of survival. I may come back as queer as a nine-bob note. But one day Saint Peter will say to me, "What did you do?" and I'll tell him. He'll say, "What did you do?" and you'll say, "I was a reporter."'

But he set out full of confidence, certain that he could beat at least one man – his old mate Ridgway.

Six days later Robin Knox-Johnston set sail from Falmouth in *Suhaili*. His little group of sponsors from the *Sunday Mirror* and, publishers, Cassell, had come down to see him off. They had become a close-knit team, very confident in their man, Knox-Johnston, who had submitted to a going-over by a psychiatrist and been judged 'distressingly normal'. He was sure that even though his boat was not fast enough to make the quickest circumnavigation he would most certainly get round. He also displayed a healthy aggressiveness when, irritated by a *Sunday Times* reporter, he threatened to throw him into the harbour. It is unlikely that Knox-Johnston would have allowed any of the media's boats to get close enough to collide with him as he sailed for the line outside Falmouth harbour.

It would be over two months before anyone else set sail, but these three contestants needed all the time they could get if they were to stay ahead of the bigger and faster boats that were to set out later on in the season. They settled down in their different ways to the long run in down the Atlantic which provides the introduction to the rigours of the Southern Ocean.

John Ridgway found the solitude difficult to cope with, becoming almost obsessively worried about the damage done in the collision at the start.

> I found myself far too tense after a day in the cabin; only active physical work on deck could ease the tension . . . My problem was that after the collision it was as if I had a kind of mental bruise, which I forced myself to ignore. The result was that I just could not relax and recharge myself; somehow I felt off-balance.

As the days rolled by and Ridgway sailed down past Madeira, where he had a rendezvous with a reporter from the *People* Sunday newspaper, and then on down over the Equator into the Southern Atlantic, he found the stress of solitary sailing no easier to bear. Each crisis took its toll. Caught in a squall, he wrote:

> A bitter struggle began on the foredeck as I fought to recover both sails; the wind shrieked with glee. In the end it was down and I crept below and burst into tears; for some reason I could not shake off the emotional strain of the loneliness. I noted that I had cried at some point on each of the twenty-seven consecutive days. Something surely must be wrong – I was just unable to relax.

He kept going all the same, down through the oily seas of the Doldrums, into the South-East Trades that he would have to fight his way against on the 1,500-mile run to the Cape of Good Hope. The boat slammed into the South Atlantic swell, juddering with the impact of each wave. Ridgway had already noticed some hairline cracks in the deck around the after shroud plate, which held one of the stays; but now the deck around it was bulging while the cracks opened and closed, bubbling spray. If it should pull away, the mast would probably go as well; not a pleasant prospect in the empty reaches of the Southern Atlantic. Even more serious, his wireless transmitter had failed so that there was no chance of calling for help. He did his best to repair the damage, replacing and strengthening the plate, but the deck continued to bulge ominously and the prospects of entering the Southern Ocean with a damaged boat, without wireless communication, became increasingly intimidating.

At last, on the 16th July, some 600 miles south of the Equator, Ridgway admitted defeat and swung westward for Recife, on the Brazilian coast, overwhelmed with a profound sense of failure. He wrote in his log: 'I don't think I have ever given up in my life before. Now I feel debased and worthless. The future looks empty and, and, I won't write anymore, there must be something to fill this vacuum.'

There was. On his return to England he plunged into plans to start his adventure school at Ardmore. Ridgway, who is very honest with himself, told me, 'I don't think I'd have got round the world anyway, not with that boat and probably not with myself at the time, I don't think I was sure enough of myself.' To admit that, in some ways, needs more courage than just trying to press on.

Chay Blyth got further than Ridgway, sailing *Dytiscus III* into the great Southern Ocean round the Cape of Good Hope, but on the way down his self-steering gear was damaged and in order to radio South Africa for spare parts to be sent out from England, he took on some fuel for his generator from a yacht, *Gillian Gaggins*, which he passed near Tristan da Cunha. He reached East London, on the South African coast, on the 13th September, to be told that he was disqualified from the race. He replied, 'I don't see how the *Sunday Times* can disqualify me when I never entered the race.' He was determined to go on and, having repaired his self-steering gear, set out into the Southern Ocean.

Quite apart from lacking experience, his boat was not suitable for the huge seas he encountered. He told me:

The boat was similar to John's in that she had a bilge keel but mine was much more buoyant in the stern; she was fine until we reached the Roaring Forties. What used to happen was that the buoyancy would lift the arse end up and so she'd go down a wave and start burying her nose. Two things can then happen; you can either pitchpole, which means the boat does a somersault, or you can broach, which means the boat swings ninety degrees to the on-coming wave and is then pushed along sideways and can go right over so that it capsizes. At least with a monohull you always come up again since there is so much weight underneath you.

Chichester talks about being capsized once; well, I was absolutely hopeless really, hadn't a bloody clue. I capsized three times in one hour and eleven times in a day. And I thought this was part and parcel of sailing – I really did! The boat would go BANG and you'd get thrown all over the place; kit would go everywhere and I'd say, 'Geez, that was pretty tough', and then you'd get up. The steering gear went again and then I thought, 'You've got to make a decision.' And the decision to pack it in is always much worse – I think it's easier to die really. The decision to pack up is bloody terrible.

Chay Blyth swung back to East London, the second competitor to fail.

By this time Robin Knox-Johnston, in *Suhaili*, had caught up and passed Blyth. His trip down the Atlantic had been full of event, some of which might easily have forced him out of the race. On his sixteenth day out from Falmouth, on the 30th June, he noticed that *Suhaili* was taking in much more water than she should. He got past the Cape Verde Islands, then donned snorkel and flippers and went over the side to discover exactly what was wrong. He found a frightening gap, about two and a half metres long, along the seam where the keel was joined on to the hull; it opened and closed as *Suhaili* pitched and rolled in the water. It was easy to imagine what would happen in the ferocious seas of the Southern Ocean.

He swam back to the surface, lit a cigarette and thought out a problem that I suspect would have defeated most of the contestants in the Golden Globe race. He described his repairs in his book, *A World of my Own*.

Having decided that caulking was the answer, I had to think of some way of doing it five feet below water. Normally dry twisted raw cotton is hammered into the seam, stopped with filling compound and painted over, but I could not do that. I decided to try and do the job with cotton anyway and hope that the fact that it would be wet would not make too much difference. We had had to do just the same thing when in the middle of the Arabian Sea, but it had not been easy, and at least I had had two other people helping me and keeping a lookout for sharks. This time I would have to do the job on my own and hope that I would notice any sharks whilst they were still circling.

I got out the cotton and twisted up some pieces in 18-inch lengths, a convenient length to handle although ideally I should have done the job with one piece. Next I put a long length of line on a hammer and lowered it overside near where I had to work. Finally I dressed myself in a blue shirt and jeans to hide the whiteness of my body, something that sharks, great scavengers, always associate with refuse, and strapped my knife to my leg. I put the cotton on deck where I could reach it from the water and taking my largest screwdriver as the most convenient caulking instrument, I went overside.

The job was impossible from the start. In the first place I would run out of breath before I had hammered enough cotton in place to hold it whilst I surfaced, and each time I came up for air I lost all the work done. Secondly, the cotton was just not going in properly, and even when I changed the screwdriver for a proper caulking iron I made no progress. After half an hour of fruitless effort I climbed back on board and tried to think of some other way of doing the job.

A while later I was busily engaged in sewing the cotton onto a strip of canvas 1½ inches wide. When the whole strip, about seven feet of it, was completed I gave it a coating of Stockholm Tar and then forced copper tacks through the canvas about six inches apart. I went into the water again and placed the cotton in the seam so that the canvas was on the outside: I then started knocking the tacks into the hull to hold the whole thing in place. The finished job did not look too bad but it was a bit ragged at the edges and I thought that it

Suhaili *fights it out.*
Every lone sailor venturing
into the Southern Ocean has his
boat knocked down sooner or later.

might be ripped off when the *Suhaili* got moving again, so I decided to tack a copper strip over the canvas to tidy it up. The copper strip was, in fact, left on board by the Marconi engineers when they fitted the new radio, and I am afraid that I had not drawn their attention to it when they finished.

So far, although I had kept glancing nervously about me whilst I was in the water, I had seen no fish at all. But whilst I was having a coffee break, having prepared the copper strip and made holes for the tacks so that I would have an easier job under water, I suddenly noticed a lean grey shape moving sinuously past the boat. The sharks had found us at last. I watched this one for ten minutes hoping it would go away as I did not want to have to kill it. I was not being kind to the shark; if I killed it, there would be quite a lot of blood in the water and the death convulsions would be picked up by any other sharks near at hand who would immediately rush in, and I would not be able to get the job finished. After ten minutes though, during which the shark kept circling the boat and showing no signs of leaving, I got out my rifle and, throwing some sheets of lavatory paper into the water, waited for the shark to come and investigate. On its first run round the shark passed about three feet below the paper, but then he turned and, rising slowly, came in again. I aimed the rifle at the shape and, with finger on the trigger, followed it as it came in. Three feet short of the paper the top of the head broke surface and I squeezed the trigger. There was an explosion in the water as the shark's body threshed around but within half a minute the threshing ceased and the lifeless body began slowly to plane down until it disappeared into the blue. For the next half hour I watched carefully to see if any other sharks would appear, but apart from two pilot fish, which, having followed their previous protector down until they realised he would never feed them again, now decided to join a larger and apparently stronger master, *Suhaili* and I had the sea to ourselves. I went overside and in an hour and a half had the copper tacked over the canvas on the port side. A light wind getting up forced me to leave the starboard side until we were next becalmed. But in any case I was quite chilled from four hours' immersion, and also a little tense from constantly glancing around expecting to see a shark coming in behind me, and I was quite glad to give the job a rest for a while.

Two days later he caulked the other side. Throughout the voyage down the Atlantic he went swimming, showing a confidence and knowledge of the sea that was to help him throughout the trip. He would dive in off the bow and swim as hard as he could, as the boat pulled ahead of him and then, in the nick of time, pull himself up on the stern stanchions. It took fine calculation not to be left alone in the middle of the ocean.

There were other crises. His battery-charging motor failed and he took the magneto to pieces, trying to find the fault. It was only when he came to re-assemble the engine that he realised he had forgotten to bring a feeler gauge for setting the gap between the points. 'I eventually got round this by counting the pages of this book – there are two hundred to the inch, therefore one page equals 5/thousandths. I wanted a gap of between 12–15/1000, thus three thicknesses of paper.' And the charging motor worked again.

But there were moments of doubt, when he was tempted to abandon the voyage at Cape Town. He describes his feelings:

This, I think, was the second period of my adjustment. When I had got over the initial problems and doubts, a short period of acceptance of the new environment arrived. This was followed by a second, longer stage of deeper and more serious doubts. Surviving this, I had my second wind, and was able to settle down to things. I got through it by forcing myself to do some mental as well as physical work. For example, I began to write out a description of the Admiral [his self-steering gear, devised by himself]. The self-steering seemed simple enough, but trying to write out a description was far from easy. Anyway, the effort took me out of my depression.

Almost every sailor venturing into the Southern Ocean has his boat knocked down sooner or later; it happened to Knox-Johnston almost immediately, just three days after getting down into the Roaring Forties. His description of the event, like that of all his fellow solitary sailors, was amazingly matter-of-fact.

It was the evening of the 5th September. The wind had changed during the day, blowing with increasing strength from the west, quickly building up the waves to meet the old seas created by the early wind direction. It was a conflict of waves that created a savage cross sea, with waves coming in from every direction. As night fell, Knox-Johnston reefed the mainsail down and left the boat under the tiny storm jib, which drove her along, under the guidance of the Admiral. He lay on his bunk, fully dressed, his damp waterproofs still on, with just a sheet of canvas to cover him. At last he dropped off to sleep, lulled by the roaring of the wind in the rigging and the crash of waves against the hull.

He was woken cruelly in the pitch dark, as heavy objects crashed down upon him and he became aware that the boat was lying on its side. He struggled to get out of the bunk but was pinned, as if in a strait-jacket, by the canvas sheet weighed down with the debris hurled upon him. Just as he struggled from under it, the boat heaved itself upright, throwing him across the cabin in the opaque darkness. Picking himself up, he fumbled for the hatch leading out onto the deck, dreading what he was going to find, convinced that the mast had been carried away when the boat lunged back up again against the immense clinging force of the sea. He pulled the hatch open, pushed his head out into the darkness through the wind-driven spume and could just discern the mast and boom; he could hardly believe that they were still there.

The boat was bucking like a wild stallion in the cross seas; he could see the angry gleam of the foam against the dark of the night but could barely discern the deck on which he was standing. He never used a safety harness, feeling that it restricted free movement. As he hauled himself from stay to stay, up the tossing deck, he felt every piece of rigging to make sure it was in place and got half-way up to the bow when another huge wave smashed into the boat, covering him, lifting him off his feet; all he could do was to cling on to the rigging as the roaring black waters tried to tear away his grasp. Once the freak wave had swept on its way he struggled back to the cockpit and adjusted the self-steering; he could not see in the dark whether or not it had been damaged and climbed back down into the shambles of the cabin, which was ankle-deep in water, with tins and packets of food, books, articles of clothing sloshing around in it.

The first priority was obviously to reduce the water level. He was reassured by the familiar effort and motion of pumping out the bilges; the adrenalin generated in the last few moments began to settle. Once he had pumped out most of the water he started to tidy up the appalling mess of soaked food, clothing and equipment. It was while doing this that he noticed a torrent of water pouring down from the side of the coach roof, where it joined the deck of the boat. On closer inspection, he was horrified to find that there were cracks all the way round, that the huge impact of the waves was slowly tearing the coach roof from the deck, with the frightening prospect of leaving a gaping hole nearly four metres by two for the waves to thunder into. If this happened there was no way he could have saved the boat from foundering. There was nothing he could do in the dark or while the storm was at its height. He could only wait patiently for the wind to drop. The following morning, after a good breakfast while waiting for the seas to quieten down, he went through his stock of tools and spare parts to find some long bolts with which to strengthen the cabin. He spent the rest of the day painstakingly drilling through the hard teak of the deck and cabin sides to reinforce the fastening of the cabin. It was another two days before he could start repairing the self-steering gear, and even then he was completely immersed by the waves on several occasions.

Life was lonely, acutely uncomfortable and very dangerous but, more than that, it stretched out in front of him, as to any solitary sailor, for such a long time – very different from the experience of a mountaineer who, at times, is probably under greater risk but over much shorter periods of time. An expedition rarely lasts more than two or three months, of which the climb above the relative comfort of Base Camp is measured in weeks at the very most.

On the 9th September, still just short of the Cape of Good Hope, Knox-Johnston summed it up in his log:

> I have bruises all over from being thrown about. My skin itches from constant chafing with wet clothes and I forget when I last had a proper wash so I feel dirty. I feel altogether mentally and physically exhausted and I've been in the Southern Ocean only a week. It seems years since I gybed to turn east and yet it was only last Tuesday night, not six days, and I have another 150 days of it yet. . . . Why couldn't I be satisfied with big ships?
>
> The life may be monotonous but at least one gets into port occasionally which provides some variety. A prisoner at Dartmoor doesn't get hard labour like this; the public wouldn't stand for it and he has company, however uncongenial. In addition he gets dry clothing and undisturbed sleep. I wonder how the crime rate would be affected if people were sentenced to sail around the world alone instead of going to prison. It's ten months solitary confinement with hard labour.

Every adventurer must question his motives when the going gets rough. There was little let-up in the next 150 days, but Knox-Johnston kept going, pushing the boat as hard as he dared because he knew that he could finish the course, but he wanted to do more than that – he wanted to win. Just south of Australia, the self-steering gear finally packed in completely. Once again he thought of giving up. But his natural optimism soon bubbled back. He had come so far, was so far ahead of the field, it would be a pity to give up. He resolved to push on to New Zealand before coming to a decision. His fellow competitors were a long way behind. Moitessier and Loick Fougeron had set out on the 21st August, Bill King three days later. It is interesting to note the way the younger men, all in their twenties, had set out at the earliest possible moment, fully aware that they would be entering the Southern Ocean in the final throes of the Southern winter, while the older men, in their forties and, in Bill King's case, his fifties, had chosen the later departure date which hopefully would give them an easier passage through the Roaring Forties. In addition, Moitessier and King had larger boats, being forty feet long, though Fougeron's thirty-foot cutter was no bigger than those of the younger men. Neither Fougeron nor Moitessier would carry transmitters, wanting, for aesthetic reasons, to sever all links with the land; Fougeron did start, however, with a companion, a wild kitten from Morocco called Roulis. It did not last long, for the kitten made mayhem of his cabin, pirating food and even chewing the plastic covering the wires leading to the aerial of his radio. After a few days he put it aboard a passing ship and returned, with some relief, to a solitary life. He and Moitessier were undoubtedly the most experienced long-distance solitary sailors, but Fougeron did not even reach the Roaring Forties. He was caught by a severe storm, knocked down during the night in much the same way that Robin Knox-Johnston had experienced. Afterwards he wrote:

> I curl up in the cramped bunk and wait for the unbridled sea to win its victory over me. What to do? The boat lunges sideways, driven by a frightful force. I am flattened violently against the side and then in the middle of the bubbling waters everything goes black. A cascade of kitchen materials, books, bottles, tins of jam, everything that isn't secured and in the middle of this song and dance I am projected helter-skelter across the boat. At this moment I believe that it is the end, that the sea will crush me and prevent me ever coming to the surface again.

The distinctive junk rig of Galway Blazer II *was easier for a single-handed sailor to control but had inherent weaknesses.*

The boat recovered and the mast was intact, but Fougeron had had enough; he resolved to head for the nearest port, and called in at St. Helena, abandoning the voyage.

Commander Bill King did get down into the Southern Ocean, but his speed down the Atlantic had been slow. He lacked the ferocious drive that had kept Chichester racing against himself, even when exhausted, and complained in his dispatches of feeling a lack of vitality; but it was the design of his boat that finally forced him out. The junk rig, which made it much easier for a single-handed sailor to control, had inherent weaknesses. The masts were not supported by stays and therefore terrific strains were exerted on the housing. When his boat was knocked down by a wave about a thousand miles south-west of Cape Town, the main mast was twisted by the force of the water, so he had no choice but to return to Cape Town.

This left Bernard Moitessier, who had already gained 2,000 miles on Bill King's *Galway Blazer*, and was undoubtedly going faster than Robin Knox-Johnston. The *Sunday Times* even began to postulate whether Moitessier could catch *Suhaili*, whose progress so far had been steady, but slow. It is extremely unlikely that Moitessier was ever particularly interested in the voyage as a race. He commented just before setting off: 'The people who are thinking about money and of being the fastest round the world will not win. It is the people who care about their skins. I shall bring back my skin, apart from a few bumps on my head.'

He took everything the sea could do to him in his stride, even when a cargo ship, which he had closed with to hand over some mail, collided with him. He simply repaired the damage and sailed on, completely at ease with the sea, happier to be alone in the middle of the ocean than on dry land. In this respect he was different from Knox-Johnston who, though equally a seaman, was not a natural loner. Knox-Johnston was able to adapt to the situation he was in from necessity, because he had to reach his goal of being the first man round the world single-handed; but he looked forward to his return to everyday life.

Moitessier, on the other hand, embraced the experience of being alone on his boat for its own sake. He wrote: 'The days go by, never monotonous. Even when they appear exactly alike they are never quite the same. That is what gives life at sea its special dimension, made up of contemplation and very simple contrasts. Sea, wind, calms, sun, clouds, porpoises. Peace and the joy of being alive in harmony.'

Robin Knox-Johnston was approaching New Zealand as Moitessier sailed down into the Southern Ocean. Having come to terms with the total loss of his self-steering gear, in a short period free from storms Knox-Johnston had refined his system for balancing out the boat so that she would sail herself, both when running under reduced canvas and also when reaching. He had nearly crossed the Tasman Sea and was coming up to Foveaux Strait. Soon he would be in the South Pacific, with the long clear run to Cape Horn before him. He always listened to the weather forecasts from the nearest radio station and, on the evening of the 17th November, at the end of it came another message for the Master of the *Suhaili*: 'Imperative we rendezvous outside Bluff Harbour in daylight – signature Bruce Maxwell.'

Knox-Johnston knew that a cold front with its accompanying storm was on the way, but reckoned he would be able to meet Maxwell, a journalist from the *Sunday Mirror*, before it arrived, hand over his story and, perhaps even more important, actually talk to someone in the flesh – an attractive thought after all the lonely weeks in the Southern Ocean. But the front rolled in faster than he had anticipated. The following evening, just off the Foveaux Strait, force ten winds, heavy rain and poor visibility were forecast; all this and he was being blown onto a lee shore. He made ready the warps that would keep *Suhaili*'s stern pointing into the waves to prevent

Loick Fougeron, like Moitessier, refused to carry a radio transmitter but, after a severe storm, abandoned the race at St. Helena.

her broaching, took a compass bearing on a light he identified as the Centre Island lighthouse and then waited for the storm to strike. He wrote: 'I put the kettle on; it was still quiet outside, although as black as pitch, and I thought of Bruce sitting in a comfortable hotel lounge with a large beer in front of him. Perhaps we'd be drinking together in twenty-four hours. This last thought stuck with me and I had even begun to welcome the idea when it struck me how disloyal I was being to *Suhaili*.'

The clouds rolled in, the rain lashed down, the waves started to race past as he sailed into what he thought was the middle of the strait. He was uncomfortably close to land in this kind of weather and was being driven inexorably closer. Somehow he managed to claw his way round a headland into calmer waters; the immediate danger was over; but he still wanted to make his rendezvous with Maxwell, though he realised that he would not be able to reach Bluff Harbour in those wind conditions, especially as his engine was now completely seized up. He resolved, therefore, to head for Otago harbour, which looked as if it would be more sheltered. He reached it the following day, nosed his way cautiously round the headland and then, to his horror, realised he had run aground. He reacted immediately to the crisis; it was a sandy bottom, so would not damage the boat and, hopefully, when the tide rose again *Suhaili* would float herself off. He dived below for the anchor, grabbed it and leapt into the shallow water, walking along the bottom carrying the thirty-pound anchor. As it got deeper and the water went over his head he jumped up every few paces to get a quick breath of air, until he felt he had gone far enough and was able to dive to the bottom, to dig in flukes. He could now rest assured that the boat would not be driven further up the sand as the tide came in, though he was still faced with the problem of getting her out again. At least it was going to be easy to make his rendezvous. Some boats came out to investigate the lonely yacht, but Knox-Johnston kept them at a distance, refusing all offers of help. He was determined not to break any of the race regulations.

That night, when the tide came in, he was able to haul himself off the sandbank by pulling on the warp attached to the anchor. All he needed to do now was wait for Bruce Maxwell to find him. He arrived the following day, with plenty of news but, to Knox-Johnston's immense disappointment, no mail. Maxwell told him that since Knox-Johnston had set out, the Race Committee had got round to making some rules, one of which was that none of the competitors should be allowed to take anything on board throughout the voyage. Maxwell had read this to include mail. It seemed an extraordinarily petty restriction to Knox-Johnston and, in some ways highlights the artificial nature of the voyage. A mountaineer, in climbing a mountain, has no easy alternative. He must keep going until he reaches the top and, having decided to climb, doing it on foot is probably the easiest, probably the only, feasible way. An Italian expedition raised a certain level of controversy by using a helicopter to help ferry supplies on Everest but, in the event, its payload at altitude was so poor that it was no more effective than muscle power and, in the end, it crashed near the head of the Everest Icefall. A sailor, on the other hand, is choosing to make life difficult for himself, firstly by selecting a sailing vessel rather than an ocean liner to make his journey, and then by denying himself the right to call in at ports on the way or, in this instance, the solace of mail from family and friends.

Even so, Knox-Johnston did get news of his fellow competitors and learned, for the first time, that three more had started – though one of them, Alex Carozzo, was already out of the race and the other two, Lieutenant-Commander Nigel Tetley and Donald Crowhurst, were still in the Atlantic, a long way behind.

Nigel Tetley first heard of the Golden Globe race in March 1968. He was a Lieutenant-Commander in the Royal Navy, based on Plymouth, and was using his

Victress was a production model trimaran, able to achieve speeds of up to twenty-two knots, but unable to right itself if capsized. The Southern Ocean would be its moment of truth.

The cabin of Nigel Tetley's Victress was fitted out with a splendid hi-fi system and tape library.

trimaran, *Victress*, as a floating home for himself and his wife, Evelyn, to whom he had been married for eighteen months. Tetley was forty-five, with two sons, aged sixteen and fourteen, from his first marriage. He was approaching a critical phase of his life; he had had an enjoyable Naval career which had given him command of a frigate, a great deal of exciting and interesting travel and also the leisure to pursue his own hobby of sailing. Having entered *Victress* for the Round Britain race, he had come in a very respectable fifth place. But only a certain number of officers gain promotion to Commander and Tetley had not made it; as a result he was automatically due for retirement at the age of forty-five – a fairly traumatic period in the lives of most Service officers.

One Sunday morning Eve slipped out, a coat over her nightdress, to buy the Sunday papers. When she got back Tetley picked up the *Sunday Times*, leafed through it and then was rivetted by the announcement of the Golden Globe race.

'Round the world non-stop. To solve the problem of perpetual motion. Why had the idea always fascinated me? To sail on and on like the Flying Dutchman. An apt simile even two years back; but the lost soul had since found its mate. A challenge from the past? It was now or never, like one's bluff being called in poker.'

He started to make plans immediately. Ideally, he would like a new boat designed for the rigours of the voyage; he wrote around to all the likely sponsors but, like Knox-Johnston, was turned down. He therefore resigned himself to using his own boat, even though it was an ordinary production model, designed more for family cruising than for solitary circumnavigation. In a trimaran the centre hull holds the living quarters, while the two outer hulls are little more than balancing floats which can be used for storage. Whereas the monohull has a heavy keel which, combined with the boat's ballast, will always bring the boat back upright even in the event of a complete capsize, the trimaran is much more lightly-built and has no keel. The boat is a platform resting on three floats. This design gives it great stability and almost limitless speed, for before the wind it literally surfs on the crest of the waves, achieving speeds of anything up to twenty-two knots –much faster than the speed a monohull could ever achieve. There are snags, however, for should the boat be capsized it will not right itself. The risk was highlighted by the fact that two leading multihull exponents and designers, Hedley Nichol and Arthur Piver, had recently been lost at sea.

Tetley was not deterred by the risk; he was fully committed to multihull sailing and showed an almost evangelistic zeal in his desire to prove the capabilities of his trimaran. Eve, his wife, gave him her total support, devising for him by far the most palatable and, I suspect, nutritious menu of all the sailors. Ridgway had taken, for simplicity's sake, a uniform diet of Army rations; Knox-Johnston's was fairly limited, but Tetley's was a gourmet's delight, with braised kidneys, roast goose and duck, jugged hare, oysters, octopus and Yarmouth bloaters. He also had a good hi-fi system in his cabin and set out with a magnificent tape library. It was very appropriate that he obtained the sponsorship of a record company, Music For Pleasure. The only thing he neglected was books, and he complained on the way round of how limited was his reading matter.

He refitted the boat himself, experienced all the usual crises, but was ready to sail in good order on the 16th September. Good-looking in a clean-cut, rather Naval way, he was excellent company, fitting easily into a group, and yet there was a definite reserve in his character, moulded in part, no doubt, by public school and his Naval career. This reserve is certainly perceptible in his book *Trimaran Solo*, for it reveals very little of his innermost feelings or reservations. The log of his voyage is equally inhibited, tending to cling to the surface of day-to-day sailing problems, accounts of the menu and the daily programme of music.

His achievement, though, was remarkable. Sailing down towards the Southern Ocean he must have been acutely aware of the risk he was taking. His boat was an ordinary production model; the comfortable cabin and raised wheelhouse undoubtedly made her the most comfortable boat going round the world, but they represented potential weaknesses in the structure which could prove fatal. Every solitary sailor has his moments of doubt and Tetley was no exception. The solitude and stress bore heavily upon him. This was reflected in his entry on the 2nd October, seventeen days out:

> Thoughts of packing it in came into my mind for the first time today, brought on I think by too much of my own company. It would be so easy to put into port and say that the boat was not strong enough for the voyage or unsuitable. What was really upsetting me was the psychological effect – of possibly twelve months – this might have. Would I be the same person on return? This aspect I knew worried Eve too. I nearly put through a radio call to talk over the question in guarded terms. Then I realised that though she would straightaway accept the reason and agree to my stopping, say at Cape Town, we would feel that we had let ourselves down both in our own eyes and those of our friends, backers and well-wishers. It was only a touch of the blues due to the yacht's slow progress.

Like Knox-Johnston, he overcame depression by some practical work; in this instance having a hair cut. There is never a shortage of things to do on a long distance voyage; quite apart from sailing the boat, there is a constant round of preventive maintenance on rigging and equipment and, however thorough the sailor may be, wear and tear is relentless. Tetley had an elaborate workshop with an electric drill; a practical man, again like Knox-Johnston, he kept on top of maintenance problems as he nursed his boat down the South Atlantic and into the Southern Ocean where she was to meet her greatest test.

After failing to charter *Gipsy Moth IV*, Donald Crowhurst also decided to go for a trimaran, even though he had never actually sailed one. Since it was obvious that he would not be ready to start before the end of October, the last possible date for entering the race, it was also unlikely he would catch up with the sailors who had started earlier. He would, therefore, have to go for the fastest time if he wanted to achieve distinction, and for that he needed a really fast boat. He decided to have a trimaran built to the same basic design as *Victress*, Tetley's boat, but with a streamlined, strengthened superstructure and a host of electronic aids to increase the boat's safety. All this needed money, though, and it was here that he effected his greatest coup. The most important creditor of his failing business was Stanley Best, a down-to-earth businessman, not easily impressed by romantic ideas. Crowhurst nevertheless succeeded in persuading Best that his surest chance of recovering his investment was to increase this still further and foot the bill for the new boat.

Now he could get started, but it was mid-May – all too little time to build a boat, especially one which was to include all the revolutionary ideas thought up by Crowhurst. It was to have a buoyancy bag hanging from the top of the mast; electronic sensors in the hull would automatically inflate the bag from a compressed air bottle if the boat was blown over. Hopefully this would stop it capsizing. There were many other electronic aids, all to be controlled by a 'computer' installed in the cabin. Crowhurst's ideas were certainly original and might have worked; unfortunately, however, he lacked both the time and also the temperament to put them into effect. He was rushing about constantly, between the boat-builders, his own home in Bridgwater and around the country chasing all the loose ends, drumming up further sponsorship and talking to the press. He had all too many bright ideas, but seemed unable to carry them through to the end and often ignored the less exciting, but essential, minor details. As a result of this and the inevitable teething troubles suffered during any form of boat construction, everything slid behind schedule. October 30th came all too quickly and Crowhurst was barely ready. The interior of the cabin was a mess of unconnected wires; there was no compressed air bottle to feed the unsightly flotation bag which hung from the masthead. More serious still, several short cuts had been taken in the construction of the boat which undoubtedly affected her seaworthiness. A team of friends helped him to get everything ready in time to beat the deadline, but it was chaotic. Crowhurst did not seem able to co-ordinate their efforts, was prey to too many conflicting demands – not least those of his energetic press agent, Rodney Hallworth, a big man with a powerful personality who handled Teignmouth's public relations.

At two o'clock on the morning of the 31st October the decks and cabin were still piled high with stores, many of which had been bought at the last minute. Exhausted, Donald Crowhurst and his wife, Clare, returned to the hotel where they were to spend what was to be their last night together. Most adventurers have moments of agonising doubt, particularly on the brink of departure, but those of Crowhurst were particularly painful. He admitted to Clare that the boat was just not up to the voyage and asked whether she would go out of her mind with worry. With hindsight she realised that he was asking her to stop him going, but she did not see it at the time and did her best to reassure him. He cried through the rest of the night.

It was three o'clock in the afternoon of the 31st, just a few hours before deadline, that he set sail. It was a messy departure; almost immediately Crowhurst discovered that the buoyancy bag, which had been hurriedly lashed to the mast the previous day, had been tied round two halyards as well, so that neither the jib nor the staysail could be raised. He screamed invective at his accompanying escort and asked to be towed back into harbour so that the rigging could be cleared. He then managed to get away, tacking into Lyme Bay against a strong south wind, until he vanished into the misty drizzle.

As he sailed down the Channel he sorted out the shambles on deck and in the cabin, but in the next few days the hopelessness of his voyage became increasingly evident. The Hasler self-steering gear, ideal for a monohull but not really suitable for a trimaran, was giving trouble; then, even more serious, he discovered that the port bow float was shipping water. The hatches to the floats were not fully watertight. This probably brought on a further realisation. He had a very powerful pump for bailing but in the last-minute rush they had failed to get the length of Helliflex hosing needed to bail out all the different compartments. The only way he could do it was by hand, a slow and exhausting process which would be impractical in a really heavy sea because almost as much water would pour back in through the opened hatch as he would be able to bail out. (Tetley had anticipated this problem by putting permanent piping into the forward compartments of *Victress*.) Also, he discovered that a pile of spare parts and plywood patches that he would need for repairs en route had somehow been taken off the boat, even though he knew he had put them on board.

The winds across the Bay of Biscay and down the coast of Portugal were mainly against him but, even so, his progress was slow, even erratic. It was as if he were shying from commitment, trying to make up his mind what to do. The BBC had given him a tape recorder and a huge pile of tapes on which to record his impressions during the voyage. Whatever his doubts or secret thoughts, he was obviously very aware, whenever he made a recording, that this was eventually going to a wide audience and there was often a tone of bravado in his monologue which, somehow, struck a false note, when the reality was so different. For a start the boat was very bad at sailing into the wind but, much more serious, there were hosts of potentially disastrous structural faults. At last, on the 15th November, he summed up the problem in his log, stating, 'Racked by the growing awareness that I must soon decide whether or not I can go on in the face of the actual situation. What a bloody awful decision!'

He went on to write a very clear, carefully thought-out assessment of his situation, listing the many faults and omissions, all of which pointed to the seeming inevitability of failure in the Southern Ocean, failure which, in all probability, would be accompanied by his own death. He then questioned whether he should abandon the voyage immediately or try to salvage something from it by going on to Cape Town, or even Australia, so that he could withdraw with greater honour and at the same time give his backer, Stanley Best, a little more mileage for his investment.

Yet on the 18th November, when he managed to make a radio link-up with both Clare and Stanley Best, he did not mention the possibility of abandoning the voyage. He asked Best to double-check whether or not the Helliflex hosing had been put on board and complained of his slow progress, giving his position as 'some hundred miles north of Madeira'. Talking to Best again a few days later, he still did not mention the possibility of pulling out of the race, but he did warn that he might be forced to go off the air because of problems with the charging motor. It was as if he could not bring himself to admit failure and return to the enormous problems which he knew faced him at home.

Crowhurst's fellow late entrant, Alex Carozzo, had no such inhibitions or, for that matter, very much choice. A thirty-six-year-old, flamboyant Italian, he was a very experienced sailor. Like Knox-Johnston he had a Merchant Navy background and had built a thirty-three-foot boat in the hold of his cargo ship on the way to Japan. There he had launched the boat and had sailed single-handed to San Francisco, surviving a dismasting on the way. His entry to the Golden Globe race was equally bizarre. Having already entered the *Observer* single-handed race, he set out from Plymouth and in the vast emptiness of the Atlantic, by an incredible coincidence, met up with John Ridgway who had just set sail on his voyage. They exchanged greetings and it was this, perhaps, that influenced Carozzo in turning back for England so that he could build a boat specially for the circumnavigation. There was little time left and he had the boat built in a mere seven weeks. It was a revolutionary design, with two steel rudders and, in front of the main keel, a three-foot centre plate which could be used to adjust the boat's trim. She was by far the biggest boat to start out on the long, single-handed voyage. Provided he could manage her alone, she should have been the fastest of all the contenders. Unfortunately, however, he was overtaken by severe stomach pains whilst in the Bay of Biscay; these were diagnosed as stomach ulcers and, in the end, he had to be taken in tow to the Portuguese coast at Oporto. No doubt the nervous stress of putting together the enterprise so very quickly had been too much for him.

This was the news that Bruce Maxwell passed on to Knox-Johnston. The only serious threat seemed to be that of Moitessier, who had been making good progress as far as the Cape of Good Hope where he had last been seen on the 26th October. The pundits had calculated that at his present rate of progress he could challenge Knox-Johnston to a neck-and-neck finish and would undoubtedly win on the elapsed time basis. Knox-Johnston commented, 'that was just the sort of news I needed to spur me on.'

He raised sail once again, his next sight of land to be Cape Horn. Even though he had worked out a series of sail patterns to cope with the loss of his self-steering, he

Alex Carozzo had already entered the Observer *single-handed Atlantic race when he met John Ridgway and decided to return to enter for the Golden Globe instead. His revolutionary new boat, Gancia Americano, was by far the biggest boat in the race.*

still had to take the helm while sailing before the wind. This meant long hours, sixteen and seventeen at a time, sitting exposed to the elements in his tiny cockpit. *Suhaili* did not have a wheelhouse or even a canvas dodger to protect the helmsman; Knox-Johnston did not believe in them, feeling that he had to be completely exposed to the winds and to have a real feel of what they were doing to his sails and boat. He spent the long hours clutching the helm, meditating about the world and his own future, or learning and reciting some of the poetry he had on board. He never relaxed his efforts to nurse *Suhaili* along, to get the very best he could out of her and yet to avoid straining her to the point of irreparable damage. By now his radio transmitter was out of action, so he had no chance of calling for help nor of reporting his position, though he could pick up the coastal radio stations back in New Zealand and then, as he crept across the South Pacific, on the South American coast.

There was a constant drudgery and discomfort – of damp clothes, of insufficient sleep punctuated by crises, a hand badly scalded by boiling porridge, the failure of a succession of parts on the boat, the struggle with contrary winds which came in against him from the east almost as often as they swept round from the west.

Cape Horn, which he reached on the 17th January, was almost an anticlimax – he coasted past it in an almost dead calm. There was no-one to meet him, no aircraft flying out from the land: he slipped past unnoticed up into the South Atlantic, past the Falkland Islands and on up the coast of South America towards the Equator. He was on the home stretch, though still had a long way to go. The only person who had any chance of catching him up was Moitessier, who had handed some letters to a fisherman in a bay near Hobart, Tasmania, on the 18th December. Moitessier was next spotted off the Falkland Islands on the 10th February, but had the variables where he could expect contrary winds before him, while Knox-Johnston had reached the South-East Trades. It is unlikely that Moitessier would have caught up with Knox-Johnston, but he almost certainly would have had a faster time round the world, having set out more than two months after him.

The question was to be academic. The next time Moitessier was sighted was off the Cape of Good Hope, when the rest of the world believed he was somewhere in mid-Atlantic approaching the Equator, nearing the final run for home. He sailed into the outer reaches of the harbour and, using a slingshot, catapulted a message for the *Sunday Times* onto the bridge of an anchored tanker. It read: 'The Horn was rounded February 5, and today is March 18. I am continuing non-stop towards the Pacific Islands because I am happy at sea and perhaps also to save my soul.'

His message was received with incredulity. How could anyone, with success and glory in his grasp, reject it like this? The *Sunday Times* tried to get a message from his wife through to him by having it broadcast on South African news bulletins: 'Bernard – the whole of France is waiting for you. Please come back to Plymouth as quickly as possible. Don't go round the world again. We will be waiting for you in England, so please do not disappoint us – Françoise and the children.'

Moitessier never heard this message, and it is impossible to guess how he would have responded if he had. He had contemplated calling in at Plymouth to claim the reward, collect all the equipment he had left there and reassure his family, but then he rejected the thought, afraid that he would be drawn back into a way of life he felt was false and into a society that he considered was destroying itself with materialism, pollution and violence. Sailing on round the Cape of Good Hope for the second time, into the savage winds and seas of the Southern winter, it was a much rougher voyage than his first through the Southern Ocean. He was knocked down on four different occasions as he sailed past Australia, past New Zealand and then on up into the Southern Pacific towards Tahiti.

Moitessier finally reached Tahiti on the 21st June 1969, having sailed one and a half times round the world, further than anyone had ever done single-handed. On arrival he told journalists that he had never intended to race:

> Talking of records is stupid, an insult to the sea. The thought of a competition is grotesque. You have to understand that when one is months and months alone, one evolves; some people say, go nuts. I went crazy in my own fashion. For four months all I saw were the stars. I didn't hear an unnatural sound. A purity grows out of that kind of solitude. I said to myself, 'What the hell am I going to do in Europe?' I told myself I'd be crazy to go on to France.

To him, the voyage was sufficient in itself; he did not need the embellishments of competition, rejected both the material rewards and the accolades of fame. There had even been talk of him being awarded the Legion of Honour in France. He displayed an independence that is rare. Most mountaineers, for instance, have consistently rejected formalised competition but, in most instances, have accepted any plaudits bestowed on them on their return to their homeland. Moitessier, however, was not so much rejecting the rewards of a society wanting to adulate its heroes; rather, he was saying, 'I am not going to play your games. I am going to do exactly what I want and lead my own life in the way I choose.' He preferred the simplicity of life in the Pacific Islands, the freedom to sail where and when he would.

With Moitessier out of the race there were only three left. Knox-Johnston had last been seen at Otago and now, in mid-March, should be somewhere in the Atlantic, though his family and sponsors were becoming increasingly worried about his survival; ships and 'planes in the mid-Atlantic were asked to keep an eye out for him. Crowhurst also had gone off the air. The only competitor still in contact was Nigel Tetley. He had made steady, but nerve-wracking progress across the Southern Ocean, nursing his trimaran through the gigantic rollers that all too easily could have capsized him with fatal results. It appears that he picked the ideal time to sail through the ocean, for the weather seems to have been kinder to him than to the others, particularly around the Cape of Good Hope where all other circumnavigators experienced the appalling storms which forced Blyth and King to abandon their voyages and which very nearly scuppered Knox-Johnston. Tetley had his narrowest escape when nearing Cape Horn; caught by a storm with sharp, choppy waves, he was very nearly pitchpoled, the cabin damaged and one of the windows smashed. In the aftermath he thought of giving up, sailing for Valparaiso, but then obstinacy set in and he turned the boat to head for Cape Horn. His passage round the Horn also was anticlimactic – he was almost becalmed.

He now turned north-east to pass the Falklands on the east, for the long run home. Tetley's achievement in sailing a trimaran through the Southern Ocean was considerable, but the stress on his boat was now beginning to tell. Both the floats and the main hull were letting in water, sure signs of structural damage caused by the months of hammering but, provided he nursed *Victress* carefully, she should get back to England and might even be the only boat to complete the voyage. Then, on the 5th April, the tanker *Mobil Acme* sighted *Suhaili* to the west of the Azores. Knox-Johnston was on the home stretch and would undoubtedly be first home. Tetley, on the other hand, had a better average speed and – in all probability – would win the prize for the fastest voyage, even if he had to nurse *Victress* very carefully those last few thousand miles up the Atlantic.

Nobody had heard anything from Donald Crowhurst since the 19th January, when he had reported his position a hundred miles south-east of Gough Island in the South Atlantic to the west of the Cape of Good Hope. It could be assumed,

Instead of finishing the race, Bernard Moitessier sailed Joshua *one and a half times round the world 'because I am happy at sea and perhaps also to save my soul'.*

111

therefore, that by this time he should be somewhere in the Southern Ocean between New Zealand and Cape Horn. In fact, he was still in the South Atlantic and had never left it.

We shall never know exactly what went through Crowhurst's mind as he dallied hesitantly down the Atlantic through December 1968 and the early months of 1969. The only evidence are the logs and casual notes he left in *Teignmouth Electron* and which Ron Hall and Nicholas Tomalin, two *Sunday Times* writers, sifted and analysed in a brilliant piece of detective work, described in their book *The Strange Voyage of Donald Crowhurst*. It seems unlikely that he planned his deception from the very start of the voyage – or even from the moment when he concluded that there was no way his boat could survive the seas of the Southern Ocean. Both Tetley and Knox-Johnston had had moments when they decided their voyages were no longer possible, had resolved to give up, then decided to keep going until the next landfall and to take a decision there. The big difference was that their decisions were all in the open; it never remotely occurred to either of them to practise any form of deception.

With Crowhurst, the deception seems to have built up over a period, from the original germ of the idea to final, absolute commitment. It started in early December with a spectacular claim to an all-time speed record of 243 miles in the day. (This almost certainly would have been a record, since the best run previously publicised was that of Geoffrey Williams who had logged about 220 miles in the *Observer* single-handed Atlantic race.) It certainly got Crowhurst the headlines he probably sought and was accepted without comment by nearly all the media, though Francis Chichester was suspicious, 'phoning the *Sunday Times* to advise them that they should watch out for Crowhurst – he could be 'a bit of a joker'. At this stage it is possible that Crowhurst was still thinking of abandoning the voyage at Cape Town; the claim, which the calculations found in his cabin show was false, would have given him a little bit of glory with which to face his backers on return to England.

But then, as he sailed on down the Atlantic, the moment of irreversible commitment came ever closer. He had already started a new log book, even though his existing one still had plenty of empty pages, the inference being that he intended, at a later date, to write out a false log of his imagined circumnavigation through the Southern Ocean, while he used his second log book for his actual calculations which, of course, he needed to know from day to day. He also started to mark out on his chart a series of false positions, well to the east of his actual route, which was taking him down the South American coast. He could still, however, have brought his actual route and faked course together at Cape Town and it is unlikely that anyone would have bothered to scrutinise his calculations sufficiently closely to see that there were discrepancies.

There would come a point soon, however, when if he tried to fake his voyage through the Southern Ocean there was no way that he could suddenly appear at a port in South Africa or South America without exposing his fraud. He must have devoted hours to working out all the pros and cons of trying to carry out the deceit. For a start he would have to close down his radio since any call he made would give a rough indication of where he really was. But the biggest problem of all was that of writing up the false log with all the navigational calculations he would need, in a way that would satisfy the examination by experts on his return to Britain.

There have been challenged claims in the past. There is doubt about the claims of both Cook and Peary to have reached the North Pole in 1908 and 1909. The claim of the former was widely rejected, while the latter was generally accepted, even though there were several contradictions in his account. The distances Peary claimed to have made each day in his dash for the Pole seem far-fetched. If he did fabricate, however, it was a relatively simple operation, since it represented only a few days and, after all, nobody could challenge conclusively whether or not the bit of featureless ice on which he had stood was or was not the North Pole. There have also been several cases of disputed mountaineering ascents, but these also have usually involved a push from a top camp towards a summit, as often as not in cloud or storm. One of the most notorious is that of the first ascent of Cerro Torre by Cesare Maestri and Toni Egger. They were gone from Base Camp for a week; on their way down, in a violent storm, Egger slipped and fell to his death, Maestri staggered back down and was found semiconscious and delirious. He claimed they reached the top, though this was disputed. Whether he did or not can never be proved conclusively, but if he did fabricate the story, again, it was comparatively easy to do, since he only had to imagine a few days' climbing and could be excused lapses of memory in the struggle he had had for survival.

But Crowhurst was embarking on a massive fraud. He would have to spend several months circling the empty wastes of the South Atlantic, carefully avoiding all shipping lanes, while he forged a log, day by day, across the Southern Ocean. On his return he would have to sustain the lie in all its details. From the scrap sheets he left in his cabin, he had obviously spent a great deal of time and thought in faking his speed record. Falsifying a circumnavigation represented an infinitely greater challenge. Doubtless he must have been wrestling with this as he sailed down the South Atlantic. His radio reports were consistently vague, but by the 19th January he realised that the distance between his actual position, a few hundred miles east of Rio de Janeiro, and his claimed position approaching the Cape of Good Hope, was becoming too great and that it was time to close down his radio. He sent a message to Rodney Hallworth, his agent and promoter back in Teignmouth, for once giving a positive position a hundred miles south-east of Gough Island and, at the same time, warned him that the generator hatch was giving trouble, to create a reason for going off the air. This was his last call for three months – three months of complete isolation, denied the stimulus of pushing a boat to its limit or of a real goal.

He had started the journey with four log books; the first had entries up to mid-December and then, even though there were still plenty of blank pages, had been abandoned. The second was a working log, giving the day-to-day details of his actual voyage. In it he had recorded his thoughts as the voyage progressed, and it is these which give the clearest indication of his state of mind. He used the third book as a wireless log, in which he recorded not only his own messages but also detailed weather reports from stations in Africa, Australia and South America, presumably to help him falsify his log in a convincing manner. The fourth book was missing when the boat was eventually recovered. It is possible that he kept this as the false log book. On a practical level, working out the false sun sights in reverse would take considerably longer than doing it for real; also, of course, it would only be by doing it from day to day that the appearance of the log could have been at all convincing.

The nervous stress of living out this solitary world of make-believe must have been immense, but there are few records of direct introspection in his log book over this period; it is full of observations of the sea life around him, of the birds and porpoises that kept him company, and yet through these emerge glimpses of his state of mind. On the 29th January an owl-like bird, which was almost certainly from the land, managed to reach the boat. He wrote a short piece around it, entitled 'The Misfit':

> He was unapproachable, as a misfit should be. He flew away as soon as I made any effort to get near him, and on to the mizzen crosstrees where he hung desperately to the shaky stays with claws useless for the task he had set himself.

. . . Poor bloody misfit! A giant albatross, its great high-aspect wings sweeping like scimitars through the air with never a single beat slid effortlessly round the boat in mocking contrast to his ill-adapted efforts of survival.

And then a poem:

Save some pity for the Misfit, fighting on with bursting heart;
Not a trace of common sense, his is no common flight.
Save, save him some pity. But save the greater part
For him that sees no glimmer of the Misfit's guiding light.

It is a poignant cry for understanding and sympathy, stripped of all the shallow bravado that appears in his taped commentaries for the outside world.

And then a real crisis presented itself. The starboard float of *Teignmouth Electron* was seriously damaged, letting in the water. The spare pieces of plywood he needed for repairs had been left behind. There seemed no choice; he would have to put into port to get the boat repaired. This presented a huge problem. Even had he wanted to use this as an honourable excuse for retiring from the race, he was now so far from where he had said he was, that his fraud would inevitably have been exposed. He seems to have dithered for several days, zig-zagging off the coast of Argentina, before finally summoning up the resolve to put into port, and then he chose the obscure anchorage of Rio Salado, near the mouth of the River Plate. He arrived on the morning of the 8th March, repaired the damage and left two days later. Although the arrival of *Teignmouth Electron* was noted in the coastguard log, it was not passed on; but Crowhurst could not be sure of this and it must have been yet another source of worry.

As he set sail from Rio Salado, in his pretended voyage he should have been somewhere between New Zealand and Cape Horn. The time was coming close when his real self could join up with the fantasy self and, with this in mind, he started sailing south towards the Falkland Islands and the Roaring Forties. It is ironic that from the 24th March, on his way south, he must have passed within a few miles of Tetley going north. He sailed to within sight of the Falklands on the 29th March, but it was still too early to radio his false position approaching the Horn, and so he veered off to the north for a further ten days, zig-zagging back and forth, before sending out his first radio message for three months:

DEVONNEWS EXETER = HEADING DIGGER RAMREZ LOG KAPUT 17697 28TH
WHATS NEW OCEAN-BASHINGWISE

The broken log line covered any contradictions there might be between his actual mileage and the one he declared, while he still avoided giving a precise position, though definitely inferred that he was approaching the small group of islands named Diego Ramirez, to the south of Cape Horn. His radio call arrived just five days after Knox-Johnston had been sighted near the Azores and inevitably the world's press were concentrating on him, saving Crowhurst from a closer scrutiny that might have picked out some anomalies both in the apparent speed of his crossing the Southern Ocean and the timing of the resumption of radio communications. Once again, Francis Chichester was one of the few people to make sceptical comment.

Tetley was approaching the Tropic of Capricorn, well off the coast of South America, when he heard that Crowhurst was back in contact and heading for Cape Horn. It was unlikely that Crowhurst could get back to England before him, but of course he had set out over a month later and seemed, from his report, to have caught up dramatically. If Crowhurst kept up his present rate of progress he would have the fastest time round the world. Tetley had been stoical about Robin Knox-Johnston's reappearance, writing in his book *Trimaran Solo*:

> Robin's arrival would hive off most of the publicity and his position where expected made glad tidings. Donald Crowhurst's challenge to me from the rear was a different matter. Even so, I could by then regard the possibility of his winning without envy. At the same time, I still wanted to win; or put in another way, I didn't want anyone to beat me . . . least of all in a similar type of boat.

Tetley undoubtedly started to push *Victress* very much harder, keeping as much sail up as possible: in his words, he was now racing in earnest. But the boat was not up to it. In the early hours of the 20th April, just short of the Equator and the point where he would cross his outward track, disaster struck. A frame in the bow had disintegrated, leaving a gaping hole. His first reaction was that it was all over and he started working out the nearest port he could reach, but once again his stubborn determination won through. He patched up the damage as best he could and was soon pushing his boat to the limit once again, his eyes set on Plymouth.

At the time Tetley was struggling to repair and then nurse his battered boat towards home, Crowhurst, in the South Atlantic, was still marking time; he had to calculate very carefully the moment when his false voyage could actually catch up with his real progress, when the two logs could become one, when fantasy became reality. During this period he tried, unsuccessfully, to get a telephone link-up with Clare. This was obviously tremendously important to him – not only the result of his isolation, but also of the massive strain he must now have been under. The period without any contact with the world might have enabled him to relax in his fantasy, but he was now back in contact, was perhaps beginning to wonder about the practicalities of carrying through his deception.

Robin Knox-Johnston had no such problems. He was very nearly home in his dirt-streaked, old-fashioned-looking ketch, *Suhaili*. As he came into the Channel, 'planes dipped low over him, getting the first shots of film showing his arrival; two boats came out to greet him – one carrying his mother and father which, to the embarrassment of his sponsors, the *Sunday Mirror*, had been chartered by the *Daily Express*, and the other carrying reporters and photographers of the *Sunday Mirror*. As *Suhaili* neared Falmouth the escort increased, with a Royal Naval Reserve ship to give him a formal escort and a host of yachts and small boats whose crews wanted to pay tribute to his achievement. *Suhaili* crossed the bar at 3.30 in the afternoon of the 22nd April. The finishing cannon fired. Robin Knox-Johnston was the first man to sail round the world non-stop single-handed. He had taken 313 days to sail the thirty-odd thousand miles. It wasn't a dramatically fast time, but in many ways the speed was meaningless. The reason why Knox-Johnston had finished at all was because he had known how to care for his boat as well as how to push her.

The first people to board him were the Customs officers with the time-honoured question, 'Where from?'

Knox-Johnston replied, 'Falmouth.'

This would have made a nice, tidy end to the story, but of course the race was not yet over and the competition, created by the *Sunday Times*, was still very open. Crowhurst, who had now united his fake position with that of his real position, sent off a jaunty congratulatory cable:

NEWSDESK BBC = TICKLED AS TAR WITH TWO FIDS SUCCESS KNOX JOHNSTON BUT KINDLY NOTE NOT RACEWINNER YET SUGGEST ACCURACY DEMANDS DISTINCTION BETWEEN GOLDEN GLOBE AND RACE = OUTRAGED SOUTH ATLANTIC OTHERWISE CROWHURST

*Robin Knox-Johnston,
very nearly home in his tiny,
old-fashioned ketch.*

*Falmouth to Falmouth.
Robin Knox-Johnston is first home
because he knew how to care
for his boat as well as when
to push her.*

But Crowhurst's actual log shows that he continued to sail southward for a further four days and then, even when he did turn north, his progress was spasmodic, as if he wanted to ensure that Tetley was first home, with himself sufficiently close behind to get a good share of the honour, yet be spared the close scrutiny that his logs and story would receive were he the winner. He did get in a few good days' sailing and his log even registered one day's run of 243 miles – by coincidence the same as his false claim of a record the previous year.

Tetley meanwhile continued to push his damaged boat to the limit and by the 20th May had reached the Azores, only a thousand miles from home. A force nine gale had blown up through the day and, as dusk fell, he took down all his sails and hove to. It was midnight when he was woken by a strange scraping sound forward. He realised instinctively that the bow of the port float must have come adrift but, when he switched on the light, he was appalled to see water flowing over the floor. He went up on deck to find a gaping void where the float should have been, but somehow, in tearing away from the hull, it had left a huge hole in the main hull as well. *Victress* was sinking fast. He only had time to send out a quick emergency call on his radio, grab his log books and a few instruments and clear the life raft from the deck, before the boat sank under him in the pitch dark. For a hideous moment the raft's automatic drogue snagged something, pulling him under the three wildly rearing sterns of the boat. He managed to cut the line only just in time, shouting, 'Give over, Vicky, I have to leave you . . . Then the pangs set in. I had fleeting glimpses of her hull above the jagged silhouette of the waves, then all I could see was her riding light waving bravely amongst the tumult. As I watched, the sea reached her batteries, the light grew suddenly bright, flickered and went out.'

He spent the rest of the night, protected by the cocoon-like canopy of the rubber dinghy, tossed like a piece of flotsam by the dark waves. In the morning an American Hercules rescue aircraft flew overhead and later on that afternoon an Italian tanker, guided by the 'plane, picked him up. He had completed his circumnavigation, had come so close to completing the voyage; he was like the marathon runner who, having almost completed the course, collapses at the entrance to the stadium, a mere lap from the finish.

This now left Crowhurst in an agonising predicament. His spasmodic progress up the South Atlantic indicates that he intended to ensure that he came in second to Tetley. But now, if he kept going at his present rate, he would almost certainly beat Robin Knox-Johnston's time round the world and be subject to the inevitable close scrutiny of his logs and story that this would entail. On the other hand, if he were to slow down, this in itself would appear suspicious – particularly in comparison with the very fast passage he had claimed for crossing the Southern Ocean. In addition, the radio messages from England were beginning to indicate both the scale and the closeness of the reception he would have to face on getting back to Teignmouth. The stress was increased still further by the failure of his transmitter – he was unable to get any messages out. He now devoted all his energy to trying to repair the transmitter, leaving the boat to sail herself while he stripped and then tried to rebuild it. The cabin must have been unbearably hot, for he was now sailing through the Tropics; it also became an untidy shambles, with bits of wire and transistors scattered everywhere. And yet, in a way, it was probably therapeutic. Even back in England, Crowhurst had frequently locked himself away for hours as he wrestled with electronic problems. This was something that he knew he could do well and, after several days' work, he managed to make the transmitter work for morse. He did not manage to make it work for voice and this meant that he was unable to get the telephone link-up with Clare that he so desperately wanted. Even so, during this period he still kept up the public front of his deception with morse messages to England and a series of passages recorded on his tape-recorder. His last recording was on 23rd June.

> I feel tremendously fit . . . I feel as if I could realise all those ambitions I nurtured as a boy like playing cricket for England. I feel on top of the world, tremendously fit. My reflexes amaze me. They're so fast you know. I catch things almost before they start falling. It's really very satisfying.

And the tape ran off the spool. He did not reload it. He had had a second go at making a high-frequency speech transmitter but did not have the parts. He had even telegrammed the Race Committee to ask for dispensation to have the necessary parts sent to him, but they had stuck to the rules. There was nothing more he could do with the radio, it is easy to surmise why he could not bring himself to reload the spool. The reality of his position must now have been too appalling for almost anyone to have borne. Crowhurst seems to have turned away from it, into the therapy of the kind of philosophical discussion that he had always enjoyed at home, particularly amongst his close friends. He started it in his second log book – a series of passages which, over the next few days, stretched into 25,000 words, some of which represented a reasoned, philosophical analysis, some a tortured, indirect self-justification and, towards the end, it all became increasingly obscure with more and more deletions and repetitions. His first thoughts were strongly influenced by Einstein, whose work on relativity was one of the very few books which Crowhurst had brought with him to while away the months of solitude. He gave his exposition the title 'Philosophy' and went on:

> Man is a lever whose ultimate length and strength he must determine for himself. His disposition and talent decide where the fulcrum will lie.
> The pure mathematician places the fulcrum near the effort; his exercises are much more mental than physical and can carry the 'load' – his own ideas – taking perhaps nothing but his own and kindred minds along the route. The shattering application of the idea that E = mc² is one extreme example of this activity.

Crowhurst developed and expanded this theme to the point where he made his great discovery, that Man – and Crowhurst in particular – could escape from his body:

> And yet, and yet – *if* creative abstraction is to act as a vehicle for the new entity, and to leave its hitherto stable state it lies within the power of creative abstraction to produce the phenomenon!!!!!!!!!!!!!! We can bring it about by creative abstraction!

Not only could he escape from his body and from the appalling predicament in which he found himself, he could become one with God. He continued to explore this thesis and to study the last 2,000 years of history, showing how some exceptional men have managed to make their impact on the world, shocking it into change. He was also becoming aware of how important were both his words and discoveries, observing: 'Now we must be very careful about getting the answer right. We are at the point where our powers of abstraction are powerful enough to do tremendous damage . . .

But the outside world still intruded. On the 26th June he received a cable from Rodney Hallworth:

BBC AND EXPRESS MEETING YOU WITH CLARE AND ME OFF SCILLIES YOUR TRIUMPH BRINGING ONE HUNDRED THOUSAND FOLK TEIGNMOUTH WHERE FUND REACHING FIFTEEN HUNDRED PLUS MANY OTHER BENEFITS PLEASE GIVE ME SECRETS OF TRIP NEAR DEATH AND ALL THAT FOR PRE-PRESS SELLING OPPORTUNITIES MONEY OUTLOOK GOOD REPLY URGENT THINKING ABOUT ADVERTISING

He was still able to project his public self through his morse key: on the 28th he told off the BBC and Hallworth for demanding an exact time of arrival, with the admonishment:

BECALMED THREE DAYS PUFF BOATS HAVE DESTINATIONS NOT ETAS

He was also disturbed by the thought of Clare coming out to meet him and on the 29th sent a message, through the operator at Portishead, that under no circumstances was Clare to come out to the Scillies. This was his last message, his last direct contact with the outside world.

Another subject that fascinated him was that of 'the game' as one's approach to living, but with a strong sense of self-justification of how he had played and manipulated 'the game' of the round the world race. He now began to jump from one idea to the next, at times very obviously in agony, as shown by these lines which filled a single page:

> Nature does not allow
> God to Sin any Sins
> Except One —
>
> That is the Sin of Concealment
>
> This is the terrible secret of the torment of the soul
> 'needed' by a natural system to keep trying
>
> He has perpetuated this sin on the tormented . . .

He had lost all awareness of the passing of time, had not wound up either his watch or chronometer. There had been no practical entries into his log, no sights or positions. And then, on the 1st July, he reopened the log, annotating his thoughts with the passage of time. His first problem was to work out the passage of days, in which he had ignored the time, and then to calculate the time itself. He did this by taking a sight of the moon. Initially, he made a mistake of both the day – forgetting that June has only thirty days, and of the time, but then he realised it and made his correction. There followed his final testament which amounted to both a confession and also a conflict in his own mind. He seems to have determined to take his own life or, perhaps as he saw it, simply to leave his physical body but what was he to leave? He could destroy all evidence of his fraud and leave the falsified log, which he is assumed to have kept throughout the voyage. In all probability his story, at least publicly, would have been accepted; Clare, and more particularly his children, would have had a hero to mourn and remember. But to do this he would have had to destroy his testament, something that had become the very centre of his world; but most important of all, he probably needed to make his atonement and to do this he had to leave what amounted to his confession. His last lines, still annotated with the time were:

> 11 15 00 It is the end of my
>   my game the truth
>   has been revealed and it will
>   be done as my family requires me
>   to do it
>
> 11 17 00 It is the time for you
>   move to begin
>
>   I have not need to prolong
>   the game
>
>   It has been a good game that
>   must be ended at the
>   I will play this game when
>   I will chose I will resign the
>   game 11 20 40 there is
>   no reason for harmful

These were the last words he wrote. He only had two and a half minutes before the self-appointed moment of his departure. One can speculate what he did next, but the three log books and the navigational plotting sheets, on which he had fabricated his run the previous December, were stacked neatly on the chart table in a place where they would easily be found. There was no sign of the fourth log book and so, presumably to wipe away his deceit, he either threw it into the calm waters of the ocean or, clutching it, plunged over the side to watch *Teignmouth Electron* gently slide away from him at around two-and-a-half knots – a speed which, even if he had had second thoughts, he could never have attained by swimming.

Teignmouth Electron was spotted on the 10th July by the lookout on the Royal Mail Vessel *Picardy*, bound from London to the Caribbean. She was like the *Mary Celeste*, ghosting along under her mizzen sail, no-one on board; the cabin was untidy with a lived-in look, dirty pans in the sink, tools and electronic gear scattered over the work table as if they had only just been put down, and the logs, with their damning testimony, lying waiting on the chart table.

All nine contestants in the Golden Globe race had now been accounted for; only one had finished the voyage. Viewed as a single entity, the expectations, tribulations and interlinking tragedy of their stories has a quality of escalating drama one would expect to find in a classic tragedy; at the same time can be seen elements of a moral fable.

Teignmouth Electron *is sighted at last, ghosting along under her mizzen sail.*

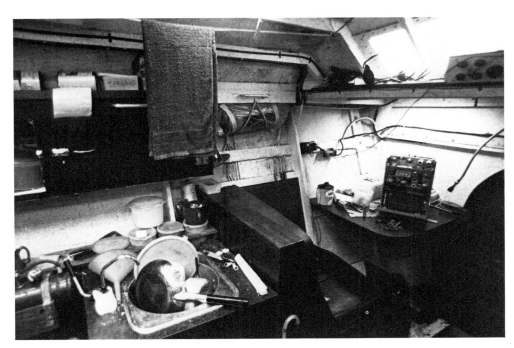

Teignmouth Electron and her abandoned galley.

A deserted Teignmouth Electron *being off loaded from* RMV Picardy.

Robin Knox-Johnston, the one who finished, showed a single-minded determination combined with fine seamanship and a level-headed judgement. He had been pronounced 'distressingly normal' on setting out; the verdict was the same on his return. One can assume that the psychiatrist meant that he was extraordinarily well-balanced and, at the same time, was adjusted to our own everyday life in an urbanised, consumer society. Looking at Robin Knox-Johnston's career as a whole this would certainly seem to be the case. With that spark of adventure that exists in many people, he simply took it to extremes by sailing round the world single-handed, but even this act was carefully thought out, based on his own background as a sailor and his knowledge, both of himself and an awareness of what it might lead to. He had no trouble in adapting to everyday life; in fact he plunged into it, exploiting his success to the full, without letting the ephemeral glory go to his head. He applied his spirit of adventure and initiative to running yacht marinas and at the same time balanced this out with the excitement and satisfaction of sailing, winning the Round Britain yacht race on two occasions and still holding the record of ten days, six hours, twenty-four minutes. He also skippered *Heath's Condor*, a big ocean racer, on three of the legs of the Whitbread round the world race in 1977–8. His family life is back on an even keel; he remarried Sue in 1972, and with his daughter Sara, they are a close-knit and very happy family.

As Tomalin and Hall observed in their book, it is doubtful whether anyone would describe Moitessier as 'distressingly normal'. In sailing on round the world to Tahiti he rejected the behaviour patterns that society expects of its heroes. He did not want to face the razzamattaz of the media's welcome back to Europe, despised the very business of racing across oceans and, most important of all, did not wish to return to our ferociously competitive society, preferring the peace of a South Sea Island.

In some ways the saddest outcome of all was Nigel Tetley's failure to finish, a failure that was undoubtedly influenced by the apparent competition offered by Crowhurst. He desperately needed to complete and, ideally, win the race; on his return he maintained a very sportsmanlike front but, only two years later, committed suicide. It is impossible to tell for certain how far this was influenced by what he felt was a failure, a failure which was only relative, since his achievement in nursing his trimaran through the Southern Ocean to complete a circumnavigation of the globe was quite extraordinary. He had shown the same high level of seamanship as that displayed by Knox-Johnston, on a boat that was less suited for the task in hand.

Of the others who withdrew from the race, three tried again, Bill King, in his revolutionary boat, *Galway Blazer*, with seven stops on the way, and John Ridgway skippering his own boat in the Whitbread round the world race, while Chay Blyth actually sailed round the world against the winds of the Roaring Forties from east to west. For them, the experience of the Golden Globe race, however painful at the time, had been a formative one from which they had been able to learn lessons and apply them as part of their lives.

Crowhurst, on the other hand, was engulfed by the experience. Enamoured of a venture that was beyond him, he found himself on an escalator built by the media and other people's expectations from which he could not escape. He had set out in a boat that was ill-prepared and, in all probability, would have foundered in the Southern Ocean, but while Ridgway and Fougeron, who had found themselves in similar circumstances, had retired with honour, Crowhurst could not bring himself to admit that his dreams of glory were over. Having allowed fantasy to lead him into fraud, when it became inevitable that his deception would be discovered, his mind escaped from reality and he committed suicide.

The way in which the ambitions of a few sailors to out-sail Chichester developed into a formalised race undoubtedly added extra pressures. It also attracted others who might never have set out without the focus given by the race and its associated publicity. There is a temptation to condemn the very concept of a formalised race, as something that sullies the purity of adventure, and yet this is an almost inevitable manifestation of the compulsive competitiveness built into so many people. The sailor or, for that matter, most adventurers, has an ego that requires the approval of others; he also needs money just to launch the venture and one way of getting it is through sponsorship or the media. They, in turn, need a story, look for ways of building one, whether it be a round the world race, the first to the top of Everest or the first across one of the Polar ice caps. And so the merry-go-round of the big adventure is built.

Some, like Robin Knox-Johnston, can ride it to attain their ambitions. Others, like Crowhurst, are not strong enough, and are destroyed.

Ice Bird

The waves reared up, chaotic, boiling white, like huge breakers on a reef; foam and windblown sleet made it difficult to tell where ocean ended and sky began. The roar of breakers intermingled with the high-pitched scream of wind in the rigging, as the little boat was hurled up onto the crest of a wave, before lurching crabwise down into the trough, where for a few strange moments she was becalmed, sheltered by the breakers around her from the noise of the wind. But somehow that only amplified the crash of collapsing rollers; sooner or later one of these must hit *Ice Bird*.

Once already, the boat had been knocked down; the self-steering vane had vanished and what little sail he had left up had been ripped away. David Lewis was now crouched, braced on the wet bunk in the cabin, his state of mind not so much fearful as beyond fear, for there was very little he could do to control his fate. He still clutched the tiller lines, which he could operate from within the shelter of the cabin, but the boat barely answered to their call.

Then suddenly, at about two in the morning, it happened. It was like a gigantic hand that picked the boat up, tossed and then rolled it; everything went black, water roaring in, clothes, tins, books tumbling around him; he was lying on the roof, then almost in the same instant on the floor amongst the swilling waters and flotsam of what had been his home. By the light of the sub-Antarctic dawn he saw that the fore hatch had been ripped away, but when he struggled from under the table that had collapsed on top of him and poked his head out of the hatchway, his worst fears were confirmed. The mast had been ripped out of its seat in the huge vortex of the roll and was trailing over the side, held only by the festoons of knotted rigging.

David Lewis was as alone as anyone has ever been on this earth. He was on his way to the Antarctic Peninsula, the first solitary yachtsman ever to attempt to reach the most inhospitable coast on earth. Six weeks out from Sydney, he was about half-way there, far south of the route taken by round-the-world sailors, on the sixtieth line of latitude, nudging down towards the Antarctic Circle where cold and ice compound the threat of 100 mph winds and freak waves thirty metres high. His boat was now a wreck; he was without a mast and his chances of survival, judged by any rational level, were minimal.

David Lewis was born in Plymouth in 1917, but his parents emigrated to New Zealand when he was only two. Agonisingly shy as a child, awkward at organised games, he naturally turned to the untracked forests, mountains and white water rivers of this exciting, only partly-tamed land. At the age of seventeen he built a canoe and paddled home from his boarding school, 450 miles by river, portage and lake. He was bright academically and studied medicine; he joined the university mountaineering club and made nineteen first ascents in the New Zealand Alps.

At the start of the Second World War, like most of his generation, any adventurous instincts were absorbed by the ugly, compulsory adventure of war and he took part in the Normandy landings as a member of an airborne ambulance unit. The war left him with the compulsive need to do something socially useful so, after a short period in the West Indies, he went into practice in the East End of London. Now married with two children, he worked hard and conscientiously at his practice and regained a touch of adventure with a sailing dinghy he built himself. It was the conventional pattern of the professional man and weekend sailor but, in David Lewis, part Welsh, part Irish, the pent-up, restless passion was too great. It exploded with the break-up of his marriage, and saw him acquiring the twenty-five-foot yacht, *Cardinal Vertue*, and entering the first *Observer* single-handed trans-Atlantic yacht race. Fourteen miles from the start his mast broke, but he returned to Plymouth with a makeshift rig, had the mast repaired and set out once again, finishing third behind Francis Chichester and Blondie Hasler in fifty-four days. He next put everything he had into building a catamaran of revolutionary design, *Rehu Moana*, sailed her to the Arctic, then entered her in the second *Observer* race and sailed on to New Zealand with his second wife and two infant daughters, down through the Magellan Straits and on across the Pacific.

In Lewis there has always been the combination of extreme adventurer and romantic scientist. He was not content just to sail or venture for its own sake or aim towards a purely competitive goal; even the single-handed race had been for him as much an exploration of solitude as it had been a race. Finishing, and what he learned from the experience, was more important than winning. His main purpose in crossing the Pacific was to try to emulate the navigational methods of the Polynesians, who had neither compass nor sextant and guided their great canoes by star paths, the pattern of ocean swells and the birds that signpost the way to land.

In many ways, the course of his life has been very close to that of Thor Heyerdahl, but in Lewis there is a harder, wilder streak of a man who courts the extreme. He had settled in Australia and was a research fellow with the Australian National University, studying the methods of the traditional star path navigators of the Pacific. He had always been fascinated by the harsh empty wastes of the Poles, and dreamt as early as 1964 of making a solo circumnavigation of the Antarctic continent. His motives were twofold, as in the case of almost every adventurer – the competitive urge to be first and the need to plumb his own personal unknown.

He had what appeared a suitable boat, a thirty-nine-foot yacht, *Isbjorn*, which had replaced his catamaran, *Rehu Moana*. *Isbjorn* was based on Tarawa, in the Gilbert Islands, under the command of Lewis's son, Barry, who was doing a bit of trading between the islands and also preparing her for the Antarctic for his father. By coincidence, Barry had met and helped John Fairfax and Sylvia Cook when they were wrecked on Tarawa. Bringing *Isbjorn* back to Sydney, Barry was caught in a severe gale and the boat foundered. The insurance had just lapsed and David Lewis had to start again from scratch.

He wanted an all-steel boat that would stand up to the huge seas and ice of Antarctica, but very few are built and Lewis had neither the time nor the money to have one specially designed. But his luck changed at last when, after searching every yard in Sydney, he stumbled upon the perfect boat. A thirty-two-foot sloop, built throughout of ⅛"-steel, she was tiny and yet ideal for what he wanted to do, being compact, immensely strong and easy to sail single-handed. Even more important, she was comparatively cheap – just under £4,000. If one compares this to the £60,000 that Chay Blyth's *British Steel* had cost a couple of years earlier, one can see just how

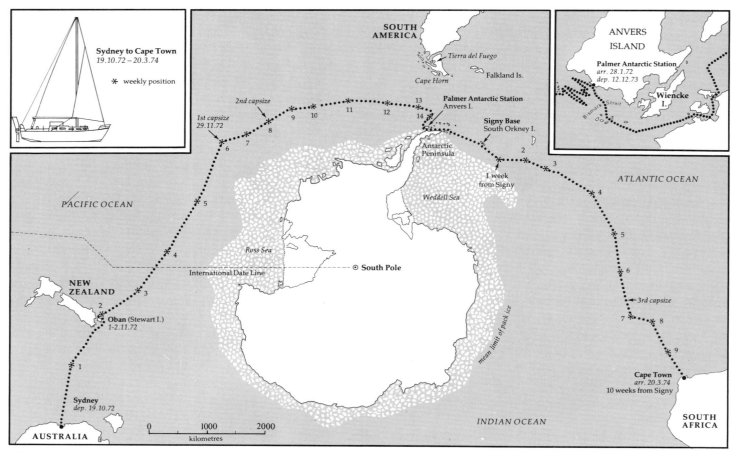

Voyage of Ice Bird

*David Lewis as he arrived
at the Palmer Antarctic Station
after a gruelling hundred days.*

small a budget David Lewis was working on. Everything had to be skimped, improvisation being the order of the day, but this was something that Lewis both excelled at and enjoyed. There were no luxuries, no heat for the cabin, the most basic of galleys, a complete dearth of electronic gadgets, except for a powerful radio transmitter and receiver. He ensured, however, that the boat herself was sound. The hull was inspected and strengthened, every wire and rope checked and replaced where necessary, extra-strong sails specially made. Every window was covered by an ⅛"-steel plate, leaving only tiny perspex rims, so that the interior of the cabin was in permanent gloom, apart from a small perspex viewing dome, fitted so that he could actually steer from within the cabin, pulling on lines attached to the tiller.

Lean, muscular but slight of build, David Lewis at fifty-five was a grizzled leprechaun of the sea, with a fey quality accentuated by a dark pointed beard and deep set eyes. Softly-spoken, very intense yet diffident, he has a lurking sense of humour. There is a modest, yet charismatic quality to him that people find difficult to resist. Every expeditioner is indebted to a mass of voluntary helpers, and David Lewis never had any difficulty in finding and using these. It was largely due to their help that he was ready to sail on the 19th October 1972.

He settled quickly to the routine of solitary sailing, irregular sleep, the constant round of make and mend, and was at one with the sea. But only a hundred miles out of Sydney, he found his new Racal radio was barely getting through, even though he had installed heavy-duty batteries to power it. So he called at Stewart Island, off the southernmost tip of New Zealand's South Island, where he replenished water and fuel, and called Sydney, warning them it was unlikely he would be able to maintain radio contact. He could not find anything wrong with his set, yet his engine failed to generate even enough power to make contact with radio stations in the South Island. When he set sail once again, his next landfall was to be the Antarctic Peninsula, 5000 miles away.

Much more serious than the lack of radio contact was his next discovery, that his bilge pump would not work. He had fitted a new one in Sydney but, in the rush to get ready, had not tried it out. In Lewis's life there is a recurring theme of disasters, some great, some small, but all of which – admittedly at the cost of vast discomfort and danger – he overcomes, almost as if he wanted the challenge to his ingenuity presented by each calamity. The solution to the bilge pump failure was irksome and potentially dangerous. The wells beneath the floorboards were packed with his tinned food. This meant he had to clear the deepest well, repacking the tins into the forepeak lockers, so that he could bail out the water with a bucket. This then had to be carried down the companionway, rested on the bottom step and then heaved up at just the right moment to coincide with the roll of the boat, to be emptied into the cockpit – a slow, laborious process.

But he sailed on into the west, forever edging southward towards the Antarctic continent. It got progressively colder, flurries of snow replacing the squalls of rain. Storm followed storm and the seas got ever higher. He wrote in his log:

> I have been running undercanvassed, being awed by the latitude – but not too over-awed, I know now. I was reading, the moan of the wind muted in the cabin. It rises to a shriek; we are pushed gradually but firmly over, as if by a hand and race ahead, luffing (storm trysail and storm jib only). I put the helm up from the cabin with the tiller lines, gasping in the spray showers even here. *Ice Bird* tore crashing along until the squall was past. Then I shook with reaction.

David Lewis devised a system of tiller lines which enabled him to steer from inside the comparative shelter of the cabin.

Looking forward after the first capsize, with Ice Bird's *mast and rigging trailing over the side.*

But Lewis was still in control; *Ice Bird* was making good, if uncomfortable, progress towards her goal; but everything changed on the 27th November. That was the date of the capsize. The barometer had dropped so low that it went off the scale; it was a hurricane more fierce than anything Lewis had experienced in his long years at sea. In the immediate aftermath of the capsize there seemed little chance of survival. He was dismasted, *Ice Bird*'s shell ruptured by the colossal force of water, and 2500 miles from the nearest port, which was only a tiny Antarctic base on a rocky, ice-bound coastline. And yet the instinctive will to survive immediately took over.

Lewis stuffed some rags into the split in the cabin wall, searched around for his gloves but failed to find them in the appalling shambles of the waterlogged cabin, so started bailing without them, bucket after bucketful, stumbling over the debris, trying to avoid spilling the painfully collected water in the wildly bucking boat. After five hours' continuous bailing, at last the boat was nearly empty and then – crash! *Ice Bird* had been smashed down once again, the ice-cold sea gushed in through the damaged hatchways and the partly repaired gash in the side. He had to start all over again.

At last the storm moderated to a mere force ten and Lewis collapsed in his sodden clothing onto the bunk. He had been bailing, non-stop, for ten hours. But he did not rest for long; the smash and crash of the mast against the hull got him back on deck. He had to clear the mast before it did real damage. There was no way he could recover the mast by himself; releasing it with his numbed fingers on the tossing, wave-swept deck was difficult enough. The mast was imprisoned by a tangle of stainless steel wire rigging, anchored to the deck by split pins that were now twisted and jammed. Hammering and levering at them, he managed to clear all but two of the wires which fortunately sheared. His hands were torn, but he did not feel anything. He could do no more and staggered back into the ruin of the cabin.

It was only the following morning that he realised that his hands were badly frostbitten. He could now take stock and his findings were appallingly bleak. His radio receiver had packed up completely, which meant that he could not get any time signals, essential for accurate navigation. He had only the one Omega wrist-watch, knew that it was gaining time, but was not sure just how much. With his frostbitten fingers he was barely able to manipulate the winder or, for that matter, use his hands effectively for the many other functions vital to his survival. He could neither handle the sextant nor even pick up a match dropped on the floor.

By now his boat was a piece of flotsam, adrift in the Southern Ocean. Somehow he had to find a way of building a jury mast. Protecting his hands with wet woollen gloves, he salvaged a ten-foot-long spinnaker pole, somehow erecting it, and staying it with what was left of the rigging and some old climbing rope. But it could only take a pathetic amount of sail, barely enough to keep him under way, as *Ice Bird* plodded, crabwise, towards his haven of the Antarctic Peninsula. It was a desperate, yet hopeless struggle for survival, for he still had 2500 miles to go and, at that speed, he would have run out of water long before he got there. And yet he kept struggling on, spending up to fourteen hours at a time operating the tiller lines from the shelter of the cabin, to claw his way in the right direction, tacking painfully, first north-east, then south-east, to gain a few precious miles. The numbness of his hands had now given way to intense and growing agony. They were soft, swollen, beginning to suppurate. He took massive doses of antibiotics to stop them becoming gangrenous but even touching anything was agonisingly painful. Despite this he had to bail out twenty or thirty bucketfuls of bilge water each day, struggle with the Primus stove, go out on deck to readjust his pathetically inadequate sail or repair the fragile mast. The position was hopeless. He commented in his log:

> A shutter has closed between a week ago when I was part of the living and since. Chance of survival negligible but effort worth it in spite of pain and discomfort. These last are very great. Must go on striving to survive, as befits a man. Susie and Vickie without a daddy is worst of all.

He continued to strive, even though the aluminium jury mast was slowly buckling and then, a week later, the barometer dropped once again. He battened down for another storm, stowing everything away, tying down the table, stuffing the ventilators with rags, and then waited.

> After watching in helpless misery while the remains of the self-steering gear broke up and was swept away, I made one more attempt to steer. It was hopeless. We lay helplessly, starboard side to, rolling the decks under. I cowered down on the port bunk, back braced against the cabin bulkhead – as if to seek companionship from the kangaroo and kiwi painted there – about as far into the depths of the cabin as it was possible to get.

He did not have to wait for long; it was almost inevitable that sooner or later one of the huge waves would break over the helpless boat. Once again she was smashed and tumbled over, but Lewis's preparations had paid off; his sleeping bag was soaked and his typewriter smashed into pieces in a corner of the cabin, but most of the gear and food had been held in place. Most important of all, his jury mast was still standing; the hatches and roof of the cabin had withstood yet another hammering. The most serious damage was to the main hatch, which would only open a foot before jamming. For a second he was caught by panic; he was entombed in the cabin, but then common sense took over, for he could always escape from the fore hatch. But with a struggle he found that he could just wriggle through anyway. He was unable to clear the hatch, however, so his bailing problems were compounded:

How on earth could I lift a bucket of bilge water past me when I was wedged in the hatchway, not to mention the far more delicate manoeuvre of lifting the toilet bucket out into the cockpit? The answer was found by trial and error. I was able to evolve a set of co-ordinated movements that, when I removed my parka and exhaled deeply, just sufficed to squeeze the bucket up past my chest and, balancing it precariously above my head lift it out of the hatch. Bilge water could then be unceremoniously tipped into the cockpit, though the toilet required further contortions before I could gain the bridge deck and empty it safely overside.

It was so difficult to light the cooking stove and then prevent the pot on top of it being hurled to the other side of the cabin, that Lewis had hot food or drink only at intervals of several days. The temperature of the cabin was barely above freezing and his clothing and sleeping bag were permanently damp, and yet he still struggled on with a dogged, Herculean ingenuity, buoyed by his own fierce spirit of survival and the thought of his two young daughters who so depended on him. It was the kind of desperate situation in which almost anyone would be tempted to look for help from a source outside himself. Lewis wrote: 'Did I pray? people ask. No, I longed to be able to but, not being religious at other times, I had just enough dignity left not to cry out for help when the going got a bit rough. A higher power, should one exist, might even appreciate this attitude.'

But he was in a situation that seemed to be steadily, inexorably deteriorating. He often omitted to wear his safety harness; there did not seem much point when the boat was almost certainly doomed anyway. While he was trying to patch up the jury mast, a breaking wave caught him unawares from behind. He was picked up off his feet and dashed across the deck in a maelstrom of foaming water. The guard wires had vanished with the loss of the mast, so there was nothing to save him from being swept overboard. Then, with an agonising crunch, he smashed against one of the stanchions, and was held in place as the wave poured over the side. It was a miraculous escape, but he paid a heavy price for it. Some ribs were almost certainly broken and his right arm was numb:

> I dragged myself, moaning and groaning and making a great to-do, along the side deck and down below. As the wind was from the south-west, there was no need to steer. Bilge water was overflowing the floorboards, though. Cursing mentally – drawing each breath meant stabbing pain enough without aggravating it by speech – I prised up the floor and scooped up twenty-two buckets from the well to tip them into the cockpit. The rest of that pain-fringed day and a restless, chilly night I spent on my bunk, increasingly aware of the vast difference between a merely damp sleeping bag and one still soaked from the recent capsize.

The effort to squeeze out of the jammed hatchway and expose himself to the bitter wet and cold above decks was becoming increasingly onerous. He delayed it until the last possible minute, sought solace in an escape world of the novels he had brought with him. He could see that the jury mast was on the verge of disintegration, but put off the moment of actually doing anything about it. Another storm, another sail torn to bits, it was becoming increasingly obvious that at this rate he would run out of water, even if the boat did not founder first, before he reached any kind of haven.

But Lewis never stopped thinking out every conceivable possibility for survival. The spinnaker pole mast was obviously hopeless. He did have one other possibility, the eleven-foot-six-inch wood boom, but he had seen no way that he could possibly have raised it into position on his own in the tossing boat. Then suddenly, at his lowest moment, when he had almost given up all hope, he saw how it could be done by rigging a system of pulleys to give him some mechanical advantage. He waited for a slackening in the weather, laid out his system of tackle and ropes, eased the boom into position and was at last ready for the crucial test. It had taken him eight and a half hours of non-stop work just to get this far. Tense with anxiety, he began to turn the winch handle:

> Was the 15° angle at which the boom lay, hopefully pivoted at the mast step and supported upon the crutch at its other end, suffient to give purchase? Yes. The boom rose a foot out of the crutch, then it slewed as the yacht lurched sharply to port and stuck fast. I could have cried. But, thank goodness, its foot had only jammed in the pin rail. On the second attempt the boom mounted steadily inch by inch to the vertical.

The new mast was still stunted, but it was sufficiently strong to hold enough sail to attain a reasonable speed. He now had a sporting chance of reaching safety; the most obvious course was to head north, for warmer climes and kinder seas, and then to try to reach Tierra del Fuego. Lewis gave it a thought but quickly dismissed it. He did not have the charts, but, more important, he was still determined to reach the Antarctic Peninsula. The charts and pilot tables he did have had been turned into a soggy mess by constant soakings, but he dried them out carefully, and decided that a small American station, Palmer Base, on the south side of Anvers Island, gave him the best chance of survival.

His water supply still represented a problem. He decided on a drastic economy campaign, reducing his liquid intake to just over a pint a day. To accustom his kidneys to such a harsh routine, he went without any liquid at all for twenty-four hours and, after this, adjusted his fluid intake to maintain a concentrated dark urine. Whenever it became a normal yellow colour, he knew that he was wasting liquid. It was a question of disciplining his body to exist on the very edge of survival, an accomplishment at which David Lewis excelled and, one suspects, enjoyed in a strange way.

At last he was making good progress. The long hours at the tiller lines were worthwhile. And slowly his body, even under these appalling conditions, was mending. His finger nails dropped off, one by one, making his hands even more tender, but also showing that the tissue was healing. His ribs became less painful and the greatest enemy now was boredom, as day followed day, with hardly an intermission of dark to mark the passage of time. He had finished most of his books, and faced hour after hour at the tiller, in a race against the steadily diminishing level of his water containers.

As the weeks went by, he became increasingly anxious about his landfall. He had no way of knowing how accurate his only watch was. The compass had a deviation of around 20°E, because the steel framework of the cockpit had been buckled over it in the storms. If he made a quite small navigational error, he could miss Palmer Base altogether.

As he got closer to land the nervous and physical strain became progressively worse. He spent longer and longer hours at the tiller, often peering into a near white-out of driving snow. He sighted land on the 26th January, piled snow peaks, rising out of chaotic glaciers that swept down to the sea, spawning great icebergs in the dark waters. It was a sight of austere, forbidding beauty, of black, ice-veined cliffs, green, gleaming walls of ice and a total lack of human life. He had had the shadowy ice birds for company for much of the voyage; he had seen whales and porpoises but, looking at that bleak coast, it was difficult to believe that there could be a human being within a thousand miles. And yet he was looking at Anvers Island, had made a perfect landfall after over 5000 miles at sea. His logic told him that the Antarctic base must be on the other side of that empty island. He was so close to warmth, comfort, the company of other people, and yet they were almost impossible to comprehend. In addition, he had entered the most dangerous phase of the entire voyage, even more so than that moment of capsize when the mast had been swept away.

For two days of increasingly wearied concentration at the tiller he dodged the jagged teeth of islands, the part-hidden threat of reefs and the more obvious ones of icebergs. He was only eight miles from safety, could even see the light of Palmer Base, but now a gale blew up with the speed and ferocity that is so typical of those climes. Close to land, particularly one so forbidding, it was infinitely more dangerous than out at sea. *Ice Bird* weathered the gale and, as the wind dropped, Lewis could keep his eyes open no longer and collapsed onto the bunk, to wake shortly afterwards by some sixth sense, just in time to see a jagged rock skerry puncturing the sea only a few yards away on his beam.

Another day and night at the tiller, tacking exhaustingly towards his goal, and he seemed nearly there – just a mile to go, when suddenly *Ice Bird* took off, tossed by a breaking wave into a chaos of spurting foam. Lewis leapt for the cockpit, but could do nothing but cling to the tiller as the boat was hurled on the crest of breaking waves over what was obviously a shoal. The keel had only to be caught once on a hidden rock and they would be tumbled, smashed, ruptured in the boiling waters. The people at Palmer Base might never even know that a yacht had come so close. And then *Ice Bird* was in smooth waters again. Somehow, she had come through the maelstrom. Another hour or so and she was in the sheltered waters of Arthur Harbour. It was 28th January 1973. The buildings, with that impermanent prefabricated look common to all structures in the far south and north, were still and silent as if they had been abandoned. A small converted minesweeper was moored to the pier. This, also, was lifeless, as *Ice Bird,* rusted, battered and dirty, sidled in under her rags of sail, to drop anchor a few yards from the sleeping vessel. It was only fear that the anchor might slip that made Lewis call out, 'Is anyone awake? Do you mind if I tie up alongside?'

People erupted out of the saloon door, to see the incredible·apparition. Lewis himself was even more battered than his boat, with clothes in tatters, stained with grease and petrol: matted hair and roughly trimmed beard framed a hollow, emaciated face dominated by eyes that were bright yet haunted by three months of constant struggle. David Lewis was the first man ever to sail single-handed to the Antarctic; he had also come through a battle for bare survival in which, somehow, he had never relinquished his goal. Of all the stories of the sea, this is one of the most remarkable.

No less noteworthy was the sequel to the voyage. Even before reaching Anvers Island, David Lewis had begun to plan the repair of his boat so that he could continue the voyage. Within days of arrival, he had started work, repairing, improvising, replacing what was little more than a robust shell of a yacht. Once again, his magnetic personality enlisted help, so that almost the entire staff of Palmer Base became involved in the recovery operation. The engine was stripped, cleaned and coaxed into working; two lengths of timber, used for battening down cargo, were shaped and glued together to make a longer mast; the temperamental cooking stove was stripped and cleaned. Even the bilge pump was repaired.

At this point the *National Geographic Magazine* got in touch with him, offering commissions too lucrative to turn down, so Lewis left *Ice Bird* in the Antarctic, returning to Anvers Island at the end of the year. He spent a hectic month in the final refit of his boat and set out once again on the 12th December 1973. There were plenty more narrow escapes. To start with it was no easy matter coaxing a small yacht through the ice-jammed channels of the Antarctic Peninsula and then, clear of land,

Refitting in the Antarctic.

he was exposed once again to the fury of the Southern Ocean. He was caught in the eye of a hurricane at the end of his sixth week out, once again was capsized, once again lost his mast. Now, running out of time before the start of a new academic job, he decided to run for Cape Town. At least he would have completed his voyage, sailing both to and from the Antarctic continent, totally under his own way. He reached Cape Town on the 20th March 1974, slipping unostentatiously into the Marina of the Royal Cape Yacht Club. There was no naval escort, no civic dignitaries or crowds. He would not have wanted it that way, and yet his voyage represents the most outstanding achievement of endurance, ingenuity and superb seamanship in the history of small boat sailing.

David Lewis flew back to Australia, but Barry, his son, finished off the long voyage of *Ice Bird*, sailing her single-handed across the Southern Ocean back to Sydney later on that year. For David Lewis this participation by his son was as important as his own incredible saga.

The Empty Quarter

It is not just the thrill of the unknown that has enticed Wilfred Thesiger back to unspoilt, wild country throughout his life; it is a fascination by and love of the people themselves, particularly the Bedu, who live on the edge of the savage Empty Quarter, that desert-within-a-desert in southern Arabia. He loved the harsh emptiness of the slow-moving waves of the sand dunes and the bleak plains of sun-blasted salt flats, was challenged by the prospect of crossing regions where no white man had been before, not so much for scientific discovery or research but rather for the pure adventure. But having crossed it once he came back to it again by another route, and then again and again, just to live and travel with the Bedu whose life-style he admired and enjoyed so much until, finally, he was forced to leave southern Arabia by the rulers and also by their English advisers who feared he might upset an already delicate balance between the nomadic, sometimes warring, tribes.

Wilfred Thesiger is the archetypal English gentleman adventurer born, perhaps, a hundred years later than ideally he would have liked. In the Victorian era there were so many more unexplored, unspoilt empty spaces; he would have been with Speke and Burton or perhaps, like Sven Hedin, would have wandered across Central Asia. Though in some ways he was born into the way of life that he eventually pursued. Son of the British Minister to Abyssinia, his infancy and early childhood were spent in that wild and colourful upland country (now Ethiopia), the only one to retain complete independence in the face of colonial domination by the great European powers. He had vivid memories of plumed warriors, rich barbaric pomp, rugged mountains and deep gorges.

Through Eton and Oxford he dreamt of African adventures. His opportunity came in 1930, when he was invited, as his father's eldest son, to attend Haile Selassie's coronation as Emperor of Ethiopia. Then, as soon as the coronation was over, he took off to the wild and lawless Danakil country to the south of Addis Ababa.

> I had everything I wanted, even more than I had dreamt of as a boy poring over *Jock of the Bushveld*. Here were herds of oryx and Soemering's gazelle on the plains, waterbuck in the tamarisk along the river, lesser kudu and gerenuk in the thick bush and greater kudu, trophy of trophies, among the isolated mountains. Here were the camp fires and voices of the night, the voices of my Somalis, the brilliant African stars, the moonlight on the river, the chill wind of the dawn, the hot still noons, mirages transforming the parched plains into phantom lakes, dust devils spiralling through the bush, vultures circling over the camp, guinea fowl calling among the trees and the loading and unloading of the camels.

There was risk as well. The Danakil tribesmen, who gathered round their campsite at night to view the white stranger with his valuable weapons and other gear, all wore large curved daggers from which hung leather thongs, one for each man they had killed and castrated. On that first trip he reached the edge only of the Danakil desert, but it was on this little expedition that his love of adventure and the open desert spaces was formed.

On his return to Oxford he spent much of his time dreaming of the Danakil and planning another expedition, once he had graduated. In 1933 he set out with a friend hoping to follow the river Awash, which flows into the Danakil desert but then vanishes, never reaching the sea. Three expeditions had ventured into this region at the end of the nineteenth century, but they had all disappeared without trace, presumably murdered by the Danakil tribesmen. Nesbitt, an English venturer, had managed to cross the desert from south to north in 1928, but his party also had been attacked and three of their retainers killed.

Thesiger's companion was forced to drop out at an early stage in the expedition, but this in no way deterred Thesiger:

> I was glad to see him go for, though we never quarrelled, I found his presence an irritant, and was happy now to be on my own. This was no fault of his, for he was good natured and accommodating. Like many English travellers, I find it difficult to live for long periods with my own kind. On later journeys I was to find comradeship among Arabs and Africans, the very difference between us binding me closely to them.

This was to be the pattern of nearly all his future ventures; it was what gave him such a close understanding of the people amongst whom he lived. I have often been conscious of the barrier that we mountaineers inevitably erect between ourselves and the mountain people whose country we pass through, simply by being an expedition and carrying our own customs and interdependence within our own tiny, inlooking world, through Himalayan or Andean foothills.

Later Thesiger realised that on that first trip to the Danakil, where he had penetrated country from which no European had ever returned alive, 'I still had a sense of racial superiority, acquired in my childhood, which set me apart from the men who followed me. Even Omar, my Somali headman, on whom I was utterly dependent, was in no sense a companion.'

But this attitude was to change. After completing his journey down the Awash river, he made a leisurely return to Britain and the problems of following a career. He joined the Sudan Political Service, managed to get himself posted to the most isolated and undeveloped district in the Sudan, and settled down to the life of the dedicated outback colonial civil servant, using his periods of leave not to rush to the fleshpots of Europe, but to make long desert journeys into the Sahara. With the war came more ventures; involvement in the liberation of Ethiopia, frustration at the inevitable wastage and bureaucracy that accompanies the massive war machine and then a period in the Long Range Desert Group. At first glance, this seemed immensely adventurous and very risky as they operated in jeeps far behind the German lines, shooting up convoys, raiding supply dumps, but Thesiger found it strangely unsatisfying. 'We carried food, water and fuel with us; we required nothing from our surroundings. I was in the desert, but insulated from it by the jeep in which I travelled.'

It was in the aftermath of war, by chance, as so often happens, that the opportunity arose which was to lead him to the Empty Quarter of Arabia and a way of life he has pursued ever since. He was in Addis Ababa, just having resigned from the post of political adviser to the Ethiopian Government, when he met O. B. Lean, a desert locust specialist. Lean wanted someone to venture into the Empty Quarter to look for locust outbreak centres. Thesiger knew nothing of entomology, but was immediately attracted by the venture and accepted on the spot.

Thesiger arrived in Dhofar on the southern coast of the Arabian peninsula in October 1945. Already he spoke Arabic and was accustomed to desert travel. He also knew what he wanted to do – to explore the Empty Quarter which had been penetrated by only two Europeans, Bertram Thomas in 1930–1 when he had made a crossing from south to north, and by H. St. John Philby who, in 1932, had ventured into its centre from the north and had escaped from it to the north-west. Thesiger was attracted to the ways of the desert Arab and sought to become one of them. But the barriers confronting him were formidable. In 1945 southern Arabia was still comparatively undeveloped; oilfields clung to the coast of the Persian Gulf while the desert tribes lived as they had always done, herding their goats and camels from one oasis to the next, warring and feuding with each other. Theirs was amongst the hardest livings in the world, comparable with that of the bushmen of the Kalahari, the aboriginals of the Australian desert, or the Eskimos.

Thesiger spent the end of 1945 and the early months of 1946 travelling on the southern edge of the Empty Quarter. He was getting to know the land and its people, finding the travelling companions for his ambitious, still secret plans. On arrival, he found that he had been apportioned a retinue of thirty of the Bait Kathir tribe, on the pretext that he would need a large party both for his safety and also as recognition of his importance. He soon realised that he was regarded as 'the rich infidel milch cow' to be milked to the very limit. Thesiger commented: 'At first glance they seemed little better than savages, as primitive as the Danakil, but I was soon disconcerted to discover that, while they were prepared to tolerate me as a source of welcome revenue, they never doubted my inferiority.'

To the Bedu, he was an Infidel or Christian; the fact that he was English had no relevance. The world beyond their arid mountains and the sea that bounded them was of little importance. They had never been colonised or conquered, though the Aden levies had made the occasional and comparatively ineffective punitive expedition against inland tribes in the Hadhramaut. As far as they were concerned this represented the total might of the Infidel, and they were not impressed. Thesiger quickly realised that he would have to capture their respect and friendship if he wanted to get away from the beaten trails and venture into the Empty Quarter.

> Anxious to prove their equal, I wanted no concessions and was irritated when pressed to ride while they still walked, or when they suggested I was thirsty and needed a drink. I wore their clothes – they would never have gone with me otherwise – and went barefooted as they did. In camp, especially when we had visitors, I sat in the formal way that Arabs sit, and found this unaccustomed position trying. I thought many of their formalities irksome and pointless. Sometimes we shot a gazelle or oryx and then fed well, but our usual fare was unleavened bread, brick hard or soggy, depending on how long it had lain in the embers of the fire. On the gravel plains the water from the infrequent wells tasted of camel's urine, but it was even worse when we reached the Sands, where it resembled a strong dose of Epsom salts, fortunately without the same effect.

At the end of this period he had earned the respect of his travelling companions and had begun to master the dialect of the Bait Kathir and other tribesmen of southern Arabia. He had also started to build up the strong friendships which were to play an important part in his travels later on. Particularly important was his meeting Salim bin Kabina, a young member of the Rashid tribe, who lived on the edge of the Empty Quarter and were familiar with its sands.

> He was to be my inseparable companion during the five years that I travelled in southern Arabia. He turned up when we were watering thirsty camels at a well that yielded only a few

gallons of water an hour. For two days we worked day and night in relays. Conspicuous in a vivid red loin-cloth he helped us in our task. On the second day he announced that he was coming with me. I told him to find himself a rifle and a camel. He grinned and said he would find both, and did. He was sixteen years old, about five foot five in height and lightly built. He was very poor, so the hardship of his life had already marked him. His hair was long and always falling into his eyes, especially when he was cooking, and he would sweep it back impatiently with a thin hand. He had very white teeth which showed constantly, for he was always talking and laughing. His father had died years before and it had fallen on bin Kabina to provide for his mother, young brother and infant sister. I had met him at a critical time in his life. Two months earlier he had gone down to the coast for a load of sardines; on the way back his old camel had collapsed and died. 'I wept as I sat there in the dark beside the body of my old grey camel, the only one I had. That night death seemed very close to me and my family.' Then he grinned at me and said, 'God brought you. Now I shall have everything.' Already I was fond of him. Attentive and cheerful, anticipating my wants, he eased the inevitable strain under which I lived. In the still rather impersonal atmosphere of my desert life his comradeship provided the only personal note.

Thesiger had to return to Britain to report his observations on the movement and habits of the locusts. Dr. Uvarov, the Head of the Locust Research Centre, wanted to know more about locust movement in Oman, at the south-east end of the Arabian peninsula, but the Sultan of Oman had already refused permission for Thesiger to enter his country. He immediately saw the chance of slipping illicitly into Oman by the backdoor and, at the same time, realising his ambition of crossing the Empty Quarter. He told Dr. Uvarov to get him permission to visit Mughshin, on the southern edge of the Empty Quarter, and returned to Salala in October 1946, to find twenty-four of his former companions of the Bait Kathir waiting for him.

Salim bin Kabina of the Rashid tribe was Wilfred Thesiger's travelling companion through five years of journeys in southern Arabia.
His most treasured possession, his rifle, is protected against the desert sand.

Thesiger adopted Arab dress, went barefoot and sat in the formal Arab way, but he was still an Infidel to the Bedu, and by definition inferior. This photograph was taken by Salim bin Kabina.

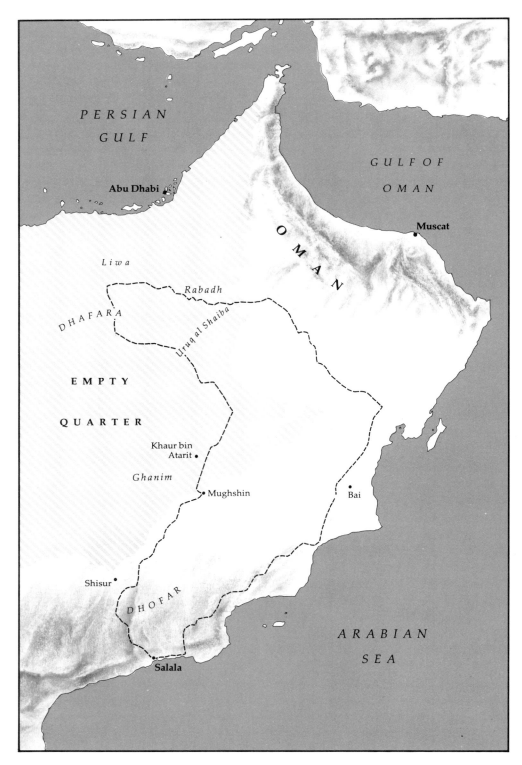

The Empty Quarter of southern Arabia

The problem, however, was that the Bait Kathir were not really suited to the Empty Quarter, for they rarely ventured into its vastness. The Rashid were very much more at home in the empty desert and would have been ideal companions for Thesiger's scheme, but somehow he had to get a message to them. It was no use asking the Bait Kathir to do this, for they were jealous of the Rashid and wanted him to themselves. He was shopping in the bazaar one day when he met a young Rashid who had travelled with him the previous year; he sent a message for bin Kabina to meet him at Shisur, on the edge of the Empty Quarter, though he had no way of knowing if it would be delivered. A few days later he set out with his party of the Bait Kathir.

Thesiger, in Arab dress, was an impressive sight. After a few weeks under the desert sun, he was nearly as bronzed as an Arab; his beard was dark and his curved, slightly fleshy nose had a semitic look to it, but there the resemblance ended. His eyes are a pale, greyish blue and at six-foot-two inches he towered above his companions with a natural air of inbred authority.

With their camels they trekked through the foothills, at first through grazing downs, green jungles and shadowy gorges on the southern side and then, as they passed through the mountains, it changed to a lunar landscape of black rocks and yellow sands. The inhabitants were as hard and wild as the land itself. Government control barely reached beyond the bounds of the towns on the coastal strip. Here, in the desert, every man went armed; disagreements were settled with the gun and tribe fought tribe in an endless circle of feud and counter-feud.

They reached Shisur without incident and began watering the camels. It was a bleak, ominous spot. The ruins of an old fort, perched on a rocky mound, guarded the well which was at the back of a large cave that undercut the mound. It was the only permanent water to be found in the central steppes and consequently had been the scene of many a savage fight, when rival raiding parties had surprised each other. They left a sentry high on the mound while they went to work, under the blazing sun, watering the camels:

Watering camels. Camel urine added to the bitterness of the already brackish water.

When we arrived at the well, the water was buried under drifted sand and had to be dug out. I offered to help but the others said I was too bulky for the job. Two hours later they shouted they were ready and asked us to fetch the camels. In turn they scrambled up the slope out of the dark depths of the cave, the quaking water-skins heavy on their shoulders. Moisture ran down their bodies, plastering the loin-cloths to their slender limbs; their hair, thick with sand, fell about their strained faces. Lowering the water-skins to the ground, they loosed jets of water into leather buckets, which they offered to the crowding camels, while they sang the age-old watering songs. Showers of camel droppings pattered on to the ground and rolled down the slope into the water, and small avalanches of sand, encrusted with urine, slipped down to add more bitterness to water that was already bitter.

The sentry, just above them, gazing over the shimmering plain, caught sight of distant, dark shapes moving across the sand, and called the alarm. No-one could ever relax in the desert; the approaching riders could be a hostile raiding party or members of a tribe with an age-old blood feud. Quickly the camels were herded together and the Bait Kathir, rifles ready, crouched behind rocks around the well. The other party approached cautiously; there were seven riders. A couple of shots were fired over their heads; they came on steadily, waving their head cloths. Then someone called out, 'They are Rashid' – 'I can see bin Shuas's camel.' Everyone relaxed, coming out into the open and forming a line to greet the newcomers. Thesiger's message had reached bin Kabina and he had come with six other members of his tribe.

That evening he told bin Kabina of his ambition to cross the Empty Quarter, to which Kabina replied that he thought the Rashid would go with him and that al Auf, who was one of their number, was the best guide in the tribe. It was an eight-day ride to Mughshin, the last sizeable oasis before the sands of the Empty Quarter, and the journey went without incident until the day they arrived there; the camels suddenly bolted and Mahsin, one of the Rashid, was thrown to the ground. He already had a damaged leg and this was broken in the fall as it twisted under him. Fortunately, Thesiger carried with him a small first-aid kit, gave Mahsin an injection of morphine, straightened the leg and made a rough splint for it. They were close to the shelter of the few trees grouped around the well, so that they could at least take stock of the situation. Suddenly, Thesiger's scheme was threatened. There was no question of Mahsin being able to go with them. The Rashid were equally unwilling to leave him because of the risk of hostile tribesmen hearing of his predicament and coming to finish him off. He had killed many men and made many enemies in the course of his life. The Rashid said that they could not move Mahsin and they would have to wait there until he either recovered or died.

After a night's sleep, however, they became more optimistic and agreed that al Auf and bin Kabina should go with Thesiger, provided he loaned the others two of his modern service rifles to guard their friend. Thesiger was delighted, and promised to stay until Mahsin's recovery was assured. He was quite glad at the reduction in the party. The fewer they were, the more unobtrusive they would be and small numbers give a greater feeling of adventure. It is perhaps a similar feeling to that of the climber who prefers to climb in a small compact party, which brings him that much closer to the mountains than he would be as a member of a massive expedition. Thesiger assumed that the Bait Kathir would not want to accompany him into the desert, but was immediately engulfed in protests. Whether it was pride or the thought of what wages they might miss, they did not want to be left out. After a lot of argument, spread over the next nine days while they waited by the well, it was decided that ten of the Bait Kathir should accompany the two Rashid and Thesiger across the Empty Quarter, while the remainder would head for the coast and meet them on their return.

*Muhammad al Auf was famous among the Rashid for his knowledge of the Empty Quarter.
He sits in the typical riding posture of the southern Bedu.*

At last, on the 24th November, they set out from Mughshin to cross the eastern end of the Empty Quarter. They had four hundred miles of trackless, unmapped desert before them. If they ran out of water, or if the camels collapsed and died, they also would almost certainly perish. And even if they succeeded in making the crossing and reached the wells of Liwa on the other side, they might well be attacked and killed by the tribes who lived there, particularly as Thesiger was unmistakably an Infidel. The problem was compounded by the fact that the Bedu, improvident with their food as they always were, had eaten most of the rations for the crossing. The Bait Kathir were now frightened at the prospect of venturing into the Empty Quarter and looking for an excuse to withdraw. Four days' march took them to Khaur bin Atarit, the last well they would encounter on the southern side of the Empty Quarter. There were no trees to give them shelter from the sun, and the well itself, little more than a depression in the sand, had been drifted over, but there was good grazing; it had rained there two years before and there was still a low ground covering of green plants, succulent forage for the camels. Because of this, a group of Bait Musan, a friendly tribe, were encamped nearby. That afternoon they dug out the well and watered the camels. The water was brackish, almost undrinkable, but this was something that Thesiger was learning to accept.

The next morning he could see that something was wrong. The Bait Kathir had gathered into a circle, arguing and talking, for decisions amongst the Bedu were always reached democratically with everyone from the youngest lad to the oldest having his say. The leader of any group was informally recognised because of his experience and personality rather than by appointment or birth. In this case a Bedu called Sultan was the undoubted leader. He had served Thesiger well on their previous trips, was courageous and wise, but he was uncertain of himself in the empty expanses of the deep desert and told Thesiger that it would be lunacy to go on; their camels were not up to it; there was insufficient food and water.

Thesiger sympathised, understood his feelings and knew how to handle the delicate politics of this little group of tribesmen. He was still dependent on the Bait Kathir since they owned the camel he was riding, and anyway, even though al Auf and bin Kabina had expressed their determination to take him across the Empty Quarter, he now realised they would be better off with a slightly larger group. Thesiger knew that Musallim, who owned the camel he was riding, was jealous of Sultan's position in the group. He therefore asked Musallim if he would be prepared to go on with them. Musallim agreed and suggested that as Mabkhaut bin Arbain was his friend he should come too. And so the team was now down to the compact size that Thesiger had wanted at the very beginning. His role had been not so much that of leader as a catalyst whose presence and will kept the venture on its course, though it was the leadership and skill of al Auf that would take them across the Empty Quarter.

They divided the food and water once again, keeping four of the best waterskins for the journey. They also bought a powerful bull camel from the Bait Musan, to help carry their supplies and act as a spare. The little party set out into the rolling dunes of the desert the following morning. They had not gone far before al Auf suggested they halt at the last vegetation to give their camels a final strengthening graze. That night they

The sands were like a petrified ocean of great waves.

stopped with some camel-herders of the Bait Imani tribe and benefited from the chivalrous hospitality of the desert. Their hosts had nothing but the milk of their camels, and little enough of that, but they insisted on Thesiger's party having it all, going without themselves, for they were the hosts.

They would meet no-one else until they reached the other side of the sands. The Bait Kathir had been full of stories of parties that had vanished, never to be seen again, but al Auf was quietly optimistic. When asked by Thesiger how well he knew the sands, he simply replied, 'I know them.' He had no map or compass, had only crossed the sands on two previous occasions, each time incredibly on his own, but in his mind was implanted a sense of direction, a recognition of tiny landmarks that no-one who had lived outside the sands could ever have. He knew where to find grazing for the camels in the seeming arid wastes, knew the exact whereabouts of the few waterholes on which their lives would depend.

The sands were like a petrified ocean of great waves that marched haphazardly from one horizon to the next; there were stretches of calm, of flat level salt flats, and there were storm-wracked dunes that towered 180 metres into the sky, each one of them with a long even slope on one side leading up to the crest, which then dropped away steeply into the next trough. The little party was dwarfed by its gigantic scale, creeping so slowly across its vast expanse.

At night it was bitterly cold; on his first trip Thesiger had brought three blankets with him, but the Bedu share everything and, since his companions had only a few rags to wrap round them at night, he had ended up surrendering two of the blankets and shivering through the night with them. This time, therefore, he brought out a sleeping bag which he could keep to himself so that at least during the night he was warm and comfortable.

The party began to stir at the first glimmer of dawn, anxious to push on while it was still cold. The camels would sniff at the withered branches of the tribulus shrub which was their main forage and which grew in hollows of this seemingly dead land, nurtured by rains that might have fallen some years before. As the journey went on they would become too thirsty to eat and once this happened their strength would wane rapidly. The men had nothing to eat or drink, just crept from under tattered blankets, saddled the camels, fastened in place their few belongings, the fast-shrinking sacks of flour and the vital, life-preserving waterskins, and set out across the desert. At first it was bitterly cold; the sand chilled their bare feet, causing the soles to crack – a source of pain and irritation, particularly when the sun heated the sands to an almost unbearable heat. Pain and discomfort filled their bodies through the day, the blazing sun being a harsher tormentor than the cold of the dawn. Thesiger could see the dew-covered bags full of water – water that was being lost by condensation, as the bags heated in the sun. He longed for the one moment in the day that he could take a drink, tried to ignore the length of time that he would have to wait for the evening meal, as he plodded through the sands, leading his camel or, after a few hours' walking, mounting it and swaying to the ungainly rhythm of its progress.

We went on, passing high, pale-coloured dunes, and others that were golden, and in the evening we wasted an hour skirting a great mountain of red sand, probably six hundred and fifty feet in height. Beyond it we travelled along a salt flat, which formed a corridor through the sands. Looking back I fancied the great red dune was a door which was slowly, silently closing behind us. I watched the narrowing gap between it and the dune on the other side of the corridor and imagined that once it was shut we could never go back, whatever happened. The gap vanished and now I could see only a wall of sand. I turned back to the others and they were discussing the price of a coloured loin-cloth which Mabkhaut had bought in Salala before we started. Suddenly al Auf pointed to a camel's track and said, 'Those were made by my camel when I came this way on my way to Ghanim.'

To them it was commonplace. There was nothing strange about recognising one's own camel track made two years before near the middle of this pathless wilderness. To them the price of a loin-cloth was much more interesting. They were obsessed by money, were immensely avaricious and yet incredibly generous. Their ways and values were so totally different from those to which Thesiger had always been exposed, that however much he admired and liked their way of life, the strain of becoming absorbed into it was considerable. He wrote:

> I knew that for me the hardest test would be to live with them in harmony and not to let my impatience master me; neither to withdraw into myself, nor to become critical of standards and ways of life different from my own. I knew from experience that the conditions under which we lived would slowly wear me down, mentally if not physically, and that I should often be provoked and irritated by my companions. I also knew with equal certainty that when this happened the fault would be mine not theirs.

And at last, at the end of the day, as the sun dropped below the crest of one of the dunes, they halted for their only drink and meal in twenty-four hours. They mixed a little sour milk with the brackish water, in an effort to make it more drinkable, sipped it slowly and carefully, trying to prolong the sensation of moisture, though within minutes their mouths were as dry, their tongues felt as swollen as they had been before. The evening meal was no more satisfying than their drink, just four level mugfuls of flour – around three pounds – to be divided between five men. They mixed the flour with a little water and milk to bake unleavened bread, burnt on the outside, soggy in the middle, over the fire they had built. Wherever they went in the desert they were able to find wood, even if it meant digging up the roots of long-dead shrubs that might have been nurtured by a rainfall some thirty years before. They would finish the meal with a few drops of sharp, bitter coffee. They would not eat or drink again for another twenty-four hours.

The principal barrier was the Uruq al Shaiba, a range of huge sand dunes through which there were no defiles or easy ways round. Towards the end of their second day they reached a high, unbroken sand dune that stretched across their route like a huge mountain range:

> Several of the summits seemed at least seven hundred feet above the salt flats on which we stood. The face that confronted us, being on the lee side to the prevailing wind, was very steep. Al Auf told us to wait and went forward to reconnoitre. I watched him climb up a ridge like a mountaineer struggling upwards through soft snow, the only moving thing in all that empty landscape. I thought, 'God, we will never get the camels over that.' Some of them had lain down, an ominous sign. Bin Kabina sat beside me, cleaning the bolt of his rifle. I asked him, 'Will we ever get the camels over those dunes?' He pushed back his hair, looked at them and said, 'Al Auf will find a way.' Al Auf came back and said, 'Come on,' and led us forward. It was now that he showed his skill, choosing the slopes up which the camels could climb. Very slowly, a foot at a time, we coaxed the unwilling beasts upward. Above us the rising wind was blowing streamers of sand. At last we reached the top. To my relief I saw we were on the edge of rolling dunes. I thought triumphantly, 'We have made it, we have crossed the Uruq al Shaiba.'
>
>   We went on, only stopping to feed at sunset. I said cheerfuly to al Auf, 'Thank God we are across the Uruq al Shaiba.' He looked at me for a moment and answered, 'If we go well tonight we shall reach them tomorrow.' At first I thought he was joking.

The terrible dune mountains of the Uruq al Shaiba through which there is no defile, previously known to western travellers only by repute.

They kept going through the night, hungry, tired and above all desperately thirsty. The camels had had nothing to drink for three days, were so thirsty that they would no longer eat the dried-up, desiccated foliage in the hollows of the dunes. If the camels collapsed and died, that would be the end. They stopped at midnight and Thesiger dropped into a troubled sleep, dreaming that the Uruq al Shaiba towered above them, as high and steep as the Himalaya.

*Al Auf showed his skill
in chosing slopes the camels
could negotiate.*

*One of the oases of Liwa
and the end of the crossing of
the Empty Quarter.
In 1946 Thesiger had to camp
at a safe distance to avoid
local hostilities.*

Next morning they set out while it was still dark, and soon the line of sand dunes, even higher and more formidable than on the previous day, barred their route. Beyond the first wave ran another and yet another, each one higher and steeper than the last. The camels wallowed and slipped on the fine grains of sand, pulled and pushed, cajoled, but never shouted at or beaten, by the five men as they struggled up the seemingly endless, shifting slopes.

We went down into the valley, and somehow – I shall never know how the camels did it – we got up the other side. There, utterly exhausted, we collapsed. Al Auf gave us a little water, enough to wet our mouths. He said, 'We need this if we are to go on.' The midday sun had drained the colour from the sands. Scattered banks of cumulus clouds threw shadows across the dunes and salt flats, and added an illusion that we were high among Alpine peaks, with frozen lakes of blue and green in the valley, far below. Half asleep I turned over, but the sand burnt through my shirt and woke me from my dreams.

This time they really were over the Uruq al Shaiba; the dunes in front of them were just as high, but Al Auf knew the way through them. Winding sinuously through the valleys, they were now travelling with the grain of the country. It was just a question of plodding on, keeping going through the day and late into the night, to reach the nearest well before the camels collapsed. One day they caught a hare; divided between five, there was little more than a morsel each, but it tasted like a feast. Two days later, they were suddenly challenged by an Arab lying hidden behind a bush. Had he been a member of a hostile tribe he could have gunned them down before they could grab their rifles, but he recognised they were Rashid and therefore friends. They all sat down, made coffee and swapped news. He was out looking for a stray camel. He warned them, however, that raiding parties were on the rampage and that King Ibn Saud's tax collectors were in Dhafara and the Rabadh, collecting tributes from the tribes. If they ventured into any of the settlements around the oases there was a good chance that Thesiger would be arrested, imprisoned at best, but he could well be killed.

They carried on through the desert towards the Liwa oases, but resolved to turn away just short of them and to avoid any contact with other Arabs. The following day, fourteen days after leaving the last waterhole of Khaur bin Atarit, they stopped just short of the oasis of Dhafara; they had completed the first ever crossing by a European of the eastern, and by far the wildest part of the Empty Quarter.

> To others my journey would have little importance. It would produce nothing except a rather inaccurate map which no-one was ever likely to use. It was a personal experience, and the reward had been a drink of clean, nearly tasteless water. I was content with that.

Thesiger still had to get back to Oman – without being identified as an Infidel, arrested or killed. They picked their way surreptitiously through the eastern foothills of the mountains of Oman and then back down the coast of the Arabian Sea to meet up with the rest of the Bait Kathir at Bai. In subsequent years, Thesiger made another crossing, of the western part of the Empty Quarter, a venture in some ways even more dangerous than his first, not so much because of the difficulty of the terrain as the hostility of the tribesmen. But it is his first crossing that he remembers with the greatest affection, for this had all the exciting novelty of the unknown.

Thesiger travelled through the breadth of southern Arabia, living with the Arabs, from 1945 to 1950, when the authorities, both Arabian and British, decided to put a stop to his journeys through this increasingly sensitive, oil-rich wilderness. As he was forced to leave the land and people whom he had come to love, Thesiger felt a deep sense of loss:

> I had gone to Arabia just in time to know the spirit of the land and the greatness of the Arabs. Shortly afterwards the life that I had shared with the Bedu had irrevocably disappeared. There are no riding camels in Arabia today, only cars, lorries, aeroplanes and helicopters . . . For untold centuries the Bedu lived in the desert; they lived there from choice . . . Even today there is no Arab, however sophisticated, who would not proudly claim Bedu lineage. I shall always remember how often I was humbled by my illiterate companions, who possessed in so much greater measure generosity, courage, endurance, patience, good temper and light-hearted gallantry. Among no other people have I felt the same sense of personal inferiority.
>
> Bin Kabina and bin Ghabaisha accompanied me to Dubai, and there we parted. 'Remain in the safe-keeping of God.' 'Go in peace, Umbarak,' they replied. As the 'plane climbed over the town from the airport at Sharja and swung out to sea, I knew how it felt to go into exile.

The Blue Nile

The Blue Nile starts with a deceptive quietness, flowing low-banked, oily-smooth and brown between the tossing plumes of papyrus reeds as it leaves the wide waters of Lake Tana. A few miles on a rumble from round a bend heralds the first cataract; the river narrows, drops a few feet and suddenly the smooth waters are turned into a boiling chaos of foaming waves. For the next 470 miles to the Sudanese border the river cleaves its way into a deep-set valley that drives in a giant half-circle through the Ethiopian Highlands. Cataracts alternate with long stretches of smooth waters, whose every eddy holds its own family of crocodiles. The two-legged variety are probably the more dangerous, however, for it is a lawless region where almost every man carries a gun or spear and several parties descending the Blue Nile have been attacked by Shifta bandits.

The combination of wild water and cataracts, crocodiles and bandits, make it one of the most exciting river challenges in the world. The story goes back to the early 1900s, when an American millionaire called W. N. McMillan attempted a descent in 1903 with three specially constructed steel boats. He launched them at the Shafartak bridge which carries the main road from Addis Ababa to Debre Markos and crosses the Blue Nile about a third of the way down, between Lake Tana and the Sudanese frontier. It is a convenient division, for some of the most precipitous rapids are above the bridge. McMillan did not get very far, as the boats sank in the first cataract.

The river was then left well alone until after the Second World War, when a series of abortive, at times bizarre, attempts were made to descend it. On one occasion a young Austrian sculptor built himself a raft of petrol drums lashed to wooden planks, but did not get very far. In 1962 a group of Swiss canoeists started down from the Shafartak bridge and very nearly reached the Sudanese frontier, when they were attacked by Shifta bandits. Two of the team were killed but the rest managed to escape. In 1964 Arne Robin, a Swedish economist working for the United Nations, set out on his own from the Shafartak bridge and succeeded in canoeing all the way down to Khartoum in eight days. He was attacked by crocodiles, never lit a fire and only stopped when it was dark. Two years later he attempted the upper part of the river with a companion, Carl Gustav Forsmark, in a two-seater canoe. They managed only fifteen miles before being capsized in a whirlpool and very nearly lost their lives.

Then, in 1968, came the biggest and most highly organised venture so far. It was led by Captain John Blashford-Snell and was essentially an Army expedition. On the stretch of river below the Shafartak road bridge, they used big flat-bottomed Army assault boats powered by outboard motors, and on the river above they had four Avon Redshank rubber dinghies powered by paddle alone. I was closely involved,

148

The most highly organised expedition down the Blue Nile was a team of fifty-six led by Captain John Blashford-Snell in 1968. They used big flat-bottomed Army assault boats, with four Avon Redshank rubber dinghies for the white water sections, and were supported by Land-Rovers, radio communication and a single-engined Beaver aircraft.

for I went out as the *Daily Telegraph* correspondent and photographer, accompanying them down most of the river. Four years later a very different party attempted a complete descent of the river; just four men in single-seater kayak canoes, led by Mike Jones, a twenty-year-old medical student. The stories of these two expeditions make an interesting contrast.

John Blashford-Snell is a big, well-fleshed man with a heavy jaw and close clipped military moustache. He sports a sola topee, Sam Browne belt with holstered pistol, and always wears his badges of rank. He is perhaps a frustrated Victorian who would have been most happy in command of an expeditionary force venturing into darkest Africa but even today, as a comparatively junior officer, he has been extraordinarily successful in creating a series of ventures under his own autonomous command that bear a close resemblance to their nineteenth-century forbears. On the Blue Nile he had a team of fifty-six, supported by a military single-engined Beaver

aircraft, Army Land-Rovers that had been specially flown out, a radio set up to make contact with headquarters in England and a flotilla of boats.

The expedition was in the best tradition of African exploration, having aims that were both adventurous and scientific. During the first part of the trip the four big assault boats were going to ferry a band of zoologists, accompanied by an archaeologist, down the lower part of the river from the Shafartak road bridge. Once this had been achieved, a white water team was to attempt the upper part of the river in rubber dinghies. It was in this latter part of the expedition that the adventure really started. I, certainly, was more frightened and came closer to losing my life in a whole series of different ways than I have ever done in the mountains, before or since.

The white water team which set out from the source of the river at Lake Tana on the 8th September 1968 numbered nine, in three Redshank dinghies named *Faith*, *Hope* and *Charity*. Leader of the group was Roger Chapman, a regular captain in the Green Howards. A quiet, serious and very thoughtful man who had done a certain

The Blue Nile

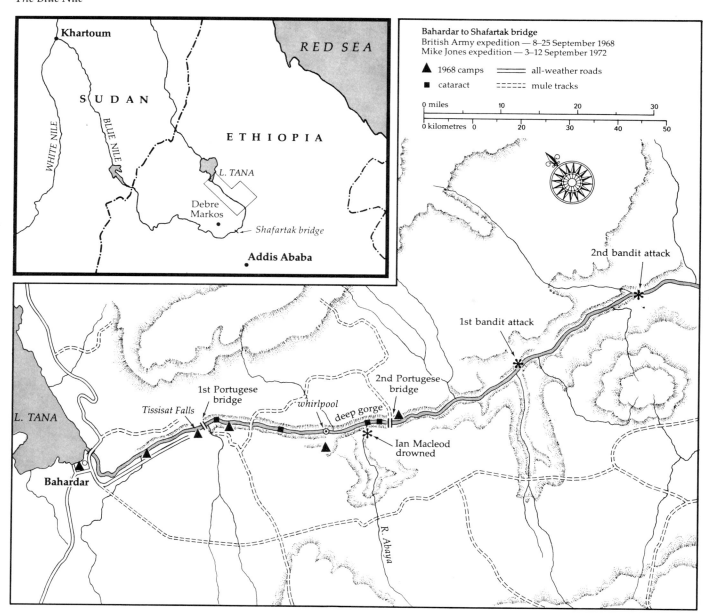

amount of sea canoeing, he had very limited experience of white water – a lack we all had in common. We had had a few days' practice on rivers in Wales, but these were mere trickles compared to the Blue Nile.

The heavily laden rubber dinghies behaved sluggishly in the smooth waters immediately below Lake Tana but when we hit our first cataract, six miles down the river, they were like pieces of flotsam at the mercy of the waves. Even so, it was quite incredibly exhilarating. As walls of white water lunged above and around us, smashing into us with a solid force, there was no time for fear – just an intense excitement. It was like skiing, surfing and fast driving, all rolled into one – a roller-coaster ride down an avalanche of white water. On that first cataract Roger Chapman's boat, the first down, capsized, thrown on its back by one of the big standing waves. There was very little skill in getting down the cataracts, our paddle power was so puny against the volume of the waters. It was a matter of luck which waves we hit.

That night we camped by the bank, just the nine of us, in an open meadow surrounded by low brush. Exhilarated by the day's run, I felt a profound sense of contentment as we sat under an almost full moon, boiling pre-cooked rice and a curried meat bar which we further seasoned with garlic and chillies. Up to this point the trip had resembled a cross between a military operation and a Boy Scout jamboree, the adventure a carefully fostered illusion, but after that day on the river the adventure now seemed real enough. The following day, it was to become all too real. My feelings at this point were very similar to those of Doug Scott when, on our 1975 Everest expedition, he had experienced the frustration of being a pawn in someone else's game until he found himself fully involved with the core of the adventure – in his case being out in front, near the summit of Everest. On the Blue Nile this came for me from being part of a small group that now formed the spear point of the expedition's effort to descend the river throughout its upper reaches.

I could even forget my irritation at Roger Chapman's firm, almost maternal authority. His leadership was excellent, but it was that of the platoon commander with absolute authority, rather than the much more free and easy style to which I had become accustomed in mountaineering circles since leaving the Army. I got on well with the other two crew members. Ian MacLeod, a lean, slightly-built Scot, was a corporal in the Special Air Service Regiment, Britain's crack commando and counter-insurgency force. Although one of the most junior ranks on the expedition he had the quiet authority of experience and competence that everyone from John Blashford-Snell downwards respected. My other crew-mate was Chris Edwards, a young second-lieutenant from the Infantry; six foot seven inches tall, he played rugby for the Army, was immensely powerful but also had a gentleness and breadth of imagination.

Next day we started by pushing the boats through an archipelago of tree-covered islands with spiky palms overhead and dank undergrowth blocking the stream bed. It was midday before we reached the open channel where the current raced wide and shallow over a series of cataracts, each one more dangerous than the last. There was no chance of making a foot reconnaissance, for the banks were covered by dense scrub and tentacles of marsh. We had to press on and hope for the best. In one of the cataracts the crew of *Hope* were flipped out of their boat by a wave. Jim Masters, at forty the eldest member of the white water team, was dragged under water by the undertow and only got back to the surface by inflating his life jacket. As we paused on the bank to repair the bottoms of the boats, he sat very quiet and tense, slightly away from us. At that stage we could not conceive what he had experienced nor fully understand why he was so badly shaken.

Sometimes the dinghies had to be man-handled around obstacles, such as this archipelago of tree-covered islands whose dank undergrowth blocked the stream bed.

Protecting the vulnerable rubber dinghies in a boulder-strewn channel.

Worried by Jim Masters' narrow escape, we roped the boats down the next cataract from the bank, but this was a slow process and everyone became impatient. We could hardly see the next fall – it was just a shimmer of water in the distance, but we decided to take it. Roger Chapman went first and vanished from sight with a frightening suddenness. There was a long pause and then we saw the green mini-flare which was the signal for the next boat to follow. We let *Hope* go a few yards in front and followed immediately. They managed to get through without tipping up but were carried, barely in control, over several more cataracts before pulling into the bank.

We were less lucky: we could not see the fall until we were right on top of it. It was a shoot of foaming water, rather like a weir, leading down into the trough of a huge stopper wave – a standing wave caused by the force of water pouring over an obstacle and then rolling back on itself. The boat seemed to teeter for a second on the brink, then shot down. We were all shouting. It hit a rock, slewed round and the next moment I was under water. I came to the surface, got a glimpse of the boat, bottomside up, and was then pulled under again. Instinctively I pulled the release of the gas cylinder for the life jacket, came to the surface, grabbed a gasp of breath and then went under. It was like being tumbled round in a huge washing machine. I had no sense of fear, just an instinctive determination to breathe when I could, but then came the realisation that I was probably going to drown. A gentle feeling of guilt at having betrayed my wife, Wendy, was replaced by one of curiosity – 'What will it be like when I'm dead?'

There was very little skill in getting down cataracts. It was entirely a matter of luck which waves we hit.

A shaken group recovering from the first experience of being totally out of control in the cataracts. From the left, Ian Macleod, Jim Masters, Roger Chapman and John Fletcher.

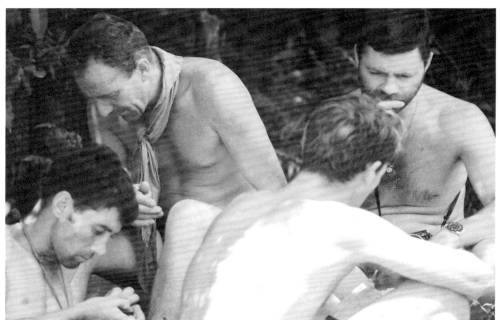

With equal suddenness the water released me and I found myself being swept onto some rocks just below the fall. All three of us had narrow escapes. Ian Macleod somehow hung on to the up-ended boat and was swept down through some huge falls before managing to grab an overhanging branch on the bank and pull himself to safety. Chris Edwards was swept down on to the brink of another fall, and was only rescued with difficulty and considerable risk by another member of the team going out to him on the end of the line.

It took twenty-four hours for the full shock of our narrow escapes to hit me. Wendy and I had lost our first child by drowning only two years earlier and this compounded the horror. I was so badly shaken that I asked Roger Chapman to drop me from the white water team. Another member of the group also withdrew and Chris Edwards was so badly lacerated that there was now no question of his going on. Both Roger Chapman and John Blashford-Snell were faced with a major crisis. The day's events had highlighted the very real dangers of the river and the inadequacy of the rubber boats in the rapids. Roger Chapman took off on foot to make a lightning reconnaissance of the river below the Tissisat Falls, where the rapids seemed even more dangerous, while the rest of us were left to work the boats down, close to the bank, to the head of the falls. The Tissisat Falls are as impressive as Niagara, plunging in a great curtain interspersed with forested islands over a sheer wall that bounds the side of a narrow gorge, opening into a wide valley below. A modern hydro-electric station lies just below the falls, and just below this is an old bridge, one of two built by the Portuguese in the eighteenth century.

Since we were short of manpower I had agreed to help bring down the boats and while edging them through narrow channels, often dragging them over water-logged grass to avoid the worst of the falls, I began to recover my peace of mind. I could not help worrying over my decision to pull out, particularly as two other members of the team who were married had elected to carry on. When Roger returned from his recce, I asked to be reinstated in the white water team, but he had already found a replacement for me and, anyway, I suspect he was quite relieved to lose an argumentative and troublesome subordinate who used his power and independence as representative of the press to get his own way.

Roger Chapman had now reduced his white water team to six, spread between two boats. As a result of his lightning recce, he had decided that a number of stretches of the river were too dangerous. They portaged the boats to a stretch of river some miles below the Tissisat Falls, then paddled about twelve miles to a point where the banks closed into a narrow neck, through which the entire volume of the Blue Nile was squeezed, hurtling into a cauldron of bubbling effervescent water. Below this the river plunged into a sheer-sided gorge that stretched for six miles to the second Portuguese bridge, below which things appeared to become a little easier. Roger Chapman, therefore, decided to send the boats down by themselves to be picked up by a party already in position at the Portuguese bridge, while the two crews walked round the top.

It is one of those tragic ironies that our SAS man, Ian Macleod, lost his life while taking what had seemed the safest course. We had nearly finished our march to the Portuguese bridge and had to cross the river Abaya; it was only thirty feet wide, but very deep and fast-flowing, opaque brown waters swirling past the sheer rocky banks in the bed of the gorge. Macleod went across second after tying on a safety line. He was so proficient in everything he did, we just assumed he was a strong swimmer, but before he was half-way it became obvious that he was in difficulties. The rope around his waist tended to pull him under and sweep him further downstream. Soon, it was all he could do to keep his head above water. The others paid

Crossing the fast-flowing river Abaya. It was here that Ian Macleod drowned while trying to take a line across.

out the rope as he was swept along but in a matter of seconds they came to the end of it. If they held on, he would be pulled under; if they tried to pull him back the same would happen. Someone shouted, 'Let go the rope!' They did, and at the same time Roger Chapman, with considerable heroism, his boots still on, dived into the river to try to help Macleod. He managed to grab hold of him and towed him to the other side, reaching it just in time before the river plunged into the next cataract. But the rope tied round Ian's waist now acted like an anchor and he was torn from Roger's grasp and dragged under. We never saw him again and his body was never recovered.

John Blashford-Snell, blancoing his pith helmet, was waiting for us when we rejoined the main party.

John Blashford-Snell was waiting for us at the Portuguese bridge. The flotilla was now to be enlarged to three Redshanks and two inflatable Army recce boats powered by outboard motors. Blashford-Snell was to assume command once more and I had elected to return to the river. Though still badly shaken, I could not possibly cover the story from the bank.

The water was never as bad as it had been above the Tissisat Falls, but it was like going down a liquid Cresta run, never sure what was round the next bend and barely able to stop. There was no more exhilaration, just a nagging fear and taut concentration as we spun the boats out of the way of boulders or edged round the worst of the waves.

Now the river began to take on a new character, hurrying in a solid smooth stream between sheer rock walls. It was at last possible to relax and marvel at the rock architecture around us. Slender towers jutted hundreds of feet out of the river bed, while huge natural arches spanned its tributaries. We stopped that night in an idyllic campsite by the tree-covered banks of a side stream. The walls of the gorge towered forty-five metres above us.

We were intrigued by two caves in the sheer cliff opposite, which had obviously been inhabited at one time. Next morning we succeeded in climbing to them from the boat, and discovered a number of broken pots and old grain silos well covered in bat dung. We were all excited by the discovery as we packed up camp. I was drinking a cup of coffee when John ran into the camp and shouted, 'Hurry up, it's time we got out of here.' At the same time, there was a sudden, high-pitched keening from above, followed by a volley of rifle fire. We were completely taken by surprise, finding it impossible to believe that people were actually trying to kill us.

My first reaction was that perhaps they just wanted to warn us off. John Blashford-Snell ran out with the loud-hailer shouting, '*Ternasterling, ternasterling,*' the conventional form of greeting, but one of the men on the cliff opposite replied by firing at him. I can remember running out myself, trying to wave to them, and then noticing a rifle pointing straight at me.

While some of us tried appeasement others raced out from cover to load the boats.

People were actually trying to kill us. John Blashford-Snell got out his service revolver and took potshots at our Shifta bandit attackers as we beat a hasty retreat.

We were still arguing in the shelter of the trees about what we should do, but no-one recommended firing back at this stage. One party wanted to make a break for it; the other, of which I was one, felt we should stay put and try to reason with our attackers, or call up support on the wireless. The deciding factor was a huge rock, the size of a kitchen table, that came hurtling down from above.

'Gentlemen, someone has got to make a decision,' said John Blashford-Snell, in a remarkably cool voice. 'When I say "go", run for the boats.'

The next thing I remember is pushing our boat through the shallows. Glancing up, the whole sky seemed full of rocks; bullets spurted in the water around us. We were gathering speed in the main current when I suddenly felt a violent blow on my back and was hurled across the boat. I had been hit by a rock.

John Blashford-Snell had now got out his revolver and was taking potshots at our attackers, though the chances of hitting anyone with a pistol at a range of forty-five metres, shooting upwards from a moving boat, must have been slight. It did, perhaps, cause them to duck, for it seems a miracle that not only were none of us hit but neither were the large targets presented by the boats. If an inflated side had been punctured it could have been serious.

Fortunately we travelled much faster on the river than they could possibly manage on the banks and as a result were soon out of range. That night we stopped on an island off the Gojjam shore. Just before dark a youngster swam the channel, chatted with us and no doubt had a good look at all our possessions. We were all nervous and, before going to bed, I made sure I had everything to hand, even contemplating keeping my boots on. Roger Chapman was standing sentry in the middle of the night. He had just walked out of the camp to check the boats and shone his torch casually at the water's edge. The light picked out the head of someone swimming across from the other bank. Then he heard a rattle of stones and swung the torch on a group of men gathered on the water's edge, spears clutched in their hands. He shouted out; one of them fired at him and suddenly it was bedlam.

I can remember waking to the shrill war-whoops of our attackers. I did not feel afraid, just keyed to a high pitch. I had been worried the previous night about the boats, which were pulled up onto the beach about fifty-five metres from our camp. If the bandits managed to release or capture these, we should have no chance of survival. Grabbing my pistol and my box of cameras and exposed film, I shouted, 'For God's sake get down to the boats,' then started running, crouched, towards them. Roger Chapman heard me and did the same, whilst the others formed a rough line across the island, firing back at our attackers. It was a confusion of shouts and yells, of gun flashes and the arc of mini-flares which John Blashford-Snell, with great resource, was aiming at our attackers. I paused a couple of times, pointed my pistol at some of the gun flashes and fired. There was little chance of hitting anyone and suddenly I realised that only two bullets were left in the chamber and there were no spare rounds in my pocket. What on earth would I do if some of our attackers had sneaked up on the boats? I ran on down to them and was greatly relieved to find no-one there.

Then, as suddenly as the noise had started, there was silence – just an occasional rustle from the bank showed that our attackers were still there. We packed up in the dark and withdrew to the boats. We stayed there for a couple of hours, hoping to wait until dawn before descending the river, but at 3.30 a.m. a bugle blared, almost certainly heralding another attack. John Blashford-Snell was worried about our shortage of ammunition and gave the order to cast off.

In complete silence we drifted into the main stream – it was an eerie experience, for we were able to see only the sheen of water and the dark silhouette of the banks.

Then we heard the thunder of a cataract ahead, tried to pull into the bank, but were helpless in the current. Suddenly, we were in white water; we climbed a huge wave, came down the other side and were through, but the other two boats were less lucky.

'We seemed to stand on end,' Roger Chapman told me afterwards. 'I jammed my leg under the thwart and somehow managed to stay in the boat, but the other two were thrown out. I realised immediately that if I couldn't grab them we should never find them in the dark. They came to the surface just alongside the boat, and I dragged them in.'

Meanwhile, the boat which had us in tow, was sinking; the air valve had developed a fault and the front compartment was completely deflated. They had no choice but to release us and we drifted away in the dark. It was a good half-mile before we managed to pull on to a sandbank in the middle of the river where we sat until dawn, feeling very lonely and vulnerable.

The drama never seemed to end. John Fletcher had damaged the propeller of his boat immediately after being thrown out in the cataract. As soon as they reached a sandbank he got out his tool kit to change propellers while the party waited for the dawn. A few minutes later he walked over to Roger Chapman.

'A terrible thing's happened. I've lost the nut holding the propeller,' he whispered.

The outboard motor was essential for our escape and they tried fixing it with a bent nail, but that was no good. Then, as a last resort, they mixed some Araldite glue and stuck it back on the shaft, but the glue needed at least an hour to stick and by now it was beginning to get light.

John Blashford-Snell waited as long as he dared before giving the order to move. John Fletcher tied a polythene bag round the propeller in an effort to keep the glue dry and the boats were pushed off and drifted down the river.

The only noise was the gurgling of smooth, fast-flowing water. The wan light of the dawn coloured the fluted rocks and pinnacles on either side of the gorge a subtle brown. In contrast to the night's violence it was unbelievably beautiful. As we swept down the river, it was all so peaceful and yet so full of lurking threats.

Later on that morning we met up with one of the big flat-bottomed assault boats that had driven up against the current to escort us down to the Shafartak bridge. Our adventures were nearly over and, that afternoon on the 25th September, we pulled the boats up onto the shore just below the bridge. We had descended most of the upper reaches of the Blue Nile, though had avoided two long sections of difficult cataracts.

The expedition had achieved a great deal, covering more of the river than any previous expedition and completing some useful zoological work. It had also proved more adventurous than any of us had anticipated. John Blashford-Snell had tried to foresee every possible eventuality, running the expedition like a military operation with the back-up of support parties and the Beaver aircraft, but once on the waters of the upper river the back-up could have been on another continent for all the help it could give. In some ways his approach was that of the leader of a large, siege-style expedition in the Himalaya, with the security of fixed ropes and camps. His management was that of a military commander with a clear chain of command, with orders being given and obeyed. It undoubtedly worked well, both in the general running of the expedition and at the moments of crisis on the river itself. It could be argued, however, that the very size and ponderousness of the party created some of its own problems. In addition, the Redshanks proved totally inadequate for the task in hand. They were too easily capsized and also insufficiently manoeuvrable to pick their way down the rapids with any kind of control.

A very different style of expedition was to attempt the Blue Nile in 1972. I became involved indirectly, when a group of young white water canoeists came to a lecture I gave on our descent of the river in 1968. They wanted to canoe down the upper reaches of the river Inn, and hoped that I would be able to gain them the support of the *Daily Telegraph* Magazine. I took to them immediately. They had a boyish enthusiasm yet, at the same time, seemed to know what they were talking about. Next day I watched them canoe down some small rapids in Yorkshire and was impressed by the way they handled their craft. Whereas we had been bits of flotsam at the mercy of the Blue Nile, they were like water animals or mermen, encased in the shells of their canoes, flitting in and out from one eddy to the next, choosing their course down a section of rapids, capsizing just for the hell of it, and then rolling back effortlessly into an upright position.

I persuaded the editor of the *Telegraph* Magazine to back them and spent an invigorating and at times inspiring week in Austria, photographing them as they shot the most terrifying rapids I had ever seen and the most difficult water any of them had ever attempted. Of the five who started down the river Inn, only two got all the way down to the end of the difficult section – Dave Allen, the oldest and most experienced of the five, and Mike Jones, the youngest.

Mike was only sixteen at the time, had just finished doing his GCEs at school and was treated by the rest of the team as the apprentice and tea boy; but they could not keep him down. He had an irrepressible quality and this combined with a powerful physique and complete lack of fear got him all the way down the river, when some of the others were forced out either through their boats sinking or a healthy sense of caution. This tremendous feat has not, and never could be, repeated, owing to the diversion of the river from these gorges.

Four years after John Blashford-Snell's powerful Army expedition, four young men in single-seat kayak canoes set out from Lake Tana to see how far they could get. They were led by a twenty-year-old medical student, Mike Jones.

After leaving school Mike decided to become a doctor, going to medical school in Birmingham; but he did not allow this to interfere with his canoeing. He was in Division 1 slalom racing, but though his canoeing was extremely powerful and completely fearless he lacked the precision to get into the British team. Essentially he was an adventurous canoeist. In 1971 he joined Chris Hawksworth, an outstanding Yorkshire canoeist, on another white water adventure, this time to canoe down the Grand Canyon. It was a big team numbering fifteen canoeists. As soon as this was over he began to look round for new challenges and was immediately attracted by the lure of the Blue Nile. He was now twenty, in the middle of an exacting degree course, and yet plunged into the organisation of a full scale expedition with the same drive and enthusiasm that had taken him down the river Inn.

He was in his element, an extrovert, a born showman with immense self-confidence and boundless energy. He wanted a lightweight trip, both for the aesthetic reason that it would be more of an adventure and also for the practical one that it would cost less. He settled on a team of six. There were to be five canoeists, three of whom were top-class white water men who had been with him to the Grand Canyon, also Mick Hopkinson, another competitive slalom canoeist from Bradford who was making a name for himself on British and Continental white water rivers. Glen Greer, a less powerful canoeist and a friend of Mike's at Birmingham University, was to be the one-man support team.

Mike flung the expedition together in six months, doing practically all the work himself, but with remarkable family support. Reg and Molly Jones, his parents, became deeply involved in Mike's adventures, supplying encouragement and practical secretarial back-up to his mercurial schemes. He was very much a one-man-band, conceiving an idea and then carrying it through with an explosive enthusiasm which made it very difficult for him to delegate jobs to others. But it was the very force of this drive, however exasperating it might have been to his team members, that overcame a whole series of hurdles which could have stopped a more meticulous and thoughtful planner.

First of all there were the problems of getting the canoes out to Ethiopia, obtaining permission to descend the river, buying firearms and pistols and finding some kind of transport in Ethiopia for the support party. He managed to get a Winston Churchill Fellowship which gave him both a cash base and an air of respectability. He also had the promise of a Land-Rover from British Leyland but was unable to get clearance to drive overland into Ethiopia. He sought help from the Royal Air Force and in a letter to the Chief of Air Staff his response to their refusal is quite revealing:

> I requested air transport out for five canoeists, (one in the Fleet Air Arm, one in the Army and myself in the RAF (University of Birmingham Air Squadron)) and, if possible, the Land-Rover.
>
> The application was turned down. The enormity of the task we are attempting, the generous support we have received from educational and charitable trusts and, above all, the fact that at twenty I should be mature enough and have the ability to set up an international expedition of this kind disgraces the RAF in their refusal, despite their vast resources, to help me explore this little-known area.
>
> To quote from the letter received from the Winston Churchill Trust informing me of my successful application: 'Sir Winston – war leader, historian, adventurer, soldier, painter, writer, politician and statesman, had no patience with formality or red tape; he believed in action.'
>
> In emulating Sir Winston, I hope to see more of the action and less of the Red Tape.'

He received neither reply nor the flights he wanted, but this did not deter him and he managed to get some concessions from Egypt Air. At the same time as organising the expedition he was studying for his exams and organising a tour of the British Junior Canoe Team in Europe. Then, just three weeks before departure, he was confronted with a major crisis. The Services refused clearance to join the expedition for two of his canoeists, on the grounds that the venture was too dangerous and that the political situation in Ethiopia was uncertain. The latter reason seems curious, since an expedition of Sandhurst cadets were in Ethiopia at the same time as Mike Jones and his team. Then a third man also withdrew. The reasons he gave were pressures of business and his unhappiness with Mike Jones's organisation. He had talked to John Blashford-Snell about the enterprise and felt that a stronger back-up was needed.

But Mike was not going to be beaten; he chased around and found two substitutes. Dave Burkinshaw, a Rotherham schoolteacher who had canoed with Mike on the slalom circuit, was, in fact, more highly-placed in the ratings than either Mike or the only survivor from the original team, Mick Hopkinson; and Steve Nash, an electronics engineer from Reading, was in the British white water team and, at twenty-seven, would be the oldest member of the expedition.

Mike set out for Ethiopia with all the gear on the 24th July. The others were going to follow a fortnight later. Looking more like a mercenary than a Winston Churchill Fellow, he arrived at London Airport with two revolvers and a shotgun under his arm. He also had the four canoes and all the expedition gear, fourteen packages in all, which Egypt Air had agreed to carry out free as accompanied luggage. He managed to get everything on the 'plane, surrendering the guns to the pilot for his safe-keeping.

He had to change 'planes at Cairo and tried to persuade the pilot to carry the guns over to Customs, but the pilot wouldn't touch them. By this time the rest of the passengers had already left the 'plane and were in the airport bus. Mike, feeling very much on his own, tucked the guns under his arm and walked out onto the tarmac; he had taken only a couple of steps when there was a yell and a guard came rushing up, gun pointed at Mike. Soon he was surrounded by excited guards, disarmed, beaten up and hauled off to a detention centre. He never discovered whether they thought he was a mercenary on the way to the wars or a potential hijacker, but it took him eight hours of hard talking before he had convinced them that he was a peaceable canoeist on the way to the Blue Nile.

His troubles were not over, for when they came to change 'planes, he discovered that the canoes would not fit into the cargo bay of the Comet which flew from Cairo to Addis Ababa. He had no choice, therefore, but to leave them behind at Cairo, hoping to have them sent on by some alternative means. On arrival at Addis, he found himself plunged into a lone struggle with Ethiopian bureaucracy to get all the gear through Customs. He managed to do this in the comparatively short time of two weeks; it had taken very nearly two months for Blashford-Snell's expedition to clear Customs. But the canoes were still sitting in Cairo Airport.

When the rest of the team flew out to join him, Steve Nash took the precaution of sealing his .38 into the bottom of the metal box containing one of the radios and, as a result, got it through undetected. They were just about to board the 'plane at Cairo, when Mick Hopkinson noticed the four canoes which Mike Jones had brought out, lying on the tarmac where they had been dumped a fortnight before. Hopkinson insisted on the 'plane delaying its departure and Steve Nash even tried to unscrew one of the pressurised windows of the 'plane, hoping to get the canoes in that way and then to lay them in the gangway. He was stopped, very forcibly, by the pilot. In the end they left Dave Burkinshaw in Cairo, while they flew to Addis. Eventually the canoes caught up with them by Ethiopian Airlines.

It was nearly six weeks from the day Mike Jones had set out from Heathrow before they were ready at last to launch their boats in Lake Tana. Inevitably the delays had got on their nerves. Although the group had met each other in the canoe circuit, they did not know each other well. For all except Mike Jones this was their first expedition and even for him there was a vast difference between joining a group canoeing down the Grand Canyon and being in Ethiopia in charge of everything.

Mike Jones was in a hurry to get going. The rainy season lasts from June to September and it was now very nearly over. As soon as the flood level began to drop, the submerged rocks would begin to reappear and the risk of tearing out the bottoms of the canoes would be very much higher. Dave Burkinshaw and Steve Nash, on the other hand, were anxious to get everything soundly organised before committing themselves to the river. Dave had spent most of the night of their arrival at Bahardar, the small town on the banks of Lake Tana by the start of the Blue Nile, fastening into position the knee clamps which would help to jam him into his canoe, to enable him to paddle and – even more important – to roll effectively. He was worried about how well he would manage to fit these and whether the fibreglass had had time to set. Steve Nash was anxious to test all the wireless equipment and opted to stay out of the water on the first day to give himself time to do this.

They pushed the canoes into the water at the Bahardar bridge on the morning of the 3rd September. Glen Greer had decided to paddle Steve Nash's boat that day, since the stretch down to the Tissisat Falls did not look too serious. Nash, with the Land-Rover, was going to meet them just above the falls that evening. At first everything went well. On the first big cataract, down which we had been swept out of control in 1968, they were able to pick their way. The waters were big and powerful but nothing like as difficult as some white water in Britain. Below the cataract, however, they ran into the same problems that we had encountered in 1968. Because of the number of different channels and heavily overgrown islands they were unable to inspect each cataract on foot, before going down. They had no choice but to take them blind. Mike Jones and Mick Hopkinson were out in front, taking one cataract at a time and then waiting for the others. Dave Burkinshaw and Glen Greer, less confident, were well behind. Greer was finding it particularly difficult, less at ease than the others in wild water, less adept at rolling back up once he had capsized.

The river was wide and shallow for long stretches, but then as they swept round a bend there was a roar of water; they could not see anything until they were on the very brink of the fall and completely committed. Jones, Hopkinson and Burkinshaw managed to shoot the fall, plunging down it to skirt a huge whirlpool, but Greer was sucked in, canoe and all, and vanished from sight. It seemed an age, though was probably less than a minute, before a paddle came to the surface well below the whirlpool, then the canoe itself, badly smashed, popped vertically from out of the water. And still there was no sign of Glen Greer. At last he surfaced, almost a hundred metres downstream, badly shaken.

He insisted on carrying on, even though he was capsized and forced to swim for it on several more occasions. At the end of the day, still five miles short of the Tissisat Falls, they pulled into the bank and struggled for half a mile through the under-growth to the road, where Steve Nash eventually found them and took them back to the hotel.

Dave Burkinshaw was becoming more and more worried about the whole venture. He had managed the first section without too much difficulty but was very aware that they had been paddling unladen canoes. Below the Tissisat Falls the river plunges through a series of gorges for the next 200 miles. They would have to carry

The river flowed between inhospitable barren uplands and a row of figures on the skyline could present a menacing aspect. All the local people seemed to be armed with rifles.

their food, sleeping bags, radios and guns with them, all of which would make the canoes heavy and difficult to manoeuvre through cataracts which were probably going to be faster and more dangerous than anything they had faced before. On top of that were the threats of crocodiles and the Shifta bandits. He wanted time to think and insisted on staying out of the river the next day to go down and look at the waters below the falls. Steve Nash also stayed out and Glen Greer had had enough of canoeing; his role, anyway, was that of shore party.

The next morning Mike Jones and Mick Hopkinson returned to the river. In spite of its volume they were enjoying themselves. They made a good team, paddled at the same standard and had a similar attitude to risk. They picked their way through winding channels, past tree-clad islands, shot tumbling cataracts and saw their first crocodile – a dark shape in the murky brown water.

It was late afternoon before they reached the top of the Tissisat Falls, hauled the boats out of the river and carried them to the road. Mike wanted to return to the water at the Portuguese bridge below the hydro-electric station. Pleased with the day's canoeing and full of optimism, they rejoined the team to face a crisis. Dave

Burkinshaw announced that he was not prepared to go any further since he was convinced that they would be unable to control heavily laden canoes in the rapids. Jones disagreed and a furious argument ensued, culminating in Burkinshaw stating that he was going to return home.

The following morning Jones, Hopkinson and Nash, watched by Burkinshaw, Greer and a large group of local dignitaries, set out just below the Portuguese bridge. At this point the river races down in a series of furious rapids. Heavily laden, it was difficult to manoeuvre the canoes through the torrent and they had gone only 275 metres when Nash hit a rock, ripped the bottom out of his canoe and was forced to bail out. The other two pulled into the bank. It was obvious that they could never get down these waters heavily laden.

Jones decided that the only course they could take was to dump as much as possible and travel down really light, living off the land – or just going hungry. After all, they should be able to reach the Shafartak road bridge in four days. Nash thought this ridiculous; the risks were altogether too great. Hopkinson was happy to go along with Jones, but kept out of the argument. In the end they arrived at a compromise. Nash suggested that he and Burkinshaw should act as a bank party, carrying their canoes and all the supplies round the difficult stretch of river – which they knew to be about twenty miles – while Jones and Hopkinson, travelling light, tried to canoe it. They would meet up again at the second Portuguese bridge. It also had the advantage of bringing Dave Burkinshaw back into the expedition. He agreed to join Nash on the walk and to canoe the river from the second Portuguese bridge.

It was now the 6th September. Mike Jones and Mick Hopkinson returned to the river with just their sleeping bags, a radio, a cine camera, a pistol each and a little food – a bar of Kendal Mint Cake, an oatmeal block and a Rowntree's jelly. Both admitted to being scared, but were determined to complete the river. The canoes, although lighter than the previous day, were still unwieldly. Fierce cataracts alter nated with stretches of brown swirling waters which gave a feeling of unpredictable power. On the banks cultivated fields were interspersed with patches of forest and scrub. After twelve miles they reached a point where the huge volume of the Blue Nile was compressed into a rocky passage a bare metre and a half wide that led into a boiling cauldron. This was the place where the white water team of the previous expedition had pulled their rubber boats out of the river. Hopkinson and Jones did the same, but paid some men who were working in the fields to carry the canoes a short distance round the obstacle.

They returned to the river at the start of the long gorge contained by sheer walls, thirty metres high, which we had avoided in 1968. It was the most committing stretch of water that Jones and Hopkinson had ever ventured on. There was no possibility of any reconnaissances of the cataracts from the bank; they could not escape from the river, for the racing waters had carved away the black volcanic rock of the gorge walls into a continuous overhanging lip. There were hardly any eddies for them to rest in; they had to keep going, weaving their way through the cataracts, trying to read the maze of foaming waves and tumbling water, cutting their way across the troughs of giant stoppers, skirting boiling whirlpools. They took turns in going out in front, never knowing what was going to face them round the next bend. Their necks ached from the continuous craning to see over the crests of waves; there was no release from the tension, no chance to relax. Mick Hopkinson admitted to being more frightened in this section than he has ever been before or since – they were so completely committed to a stretch of river they knew nothing about.

It was five o'clock in the afternoon; the tropical dusk was getting close when they noticed a slight bay on the right. There was some slack water and a steep water-course cutting its way through the wall of the gorge. They swung into it, had a desperate struggle to heave the boats out of the water and then started to scramble up the boulder-strewn slope, canoes balanced precariously over their shoulders. Out in front, Mike Jones stumbled on a huge boulder; it started rolling, bounding down towards Hopkinson coming up behind. He dived out of the way and just managed to avoid it. Shaken, exhausted, they reached the top of the slope and found a thicket in which to get some shelter for the night. It started to rain, quickly soaking their clothes and sleeping bags, but they dared not light a fire for fear of attracting bandits. Munching Kendal Mint Cake and chewing through some jelly, they joked about the fact that it was Mike Jones' twenty-first birthday, then tried to settle down for the night. They both slept lightly, shivering in wet sleeping bags, frightened by every rustle in the undergrowth. Mike woke up on one occasion to find himself holding his cocked and loaded pistol, finger on the trigger, pointed at Hopkinson's head.

At last the dawn came. They could not bring themselves to put the canoes back into the gorge, particularly as the cataracts just ahead were even worse than those they had been through the previous day. Instead they decided to carry them for about a mile, round the top of the gorge, struggling through undergrowth, up and down over stream beds until the walls of the defile began to relent and they were able to return to the water. It was still very fast and threatening; they were both very tired and as a result both had narrow escapes.

Mick Hopkinson was in front as they came to the top of a fall. At first glance it did not look too bad, a shoot of brown water leading to swirling brown waters below. It was only when he was on the very brink that he realised that the water was thundering over a sheer drop of nearly five metres. As he plummeted down he stood on his foot rest, leaning back against the canoe to reduce the impact when he hit the water below. Fortunately there were no rocks and he arrowed down into the middle of the pool of boiling water, completely submerged, and then shot out just beyond it, his close-fitting spray deck keeping the water out of the canoe, managed to skate past the top of the fall and find an easier way down, further across. A few hundred metres further on Jones was caught in a huge whirlpool; he was spun round and round, helpless in the huge vortex before several minutes of frantic paddling enabled him to escape.

They reached the second Portuguese bridge that same afternoon. There was no sign of their bank support party and so they set up camp a few hundred metres above the bridge. They were careful to hide the guns and their very obvious poverty was probably their best defence. What little money they had left had been spent in paying the local people to carry their canoes round the start of the gorge. In the next two days, while awaiting the arrival of the others, they bartered the few scanty articles of clothing they had with them for potatoes. In the afternoon of the second day Nash and Burkinshaw, with nine porters, reached the bridge. They were all exhausted, for they had had to walk about ninety miles of very steep and difficult going; the porters had become increasingly nervous as they got further away from home and at one point Nash had been forced to threaten them with his loaded revolver to stop them dropping the canoes and deserting.

Mike Jones could sense an almost immediate change of atmosphere amongst the rapidly-growing crowd of local people, all of them armed with rifles, now that they saw the size of the team and the amount of gear they carried. It did not seem wise to hang around longer than was absolutely necessary and so that very afternoon they loaded the canoes and pulled out into the river.

It was now both wide and deep – comparatively easy canoeing, even when heavily laden. That day they paddled a few miles downstream and stopped for a big celebration tea, lighting a fire and gorging themselves to the full and then set off once again paddling until it was very nearly dark before slipping into a slight inlet and bedding down amongst the bushes without lighting a fire. In this way they hoped to avoid being discovered by the local people. Using this technique they managed to get down to the Shafartak bridge in four days. They were fired upon once by a group on the bank, but their progress was so swift and surreptitious that they avoided the trouble we had encountered in 1968.

Crocodiles, on the other hand, gave them some severe frights. We had been towed down the slower, more meandering section of the river by one of the big assault boats and, as a result, had hardly noticed the crocodiles. They, however, were paddling at about the same speed as a crocodile swims and, to a crocodile, a canoe must closely resemble a very large fish. They had heard tales of crocodiles biting canoes in half and, sitting in a fragile, fibreglass shell, you don't feel like taking any chances when a five-metre crocodile comes cruising though the water to take a look at you.

Dave Burkinshaw was some hundred metres in front of the others when he noticed the distinctive V-wave coming up fast behind him. He put on speed, hoping that he could out-paddle it, having heard that crocodiles lack stamina. After about a hundred metres he was beginning to tire and he glanced round to see that the crocodile seemed to be gaining on him. By this time he was naturally very, very frightened. He turned for the bank and paddled flat out for it. He was, of course, fastened into the canoe by his spray cover and, to make himself even more secure, he had doubled up with a second one. This meant it was always quite a struggle to free himself from the canoe, but now – with the strength of desperation, he succeeded in tearing off the covers with one hand between racing strokes of the paddle, leaping out of the canoe in a single movement as it ran aground and in three bounds reached the foot of the four-metre high wall of the bank and climbed it.

The crocodile was more interested in the canoe and, as it drifted off, he followed it downstream. The others had seen Dave's sprint for the bank and followed as quickly as they could. Steve, who wore his pistol in a shoulder holster, was the only one with a gun readily available. With considerable courage, realising that he had to recover Dave's canoe, he paddled right up to the crocodile and emptied the magazine of his revolver into it at point blank range. The crocodile sank from sight, so they could not be sure whether it had been killed or not.

From this point, every stretch of slack water had its resident crocodiles who came out to investigate the intruders. Jones and Hopkinson now kept their guns at the ready, but Burkinshaw was unarmed and had to content himself with a little pile of stones. They now kept close together, but had several more encounters and had used up most of their ammunition by the time they reached the Shafartak bridge.

They arrived there on the 12th September, tired and very tense from twelve days of nerve-wracking canoeing, the threat of crocodiles and the danger of possible attack by local people. They had originally planned to go all the way to the Sudan, but now all of them, I suspect, were beginning to have second thoughts. They had to wait a day at the bridge, both for Glen Greer with the support Land-Rover and also for a Reuter correspondent who had arranged to meet them there. It was a period of relaxation after tension; the bridge was somehow a natural bound to the venture and yet there was the pressure of their expressed intentions. Mike Jones, perhaps, felt obliged to urge them on, down past the bridge; after all, the expedition had been his concept. At first the other three were doubtful. Dave Burkinshaw had definitely had enough; Mick Hopkinson observed that they had very nearly run out of ammunition and that there would be even more crocodiles below the bridge than there had been above. It was not as if the river itself would provide a challenge – they knew they could manage the water. It was the threat of crocodiles and Shifta bandits and the fact that there was no road from the river once they had reached the border that deterred them now. They were not a closely-knit team, had never been away on expeditions before and this, of course, was their first venture into really wild country. Steve Nash, after a night's rest, came round to wanting to complete the journey, but by now Mike Jones had swung away from it, saying that there was no point in going on if they were not united. This, I suspect, was the crux of the problem and in the end they piled their canoes into the Land-Rover and drove to Addis Ababa.

They may not have completed their objective, but they had descended more of the upper part of the Blue Nile than anyone else has succeeded doing to this day and, in so doing, had tackled some of the most dangerous white water that anyone has ever attempted.

Mike Jones went on to organise and lead an expedition which canoed down the

Dudh Kosi, the glacier torrent that runs down from the Khumbu Glacier on Everest. Mick Hopkinson went with him. It was a slightly larger team than he had had on the Blue Nile and, although the waters in places were technically more difficult than those encountered on the Blue Nile, there were none of the extra risks of attacks by bandits or crocodiles. In addition, a bank support party was able to follow the river much of the way and Nepal today is becoming as much a holiday area as the European Alps. Nevertheless, this was a fine achievement which confirmed Mike Jones as the most outstanding white water expedition organiser in the world. In the course of the descent he saved the life of Mick Hopkinson, who had fallen out of his canoe, by towing him to the side through a serious of dangerous rapids.

He next went off to the Orinoco in South America and then, in 1978, with the bulk of the Dudh Kosi team, on the Braldu river running down from the Baltoro Glacier in Pakistan. Here he was drowned – once again going to the help of a member of his team who had fallen out of his canoe in a practice session. It was typical of Mike Jones that he did not think of his own safety in going to someone else's assistance. He was still only twenty-six. His immense enthusiasm and drive, combined with his boldness and physical strength, would have taken him through many more adventures had Fate spared him. Mick Hopkinson plans to return to the Braldu river with the rest of the team, to finish what they had started. Neither Steve Nash nor Dave Burkinshaw have joined any other expeditions, though Glen Greer went with Mike Jones to the Orinoco.

Of the 1968 expedition, John Blashford-Snell went on to organise a series of even more ambitious projects, manhandling Range-Rovers across the Darien Gap, the pathless jungle swamp that divides North America from the southern continent; descending the Zaire river with another large waterborne expedition of scientists and soldiers and, most recently, organising Operation Drake, a global project to give youngsters a taste of field scientific work and adventure. In doing this he has given a large number of people a great deal of enjoyment and excitement and has made possible some useful scientific work.

There is a vast difference between the approach Mike Jones adopted and that of John Blashford-Snell on the Blue Nile. In climbing terms, it is the difference between the massive, carefully organised siege attempt on a mountain and a small party making an Alpine-style ascent. It was ironic that the big and very carefully organised party had a fatal casualty and, because of the very size and therefore somewhat ponderous descent down river, attracted two full-scale bandit attacks, while the comparatively unorganised, lightweight dash by canoeists who really understood white water, and were using suitable boats for the upper reaches of the river, got away unscathed. It is possible that audacity has a momentum that sometimes carries its own protection.

The Karakoram and the Himalaya

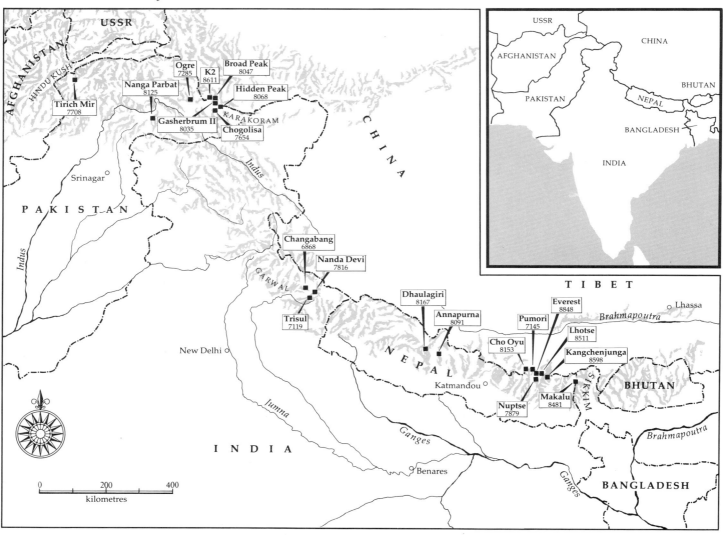

Annapurna, the first 8000

One's first visit to the Himalaya is always immensely exciting. There is the anticipation of the climbing on mountains higher than one has ever been before, the anxiety of how one will adapt to altitude or, on larger expeditions, whether one will be a member of one of the teams to reach the top. But beyond that is the fascination of the country itself, not just the mighty snow peaks that can be glimpsed, often half hidden, elusive, mysterious through the haze from the ever ascending crests of the foothills, but of a new and different people, the women in their long cotton skirts, heavy ear-rings and gold stud in one nostril, often beautiful in a subtle, gentle way, the men, lightly built, lean from hard work, but laughing and friendly. Every inch of fertile ground is intensely farmed in terraces carved from the steep hillside, the houses, with mud walls, often with elaborately carved window frames and either thatched or slated roofs, nestle into the country with the same feeling of belonging that I've seen in English Lakeland farmhouses or the old Swiss mountain chalets.

But for Maurice Herzog and his team of eight, the excitement was especially intense. It was 1950. Only one of them had ever been to the Himalaya before. Nobody had ever climbed a peak of over what has become the magic height of 8000 metres; and only one solitary mountaineering expedition had ever been into Nepal (to Kangchenjunga back in 1930), for that mountain kingdom which straddles the spine of the Himalaya for about 400 miles and which contains eight of the fourteen highest peaks of the world had kept its borders closed to almost all foreigners until 1949. The pre-war British expeditions to Everest had all made their approach through Tibet. Now, in the post-war period, the position was reversed. With the Chinese taking over in Tibet, that country was closed to outsiders, whilst Nepal was beginning to open up.

The French had played a minor part in the expeditions that had attempted the highest peaks of the world before the Second World War. But the 1950 Annapurna expedition was to be the first of a series organised centrally by the French Alpine Club which were to have a remarkably high level of success. A committee nominated both the leader and all the members of the team. Their selection was the more difficult because so few French climbers had been to the Himalaya and of course, with the gap of the war, the few that had, were probably over their prime. The younger French climbers had, however, been undergoing a renaissance of hard Alpine climbing. Before the war, pioneering the steep and difficult face routes of the Alps had been a preserve of the Germans, Austrians and Italians, who had claimed the North Faces of the Eiger, Grandes Jorasses, Matterhorn and Badile. The French approach, like the British, had been rather conservative, rejecting the techniques needed to scale the steepest walls of the ice, techniques that had been developed on

*Maurice Herzog, leader of
the French attempt on Annapurna
in 1950, on the party's
reconnaissance.*

*Lionel Terray, pictured here
at Camp 2, with Louis Lachenal
(below), were members of the new
post-war breed of French climbers.*

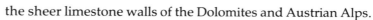

the sheer limestone walls of the Dolomites and Austrian Alps.

After the war, however, a new breed of French climbers had emerged, keen to catch up with modern Alpine trends. Lionel Terray and Louis Lachenal had made the second ascent of the North Wall of the Eiger. French climbers were repeating the hardest routes put up before the war and were beginning to pioneer technically hard rock routes in the Mont Blanc region. Terray and Lachenal must have been obvious choices for the team. They were very much the modern post-war climber; both had been keen and talented amateur climbers and had then decided to base their lives around climbing, becoming Chamonix guides, no easy feat for men not born in the Chamonix valley. Gaston Rébuffat came from a similar background, though born and brought up in Marseilles. He had learnt his climbing on the sun blazed rocks of the Calanques sea cliffs, but had gone on to do many of the most difficult climbs in the Alps. Jean Couzy and Marcel Schatz on the other hand were talented young amateurs, both coming from the traditional middle-class backgrounds which were the hallmarks of the pre-war and immediate post-war mountaineers, certainly the ones who were invited on Himalayan expeditions in both France and England at this time.

The leader, Maurice Herzog, was also an amateur climber. His appointment caused a good deal of argument, his critics pointing out that Herzog was not at the forefront of hard climbing in the Alps. He had, on the other hand, got a broad Alpine background, was secretary of the elite Groupe de Haute Montagne, was a good organiser and committee man and acceptable to the French climbing establishment. He had climbed with all the members of the team and had the force of personality, combined with tact and sympathy, to co-ordinate the efforts of a group of individualists. The team was made up by three climbers who had more of a support role, Jacques Oudot, the doctor, Marcel Ichac as climbing camera man and Francis de Noyelle, a young French diplomat who came along as liaison officer, and in effect was their Base Camp manager.

Herzog got his first glimpse of the great peaks of the Himalaya on the 10th April, from the brow of a hill above the small town of Tansing. He wrote:

> The sight which awaited us at the top of the hill far exceeded anything we had imagined. At the first glance we could see nothing but filmy mist; but looking more closely we could make out, far away in the distance, a terrific wall of ice rising above the mist to an unbelievable height, and blocking the horizon to the north for hundreds and hundreds of miles. This shining wall looked colossal, without fault or defect.

This was Dhaulagiri. They had permission for both Dhaulagiri, 8167 metres (26,795 feet), and Annapurna, 8091 metres (26,545 feet), but first they had to find the way to the foot of their mountains. The maps of the Nepal Himalaya were particularly inaccurate, for the Survey of India had not been allowed into Nepal and consequently most of the mapping had been done from a distance. They reached the village of Tukucha on the 22nd April and immediately split up into reconnaissance parties to determine which mountain to attempt and then the route that would give the greatest chance of success.

Initially they were attracted to Dhaulagiri. Higher of the two and by far the most obvious, it rises in a huge isolated hump above the Kali Gandaki, steep on every side. They made three reconnaissances but were discouraged by what they found. They had judged the appearance of the difficulties by their own Alpine standards, but once they attempted the long steep ridges they quickly discovered how much greater was the scale of everything, combined with the insidious effects of the greater altitude. They then turned to Annapurna, whose upper slopes they could see were less steep, but first they had to find a way to the foot of the mountain. The map was particularly misleading, putting both the Tilicho Pass and the range of mountain peaks that sweep to the north of Annapurna in the wrong place. As a result it took two further exploratory trips to find a way to its base.

Time was now slipping past all too quickly. In a spring or pre-monsoon attempt the time available for climbing in Nepal is bounded by the end of winter and the thawing of winter snows towards the end of March and the arrival of the monsoon towards the end of May or early June, and now it was the 14th May. They had spent very nearly a month on reconnaissances.

At Tukucha Herzog held a meeting. He asked everyone their opinion, let them all have their say, before summing up the consensus that Dhaulagiri was impossible, at any rate as far as they were concerned, but that Annapurna offered a chance of success. It was an agonising choice. Dhaulagiri was a magnificent challenge; they could at least see the way onto it, hard though it obviously was. They had still only had glimpses of the elusive Annapurna, by penetrating the precipitous Miristi Khola, which seemed to give the only feasible approach to the North Face, but they

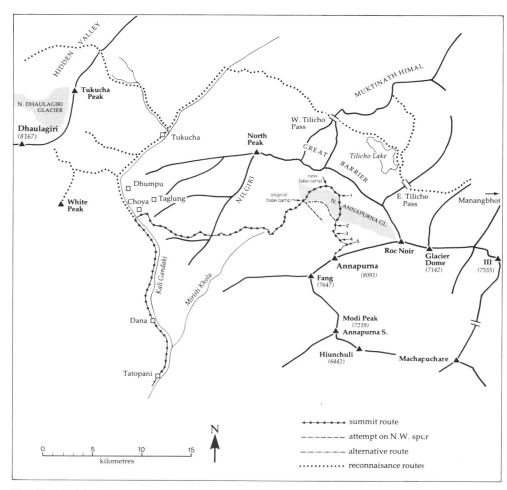

The Dhaulagiri and Annapurna massifs

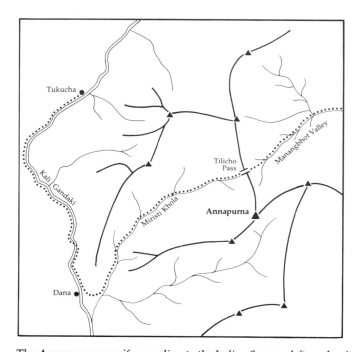

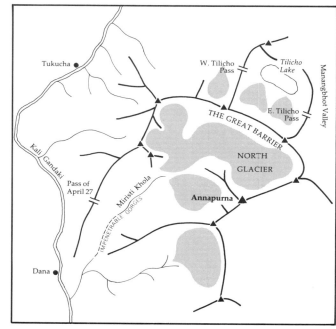

The Annapurna massif, according to the Indian Survey, left, and as it really is

Herzog's party first had to find their mountain. The Indian Survey maps of the period were particularly misleading, putting the Tilicho Pass, pictured here, and the mountains to the north of Annapurna in the wrong place.

had only had a limited view of this and of the North-West Ridge, though these seemed less steep than those on Dhaulagiri. It was Herzog's ultimate responsibility. In Terray's words, 'Maurice Herzog hesitated before the choice. Should he abandon a prize, however doubtful, in favour of a mystery so insubstantial? Could he expose men who had sworn to obey him to mortal danger?'

In some ways I envy the level of authority that Herzog had vested in him. On my own Annapurna South Face Expedition in 1970 the members of the team had signed an agreement which included a promise to obey their leader, but I always had a feeling that this was something that would be ignored in the stress of the moment if ever my own commands were far out of line with the consensus of the expedition. In fact the authority of a leader of an expedition does not depend on a scrap of paper, or even on a formal oath, but rather on the personality of the individual concerned. Climbers tend to be individualists, accustomed to taking their own decisions and as a result they do not respond to authoritarian leadership. A group of two or four people climbing together in the Alps, or for that matter the Himalaya does not need a formal leader, though interestingly enough someone nearly always emerges as a natural undeclared leader in any particular situation. With a larger group, however, particularly one where the members are scattered between different camps, some kind of positive co-ordination which is accepted by the other members of the party is necessary

It is interesting to surmise how much stronger Herzog's authority was in 1950 than that of the expedition leader of the 'eighties. The mood of the early 'fifties, even

Camp 2 of the 1978 American women's expedition, which was in approximately the same place as Herzog's, with the North Face towering above in the moonlight.

Annapurna, North Face

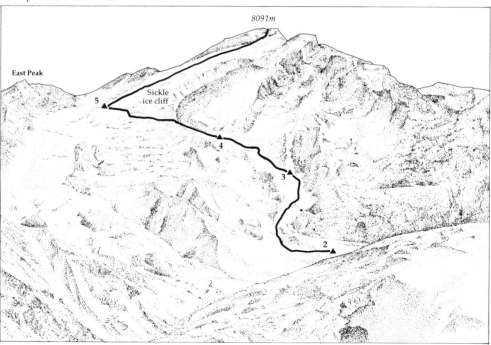

8091m

East Peak

Sickle
ice cliff

5

4

3

2

A Sherpa crossing the ice slope above Camp 2. The monsoon was almost upon them and they were running out of time.

amongst mountaineers, was more amenable to the concept of authority than it is today. Even so, the morale of the team depended on very much the same ingredients as that of a modern expedition, and in this respect Herzog's approach to leadership was similar to that of John Hunt on Everest in 1953 or my own today. He believed in keeping in close touch with the feelings of his team, took an active part in the climbing and yet, when it came to decision making, took them himself rather than put the question to the vote.

The first problem was to reach the base of Annapurna. On the 15th May, Terray, Lachenal and Schatz, with three Sherpas, set out up the Miristi Khola. It is an incredible switchback along forest and scrub-covered terraces, around rocky bluffs, along a series of tenuously interconnecting ledges that weave their way between the dizzy snow-clad summits of the Nilgiri peaks and the dark gorge of the Miristi Khola, 1500 metres below. They could barely hear the thunder of the torrent that hurtled down its bed, and then at last at the end of the switchback, a steep but easy couloir led down to the open sweep of the Annapurna Basin.

Annapurna was before them, but they still had to find a way up the mountain and the uncertainties weren't over. By far the safest route seemed the North-West Ridge because of being free from avalanche danger, but it was long and gendarmed. Herzog once again wanted to recce every alternative, sending parties both to the ridge and the heavily glaciated North Face. The ridge proved to be more difficult than they had anticipated, whilst the face proved to be easy, though threatened by huge avalanches that came sweeping down it from a great sickle of ice cliffs above. So they accepted the dangers of the easier route. It was now the 23rd May; the monsoon would be upon them in another fortnight and most of the expedition baggage and part of the team were still scattered between Tukucha and their newly established Base below the mountain.

They wasted no time and started to push the route out in the manner that had already become customary on most Himalayan climbs. There are two ways of climbing a mountain, either Alpine-style, where the climbers carry everything with them and make a single push towards the summit, bivouacking or camping as they go, or by siege tactics, where a series of camps are established up the mountain and all the gear needed to make a summit bid is slowly ferried upward, the aim usually being to put two men into a top camp to make the summit bid. This pyramid approach was developed in the face of the great scale and altitude of the Himalaya, once climbers found that they were unable to carry everything they needed on their backs for a single push. The number of camps and the distance between them is determined by how far a man, usually a Sherpa, can ferry a load in a day. The Sherpas therefore filled a vital role in this siege approach to mountaineering. Ferrying loads is both exhausting and monotonous work; much pleasanter to pay someone else to do this, while the climbers concentrate on the exciting business of finding the route. On pre-war Everest expeditions the British climbers very rarely carried a load.

Back in France, Herzog and his team had discussed the possibility of making an Alpine approach, of moving swiftly, lightly laden up the mountain, as they had done on many multi-day climbs in the Alps. It seemed aesthetically more pleasing and, on a practical level, would have meant that they could complete the climb much more swiftly. But they were ahead of their time and now, in the great bowl of Annapurna, they were confronted with the realities of Himalayan climbing, the savage heat of the midday sun, the afternoon snowfall that covered their tracks each day, but most of all the effects of altitude, exaggerated by the fact that it was their first visit to the Himalaya. With subsequent visits the speed of acclimatisation undoubtedly improves.

They found that they had no choice but to resort to siege tactics – though they approached it with considerable élan, sharing the task of load carrying with the Sherpas and pushing the route out as fast as possible.

The six climbers alternated out in front, picking their way across the dangerous basin below the Sickle ice cliff, up the steep gully that led into the upper reaches of the mountain. They were full of optimism, yet their differing abilities and characters began to emerge. Herzog, probably the least capable technical climber of the six, emerged as an extremely strong goer at altitude. The other driving force of the team was Lionel Terray, dogmatic, single-minded, immensely determined, not so much for himself, but for the expedition as a whole. He was prepared to do that little bit extra, to go back down with the Sherpas, to escort them through a dangerous stretch of glacier, rush back up with a heavy load the next day, push the route out a little bit further when others were exhausted. They had already heard that the monsoon had reached Eastern India, and was expected to hit Nepal on the 5th June. May was now very nearly spent and they were running out of time.

At last, on the 2nd June, they seemed poised for their bid for the summit. Who goes for the summit depends as much on their position on the mountain at the time as their fitness. Herzog had hoped to make his bid with Lionel Terray, but they had got out of phase with each other, through Terray doggedly stocking Camp 4, knowing it had to be done, even though it would mean he would be in the wrong

Climbers just below the Sickle ice cliff.

place to make the summit bid with Herzog. As a result it was Terray's closest friend, Lachenal, who teamed up with Herzog to climb up to the top camp. Lachenal, a volatile, impetuous personality, was always restless, at times wildly optimistic, he could also be easily depressed. On Annapurna he had swung from demonic pushes to moments of pessimism, but now, making his way with Herzog and two Sherpas, above the Sickle ice barrier, across the long slope that stretched up towards the summit, it didn't look as if anything could stop them. They were climbing at over 7300 metres; every step took a separate effort of will as they ploughed through the freshly fallen snow; high above, the snow-laden wind blasted through the crenellated summit ridge as through the teeth of a comb, trailing long streamers of mist across the sky above them. They plodded on through the afternoon, the ridge never seeming to get any closer, and then, almost before they were aware of it, it was there in front of them, smooth ice-plastered rock.

They hacked out a tiny ledge in the hard snow, erected the tent and, wishing them luck, the two Sherpas hurried back down to the security of the lower camps. The tent was barely big enough for two; already, before dusk, the spindrift hissing down the slope, had started to built up between the snow and the tent wall, inexorably pushing them towards the abyss. At altitude there is a terrible lethargy that makes every movement, every task an almost insurmountable challenge. That night they couldn't face cooking any food, just brewed some tea and swallowed the array of pills that Oudot had prescribed. Through a combination of excitement and discomfort they didn't sleep much. It had now begun to snow and the wind was tearing at the tent, threatening to pluck it from its precarious perch. By morning the tent had very nearly collapsed; they were both half suffocated, the rime-covered walls pressed down on to their sleeping bags. Dulled by the altitude, it was just too much trouble to even light the stove; it was hard enough wriggling out of their sleeping bags, forcing on frozen boots.

And so they set out, having had only a cup of tea the previous night and nothing at all to eat or drink that morning. The slope looked straightforward so they left the rope behind, but Herzog did push into his sack a tube of condensed milk and some nougat. They struggled upwards through the day, one foot in front of the other, several pants for every step.

Lachenal insisted on stopping and took off his boots to massage his feet; he had lost all feeling, they were so cold.

'What'll you do if I turn back?' Lachenal asked Herzog.

'Go on by myself,' was the reply.

'I'll keep going then.'

And they plodded on, the mountains around them slowly dropping away below their feet, each of them in a world of his own. Herzog, in a state of euphoria, described it. 'I was living in a world of crystal. Sounds were indistinct, the atmosphere like cotton wool. An astonishing happiness welled up in me, but I could not define it. Everything was so new, so utterly unprecedented.'

And at last the summit rocks came in sight; there was a short gully leading through them; they climbed it and suddenly the savage wind was tearing at their clothes and faces, the slope dropped away on all sides. They had reached the summit of Annapurna; they were the first men to climb a peak of over 8000 metres. Herzog had a wonderful sense of joy as he gazed across at the new vistas, now unfolded. The South Face of Annapurna dropped away dizzily below his feet; he could gaze down at the shapely fish-tailed summit of Machapuchare, nudging through the dark, banked clouds marching in from the south. They had got there only just in front of the monsoon.

Maurice Herzog on the summit of Annapurna, the first 8000-metre peak to have been climbed, 3rd June 1950.

Already Lachenal was impatient to start down, but Herzog, wanting to savour their moment of victory, dug a tiny silk flag from his rucksack, tied it to the ice axe and handed it to Lachenal for the vital photograph. Herzog stayed on the summit for another few moments after Lachenal had started descending the gully and then, almost in a dream, began to follow him down. It was all so miraculous, after being rebuffed by Dhaulagiri, the long search for the way onto Annapurna, and then their race up the mountain. He was hurrying to catch up with Lachenal who was already a tiny dot making the long traverse below the summit rocks. Out of breath, he paused, took off his sack and opened it, he could never remember why. To do this he had taken off his gloves; suddenly, out of the corner of his eye he saw two dark shapes roll and bounce down the slope – his gloves. He watched them with a growing awareness of the significance of their loss as they vanished into the dazzling white of the snows around him.

He had a pair of socks in his rucksack, but it never occurred to him to use them as gloves. Terray and Rébuffat should be at the top camp by now; they'd look after him; he had to get there as quickly as possible and he set off once more. He felt as if he was running, but in fact he was desperately slow, a few slow motion steps, sit down in the snow for a rest, then a few more in the daze of euphoric exhaustion. The clouds were now racing over the top of Annapurna, a bitter, penetrating wind lashing down the slope but his hands were no longer cold, there was no feeling at all.

The tendrils of cloud wrapped around him. Lachenal had been somewhere in front, but his tracks were covered; Herzog kept going, and at last the tents came in sight. Two tents, when there had only been one that morning. Terray and Rébuffat must be there; his problems were over. He plunged into the tent with a shout of relief, excited to tell them of their successful ascent. They were as delighted as he, but then they noticed his hands; they were like blocks of ice, white, hard and cold. Where was Lachenal? He should have been down in front of Herzog, but he hadn't arrived. Terray poked his head out of the tent and listened, but heard nothing beside the howling of the wind, and then there was a distant cry.

He got out of the tent and gazed around him, but the cloud had closed in and he could see nothing. He shouted into the mist but there was no reply. Lachenal was one of his best friends, they had done so many hard climbs together. He broke down crying, and then the mists parted, and about a hundred metres below, he saw the body of his friend lying motionless in the snow. He didn't wait to put on his crampons, just grabbed an ice axe and leapt into a glissade down the steep, hard snow, stopping himself with a jump turn as he came level with Lachenal. It was a rash, but incredibly courageous act.

Fortunately Lachenal had not broken any bones in his fall but he had lost a crampon and his ice axe, and was obsessed with worry about his feet which were now frozen hard. He wanted to go straight down that night to reach the doctor, terrified at the prospect of amputation and never again being able to climb. It was all Terray could do to persuade him to climb back up to the tents.

They had a terrible night, Terray and Rébuffat spending most of it massaging and beating the frostbitten limbs of Herzog and Lachenal. In fact they probably did quite a lot of damage, for it has since been found that it is better to avoid any kind of abrasion on frostbitten areas and to use steady body heat to warm up the injured parts. It would in fact have been better to have left the limbs frozen until they got back down to Base Camp. Even so by the morning some life had come back to their limbs but with it also came inflammation and swelling. The storm had now built up to a furious crescendo, spindrift avalanches pouring down the face, crushing the tents, penetrating every chink in the entrance and ventilators. Getting ready in the morning is bad enough in perfect conditions. In a storm with two exhausted, injured men, it must have been desperate. In these circumstances, someone nearly always assumes command; in this instance it was Terray. He shouted at the others to get ready, started to dress Lachenal for the descent and was immediately confronted with an appalling problem. In thawing out his feet, they had now swollen and he couldn't force them into his boots. There seemed only one solution; Terray's were two sizes larger, and Lachenal could get these on, but then, what about Terray? It would mean forcing his feet into boots that were much too small. He realised the significance of what he was doing, probably condemning himself to severe frostbite but he didn't think twice, and taking off his spare socks, managed to squeeze into Lachenal's boots. He stuffed their sleeping bags into the rucksacks and climbed out of the tent, shouted at Rébuffat to hurry up, and then at last they were all ready and started down the slope.

It was a white out. They couldn't see where they were going, couldn't recognise the séracs and crevasses through which they had weaved on the way up. Herzog was terribly weak, but kept going; Lachenal was almost hysterical with worry about his feet; his natural impatience exaggerated by the crisis. At one moment he fought with Terray to keep rushing downwards, no matter if it was in the wrong direction, and the next, demanded they stopped where they were and waited till the weather cleared. The day crept by; no sign of the tent at Camp 4; no sign of the vital gully that led back down through the Sickle ice wall. They were lost, exhausted and almost helpless, faced with the prospect of a night out in the storm without any kind of shelter. Terray began trying to dig out a snow cave with his ice axe; Lachenal had wandered off to look at a part-covered crevasse a few metres away. Suddenly there was a yell; he vanished from sight. They raced over, and there was a shout from its dark depths.

'It's all right. I've found just the place. There's a bloody great cave in here.'

Soon they were all down in the cave, sheltered from the tearing wind and cold above. At least they had a chance of surviving the night. Terray pulled out his sleeping bag, longing to snuggle into it, looked across at the others. Rébuffat and Herzog had that look about them that told him they didn't have their bags; in the rush to get down that morning they had wanted to travel as light as possible, convinced that they could get all the way down that day. Terray shared his bag with the other two, all three squeezing their legs into it.

They shivered and dozed through the night, as the spindrift seeped down into the cave, covering them and all their equipment. At last the dawn arrived. In an ice cave you can't tell what is happening outside; you can't hear the howl of the wind and the light filtering through the snow gives no indication of whether it is bright sunlight or thick cloud. Lethargically, they started to hunt for their boots and other gear, hidden under the mantle of icy spindrift. Rébuffat was the first to find his boots, get them on and climb out of the cave, but he could only report that it was savagely cold and windy; he could see nothing. It took him a moment to realise that he was snow blind; the previous day, he and Terray had removed their goggles in an effort to see through the driving snows of the white out. They were now paying the price for their mistake.

Their spirits dropped; they must all have secretly wondered about their chances of survival. It was a case of the blind leading the lame. Lachenal was the next out; as he poked his head out of the hole he let out a cry of joy. It was a fine, clear day. They might yet survive. Terray also climbed out but Herzog stayed below searching for all their boots and belongings in the snow, digging away with his bare, feelingless hands. At last he found all the vital items and then Terray had a desperate task trying to haul him up the steep snow shoot that led out of the cave. Herzog had lost the use of his hands; his fingers were frozen sticklike talons. There was no feeling at all in his legs. With an enormous struggle he managed to crawl out of his icy tomb.

'I'm dying,' he told Terray. 'You'll have to leave me.'

Terray did his best to reassure Herzog, and then suddenly there was a shout. It was Schatz; the Sherpas were there too. The previous night they had stopped only a couple of hundred metres short of the camp. They were saved, but their adventures were by no means over. They had a long way to get down. They were involved in an avalanche and only saved because Herzog fell into a crevasse and was caught like an inert anchor, holding the others from the rope tied round his waist. At last, that afternoon they staggered into Camp 2. The other members of the team and, most important, Oudot, the doctor, were there. They had come through it alive, but the pain had only just begun; the agony of intravenous injections given by Oudot in the

cramped confines of a two-man tent, of being manhandled down the mountain, and then, in the monsoon rains, back over the switchbacks of the Miristi Khola, down through the foothills; days of pain and worry, of amputations by the wayside without the benefit of anaesthetic, wondering how they would adapt to lives without fingers and toes, deprived of the joy of climbing.

Lionel Terray and Gaston Rébuffat had escaped with no more than frost-nipped fingers and toes, and snow blindness that soon wore off. It was undoubtedly a miracle that the four survived at all; there had been so many narrow escapes. With the hindsight of the present day it is easy to pick out mistakes, to observe that the north side of Annapurna was technically easy, but this is to forget how little was

Bringing the badly frostbitten Herzog down to Base Camp after a desperate descent involving a bivouac in a crevasse. Lachenal was also suffering from frostbite, Terray and Rébuffat were badly snow-blinded. It was a miracle the four survived at all.

Quest for Adventure

known of Himalayan climbing in 1950, how sparse was the level of success up to this time. Considering the problems they had had in trying to find a way onto the mountain and then the limited time they had to climb it, their achievement was all the greater. They displayed élan in their approach to the climb that in many ways was ahead of their time. The team had worked well together. One can't resist wondering what would have happened had Terray not sacrificed his chance to be on the summit bid. He might well have stayed with Herzog, given him a spare pair of gloves to ensure he got back to their top camp without frostbite, but that is pure conjecture.

After getting back, Herzog ended his book with the following words:

'Annapurna, to which we had gone empty-handed, was a treasure on which we should live the rest of our days. With this realisation we turn a new page: a new life begins.

'There are other Annapurnas in the lives of men.'

Herzog found his Annapurnas in spite of losing all his toes and fingers. He could never climb again but he sublimated his energies in his business and the work of the French Alpine Club, eventually becoming Minister of Sport for France. Today he is an urbane, relaxed man who one feels has led a full and profoundly satisfying life. There are no signs of discontent or frustration.

Lachenal, on the other hand, found it less easy. Terray described it:

The curtailment profoundly changed his character. Once he had seemed magically immune from the ordinary clumsiness and weight of humankind and the contrast was like wearing a ball and chain. This slower kind of mountaineering no longer gave him the old feeling of moving in a fourth dimension, of dancing on the impossible and he sought desperately to rediscover it elsewhere.

He had always been a fast driver, as many climbers are, the recklessness of his driving became legendary, and he died four years later in a skiing accident.

Terray was killed in 1965 on the limestone cliffs of the Vercors in Central France. Only a few weeks before, I had climbed with him and the famous Belgian solo climber, Claudio Barbier, on the very same cliff. It had been a joyous, light-hearted day, climbing on the sun-warmed limestone, the wooded valley with its nestling fields and rambling farmhouses, down below. It all seemed so peaceful, so free from threat. Terray's death brought home to me how constant is the risk in climbing, not so much in the moments of acute and obvious danger, as on Annapurna, when fighting for life, every nerve stretched to the limit, but in the moments of relaxation on easy ground, when a loose hold, a falling stone, can cause a slip which might end in a long and fatal fall.

'Tell me if it hurts.'
Dead tissue didn't hurt, but it meant Oudot amputated the ends of all Herzog's fingers and toes without anaesthetic during the retreat from the mountain.

The challenge of Everest

From the south Mount Everest (8848 metres/29,028 feet) resembles a mediaeval fortress – its triangular summit, the keep, guarded by the turreted walls of the outer bailey; Lhotse, fourth highest mountain in the world, is a massive corner tower linking the high curtain wall of Nuptse. The gateway to this fortress is the Khumbu Icefall, portcullised with séracs, moated with crevasses. Few mountain peaks are better guarded or have resisted so many assaults. There was no doubt concerning the whereabouts of the mountain or even of how to approach it from the south, as there had been in the case of Annapurna and Dhaulagiri, but there was a great deal of doubt as to whether it could be climbed from this direction.

British climbers had reached the Lho La before the war and had seen the entrance to the Khumbu Icefall, but the way to the peak itself was barred by the outlying spurs of the West Ridge and the South-West Face. The first westerners to approach Everest from the south were Bill Tilman and Charles Houston, who had attempted Everest and K2, respectively, in 1938. As members of a small trekking party, for them it must have been like venturing into an incredible Aladdin's cave of treasures, of unknown, unclimbed peaks, of unspoilt villages that were the homes of the Sherpa people, or turbulent glacier torrents, lush vegetation, high pastures, *mani* walls and prayer flags. It is hardly surprising that they took little more than a cursory glance at the approach to Everest, walking a short way up the Khumbu Glacier to peer round the shoulder of Nuptse into the Icefall and Western Cwm. They could only see the steep buttresses of the South-West Face of Everest, which appeared to reach the South Col; as a result, their report was discouraging.

But even as they made their reconnaissance, a young, unknown climber of the post-war generation was also thinking of Everest. Mike Ward had started climbing in North Wales during the war, while still at school, had gone to Cambridge in 1943 to study medicine and climbed at every possible opportunity. With the end of the war, he was able to go out to the Alps. He had already shown himself to be a brilliant natural rock climber, and the thoroughness and persistence with which he re-searched and then pushed through his plans for a further Everest reconnaissance, despite Tilman's unfavourable report, displayed his capacity as an organiser as well as a climber. Yet he was in the traditional mould of pre-war climbers, essentially amateur, knowing that however great his enthusiasm for climbing his career in medicine would always take priority.

He realised he was short on big mountain experience and therefore invited Bill Murray, a Scot who had led an expedition to the Garhwal Himalaya the previous year, and had climbed extensively in Scotland both before and after the war. Murray's books *Mountaineering in Scotland* and *Undiscovered Scotland* have become climbing classics. The other member of the team was to be Tom Bourdillon, one of the most outstanding of all the post-war young climbers.

Pre-war expeditions to Everest had been sponsored through an organisation called the Everest Committee, formed from members of both the Royal Geographical Society and the Alpine Club. It was coming into existence once again, under the name of the Himalayan Committee, and was to play a very important role in the Everest expedition, but for the time being Mike Ward simply wanted its approval and blessing which, after some hesitation because of Tilman's unfavourable reaction, was finally given.

Only a short time before they were ready to depart, Eric Shipton came onto the scene. Undoubtedly Britain's most eminent mountaineer at this time, he had established himself, with Tilman, as an outstanding mountain explorer, surveying and exploring the Himalaya with small, lightweight expeditions. Shipton was more mountain explorer than technical climber for whom reaching the top of a mountain was just part of the experience as a whole and not an end in itself. Of average height and build, with bushy eyebrows shielding piercing blue eyes, he seemed to gaze straight through you to some distant mountain range. There was also a slightly absent-minded distance in his manner, not cold or aloof, for he was essentially a kind man, but a distance born, perhaps, of shyness, a certain inhibition of emotion. He did not enjoy the hurly-burly of big expeditions, their politics and ponderous slow movement, but he had been unable to resist the lure of Everest and had taken part in four pre-war Everest expeditions, while his books were an inspiration to countless youngsters, including myself, who were just starting to climb. During the war he was British Consul-General in Kashgar, in Sinkiang, and had gone on to Kunming in China, but this had ended with the victory of the Communist forces and he arrived back in Britain, not at all sure what to do next. He was promptly invited to lead the Reconnaissance expedition.

Mike Ward and Bill Murray had already set out by sea when Shipton received a telegram from the President of the New Zealand Alpine Club, saying that four of his countrymen were climbing in the Garhwal Himalaya and asking if two of them could join the Everest Reconnaissance. Up to this point Shipton, who always favoured the smallest possible numbers, had resisted several applications to join the expedition, but on impulse, mainly because of good memories of climbing with New Zealander, Dan Bryant, on Everest in 1935, he accepted the proposal – even though it meant taking on two climbers whom none of them knew.

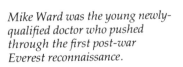

Mike Ward was the young newly-qualified doctor who pushed through the first post-war Everest reconnaissance.

Eric Shipton, undoubtedly Britain's most eminent mountaineer and mountain explorer, pictured here in 1951 when he led the Everest Reconnaissance.

This also gave the four New Zealanders a very real problem – which two of the four should accept this opportunity? Ed Hillary, a big, raw-boned bee-keeper, was an obvious candidate. Although having only started climbing at the comparatively late age of twenty-six, his physique was superb and, on the expedition in the Garhwal, he had been outstandingly the strongest. The second place in the team was open to question, however. The leader of the party, Earle Riddiford, was determined to go, even though George Lowe, a primary school teacher who combined a rich sense of humour with a great deal of climbing ability and determination, felt that not only was he stronger, but also that he and Hillary made a particularly good team. Nonetheless, it was Riddiford and Hillary who joined Shipton.

And so there were six climbers on the Everest Reconnaissance. They had a tough approach through the height of the monsoon from Jogbani in the south to reach the Upper Khumbu Valley on the 29th September 1951. Bourdillon, Riddiford and Ward ventured into the Icefall, while Shipton and Hillary climbed a spur of Pumori to look into the Western Cwm. The view they got showed that Everest was undoubtedly climbable from the south, for they could now see right up the Cwm, the long easy slope of the Lhotse Face and the comparatively easy angle of the South-East Ridge leading down to the South Col. The way into the Western Cwm, however, lay through the daunting obstacle of the Khumbu Icefall.

This Icefall descends about 800 metres, a maze of tottering ice towers and blocks, of crevasses and huge holes, all of it shifting under the relentless pressure from the glacier above, and threatened by avalanche from the steep slopes on either side. It has always been one of Everest's major hazards. It was a particularly formidable barrier for the first men to set foot upon it, being considerably larger and more complex than any icefall they had experienced, though the two New Zealanders were at some advantage, since they had been climbing all summer and the icefalls of the New Zealand Alps are both bigger and more difficult than anything in Europe.

Their progress must be judged against this background. On their first attempt they got about three-quarters of the way up when they were hit by an avalanche and were lucky to escape without serious injury; they decided to leave the Icefall for a fortnight, in the hope of letting the snow settle. This also gave Shipton an opportunity to explore the mountains to the south of Everest, which I suspect he found much more intriguing than the challenge of the Icefall.

Returning to the fray, on the 19th October, they were undoubtedly shaken when a complete section, that had seemed fairly stable, collapsed during the night, leaving behind an area of chaotic debris. When, at last, they reached the top of the Icefall they found that the way into the Western Cwm was barred by a huge crevasse that stretched from wall to wall. This was the place where Camp 1 is usually situated. Now a long way above their last camp, they were tired, stretched to the limit by the very level of the unknown, but the younger members of the team were keen to press on, while the older and more experienced decided that the risks were too high and that they had seen enough. In retrospect, Shipton regretted this decision but, at the time, it seemed sensible. They had proved that Everest was feasible by this route.

Unfortunately, however, the British had lost the opportunity to confirm it. The Himalayan Committee, perhaps over-confident that Everest was a 'British' mountain, had not applied for permission for 1952 in time. A Swiss expedition had got in first. There was some discussion about making it a Swiss–British effort under joint leadership, but this came to nothing. The Swiss were given first chance and they nearly made it, with what was really a very small expedition. Although the team numbered twelve, only six of them were hard climbers; the rest were scientists or had a support role such as doctor or camera man.

Previous page]
Mount Everest lit with sunset
fire, as seen by Doug Scott
from neighbouring Nuptse.

The Sherpa force numbered twenty, led by Tenzing Norkay, who had already gained a considerable reputation not only as a sirdar, or foreman, of the Sherpas, but as a climber in his own right. He was thirty-eight years old, tall and heavy by Sherpa standards, weighing over ten stone. With his swept-back hair, strong, square-cut chin and broad smile, he had an almost European look which was reflected in his attitude to the mountains. Most of the Sherpas still regarded mountaineering purely as a job; Angtharkay, Herzog's sirdar on Annapurna, whose experience was even greater than Tenzing's, declined an invitation to go to the summit of Annapurna. His job was to supervise the efforts of the high-altitude porters and he saw no point in the struggle and risk to reach the top. Tenzing, on the other hand, had the same driving ambition as a European climber to reach the summit. Already he had been to the top of Nanda Devi East with the French in 1951; he wanted to reach the summit of Everest in 1952. With the Swiss, Raymond Lambert, he got within 250 metres, high up on the South-East Ridge, just 165 metres below the South Summit.

The Swiss had shown the way to the top; almost all the route was known. Their failure to finish was partly the result of the comparative lightness of their assault, in the face of the huge gulf of the unknown that they had to penetrate, through the mysteries of the Western Cwm, the Lhotse Face and the final Summit Ridge; but, most of all, it was because the oxygen sets used by Lambert and Tenzing were ineffective, feeding them insufficient oxygen to compensate for the weight of the cylinders they were carrying. The sets were so primitive, they could only use them while resting, which meant having to carry the extra load of the oxygen bottles without getting any benefit from them whilst actually climbing. The Swiss did not give up; they made another attempt in the autumn, after the heavy snows of the monsoon, but the savage cold and high winds of the winter overtook them and they got no higher than the South Col.

Meanwhile, the British had to sit it out, praying secretly that the Swiss would not succeed. This did at least give them more time to work on some of the specialised equipment, particularly oxygen systems which seemed a vital ingredient for success, and a rather abortive expedition to Cho Oyu (8153 metres/26,750 feet) under Shipton's leadership gave further altitude experience to some potential members of the next British attempt on Everest, which was now scheduled for 1953.

It was generally assumed that Shipton would lead this attempt, but he himself had some doubts about the suitability of his temperament for such a role, as he confessed in his autobiography, *That Untravelled World*:

It was clear that the Committee assumed that I would lead the expedition. I had, however, given a good deal of thought to the matter, and felt it right to voice certain possible objections. Having been to Everest five times, I undoubtedly had a great deal more experience of the mountain and of climbing at extreme altitude than anyone else; also, in the past year I had been closely connected, practically and emotionally, with the new aspect of the venture. On the other hand, long involvement with an unsolved problem can easily produce rigidity of outlook, a slow response to new ideas, and it is often the case that a man with fewer inhibitions is better equipped to tackle it than one with greater experience. I had more reason than most to take a realistic view of the big element of luck involved, and this was not conducive to bounding optimism. Was it not time, perhaps, to hand over to a younger man with fresh outlook? Moreover, Everest had become the focus of greatly inflated publicity and of keen international competition, and there were many who regarded success in the coming attempt to be of high national importance. My well-known dislike of large expeditions and my abhorrence of a competitive element in mountaineering might well seem out of place in the present situation.

I asked the Committee to consider these points very carefully before deciding the question of leadership and then left them while they did so.

The Chairman, Claude Elliott, and several members of the Committee already had doubts about Shipton's leadership, particularly in the light of his failure to push through into the Western Cwm and his seeming lack of determination on Cho Oyu, but they could not bring themselves to dispense with him altogether – the main problem being that there was no other obvious candidate. It was felt, however, that a more forceful climbing leader was needed for the final push on the mountain, together with a good organiser to co-ordinate preparations in Britain, so that Shipton could remain a figurehead for the expedition whilst the two most vital executive functions of leadership were hived off. It was a compromise decision with all the weaknesses that this involved.

The Committee liked the idea of a military man with a proven ability in organisation and management. Two soldiers were particularly discussed – Major Jimmy Roberts, a Gurkha officer who had climbed extensively in the Himalaya, and Colonel John Hunt, who had also served in India, and had had both Alpine and Himalayan expedition experience, but was almost completely unknown in British climbing circles. The previous summer, however, Hunt had climbed in the Alps with Basil Goodfellow, who was secretary at this time of both the Alpine Club and the Himalayan Committee. Impressed by Hunt's ability as a mountaineer, combined with his obvious drive and capability as an organiser, Goodfellow pushed Hunt's case very strongly and it was decided that he was the ideal choice as assault leader and organiser.

Colonel John Hunt,
almost completely unknown in
British climbing circles,
but the man for the job.

On being told of the Committee's suggestion that there should be an assault leader, Eric Shipton concurred but suggested that 'deputy leader' would be a better title and that Charles Evans who had been on Cho Oyu with him could best fill this role. There was no question of Evans, a busy brain surgeon, being able to take on the job of full-time organiser, however, so this left an opening for Hunt.

But Elliott and Goodfellow were determined to go much further than this and, the day after the Committee meeting, without consulting Shipton, Elliott wrote to Hunt asking whether he would be available for the expedition as assault or deputy leader, and also to act as full-time organiser. A few days later Goodfellow telegrammed Hunt, inviting him to come over to England to discuss his role with Shipton. It must have been downright embarrassing for all concerned. Shipton was under the impression that he was interviewing Hunt for the job of expedition organiser, while Hunt had been given the impression that he was to be deputy leader – a role that Shipton considered was already held by Charles Evans. The meeting was a failure and Hunt returned to Germany where he was serving at the time. Charles Wylie, another Army officer, was made full-time organiser and set up an office in the Royal Geographical Society building.

But Goodfellow, convinced that Hunt was essential to the success of the expedition, was not prepared to let the matter drop. At the next Committee meeting on the 11th September, the question of deputy leadership was at the top of the agenda. Shipton was asked to leave the room – an extraordinary slight to the leader of the expedition – while the Committee discussed it. When Shipton was asked back in, he was told that the Committee had decided to make John Hunt, not deputy leader, but co-leader, something that they must have realised would have been unacceptable to Shipton who felt he had no choice but to resign.

Inevitably there was uproar throughout the mountaineering world and within the team. Eric Shipton was by far the best-known and most popular mountaineer in Britain at that time. Nobody had ever heard of John Hunt. Bourdillon, loyal as always, said he was going to withdraw from the expedition and it was Shipton who persuaded him to stay on. Evans was very distressed though, ironically, received the title deputy leader. Hillary, first hearing about it in a newspaper report, was indignant, saying that Everest just wouldn't be the same without Shipton, but he never thought of withdrawing from the expedition.

Were the Committee right? Would Everest have been climbed under Shipton's leadership? Certainly several members of his team thought so, arguing that Charles Evans and Charles Wylie would have ensured that the organisation was sound and that the determination of the climbers out in front, men like Hillary and Lowe, would have carried the expedition with its own momentum, even if Shipton had left it to look after itself. I experienced something like this when I went to Nuptse, the third peak of Everest; the leader of the expedition believed in letting the climbers out in front make their own decisions, without actually appointing anyone in authority. We had no radios, but left each other little notes at the various camps with the plans that each member had made. We climbed the mountain in a storm of acrimony, that might have had a certain dynamic force of its own. But in the case of Everest, I suspect that the problem was so huge and complex, the need for careful co-ordination so great, that it required a firm and positive overall leadership. This can only come from one person who has this responsibility vested in him, is prepared to use it, and at the same time has the acceptance and respect of his fellow team members. From this point of view, the expedition almost certainly had a higher chance of success under John Hunt's leadership than it would have done under Shipton who, apart from anything else, never seemed totally committed to the enterprise or happy directing a single-minded thrust up a mountain. It was very unfortunate, however, that the decision was made in such a messy, indecisive way.

Shipton was cruelly hurt by this rejection. It is one thing to be allowed to stand down from an expedition, quite another to be manoeuvred into an impossible position. It triggered off a series of personal crises that had a traumatic effect over the next five years and it was only in 1957, through an invitation by a group of university students to lead their expedition to the Karakoram, that he returned to the mountains and then, in his fifties, had a renaissance, which he described as the happiest years of his life, exploring the wild, unmapped glaciers and mountains of Patagonia in the southern tip of South America. This was the style of mountaineering in which he excelled and in which he could find complete commitment and happiness.

In the meantime, John Hunt had been given the opportunity of his life. Shipton and Hunt, who were so very different in personality, had very similar backgrounds. Both were born in India, Shipton in Ceylon in 1907, the son of a tea planter, Hunt in Simla in 1910, the son of a regular Army officer; both lost their fathers at around the age of four; both were sent to prep schools in England, but here the similarity ended. Shipton was a slow learner, perhaps suffered from dyslexia, for he was a very late reader. As a result, he failed the common entrance examination to public school, and after a sketchy schooling took up tea planting in Kenya; for him, this led naturally to a life of individual adventure.

The young Hunt, on the other hand, was brought up from a very early age to the idea of a life of serious and dedicated public service. He went to Marlborough, then followed family tradition by going to Sandhurst where he distinguished himself, becoming a senior under-officer and winning both the Sword of Honour and the Gold Medal for Top Academic Attainment. He was commissioned into the fashionable Rifle Brigade and posted to India. But here he ceased to be the stereotyped young subaltern; he was not happy in the claustrophobic pre-war Army officer's life of polo, cocktail parties and mess gossip. He preferred playing football with his soldiers, and already had a sense of social responsibility combined with a strong Christian belief that made him much more progressive in his political and social attitudes than the average Army officer. Tiring of the fairly aimless routine of garrison life, he applied for a temporary transfer to the Indian Police to work in intelligence and counter-terrorism. Already he was addicted to mountaineering, having had several Alpine seasons before going out to India. With the Himalaya on his doorstep, he took every opportunity to escape to the mountains with adventurous ski tours in Kashmir and more ambitious climbs on Saltoro Kangri and in the Kangchenjunga region. Hunt was considered for the 1936 Everest expedition but, ironically, failed the medical test because of a slight flutter in his heart-beat. He saw active service during the war, commanding a battalion in Italy, where he was awarded the Distinguished Service Order, and then getting command of a brigade in Greece at the end of the war. He went to Staff College and served on Field-Marshal Montgomery's staff at the end of the 'forties, at Fontainebleau, getting to know French climbers and being invited to join the Groupe de Haute Montagne. He married Joy, who was a Wimbledon tennis player, in 1935. Theirs is a very close relationship and between an exacting career and raising a family, they have done much of their mountain adventuring together.

Hunt certainly looked the part of the professional soldier, but he was no martinet. He plunged into the job of organising the expedition, but in doing so fully involved everyone around him, overcoming any initial resentment. One commentator, Ingrid Cranfield, summed up what has become a popular interpretation of Hunt's approach, writing: 'To Hunt an "assault" merely meant a concerted, military-style operation; whereas to Shipton "assault" sounded more like a criminal offence.' In fact, this was hardly fair, for Hunt's approach to climbing was essentially romantic, with an almost spiritual undertone. Wilfrid Noyce remembered Hunt commenting how mountains made him want to pray. Hunt undoubtedly saw Everest as a romantic, perhaps even spiritual, challenge, but used his military training to approach a task that needed careful planning. He could see the basic principles of ensuring success on a mountain are very similar to those of success in war and one finds oneself using similar terminology.

Dr. Griffith Pugh, the physiologist who had accompanied the Cho Oyu expedition, played a very important part in the preparations. The way the human body adapted to altitude was still a mystery and it was largely Griff Pugh's work that determined the need for acclimatisation to altitude and, perhaps even more important, the need to drink a lot to avoid dehydration. The diet of the expedition was carefully worked out and the equipment, with specially-designed high-altitude boots, tentage and clothing, was better than anything that had been used before.

There were plenty of strong incentives demanding success; the fact that the French had permission for 1954, the Swiss for 1955, so that if the British failed this time they were most unlikely to have another chance; the fact that it was the year of the Queen's Coronation; the amount of money and effort involved; the controversy over the change in leadership; but, most important of all, Hunt – and for that matter most of his team – wanted success for its own sake. If you set out on a climb, there is a tremendous drive to succeed in what you are attempting. On Everest, certainly in 1953 when six serious attempts had failed (five on the north side and one on the south), the chances of success seemed slim, however large and well-equipped the expedition might be.

Hunt settled on a slightly larger team than perhaps Shipton would have taken, making it up to a total of twelve climbers, plus thirty-six high-altitude porters. Evans, Bourdillon, Gregory, Hillary and Lowe had been in the Cho Oyu party, Michael Ward, who had been on the 1951 Reconnaissance as doctor, and George Band, Wilfrid Noyce, Charles Wylie and Mike Westmacott were newcomers. Even the Cho Oyu men were thin on real high-altitude experience; Charles Evans had reached 7300 metres on Annapurna IV in 1950, while Hillary and Lowe had collected a fine crop of peaks around 6400 metres and had been to about 6850 metres on both Mukut Parbat and Cho Oyu, but they had not climbed any really high mountains. In this respect John Hunt was the most experienced, for he had been to 7470 metres on Saltoro Kangri and had made a bold solo ascent of the South West Summit of Nepal Peak (7107 metres/23,350 feet) in East Nepal. It was Tenzing Norkay, however, who had more high-altitude experience and knew Everest better than any of the other members of the party and, because of this, he was made a full team member as well as being sirdar of the porters.

The British part of the expedition came from traditional Oxbridge or military backgrounds, the only exception being Alf Gregory, who was a northerner, running a travel agency in Blackpool. The selection, however, was a natural one, for the climbing explosion that hit Britain in the early 'fifties, spearheaded by the tough Mancunians of the Rock and Ice Climbing Club, had only just got under way. In completing the selection of the team, Hunt had looked for compatibility as much as a record for hard climbing. This certainly worked out, for the team functioned well together under Hunt's firm, but tactful direction.

Preparations were complicated by the fact that the Swiss were having their second try for the mountain that autumn, which meant that Hunt and his team could not let go at full bore until the end of November, when the Swiss finally admitted defeat.

The British had just three months to put the expedition together; much of the equipment had to be specially designed and manufactured and, although some work had already been started, they had not been able to place any firm orders until they knew the outcome of the Swiss attempt. It is unlikely that they would have been able to raise the financial support for a second ascent of the mountain.

All the gear and food was ready to leave by sea on the 12th February 1953. The team reached Thyangboche, the Buddhist monastery a few miles south of the Everest massif, on the 27th March. This was early in the season, but Hunt was determined to allow an acclimatisation period before the start of the serious climbing. This was a concept fashionable in pre-war expeditions and in those of the early 'fifties, though later expeditions tended to concentrate all their efforts on the climb itself, acclimatising by working on the lower slopes of the mountain.

Acclimatisation camp at Thyangboche, showing just part of the array of stores and manpower needed by a siege-style expedition.

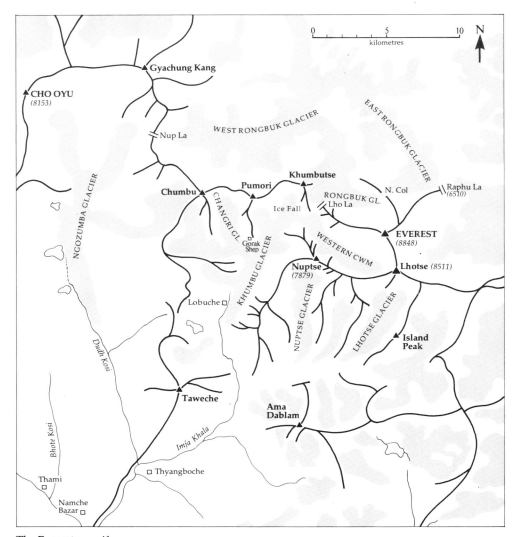

The Everest massif

The story of the Everest expedition, like that of all siege-type expeditions, is a complex yet stereotyped one, of establishment of camps and different parties moving up and down the mountain, as the route is slowly pushed towards the summit.

The first barrier is the now famous Khumbu Icefall; the route then relents through the Western Cwm; it is a long walk, skirting crevasses which tend to force the climber into the sides, and the consequent threat of avalanche from the steep, crenellated walls of Nuptse. At the head of the Cwm is the Lhotse Glacier, a giant series of steps, steep ice walls alternating with broad platforms, leading up towards the summit rocks of Lhotse. From near the top of the glacier, a long traverse across snow slopes leads to the South Col of Everest, the springboard for a summit bid up the South-East Ridge, soaring for 860 metres past the South Summit which, deceptively, looks like the top from the South Col, and then beyond it to the summit itself.

Throughout, John Hunt pressed himself to the limit, determined to be seen to be working as hard, if not harder, than anyone else on the expedition, either in carrying a load whilst escorting porters, making a reconnaissance in the Western Cwm or on the Lhotse Face, as well as coping with the detailed planning and day-to-day administration needed for the expedition. On several occasions he pushed himself

A climber crosses a crevasse in the immensity of the Everest Icefall, gateway to the Western Cwm and one of the most dangerous parts of the mountain.

too hard, as he struggled, grey-faced, to complete the day's task. There was a strong competitive element in his make-up, noticed by Hillary on the approach march and recorded in his autobiography:

> I learned to respect John even if I found it difficult to understand him. He drove himself with incredible determination and I always felt he was out to prove himself the physical equal of any member – even though most of us were a good deal younger than himself. I can remember on the third day's march pounding up the long steep hill from Dologhat and catching up with John and the way he shot ahead, absolutely determined not to be passed – the sort of challenge I could not then resist. I surged past with a burst of speed, cheerfully revelling in the contest, and was astonished to see John's face, white and drawn, as he threw every bit of strength into the effort. There was an impression of desperation because he wasn't quite fast enough. What was he trying to prove, I wondered? He was the leader and cracked the whip – surely that was enough? I now know that sometimes it isn't enough – that we can be reluctant to accept that our physical powers have their limits or are declining, even though our best executive years may still be ahead of us.

Mike Ward had an uncomfortable feeling in his presence, noting, 'My first impression of John was of some disturbing quality that I sensed but could not define. Later,

I understood this to be the intense emotional background to his character, by no means obvious, and yet an undercurrent came through.' George Lowe commented, 'He greeted me most warmly and said how much he was depending on *me* – his assault on personal susceptibilities was impossible to resist.'

This was an experience that everyone I have talked to remembered. At the same time, however, both through his own personality and also from his position as leader, he kept a certain distance from his fellow members and had an air of authority, very similar to that Thor Heyerdahl inspired in his crew on *Kon-Tiki*. Even when members of the team disagreed with him they always ended up complying with his wishes.

From the very start Hunt had thought Hillary and Tenzing potentially his strongest pair, though they had never met before the expedition, and climbed together for the first time in the lower part of the Western Cwm. Hillary was immediately impressed by Tenzing's energy, competence, enthusiasm and, above all, his determination. He wrote later:

> If you accept the modern philosophy that there must be a ruthless and selfish motivation to succeed in sport, then it could be justly claimed that Tenzing and I were the closest approximation we had on our expedition to the climbing prima donnas of today. We wanted for the expedition to succeed – and nobody worked any harder to ensure that it did – but in both our minds success was always equated with us being somewhere around the summit when it happened.

Charles Evans (above) and Tom Bourdillon whose father had designed a closed-circuit oxygen system intended to avoid the wastage of the conventional open-circuit set.
Evans and Bourdillon commited themselves to proving its value on Everest.

Another strong pairing was that of Charles Evans and Tom Bourdillon. Although Bourdillon was younger than Evans and had climbed at a much higher standard in the Alps, they had much in common. Both had a scientific background and Evans, though initially sceptical, became deeply involved in Bourdillon's brainchild, the closed-circuit oxygen system, which his father had specially developed for the 1953 expedition in the hope of avoiding the wastage of the conventional open-circuit set. In theory it should have been the best system, but in practice it proved to be less reliable than the open-circuit system and the other members of the team were not impressed. Privately, Hunt felt the same way, but gave his support to the closed-circuit trials all the same. Bourdillon and Evans had been the two members of the team closest to Eric Shipton, Bourdillon having actually resigned from the expedition, and only brought back in after a great deal of persuasion. Hunt had been very touched on the walk in, when Bourdillon had told him how happy the expedition seemed to be. He wanted to keep it that way.

Hillary, down-to-earth and practical, preferred the look of the open-circuit oxygen system and felt that too much time was being expended in trying to prove the closed-circuit equipment. At 6.30 a.m. on the 2nd May, Hillary and Tenzing set out from Base Camp, using the open-circuit set, carrying a load that totalled forty pounds. They reached Camp 4, the Advanced Base in the Western Cwm, 1525 metres of climbing with about four miles in lateral distance, breaking trail most of the way through soft snow. It was as much an affirmation of their fitness and suitability for the summit as a vindication of the open-circuit system. Hunt was already thinking of them as his main summit hope, and this confirmed his choice.

By modern standards, Hunt's approach to the assault was slow if methodical, not so much a blitzkrieg as a steady siege. But there was a great deal more that was unknown in 1953 than there is today. Only one mountain of over 8000 metres had been climbed and Hunt had no desire to repeat the desperate, ill-supported summit bid, followed by the near disastrous retreat from Annapurna experienced by Herzog's expedition, nor the failure through an inadequate oxygen system and

Everest from the Western Cwm

cumulative exhaustion of the Swiss. It was believed climbers deteriorated physically, even while resting, at heights of over 6400 metres, and it was not known how long anyone could survive and function effectively above this height. Hunt, therefore, was determined to nurse his team, particularly the climbers he was considering for the summit.

It was on the 7th May, with most of the team down at Base Camp, that he laid before them his final plan of assault. He felt that he had only the resources, both in materials and man-power, to mount one strong attempt on the summit. If this failed they would all have to come back down, rest and think again. But his thinking for the summit bid was consistent with his policy up to that point; it was one of reconnaissance, build-up of supplies and then the thrust forward. To do this, he first had to reach the South Col and he gave this job to George Lowe who, with Hillary,

George Lowe, who with Hillary, his New Zealand climbing partner, probably had the greatest all-round snow and ice experience of the party, was chosen by Hunt to push the route out up the Lhotse Face.

probably had the greatest all-round snow and ice experience of the expedition. With him were to be George Band and Mike Westmacott, two of the young newcomers to the Himalaya, and a group of Sherpas. Once the route was made to the South Col, Hunt planned a big carry to the Col, supervised by Noyce and Wylie, after which Charles Evans and Tom Bourdillon would move into position and make a bid for the South Summit, using the closed-circuit sets. Since, in theory, these sets were more effective and had greater endurance than open-circuit sets, they should be able at least to reach the South Summit from the South Col, a height of around 780 metres, and it was just conceivable that they could reach the top. In this way Hunt could satisfy the two exponents of the closed circuit system as well as making what he felt was a vital reconnaissance, opening the way for the main summit bid. In this respect one must remember just how huge a barrier that last 250 metres on Everest appeared to be in 1953. Just one day behind them would be Hillary and Tenzing, with a strong support party consisting of Hunt, Gregory and two Sherpas. They would establish a camp as high as possible above the South Col on the South-East Ridge, and then Hillary and Tenzing, using open-circuit sets, would make their bid for the summit – hoping to benefit from the first party's tracks and with that indefinable barrier of the unknown pushed still higher up the mountain.

Subsequently Hunt modified his plan so that he, with two Sherpas, would move up with Evans and Bourdillon to give them direct support just in case anything went wrong and, at the same time, to make a dump for the high camp. Hunt hoped to stay up on the South Col throughout the period of the summit attempts, since this was obviously the place of decision and the only place from which he could effectively influence events.

It must have been a tense moment for the entire team when they assembled for the meeting that was to give them their roles in the final phase of the expedition. Up to this point, Hunt had used a low-key approach to leadership, consulting with people as far as possible, often sowing the germ of an idea in others' heads so that they could almost believe that it was their own; but now he had to lay down a series of roles for the team, knowing all too well that some members would be bitterly disappointed.

Ward came out very strongly against Hunt's plan on two counts. He could not understand the logic of making an initial bid from the South Col, when only a slightly greater porter effort would be needed to establish a high camp for Evans and Bourdillon's attempt which, of course, could also be used by Hillary and Tenzing. He also challenged Hunt's plan to take charge of the carry to the top camp himself on the grounds that he was not physically fit for it – a heavy charge, coming from the expedition medical officer. But John Hunt weathered both attacks, which were delivered with great vehemence, and stuck to his guns.

I myself have always wondered at the thinking behind John Hunt's decision to allow Bourdillon and Evans to make their attempt from the South Col which meant, in effect, that there would be only one strong attempt on the summit itself. Had Bourdillon and Evans been granted that top camp, in all probability they would have been the first men on top of Everest. It is easy, however, to be wise after the event. Hunt was probably the only member of the team fully aware of just how thin was the ferrying capability of his Sherpas, particularly once they were above the South Col. Had Hillary and Tenzing failed in their summit bid, and the British team not climbed Everest in 1953, then no doubt the post-mortems would have been long and furious – but no-one is too interested in a post-mortem after success.

Whatever reservations some members of the team might have had, they all settled into their roles and worked themselves to the limit in the next three weeks. But things began going wrong almost from the start. It needs ruthless determination to keep the momentum of a climb under way. At altitude time seems to be slowed up by the very lethargy of the climber himself; the chores of struggling with a recalcitrant Primus, washing up dirty dishes in cold snow water, fighting with frozen crampon straps, can eat into a day and somehow dominate it so that the real aim of the climber, in this case to reach the South Col, becomes obscured. This is what happened now.

At Camp 6 on the night of the 15th, Lowe took a sleeping tablet for the first time. It had a disastrous effect. The next morning he just couldn't wake up. Noyce pleaded with him, cursed him, pummelled him, but it was not until 10.30 that Lowe staggered out of the tent and they were able to start up the tracks he had made the previous day. They didn't get far; he was falling asleep while he walked; they had no choice but to return, a precious day wasted. On the 17th, fully recovered and now well-rested, Lowe went like a rocket and at last they established their seventh camp, about half-way up the Lhotse Face at a height of 7315 metres. They still had 670 metres to go to the South Col. Noyce now dropped back, for he was going to be responsible for supervising the first big carry up to the South Col. Mike Ward went up to join Lowe that day, but he had a struggle just reaching the camp. Next day an icy wind blasted across the slope; Ward felt the cold bite through him. He went more and more slowly before being forced to turn back after less than a hundred metres' progress. They stayed in the tent on the 19th and barely reached their previous high point on the 20th. The forward drive of the expedition seemed to have come to a grinding halt.

Hunt now made a bold decision, pressured no doubt by desperation. Even though they were still far short of the South Col, he resolved to send Wilfrid Noyce up to Camp 7 with the Sherpa carrying party to try to push the route out and make the carry at the same time. In Hillary's view, Wilf Noyce was the best and most determined mountaineer of all the British contingent. A school master and a poet, he had a diffident manner, but once on the mountain was a very different person, with a single-minded drive and the immense determination of a man who had been one of Britain's most outstanding young rock climbers before the war.

Hunt, still desperately worried, uncharacteristically snapped at Lowe when he came down after his marathon ten days out in front on the Lhotse Face. In Mike Ward's words 'he was excessively rude' – an outburst caused by strain, and very quickly rectified. Hunt now realised, though, that he had to reinforce the push for the South Col; but who to send without weakening his summit assault? That night he resolved to send two more climbers up to Camp 7 the following day.

On the morning of the 21st things looked bad at the top camp. The Sherpas with Noyce had eaten something that disagreed with them and were all sick. There seemed little chance of getting up to the South Col, particularly on a route that was still unclimbed. Noyce, therefore, decided to set out with Anullu, a powerfully-built young Sherpa who chain smoked and enjoyed his *chang*, the local beer, brewed from fermented rice, maize or barley.

Back at Advanced Base, Hunt watched the slow progress of the two tiny dots and decided that Hillary and Tenzing would have to go up to the front and lend a hand. Hillary had come to the same conclusion already. Tenzing, more than anyone, would be able to encourage the Sherpas and Hillary had a huge vested interest in getting the camp on the South Col established. In addition, he was confident that he had the fitness to make this lightning push up to the Col, come back down, rest a day or so, and then make his summit bid. So Hillary and Tenzing set out from Advanced Base that afternoon and surged straight through to Camp 7.

Meanwhile, Wilf Noyce and Anullu had passed the high point reached by Lowe

Wilf Noyce achieved his own personal summit by completing the route to the South Col.

and Ward and were now working their way across the steep snow slope that swept down in a single span to the floor of the Western Cwm 900 metres below. They reached a crevasse that stretched its barrier right across the slope, and cast in either direction to find a snow bridge; but there was none:

> I looked at Anullu, and Anullu, behind his mask, looked back at me. He was pointing. Where he pointed, the crevasse, some eight feet wide, had narrowed to perhaps three. The cause of narrowing was the two lips, which had pushed forward as if to kiss over the bottle-green depths below. The lips were composed, apparently, of unsupported snow, and seemed to suspend themselves above this 'pleasure-dome of ice', into whose cool chasms, widening to utter blackness, it would at other times have been a delight to peer. I walked right once more, then left. Nothing. I signed to Anullu that he should drive his axe well in and be ready for me. Then I advanced to the first unsupported ledge. I stood upon this first ledge and prodded. Anullu would have held me, had one ledge given way, but he could not have pulled me up. As the walls of the crevasse were undercut to widen the gap, I would have been held dangling and could not have helped myself out. It would be silly to face such a problem in the Alps without a party of three. But I cannot remember more than a passing qualm. Altitude, even through oxygen, dulled fears as well as hopes. One thing at a time. Everest must be climbed. Therefore this step must be passed. I prodded my ice axe across at the other ledge, but I could not quite reach deep enough to tell. I took the quick stride and jump, trying not to look down, plunged the axe hard in and gasped. The lip was firm. This time the Lhotse Face really was climbed.

Slowly, they plodded on towards the wide gully that led to the crest of the Geneva Spur, which in turn would lead them easily to the South Col:

> Strange, how breathless I could feel, even on four litres a minute. Anticipation was breathless too as the crest drew near, backed by the shadow of Everest's last pyramid, now a floating right-handed curve from which snow mist blew. I was leading again, and hacked the last steps on to the crest. Still no view, and no easy traverse; we must go on up to the widening top. First boulders, up which we stumbled easily, then more snow, the broad forehead of the Geneva Spur, and then suddenly nothing was immediately above us any more. We were on a summit, overlooking in this whole scene only Lhotse and Everest. And this was the scene long dreamed, long hoped.
>
> To the right and above, the crenellations of Lhotse cut a blue sky fringed with snow cloudlets. To the left, snow mist still held Everest mysteriously. But the eye wandered hungry and fascinated over the plateau between; a space of boulders and bare ice perhaps four hundred yards square, absurdly solid and comfortable at first glance in contrast with the sweeping ridges around, or the blank mist that masked the Tibetan hills beyond. But across it a noisy little wind moaned its warning that the South Col, goal of so many days' ambition, was not comfortable at all. And in among the glinting ice and dirty grey boulders there lay some yellow tatters – all that remained of the Swiss expeditions of last year.

Wilf Noyce had achieved his own personal summit; he knew that for him the expedition was probably over. He had fulfilled his role in John Hunt's master plan, had established one vital stepping-stone for others to achieve the final goal, but that goal was denied him, as it is to the vast majority of members of a large expedition. Some are better than others at suppressing ambition and envy; in his book, *South Col*, Wilf Noyce only allowed: 'Yet when I looked up and saw John's trio setting out for the Face, a demon of suppressed envy pricked me, now that my job was done.'

On the 22nd May, Ed Hillary and Tenzing helped cajole and encourage Charles Wylie's carrying party to the South Col; Charles Evans and Tom Bourdillon with John Hunt in support, were on their way up to the Lhotse Face to put in the first tentative assault or reconnaissance of the South Summit, though I am quite sure that as Bourdillon and Evans plodded up the long slopes, enclosed in the claustrophobic embrace of their chosen oxygen sets, they were dreaming and hoping for the summit. In theory, the closed-circuit system should give them the speed and have

The South Col from the top of the Geneva Spur. The main summit of Everest is hidden in snow mist.

the endurance to get them to the top, but what if it failed or ran out near the summit? They had talked endlessly about this eventuality. The sudden withdrawal of a flow of almost pure oxygen could have disastrous effects. Would it be like running out of oxygen in a high-flying aircraft? Could they adjust to the complete loss of oxygen in time to get back down the mountain? There was no way of knowing for certain.

Until now, Wilf Noyce, George Lowe and all the others had been pursuing a series of limited adventures, limited not so much by their own strength, determination and acceptance of risk, as by the roles imposed upon them by the leader of the expedition. Bourdillon, however, had been given the opportunity of seeking out adventure in its fullest sense, for not only had he an outside chance of getting to the top, but also he was putting on trial his own oxygen system.

It is often argued that the use of artificial aids reduces the level of adventure; it certainly does with the indiscriminate use of expansion bolts, drilled and hammered into a rock wall to aid an ascent, for this dramatically reduces the level of uncertainty experienced by the climbers. In this respect, perhaps, had the closed-circuit oxygen system been perfect in every respect, lightweight and reliable, reducing Everest's summit to the height of Snowdon or Scafell, the feeling of adventure would have been lessened, though no doubt the satisfaction to Bourdillon the scientist would have been enormous. As it was, the system was by no means perfect. With fully-charged bottles and spare soda lime canisters (which absorbed the carbon dioxide), it weighed fifty pounds: it was temperamental in the extreme and uncomfortable to use. Charles Evans went along with Bourdillon out of friendship, coupled with his own scientific interest in the outcome of the experiment. It was a loyalty and enthusiasm that was to be severely tried.

Initially, their route went up a snow gully on the side of the ridge. They reached the crest, at a height of around 8290 metres, just after nine o'clock, having taken only an hour and a half to climb 400 metres. At that rate they had a good chance of not only reaching the South Summit, but getting to the top; but the going now became much more difficult. Fresh snow covered the rocks of the ridge; the clouds rolled in and soon it began to snow; their pace slowed down and it took two hours to cover the next 245 metres. They had now reached the high point achieved by Lambert and Tenzing the previous year and were confronted by a difficult decision. The soda lime canisters had a life of around three and a half hours; they were slightly awkward to change and there was always a risk of valves freezing up immediately after the change. At this point the angle had eased and it would be safe and easy to make the change. On the other hand, they could probably get another half hour or so out of the canisters that were in place – something that could make a big difference later on. They had a muffled conversation through the masks clamped around their faces. They decided to make the change.

Once again, they set out, now on new ground. The cloud swirled around them, the angle steepened and the snow was unstable, a fragile crust overlying loose deep snow beneath. There was a serious risk of avalanche. Even more serious, Evans' set now developed a fault which caused laboured, rapid breathing. Slowly, they forced their way upwards and, at last, reached the crest of the South Summit. The cloud was milling around them, clinging to the eastern side of the ridge like a great banner, but the crest of the ridge was clear.

Now higher than any man had ever been before, for the first time they were able to examine the final ridge to the summit of Everest. It did not look encouraging. Looking at it head-on made it appear much steeper and more difficult than it actually was; it also looked very much longer, a phenomenon noticed by Doug Scott when he arrived just below the South Summit in 1975. It was one o'clock in the afternoon; they had already been going for five and a half hours; they were tired and were now well into their second canister. To go on or not? The summit was within their grasp; they could almost certainly reach it, but could they get back? They would un-doubtedly run out of oxygen, might well be benighted. Bourdillon was prepared to risk all; he had that kind of temperament, had made a whole series of very bold and committing climbs in the Alps. Evans, however, whom John Hunt had put in charge of the pair and who was that little bit older, resolved that the risk was too great. They had a furious argument, muted no doubt by their oxygen masks, but Evans stuck to his point and Bourdillon, reluctantly, agreed to retreat. They only just got back,

Bourdillon and Evans return from the South Summit. They had been higher than any climber before. The main summit had been within their grasp, but their oxygen supply was low and they could not risk the return.

falling in their exhaustion on several occasions and tumbling, almost out of control, down the final gully leading back to the South Col, only saved by Bourdillon taking braking action with the pick of his axe. Had they pushed on to the summit, it seems most unlikely that they would have managed to get back alive.

Back on the South Col, there had been a moment when the onlookers, who now included Hillary and Tenzing, thought that Bourdillon and Evans were going to be successful. It was something that Hillary and Tenzing must have watched with mixed emotions. Whatever he felt, Hillary was able to muster a show of Anglo-Saxon team spirit. Tenzing, however, was both visibly and vocally agitated as he saw his chances of being the first man on top of the world starting to vanish.

Bourdillon and Evans, lying exhausted in their tents, had done a magnificent job; had they started from a higher camp they would almost certainly have reached the summit of Everest. As it was, they had opened the way for Hillary and Tenzing, though the story they brought back, understandably, was not encouraging.

John Hunt, who was also exhausted after his carry, felt a deep sense of satisfaction. His oxygen set had given trouble and, as a result, he had received a flow rate of only two litres per minute – half of what he really needed to make up for the weight of the oxygen cylinders and then to give him real help. Even so, he had struggled on to a height of around 8336 metres before dumping his load. For the leader of an expedition it is very important psychologically to make this carry to the top camp; in doing so he can feel that everything possible has been done to make the ascent viable and in some measure, I suspect, have a stronger sense of vicarious involvement in the final summit bid. The expedition as a whole becomes an extension of the leader's personality and ego and, because of this, it is not a huge sacrifice to forego the summit bid, for the success of the expedition overall is very much his handiwork, bringing a satisfaction that is as much intellectual as purely egotistical. On the other hand, the other expedition members inevitably experience frustration on many occasions because they are being held back, or given humdrum tasks, or are denied the chance of going to the summit. On a large expedition, some can lose the sense of personal adventure they would have experienced on a smaller venture.

John Hunt's ambition was to establish the top camp for Hillary and Tenzing's summit bid. This is the point at which he and Da Namgyl, pictured here, established a dump of stores at around 8326 metres.

Not so the irrepressible George Lowe who, as Hunt returned to the Western Cwm, had bobbed back up to the South Col, after the very minimum of rest from his herculean efforts on the Lhotse Face. He had no thought and little chance of making a summit bid himself; he just wanted to get as high up the mountain as he could, and was all too happy to do this in a support role.

After a day of storm the 28th dawned fine, though bitterly cold at −25°C, and still very windy; but they had no choice, they had to start the final push for the summit. Of their two Sherpas, only Ang Nyma, another hard-drinking, chain-smoking young man, was fit, so Gregory, Lowe and Ang Nyma had to take on heavy loads, but the heaviest of all were those carried by Hillary and Tenzing, who each took around fifty pounds. They reached the place where John Hunt and Da Namgyl had dumped their loads, but decided that this was too low and therefore picked up everything, sharing it out amongst themselves. Hillary was carrying the heaviest load – over sixty pounds.

Hillary and Tenzing at the top of the Lhotse Glacier. Tenzing, behind, has the summit flags wrapped confidently round the shaft of his ice axe.

Slowly, they clambered on up the ridge to a height of around 8494 metres, before finally stopping. Hillary and Tenzing started digging out a platform for their tent, while the others dropped back down towards the South Col. Both Hillary and Tenzing were in superb condition, finding they could work at the platform and put up the tent without using oxygen. That evening they dined well off endless cups of hot, sweet lemon water, soup and coffee, which washed down sardines on biscuits, a tin of apricots, biscuits and jam.

They woke up at 4 a.m. on the morning of the 29th May. It was a brilliant, clear dawn and, even more important, the wind had almost vanished. Tenzing was able to point out the Thyangboche Monastery, 5180 metres lower and twelve miles away. It took them two and a half hours to get ready for their bid for the summit, melting snow for a drink, struggling with frozen boots and fiddling with the oxygen sets. At 6.30 they set out. In the event, they got little benefit from the previous party's tracks. They did not like the look of the route taken and therefore waded up through steep, insubstantial snow that felt as if it could slip away with them any minute. It was only nine in the morning when they reached the South Summit, and the view from it was magnificent. Makalu in the foreground, Kangchenjunga behind, were almost dwarfed from their airy viewpoint; little puffballs of cloud clung to the valleys, but above them the sky was that intense blue of high altitude, while to the east it was traced with no more than light streamers of high cloud. Hillary looked with some foreboding at the final ridge, about which Evans and Bourdillon had made such a gloomy forecast.

At first glance it was an exceedingly impressive and indeed frightening sight. In the narrow crest of this ridge, the basic rock of the mountain had a thin capping of snow and ice – ice that reached out over the East Face in enormous cornices, overhanging and treacherous, and only waiting for the careless foot of the mountaineer to break off and crash ten thousand feet to the Kangshung Glacier. And from the cornices the snow dropped steeply to the left to merge with the enormous rock bluffs which towered eight thousand feet above the Western Cwm. It was impressive all right! But as I looked my fears started to lift a little. Surely I could see a route there? For this snow slope on the left, although very steep and exposed, was practically continuous for the first half of the ridge, although in places the great cornices reached hungrily across. If we could make a route along that snow slope, we could go quite a distance at least.

They had a short rest and Hillary changed both his and Tenzing's oxygen bottles for full ones. Then they set out, Hillary out in front cutting big steps for their ungainly, cramponned high-altitude boots, down a slope of good firm snow leading to the col between the Main and South Summits. Tenzing kept him on a tight rope, and then followed down. From the col they followed the heavily corniced ridge, moving carefully, one at a time. Hillary noticed that Tenzing had slowed down badly and was panting hard; he checked Tenzing's oxygen mask and saw that one of the valves was iced up so that he was getting hardly any oxygen. Quickly, he cleared it and they carried on, cutting steps, edging their way round ledges, ever-conscious of the dizzy drop down into the Western Cwm, 2438 metres below.

Hillary and Tenzing whose achievement caught the imagination of the world. 'Well, we knocked the bastard off!' Hillary greeted his compatriot, Lowe.

The summit ridge, looking up from the South Summit.

The most serious barrier was a vertical rock step in the ridge. At first glance it looked smooth and unclimbable, but then Hillary noticed a gap between the cornice that was peeling away from the rock on the right of the ridge and the wall of rock itself.

> In front of me was the rock wall, vertical, but with a few promising holds. Behind me was the ice wall of the cornice, glittering and hard but cracked here and there. I took a hold on the rock in front and then jammed one of my crampons hard into the ice behind. Leaning back with my oxygen set on the ice, I slowly levered myself upwards. Searching feverishly with my spare boot, I found a tiny ledge on the rock and took some of the weight off with my other leg. Leaning back on the cornice, I fought to regain my breath. Constantly at the back of my mind was the fear that the cornice might break off, and my nerves were taut with suspense. But slowly, I forced my way up – wriggling and jamming and using every little hold. In one place I managed to force my ice axe into a crack in the ice, and this gave me the necessary purchase to get over a holdless stretch. And then I found a solid foothold in a hollow in the ice, and next moment I was reaching over the top of the rock and pulling myself to safety. The rope came tight – its forty feet had been barely enough.

Tenzing then followed.

> As I heaved hard on the rope Tenzing wriggled his way up the crack and finally collapsed exhausted at the top like a giant fish when it has just been hauled from the sea after a terrible struggle.
>
> I checked both our oxygen sets and roughly calculated our flow rates. Everything seemed to be going well. Probably owing to the strain imposed on him by the trouble with his oxygen set, Tenzing had been moving rather slowly but he was climbing safely and this was the major consideration. His only comment on my enquiring of his condition was to smile and wave along the ridge.

They had now overcome the last real barrier and at last, at 11.30 in the morning, Hillary, with Tenzing just behind him, reached the highest point on earth. Suddenly everything dropped away around them. They could gaze down the North Ridge of Everest, across the endless, arid brown hills of Tibet, across to Kangchenjunga in the east and the serried peaks of the Himalaya to the west. They shook hands, embraced, flew their flags in those few moments of untrammelled delight, of complete unity in what they had achieved. Then they started the long and hazardous way down.

The first ascent of Everest caught the imagination of the entire world to a degree as great, if not greater than, any other venture before or since. Only the arrival of the first man on the moon, a victory of supreme technology, perhaps surpassed man's reaching the highest point on earth. But the very scale of the interest and adulation brought its accompanying problems the moment the expedition reached the Kathmandu valley. Nepalese nationalists wanted to adopt Tenzing as a standard-bearer for their own cause; the adulating crowds pounced upon him, shouting, *'Tenzing zindabad'*, long live Tenzing! They ignored Hillary and waved placards which depicted Tenzing arriving at the summit of Everest hauling behind him a fat and helpless white man. Hunt and Hillary were awarded knighthoods, Tenzing the George Medal. The fact that, as an Indian or Nepalese citizen, he was not allowed to accept a foreign title was ignored and, inevitably, the Indian and Nepalese press tried to exploit what they described as a racist slight to Tenzing. Hillary, perhaps extra-sensitive to the implications that he was hauled to the summit by Tenzing, wrote a frank description of what he thought happened on the day of the summit bid. Tenzing was affronted by the suggestion, which I suspect was true, that Hillary took the initiative on the push to the summit, particularly from the South Summit onwards. In his autobiography, *Man of Everest*, compiled by the American novelist, James Ramsay Ullman, Tenzing stated:

I must be honest and say that I do not feel his account, as told in *The Ascent of Everest*, is wholly accurate. For one thing, he has written that this gap up the rock wall was about forty feet high, but in my judgement it was little more than fifteen. Also, he gives the impression that it was only he who really climbed it on his own, and that he then practically pulled me, so that I 'finally collapsed exhausted at the top, like a giant fish when it has just been hauled from the sea after a terrible struggle'. Since then I have heard plenty about that 'fish' and I admit I do not like it. For it is the plain truth that no one pulled or hauled me up the gap, I climbed it myself, just as Hillary had done; and if he was protecting me with the rope while I was doing it, this was no more than I had done for him.

In their own ways both accounts are probably true, but it is noticeable that Hillary toned down his account of how Tenzing climbed the step, both in his own personal story of the expedition, *High Adventure*, and in his autobiography, *Nothing Venture, Nothing Win*.

The other members of the expedition, who had helped Hillary and Tenzing reach the top, got only a fraction of the acclaim. The public needs easily identifiable heroes and is little interested in whole teams. The team itself, however, have held together, meeting regularly for reunions and, in various combinations, joining each other for other climbs or expeditions. Perhaps this is the ultimate tribute to John Hunt's leadership.

Charles Evans avoided the fanfares of the return journey, going off trekking to the south of Everest. Two years later he led a small, low-key expedition to Kangchenjunga, third highest mountain of the world, and George Band, the youngest of the Everest team, who had had difficulty in acclimatising, reached the summit with Joe Brown, the Manchester plumber who was the representative of a new driving force in British climbing. Wilf Noyce, also, went on to climb other mountains in the Himalaya, until he was killed in the Pamirs in 1962 with the brilliant young Scottish climber, Robin Smith. George Lowe made the Antarctic crossing with Vivian Fuchs, meeting Ed Hillary who led the New Zealand contingent coming in the opposite direction, and ended up marrying one of John Hunt's daughters. John Hunt's career was undoubtedly helped, as in fact was that of most of the others, by his experience on Everest, but he has always remained a distinguished public servant rather than an adventurer. After retiring from the Army, he ran the Duke of Edinburgh's Award Scheme for some years, before becoming Chairman of the Parole Board. He has also taken part in several public enquiries and became a Life Peer in reward for his many and varied public services. Hillary, also, has put a great deal back. His greatest work and contribution has undoubtedly been with the Sherpas, running a Sherpa Trust which has brought them small hospitals and schools, helped them build bridges and adapt in general to a changing world.

Everest has held its fascination, attracting climbers from every climbing country in the world, to repeat the route made by the 1953 expedition, or to try to find a new way to the highest point on earth. It is a focal point of adventure that draws the participant as much as the onlooker, through the irresistible attraction of its supreme height, in which the sense of discovery, the challenge of risk, the sheer beauty of what can be seen from so high and the drive of ego-satisfaction all play their parts.

Cho Oyu

The Cho Oyu expedition was born in a terraced field on the banks of a small river in West Nepal. Herbert Tichy, a forty-two-year-old Austrian geologist, scholar, wanderer, mountaineer and philosopher, was on his way back from a four-month trek in the wild, little known mountains of West Nepal. For companions he had four Sherpas; they had climbed several virgin summits of around 6000 metres, had penetrated valleys where no European had ever been before and now they were on that saddening brink of the end of a journey, of returning to the bustle of civilisation. The Sherpas started talking about what they could perhaps do next year. Why not try a bigger peak? Couldn't they climb an 8000 metre one? Tichy was immediately attracted, as much at the prospect of climbing with his little group of Sherpas, as by the mountaineering challenge imposed by one of the Himalayan giants.

Everest and Nanga Parbat had been climbed earlier that year, but in each case by large, highly-organised expeditions. Tichy was essentially a romantic explorer; before the war he had travelled overland to Afghanistan on a motor bike, had spent seven years in China, part of the time studying Buddhism and Tibetan culture in a border monastery, making the pilgrimage round the sacred mountain of Kailas disguised in local dress; and he had made a two-man attempt with just one Sherpa companion on the high Tibetan peak, Gurla Mandhata.

Over six feet tall, with a prominent nose and the round, thin-rimmed spectacles that have become fashionable with our own hip generation, Tichy has gone through life, very much an individual, melding into a group or society, becoming part of it, both giving and taking but then always moving on to other places, other people. But he is no ascetic, smokes prodigiously, enjoys a drink, and has a rich sense of humour.

Sitting in the late afternoon of that December day, they talked round the possibilities of an expedition. Tichy demurred that they would have to get permission from the Nepalese Government, but Pasang, the most experienced of the four Sherpas, assured him that this would offer no problem. Pasang was one of the most distinguished of all the Sherpa high-altitude porters. He had been on many pre-war expeditions, had climbed with both John Hunt and Ed Hillary, but his greatest achievement was undoubtedly on K2, second highest mountain in the world, when he spent nearly ten days at over 7620 metres with the American climber, Fritz Wiessner, and made two extraordinarily determined attempts at the summit without using oxygen, getting to within 300 metres of the top on each occasion. It was Pasang who suggested attempting Cho Oyu, the peak attempted unsuccessfully by Eric Shipton's expedition in 1952. At 8152 metres (26,750 feet) it was the eighth highest peak in the world.

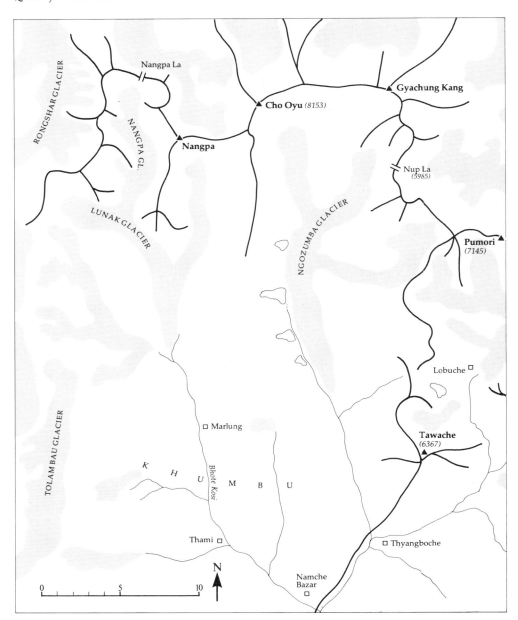

Cho Oyu

Cho Oyu from the south, at 8152 metres the world's eighth highest peak.

Tichy was determined to keep the team as small as possible; apart from anything else he undoubtedly preferred the company of Sherpas to his fellow Europeans. He finally resolved on a team of three Austrians of whom Sepp Jöchler, a thirty-two-year-old engineer, was to be the hard climber, and Helmut Heuberger, who was the same age, the expedition scientist. Jöchler had climbed some of the most difficult routes in the Alps, including the notorious North Wall of the Eiger with Hermann Buhl in 1952. The team was to be made up with seven Sherpas, but these seven were to be team members, albeit paid, and were to take a full part, not only in the climbing, but also in the policy-making of the expedition as it tackled the mountain.

Tichy returned to Nepal with his two companions in the autumn of 1954. They marched through the monsoon rains to Sola Khumbu, home region of the Sherpas, where they were fêted as old friends. Even Pasang, who had been teetotal for several years, succumbed to his native *chang*. It slides down with deceptive ease, milky-

white or creamy in colour, with an agreeable thirst-quenching taste that gives little forewarning of its alcoholic power; it's not difficult to get very drunk on *chang*, as many climbers have found to their cost.

All too easily an expedition can insulate itself from the people and country it passes through, travelling in a cocoon of taped western music, in-jokes, alien language, and pre-packed processed foods to avoid the risk of dysentery. Tichy's years wandering through the Far East had, however, lined his stomach with anti-bodies against this last hazard and he planned the expedition from the start on a lightweight principle, buying almost all the food in India and Nepal and living as far as possible off the land on the approach march.

The autumnal post-monsoon period is potato time and the Sherpas live on them almost exclusively at this time of year – great pots of boiled new potatoes, as succulent as any I have discovered anywhere else in the world. As Tichy observes:

> When you are being spoilt as a guest, there is no need to peel your own hot potatoes; your hosts fight for the honour of doing it for you. If you watch them for a short time as they dig in their nails and strip the potatoes of their jackets you will soon see that their fingers, at first black from the day's work, acquire a spotless flesh tint, while the potatoes they hand you are not white but grey.
>
> One might, of course, on trivial pretexts, insist on peeling one's own potatoes, but only at the cost of giving offence.

They pressed on past Namche Bazar and Thami, towards the Nangpa La, the main trading pass between Sola Khumbu and Tibet. It was the presence of this frontier which had inhibited Shipton in 1952; he had not cared to risk establishing a full scale Base Camp on the other side of the pass within Chinese territory, although he had compromised with a light push which, in fact, was stronger both in terms of numbers and material than the total strength of Tichy's expedition. Tichy had no such inhibition and resolved to press on ahead with Sepp Jochler over the pass to find a suitable site for their Base Camp.

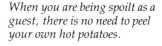

When you are being spoilt as a guest, there is no need to peel your own hot potatoes.

The rivers were high after the monsoon and the skeletal Nepalese bridges frequently presented problems.

I looked forward to accompanying Sepp, who was sparing of words and liked to have a hundred yards between himself and the next man. I sympathised and looked back with longing to the lonely treks of the previous year, when I had none of the worries of organisation and manpower entailed even by so small an expedition as ours . . .

A year ago there had been no gap. We were a little party, all dependent on one another. I relied on the Sherpas' practical experience and they without me would never have been exploring these unknown regions. We were close friends and the comfort of the night ahead of us depended on the way we complemented one another. But we were not friends for the sake of our comforts; we were friends first and our success followed from it. Now we formed an expedition, a great undertaking; there were sahibs, the sirdar, the Sherpas and the porters. The hateful and perhaps inevitable distinctions that life imposes had got hold of us. I was often sad: I find many entries like this in my diary: 'It is not as it used to be. Has Pasang become the manager of an expedition? Have I changed?' There was nothing to be done about it. We were bound for a lofty aim and perhaps lofty aims demand the sacrifice of personal principles.

Tichy's feelings were similar to those of many climbers; the conflict between his own individuality and the need to form part of a team. In many ways Tichy had much in common with Eric Shipton; he was happy wandering through the mountains, mingling with the mountain people, but whereas Shipton had committed himself to an expedition on Cho Oyu and then held back, partially through sickness but as much from a lack of enthusiasm for the single end of trying to climb a mountain, Tichy had committed himself to the challenge of climbing Cho Oyu and, though he frequently agonised over the constraints set by so limited an objective, he never wavered from his original aim, even though he did not consider himself to be a mountaineer.

215

*A porter crossing a bridge
on the way to Namche Bazar.*

I am no mountaineer in the strict sense. Mountains, strongly as they have always attracted me, are not for me aims in themselves, tests of technical accomplishment and physical strength; they are only part of that great world in which I feel so much at home. I love mountain peaks as I love people, because they are equivalent parts of a greater whole.

On reaching the crest of the Nangpa La, it was not Cho Oyu that caught his eye and imagination, it was the view to the north:

> There the glacier fell away and the grey-brown vales of Tibet closed in, wave after wave. Beyond there were more hills, faint outlines of snow peaks, and again hills upon hills. The best of the view was the peaceful harmony between earth and sky, whereas looking south what one saw was the wild commotion between the two.

I can remember the same almost magnetic fascination that this endless vista of brown hills, with the occasional snow cap of white, had for me on Nuptse in 1961. We had spent two months climbing its South Face and at last were making our bid for the summit. I was a technical climber who revelled in the difficulties presented by the steep face of Nuptse, but as I crested the summit ridge and suddenly the view to the north was opened, it was not the black pyramid of Everest, towering on the other side of the Western Cwm, but these same purple brown hills that grasped my imagination and have remained in my mind ever since.

The technical climber and the mountain philosopher need not be that far apart. Tichy's eyes were drawn from the great expanse of sky and cloud over the rolling hills of Tibet to his objective, Cho Oyu. Now squat and foreshortened, it seemed almost to lean over him; the original attraction of the expedition had been an intellectual desire to show that a big mountain could be climbed by a small team without 'organising the matter on a scale which seemed to me to disturb the harmony of creation'.

> But now that I gazed into the vastness of the sky above Tibet, I suddenly felt different. I wished to press forward into that sky recklessly and even though it would suffer us only on its circumference. It had dawned on me for so many years and never once proved a disillusionment and I wanted now to get as close to it as my limited powers allowed. There before my eyes was Cho Oyu, and its ridges were ladders into that longed-for sky. Suddenly I had become a fanatic to climb them.

Tichy certainly did not waste any time; the next day they established Base Camp and immediately started to find their way up the mountain. Heuberger was the first to feel the effects of altitude but he had never been intended to fulfil more than a support role. So Tichy and Jöchler, with the Sherpas, began pushing the route up the mountain in the traditional manner of reconnaissance, followed by humping loads to the site of the next camp, moving up to it and repeating the process all over again. What was different was Tichy's approach to the question of leadership. 'I was supposed to be the expedition's leader, but we were not disciplined on military lines, and when a decision had to be made we sat down and discussed the matter. Usually Pasang's greater experience turned the scale. None of us, I hope, had the feeling that I was "Leader of the Expedition".'

Nonetheless, it was Tichy who provided the driving force behind what they were all doing. Within a few days they had established their third camp at 6590 metres, moved into it and were ready to tackle the Ice Barrier which had defeated Eric Shipton's party in 1952. Ed Hillary, who had been out in front, had reckoned that it would take at least a fortnight to force. Sepp Jöchler, on his first visit to the Himalaya, was now suffering from the altitude and had turned back at Camp 2. Tichy, therefore, was alone with his trusted little band of Sherpas.

8153m

4 *(7000m)*

3 *(6590m)*

2 *(6446m)*

Base Camp

Cho Oyu, North-West Face

The ridge between Camps 2 and 3, just below the ice cliffs which turned back Shipton's 1952 expedition.

On arriving at the camp site on the ridge, he, too, was beginning to feel the altitude, longed to put up his tent, crawl into it and rest for the remainder of the day. But Pasang had other ideas and, while the Sherpas carved out platforms for the tents, he was already rummaging through the rucksacks for some ice pitons and a climbing rope. Tichy resigned himself to a hard afternoon's work and followed with the Sherpa Adjiba in Pasang's wake up towards the wall of ice that seemed to bar their way into the upper part of the mountain.

It was not the first time we had faced such icefalls together with the peak we were after, above us, beneath us the great desolation, parting us from all mankind, and within us that tried friendship which alone makes the invasion of such altitude possible.

I felt then that we had never been untied from that rope and all that I had been through and the people I had seen since our last climb were forgotten. It was not that those things and those people were in any way diminished, but now the rope, on which our lives and our comradeship depended, was all in all.

It was Pasang who had the initiative, out in front; he was picking his way below the Ice Wall, ferreting into ice chimneys, trying to find a chink in its defences. Tichy was happy to pay out the rope as Pasang pulled over an ice step and disappeared from view. The rope ran slowly through Tichy's hands and then there was a shout: 'Come on up.'

He followed, along a gangway sliced across the Ice Wall, up through a cornice, and reached a broad ledge. It took some moments for him to realise that they had solved the great problem of Cho Oyu in little over an hour.

The summit now seemed within their grasp. On the way down Pasang and Adjiba fixed a length of rope in place and cut steps to aid their passage when they returned carrying tents and gear for the next camp. Tichy, exhausted, staggered down to Camp 3, needing all his concentration, just to put one cramponned foot in front of the other. The following day they were pinned down by the violent autumnal gales that tear out of a clear blue sky. It was the 4th October. In his diary Tichy noted:

> Enjoying tent to myself. Final preparations were planned for early morning. At dawn all three tents flattened by terrific storm. Never known anything like it. Lie like a fish in a net, or a corpse under a shroud. Cloudless sky and tearing wind all day. Two Sherpas from Camp 2. When it strikes the canvas it is like a punch of almost human, brutal strength. Have never encountered such violence in such contrast with the beauty of the landscape.

On the 5th the weather relented only very slightly, but the five Sherpas and Tichy set out to establish their fourth camp. Hammered by the wind, affected by altitude, their progress was painfully slow and it was late afternoon before they had slowly plodded up to a spot just above the icefall, at a height of around 7000 metres. The two youngest Sherpas went back down, leaving the remaining four men to dig platforms in the hard wind-packed snow and put up their two tents. That night Tichy was full of optimism that they would reach the summit the next day. It was a long way, but they could see that there were now no more difficulties.

He was woken by what at first he thought had been a nightmare. It was pitch dark; something cold, wet and heavy was pressing down upon him, stifling, imprisoning. The scream of the wind was muffled. It took him a few seconds to realise where he was, several minutes to work out what had happened. The guylines of the tent had obviously been torn out by the force of the furious wind and the tent had collapsed. It was only his and Pasang's weight that was keeping it down, preventing them from being blown like a snowball down the steep slope into Tibet. Pasang muttered and groaned. There was nothing they could do in the dark and they seemed stable enough. Tichy cleared a small space round his mouth so that he could breathe and dropped off into an uneasy doze.

They lost all sense of time; Tichy became aware of light glimmering through the walls of the collapsed tent, then the glare of sunlight in strange contradiction to the screaming wind and fierce cold.

'Wait? Go down?' Pasang asked him; but Tichy did not know; wasn't sure if it was dawn or dusk. Had they spent all day pinned under the tent? The cold, the altitude, but most of all the incessant scream and hammer of the wind had frozen their perception of time and space. But they had to do something, and Tichy started to struggle out of his sleeping bag and then out of the tent – no easy matter, pinned down as it was over their prostrate bodies. Soon they were crouched in the snow. The other tent was in no better shape and the Sherpas had reached that state of numbed resignation that destroys the will to struggle for survival. It seems to hit the Sherpa earlier than the westerner, something that has been brought out in several accounts of crises in the Himalaya and from my own experience. The previous day, there is no doubt that it was Pasang who was in charge, taking the lead, selecting the campsite, but now he had lost that initiative, was crouched grey-faced by the collapsed tent.

'Never known a storm like this,' he shouted. 'All die.'

He repeated it over and over again. It was the force of the wind that dominated them, a wind that tore out of a cloudless blue sky, picking up snow and ice from the slope, driving it like a thousand daggers into their faces. They couldn't look into it, couldn't move for fear of being blown away, couldn't even think straight. Tichy recorded:

> Like Pasang and Adjiba and Ang Nyima, I was a poor wretch, tortured by cold and the fear of death, whose only comfort in face of the final and utter solitude was derived from the presence of my three companions. And at the same time the other part of me looked down without the least emotion, almost with irony, on the four of us . . . This split personality persisted throughout the events that followed; one part acted instinctively and suffered in the flesh, and the other followed events without feeling or pity, merely as a critical observer, coldly making his own comments upon them.

Tichy was shaken out of his reflection by the threat of their tent taking off in the wind. Without thinking, he dived over it to pin it down, plunging his hands deep into the snow. In the crisis of the moment, he had forgotten that his windproof mitts had somehow come off in his struggle to escape from the tent. He had been huddled in the snow with his hands in his pockets, and had hardly been aware of them: 'They were well off compared with the rest of my shuddering body.'

The Sherpas, now shaken out of their bemusement, grabbed the tent and bundled it up. While they did so, Tichy became aware of his hands; it began with a burning sensation that became progressively more intolerable. He chafed them, beat them against his sides, but it did no good; it was as if they had been on fire – the injuries caused by fire and frost are similar – he started shouting uncontrollably and the Sherpas crawled over to him, put his hands through their open flies to warm them between their thighs. But it was too late; the damage had already been done.

> My watching, critical self showed up again. I saw it all before my eyes as a picture; Pasang and Ang Nyima with their backs pressed against the wind and myself kneeling crucified between them, my hands outstretched and hidden within the remnants of warmth which might still be my salvation. My animal self relished these few seconds of warmth and shelter but that other self thought: 'What a subject for Kubin to paint! The Crucifixion or Journey's End.'

And then Adjiba brought him his mitts, which he pulled over his white and swollen hands. This action brought him back to the immediacy of their predicament. Suddenly he realised just where they were, how close to death and how much he wanted to live. He shouted: 'If we mean to live, we must go down, not sit here.'

The Sherpas were shaken into action, began to grab up pieces of gear that were worth taking down, leaving the tents where they were. Tichy was almost completely helpless, unable to strap on his own crampons or even hold an ice axe, and yet tied into the rope of four he felt extraordinarily secure, convinced that somehow they would get him down.

As they lost height the wind relented slightly. At Camp 3 they found Sepp Jöchler, who had fought his way up against the wind, being lifted bodily on one occasion and blown down fifty metres, fortunately into soft snow. They continued down to the site of Camp 2; Heuberger was there and able to give Tichy some injections to improve his circulation. There was little, however, that he could do for Tichy's hands, which were now swollen to twice their normal size and covered in huge blisters. At first glance, the state of his hands was as serious as those of Maurice Herzog and there seemed a very real danger of his losing all his fingers. In the next twenty-four hours he swallowed down eighty pills to improve his circulation; the correct dose was sixteen, but there was no doctor to advise against it.

They did something else which could have been much more serious. Sepp Jöchler was in favour of leaving Tichy's hands alone, but Pasang, who had had experience of frostbite before, was convinced they should cut the blisters, thus opening the injured hands to the risk of infection. Probably, what saved him was his decision to stay on at Camp 1 which, being above the snow line, was comparatively germ-free.

Amazingly, their spirits were already beginning to recover. They had been so close to success; surely Jöchler could reach the summit with Pasang, once the winds had dropped and they had had a chance to rest. Tichy wanted to see, and perhaps even help them to success, though at this stage he could not conceive taking more than a very minor support role.

They had left much of their food and fuel at Namche Bazar, hoping for a quick ascent. They were now low in all supplies and so Tichy told Pasang to go down to Namche and bring up their reserve food and fuel while the rest of them waited and rested below the mountain. Tichy spent his days recuperating, lying out in the sun in his sleeping bag, sucking in its warmth, gazing up at the great mass of Cho Oyu, his own ambition for a greater involvement in their next attempt growing with the physical strength that was beginning to return to him. The other two members of his team quickly became restless and went off to explore the western side of Cho Oyu and then, on the third day of their rest, Tichy saw some figures approaching from the direction of the pass. At first he thought that these were perhaps Tibetan soldiers, coming to arrest them, but then as they came closer he could see the visitors were climbers, armed with ice axes rather than rifles and that one of them was a woman.

The two visitors were Claude Kogan and Dennis Bertholet, members of the Swiss Gauri Sankar expedition. After the first greetings, it soon became obvious that the Swiss were planning to try Cho Oyu. They had found Gauri Sankar too difficult and wanted an easier option, suggesting that the two expeditions might join together, with the strong implication that the frostbitten Tichy and his two companions had no hope of climbing the mountain by themselves. Tichy found two European companions, however congenial, more than sufficient, and had no desire to become involved in a larger expedition. He pointed out that he had exclusive permission for Cho Oyu and suggested that the Swiss look at some other mountain in the area – after all, there were plenty of them. The Swiss were obdurate; the train of baggage, carried by yaks and porters, was on the way and could not be stopped. They were determined to try Cho Oyu with or without Tichy's participation. The Swiss team was led by Raymond Lambert who had got so close to the summit of Everest just two years earlier. After a long, at times heated, discussion, they reached a compromise: the Swiss would start establishing camps on the mountain, but would not make a summit bid until the Austrians had had another try from their top camp above the Ice Cliff.

There was now no question of waiting for Pasang. The Austrians had a very small quantity of food stocked in their camps on the mountain. At Camp 3 there was some cocoa, cheese, jam, ten pounds of *tsampa* (barley flour), a cooking stove and some fuel. At the site of their top camp there were a few tins of meat and fish, some milk, porridge and a couple more stoves – all too little for an assault on an 8000 metre peak.

Tichy hesitated; their team was so weak, their provisions for six Sherpas and three Europeans so ludicrously insufficient, but then one of the Sherpas reported that the Swiss were starting up the mountain. Tichy wavered no longer and they set out from their Camp 1, going straight up to the site of Camp 3. It was now the 17th October and the autumnal winds were tearing past the mountain. To avoid having their tents blown away once again, they dug a snow cave, by far the safest and most comfortable kind of shelter on a mountain. At this stage they were planning for Sepp Jöchler

After leaving off his windproof mitts in the storm at Camp 4, Tichy's frostbitten hands were now swollen to twice their size and covered in huge blisters.

The ice cave at Camp 3, at 6590 metres, dug on the second attempt as some protection against fierce autumnal winds.

and three of the Sherpas to move up to Camp 4, and then for Jöchler and Adjiba to make a bid for the summit. Tichy's hands were still badly swollen and he was unable to put on his own boots or even fasten the buttons on his clothing without help.

Jöchler and the three Sherpas tried to reach the site of Camp 4, but were driven back by the bitter cold and savage wind. Tichy had mixed feelings, part worried that they might not have another chance of making a bid for the summit, and yet part relieved, since with a delay there was just a faint chance that he might be fit enough to go for the top.

The storm raged for two more days, pinning them down in the snow hole. Each day Tichy was given an injection in the thigh by Heuberger, to help his circulation. The frozen ampoules had to be thawed out over the stove before they could be fed into the syringe, and then Heuberger had to find a vein quickly before the solution froze in the syringe. It was a desperately cold, painful business, the temperature in the snow cave being permanently just below freezing, but Heuberger persevered and Tichy stuck it out, determined to see the climb to its end, even if it meant losing his fingers in the process.

While they were pinned down by the savage wind, the Swiss – fresher, stronger in numbers – forged their way up the mountain, reaching the Ice Cliff and putting in a fixed rope of their own, parallel to that of the Austrians.

The morning of the 18th dawned fine but, most important of all, the wind had dropped. They resolved to make another attempt to reach the site of Camp 4. Just as they were getting ready, they saw three figures coming up from below. These must be the Swiss, now ready to forge ahead of them. And then as the figures came closer, to their delighted amazement they saw that it was Pasang and two of their Sherpas. Pasang, his face grey and lined with fatigue, gasped:

'Have the Swiss reached the summit?'

'No.'

'Thank God; I'd have cut my throat if they had.'

And he sounded and looked as if he really meant it! He had heard the news of the Swiss incursion the previous morning at Marlung, at just under 4000 metres, one of the last villages on the other side of the Nangpa La, some thirty miles away, much of the route over pathless moraines which make for slow and exhausting walking. The three Sherpas had packed their belongings immediately and, heavily laden with provisions, had kept going through the day to reach Base Camp late the previous evening. Setting out before dawn, still heavily laden, they had reached Camp 3 that morning. This in itself was an incredible achievement, but much more was to follow.

Pasang would not think of resting, but immediately volunteered to carry on with

Tichy at about 8000 metres.
His hands are useless.
He could not even hold his ice axe.

the others up to the site of Camp 4. He was determined to share in the summit bid. Tichy, inspired by Pasang's achievement and hating the thought of being left behind, resolved to go at least up to the site of the top camp. He had to have his boots and crampons placed on his feet by the Sherpas, was unable to handle a rope, but slowly, doggedly, he plodded on, in the wake of the others. The ice barrier was a desperate struggle; he could not handle the fixed rope and had to be heaved up it on the end of the climbing rope. Half-way up one crampon became loose, but he could not tighten it himself. He almost cried, not just from the throbbing agony of his injured hands, but from the sense of helplessness and guilt at being such a burden, perhaps an added danger, to his comrades. But once above the ice barrier they were able to unrope; it was just a question of putting one foot in front of the other and slowly, laboriously, he was able to keep going. There was now no sign of other tracks; the Swiss were somewhere safely below and out of the way. The wind was bearable, the snow firm under foot. They had perhaps found that elusive window, between the end of the post-monsoon storms and wind and the beginning of the real winter, when there are the odd few days of still, clear weather.

But the still period was all too short; by mid-afternoon, when they were still below the site of their previous high camp, the wind returned in all its fury, tearing out of the sunlit, blank, pale blue sky, hammering at their clothes, whipping particles of snow from the now hard-beaten surface and driving them against every patch of exposed skin. They climbed forty-six metres above their previous camp before stopping for the night. There was no question of digging a cave; the snow was much too hard. It was all they could do to level the small patches they needed for their two tents. Tichy's hands were agonisingly painful as he crouched, helpless in the snow, waiting for the tents to be erected. They tied the tents together, guying them out as well as possible, all too mindful of what had happened on their previous attempt. There was little comfort, even once the tents were up, for six were staying at Camp 4, and with three in a two-man tent, it is almost impossible to cook, lie down or move without disturbing one's companions.

They were not quite sure how high their camp was; according to the photographs they had, they were at a height of around 7000 metres, but according to their altimeters they were only at 6862 metres. Whichever was right, they had over 1200 metres to go to the summit, a seemingly impossible feat, particularly without the help of oxygen. The idea was for Jöchler and Pasang to make the attempt the following morning, whilst the rest of them would follow on behind and establish a higher camp for them to reach on their descent. But through the late afternoon, Tichy's mind turned once again to the summit. The thought of just sitting, waiting, while the pair headed for the top, was unbearable.

> I should never be able to endure such a day as that. I had staked all on Cho Oyu since that talk a year ago, and now at the last moment my stake was disallowed. I had to sit and do nothing, to leave the crucial moment to others and stay safely in the tent. The prospect filled me with a gloom such as I had never experienced. It was so painful that I forgot the pain in my hands.

It was a feeling that many climbers have felt; the immense, all-powerful magnet that a summit imposes. On an expedition, the world vanishes; one's horizon becomes encompassed by the surrounding peaks, but one's eye is drawn constantly to the summit that looms, elusive, above. Throughout the climb Tichy had been in a state of conflict, part of him in revolt against the minimal social structure and discipline needed to ensure climbing a single objective and yet, at the same time, in this one case he really wanted to reach the summit of Cho Oyu, had all the fixated

224

ambition of the dedicated technical climber, with the same drive as a Buhl or a Messner or a Bonatti. This was undoubtedly heightened by the fact that the expedition was his concept and, of course, the thought of somehow getting to the top had been in the back of his mind, ever since he had gone down with frostbite, rejected by his logical faculties, but secretly embraced, like some illicit love, by his emotions. And now he brought his decision into the open, announced it across Gyalzen's feet, to the patient and long-suffering Heuberger, and then crawled over to the other tent to tell Sepp Jöchler, who merely said: 'Fine, that's what I wanted.'

None of them slept much that night; you rarely do before a summit bid, the excitement is so intense and, on top of that, they were all acutely uncomfortable, with the wind beating on the tents throughout the night, shaking the hoar frost caused by condensation down on to their frozen sleeping bags. In Tichy's tent, only Gyalzen, untroubled by pre-summit excitement, slept deeply, emphasising the wakefulness and discomfort of the two Europeans on either side of him.

It was still dark when Adjiba, in the other tent, started to make breakfast, handing in to Tichy a bowl of porridge and a cup of cocoa. Gyalzen had to force Tichy's feet into his frozen boots, fasten on his crampons and then, in the early dawn light, they were ready.

As they plodded unroped up the long slopes that led to the distant summit, it was bitterly cold and windy. They were still in deep snow. Jöchler quickly lost all feeling in his feet which had been frostbitten on his ascent of the North Wall of the Eiger. He tried beating them with his ice axe but to no avail. Tichy felt his responsibility as leader of the expedition:

> I might have said: 'It won't do. Turn back.' It would have been good advice. Yet I should never have got rid of the suspicion that beside the solicitude for Sepp there might have been lurking ambition to be the only European to reach the top.
>
> I might have said: 'Pull yourself together, Sepp. You'll make it.' But how could I take the responsibility for his losing a foot?
>
> It was a case when each man must decide for himself. Pasang knew his own resources; I should know if I had to turn back; Sepp, too, must know best what to ask of himself. What I said to him was: 'In your place I should turn back, but do as you think right.'

Jöchler loosened his boots and carried on; it was the same attitude that had brought Tichy this high on the mountain. They were going slowly, with several pants to each step, but they made steady progress, reaching a steep section through which rocky outcrops obtruded. Tichy was unable to grasp the rocky holds; his hands were useless lumps and the pain unbearable. Pasang got the rope out and with a few pulls he was up the rocky section. The slope now swept at an easy angle up to the top. They left the rope behind and plodded upwards, each one of them lost in his own world. Tichy did not hallucinate, as several people at altitude have done, but he did undergo a profound emotional and intellectual experience:

> The world seemed to me to be instinct with a hitherto unknown benevolence and goodness. The barrier between me and the rest of creation was broken down. The few phenomena, sky, ice, rock, wind and I which now constituted life, were an inseparable and divine whole. I felt myself – the contradiction is only apparent – as glorious as God and at the same time no more than an insignificant grain of sand . . .
>
> I had broken through a metaphysical barrier and entered a world where other laws were in force. I recalled Blake's words: 'If the doors of perception were cleansed everything would appear to men as infinite.'
>
> Here the doors were all thrown wide open and an indescribable, impersonal bliss filled me. It did not prevent my believing that we should all die that very day. My waking mind was convinced of this. We should reach the summit very late and never get back either to Camp

In the space of three days Pasang had covered over thirty miles and gained over 4000 metres to stand beside Tichy on the summit of Cho Oyu, with Everest behind them to the left. His was one of the most remarkable speed climbing achievements of all time.

4, or to the tent with which Helmut and Adjiba would come to meet us. We should have to bivouac in the open and we should be frozen. This belief was also part of the unfolding bliss; it had nothing heroical in it, or menacing, and it did not make me hurry.

As nearly all religions strive to take away the fear of death and to make it seem acceptable, I may claim to have had a genuine religious experience.

And they got ever higher on the mountain, till suddenly the slope was dropping away on all sides; they could see around them, across to Everest, the peaks of Sola Khumbu, to the cloud-girt valley of Namche Bazar, where Pasang had been just two days before. In the space of three days he had covered over thirty miles and gained over 4000 metres to stand on the summit of Cho Oyu, probably one of the most remarkable feats in the history of mountaineering – a feat equalled only by Tichy's extraordinary determination that had held him on the mountain and then slowly taken him up it until, now, he too stood on top of this mountain of his dreams. They all wept with the joy and sense of unity that the moment gave them, but even here Tichy was aware of a greater immensity than just being on the top of that high mountain peak: 'The endless blue sky fell steeply all round us like a bell. To have reached the peak was glorious, but the nearness of the sky was overwhelming. Only a few men have been nearer to it than we were that day. It was the sky that dominated our half hour on the summit.'

They managed to get back to Camp 4 with the last rays of the setting sun and then underwent that slow, at times painful, transition from mountain to civilisation.

The Swiss never made it to the top; the winds were too high. Whether the wind was much worse than that encountered by Tichy, it is difficult to tell, for there is something anticlimactic about a second ascent. The Swiss had not got the same level of commitment; for them, Cho Oyu was a second-best after already having had one failure. They had not been through the same Armageddon. As for the victors – Pasang went down to Sola Khumbu to get married to a young Sherpa girl. He was the hero of the day. Tichy returned to Vienna, also to a hero's welcome, one that slightly surprised, even bewildered him. In spite of the extent of his injuries, he had only minor long-term damage to his fingers. (He attributed this to the amount of *chang* and *rakshi* he consumed on their return to the valley, claiming that it had kept his blood vessels well dilated. 'We were either tipsy or completely plastered for two whole weeks.') He has not undertaken any more major climbs since Cho Oyu, but this has been not so much because of physical inability as a broader, wider sense of discovery that has taken him all over the unspoilt world to experience people, places and other philosophies. Pasang, also, was nearing the end of a long and distinguished mountaineering career, though he did climb Cho Oyu once again, this time guiding an Indian expedition to its summit.

Tichy's expedition to Cho Oyu was unique in many ways. The mountain itself is not a difficult one by modern standards, but at the time it was the third highest peak to be climbed; it had already defeated one expedition which, at first glance, was very much stronger and more experienced than that of Tichy. There had been equally small and even smaller expeditions to the Himalaya, but none had succeeded on a mountain as high as Cho Oyu. Also unique was the relationship between Sherpas and climbers, where they genuinely became a single team working on an equal footing. For much of the time, Pasang had been the effective leader, both breaking trail and providing the upwards impetus, but in the manner of the small modern expedition each member of the team was able to influence events and, in effect, take the lead at different times. It had been Sepp Jöchler who had been the most vehement in turning down any suggestion that they should join up with the Swiss, but it was Tichy who had held the expedition together, to whom both Pasang and Jöchler had looked in moments of serious crisis.

Most remarkable was Tichy's indomitable determination in the face of serious frostbite, and Pasang's incredible three-day dash to the summit which, in terms of distance and height gained, has never been equalled – even today.

After the climb, the expedition helped celebrate Pasang's wedding to a young Sherpa girl in Sola Khumba.

The Bonatti Pillar

Walter Bonatti, aged twenty-four, on the 1954 Italian expedition to K2. By ferrying the vital oxygen supply up to the top camp, he assured Compagnoni and Lacedelli of their chance to reach the summit of the world's second highest mountain, but forfeited his own.

Some three months before Herbert Tichy's impulsive decision to go for the summit of Cho Oyu, another climber, at the other end of the Himalayan range, knew black despair because the summit of his ambition had eluded him. Walter Bonatti was a member of the Italian K2 expedition, attempting the first ascent of the second highest mountain in the world. This was very much a national expedition, the team carefully selected from the best climbers in Italy, with a clearly-defined leadership structure and the support of high-altitude porters. Walter Bonatti, aged twenty-four, was already emerging as one of Italy's leading Alpinists, with several difficult and technically innovative first ascents in the Alps to his credit. This was his first visit to the Himalaya and he desperately wanted to reach the summit of K2.

The early stages of the climb were beset by bad weather, but slowly the strong team forced its way up the mountain, establishing a series of camps linked by fixed rope. Bonatti took a leading part in this phase of the expedition, felt that he was going as well as, if not better than, anyone else in the team and probably had that competitive edge that Ed Hillary described in his relationship to the other members of the British Everest expedition.

And then everything fell apart. Six of the team, including Bonatti, were poised at Camp 7 at a height of 7320 metres, ready to establish the two final camps and then make the summit bid, when Bonatti went down with some kind of food poisoning. As a result two others, Achille Compagnoni and Lino Lacedelli, were chosen to make the summit bid. In his book, *On the Heights*, Bonatti wrote:

> Now that the moment had come to watch my companions leave for the summit, the world seemed to collapse about me. I felt shaken and listless, no use to anyone, and I cursed the fate which stopped me from savouring that moment which I had so long awaited to settle accounts with K2 . . .
>
> As my five companions went further and further up the slope on which the sun was glistening I remained in the tent, a prey to depression. So intense and bitter were my thoughts that finally I was compelled to pull myself together. I decided to eat at all costs, even though I felt sick at the very thought; only thus could I recover a little energy and again take my place up there. I often had to close my eyes to swallow a little of the food available and force myself to think of something else; at times I would choke from nausea but fortunately I managed to keep down all that I swallowed.

Bonatti recovered from his food poisoning in time to give them vital support. As so often happens in any major Himalayan expedition, however strong the team, the final push to establish a top camp is a last gasp, when all the carefully laid plans collapse with the growing frailty of the expedition members. What happened on K2 was to have a direct effect on what was probably Bonatti's greatest achievement and what, to this day, represents one of the most outstanding ascents ever completed in the European Alps. It is also very revealing, not just of Bonatti's personality but also of the huge stresses that can occur on an expedition, particularly one in the siege style where, all too often, only two members of the team manage to get to the top. The rewards of reaching the summit in terms of personal satisfaction, material gain and public acclaim are so great that it is rather like an open golf tournament, but one in which the competitors have to help each other until one pair gains the final prize.

Two days later, on the 30th July, Bonatti, now fully recovered, was up at their highest camp (Camp 8) at around 7620 metres, with Gallotti and the two summitters. Things now looked pretty desperate. The previous day Compagnoni and Lacedelli had tried to establish their final assault camp, but had been turned back by heavy snow. Two of the original six who had reached Camp 7 were now exhausted and had retreated back down the mountain. Bonatti and Gallotti had been forced to leave the vital oxygen for the summit bid in a dump between Camps 7 and 8, and at Camp 8 they were very nearly out of food and fuel. They were going to have to make a bid for the summit in the next couple of days or admit defeat.

Bonatti was in an agonising position. He now felt that he was going more strongly than either Compagnoni or Lacedelli and therefore had more chance of reaching the summit, but before they could make their bid they had to recover the oxygen bottles that had been left below the previous day; at the same time it was essential to get the top camp established. This would mean that one pair would have to carry the tentage and food another 300 metres up the mountain, while the other dropped back down to pick up the oxygen before trailing all the way back up, past Camp 8 and on to the newly-sited Camp 9, that same day. Bonatti describes his dilemma:

> All that evening Compagnoni had looked obviously exhausted. Doubting if he would be able to endure the effort of the assault on the summit, I was more than once tempted to ask him to let me take his place; but in the end I didn't. I felt that such a suggestion made by me rather than by him would have been tactless. Furthermore I was worried by the fact that before the final assault we still had a very active day's work before us, full of unforeseen events. I was in fact torn between the feeling that I would have to take Compagnoni's place, the scruples which in our present situation prevented me from doing so and finally, without a shadow of presumption, the fear that in my place, Compagnoni would not succeed in bringing the oxygen up to Camp 9.

And so Bonatti resigned himself to going down for the oxygen, but he was buoyed by Compagnoni's unsolicited offer. 'If you are still in good shape tomorrow up there at Camp 9, it might well be that you will have to change with one of us.'

Bonatti dropped down to the oxygen bottles to meet up with Abram and two Hunza porters who had come up from Camp 7. One of them, Mahdi, was going particularly strongly and so he shouldered the oxygen and, with Bonatti, set out on the long trail past Camp 8, to catch up with Compagnoni and Lacedelli at Camp 9. The summit bid hinged on their ability to carry up the vital oxygen.

The day raced past but their own progress was pathetically slow. Both were beginning to tire as they took one step at a time, slumping panting into the snow before the next agonised laborious step. By half past four in the afternoon they were far above Camp 8, the tracks of Compagnoni and Lacedelli stretching on above them; there was no sign of the tent. Bonatti shouted out; there was a reply: 'We're here. Follow the tracks.' But they could still see no sign of Lacedelli or Compagnoni as they struggled on in the now fading light of the afternoon. The track, part covered in by new snow, led tenuously through a crevassed region, over shaky snow bridges, round thin snow ridges, but still no sign of the tent. They cried out again; the same

The route to Camp 9 up which Bonatti and the Hunza porter, Mahdi, had to take the oxygen bottles. This picture was taken by Joe Tasker in 1980.

reply came: 'Follow the tracks.' It was now getting dark and the tracks stretched on ahead into the shadows. There was no reply to Bonatti's calls. He could have turned back, dumping the bottles of oxygen in the snow, but this would almost certainly have destroyed their chances of climbing K2. He did his best to encourage Mahdi, who was getting increasingly worried, almost hysterical, about the dangers of being benighted, and kept doggedly on.

It was now pitch dark; Bonatti's little hand torch would not work, probably because of the savage cold. They had no bivouac equipment and the prospect of a night out at 7925 metres was appalling. To make matters worse, Mahdi was in a blind panic, screaming profanities in Hunza, completely out of control. There was no question of getting back down in the dark, no possibility of going on. In desperation, Bonatti began digging out a platform for them to sit out the night; as he did so he,

230

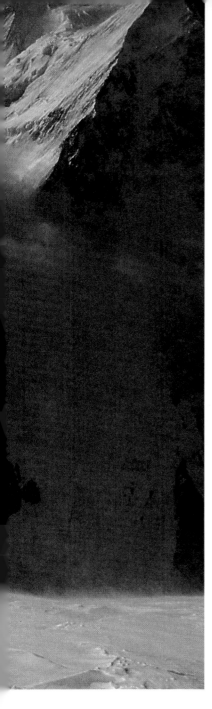

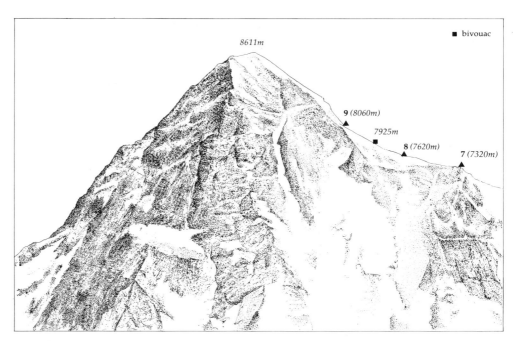

K2: Italian 1954 expedition

also, lost all control, shouting out into the darkness, 'No, I don't want to die. I must not die, Lino, Achille, can't you hear us? For God's sake help us!'

His curses fell into the cold unresponsive darkness; there was no reaction, no reply, no glimmer of light – just the dark silhouette of the mountain against a blue-black, star-studded sky, and the wind that hissed with a bitter cold over the hard-packed snow. Bonatti spent his rage; Mahdi was tearfully resigned, huddled in the snow. They were both hoarse and could raise little more than a whisper from painfully dry throats.

Then suddenly, on the other side of a steep ice slope, a light glimmered and Lacedelli called them. The voice was so clear that Bonatti could not understand how he had failed to hear their earlier agonised calls for help. But Lacedelli claims that he could barely make out Bonatti's words. Perhaps the wind direction must bear the blame for this. There are some discrepancies in their accounts; they both agree that Lacedelli told Bonatti to dump the oxygen cylinders, but then Bonatti claims that Lacedelli told him to come across to the camp, while Lacedelli says he told Bonatti to go back down and assumed that this was what Bonatti did. Whichever recollection is correct does not really matter, since Bonatti realised that there was no way Mahdi could either cross the steep ice slope between them and the haven of the camp, or descend in the dark. Bonatti could undoubtedly have reached Lacedelli and Compagnoni by himself, but it would have meant abandoning Mahdi to his fate. And so Bonatti resigned himself to sitting out the night with his crazed companion.

I have spent a night out at 7320 metres with Doug Scott, a companion with whom I had total trust and understanding. That was bad enough – I have never felt so cold nor known a night go so slowly. Bonatti was over 600 metres higher with a companion who spoke hardly any English and had lost all control. And then to cap it all, the weather broke and they were engulfed in a ferocious blizzard, the wind screaming past them, the snow penetrating every chink in their clothing. Yet somehow Bonatti managed to hold on, saving Mahdi when he tried to hurl himself down the slope in a mad, desperate bid to escape the screaming wind and snow. The storm blew itself out before dawn and in the first glimmer of light, Mahdi took off, staggering drunkenly down the steep slope. Bonatti remained where he was until the sun crept round to bathe him in its warmth before slowly, carefully, plodding down in Mahdi's wake. His hands and feet were numb with cold, but the frostbite was superficial, a tribute to his own extraordinary control over mind and body. The experience he had been through had been infinitely worse than anything that had beset Tichy, who had suffered severe frostbite through just one thoughtless moment. Bonatti, on the other hand, had nursed himself through the savage night, surviving unscathed where many would undoubtedly have died.

Bonatti's sacrifice had made Compagnoni and Lacedelli's bid for the summit possible, but when they returned, exhausted, frostbitten but successful, it was inevitably their achievement that the media – and for that matter the climbing world – latched on to. Bonatti could not escape from a profound feeling of lost opportunity. He desperately wanted to succeed and almost seems to have needed the approval and acclaim of his fellows. His background may have had a considerable influence on this.

He was an only child; his mother died while he was still very young and he was brought up by his father, a factory worker, who believed he should learn to look after himself. In the words of his close friend, Carlo Mauri: 'Each did their own thing. Living together, but leading independent lives. It wasn't a relationship of father and son, or of love; basically, it was a matter of "you're a man; I'm a man and we are here together but let's live without emotion."'

His early years, of course, were spent in the stress of deprivation of the war in the northern Italian industrial town of Bergamo. On leaving school he took a job in the local factory, but it was the mountains to the north that enabled him to escape and realise his potential, in his physical ability as a climber, his sheer imaginative scope and creative drive, for there is a creativity in climbing, both in discovering a new way up a mountain or rock face and in the way the climber actually tackles it. There is a conflict between the desire of the climber to ensure both his safety and the success of his venture, and the need to maintain a level of uncertainty and, indeed, risk which are vital ingredients of adventure.

Around the 'fifties, in the European Alps controversy raged regarding the use of expansion bolts. Some of the Italian Dolomites were being climbed by drilling holes in the rock and then hammering in these bolts, by which technique it was possible for the climber to go anywhere without any regard for the natural configuration of the rock. Providing he had sufficient endurance and patience, he could slowly hammer his way up any rock wall or mountain. Bonatti had always deplored this approach, had wanted to keep climbing as close as possible to a fundamental adventure, using the minimum of artificial aids. He was a perfectionist, renouncing any compromise of his own ethical stance, and demanding the same standards of others. Once again, in Mauri's words:

> Bonatti sees everything in black and white; there are no in-betweens. His whole life, his whole reason for existing, is to overcome the challenge of the mountains, not just mountains, but forests, deserts – anywhere. He is constantly looking for challenges to overcome. For example, when I'm in the mountains, I think of my family back home, because I have emotional ties with them, but for Bonatti, it is only the mountains that exist.

In 1951 Bonatti had made the first ascent of the East Face of the Grand Capucin on the side of Mont Blanc de Tacul – at the time one of the most difficult rock climbs to have been completed in the Alps – but the challenge that fascinated him above all was the South-West Pillar of the Petit Dru. It towers above Chamonix, a focal point amongst an array of spectacular granite peaks. It has the symmetry of the tall spire of a cathedral, its colouring and texture changing, chameleon-like, with the moods of the day. At dawn, silhouetted against the rising sun, it is stark and black, all features lost in opaque shadows and then, as the sun creeps up and round, glancing across the face of the pillar, its columnar structure is picked out in relief, emphasising rather than lessening its uncompromising steepness, showing up the bristling overhangs, the lack of ledges, the blankness of the rock. The tone is now grey, hard, forbidding and then, as the afternoon sun begins to mellow, the pillar becomes a rich brown, almost red, in the rays of the dying sun. It now beckons, almost friendly, to the dreaming climber.

The West Face of the Petit Dru was first climbed in 1952 by a French party. At the time it was an outstanding achievement, but they were forced away from the centre of the face to creep up its left-hand side, and to escape altogether towards the top. The great pillar that soared up the centre was left untouched, and it was this that fascinated Bonatti. He had attempted it with Carlo Mauri in 1953, but they had been beaten back on its lower part by bad weather. He tried again in July of 1955 with Mauri and two other friends, Oggioni and Aiazzi. Once again the weather was bad, and once again they were forced to retreat.

> This second defeat led to a great spiritual depression which was the fateful last drop which made my cup of disillusion and bitterness, which had brimmed after the conquest of K2, overflow. My spiritual crisis had already lasted too long. For a whole year one might say that I no longer believed in anything or anyone. I was nervous and irascible with everyone, sick of everyone, bewildered, without ideals, sometimes even desperate without any apparent reason. I felt that I no longer belonged either to others or to myself. Often when someone suggested that K2 had done for me, I was seized with a paroxysm of weeping and what I suffered in silence, no-one could imagine.

It was in this mood that the first glimmer of the idea of attempting the South-West Pillar of the Petit Dru by himself began to take root.

In a way solo climbing is the ultimate expression of the sport, for when climbing by himself the climber is staking his life on his judgement. Although there are techniques of self-belaying, the climber is totally dependent on his own resources, is only able to use a rope on very difficult ground, and if he does, it is both laborious, time-consuming and, in the event of a fall, of very dubious value. Most of the time the climber is moving unroped, his life literally in his hands. This in turn gives a wonderful sense of freedom of movement and mastery over one's destiny, something that Bonatti urgently needed at that moment.

But while top standard climbers frequently climbed solo, it was usually on routes that had already been climbed. Bonatti was now thinking of tackling alone a climb that was not only unknown but probably technically the most difficult route ever to have been attempted in the Western Alps. It was a truly gigantic challenge and his depression dropped away as he became absorbed in his preparations.

He made his plans secretly to avoid ridicule, confiding in only one close friend, Professor Ceresa. Deciding to make his attempt that summer, he and Ceresa arrived at Montenvers, the hotel on the west bank of the Mer de Glace, just opposite the Dru, on the 11th August. The weather was unco-operative, however, and it rained for the next four days. The tension of waiting must have been extreme. I was a member of a party that made the fifth ascent of the South-West Pillar in 1958; we were also delayed by weather at Montenvers, and I remember how the nervous tension built up for us; but we were planning to tackle a climb that had already had several ascents with a strong party of four. Bonatti was on his own, faced by the unknown.

At last, on the 15th August, the weather cleared. Bonatti set out at two in the morning, weighed down by seventy-nine pounds of food and climbing equipment. He plodded across the smooth ice of the lower part of the Mer de Glace, stumbled in the dark up the steep and crumbling moraine and then up the long rocky and grassy slopes that lead towards the base of the South-West Pillar. By eight o'clock he was at the foot of the gully that leads up to the pillar. It is a grim, frightening place, a dark gash between the wall of the Dru and the broken, crumbling rocks of the Flammes de Pierre, a ridge of rotten pinnacles sweeping in a dramatic cock's comb from the slender tower of the Petit Dru itself. The rocks at the bottom are scarred by stonefall. It is a dangerous place to be once the early morning frost loosens its grasp over the crumbling rocks above. Bonatti's progress was painfully slow. There was a lot of snow in the gully and the rocks were covered by an invisible layer of verglas. It is one of the most threatening places I have ever been in, the pillar's granite walls soaring smooth on the left, and the crumbling rocks above and around. There is a feeling of naked vulnerability, as if every stone that comes down is aimed specifically at you, with no cover, no escape. Alone, weighed down by the huge load which Bonatti was now towing behind him, it must have been a nightmare. But he kept at it for seven hours. At the end of this time he had made only 150 metres; the sack behind him kept getting jammed in the broken rocks and each time he had to climb back down to free it. But only when it started to snow did he give up.

He was no longer depressed by temporary failure; he felt he was carrying too much and abandoned some of the food and gear on the way down. He also had second thoughts about the gully. A safer approach, surely, would be to climb the Flammes de Pierre from the other side, where the angle was easier and less prone to stonefall, and then to abseil into the gully at the shoulder where the ridge of the Flammes de Pierre abutted onto the main mass of the Aiguille du Dru.

He didn't waste any time resting; next morning, with a small team of friends, he went round to the Charpoua Hut on the other side of the Dru. The following day, with the help of Professor Ceresa, he intended to carry all his supplies up to the shoulder and then to abseil the 245 metres down to the foot of the South-West Pillar. It took much longer than they had anticipated and by late afternoon they were still well below the shoulder. They dumped the gear and dropped back down to the hut for one last night in the comfort of a bed. The delays, combined with the fact that next morning he would inevitably be committed, were beginning to have their effect. He wrote:

> I envied Professor Ceresa who, on the next day, would get out of this inferno and I also envied all men who did not feel, as I did, the need to confront such trials in order to prove themselves. Filled with these thoughts I was getting ready to return to the hut when I saw a poor butterfly, lured there by the day's warmth, which fell helplessly to the snow a few feet away from me with a last beat of its wings. Poor living thing, what bad luck you had to find yourself about to die in this cruel world, whose existence you never even suspected. In that last beat of its wings I saw before me an almost human drama. Who knows, I thought to myself, with what terror your little eyes watched the last rays of the setting sun, the unexpected metamorphoses of their colours? Who knows with what horror your senses warned you of the fateful bite of the frost, the atrocious certainty of death and like me the same infinite regrets? Wretched insect, my brother in misfortune in this place of death, how much I feel for you and with you. Your tragedy is mine too: what I am searching for in the conquest of the Dru is similar to the intoxication which brought you here. The Dru which I was about to challenge was nought else for me than that last ray of sunlight which only a few minutes ago you saw set for ever. If tomorrow I do not succeed in mastering myself, I will share your end.

The South-West Pillar of the Petit Dru, the challenge that obsessed Walter Bonatti. He had attempted it twice with friends before he conceived the idea of tackling probably the most difficult route in the Western Alps solo.

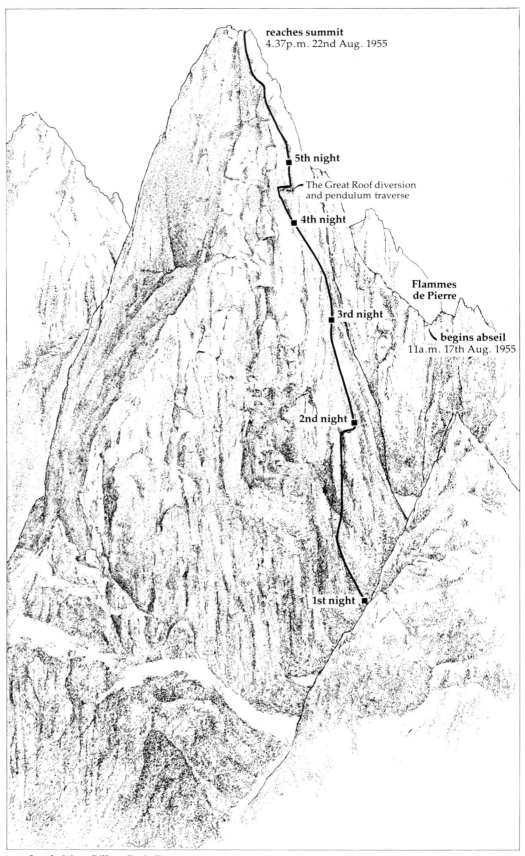

reaches summit
4.37p.m. 22nd Aug. 1955

5th night

The Great Roof diversion
and pendulum traverse

4th night

**Flammes
de Pierre**

3rd night

begins abseil
11a.m. 17th Aug. 1955

2nd night

1st night

South-West Pillar, Petit Dru

Throughout the night he was wracked with misgivings. It's not surprising. I have never been to the extremes to which Bonatti went, but I have known the same conflict, as I am sure do most other climbers before setting out on a big route. The night before I set out for the South-West Pillar of the Dru or for the North Wall of the Eiger, I knew the combination of dread and excited anticipation. There are the inevitable questions of why do we do it, assessments of one's chances of survival, accompanied by horribly clear cut images of breaking weather, falling stones, smashed, spreadeagled bodies. The lure that leads one on is the euphoria, the mastery of one's own mind and body that can be found on a high mountain wall. But for Bonatti, it was not just the joy of climbing that drove him on; he needed the extreme, totally individual pilgrimage of his solo ascent to exercise his inner pain.

He set out from the hut on his own, climbed through the chaotic jumble of the Charpoua Glacier and up the lower slopes of the South Face of the Dru, picking up his heavy load on the way. Poised on the shoulder of the Flammes de Pierre, he waved to his friends whom he could see as tiny black dots outside the Charpoua Hut. He then turned to the gully:

> The void there was absolutely terrifying, broken only by icy shadows and the sharp, vertiginous outline of the South-West Pillar. In the half hour of rest which I allowed myself before the descent, I lived through perhaps the most important moment of the whole climb. Till then every foot I advanced up the mountain had still allowed me the possibility of return, but beyond the gap that was no longer possible.

He tied his two thirty-six-metre ropes together, put them round a rock spike and tied his heavy sack to the two ends, lowering it into the void. He then abseiled down, the weight of the sack making it desperately difficult to manoeuvre his way down the steep but broken and snow-covered rocks. It was a slow, nerve-wracking business. The sack kept getting jammed and the lower he got in the gully, the greater became the danger of being hit by falling stones. This was probably the most oppressive part of the entire climb. He used spikes of rock as far as possible for anchor points, but he also had to abandon some of his precious pitons when there was no spike available. Often he could go no further than nine metres at a time, the ground was so broken.

He was about half-way down, in a particularly awkward position, jammed across an icy chimney, trying to hammer in a piton, when he missed it and smashed the tip of his ring finger against the rock. Blood poured from it and the pain was so agonising that he felt faint. Somehow he managed to hammer the piton into the crack, clipped into it and examined the damage. The entire tip of his finger had been sliced off by the blow; it took him an hour to staunch the blood and then he continued on down the gully. It was now late afternoon. He hadn't even reached the start of the climb and the entire enterprise seemed doomed. Worse, however, was to follow. He reached the snow patch at the foot of the South-West Pillar at about seven o'clock that evening; he pulled one end of the rope to recover it, but it was now so wet that it jammed solid. This is the nightmare of all climbers, for the only way to recover it is to climb back up the rope, with the constant risk of it suddenly becoming unjammed and taking you hurtling down the slope with it. Bonatti decided to leave it until morning and started sorting out his first bivouac on the face. There was no ledge, just smooth, steep ice. He had left his ice axe at the shoulder, so had no means of cutting out a ledge to sit on. He was soaked to the skin and, on opening his rucksack, discovered that his fuel bottle had leaked, contaminating most of the food. All he had left were two packets of biscuits, a tube of condensed milk, four little cheeses, a small tin of tunny, one of liver paste, a small flask of cognac and two cans of beer. Most serious of all, he had lost all his fuel and so would be unable to melt ice or snow for drinks during the climb.

*A climber on a subsequent ascent
on the slabs in the centre
of the pillar.*

There was little question of sleep or even rest that night. Bonatti was wet, shivering with cold and acutely uncomfortable, his position dangerous but, even worse, it seemed to be collapsing into yet another fiasco. The night dragged out but at last it dawned a fine day; the ropes had dried during the night and he was able to pull them down. In a way this was another moment of decision. He could have bailed out, continuing abseiling down the gulley. After all, he had been down it twice before on his earlier retreats. But the idea did not even occur to him.

The rock on the pillar was clear of snow, looked clean and inviting. He thrust behind him the fears and worries of the night and started up it. It was a slow, laborious process. The rock is ferociously steep and smooth, split by narrow cracks, the only means of upwards progress. Bonatti used a technique of self-belaying, attaching one end of the rope to the sack and the other to himself. He attached the sack and rope to a piton at the start of the pitch and would then climb for a short distance, clipping the rope into further pitons, which he used both for direct aid and also for further protection. Having completed the pitch he would then attach the rope to the top piton, slide down to the bottom one, remove it and all the intermediate pitons and then haul up the sack. This was his greatest problem, for the sack kept getting caught. He would then have to climb back down to release it, back up again, continue hauling it until it became stuck once again, and then repeat the whole process. As a result, by the time he reached the top, he had climbed the South-West Pillar three times over.

Comparing Bonatti's experience with that of the solitary yachtsman, he was alone for just six days, compared with the 313 that Robin Knox-Johnston took to sail round the world. On the other hand, the level of danger was much more acute. A single mistake at any moment of those six days could have meant a long, terrifying fall. One's life depends on one's fingers or, perhaps even more frightening, on the security of a small block of wood hammered into a crack; each time the rope gives unexpectedly with a drop of a few inches it could mean that the vital anchorage has failed and you've started your last hurtling fall to the depths below. Each time your heart seems to jump into your mouth, the adrenalin pumps through your body.

About two-thirds of the way up the South-West Pillar, a huge overhang bars the way. Bonatti reached this on the eve of the fourth night. That night he could see the lights of Chamonix spread below him, could hear his friends call him from Montenvers, 900 metres below, but somehow the very proximity of people and comfort accentuates the isolation of the sheer rock wall. By this time his hands were swollen and lacerated from the constant hauling of the heavy sack and clinging to the rough granite. His injured finger throbbed ominously. He was suffering from dehydration, his muscles wracked with cramp. After handling a piton or gripping the hammer, he had to use his teeth to straighten out his fingers.

The overhang jutted out above him in a series of huge, insecure-looking flakes. It seemed suicidal even to think of committing himself to it. He could vividly imagine the consequence of one of those huge flakes coming away, with him clinging to it, hurtling down to the dark gully from which he had so slowly struggled.

To the left a crack split the smooth bulging wall, disappearing from sight round the bulge. This, at least, went up some solid rock and was the route that Bonatti chose. He pitoned his way up the crack, a tiny figure lost in a huge blank wall. The crack curled up into a gently overhanging wall, widening until it was too wide for his pitons but still too narrow for his wedges. A small 'plane buzzed past, then came back in a wide easy swing, first above then below him, obviously trying to find him in the immensity of the pillar. Its presence emphasised his isolation even further.

Climbers in action setting out from the site of Bonatti's second bivouac.

Who could tell if they had seen me, I thought, and I was overcome by the strange feeling that the 'plane was a living part of me which was now leaving me and tearing me apart. I became aware that I would have preferred absolute solitude. Everything that happened in that short time seemed to me like a final effort to associate me with that life which no longer seemed to have any meaning for me. It had come unexpectedly and like a breeze had skimmed lightly over me several times and then vanished in the distance for ever, leaving me up here, out of the world, like a thing already dead.

He was left in the silence of the huge face, suspended from his top piton. The thought of retreat, to the foot of the overhang, was appalling. In desperation he gazed around him and noticed a long, thin crack curling up the wall over to the right. If only he could reach it – but the rock in between was smooth, sheer and blank. But if he could swing across on the end of the rope, he might still be able to surmount the obstacle. He threaded his double rope through the top piton, descended, removing the others he had put in place, until he had rejoined his sack. Then he started to pendulum back and forth across the smooth granite wall, each swing gaining momentum until he was very near the crack. His troubles were not over; the rope jammed when he tried to recover it. He had to climb and swing back along the line of the rope until he was able to pull it free, and then work his way back. He was nearly there; just twelve metres separated him from the crack line, but those twelve metres seemed insuperable. Between him and his haven was a sheer, smooth depression of rock. He could not climb any higher to get an anchor point for another pendulum. There was no way he could get back the way he had come, for he had now pulled the rope from behind him. He could not go down, for he would have ended up dangling helplessly in space. Alone, at the end of five days' struggle with insufficient food or drink, he was on the point of panic, but once again he managed to take a firm grip of himself. He saw, at the foot of the crack he was trying to reach, a small outcrop of rock shaped like a hand with five fingers extended. It was his only hope. If only he could lasso it and then swing across; he made a kind of bolas with a series of nooses and his entire stock of fifi hooks and metal rings, hoping that enough of this rope octopus would catch in the rocky encrustation firmly enough to take his weight. It took a dozen casts before the bolas seemed securely settled on the outcrop.

He gave it a trial tug; the rope broke loose. He threw the lasso again; again it broke away as soon as he pulled on it. At last it held, though he could not pull at it really hard, because his stance was so awkward. Its security could only be truly tested once he cast himself off to swing across on it. To give himself some measure of safeguard, he threaded his rope back through the piton to which he was attached. This was a desperate measure, for had the lasso pulled clear of its anchorage, he would have fallen around twenty-one metres before the piton took his weight, and that would almost inevitably have pulled it out.

A last unnerving delay, a last inner prayer for safety, and then, as an uncontrollable tremor ran through me, before my forces grew less, I closed my eyes for a second, held my breath and let myself slip into space, holding the rope with both hands. For an instant I had the feeling of falling with the rope and then my flight slackened and in a second I felt I was swinging back; the anchorage had held.

He still had to climb the rope, doing it hand over hand, but very gently, frightened that he might disturb the fragile anchorage above. A final moment of crisis came as he reached the rock outcrop; just by reaching up and out, he could have pulled the lasso from off the rocky projections, and have gone hurtling back into space. His muscles were aching, his hands had very nearly lost their strength as he gently grasped the rock and, oh, so carefully, eased himself onto the pillar that had held his weight.

The climbing remained steep and difficult; crack followed crack. There were more abseils, more crises. His hands become more and more painful; the rocky holds were spattered with his blood, but there was nothing quite as bad as that appalling pendulum. By the end of the day he was only a very short distance above the big overhang which had forced him to make his desperate diversion, but that night – his sixth – for the first time he felt that success was in sight. Now far above the ridge of the Flammes de Pierre, he could look down into the Charpoua Glacier and could see the haven of the Charpoua Hut. He could hear distant shouts and see moving lights. He lit a piece of paper and used this as a signal to show where he was.

The following morning he set out on the final stages of the climb. Although the angle now eased a little, there was a series of steep and difficult steps. To make things worse, his hands were almost useless – swollen, suppurating and very painful. He could hear the voices of his comrades who were coming up the original route on the other side of the Aiguille. Their presence encouraged him but he was still totally alone; just one mistake, in his exhausted state, and he could die. He climbed through the day; just short of the summit a huge rock came away above him. He very nearly fell with it, but somehow held on, hands wedged into the crack, as it smashed down, grazing and numbing his leg. He hardly noticed it – success was at last in sight – and, at 4.37 exactly, he arrived on the summit of the Petit Dru. There was no sign of the others. Bonatti had the summit to himself. He had exorcized the demons of K2 and could enjoy the solace of his extraordinary achievement.

Inevitably anyone who takes adventure to such extremes, who knows no compromise, becomes a target for criticism – usually by his jealous peers. Bonatti had always found it very difficult to ride this criticism. It was this that influenced him in announcing, after his extraordinary solo ascent of a new route straight up the North Face of the Matterhorn in the depth of winter in 1965, that he would no longer undertake any major climbs. He still climbs, but with a small group of close friends. In many ways he is a sad and lonely man. The problem with chasing the extreme in risk and physical adventure is that the solace it gives is ephemeral.

Broad Peak

The 'fifties have been described as the golden age of Himalayan climbing, for it was during this period that all but two of the fourteen peaks over that magic height of 8000 metres were climbed. Most of them had fallen to large expeditions in the pattern of John Hunt's Everest in 1953, using a series of camps, fixed rope where necessary, oxygen on the highest peaks and, in every case but one, high-altitude porters.

Up to 1957 practically every expedition to the Himalaya had employed high-altitude porters who, of course, had taken on the greater part of the drudgery and sheer hard work of humping loads up the mountain. It was the lack of this support, combined with the smallness of the team, that made the Austrian expedition to Broad Peak unique. Hermann Buhl wanted to pare down the size of a Himalayan expedition to the very minimum – to bring it as close as possible to the scale of a team attempting a serious climb in the European Alps. He chose Broad Peak, an unclimbed mountain of 8047 metres (26,400 feet), towering above Concordia in the very heart of the Karakoram mountains. The story of the expedition not only marks an important step in the evolution of Himalayan climbing, it also traces the pattern of tragedy that culminated in Hermann Buhl's death.

Buhl reached a peak of fame in 1953 with his incredible solo bid for the summit of Nanga Parbat, in many ways a much greater achievement than that of Hillary and Tenzing on Everest. Before that he had already emerged as the most forceful rock climber of the Eastern Alps. His book, *Nanga Parbat Pilgrimage*, published in Britain in 1956, provided me, and all my fellow climbers who had just started visiting the Alps, with an inspiration that was immensely important.

Buhl, like Bonatti, lost his mother at an early age and both were brought up by their fathers in fairly straitened circumstances. Buhl was fifteen at the beginning of the war and had started going to the mountains with his local Innsbruck youth club. Short in stature and lightly built, he was often the victim of cruel practical jokes from his more muscular companions. He was a natural target, partly because of his stature, but also because of his obsessive drive. It didn't matter how hard it was raining, Buhl was determined to get out onto the crags, nagging and cajoling his companions until he managed to find a partner.

His early years as a rock climber were similar to those of any working-class youngster. Joe Brown and Don Whillans, for instance, started their climbing in post-war Britain, sleeping in barns or leaky tents, using battered old equipment cadged or borrowed from their seniors, finding a freedom, adventure and means of self-expression in the mountains surrounding their homes, and then discovering a real ability. In Buhl's case this took him firstly on to the most difficult routes on the steep walls of the Kaiser and Karwendel and then into the unknown of new ground.

Dr. Karl Herrligkoffer, the Munich general practitioner whose obsession with Nanga Parbat drove him to lead no less than eight expeditions to the mountain.

By 1942 he had already made his mark as an outstanding rock climber, but then was caught up in the war, conscripted into the Army, where he survived the bullets on the Russian Front and a Russian prison camp before returning to Austria in 1946.

Climb followed climb at a headlong pace; his horizons expanded, first to the Dolomites, then the Western Alps – the Walker Spur of the Grandes Jorasses, the North Wall of the Eiger, first-ever complete traverse of the Aiguilles de Chamonix and then, in 1953, the Himalaya. Hermann Buhl was invited to join Dr. Karl Herrligkoffer's expedition to Nanga Parbat.

A general practitioner from Munich, Karl Herrligkoffer has had a profound influence on Himalayan adventure and his name crops up again and again. In the 'thirties Nanga Parbat had become very much a German peak in the same sense that the British had adopted Mount Everest. Four fiercely determined German expeditions to Nanga Parbat before the war had paid a heavy price – ten dying in 1934 and sixteen in 1937. But to Herrligkoffer the mountain offered a special challenge. His idolised half-brother, Willy Merkl, had been one of those who lost his life in 1934, and the young Herrligkoffer resolved then that one day he would organise a new expedition to fulfil 'a sacred trust'. Nanga Parbat obsessed him; he collected every book and journal that mentioned the mountain, dreamed and schemed of going there, though his level of climbing ability made it most unlikely that he would ever get the opportunity. He decided, therefore, to organise his own expedition and, in the face of much scepticism and even direct opposition – some of which ended in the law courts – he managed to raise the funds and put together an Austro-German team.

Herrligkoffer's biggest problem was that he was unknown and lacked experience. He got round this by appointing Peter Aschenbrenner, an established mountaineer who had been on the 1932 and 1934 Nanga Parbat expeditions, as climbing leader, contenting himself with the title of organiser. It is questionable whether Aschenbrenner was ever totally committed to the expedition. Because of his work commitment as guardian of a climbing hut, he took no part in the organisation, joining it at the last possible moment, and had to set himself a time limit of mid-July for his return to Europe. They established Base Camp at 3967 metres on the north side of the mountain on the 14th May 1953. Buhl, who was undoubtedly the most talented and forceful member of the team, felt that the leaders of the expedition lacked a sense of urgency. Buhl was out in front most of the time, forcing the route out and fretting at the slow build-up of supplies. In fairness to Herrligkoffer and Aschenbrenner, there were considerable problems, for the expedition had been unable to bring experienced Sherpa high-altitude porters into Pakistan and, instead, were using Hunzas who had neither the temperament nor the experience for the job. It is very easy for the climber out in front to feel that he has the only difficult job on the expedition when, in fact, it can be just as hard to ferry up the supplies behind the lead climbers. If the expedition is not closely integrated and controlled by a leader capable and determined to keep up with the front climbers, a rift can very easily develop between those out in front and the people in support.

By the end of June things were serious. The team were tired; they had been delayed by bad weather and Aschenbrenner had gone home. The expedition had become divided between a small group of the four strongest climbers, who were determined to sit out the bad weather on the mountain and make one last bid for the summit, and the rest of the team down at Base Camp who tended to be pessimistic and kept sending the men out in front orders which had little bearing on the actual situation and which inevitably were ignored. It culminated in Hermann Buhl's incredible solo bid for the summit on the 3rd July, from the top camp at only 6895 metres.

Otto Kempter, a climber from Munich, was meant to accompany Buhl, but at one o'clock that morning, when Buhl started getting ready in the bitterly cold, hoar frosted tent, Kempter's willpower was at a low ebb. He could not tear himself from the warmth of his sleeping bag and lay comatose, oblivious to Buhl's exhortations. I know just how he must have felt; there are few things worse than that early-morning transition, particularly when – as in Kempter's case – you realise that in all probability you are not capable of making the climb. Even so, by the time that Buhl was ready to leave, Kempter's resolve had hardened and he said he, too, would go for the summit. Buhl therefore gave him some spare food to carry and set out to break trail, hoping that Kempter would catch up. He never did; it was all he could do to stagger in Buhl's wake as far as the Silver Saddle.

Meanwhile, Buhl pressed on alone towards the summit of Nanga Parbat; at first it was little more than high-altitude walking, but that posed its own problems, for not

Nanga Parbat, Rakhiot Face

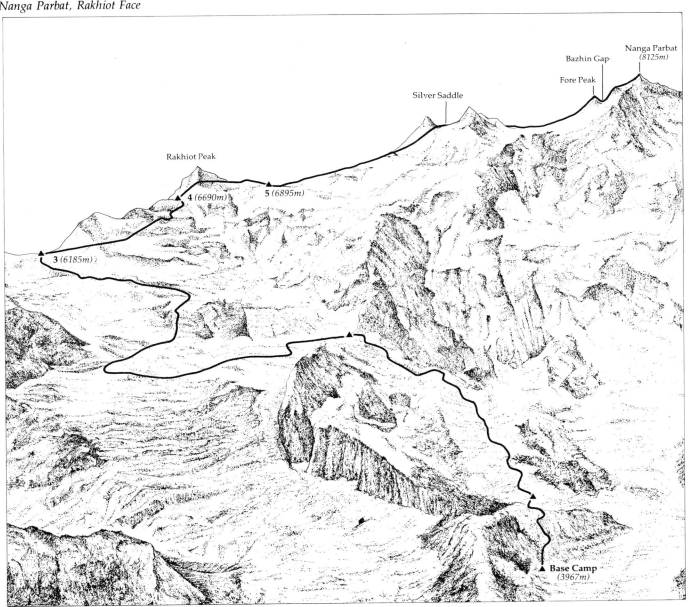

Nanga Parbat in the 'thirties was very much a German mountain and four strong expeditions paid a heavy price for attempting it.

only had he to climb around 1220 metres on the undulating ridge, but he also had to cover around five miles over the Silver Saddle and then up and down the other side of the Fore Peak to the Bazhin Gap. It was a still, breathless day and as the sun crept up the glare and heat became almost unbearable. On the subsidiary summit he abandoned his rucksack and left his heavy sweater behind. All he took with him towards the summit was the light sweater, shirt, vest and anorak he was wearing.

There was some difficult climbing past rocky pinnacles on the ridge leading up to the shoulder of the main summit. He used some Pervitin to give him energy and then, Cocatee for the final struggle up the last snow slope leading to the main summit. He was so exhausted that he crawled on all fours the last few feet to the top. It was seven o'clock in the evening. He had practically no food, nothing to drink and only a light sweater to keep him warm through the night. It was essential he got back down to the tent that night.

Bemused and exhausted, he left his ice axe on the summit, flying the flag of Pakistan; there was no way he could have reversed the difficult rock ridge and so he dropped down the steep snow slope on the Diamir side of the ridge. It was now very nearly dark; he had only his ski sticks to steady himself. His crampon fell off; he just managed to save it, but the strap had come loose and slithered down the slope into the shadows below. With only one crampon and no ice axe, he had no hope of getting down in the dark. He spent the night sitting on a rocky outcrop, at an altitude of nearly 8000 metres, not only without any kind of bivouac gear but without even adequate day clothing. He was very fortunate it was a comparatively warm night – a mere 10° or so below freezing!

Next morning he staggered back down to the top camp, badly frostbitten and in the last stages of exhaustion. The photograph taken of him when he got back shows an old and wizened man. It had been an incredible achievement, particularly when one considers that this was the first time that Buhl had ever been to the Himalaya. In the light of what later happened on Broad Peak, his physique seems to have been permanently weakened by the ordeal.

Back home, he became involved in a public dispute over the organisation and leadership of the expedition. Buhl ignored the expedition contract which he had signed and published his own version of what happened. Herrligkoffer sued him and the whole business was dragged through the law courts, inevitably tarnishing what had been a magnificent achievement; even more unfortunate, damaging Hermann Buhl's reputation.

This photograph of Hermann Buhl, taken as he staggered back down from the top after his extraordinary solo achievement, shows him as a wizened old man.

Buhl's recovery was a slow one, but by 1956 he seemed to be back in his old climbing form. That year he made a very fast ascent of the West Face of the Dru, which still ranked as one of the most formidable rock climbs in the Alps. His partner was Markus Schmuck, another very talented rock climber who was the same age as Buhl. Both were married and had young families. By this time Buhl had worked through a lot of climbing partners – partly through his edgy temperament, partly because he was so good that he burnt them off – but he got on well with Schmuck, not just on the crags, but also at home. He started talking to Schmuck of his dream of treating the Himalaya as you would the Alps, of avoiding all the trappings and complications of a big expedition and just going off as a very small group of friends and climbing one of the giants of over 8000 metres. Eventually, they picked on Broad Peak (8047 metres/26,400 feet) and decided to make it a team of three, inviting another very determined and accomplished climber, Fritz Wintersteller. At the last minute he increased the team to four, by including a young climber called Kurt Diemberger who, at twenty-five, was gaining the reputation of being Austria's most outstanding

ice climber after his recent ascent of the huge ice cornice on top of the North Face of the Königsspitze.

External pressures, however, were already building up to unbalance what should have been a simple, though very bold Alpine-style climbing trip transposed to the Himalaya. Even keeping everything down to the minimum, the expedition was going to cost more than they could possibly raise out of their own pockets. They needed sponsorship, and to get that they needed the approval and support of the Austrian Alpine Club. This is where the trouble began, for the climbing establishment distrusted Buhl; it was the distrust that most established bodies seem to have for a newly-emerging and forceful star. Buhl did not fit comfortably into a category; he wasn't an amateur climber with a trade or profession, nor was he a professional guide. At this time he was working for Sporthaus Schuster in Munich, the biggest sports and mountaineering shop in Europe. While the legal action over his book, *Nanga Parbat Pilgrimage*, had simply focused the latent distrust and resentment that any conservative body tends to feel about an individual who breaks away from the pack. The very qualities that had given Buhl his success, his obstinacy, single-mindedness that verged on the obsessional, his sensitivity to criticism, all aggravated the situation.

It came to a head when the Innsbruck Section of the Austrian Alpine Club

Broad Peak and the Baltoro Glacier

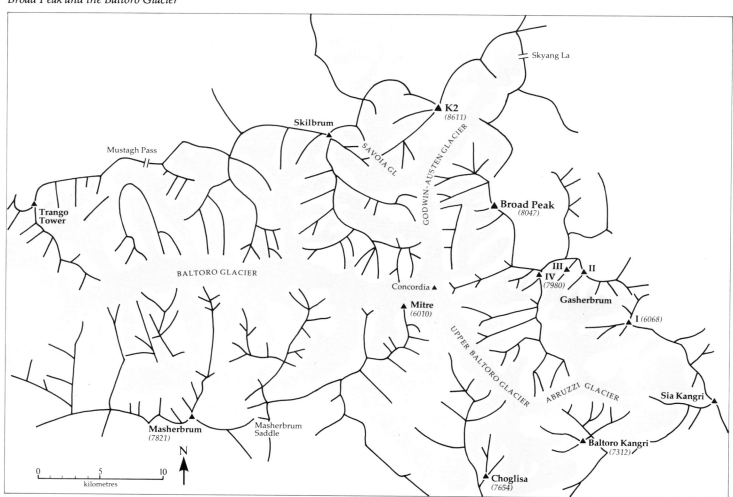

Leaving for the Karakoram from Salzburg station, nearest the camera, Hermann Buhl, left, and Kurt Diemberger, the pairing of experience and youth which was to climb together on Broad Peak and Chogolisa.

indicated that they would not support the expedition if Buhl were leader. It was agreed, therefore, to satisfy the climbing establishment, that Markus Schmuck should be over-all leader of the expedition, but he and Buhl agreed privately that Buhl would lead if necessary on the mountain.

It was the media that nearly upset this uneasy compromise. After his achievement on Nanga Parbat, Buhl was a heroic figure throughout the German-speaking world and it was very easy to whip up a public outcry against the change in leadership. The Innsbruck Alpine Club reacted by trying to force Buhl out of the expedition altogether. Schmuck stood by his friend and said that if Buhl didn't go on the expedition, nobody would, and the Alpine Club stood down. The four set out in the spring of 1957.

The Karakoram is a stern, harsh place, a mountain desert of sands merging into bare rock, ice and snow. The villages are oases of green set into this stark landscape. It is very different country from Nepal which is so much softer, lush and green in the foothills. The people reflect the land they live in; whereas the Nepalis are a gentle, smiling people, there is a tough, rapacious, volatile quality in the Balti. One moment the group can be sitting and singing round the camp fire; a few minutes later it can erupt into almost hysterical rage over some dispute or misunderstanding. An approach march is walked on a precarious tightrope of bargaining, bullying and appeasement.

On a four-man expedition there is barely any need for formal leadership, yet a leader nearly always emerges, one person who somehow has the drive, initiative and charisma to gain an often unspoken, perhaps unconscious dominance within the group. This edge of initiative can sometimes change from one person to another, depending on the qualities needed to solve a particular problem. The happy expedition is one where this process of decision-taking goes almost unnoticed, with each member of the group content with his or her degree of influence. On a large expedition, this process must inevitably be more formalised, since the number of people involved, the fact that they might be scattered in groups based on different camps up the mountain, demands the role of an effective and formal co-ordinator.

On Everest it had worked well, for John Hunt had managed to gain the respect and acceptance of his team; on Nanga Parbat in 1953, it had been less successful, since the formal leadership had never gained the acceptance of the more accomplished climbers. On Cho Oyu, where just ten men had been involved, Tichy had captured the respect of the entire team and had enough confidence in himself and the others to allow each individual to take the lead when he was most suited to do so in the decision-making process. On Broad Peak, a different pattern began to emerge on the walk in; the foursome imperceptibly polarised into two separate, at times competitive, even antagonistic pairs.

Schmuck, the organiser, the man who chased up the day-to-day administration, ensured that the sixty-eight low-altitude porters had their rations, that the loads were correctly allocated, was not just an administrator, he was also a first-class climber who approached his climbing in the same systematic, tidy manner in which he conducted his life. Buhl, on the other hand, was engrossed in the mountain, impatient of the day-to-day administration. He was used to taking his own decisions, in having the initiative on almost all the climbs he had been on.

Essentially, it was a power struggle. Schmuck, a natural leader and organiser, saw how things should be done and acted accordingly. Now that they were on the way to

Broad Peak, a magnificent triple-summited mountain of 8047 metres. Buhl chose a route up the steep snow on the right of the picture. This was the first ever lightweight expedition to a mountain over 8000 metres.

the foot of the mountain he was not prepared to step down and allow Buhl to take over. It was a situation in which the tenuous bonds of friendship quickly became frayed.

Diemberger, the youngster of the party, was captivated by Buhl's charisma and immensely flattered and excited when Buhl casually suggested they join up to get a first glimpse of their mountain:

> Hermann Buhl was well disposed towards me. I knew it from frequent small touches, such as suggestions he might throw out, and I was glad. He would sometimes explain to me, in a paternal manner, things I knew perfectly well already; but when I saw what pleasure he took in imparting the knowledge, I refrained, sometimes with difficulty, from saying anything. Certainly I came to know Hermann in a very different light from that in which many of those with whom 'he crossed swords' picture him. Of course he was a difficult man – that did not escape me either – an extrovert individualist, thin-skinned, and sensitive as a mimosa – but a man in whom there burned an eternal flame for his mountains . . . he never compromised.

Diemberger had another thing in common with Buhl (and for that matter Bonatti, another man who 'never compromised'); he, also had lost his mother while young, was brought up by his father, a geographer and explorer, but Diemberger's child-

Broad Peak, West Face

8000m

8047m

3 *(6950m)*

2 *(6405m)*

1

Base
Camp
(4910m)

GODWIN-AUSTEN GLACIER

hood had been much happer than that of either Bonatti or Buhl and this gave him, perhaps, a gentler, more romantic and less assertive dimension to his character. At this stage, Diemberger was very happy to be disciple to his guru.

Wintersteller, easy-going, practical and very capable, paired naturally with Markus Schmuck; in this little family of four, Diemberger and Wintersteller were the two in the middle, encompassed by the two extremes.

They had come out to the Karakoram at the beginning of the season; it was still early May when they reached Concordia, that incredible meeting-place of gigantic glaciers, broad rubble-covered highways of ice that penetrate the steepest, most spectacular mountains found anywhere in the world. Looking back down the Baltoro Glacier are the serried rock towers and walls of the Baltoro spires, of Trango, Paiju and Uli Biaho; to the left is Masherbrum, soaring ice ridges and sérac walls leading to the pointed rock beak of its summit. Straight ahead is Gasherbrum IV, a symmetrical wedge of snow-veined granite, to be climbed the following year by Walter Bonatti, a consolation prize for K2; it stands, a massive pyramid, at the head of the Godwin-Austen Glacier and, to the right, the Upper Baltoro Glacier is skirted by great snow peaks, voluptuous with their flowing form, Sia Kangri, Baltoro Kangri and, most beautiful of all, the Bride Peak, Chogolisa. But they were there too early; the glacier was covered in knee-deep snow. The porters, with their thin blankets, tennis shoes and ragged clothing had had enough. Blandishments, bullying and offers of more money were no longer any good; they turned round and headed for home.

Though they did not appreciate it at the time, the expedition had been extremely fortunate. They had no choice but to spend the next week ferrying loads up the Godwin-Austen Glacier to the site of their Base Camp. They couldn't have had a better way of acclimatising to the altitude. They were still at a sufficiently low altitude to build up strength steadily, yet were working hard, carrying loads much heavier than the ones they would take with them on the mountain. At last, on the 13th May, they set foot on their mountain for the first time.

Broad Peak, named by Sir Martin Conway, the first European to penetrate the Upper Baltoro region, is a magnificent mountain; massive, triple-summited, it dominates the eastern side of the Godwin-Austen Glacier. It had been attempted in 1954 by Herrligkoffer but, relying on Hunza high-altitude porters, he had chosen the easiest possible line, which turned out to be appallingly dangerous, going straight into a serious avalanche area. It was, perhaps, just as well that the wind and cold overtook them, for they had set out in the early autumn and were forced to abandon the attempt while still low down.

Buhl had chosen a much bolder, but safer, line up the steep West Ridge of the mountain. At first everything went smoothly as they ferried loads 915 metres up to their first camp, then another 610 on to a shoulder at 6405 metres, where Buhl and Wintersteller established a second camp. At this stage the team was still working as a flexible foursome, but Wintersteller was going very much faster than Buhl, something that Buhl found hard to accept. He complained that Wintersteller was always running away and that it was impossible to climb with him. Even so, together they pushed the route out, across a slight plateau and then up a smooth steep ice slope, safeguarding it with some old fixed rope, left by Herrligkoffer's expedition, which they had found buried in the snow lower down on the mountain. They also uncovered some Italian salami, which the 1954 expedition must have found and salvaged from the K2 Base Camp. Three years later it was still moist and tasty, once it had been de-frozen.

The weather now broke with a violent storm and they were driven back to Base

Camp for a few days. When the weather cleared on the 26th May, Buhl had reverted to his partnership with Diemberger, who was well content to defer to his judgement and, more important, to his pace. Buhl and Diemberger completed the route up to the site of Camp 3, just short of 7000 metres, while the other two ferried the supplies behind them. All four moved into the camp on the evening of the 28th May, planning to push for the summit the following day.

Being a west slope, it was always bitterly cold first thing in the morning; it was some hours before the sun crept over the summit ridge, far above them. They set out in the dawn, at first made good progress, but then hit deep powder snow. Their pace slowed down to a crawl as they waded laboriously through the deep morass of snow. They were not roped up, each one going at his own pace, Wintersteller and Diemberger out in front, Buhl and Schmuck about forty-five metres behind. It was mid-afternoon before they reached the saddle between the central and the main summits. Slowly, doggedly, they slogged their way up towards the top, at last reaching what they thought was the summit. The mist was swirling about them, but the summit ridge curled away. Their eyes followed it as it dropped and then started climbing to a true summit, which was undoubtedly eighteen metres or so higher than their vantage point. It was now 6.30 in the evening. They were exhausted, demoralised by the disappointment; the weather seemed unsettled and it was bitterly cold. Both Buhl and Schmuck were complaining of frozen toes. They turned round and retreated.

They had been so close – almost as soon as they got back down to Base Camp, the disappointment, the self-disgust at their momentary weakness, began to gnaw. Although their unity was fragile, up to this point the four had worked well together, but now their latent differences began to come to the surface as they faced the prospect of repeating almost the entire climb – just to finish off twenty metres.

After a few days the weather settled and they returned to their high camp, Buhl and Diemberger in one tent, Wintersteller and Schmuck in the other. Nobody slept well that night; there was a feeling of tension, almost anticlimax; there was so little that was unknown before them, just the effort and grind which they knew too well. At two-thirty on the morning of the 9th June it was unbelievably cold; −25°C inside the tent, it must have been −30° or so outside. But it was a brilliantly clear night and the weather was settled as they set out into the dark grey glimmer of the pre-dawn. Buhl and Diemberger got away first, plodding up through the dark, crampons squeaking in the hard, frozen snow. It was much easier going than on the first attempt, but bitterly cold. Buhl's feet were numb but he kept plodding on until, at last, the early morning sun crept over the summit ridge, still far above, and gave them some slight respite from the cold. Buhl stopped and took his boots off and massaged his already severely frostbitten, part-amputated toes. Wintersteller and Schmuck caught up, also took their boots off but quickly restored the circulation to their feet. They were ready to go on, but Buhl was not.

No-one likes hanging around on a mountain; there is too much at stake – the prize of the summit, the risk of frostbite, the risk of life itself. On this, their second attempt, they no longer felt a foursome; they were two pairs who happened to be on the same mountain. When Wintersteller and Schmuck pressed on, now going very strongly, Buhl resented it bitterly; whilst the others' strength had built up from their previous effort, his had waned. He no longer had the endurance – but it is a cruel thing to have to admit to oneself.

Diemberger stayed with Buhl, plodding slowly with him as the gap between the two pairs increased. The circulation restored to Buhl's injured feet, the pain was almost unbearable, weakening him still further. They reached the saddle between

*Looking out from Camp 3
towards Masherbrum at just under
7000 metres.*

the two peaks at about 1.30. Buhl was very nearly finished, and had to lie down, he was so tired. Diemberger coaxed him into eating a few dried prunes and sipping some cold tea. They rested for an hour, Diemberger restraining his impatience, to give his companion a chance to recoup his strength. And then they set out once again.

For Buhl, each step was an agony; the sun now blazed down from a cloudless sky, enervating, sucking out their strength; a few slow paces, rest, another few, another rest, each time the interval getting shorter, the rests longer, the progress more painful. And time was slipping by. There was no sign of the others, just their tracks snaking up over the slope to the false summit that had betrayed them on their first attempt. It was five o'clock and they were still far short of their previous high point; no chance of getting to the top before dark and, at that pace, little chance of getting there at all. For Diemberger, the frustration of holding his pace down to that of his partner had been cruel, but he had done it willingly. It was now so obviously hopeless, he asked Buhl if he could press on for the summit on his own. Buhl agreed and Diemberger continued by himself, his pace improving, his strength coming back with renewed hope. Reaching the false summit, he glanced back to see Buhl, sitting just as he'd left him, gazing out into nothingness. In front, the two tiny dots that emphasised the immensity of the mountain were Wintersteller and Schmuck on the summit slope.

Diemberger pushed himself along the summit ridge, panting, giddy. It took him just half an hour to reach the final slope. Wintersteller and Schmuck were still there, on the summit.

'I wanted to shake hands with the others,' Diemberger told me. 'I was just about ten metres or so away from them, but they didn't wait – they left the summit before I got there. I didn't like that.'

Diemberger had the summit to himself, and gazed around:

Hermann Buhl on the col between the Central and the West Summit where he paused, exhausted, while Diemberger went on to the summit for the first time.

Wherever I looked, a sea of peaks met my eye. Far away, over there, the Pamirs; farther to the left, all by itself, Nanga Parbat, 125 miles away as the crow flies, K2 bulked enormous, just above the subsidiary summit – 28,250 feet of it. I looked up at it in awe, realising that my 26,400-foot perch was so noticeably lower. To balance that, I looked down and far, far below me recognised a fairly hefty dwarf; it was, in fact, the proud sharp head of Mitre Peak, 20,000 feet high. Beyond, soared Masherbrum, which had lost nothing of its magnificence. Close at the feet of Mitre Peak lay 'Concordia', my eye plunging almost 12,000 feet down upon it. Then I began to look for our route up the long waves of the Baltoro. That browny-green spot at its far end must be Paiju, the last little oasis before we took to the ice. I couldn't take my eyes off it; I hadn't seen a living green thing for six weeks . . . Why, today must be Whit Sunday! At home, now, the trees must be in blossom, the meadows green with lush spring grass; at home they will be thinking of us. All about me the great peaks stood in an immense silence. I suddenly felt terribly lonely.

Yet somehow there was a sense of anticlimax. He started down:

It was all over. Was I really happy? Was that the hour of which I had dreamed ever since I first set foot on a mountain? Down there on the ridge, my rope mate was sitting, the man with whom I had hoped to climb the summit. And what about the summit itself? It had been impressive, the prospect from it overpowering; but the picture in my imagination, my fantasy summit, outshone it by far.

He hurried on down the long curving ridge, and then slowed down as he reached the short, upwards slope that led to the subsidiary summit. He was anxious to rejoin Buhl, who would now, surely, be sufficiently rested for them to make a fast descent to their tent. He crested the top, was vaguely aware of the huge bulk of K2 looming over him, mellowed in the warm light of early evening, and then down below he saw something moving. 'It was a yellow point; it disappeared, but then came again, and there he was. I shall always remember that moment; on the one hand it was unbelievable, on the other hand it was believable, because Hermann was there, coming very slowly up towards me.'

Left on the col, Buhl had lain slumped in the snow for a long time, but then his resolve had crept back. Slowly, painstakingly, he had plodded up the long slope leading towards the subsidiary summit. It would be dark before he reached the top, but no matter, he had survived one night at over 7930 metres; he would survive this one.

Diemberger waited for his partner to reach him and then, without a second thought for the consequences, turned round to follow him, back towards the summit.

Suddenly everything was so natural that I could laugh about it all; about the fears of all the others down below there, their fears about their lives, my own fear of a little moment ago. Now, for the first time, I was truly at one with the heights up here. The world down there lay bottomlessly far below, and utterly devoid of meaning. I no longer belonged to it. Even my first climb to the summit was already remote beyond words. What had it brought me? Boundless astonishment that it had all been so different from my anticipation, utter disappointment. That was all, and it was all forgotten already. But now the true summit was up there, bathed in unearthly light, as in a dream.

The shapes of the huge snow-mushrooms grew ever more ghostly, their shadows strangely like faces. Everything seemed alive; and there in front of me on the level snow went Hermann's long shadow, bending, straightening, even jumping. It was deathly still. The sun was almost down. Could anything in life be so beautiful?

I stopped for a moment, leaning heavily on my sticks, then moved on, smiling to myself. There was Hermann, going on ahead. We were going on to the top together. Yes, we were going to it in the dark; but ahead of us gleamed a radiance, enfolding every wish life could conjure, enfolding life itself.

Now was the moment of ineffable truth – the silence of space around us, ourselves silent.

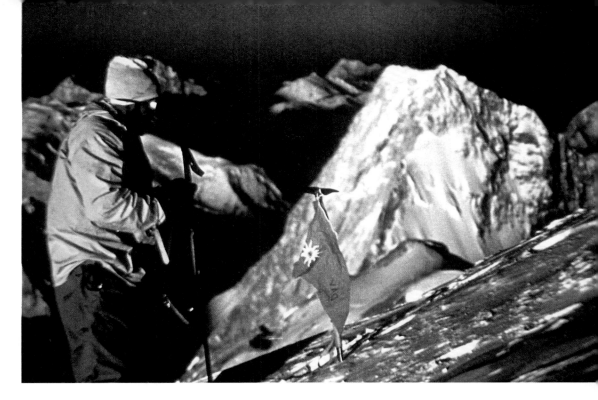

Buhl eventually drove himself to the summit, where he was photographed by his companion, Diemberger, who retraced his steps to join him in the unearthly glow of the setting sun.

This was utter fulfilment. The sun bent trembling to the horizon. Down there was the night, and under it the world. Only up here, and for us, was there light. Close over yonder the Gasherbrum summits glistened in all their magic; a little farther away, Chogolisa's heavenly roof-tree. Straight ahead, against the last light, K2 reared its dark and massive head. Soft as velvet, all colours merging into a single dark gleam. The snow was suffused with a deep orange tint, while the sky was a remarkable azure. As I looked out, an enormous pyramid of darkness projected itself over the limitless wastes of Tibet, to lose itself in the haze of impalpable distance – the shadow of Broad Peak.

There we stood, speechless, and shook hands in silence. Down on the horizon a narrow strip of sunlight flickered – a beam of light reached out above and across the darkness towards us, just caressing the last few feet of our summit. We looked down at the snow underfoot, and to our amazement it seemed to be aglow.

Then the light went out.

They still had to get down. Fortunately it was a sharply moonlit night and they were able to stagger, exhausted, back to their tent over 900 metres below.

It had been a brilliant achievement, the first time a peak of over 8000 metres had been climbed by such a small expedition, with the entire team reaching the summit. Sadly, however, it did not bring the two pairs any closer together; if anything, what happened that day widened the gap. Buhl was bitterly resentful of the way the other two had left him behind to go to the summit; Schmuck, wanting his expedition to be a tidy success, was appalled by the levels of risk to which Buhl and Diemberger had been prepared to push themselves.

By this stage the two pairs were barely communicating. They had already agreed that each couple should be responsible for clearing their own tentage and equipment off the mountain. Very much fresher, Wintersteller and Schmuck did their share of the job more quickly than Buhl and Diemberger. Then without telling the other two, Schmuck and Wintersteller went off to climb another peak. They chose Skilbrum, a magnificent, steep snow peak of around 7420 metres which they could see from their Base Camp, just opposite the vast bulk of K2, on the other side of the Savoia Glacier. It was a bold and forceful ascent, carried out in their characteristic way, methodically, fast and with the minimum of fuss. They skied to the foot of it and took just six days from Base Camp back to Base Camp.

In the immediate aftermath of their ascent, Buhl wanted only to return home; he was tired, demoralised by his failure to keep up with the others, but when he realised that the other two had slipped away to bag another peak, he felt betrayed. Diemberger, young, fit and immensely enthusiastic, was longing to get some more climbing. They had talked earlier of making a reconnaissance of the Gasherbrum peaks, of trying Mitre Peak, a beautiful but comparatively small 6010-metre peak at the confluence of the Baltoro and Upper Baltoro Glaciers, or even the Trango Tower, the 6250-metre rock spire, as steep and slender as a gigantic chimney stack which was finally climbed in 1975 by a British party. The spur of competition, undoubtedly inflamed by Diemberger's buoyant enthusiasm, rekindled Buhl's drive.

The pair now started talking of an altogether more ambitious scheme. How about trying Chogolisa, perhaps the most beautiful of all the Baltoro summits, with its

Chogolisa, the Bride Peak, perhaps the most beautiful of the Baltoro summits with its sweeping fluted ridges and gigantic cornices.

sweeping fluted ridges and gigantic cornices; in addition, at 7654 metres it was quite a bit higher than Skilbrum – a strong incentive in the competitive stakes. They wanted to get away on their little expedition before the other two returned, but Buhl still had some gear he needed on Broad Peak. Diemberger, therefore, went ahead, promising to mark his trail with marker wands so that Buhl could follow him. Wintersteller and Schmuck got back before Buhl was ready to set out but he told them nothing of his plans and slipped away from the camp that night, after they had gone to bed. He left a note saying only that Diemberger had gone to the foot of Gasherbrum to take photographs and that he was going to join him.

Diemberger was delighted to see Buhl and was even more pleased and relieved when he saw how well Buhl seemed to have recovered. It was a real renaissance; he was full of enthusiasm for the climb, going very strongly – so strongly, in fact, that he insisted on breaking trail throughout their first day on the mountain. This was to be a true Alpine-style push. There was to be no ferrying of loads as there had been on Broad Peak. They were going to start at the bottom with a tent, some food, a stove and a rope, and keep going up the mountain till they reached the top. It was the principle Wintersteller and Schmuck had used on Skilbrum, but Chogolisa is not only higher, it is also a very much bigger mountain with its great sweep of ridges.

They started out with loads of around sixty-five pounds, as they picked their way through Chogolisa's lower icefall. By the 24th June they had carried their tent and gear onto the spur. The weather was unsettled, with intermittent snow showers; they took advantage of every break to push on up the ridge, travelling tortoise-like, their home on their backs. They were completely attuned to each other and the elements, were dreaming of shared climbs for the future, a traverse of Mont Blanc in the autumn, Rakaposhi next year, perhaps, even, they might grab Baltoro Kangri, glimpsed through a break in the clouds, after they had finished with Chogolisa.

Ensconced on the shoulder of Chogolisa's South-East Ridge, at a height of around 6700 metres, they were trapped by storm on the 26th, but the following day dawned clear and calm; they felt the benefit of their day's rest, were happily confident of success. The ridge curled up into the sky, tortuous, convoluted and heavily corniced; the snow was knee-deep, the going hard and at times dangerous as they picked their way delicately over crusty windslab. But they were going well, gaining height steadily, taking it in turns to go out in front to break the trail through the deep snows. The summit was still about 450 metres above them, but they could see the whole route, winding out before them. There were no serious difficulties; it was just a question of keeping going.

But to the south a great bank of clouds was rolling up the Baltoro Glacier, swallowing up each of the great mountains in turn; a small cloud, a scout of the invading army, skirmished round the ridge below, raced up behind them, tendrils of cloud from the great cloud bank reached out to their mountain and then, suddenly, they were engulfed. Within seconds it had changed from a sunlit, sparkling day to an inferno of wind and snow, where the wind-driven snow in the air merged into the solid snow under foot. You couldn't look into it, for a million tiny darts cut and lashed at any exposed skin. But they kept going on upwards; they seemed so close to success, until eventually Buhl said: 'We've got to turn back now, the wind'll cover up our tracks and we could stray onto these cornices.'

Diemberger, younger, perhaps prepared to take greater risks, might have pressed on further, but he saw the sense of Buhl's argument and they both turned back. It was easy ground and so they had not bothered to put on the rope. In front, Diemberger imperceptibly drew ahead, all his concentration devoted to picking out the fast-vanishing trail:

I was at a loss; it was almost impossible to see anything at all. Crack! Something shot through me like a shock. Everything shook and for a second the surface of the snow seemed to shrink. Blindly I jumped sideways to the right – an instantaneous reflex action – two, three great strides, and followed the steep slope downwards a little way, shattered by what I had seen at my feet – the rim of the cornice with little jagged bits breaking away from it. My luck had been in all right. I had been clean out on the cornice. What would Hermann have to say about that, I wondered? I still couldn't fathom that extraordinary shaking sensation; had the snow really settled under my weight?

Still no Hermann. 'Hermann!' I shouted. 'For God's sake what's up, Hermann?' I rushed, gasping, up the slope. There it was, the crest . . . and beyond it, smooth snow . . . and it was empty . . . 'Hermann . . . You! . . .'

'Done for. . .'

I dragged myself up a little further. I could see his last footmarks in the snow, then the jagged edge of the broken cornice yawning. Then the black depths.

Somehow Diemberger managed to stagger down to the foot of the mountain and then the long, weary way over the glacier to their Base Camp at the foot of Broad Peak. It took him twenty-seven hours. The others had been getting increasingly worried as the days had gone by. Faced by the cataclysm of tragedy, Schmuck reacted with rage, furiously blaming Diemberger for egging Buhl on into the situation that caused his death. It was an unreasonable reaction, but in the moment of shock and tragedy people seldom are reasonable. At the time it sparked off a violent public controversy, but today the two men have healed their wounds and meet socially, though they have never become close friends.

Schmuck still believes that Buhl had overstretched himself, telling me: 'I think he felt bad about being known as the world's best and strongest mountaineer and yet to be the weakest in that group of four. He couldn't just say to me, "Well, I'm not as good as I used to be;" I don't understand why he didn't say that to me, because I really felt that we were true friends.'

It is all too easy to understand Buhl's feelings and the reasons why he and Diemberger went to Chogolisa. Diemberger might well have urged Buhl on; I am quite sure I would have done so at the same age and in the same circumstances. But I am also quite sure that Buhl did not need much urging, that he found the joy and solace he needed in those few days on Chogolisa, when once again he felt master of his own body, attuned to the mountains he loved and needed. On the way down, it is possible that he was that much more tired than Diemberger, that his concentration had flagged and that this contributed to his mistake. We shall never know.

In the story of Broad Peak there is the pathos of the story of a declining but once brilliant star. And yet all four members of the team succeeded in reaching their summit without the help of high-altitude porters, using the very minimum of set camps. In doing so they marked a major step forward in the development of Himalayan climbing.

Annapurna, South Face

We projected the two-metre-square picture onto the wall of the living room and gazed and gazed – excited and then frightened.

'There's a line all right,' said Martin, 'but it's bloody big.'

The South Face of Annapurna – I don't think I remember seeing a mountain photograph that has given such an impression of huge size and steepness. It was like four different Alpine faces piled one on top of the other – but what a line! Hard, uncompromising, positive all the way up. A squat snow ridge, like the buttress of a Gothic cathedral, leaned against the lower part of the wall. That was the start all right; perhaps one could bypass it by sneaking along the glacier at its foot – but what about avalanche risk? The buttress led to an ice ridge; even at the distance from which the photograph had been taken one could see it was a genuine knife-edge. I had climbed something like it before, on the South Face of Nuptse, the third peak of the Everest range – in places we had been able to look straight through the ridge, thirty metres below its crest. That had been frightening; this would be worse. The knife-edge died below a band of ice cliffs.

'I wonder how stable they are?' asked Nick. I wondered too and traced a line through them with only partial confidence. And that led to a rock band.

'Must be at least a thousand feet.'

'But what altitude is it? Could be at 23,000 feet. Do you fancy some hard climbing at that height?'

'What about that groove?' It split the crest of the ridge, a huge gash, inviting, but undoubtedly more difficult and sustained than anything that had ever been climbed at that altitude.

The rock band ended with what seemed to be a shoulder of snow that led to the 8091 metre (26,545 foot) summit. It was difficult to tell just how high the face was, but you could have fitted the North Wall of the Eiger into it two, perhaps even three, times. The expedition was barely conceived, and I don't think any of us fully realised then the significance of what we were trying to do. The South Face of Annapurna was considerably steeper, bigger and obviously more difficult than anything that had hitherto been attempted in the Himalaya. Our decision to tackle it, first arrived at in autumn 1968, was part of a natural evolution, not only on a personal level but also within the broad development of Himalayan climbing. It is significant that around the same time groups of German and Japanese climbers, without any contact with ourselves or each other, were planning similar expeditions – the Germans, under Dr. Karl Herrligkoffer, to the huge Rupal Face of Nanga Parbat and the Japanese to the South-West Face of Everest.

I had been a member of two conventional Himalayan expeditions, in 1960 and '61, making the first ascents of Annapurna II (7937 metres/26,041 feet) and Nuptse (7879 metres/25,850 feet). This was very much part of the first wave of Himalayan climbing, when climbers were attempting first ascents of the myriad of unclimbed peaks. By 1969, however, the Himalaya was in the same state of development as the European Alps had been in the mid-nineteenth century, with most of the highest peaks achieved and climbers now turning their attention to the challenge of harder and harder routes. In the Alps there had been a gradual development of skills and techniques, enabling pioneers to climb successively more difficult ridges and then faces, slowly filling in all the gaps of unclimbed ground.

Inevitably, however, this gradual evolution was accelerated in the Himalaya where climbers had skills developed on the rock and ice of the Alps as a reference. For political reasons, the Himalaya had been closed to climbers from 1965 to 1969. Nick Estcourt, Martin Boysen and I had been talking about going off on an expedition somewhere – anywhere, probably to Alaska – when we heard that Nepal was going to open its frontiers once again. The selection of an objective was strongly influenced by my experience on Annapurna II and Nuptse. All the highest peaks in Nepal had been climbed, and although we could have gone for an unclimbed 7500 metre one, I felt that this would have been a lesser experience than the peaks I had already climbed A big unclimbed face, on the other hand, would give an altogether new dimension – the combination of a North Wall of the Eiger with all the problems of scale and altitude. At the time I did not stop to analyse my motives; it was more a gut-feeling, a rejection of the familiar in favour of the new, unknown experience which, after all, is the very essence of adventure.

It was at this stage that I saw a photograph of the South Face of Annapurna and showed it to Martin Boysen and Nick Estcourt. During the following months the team grew as I began to put together the expedition. For me it was an adventure on two levels, both in terms of the mountain challenge and also grappling with the problems of organisation and leadership. I had never before led an expedition, had never considered myself to be the organising type. In fact, my lack of organisation was becoming a bad joke amongst my friends. I was unpunctual, forgetful and absent-minded. Although I had held a commission in the regular Army, my military career was hardly distinguished. I had detested all the administrative jobs that I had been given as a junior officer and one commanding officer had even refused to recommend me for the almost automatic promotion to captain because of my poor personal administration – there were never enough lamp bulbs in the barrack room I was responsible for.

And now I was trying to organise and lead the largest and most complex expedition since the 1953 Everest expedition. Some of my antecedents might have been similar to those of John Hunt – we had at least both been to Sandhurst, but there is a vast difference between commanding a brigade in battle and misdirecting a troop of three tanks on Army manoeuvres in North Germany. However, I did have the experience I had gained both on hard Alpine climbs and also in the past few years when I had earned a living as a freelance writer and photographer, joining projects like Blashford-Snell's Blue Nile expedition and going off to Baffin Island in the middle of winter to hunt with the Eskimoes. It had taught me to be more organised in myself and also to understand how the media worked, a thing that was essential if you wanted to finance an expedition.

There were many moments in the months of preparation when I knew a blank despair, either appalled by organisational mistakes I had made, by personality problems or, most of all, by the fear of the whole thing being a complete flop. After all, we had only seen a photograph of the face. We had been given the sponsorship

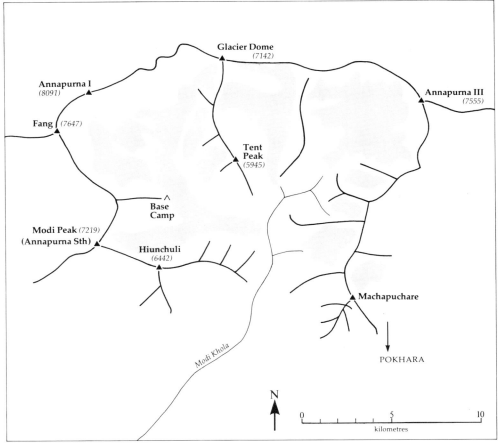

*My first choice summit pair:
Don Whillans, above, who with
Joe Brown had revolutionised
rock climbing in Britain in the
early 'fifties, was undoubtedly
the most experienced climber on
the expedition; and Dougal Haston,
the strongest of the newcomers
to the Himalaya, and already
established as Britain's
outstanding young climber.*

Annapurna from the south

of the Mount Everest Foundation, we would have a TV team with us, every move would be reported. What if the route proved impossibly dangerous, if it were swept by avalanche so that we could barely make a start on the face? Could I really control and co-ordinate this group of talented, strong, and often at times bloody-minded individuals.

I had finally settled on a team of eleven, of whom eight were hard climbers, each with the ability and drive to reach the summit, and three having more of a support role. Of the eleven I knew eight extremely well; we had climbed together, knew each other's ways, strengths and weaknesses. At the same time, though, there were elements of stress within the make-up of the team, a factor that was perhaps inevitable and even useful as a spur and irritant that was to be important later on. Undoubtedly the most experienced member of the party was Don Whillans, the tough, stocky ex-plumber from Manchester who, with Joe Brown, had revolutionised British rock climbing in the early 'fifties. I had had some of my best climbing with Don. Of all the people I have climbed with, Don had the best mountain judgement and, at his peak in the early 'sixties, the greatest climbing ability. We had got on well in our two seaons in the Alps mainly, I suspect, because I had been prepared to yield to his judgement; it was Don who undoubtedly had the initiative in our relationship. Through the rest of the 'sixties our paths rarely crossed. Don had seemed to have lost interest in rock climbing on his home crags, had little interest even in the Alps. He had been on an expedition to Gauri Sankar in 1965 and had climbed in North America, but a fondness for his pint and lack of exercise while at home in Britain had given him an impressive gut. I had had serious reservations about inviting him to join the expedition; knew that there would be tension between us but, at the same time, felt sure that once he got going he had a judgement and drive that would increase our chances of success.

The feeling was mutual, Don commented in an article after our return:

Chris had developed from an easy-going, generous, haphazard lieutenant in the Army to a high-powered, materialistic photo-journalist, to all outward appearances motivated only by money. (Chris believes we must tell the truth about each other regardless of feelings, as long as he is doing the telling!) However, I knew him well enough to know that when the crunch point is reached his sense of proportion always returns to more normal standards, so I had no real decision to make about accepting his offer.

The others were easier choices. The only other member of the team who had been to the Himalaya was Ian Clough, who had climbed the Central Pillar of Frêney with Don and myself, had been with me on the Eiger and with Don on Gauri Sankar. Warm-hearted, unselfish and easy-going, Ian was both a brilliant and a very safe climber, as well as being a perfect member of any team. Of the newcomers to the Himalaya, Dougal Haston was undoubtedly the strongest. A quiet, introverted Scot, he had a single-minded drive that had taken him to the top of the North Wall of the Eiger by its direct route and had already established him as Britain's most outstanding young climber. Mick Burke from Wigan had a very similar background to Whillans, the same dry Lancashire humour, and a readiness to speak his mind. The two frequently clashed. Martin Boysen was a brilliant rock climber, easy-going, indolent but completely committed to climbing. He and I had had many delightful days' climbing on British crags but had never been together further afield. I had also climbed a lot with Nick Estcourt, a steady rock climber and very experienced Alpinist. He was a computer programmer by profession and, unlike many of his fellow climbers, understood the need for systematic planning. He always saw my problems in trying to organise an expedition and gave me a steady, loyal support throughout our expeditioning.

So far, I knew everyone well, but my choice of an eighth climber was influenced by commercial considerations. Our expedition agent, George Greenfield, with whom I had just started to work, suggested that perhaps we could have an American climber in the team. It would be such a help in selling American book rights. Today I don't think I would agree to let such a consideration affect team selection, but back in 1970 none of us was particularly well-known, and fund-raising was a very much more serious problem. I did not know any American climbers personally but both Don Whillans and Dougal Haston knew several. Finally, we settled on Tom Frost, a brilliant rock climber who had taken a leading part in the opening up of the great rock walls of Yosemite and who also had some Himalayan experience. It was only at a later date that I discovered he was a practising Mormon, a very strict religion that forbids drinking, smoking and swearing – vices pursued to a greater or lesser degree by almost everyone else in the team. In the event he proved to be very tolerant and, though he did not succeed in converting any of us, we co-existed very happily.

I now had eight outstanding climbers in the team, it seemed essential to have someone whose sole function was to look after Base Camp and ensure that the right supplies started their passage up the mountain. In military parlance I wanted a combination of Chief of Staff and Quartermaster General, who would look after headquarters, leaving me free to get up into the front line to get the feel of the action. Who better for this role than a military man? I made enquiries through the Gurkhas, because it would obviously be a tremendous advantage to have a Nepali-speaker. As a result, Kelvin Kent, a captain in the Gurkha Signals, became our Base Camp manager. A dynamic hard worker, he took on all the organisational work in Nepal and was to fill a vital role on the expedition.

The final two members of our team were Dave Lambert, our doctor, and Mike Thompson, another ex-military man and one of my closest and oldest friends. A good steady performer, I invited him along as another support climber, someone who would be happy to help in the vital chore of humping loads between intermediate camps without expecting to go out in front to make the route or have a chance of a summit bid.

We had our share of crises in putting together the expedition. Through inexperience, I had failed to delegate nearly enough, but my worst mistake was to send out all the expedition gear by sea to Bombay with an uncomfortably tight margin for error in a boat that broke down at Cape Town. Fortunately for us a British Army expedition was attempting the North Face of Annapurna at the same time that we were trying the South. Generously, they agreed to loan us some of their rations and fly out enough gear for us to get started on the South Face while we waited for our own supplies to catch up with us.

We reached Base Camp on the 27th March. The route to the South Face of Annapurna is guarded by outlying peaks; the beautiful Machapuchare or 'Fish's tail', Hiunchuli and Modi Peak. At first glance they seem to form a continuous wall but the Modi Khola, a deep and narrow gorge, winds sinuously between Hiunchuli and Machapuchare to reach the Annapurna Sanctuary, a great glacier basin at the head of which towers the South Face of Annapurna. Don Whillans, having gone ahead to make a reconnaissance, met us in the gorge of the Modi Khola.

'Did you see the face?' I asked.

'Aye.'

'What was it like?'

'Steep. But after I'd been looking at it for a few hours, it seemed to lie back a bit. It's going to be hard, but I think it'll go all right.'

The following day we emerged from the confines of the gorge and were able to see the South Face for ourselves. It was certainly steep and difficult, but it did look climbable. ·

For the next two months we were to be involved in the complex, at times repetitive manoeuvres of a siege-style climb. For me, the juggling of logistics – devising a plan and then trying to make it work – was as fascinating as the climb itself, but for most of the team the exciting rôle, was to be out in front, actually selecting, then climbing the route up the next few feet of snow, ice or rock. The very steepness and difficulty of the face made this all the more satisfying; but only one person of the team of eleven could be out in front at any one time. The rest were either humping loads up the fixed ropes or resting at Base Camp. We had six high-altitude porters with us – a very small number by standard custom, but I had felt that the Sherpas were unlikely to be able to cope with such steep ground. As there had not been any climbing expeditions in Nepal since 1965 they would be out of practice, and it was also most unlikely that they had ever been asked to use fixed ropes on anything as steep as the South Face of Annapurna.

Most of the inevitable tensions of a siege-style expedition are caused by the frustration of spending so much time in a support role, and in worrying about one's prospects of personally getting to the top of the chosen peak. Back in England I had hoped to get over this problem by alternating the lead climbers so that everyone had a fair turn, but now reality was forcing me to adopt pragmatic courses, to abandon

8091m

6 *(7300m)*

ROCK BAND

5 *(6940m)*

ICE CLIFF

4 *(6495m)*

ICE
RIDGE

3 *(6130m)*

2 *(5335m)*

Ian Clough's accident

1

Annapurna, South Face

Ian Clough jumaring over the ice mushrooms.

the notions of equality. The problem is that people's talents are not the same, yet each person involved sees his abilities in a different perspective. Already, I felt that the two strongest climbers in their different ways were Don Whillans and Dougal Haston, even though Don, at the start of the expedition, was anything but fit. Don's canniness and Dougal's fitness, drive and climbing ability made a powerful combination but it also created an imbalance, for the other pairings just did not have the same drive or experience – at any rate in my eyes. I was never quite as confident when one of the other pairs was out in front.

At times this lack of confidence was barely justified. Martin Boysen and Nick Estcourt forced the steepest and most difficult section of the Ice Ridge that guarded the middle part of the face. It was an incredible cock's-comb of ice, to which clung great cornices of crumbling, aerated snow. Martin burrowed his way through a narrow tunnel which went right through the ridge and then climbed a stretch of vertical ice leading up into another cornice of soft snow. It was probably the most demanding lead of the entire climb.

Ian Clough and I took over from them. Perhaps through over-confidence in myself, a desire to be where the most vital part of the action was, I stayed out in front for what was probably much too long. The snow arête which linked the lower part of the face with its upper reaches proved to be a critical barrier. It just never seemed to end – fragile ice, little rock steps, endless traverses on insubstantial snow. I spent a week at Camp 4, the only place where the ridge relented into a small half-moon of angled snow. It would have been no good for an ordinary tent, but Don had designed a special box tent, based on our experience in Patagonia in 1963 where we had found that no normal tent would stand up to the savage winds. The Whillans Box, a framework of alloy tubing with a covering of proofed nylon, had the advantage of being a rigid structure that could be fitted into a slot cut into a snow slope and, unlike a conventional ridge tent, would not collapse under the weight of snow. Camp 4 was a spectacular but uncomfortable eyrie and the climbing each day was

Looking out from a Whillans Box.

Chris Bonington jumaring to the high point on a rock wall to continue the initial ascent of the Ice Ridge.

Camp 4 was a Whillans Box, a revolutionary new shape designed specifically for this style of steep face expedition.
Above on the crest Martin Boysen is tackling some of the most difficult ice climbing of the entire ascent.

both exacting and wearing. Somehow we had to make a route, up which we could ferry loads. This meant finding suitable anchor points for the fixed rope and, because our line traversed along the side of the ridge, these anchors had to be every few feet. The weather did not help. It was bitterly cold and windy, with the cloud rolling in from below and engulfing us before mid-morning; with the cloud came snow and more wind.

In many ways I was in the wrong place, for out in the lead your entire concentration is taken up with the few feet of snow and ice in front of your nose. It was difficult to take a long-term view of the climb, to keep track of the flow of supplies and people up the mountain behind us. I had become obsessed with reaching the end of the arête. My partner, Ian Clough, who had stayed behind at Bombay to escort all our late-arriving baggage across India by truck, was barely acclimatised. He was forced to go down and Don, who was now running the lower part of the mountain, sent up Dougal Haston instead of Mick Burke or Tom Frost, whose turn it was to go out in front. Don felt that neither of them was going strongly enough.

Dougal certainly brought a fresh drive to our daily struggle, though we were still making little more than thirty metres or so progress each day. But at last, on the 3rd May, Dougal Haston and I reached the top of the Ice Ridge. Back in England we had allowed a mere three days for climbing it; after all, it was only forty-five and a bit metres of vertical height, had looked in the photograph like a fragile but elegant flying buttress between the lower and upper parts of the face. It had taken us three weeks. By now I had been out in front for just over a week. It doesn't sound much, but I was desperately tired, as much, I suspect, a nervous tiredness from worrying about the climb as a whole, as the actual fatigue of the climbing. I had not yet learned how to pace myself while running an expedition.

When Dougal and I had arrived back at Camp 4, Don Whillans, with Mick Burke and Tom Frost were already there. They had dug out another notch for a box tent and were cosily installed. I dropped back down the ropes to Camp 3, hoping to stay there for a few days' rest rather than go all the way back to Base Camp. This had been Whillans' idea. Harder, more ruthless than I, he was worried by the amount of time being wasted by climbers moving up and down between camps to rest at Base Camp, and had decreed that none of the climbers should go below Camp 2. It had sounded a good idea at the time, and I was to be the first guinea pig. I spent two days lolling in my sleeping bag, and then set off for Camp 4, got about half way up but felt the strength ooze out of me. I decided to go down, turned round and slid a few feet down the rope, but the thought revolted me. How could I expect others to grind their guts out if I wasn't prepared to do it myself? A spasm of coughing hit me, and I hung on the rope, amidst tears and coughs, trying to bolster my resolve.

I turned back up the rope and made a few steps. It had taken a matter of seconds to drop back nine metres on the rope. It took me a quarter of an hour to regain those few metres. The contrast was too much. My body was screaming to go down, my logic told me that I could do no good by going up, yet a sense of duty, mixed with pride, was trying to force me on. I felt torn apart by two conflicting impulses, weakened and degraded by my own indecision. There seemed no point in stopping at Camp 3. I felt I had learnt the hard way that if you get over-fatigued, rest at 6000 metres does very little to help you recover. I therefore dropped all the way down to Base Camp.

It is interesting that on Everest in 1972 and 1975, I never went back below our Advanced Base, once it had been established. This meant staying there for periods of up to six weeks, at a height of 6615 metres, without any ill effects. On Annapurna South Face we undoubtedly pushed ourselves harder than we ever did on Everest. Wracked by coughing, I spent very nearly a week at Base Camp, watching through binoculars the drama that was being enacted on the great wall opposite.

Don and Dougal were able to make fast, spectacular progress up the long, comparatively straightforward snow slopes above the ridge. On the 6th May they established a camp just below the sheer Ice Cliffs that formed the next barrier but, on the following morning, Dougal found a gangway that led – dizzily but surprisingly easily – through them. Tom Frost and Mick Burke, impatient to have their turn in front, now went up to the foot of the Rock Band. We had always thought that this feature would prove to be the crux of the entire climb, steep rock and ice at an altitude of around 7000 metres.

Nick Estcourt ferrying loads up the Ice Ridge. The carry from Camp 4 to 5 exhausted the whole team.

Don and Dougal shot down the ropes for a rest, leaving Nick and Martin at Camp 4 with the unenviable task of supporting Tom and Mick. I was lying, frustrated, on the sun-warmed grass at Base Camp. I had tried to go back up but had only reached Camp 2 at 5335 metres, where Dave Lambert, our doctor, was staying. I had a stabbing pain in my chest every time I coughed and he diagnosed pleurisy. Clutching a bottleful of antibiotics, I returned disconsolately. There was no way that you could lead or even effectively co-ordinate an expedition from down at Base. You had no feel for what it was like high up on the rock and ice of the face, even though you had been there just a few days before. On an expedition of this kind, undoubtedly the best place for the leader is in the camp immediately behind the lead climbers. In this way he maintains a direct contact with the people out in front and, being at the penultimate point in the line of supply, can feel how effectively this is working.

The carry from Camp 4 up the Ice Ridge and then up the endless snow slopes to the foot of the Rock Band was particularly savage. The ropes were too steep and difficult for our Sherpas, and anyway we needed them for the carries between the lower camps. We were now so short of manpower that we were using local Gurkha porters, who had never been on a mountain before, for ferrying loads from Base Camp, across the glacier to our bottom camp. We even ensnared casual visitors with

the promise of a good view from the lower part of the face as a reward for ferrying a load up to Camp 1, 2 or even 3. One party of trekkers, two men and a couple of girls whom we named the London Sherpas, stayed for several weeks and became honorary members of the expedition. But it was the climbers doing the carry from Camp 4 to 5 who were becoming exhausted and it was at Camp 4 that I should have been at this stage.

The Whillans Box at Camp 5 was tucked into the bergschrund itself. This gave some protection from the spindrift avalanches that came pouring down the slopes from above, but as it also blocked out the rays of the early morning sun, the interior rapidly became an icy coffin. The ice on its walls never melted, the spindrift that had poured down each afternoon and night covered everything that had been left outside. And the climbing was hard, much harder than anything we had encountered so far.

And while those at Base Camp theorised and criticised, out there in front Mick Burke did some of the most difficult climbing that had ever been carried out at such an altitude. Icy runnels led onto steep rock. He had to take off his crampons, balancing on a tiny foothold some thirty metres above Tom Frost, as he struggled ungloved with frozen straps on the almost holdless rock.

But we were running out of time. It was now mid-May; the monsoon was close upon us and we were barely a quarter of the way up the Rock Band. I was impatient to push the route out, fully confident only of Don and Dougal as a lead climbing pair. Everyone else was beginning to tire, largely because they had all been exhausting themselves on the long carry from Camp 4 to 5. I decided to push Don and Dougal into the front as quickly as possible, even though this meant upsetting the rotation of lead pairs. I put the plan across on the radio. And then all hell broke loose. It's never easy having an argument by radio – Nick, at Camp 4, very rationally pointed out the appalling bottleneck that we now had at the start of the long carry to Camp 5. Mick Burke, at Camp 5, urged the need for Don and Dougal to make a carry from 4 to 5: 'The thing is, Chris, you don't realise what it's like up here. It's much easier to lead than to carry loads.'

274

Then Don came on the air.

'Dougal and I left that place Camp 5 a week ago. Camp 5 isn't even consolidated and the progress of all towards Camp 6 is so poor that it's had me and Dougal depressed all the way up the mountain. I don't know what Mick thinks he's playing at, but Camp 5 is short and we want to get the route pushed out and unless they get their fingers out, push it out and establish 6 or at least find a site, they should make way for someone else to try. He's had a week and progress seems very poor.'

The reaction from the two higher camps to this remark was violent. It was just as well, perhaps, that the various contenders in the argument were separated by several thousand feet of space! In fact, both parties were partly right. Ferrying loads up behind the lead climbers was a desperate problem, but if we had slowed down in an effort to build up our supplies I suspect we would have come to a grinding halt.

The following day Mick, who always responded to a challenge, particularly one set by Don, was determined to prove that he could do as much as – if not more than – any other pair on the mountain. Mick and Tom ran out 240 metres of rope up some of the steepest and most difficult climbing we had yet encountered. It was certainly the best bit of climbing that had been done on the expedition up to date, but it was also their last fling, for they were now on their way back down to Base Camp for a rest. Martin Boysen helped Don and Dougal get established in Camp 6, half-way up the Rock Band, but he also was forced to retreat, exhausted by his long stint of carrying, his morale undoubtedly dented through being passed over by Don and Dougal.

I was now on my way back up the mountain, but our effort was like a rickety human pyramid: Don and Dougal at Camp 6 at around 7300 metres, Nick Estcourt at Camp 5, Ian Clough and Dave Lambert at Camp 4, Mike Thompson and the Sherpas at Camp 2 and a growing number of exhausted climbers and Sherpas recuperating at Base Camp. I joined Nick Estcourt at Camp 5 on the 15th May, finding it all I could do to struggle up those long slopes leading up to the Rock Band. Every time I coughed I had to hold my ribs to try to control the stabbing pain.

The carry from Camp 5 to 6 was the wildest and most exhausting so far. The ropes went diagonally across the face, over a series of ice fields and rocky walls. It was impossible to build up any kind of rhythm and the ropes stretched away, never seeming to come to an end. I did that carry, and most of the other carries I made in the next week, on my own. In spite of my exhaustion I could not help marvelling at the wild beauty of the scene. To the east, in the distance, was the shapely pyramid of Annapurna II which I had climbed ten years before; to the south Machapuchare, now almost dwarfed as we looked down onto it, the great spread of the Annapurna Sanctuary, patterned with its crevasses into a crazy mosaic far below, and then round to the east the retaining walls of Hiunchuli, Modi Peak and the Fang. We were now almost level with their tops. But fatigue and altitude were taking their toll and it took me six hours to climb the 365 metres to just below Camp 6. I was so exhausted on getting within shouting distance of the camp that I dumped my load and yelled for Don to come down and pick it up; after all, he had had a rest that day.

I was at Camp 5 for over a week. Nick, exhausted by his long stint in a support role, was finally forced to drop back down to Base. I had two lonely days by myself before Ian Clough came up to join me; exhausting carries in the teeth of the driving wind and swirling spindrift; moments of hope and elation, moments of utter despair. I still had dreams of reaching the summit, was warmed by Dougal's invitation to join them after they had forced a way up a long snow gully that led to the top of the Rock Band, even set out from Camp 5 with my personal gear plus the tent, rope, spare food and cine camera that we needed to make the summit push, and got only a few feet above

Ian Clough and Don Whillans at Camp 6. Four of us spent a hideously uncomfortable night in a tent designed for two. After nine nights at Camp 6 Don Whillans and Dougal Haston went on to the summit on 27th May 1970.

the camp before realising that there was no way I could manage such a heavy load. In addition, I was using oxygen to reach them, while Don and Dougal were doing without. I could not possibly do it and so dropped back to the empty camp to dump my personal gear. In my despair I sat down and cried and then, ashamed at my weakness, shouted at the walls around me, 'Get a grip of yourself, you bloody idiot,' repacked the sack and set out once again.

In a way, it was much easier for me to suppress my own personal ambition to reach the top; after all, having conceived the idea of the expedition, having co-ordinated it and, for most of the time, held it together it was possible to sublimate my own desires in the success of the team as a whole. This was very different for the other team members. Nick Estcourt summed it up when he got back to Base Camp, saying: 'It's all very well talking about the satisfaction of contributing to the success of the team, but it's a hell of a sight better if you manage to kick the winning goal.'

Don and Dougal stuck it out at Camp 6, surviving on the trickle of food and gear we were able to funnel up to them. The monsoon now seemed to be upon us – day after day of cloud and storm, of fierce winds and billowing spindrift. Don and Dougal had one abortive attempt at establishing Camp 7, but were unable to find anywhere to pitch a tent, very nearly failed to find the way back to the top of the fixed ropes and finally struggled down to Camp 6, where Ian Clough and I had moved up in support, hoping to have a go for the summit ourselves. The four of us spent a hideously uncomfortable night crammed into one small, two-man tent, pitched precariously on a tiny spur of snow. Next morning, there was no discussion about who should stay and who should go down – Don and Dougal were so much more fit than Ian and I.

Tom Frost and Mick Burke were on their way back up, eager to have a go for the summit, prepared to support Don and Dougal up at the front, and so Ian and I dropped back down to Camp 4. We knew that we had used up most of our reserves but were determined to hang on somehow until Don and Dougal had either made their bid for the summit, or had given up. Until that happened, somehow, we all had to keep them supplied with just enough food to keep going.

On the 27th May we were storm-bound at Camp 4, the snow hammering at the box tent throughout the day. That evening I called Camp 5 and asked Dougal if they had managed to get out at all.

He replied: 'Aye, we've just climbed Annapurna.'

Don and Dougal had set out that morning, hoping to establish a top camp. Higher up on the mountain it wasn't quite so bad as it was on the lower slopes. They made fast progress on the fixed ropes up the gully, reached the top of the Rock Band where they had left the tent but, with hardly a word between them, they set out up the crest of the long ridge leading up towards the summit. They had reached a level of communication over the weeks on the mountain that hardly needed words. They were going for the top, Don out in front breaking trail and picking the route, Dougal behind carrying the rope and cine camera. They were both going superbly well; Dougal wrote: 'The wonderful thing was that there was no breathing trouble. I had imagined great lung-gasping efforts at 26,000 feet [7925 metres], but I was moving with no more difficulty than I had experienced 4,000 feet lower down.'

There was a steep wall of snow-plastered rock at the top but they climbed it unroped, and then Dougal filmed Don as he plodded those final few feet to the summit of Annapurna, to stand where Herzog and Lachenal had been twenty years before. Their descent in a storm could easily have been more disastrous than that of their predecessors, but so superbly attuned were they to their environment that they picked their way back down the mountain, still unroped, through the gusting spindrift, down over icy steps and snow-plastered rocks to the haven of the top of the fixed ropes.

There was a moment of sheer, unrestrained joy throughout the expedition; there was no more recrimination, no envy for their achievement; but for me the euphoria was very short-lived, for the expedition was not yet over. Tom and Mick, up at Camp 5, naturally wanted a go at the summit and, the following day, moved up to the top camp. I was filled with foreboding. The pair in front were very much on their own. If anything were to happen to them none of us had the strength to go back up the face to help them. I listened to the radio all day; at midday Mick Burke came on the air. His feet had lost all feeling and he had dropped back to the tent, but Tom was going on by himself for the summit. I was even more worried. Then, at last, the radio came to life again; Tom, also, had returned.

Although sorry for their sakes that they had not made it to the top, I was even more relieved that they were down in one piece. I must confess here that the feeling was not entirely humanitarian. I was guilty of a feeling that I suspect is common to almost every leader of any enterprise – of wanting the expedition as a whole, as a projection of the leader's ego, to be successful both in terms of achieving its objective and reaching a satisfactory conclusion.

Next morning it was with a profound sense of relief that I raced down to Base Camp to start the heady job of writing the expedition reports and co-ordinating our return to civilisation. I was sitting inside the tent, typewriter on an upturned box, when I heard someone rush up to the tent calling, 'Chris, Chris!' The rest of what he said was incomprehensible. I ran out and found Mike Thompson sitting on the grass, head between knees, sucking the air in great hacking gasps. He looked up, face contorted with shock, grief and exhaustion.

'It's Ian. He's dead. Killed in an ice avalanche below Camp 2.'

Everyone had run out of their tents on hearing Mike's arrival; they just stood numbed in shocked, unbelieving silence as Mike gasped out his story.

Mike, Ian and Dave Lambert had decided not to wait for Mick Burke and Tom Frost, who were on their way down from the top camp, but set out from Camp 3 early that morning, hauling down as much gear as they could manage. They passed Camp 2, and carried on down the side of the glacier, onto a narrow shelf below an ice wall. This was a spot that we had always realised was dangerous, but the most obvious threat, an overhanging ice cliff, had collapsed earlier on. There was still an element of risk from some ice towers further up the glacier, but their threat was not so obvious and it seemed unlikely that these would collapse in the space of the few minutes it took to cross the danger zone. Even so, we all tended to hurry across this section of the glacier.

Ian was in front, Mike immediately behind. Dave Lambert was about five minutes behind them. There was practically no warning, just a thunderous roar and the impression of a huge, dark mass filling the sky above. Mike ducked back into the side of an ice wall, where a small trough was formed. He thought that Ian, slightly further out than he, had tried to run away from the avalanche, down the slope. But Ian hadn't a hope and was engulfed by the fall.

'It went completely dark,' said Mike. 'I thought I'd had it; just lay there and swore at the top of my voice. It seemed such a stupid way to die.'

When the cloud of ice particles had settled and the last grating rumble had died away into the silence of the glacier, Mike picked himself up and, with some Sherpas who had been on their way up to meet them, started searching through the debris, finding Ian's body part-buried by blocks of ice. They carried him down and we buried Ian just above our Base Camp, on a grassy slope looking across at the face on which we had striven all those weeks.

Shortly after the climb, I wrote:

> I can't attempt to evaluate the worth of our ascent balanced against its cost in terms of the loss of a man's life, of the time devoted to it or the money spent on it. Climbing and the risks involved are part of my life and, I think, of those of most of the team – it was certainly a very large part of Ian's life. It is difficult to justify the risks once one is married with a family and I think most of us have stopped trying. We love climbing, have let a large part of our lives be dominated by this passion, and this eventually led us to Annapurna.

Although I had been climbing for nearly twenty years, Ian was the first close friend I had lost in the mountains, but the last ten years between 1970 and 1980 have seen a terrible toll. Mick Burke was killed on Everest in 1975 when he went for the summit on his own. Dougal Haston died in an avalanche near his home in Leysin, Switzerland, the day before I was due to meet him in Chamonix to go winter climbing. Nick Estcourt, the closest of all my friends, died on the West Ridge of K2, swept away by an avalanche, during our attempt on the mountain in 1978. Mike Thompson has compared the sadness of lost friends to being prematurely old; so many of one's contemporaries have died that one knows the loneliness of an older generation. Of the eight lead climbers on the South Face of Annapurna, four are now dead, a frightening statistic that is mirrored amongst almost any other climbing group undertaking extreme climbing over a long period of time, particularly at high altitude.

The mountaineer is exposed to some level of risk at almost all times he is on the mountain, but it is fairly rare for a good climber to be killed because the climb is too hard, or even when caught out by bad weather or some other kind of emergency. Then, his concentration is complete, with every nerve stretched towards survival. It is on easy ground that accidents occur; that momentary lack of concentration, a slip where there happens to be a long drop; a hidden crevasse and, most dangerous of all, the risk of avalanche.

And yet we go on; it has certainly never occurred to me to give up climbing – I love it too much; the challenge and stimulus of playing a danger game, the beauty of the mountains in which there is so much peace alongside the lurking threat are all tied in with the gratification of ego, the enjoyment of success, of being good at something. I do worry about the responsibility I have to a family I love, but then the pull of the mountains is so great that perhaps selfishly, I could never give up climbing – I will always want to go back to the mountains.

An aerial view of the Rupal Face of Nanga Parbat from the south-west.

Diamir – Messner on Nanga Parbat

Only the gentle roar of the gas stove disturbed the silence. The tent, with its chill moss of hoar frost festooning the walls, was sepulchral in the dim, grey light of the dawn. Yet it had a reassuring, womblike quality, for those thin walls protected him from the lonely immensity of the sky and mountains outside. And then another noise intruded; an insistent, rushing, hissing rumble that came from all around him. It sounded like a gigantic flood about to engulf his shelter. Panic-stricken, he tore at the iced-up fastenings of the entrance to see what was happening. The whole mountain seemed to be on the move, torrents of ice pouring down on either side, whilst below him the entire slope, which he had climbed the previous day, had now broken away and was plunging in a great, tumbling, boiling wave to the glacier far below, reaching out and down towards the little camp at its foot where he had left his two companions.

And then the sound died away. A cloud of snow particles, looking no more substantial than fluffy cumulus on a summer's day, settled gently, and it was as if the avalanche had never happened, the icy debris merging into the existing snow and ice. Once again, the only sound was the purr of the gas stove. Somehow it emphasised his smallness, inconsequence, the ephemeral nature of his own existence.

Reinhold Messner was at a height of around 6400 metres on the Diamir Face of Nanga Parbat. Having set out the previous morning from a bivouac at the foot of the face, he was attempting the first solo ascent of a major Himalayan peak, all the way from its foot to the summit. It meant complete self-sufficiency, carrying all his food and equipment with him, facing the physical and mental stresses of high-altitude climbing on his own, also facing the risk of accident, of falling down a hidden crevasse, with no-one to help him.

Although he could see the site of his Base Camp, some 2000 metres below and five miles away, he was as much alone as a solitary sailor in the Southern Ocean, or as isolated as an astronaut in orbit on the other side of the moon. That sense of isolation was now even more extreme; his line of descent having been swept away by the avalanche, he would have to find another way back down the mountain.

Others had, of course, reached Himalayan summits on their own. Hermann Buhl had made the first ascent of Nanga Parbat in a solitary push – an incredible achievement, but he had been part of a large expedition which had worked together to reach the top camp. It was just the final, if most challenging, step that he had to make on his own – a very different concept from that of starting at the foot by oneself. Some had tried. In 1934 Maurice Wilson had slipped into Tibet and attempted to climb Everest from the north leaving his porters behind at Camp 3. Comparatively inexperienced, he had wanted to climb the mountain for the mystic

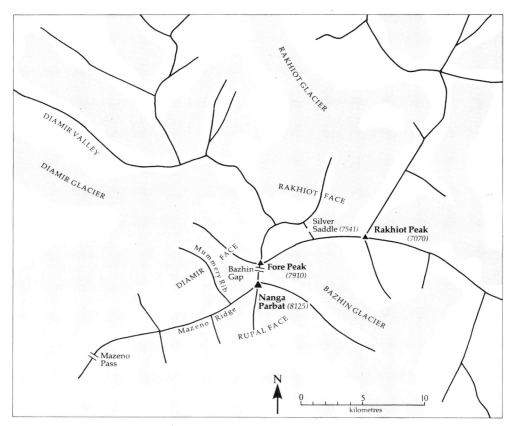

The Nanga Parbat region

experience, but perished fairly low down. The Canadian, Earl Denman, got no further than the North Col before accepting the futility of his attempt in 1947, while four years later the Dane, Klaus Becker Larson, did not get as high. Both these climbers had employed Sherpas. Messner himself had attempted Nanga Parbat solo on two previous occasions, but on the first barely started the climb before the immensity of the challenge overcame him, and on the second did not even reach the foot of the mountain.

But unlike Wilson, Denman and Larson, most of Messner's life had been devoted to the mountains, to stretching himself to the extreme, forever striving to discover new ground, new experience. Attempting an 8000-metre peak solo was a logical step in his own personal evolution.

Born in 1944 in the village of Vilnoss which nestles amongst the Dolomite peaks of South Tyrol, he was the second of eight children, seven boys and a girl. His father, the village schoolmaster, was from the same peasant stock as the children he taught. There was not much money, but it was a secure and happy, if disciplined, upbringing within the tight circle of this large family. Joseph Messner loved the mountains and each summer they moved up to a hut amongst the high pastures where they could wander and climb. Reinhold Messner was taken on his first climb, up Sass Rigais, the highest peak of the Geisler Alps, at the age of five.

As he grew older he began climbing with his younger brother, Günther, exploring the Geisler peaks around his home and steadily expanding his own climbing ability. By the time he went on to the University of Padua he was already an extremely capable and forceful climber and quickly developed his prowess, spurning the use of artificial aids, particularly the indiscriminate use of expansion bolts. He made a series of very fast ascents of the most difficult routes and also some outstanding solo ascents, amongst them the North Face of the Droites, long considered the most difficult mixed ice and rock route of the Western Alps, and the Philipp/Flamm route on the North Face of the Civetta, one of the hardest free rock routes in the Dolomites. By 1969 Messner was established as one of the boldest and most innovative climbers in Europe, with a stature very similar to that of Hermann Buhl in the early 'fifties. And once again it was Karl Herrligkoffer who was going to offer the opportunity of going to the Himalaya.

Over the years Herrligkoffer had continued to organise and lead expeditions and Nanga Parbat maintained its compulsive attraction for him. In 1961 he attempted the mountain from the west, by its Diamir Face. This is the side from which Mummery, the British pioneer who was swept away in an avalanche, made the first attempt in 1895. Herrligkoffer failed in 1961 but returned the following year, when Toni Kinshofer, Siegi Löw and Anderl Mannhardt reached the top by a difficult route skirting round the huge ice cliffs in the centre of the face.

Herrligkoffer turned next to the forbidding south aspect, the Rupal Face, at 4500 metres one of the highest mountain walls in the world. He had made three attempts on this face between 1963 and 1968, each time getting a little higher. The year 1970, however, seemed destined to be the year of the big walls in the Himalaya. It was the year our British party climbed the South Face of Annapurna and the Japanese were attempting the South-West Face of Everest. Messner had reservations about joining a large expedition, very few of whose members he knew personally, but the opportunity was too good to miss.

He approached the climb with characteristic seriousness, very different from the attitude of British climbers of this period. In Britain there was undoubtedly an ethic against formal training outside the process of climbing itself; it was a tradition of climbing by day and boozing in the pub at night. Messner, on the other hand, approached his climbing with the dedication of a competitive athlete. He trained on the walls of an old saw mill near his home, traversing along the wall, back and forth until his arms and fingers gave out. This is very similar to the climbing training undertaken by leading British rock climbers today, but in Britain this approach has been developed only in the last six years or so. Messner's training went a lot further. It encompassed a regime of cold showers in the morning, a careful diet in which he ate only fruit for one day of the week to accustom his body to food deprivation, and a routine of four hours' distance running each day and exercises designed to build up his stamina.

Before going to the South Face of Annapurna, I can remember being invited by a sports medicine research unit to submit my own group of climbers to the same series of tests for fitness as those which had recently been given to the England football team. I found an excuse for declining the invitation, knowing that we should almost certainly compare unfavourably and, if we failed to climb the South Face, could then be pilloried as unfit. As it happened Don Whillans, who had a substantial beer gut before the expedition, got himself fit during the climb and reached the top. Messner could have taken such a test with impunity and, I suspect, would have compared in lung capacity and fitness with any Olympic athlete. His pulse rate was down to forty-two beats per minute and he could gain a thousand metres of height on his training runs in under an hour. The Rupal Face was to prove a crucible in which to test his fitness and drive.

Once again, as in 1953, there was dissension between Herrligkoffer and the climbers spearheading the attempt – a dissension focused on Messner, who wanted to make a solo bid for the summit. The story around this is still clouded with

The forbidding Rupal Face, at 4500 metres one of the highest mountain walls in the world.

Reinhold, above, and Günther Messner. When Reinhold's younger brother joined him on the summit bid their success was overshadowed by the problem of finding a way down for the overstretched Günther.

confusion and, like the earlier expedition, was to end in court actions.

Just three climbers were at the top camp; Reinhold Messner, his younger brother, Günther, and a German climber and film cameraman, Gerhard Baur. They had no radio, so the previous day on the radio at the camp below Messner had made an agreement with Herrligkoffer that if the weather report were good, the three at the top camp would fix ropes in place for a summit bid to be made by Felix Kuen, Peter Scholz, Günther and himself. But in view of the lateness of the season and the approaching monsoon, if the weather report were bad, Messner should make a fast solo bid for the summit. The signal was to be a rocket fired from Base Camp – a red one for a bad weather report and a blue one for good.

It was the 26th June and that evening at Base Camp the weather forecast was good for the next few days. It should have been a blue rocket. This was to become the subject of a violent controversy, for a red rocket was fired. Apparently it had a blue marking on its cover and Herrligkoffer, assuming that all the remaining rockets were also red, did not attempt to fire any others for fear of confusing the issue still further.

To Messner it seemed quite clear. He could see the great cloud bank in the distance; the rocket signal indicated that it was rolling up towards Nanga Parbat, but his eyes and experience told him that he just had time to reach the summit and get back. It was a touch of Hermann Buhl – a challenge that inevitably part of him welcomed, daunting, huge but something that he had confronted before, on the steep walls of the Alps. He set out at three in the morning, climbed swiftly and steadily upwards, into the Merkl Gully. After a mistake in route finding he was forced to drop back and take another line and then, just after dawn, he saw a dark shape coming up from below. It was Günther, who had been unable to resist the temptation to follow his brother, and share in the summit. He had made extraordinary progress, catching Reinhold up in only four hours of climbing over a distance that was to take Kuen and Scholz a full ten the following day.

The two brothers climbed on together. It had been a bitterly cold night when they started, but now the enervating glare of the sun was their main problem. Making steady, continuous progress, they reached a shoulder on the ridge, and suddenly Reinhold realised that success was within their grasp. He could see across to the Silver Saddle, the long weary way that Buhl had crossed all those years before. The summit pyramid was just a short way beyond; nothing could stop them. And then in the late afternoon they were at the top, relishing the momentary euphoria of slopes dropping away on every side, of endless peaks around them in the warm yellow light of the late afternoon sun, but then came the nagging awareness of their position. They had to find a way down.

On the way up fear becomes anaesthetised by the summit goal, the focal point of all one's effort and desire, but once attained, reality floods back and, for the Messners the reality was daunting. They had no rope, no bivouac gear except a thin silver foil space blanket, no stove for melting snow and practically no food. Reinhold had been confident he could return the way he had come, but Günther was an unforeseen circumstance. Younger, less experienced than his brother, he had stretched himself to his limit on the way up and knew with a horrible certainty that he could not climb back down those desperately steep walls of the Merkl Gully. The Diamir Face swept away to the west, lit by the setting sun, seemingly easy-angled, inviting, less daunting than the steepness of the wall from which they had only just escaped. But it was completely unknown ground. Kinshofer, Löw and Mannhardt's route had been well to the right of the apparently easy summit slopes the brothers could see below them. But what of the route lower down? Messner had examined photographs and knew all too well how complex were the icefalls through which

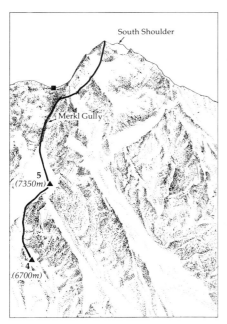

Nanga Parbat, Rupal Face

they would have to find their way. And so he compromised; there was only an hour or so before it was dark and a bivouac was inevitable. They could at least lose some height by climbing down to the col below the summit pyramid. From there it might still be possible to go down the Rupal Face and it was just feasible that someone might come to help them. It took them a long time to reach the col. Günther was desperately tired, slumping into the snow every few feet to get some rest.

Huddled into a tiny rock niche on the col, wrapped in the space blanket, they shivered through the night, exposed to the icy wind blasting through the gap. In the chill dawn Reinhold scrambled over to the ridge of the col; he could see where they had left the Merkl Crack to reach the shoulder about a hundred metres below. There was no way they could climb down without a rope. If only someone would come up from below. He shouted for help, but his voice was snatched away by the wind. For two hours he called, to no avail. And then, far below, he saw two figures slowly working their way up towards them. A great wave of relief – they were saved!

The two figures were a hundred metres below when Reinhold recognised Felix Kuen and Peter Scholz. He shouted down to them and Felix looked up, but their words were torn away by the winds. Messner took it for granted that they would climb up the steep and broken rocks leading to the col but saw that Kuen had turned away and was following their tracks leading to the shoulder. He shouted that it was much quicker for them to climb up to the col, that all he and Günther needed was the use of the rope to get down to where Kuen was now climbing, that Kuen and Scholz could then go on to the summit. But Kuen did not appear to understand or hear properly, merely shouting, 'Everything O.K.?'

Messner thought he was simply asking if they were all right, so said yes. After all, they only needed a rope. So he was stunned when Kuen turned away and continued up the shoulder. When Kuen looked back Messner pointed to the west, the Diamir side, to which he now seemed irrevocably committed.

In Felix Kuen's account, there is no mention of the wind or any difficulty in communication:

> The Merkl Gully continued vertically above. We left the gully by the right and crossed towards the South Shoulder. The traverse led over a snow slope of about fifty degrees in easy terrain, where I was able to carry on a conversation with Reinhold Messner. He stood on the ridge where the top of the Merkl Crack met the South Shoulder, some seventy to a hundred metres distant. It was ten o'clock and we spoke of the possible routes to the summit, as well as the time they would require. Reinhold reported that he and his brother were on the summit at 17.00 hours the previous day and that they were now about to descend in a westerly direction (Diamir side!). To my question whether everything was OK, he replied 'yes'. A great weight lifted from my heart for I had feared he was calling for help. As yet I had no presentiment that the tragedy had already begun the day before when Günther had followed in the wake of his climbing brother. From that moment the two were without a rope, without bivouac sack, without sufficient survival equipment. Reinhold was prepared only for a solo climb with an NRC-blanket and some food in his pocket. And now he charged me to tell the others he was going down the reverse side of the mountain and would soon be back at Base. I strongly advised him against this, whereupon he broke off with a 'Cheerio' and disappeared over the ridge.

The two versions have the bare skeleton in common but the interpretation of the detail is very different. It certainly seems unlikely that Reinhold Messner would have *chosen* to go down the Diamir Face, as Kuen implies. Although an extraordinarily bold and innovative climber, he has always displayed very sound judgement and practical common sense. Heading down an unknown face on the other side of the mountain, with no gear, food or support, accompanied by his exhausted brother, seems completely out of character.

He was in a desperate state, he stumbled and fell a few times, tearing his hand on his crampons, and eventually leant on his ice axe and cried. It was not until the exhausted Günther rallied his brother that Messner took charge of the situation.

He knew that Günther would never survive another night out at this altitude and it seemed unlikely that Kuen and Scholz would get back to the Merkl Gully before dark. There was no question of climbing back up to the summit to meet the other two, since Günther would never have made it. Reinhold suggested that he went alone, but Günther rejected this suggestion. He was desperate to get down those easy-looking slopes on the western side and so, at about eleven o'clock in the morning, they set out down the sunlit snow of the Diamir Face.

Reinhold went first, trying to pick out the best route, never easy from above, for it is impossible to see the ice cliffs until you are right on top of them. And then the afternoon clouds crept up the slope, engulfed them in their tide, flattening out all perspective as they groped their way down. Suddenly the mist parted, revealing a dark hole plunging into the depths of the Diamir Valley far below. They came to a barrier of ice, steep, sheer, impossible. Skirting it, Reinhold found a chute of smooth, polished ice at an angle of around fifty degrees. It was just possible. Facing in, kicking in with the front points of their crampons, penetrating only a few millimetres, they teetered down the hard, smooth surface.

Reinhold felt the presence of a third person with uncanny clarity, just outside his field of vision, keeping pace with him as he carefully kicked downwards. They climbed on into the dark. A few rocks appeared. They were now on the Mummery Rib. They stopped at last around midnight. Exhausted, chilled, desperately thirsty, for they had had nothing to drink for two days, they crouched on a tiny ledge.

They set out before dawn, by the light of the moon. It was ghostly, mysterious with the thin gleam of the snow and the opaque black of the shadows lit by the occasional spark of crampons striking rock. Forcing themselves through the last levels of their exhaustion, they finally realised in the dawn that they had reached the glacier at the bottom of the Diamir Face. They had come through the worst; exhausted as they were, still far from safety, they knew the momentary elation of what they had achieved – of having made the first traverse of Nanga Parbat, the first ascent of the Rupal Face, the first direct descent of the Diamir Face – and of being alive.

In a dream, they wandered on down the glacier, Reinhold out in front picking out the route, Günther coming on behind. The glacier was bare of snow, the crevasses exposed, no longer a threat, and then as the sun rose little rivulets of water began to trickle on every side. Reinhold lay down, drank and drank, then sat basking in the sun as he waited for his brother. He heard voices, saw a horse silhouetted against the sky, cattle grazing, people leaning against a wall. He focused his eyes and the horse turned into a crevasse, the cattle into great blocks of snow, the people into stones.

But there was no sign of Günther. He waited for another hour – still no sign. Increasingly worried, he forced his body back up the glacier, retracing his route, forgetting his exhaustion as he made his frantic search. There were no footprints, for it had been frozen hard as they walked down, but there was the great piled debris of an ice avalanche that had swept down only a short time after he had last seen his brother. Slowly, the realisation sank in that Günther had almost certainly been caught by it and was somewhere underneath thousands of tons of ice. Unable to accept it fully, he continued searching throughout the day, shouting himself hoarse. He slept out on the glacier, searched the next day as well, and only towards evening at last began to admit what had happened. In a daze, almost unconscious, he staggered down the glacier to its end, to spend his fourth night in the open without food or shelter.

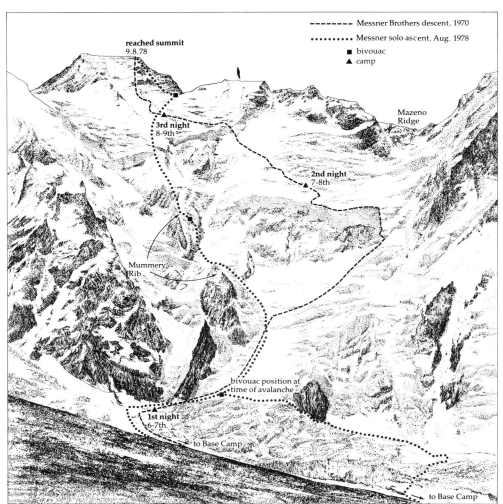

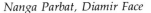

Nanga Parbat, Diamir Face

Messner filming Habeler filming him on Hidden Peak. They were prepared to carry the weight of a cine camera, but had decided against taking a rope.

The following morning was cold, clear, still and silent, the Diamir Face inscrutably in shadow, the teeth of the Mazeno Ridge just catching the rays of the early morning sun. It was as if there were no-one left alive in the entire world. Messner shouted his brother's name yet again into the silence. There was not even an echo. He left his gaiters on top of a rock in case a helicopter was sent in to search for him, and started down the long, empty valley. His progress was desperately slow. Accompanied by spectres, he staggered from boulder to boulder, spending three more nights in the open before stumbling upon the high grazing camp of local villagers. He was emaciated, burnt by the sun, with torn, frostbitten feet.

For Messner it had been an Armageddon that I suspect very few people would have survived, let alone have gone on from to even greater challenges. There were not only his injuries – the amputation of one big toe and the loss of parts of all the others except the two little ones, but also the emotional wounds. As if that were not enough, a series of law suits were brought by Herrligkoffer against Messner for breach of contract and libel. Messner described the impact of his experience in his book, *The Big Walls*: 'The Nanga Parbat Odyssey has given me the strength to face any future hazards squarely and accept or reject them, and every single hazardous enterprise I now undertake – whether it is successful or no – is an invisible ingredient of my life, of my fate.'

In every way, 1970 was a year of crisis for Messner. He was befriended by Baron von Kienlin, a wealthy German aristocraft who had played a minor role on the Rupal Face expedition and had taken Messner's side in the protracted legal wrangling which followed. He also invited the climber to convalesce at his castle in Württemberg. It was during this period that Messner and von Kienlin's beautiful young wife, Uschi, fell in love. Uschi left her husband and three children to be with Messner. They were married in 1971 and together returned to the Diamir Valley to search for the body of Günther. They did not succeed.

In 1972 Messner climbed Manaslu (8156 metres), his second 8000-metre peak, as a member of an Austrian expedition led by Wolfgan Nairz, but once again disaster struck his climbing companion. Franz Jäger, who was making the summit bid with Messner, turned back, while Messner pressed on to the top alone. On his way back down from the summit, Messner was caught in a violent snow storm, and when he reached the top camp was appalled to learn Jäger had not arrived. Two other climbers at Camp 4 immediately set out in search of him and one of these, Andi Schlick, also lost his life. Inevitably there was some controversy, though there was no way Messner could have foreseen the events that followed his decision to go for the top alone.

Around this time Messner began to dream of the possibility of climbing an 8000-metre peak solo, and the Diamir Face seemed to act as a magnet. He returned in 1973 to make his first solo attempt, described in his book, *Solo Nanga Parbat*, camping below the rocky spur of the Mummery Rib, quite close to where he had bivouacked in despair after his brother's death. But his heart was not in it. Before leaving his little Base Camp, he had confessed in his diary:

> Long after midnight and I cannot sleep. The few mouthfuls of food I managed to force down last evening weigh heavily on my stomach. I think of Uschi and sob violently. This oppressive feeling that robs me of hunger and thirst won't go away. It is not my Grand Plan that prevents me from eating and sleeping, it is this separation from my wife. I am not mentally ready to see such a big undertaking through to the end.

Even so, he had set out and, that morning of the 3rd June, he packed his sack, put on his boots and started climbing the lower slopes of the Face in the ghostly light of the dawn. He did not take the decision to turn back consciously. He simply found himself heading back down the slope. The jump into the unknown was too big and, equally important perhaps, his own ties on the ground were too strong.

No sooner did he get back to Funes than he began to dream and plan for other climbs; it is a syndrome which I, and almost every other addicted climber, have been through, the longing to be home when on the mountain, and the restless plans within a few days of getting back.

In 1975 Messner went on two expeditions which provided extreme examples of two different climbing philosophies. In the spring he joined a siege-style Italian expedition to the huge South Face of Lhotse, one of the most complex and dangerous faces in the Himalaya. So far, it has resisted all attempts to climb it. The party was led by Riccardo Cassin, one of the great climbers of the pre-war era. Messner liked and respected Cassin and, on the whole, got on well with his fellow team members. Though he had done much of the climbing out in front, he found this type of expedition uncongenial, commenting in his book, *The Challenge*:

> On the one side it offers greater safety, back-up, the possibility of substitution in case of illness, comradeship. On the other hand you must offset the restricted mobility, the long discussions and the team spirit, which under some circumstances can strangle all progress. With careful preparation and the necessary experience, a two-man expedition would not

only be quicker and cheaper, but also safer. On any quite large mountain everyone must be self-reliant. It is much easier to find a single well-matched partner than ten or fifteen.

Already he was planning a very different kind of expedition, a two-man attempt on Hidden Peak (Gasherbrum I, 8068 metres/26,470 feet) in the Karakoram. No mountain of over 8000 metres had yielded either to a two-man expedition or, for that matter, to a purely Alpine-style attempt. Hermann Buhl's expedition to Broad Peak had been extremely compact and had not used high-altitude porters, but they had ferried loads up the mountain, establishing their camps in the traditional way.

The evolution of mountaineering is influenced strongly by a conflict between basic instincts. On the one hand there is the spirit of adventure, the desire to pitch skill and judgement against the unknown, with the spice of risk to sharpen the experience, but on the other hand is the instinct for survival and also a desire to increase the chances of success. The siege approach gives a greater chance of success, with its big teams and lines of fixed ropes, and at the same time reduces the psychological commitment, though in some ways the risks are just as great, if coming in different guises. The climber on a siege-style expedition can become over-complacent, confident in his camps and ropes. But he is going back and forth over potentially dangerous ground many times, and is therefore increasing the chances of being caught by avalanche, stone fall or hidden crevasses. A weaker climber can, perhaps, get higher on the mountain than he ever would have done had he started from the bottom without the fragile scaffolding of a siege-style expedition.

And so, the move towards an Alpine approach, whilst psychologically much more daunting, had some sound, practical merit, as pointed out by Messner. He had talked this over with Peter Habeler, a talented Austrian guide with whom he had climbed in the Andes and made a very fast ascent of the Eiger. He learned that he had permission for Hidden Peak during the Lhotse expedition. The timing was tight, for it was unlikely that they would have finished on Lhotse – successfully or otherwise – before mid-May, the start of the climbing season in the Karakoram. Nevertheless, he resolved to go and, as soon as he got back to the Tyrol, plunged into preparations for the expedition. This introduced another conflict between his relationship with Uschi and his driving urge to climb. She could see only an endless series of expeditions, with the period between devoted to preparations for the next one, to lecture tours, to a constant preoccupation in which their life together would be forever subordinate. Messner could see signs of trouble, but the need to go to Hidden Peak was all-consuming; he could not give it up and Uschi would never have asked him to, knowing all too well that this in itself would forever have put a shadow over their relationship.

So a few hectic weeks after getting back to Europe, Messner was back in the Himalaya, this time in Skardu. He and Peter Habeler had a mere twelve porters to carry in the expedition gear, and reached their Base Camp below Hidden Peak near the end of July. They spent a fortnight reconnoitring the approach to their chosen route and then, on the 8th August, set out in a dramatic dash for their objective, bivouacking at the foot of the North-West Face and then, on the following day, they climbed the 1200-metre ice and rock wall. It was as steep and committing as the North Face of the Matterhorn, with all the problems of altitude thrown in. To reduce weight and commit themselves to fast movement, they had decided to leave the rope behind which meant, in effect, that each was climbing solo; a mistake would mean almost certain death. Even so, the psychological reassurance that each could give the other was tremendously important. This is what Messner had lacked in that first solo attempt on Nanga Parbat.

Hidden Peak (8068 metres). Messner and Habeler climbed the North-West Face. It was the first time a mountain over 8000 metres had been attempted by a two-man expedition.

The Diamir Face of Nanga Parbat. The fact Messner had climbed down it in the desperate circumstances of 1970 did not lessen the challenge. This would be his third attempt at an ascent.

They climbed through the day, steep ice, rocks piled loosely upon each other, with the uncomfortable knowledge in the backs of their minds that they also had to get back down. Calves ached with the constant strain of being on the front points of their crampons; their lungs ached with the fatigue of their exertion as they thrust slowly upwards from a height of 5900 metres to 7100. And then, at last, they were above the face in a great snow basin on the upper part of Hidden Peak. The summit ridge, another thousand metres high, stretched invitingly, less steeply above. They camped in their tiny two-man tent and next day set out for the summit. Never had a mountain of this height been climbed with such élan, and complete commitment.

But Messner was to pay a high price for his single-minded devotion to the mountains. In 1977 Uschi left him. He had never loved anyone in the way he loved Uschi and, for that matter, he has found no-one since who could fill her place in his emotions. On returning to Nanga Parbat later the same year, once again hoping to make the solo ascent, he did not even reach the foot of the mountain – so great was his sense of desolate loneliness.

But there were other challenges. No-one had ever reached the summit of Everest without oxygen, though people had got very close. In 1924, Colonel Norton had reached a height of about 8570 metres on the north side of Everest and then, in 1933, Wyn Harris, Wager and Smythe reached the same height. The difficulty of the ground, as much as the lack of oxygen, finally forced them to retreat. The Chinese, on their ascent from the north in 1975, made only partial use of oxygen, carrying a couple of bottles and passing one round whenever they rested, so that everyone could have a whiff. But nobody reached the top without using it at all.

There were many unanswered questions. Was the human frame capable of working at 8000 metres without the help of an extra oxygen supply? It was certainly very close to, if not above that critical height when there just is not sufficient oxygen in the atmosphere to sustain life. And what about the threat of brain damage? For Messner, however, the challenge was immensely appealing; it fitted into his philosophy of reducing all technical aids that intrude between the climber and the actual experience to the very minimum. It was also a unique dramatic statement. He described his attempt as being an attempt on Everest by fair means, implying that everyone else who had climbed the mountain had, in some way, been cheating.

But it is not easy to get permission to climb Everest. The mountain was booked for years ahead. An Austrian expedition, led by Messner's friend Wolfgang Nairz, was going there in the spring of 1978, and he agreed to Messner and Habeler joining the expedition, almost as a self-contained mini-expedition within his own. In return, Messner was able to raise funds which would not have been available otherwise.

They worked well together as a team on the climb, with Messner and Habeler helping to make the route up through the Icefall, the Western Cwm and up onto the Lhotse Face. They abandoned their first summit bid without oxygen, Habeler because of a stomach upset and Messner defeated by a storm. At this point Habeler had momentary second thoughts and tried to join an oxygen-using team for his second bid, but the rest of the party's arrangements had already been made and there was, anyway, a level of resentment among the others, since part of the deal had been that the oxygenless pair should have first go for the summit. Habeler's resolution returned and on the 8th May he and Messner reached the top of Everest without oxygen.

It was an extraordinary achievement and yet Messner felt a sense of anticlimax; he was already thinking about going back to Nanga Parbat: 'When we were back in Base Camp again and I didn't feel any joy in our success, but rather an inner emptiness, I filled this emptiness with the conception of this eight-thousander solo ideal.'

Peter Habeler, Messner's partner on Hidden Peak and Everest.

He had already applied again for permission for Nanga Parbat and he learned he had got it whilst on Everest. He returned to the Tyrol to spend a hectic month writing his account of his Everest climb, giving interviews and arranging the new trip. One advantage of making a solo attempt is that it requires delightfully little organisation. At the end of June the expedition set out. It consisted of Messner and Ursula Grether, a medical student in her final year who had trekked on her own to the Everest Base Camp where she had met Messner. She was to be companion and doctor on the expedition.

In Rawalpindi they acquired a liaison officer, Major Mohammed Tahir, bought some local food and set out for the mountain. The challenge awaiting Messner was probably greater, and certainly very much more committing, than the one he had faced on Everest. He had made two attempts already and had failed because he had not been ready psychologically for so great a commitment. This time, perhaps, he had managed the right mix. His ascent of Everest must have given him still greater confidence in his own ability to keep going. With Ursula's companionship as far as Base Camp, he would not know the debilitating loneliness that he had experienced on both his previous attempts, and he had come to terms with the break-up of his marriage, writing: 'I still suffer from depression every now and then, but it does me good to think about her. I certainly don't want to forget her.'

The approach to the mountain was delightfully relaxed; it was more like a trekking holiday than an expedition, with the little team of three becoming absorbed into the atmosphere of the society around them. Quickly they formed a close and easy friendship with their liaison officer; each took turns at cooking and the other minor chores as they walked through the foothills, and at the foot of the Diamir Glacier, where Messner had now been on three separate occasions, they set up their tiny camp and looked up at the face. The fact that he had climbed down it in 1970 did not lessen the challenge, the quality of the unknown. It is the concept of being totally alone on that huge mountain, the obvious risk of falling into a hidden crevasse or bergschrund, the less obvious one of facing the appalling upward struggle of high-altitude climbing without encouragement, without the sustaining presence of another.

They had been at Base Camp for ten days before Messner felt ready for his attempt. He had the residual acclimatisation and fitness left over from his ascent of Everest as well as the ten day approach march, going up and down between two and four thousand metres. Yet, even as he packed his rucksack that afternoon, there was a nagging doubt at the back of his mind. That night it was worse; thoughts and images galloped through his mind in that hazy, frightening realm that lies between wakefulness and uneasy sleep:

> In my torment I sit up. Suddenly the vision of a body falling down the mountainside flashes before me. It comes straight at me. I duck out of its way. Fear engulfs my whole body. As it falls, this whirling body almost touches me, and I recognise its face as my own. My stomach turns over. I think I am going to be sick. It no longer makes any difference if I fall or cling on, live or die. I must have uttered a cry for Ursula wakes.

He did not set out the following morning. Instead, he and Ursula climbed a small peak above their camp and through this he gained the self-confidence he needed, together with a feeling of being in harmony with the face that was his objective and the peaks and the sky surrounding him. A few days later he was ready to start. As on Hidden Peak, he was basing his plan on speed; the longer he was on the mountain, the more likely it was for the weather to break, the longer he would be exposed to objective dangers of avalanche or stone fall. He therefore carried with him the bare minimum – a lightweight tent, sleeping bag, ice axe, crampons, gas stove and a few days' food.

The lot came to fifteen kilos. This meant that he had to climb the 3500-metre face in just three or four days, whereas a conventional siege-style expedition might have taken as many weeks, or even longer.

Setting out from Base Camp on the 6th August, he walked up the easy dry glacier to the foot of the Mummery Rib; Ursula accompanied him and, that night, they camped beneath a large rock which Messner hoped would guard them from the effects of any avalanche from the face. The following morning he set out in the grey dawn, up the glacier guarding the lower part of the face, picking his way through the crevasses and round the steep sérac walls. As on his fateful descent with Günther eight years before, he felt another presence and could actually hear its voice guiding him, telling him to go left or right to find the best route. He was making good progress, heading for the hanging glacier that turned the huge ice wall that barred the centre of the face. To be safe, he had to get above it that day.

The face was still in shadow, the snow crisp and firm under foot and he was above the great ice wall. He had climbed 1600 metres in only six hours. Although still early in the day, he decided to stop where he was and trampled out a small platform immediately below a sérac wall which he hoped would protect it from avalanches. He put up his tent and flopped inside. At altitude the contrasts are almost as great as those on the moon. In the shade it is bitterly cold, but in the sun, particularly inside a tent, it is like being in an oven, so warm that the snow packed into the tent bag, hanging from the roof, steadily melted through the day providing him with precious liquid and thus conserving his fuel. He heated the water and made soup, swallowed some cold corned beef and was promptly sick. The heat, the fast height gain, exhaustion had all played their part; but in being sick he had lost precious fluid, something that he could not afford. He sipped the melt water through the day, had another brew of soup that night, and then snuggled down into his sleeping bag for his first night alone on the Diamir Face. So far everything was under control, progress as planned.

And then came the morning of the huge avalanche. Much later he learned that this had been caused by an earthquake whose epicentre was in the knee-bend of the river Indus in its serpentine course through the mountains. All he knew was that the route he had followed the previous day had been swept away, that if he had started just one day later, he would have been at the bottom of the face, in the direct path of the torrent of ice and snow. The size of the catastrophe emphasised his own lonely vulnerability. But it never occurred to him to start trying to find an alternative way back; his whole being was focused on the summit.

He packed his gear, neatly folded the tent and set out once again in the bitter cold of the early morning, heading for the next barrier – a broken wall of rock and ice stretching down from the crest of the ridge. He was going more slowly than on the previous day, each step taking a separate effort of will. There was no question of racing the sun, and once this crept over the shoulder the bitter cold changed to blazing heat and the snow soon turned into a treacherous morass. And still he kept going, getting ever closer to the great trapezoid of rock that marked the summit block. He stopped just beneath it. He was now at a height of around 7500 metres, another thousand metres gained, another long afternoon to savour his isolation. Intermittently he was again aware of another presence, this time a girl; tantalising, he could almost glimpse her at the extreme edge of vision. They talked. She reassured him that the weather would hold, that he would reach the summit the following day. And through the afternoon the clouds, strange mountains of cumulus, shifted and changed in shape and tone as the sun dropped down over the western horizon. That night, in the lee of the long day, Messner felt at peace with himself, but the following morning was very different:

> This sudden confrontation with such utter loneliness immediately envelops me in a deep depression. In the months after my break-up with Uschi it was often like this when I woke up. The sudden pressure which threatens to dash me to pieces, a well of despair bubbling up from deep sources and taking possession of my whole being. It is so strong I have to cry.

But action has its own quality of reassurance. He peered out of the tent to see what the reality of day would bring:

> The play of the dark clouds below me both worry and fascinate me. Now and then, between the surging clouds, a mountain top emerges. It is like being witness to the Creation. Like seeing everything from the outside. It doesn't occur to me to be surprised at the threatening bad weather. It is a strange sensation. *'Tike'* [All right] I say; just that, a word that slips into my mind unbidden. I could blow soap bubbles and suspend the tent on them. For a tiny moment something warm passes through my dog-tired body.

Now within striking distance of the top, he could hope to get there and back in the day; indeed, he had to, for he could no longer carry a fifteen-kilo load on his back; could not afford to spend any more nights at that altitude and continue to toil upwards. He therefore left his tent, sleeping bag and food and just carrying his ice axe and camera started out for the top.

He was now well above the altitude where snow thaws and then freezes. Even in the early morning cold, it was a deep slough in which he wallowed up to his thighs. After three hours' struggle, he had made hardly any progress – the day and his own strength were racing away. There seemed only one chance, to take the steep rocks leading direct to the summit, even though this meant infinitely greater insecurity. He teetered around narrow ledges, no wider than a window sill; no chance of hard rock climbing here, at this altitude, in clumsy double boots with crampons.

Messner resting at about 7800 metres on his final day, looking down on the tent of his top camp.

Reinhold Messner on the summit of Nanga Parbat.
A screw set into his ice axe shaft turned it into a tripod for delayed action photography.

The act of balancing on crampon points was bad enough. Snow-filled gullies alternated with rocky steps; his rests became more frequent as his limbs grew more and more leaden. There is no physical exhilaration in climbing at altitude; it is will-power alone that can keep you going, make each leg move forward with such painful slowness that the goal never seems to come any closer. He could hear his lungs roar, his heartbeat hammering at a furious rate and still he kept plodding on.

It was four o'clock when, at last, he reached the top. Suddenly, the snow dropped away on every side; the view was the same as he had seen eight years before and yet so different, for that ascent had been in the freshness of his experience, his first Himalayan peak and his brother had been with him to share that momentary euphoria. Messner writes:

> I wander around in a circle, repeatedly looking at the view, as if I can hardly believe I am really here. There is no great outrush of emotion such as I experienced on Everest; I am quite calm, calmer than I have ever been on any eight-thousander. I often thought about that later, and wondered why these swelling emotions which on Everest wracked me with sobs and tears, should have been absent on Nanga Parbat. I have come to the conclusion that being alone, as I was on top of Nanga, I could not have borne such a strong surge of feeling. I would have been unable to leave. Our bodies know more than we understand with our minds.

He spent an hour on the summit, and took a series of pictures with his camera mounted on a screw head specially fitted to his ice axe. Using the timer and an ultra-wide-angle lens, he could include himself in the picture. A great mass of cloud covered the Karakoram; ominous tendrils chased across the sky, reaching out towards Nanga Parbat, yet Messner felt very little anxiety about his chances of getting back down by a different route from his ascent in the face of the threatened storm. No doubt his reactions were deadened by fatigue and lack of oxygen but, more important, so at one with the mountain did he feel that the very strength of this feeling gave a calm confidence.

But it was time to descend. He picked a different route down and was able to make relatively fast, easy progress back to the lonely tent at the foot of the summit pyramid. That night he could sense the gathering storm. There was not yet any wind, but he could almost feel the cloud pressing in on the tent and then, next morning, with a banshee wail came the wind and the snow. There was no question of moving now, for he could never have found his way down in the driving snow. But the storm might last a couple of days, a week, or even longer. If he conserved his fuel and food he could last for five days, and so he settled down in his sleeping bag to try to wait it out. But it wasn't just a question of supplies, for at that altitude the body is slowly deteriorating. Already badly dehydrated, he was also exhausted and knew that he could only get worse, that even rest would do him little good. He was becoming clumsy in his movements, upset the stove a couple of times and burnt his sleeping bag. There was plenty of time in which to ponder his predicament, to try to work out the best line of descent.

All that day he was pinned down in the tent, but the following morning the cloud around him cleared, although the sky was still overcast with a high scum of grey. He realised that he had to get down that day and so abandoned tent, sleeping bag and food, knowing that if he failed to escape from the face before dark he would have little chance of survival. He set out, heading down the long snow slopes towards the ice runnel running down the centre of the face between the Mummery Rib and the great ice wall – his only hope of descent, for the rocks on the rib were plastered with a thin layer of ice. But it was also the natural avalanche line. Messner had no choice; he just had to hope for the best. He slipped on the way down, knew that once he fell he would be out of control and so raced down the slope in a series of giant strides, crampons biting into the ice as he tried to regain his balance and get back control. Lungs heaving, trembling with shock, he managed to do it. And so it went on through the day, the whole time at the edge between extinction and survival, of accepting exhaustion and forcing himself on, each step on the hard ice needing all his concentration as he teetered down, seeming to go little faster than he had on the way up.

And then he was down; almost without realising it, the angle had eased. He was on the dry glacier at the foot of the face and just had to put one foot in front of the other. Ursula came out to meet him. The climb was over.

> Somehow I have overstepped my limitations; my strength, the loneliness. A year ago feeling I was alone was my weakness. I am not saying that now I have got over it, no, I was only totally alone for a few days. But it was beautiful. I don't know everything about loneliness yet – that too, is reassuring.

The following year Messner climbed K2, this time as part of an expedition and then, in 1980, he climbed Everest solo, once again without oxygen, from the Chinese side. The pattern, in many ways, was very similar to that of Nanga Parbat. A girlfriend, this time Nena Ritchie, from Canada, accompanied him to Base Camp and, like Ursula in '78, went with him to his advanced camp. Once again he took the mountain by storm, climbing it in just three days by the North Ridge, the route attempted by the British before the war and first climbed by the Chinese in 1960. It was an amazing feat. To put it into perspective, there have been twenty-five successful expeditions to Everest since 1953, none of them with less than thirty

An exhausted Messner has an injection to aid circulation back at Base Camp.

Everest from the north, the route attempted by the British before the war. Messner climbed it solo without oxygen in three days.

climbers and Sherpas, none of them without oxygen and not one of these expeditions has taken less than a month to climb the mountain.

There is still infinite ground for climbers to stretch themselves. So far, Alpine-style attempts have achieved success only on comparatively straightforward routes where the climbers have been able to move quickly. Steep and technically-difficult walls, like the South Face of Lhotse, the western aspect of K2, have remained inviolate. But this is only a matter of time, and as climbers refine their techniques, discover just how much the human body and spirit can achieve, these will also yield.

The crossing of Antarctica

The Antarctic continent is an icy desert – the coldest, most arid place on earth. There is no grass, no vegetation except a little lichen on the rocks by the coast in summer. Inland, only the highest mountain peaks emerge from the ice and snow. The ice cap is over 4500 metres thick in some areas. The penguins and seals, the only wild life on the continent, are dependent on the sea for their sustenance. There have been no human inhabitants and, even today, the shifting population of scientists with their support staffs are totally reliant on the outside world for supplies. Yet the Antarctic can get a hold on people as tenaciously as any mountains, ocean or desert. Men who have worked in the Antarctic return again and again and, even after settling down in their own home countries with wives and families, they still yearn for that harsh, empty but incredibly beautiful land.

I am not sure whether a certain kind of personality is attracted to the Antarctic or if life in polar regions moulds the man, but a very definite type of person seems to emerge. You need a resolute, almost plodding sense of endurance to survive. Everything takes a long time. An expedition is going to take a year, perhaps longer, to complete; it is not a question of surmounting a spectacular mountain peak, but rather one of sheer survival, of just keeping alive, of plodding over endless icy wastes, carrying out a task of survey, meteorology or some other scientific aim. It may entail wintering together in one tiny hut. And so the successful polar man is a great survivor with a lot of self-control; often quiet and self-contained, immensely tenacious, a steady plodder, he is not the athletic star with whom many mountaineers could be compared.

Vivian Fuchs, who was to lead the Commonwealth Trans-Antarctic expedition, summed up the difference saying: 'I see mountaineering like a hundred yards race, where it is a quick, tremendous exertion of effort that counts; whereas the Antarctic thing I see as a cross-country race. You will always win against nature if you hold your position and then, at the right moment, press through.'

In many ways Vivian Fuchs epitomises the polar explorer. Of medium build and height, he has a compact strength, both of physique and personality. He is a singularly self-contained man who rarely shows emotion and projects an aura of complete self-control. Like Thor Heyerdahl, he sees himself not so much as an adventurer, but as a scientist whose insatiable curiosity might take him into areas of risk, but the risk of adventure is in no way an end in itself. Born in 1908, Vivian Fuchs had a classic, middle-class upbringing, going to Brighton College and then St. John's, Cambridge. At school he was reasonably good at games and fairly bright, without being brilliant, academically. From an early age he had a passion for natural history, collecting butterflies, beetles, flowers, odd-shaped pieces of wood. He was also practical and built his own radio set in the very early days of radio. As an only child, he had a close, warm relationship with his parents and, as a result, grew and developed in a very secure environment.

At Cambridge Fuchs studied geology and went on his first expedition, to Arctic Greenland. This did not lead to an instant devotion to polar regions for his next opportunity arose in equatorial Africa, with another Cambridge expedition to the African lakes. At the end of this trip there were still some unanswered questions and so other opportunities arose and he spent the period before the Second World War taking part in and leading a series of geological expeditions in Africa, collecting a PhD on the way. He would probably have become an African expert, was already negotiating for a job with the Colonial Government of the Sudan, but the war changed all that. Commissioned, he was sent to Staff College where his administrative abilities were both noticed and undoubtedly developed. With the end of the war coincidence, as so often happens, was to lead him into the career for which he was so singularly qualified.

Antarctica was still a huge, empty continent of unknown potential. The great powers and the countries closest to it had already put in their claims and Britain, even during the war, had established a few scientific outposts on the islands off Graham Land, the peninsula that juts from out of the Antarctic continent, reaching up towards the southern tip of South America. After the war the British immediately planned to widen their programme and advertised for personnel. Vivian Fuchs was one of the men who applied for a position with the Falkland Islands Dependencies Survey and, because of his qualifications gained in geological surveying in Africa and his administrative experience in the Army, was offered the post of Director in the field of all the British bases then in Antarctica. It was decidedly not a desk job and during the next three years Fuchs journeyed many thousands of miles with dog teams, learning how to travel and live in Antarctica.

It was whilst on a survey trip that Fuchs first thought of making the trans-Antarctic crossing. He told me:

> I remember the moment well. It was in a tent and we were about four or five hundred miles out from Stonington and couldn't go any further because we were running out of food and had all that way to go back. We'd been stuck there for four days by a blizzard. We could see some mountains further on and wanted to know what their geology was. I said that there must be even more peaks beyond, but we did not know at that time what happened inside the continent. There had been very little aerial survey at that stage. I said to Adie, 'The only way to do this is to make a trip all the way across the continent and then we shall know, shan't we.' I sat down then and there, with a stub of pencil and worked out that it should be a joint effort of all the Commonwealth nations with claims in the Antarctic and that it would cost a quarter of a million. In the event, it cost three quarters.

This was in 1948, but the idea lay dormant for a little longer. Fuchs was advised to wait – something he was very good at doing; and as Director of the Falkland Islands Dependencies Survey Scientific Bureau back in Britain, he remained in an excellent position to seize the right opportunity for advancing his plan.

It was not a new idea. In 1914 Ernest Shackleton had sailed into the Weddell Sea in *Endurance*, planning to winter on the coast before making his attempt to cross the continent the following summer. It was an almost unbelievably bold project, considering they were totally dependent on their dog teams and their own strength, that they would have to establish their own supply depots on the way to the Pole before setting out on their journey, and that they would have no form of radio communication with the outside world or their support party, coming in from the other side to lay depots up the Beardmore Glacier. Caught in the ice through the winter of 1914,

Endurance drifted further and further in towards the centre of the Weddell Sea and was finally crushed. They were in a desperate predicament, hundreds of miles over ice and ocean from the nearest settlement, with very little chance of anyone being able to come and look for them, since the First World War was now well under way. But for Ernest Shackleton's extraordinary powers of leadership, the twenty-seven

The crossing of Antarctica

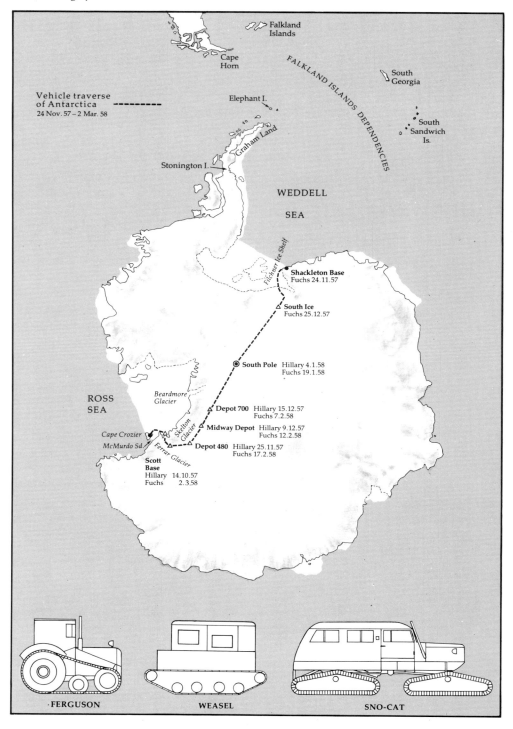

men under his command would almost certainly have died. They set out to save themselves, hauling two of the ship's boats over the ice of the Weddell Sea, through the bitter cold of the winter, till the summer thaws stopped their progress. Then they drifted on an ever-decreasing ice floe, through the long summer, towards the Atlantic Ocean until, at last, they could push the boats into open waters and row towards the dubious haven of Elephant Island, a bleak and rocky bump, buffeted by Atlantic storms. Had they stayed there they would have starved to death and so Shackleton, with five seamen, sailed one of the boats to the island of South Georgia, 700 miles away over some of the stormiest seas in the world. It took them sixteen days, half-starved, their clothes soaked and rotten, the boat covered in ice and filled with water for most of the time. And still it wasn't over. Having landed on the uninhabited side of the island, they had to cross its glaciers and mountainous terrain without maps, food or any kind of climbing equipment to reach the whaling station of Stromness. Shackleton then sailed back with the rescue party to pick up the remainder of his crew. It was an extraordinary achievement, something that the modern polar explorer, with his radios, air support, modern food and equipment, would never be called upon to perform.

Vivian Fuchs' plan was almost identical to that of Shackleton. He, also, wanted to sail into the Weddell Sea, establish a wintering base on its shore and then make his dash for the Pole with a support party to lay down depots at the other side. The plan was the same; the available equipment was vastly different. He would have a powerful, almost unsinkable ice-breaker to penetrate the Weddell Sea, aircraft to spy out a route and stock his depots, motor-driven, specially designed tractors to make the crossing. It could be argued that Shackleton's plan, with the knowledge and equipment available at that time, was a forlorn hope, but it also held the very essence of adventure, a challenge against vast odds and unknown dangers, while that of Fuchs had an element of over-kill; but then, Vivian Fuchs was not interested in adventure for its own sake. He was undoubtedly an adventurous man. He would not have chosen the course of life he had adopted had he been anything else, but he was essentially a scientist.

'I have to have a reason for everything I do,' he told me.

His main aim in making the crossing of Antarctica was to increase man's knowledge of that continent; the adventurous side of the concept, which was something he most certainly enjoyed, was still secondary to the scientific.

In 1954 Vivian Fuchs had his chance. The International Geophysical Year was going to be from 1957 to 1958, when the governments of the world would be concentrating on scientific exploration and research, and would be amenable to a project which would be extremely expensive but also prestigious. Fuchs was not the only Briton who dreamed of making a trans-Antarctic crossing. Duncan Carse, the childhood hero of my generation in the guise of 'Dick Barton – Special Agent' (in a radio series of the late 'forties and early 'fifties), had grown tired of fantasy adventure and had joined the Falkland Islands Dependencies Survey. Now he produced a plan for an Antarctic crossing which he submitted to the Polar Committee. Vivian Fuchs produced his, and from the position he held and with the backing he had from the establishment it was almost inevitable that his would be accepted. He then succeeded in gaining the enthusiastic support of Winston Churchill, presented his plans to the Conference of Commonwealth Prime Ministers in 1954, and the expedition was fully under way.

Fuchs needed a support team to come in towards the Pole from the other side and, since this was in New Zealand's sphere of influence, a New Zealand party was the obvious choice. He had already met Sir Edmund Hillary and, as New Zealand's most eminent adventurer, Hillary seemed best qualified for leader, even though he had no polar experience. The two men provided an interesting contrast, which was to cause a great deal of trouble as the expedition unfolded. Fuchs was primarily the scientist and brilliant bureaucrat, with the plodding patience and determination that so many polar explorers have developed; Hillary, on the other hand, regarded the South Pole as a mountain to be climbed for its own adventurous sake. He was extrovert where Fuchs was self-contained; Hillary spoke his mind, whereas Fuchs carefully chose his words. But in those early days of preparation they each got on with their own sides of the huge and complex job of organisation without coming over much into contact or conflict.

In November 1955, the advance party of the expedition set sail in the ice-breaker *Theron*, with both Fuchs and Hillary on board. They shared a cabin, but this did not bring the two men any closer together, perhaps even accentuated an awareness of their differences in temperament and motive. Hillary remembered:

> I was treated with an unswerving friendliness but it was made very clear that I was only an observer and I was never permitted to attend the regular meetings of his executive committee (although both of my expedition members were invited to these meetings on various occasions). I suppose I shouldn't have resented this, but I did. I felt an outsider, not to be trusted with expedition responsibilities, and this was probably an uncomfortable foundation on which to build our association over the next couple of years.

The eight-man advance party lost vital stores in a storm but survived the Antarctic winter of 1956 in their Sno-cat crate.

Most of the voyage was very relaxed, since they were little more than passengers, their only duties being to take turns in cleaning out the dogs. They played various deck games to while away the hours and maintain some level of fitness. In these

games Fuchs showed another side of his character; although fifty years old and the oldest man in the party, he was furiously competitive, would always do more skipping or press-ups than anyone else on board, was determined to win every rough game they played and was the champion arm wrestler of the voyage. He had to be leader in every respect, commanding his team by physical as well as intellectual dominance.

The object of the voyage was to establish an advance party on the permanent ice shelf of the Weddell Sea, to prepare for the main party which would set out the following year. Only one other boat had ventured into the Weddell Sea since *Endurance* had been trapped forty years before. Even with the power of modern engines and the help of their Auster aircraft, it was all *Theron* could do to penetrate the piled floes and reach the Filchner Ice Shelf. They were late in reaching their destination, barely had time to unload all the supplies onto the ice floe abutting the main ice shelf, before setting sail in a rush to avoid being trapped as *Endurance* had been.

The eight members of the advance party, under the leadership of Ken Blaiklock, an experienced Antarctic hand, had the task of ferrying all the supplies from the floe edge to the relative safety of the permanent ice. They had the advantage of tractors and Sno-cats, but even these were of little use against the power of the elements. A violent storm blew up shortly after the departure of *Theron*, broke up the sea ice on which most of the stores were still stacked and the lot were swept out to sea.

The advance party's hut was not yet built and they were still living in tents. The Antarctic winter was close at hand. Blaiklock kept his nerve, calmly suggesting that they return to the big crate which had contained their Sno-cat, and which they were now using as a living shelter, to have a cup of tea and take stock. It was a very different situation from the one that had faced Shackleton some forty years before, for the nearest base – an Argentinian one – was only fifty miles away down the coast. Even though they had lost most of the fuel for their tractors, they had plenty of fresh dog teams and could undoubtedly have reached safety. But Blaiklock quickly dismissed this option. He had had the foresight to bring up to their camp a carefully balanced selection of stores which were just enough to last out the winter. True, there was no fuel for heating but there was just enough for cooking. He was determined to get the hut built and Shackleton Base established before the return of the main party.

The discomfort and the feeling of isolation experienced by Blaiklock's party was no less acute because it was self-chosen. Several of them, particularly the ones without Antarctic experience, had difficulty in adjusting to their circumstances. Hannes la Grange, a South African meteorologist, suffered particular stress, spending long hours by the floe edge gazing out into the pack ice for a relief ship that, logically, he should have known would not be arriving until after the winter. He would shout out, 'A ship! A ship!' at the sight of a distant iceberg, only to be told by the others to shut up and not to be so bloody stupid! Then he took to walking out of earshot, so that he could shout out in the cold, empty spaces, 'A ship! A ship!' without irritating his companions.

Eventually he and the other members of the advance party overcame their troubles and settled down in their bleak environment. In talking to polar people, I gather Blaiklock ran a no-nonsense set-up, where individuals were encouraged to keep a stiff upper lip, keep their emotions to themselves and sort out their own troubles. Perhaps this was the only way for a small group to survive, living on top of each other in fair discomfort over a long period of time.

It took them most of the winter to build the hut. It was prefabricated into hundreds of pieces that bolted together. Unfortunately, however, laid out on the uneven surface of the ice with the snow constantly drifting in, few of the bolt holes could be lined up together. As a result, assembling the hut was a painfully slow process which occupied the entire winter, with the men working in temperatures which went down to −50°C and having constantly to dig out the wind-driven snows. They had no fuel for heat, slept in their tents and used the Sno-cat crate, which was also unheated, as a kitchen and living-room.

And yet, at the end of the winter, when the main party returned in the ice-breaker *Magga Dan*, their spirits were high, for the hut was built, their initial fears overcome, the small group welded into a tight team. Fuchs, with George Lowe, an easy-going New Zealander who had been a member of the 1953 Everest expedition and was now official photographer for the venture, flew into Shackleton Base in advance of the boat to bring in their mail and a few luxury items. The advance team had made a special feast for their visitors, enormous cakes, home-made biscuits and sugared dough cakes, all cooked on an oil drum stove. *Magga Dan* arrived the following day and the stores were unloaded in the next few weeks. At the same time, on the other side of the continent, Ed Hillary was establishing Scott Base on the Ross Sea, whence he was going to lay out his line of depots for the traversing party.

The pattern of polar exploration is so very much more deliberate than that of mountaineering. You arrive one summer, build a base or camp, in which to survive the winter and be poised at the beginning of the following summer to carry out an adventure or do scientific work. Antarctic bases very quickly resemble one another, each with a big living hut containing workshops and laboratories, and a work shed for the vehicles nearby. The Antarctic explorer has to be a practical man, able to set his hand to building, vehicle maintenance, sewing and taking his turn at mass catering, in this instance for sixteen hungry men. There is also a tradition of structured work and routine, established partly by the scientific disciplines that have always dominated polar adventure and partly by the fact that everyone taking part in the Falkland Islands Dependencies Survey had been doing it as a job of work, admittedly a highly vocational one, but nonetheless one for which they were being paid.

This was a difference in approach that George Lowe noticed particularly. Used to the free and easy ways of a mountaineering expedition, he began to see the difference that winter in Shackleton Base. They had a record player in the communal living-room, but the rule was that this could only be played on Saturday nights and Sundays, the argument being that it would disturb people who were working and that not necessarily everyone would want to have music – or like the music that had been chosen. It was a logical rule, but it was also a fact that Fuchs was not particularly musical, considering the music as an 'infernal din', and that the decision had been reached by Fuchs without any kind of consultation with the others. This was undoubtedly his style of leadership. A self-contained man, who knew exactly what he wanted, he governed every feature of the expedition with a firm hand. It had to be done his way. He did not encourage any kind of discussion, even casual, of expedition matters. George Lowe described one incident that brought this out.

One day, a group of three or four were listening with interest while Geoff Pratt held forth on the subject of the gloves he wore. 'These things are no bloody good,' said Geoffrey. 'I wouldn't mind betting that I could design a far more efficient glove for conditions like ours.'

Bunny glanced up sharply from his book, took off his glasses, laid them on the open pages, and spoke. 'When you know a good deal more about Antarctic conditions,' he said quietly, 'you'll also know more about gloves. These gloves have been designed after years of experience – and I think you'll find they will do the job they were intended for.'

The ice-breaker Magga Dan *unloading at a dock cut for her in the sea ice. Shackleton Base can be seen on the plateau in the middle distance.*

On the other side of the continent, Ed Hillary had no such inhibitions. He knew very little about the Antarctic, had very few preconceived notions and therefore had looked at each piece of equipment with fresh eyes. He foresaw the problems that the prefabricated huts could present and completely redesigned the ones he was going to use, having them made in very much larger sections that could be more easily bolted together. He was also flexible on the question of clothing, bringing to bear the experience he had gained in the Himalaya. Fuchs distrusted down gear, feeling that the down would get wet, then freeze and lose all its insulating properties. Hillary, on the other hand, went for down suits and jackets, since they had worked so well on Everest.

Although Fuchs' rule was autocratic, he had the personality to gain acceptance. The morale of the group was high because they felt that the venture was worthwhile and that, under Fuchs' command, they had a very good chance of success. He was totally competent, consistent and quietly determined; also, equally important, his team were accustomed to this kind of discipline and were, in Lowe's view, very much more amenable than a group of mountaineers would have been.

The period before the arrival of winter had been spent in organising both the Shackleton Base and establishing their forward depot, to be known as South Ice; it was on the Antarctic plateau, about 300 miles south of Shackleton and 500 miles from the Pole. This was done entirely by air, using the single-engined Otter, to make both the initial reconnaissance and then to ferry in the parts of the prefabricated hut. Three members of the team, led by Ken Blaiklock, whose appetite for lonely outposts was in no way diminished by his experience of the previous year, were to stay there through the winter, to carry out a scientific programme.

Winter and summer in Antarctica are merely relative terms. Summer means continuous glaring light, cold, snow and wind. Winter is continuous, unrelenting dark, even greater cold, with yet more winds and snow. Fuchs and his party sat out the winter, filling their time with scientific research and the preparations for their long journey next year. The vehicles were overhauled, modified and improved in a large engine shed which was even heated. The huts, partly buried in drifting snow, had an ugly, impermanent look, as if they did not belong to this pure, bleak, empty land. Their occupants were able to maintain an improbable contact with the outside world, having a radio that was sufficiently powerful to reach England, with an arrangement to link in with the telephone network. This meant that they could call anyone in Britain for a modest ten shillings and six pence a minute. It was a strange mixture of the traditional and the new – on the one hand the huge, empty continent, a hut which was very similar in design to the ones built by Captain Scott or Shackleton at the beginning of the century, a diet that was very similar to the one that the early explorers had had, even a rhythm of life that was not so very different, and yet combined with this were the aircraft, the big, powerful Sno-cats, wireless communication that could reach anywhere in the world and the knowledge that there were other, similar bases littered over the continent, even at the Pole itself.

The sun nudged over the northern horizon towards the end of August, a sign that they would soon have to start moving, but although it crept higher each day, there were few other signs of a let-up in the winter. The temperature dropped to −50°C and there were winds of up to sixty-three miles per hour. Fuchs had prepared an ambitious programme of reconnaissance, aerial exploration and survey work in the area before the departure of the main party on the traverse, but this very soon had to be modified. Most important was the reconnaissance on the ground of the terrain between Shackleton and South Ice.

It was the 8th October before Fuchs, with deputy leader David Stratton and his two engineers, David Pratt and Roy Homard, set out with four vehicles to make the reconnaissance. They had three types of vehicle on the expedition, the largest and most sophisticated of them, the Sno-cat, rode on four-tracked pontoons; then there was the Weasel, an oblong box on two tracks, and finally some modified tractors. One of the Weasels, driven by Roy Homard, broke down within eight miles of Shackleton Base and, although they managed a temporary repair, there was no question of taking the vehicle all the way. Roy Homard drove it back to Base, leaving the others to press on.

It was discouraging, nerve-wracking work as they edged their way over the crevassed ice shelf. Walking across a crevassed region is bad enough, but cooped in the cabin of a vehicle it must have been much worse, with the ever-present thought of hurtling downwards into the black pit of a crevasse, trapped in the cockpit. Roped together, it needed precise driving to ensure that there was enough slack cable to allow the front vehicle to surge forward if it started to go into a hidden chasm (and thus, perhaps, manage to bridge it), and yet not so much slack that it could fall into the crevasse and become irretrievably jammed or perhaps even break the rope. The cabins of the vehicles were unheated, for Fuchs believed that the interior should be a similar temperature to the outside to avoid the driver becoming cocooned from the environment, but it meant being perpetually cold, encumbered in furs or down clothing at all times. Some days they made little more than two or three miles' progress, spending most of the time hauling vehicles out of crevasses or back-tracking to find a better way round a particularly bad area. Time was now slipping by. They had set out a week late anyway, and were now badly over time. It took them thirty-seven days to reach South Ice; they had lost one vehicle and were forced to abandon another temporarily.

Back at Shackleton Base, the morale of the team had reached a low ebb. In the absence of the two most experienced engineers, they were badly behind in their maintenance programme and several of the vehicles were still buried in the snow. Several members of the crossing team had never even camped on Antarctic ice before; there was a feeling of unpreparedness and even of a haunting failure, not eased by the constant barrage of queries over the radio from the world's press, asking when they were going to start, or for news of Hillary's progress on the other side of the continent.

With three modified Ferguson farm tractors and a Weasel loaned by the American polar station, Hillary's party had climbed the Skelton Glacier, the major obstacle barring their way to the polar plateau, and had established their second depot for Fuchs' polar crossing. Viewing the efforts of the two parties, there seems a dynamic energy about everything that the New Zealand support party did, while the main party seems to have had a slow, cumbersome quality about its approach and progress. The difference was noticeable from the very start. Whilst it took most of the energies of the main party just to erect their complex jigsaw of pre-assembled huts, Hillary's simplified structures left his team with the time and the energy to start their reconnaissance programme before the arrival of winter. He wasted no time in getting his dog teams out to find a way up onto the Antarctic plateau. First they looked at the Ferrar Glacier, but the lower part was too badly broken up by crevasses and ice towers, so they turned their attention to the Skelton Glacier and, in spite of deep snow, managed to climb it before winter. They established a depot at the top of it which was stocked by air. Hillary was still not content, however. He wanted to try out his farm tractors and decided to make a journey to Cape Crozier, repeating the incredible winter journey made by Wilson and described by Apsley Cherry-Garrard on Scott's expedition in 1910.

A Weasel and the caboose on runners in which Hillary's team could sleep and cook.

They had set out in the middle of winter to investigate the nesting habits of the emperor penguin. In Cherry-Garrard's words, 'And so we started just after mid-winter on the weirdest birdsnesting expedition that has ever been or ever will be.' For nineteen days three of them had hauled a heavily-laden sledge through the bitter cold and dark of the Antarctic winter. They had then built a tiny stone hut at Cape Crozier as a shelter while they observed the penguins. I remember reading the account while I was on an expedition to Nuptse, the third peak of Everest. Whenever I thought the climbing was getting at all rough, all I had to do was to read Cherry-Garrard's description to know that our Himalayan expedition was a holiday compared to what they had gone through.

Hillary's experience was also very much easier. Having set out on the 19th March with two tractors, they took three days to cover the distance that had taken Wilson and his party nineteen. It did give them an insight, however, into some of the drawbacks of the tractors and produced ideas for modifications to improve both their performance and comfort. As a result of their experience, Hillary built a canvas shelter for the driver of each tractor and a caravan or caboose on runners, so that the team could use it for cooking and sleeping in during their journey the following year. As on the other side, the New Zealand team spent the winter preparing for the summer's activities and doing scientific work. Hillary, in consultation with the scientists, had prepared an extensive programme for the following year but was then amazed – indeed, outraged – when the Committee of Management back in New Zealand vetoed many of his plans as being too ambitious or risky.

> I had no particular desire to offend the committee but I was confident that the programme was well within our powers. I continued as though the exchange of messages had never occurred, made a few worthwhile modifications to the plans and reintroduced the idea of a push towards the Pole if I could get enough extra fuel at Depot 700. It was becoming clear to me that a supporting role was not my particular strength. Once we had done all that was asked of us and a good bit more – I could see no reason why we shouldn't organise a few interesting challenges for ourselves.

Hillary's approach to his venture was as a mountaineer. The summit was the South Pole and he wanted to get there. His three team members, like himself, had had no previous Antarctic experience. Pete Mulgrew was a petty officer in the New Zealand Navy and an expert on wireless communications. He was also a climber and he and Hillary formed a close friendship from the very start. Mulgrew's original role had been to remain at Base, controlling the rear link back to the outside world, but he had set his heart on the Pole from the very beginning, was irrepressibly adventurous and, anyway, Hillary needed a good wireless operator for their polar journey. The other two members of the 'Old Firm', as they called themselves, were Jim Bates, a brilliant mechanic and inventor who was also an expert skier, and Murray Ellis who was an engineering graduate with sound mechanical knowledge. Hillary was the only member of the team who knew anything about celestial navigation, and so he would have the sole responsibility for pointing them in the right direction.

One of the three modified Ferguson tractors which Ed Hillary's Scott Base support party drove to the South Pole. The canvas shelter was added to protect the driver.

Mount Erebus, Antarctica's only known active volcano was climbed by members of Shackleton's party in 1908. Hillary drove around it while trying out his transport.

Transport old and new: Hillary's dogs arrive at the foot of the Skelton Glacier to lead the route.

They set out from Scott Base on the 14th October with their one Weasel and three tractors towing the cumbersome caboose they had made and the heavily laden sledges. No-one had much confidence in the tractors, since they had not been designed for the task in hand and the modifications were of a makeshift character. Two dog teams, with Bob Miller and George Marsh, one of the two English polar experts with the expedition, were flown in to the foot of the Skelton Glacier, so that they could lead the route which they had already completed the previous year. With the constant threat of concealed crevasses, the four drivers took turns in going out in front to make the route, each trusting the ability of the others. This was in marked contrast to Fuchs' approach. He insisted on being out in front the whole time, physically leading the expedition, taking the major risk, but also taking the satisfaction of actually finding a route. Hillary's policy of sharing the lead amongst the team certainly increased the enjoyment of the individual team members and also enabled them to make better progress. In a matter of days, Hillary had reached the Antarctic plateau, ready to establish his depots and then, once free of this responsibility, make his push for the Pole. He set out across the plateau on the 12th November, just one day before Fuchs reached South Ice – still on the reconnaissance. The main party had not even left Shackleton Base, and were still not ready for their part of the expedition.

Vivian Fuchs now announced that, come what may, they would set out on the 24th November. It meant working round the clock to get all the vehicles ready in time but, on the 24th at 6.45 p.m., they were ready at last and set out with three Sno-cats, two Weasels and a converted Muskeg tractor. There were eleven men in the party and they were going to pick up the vehicles used in their recce at South Ice, also the two dog teams which had found the route up on to the plateau. It was a very much larger team than Hillary's and, of course, had further to go. The atmosphere and discipline of the party was also very different. Fuchs made the decisions. The only person with whom he consulted closely was his deputy leader, David Stratton, an Antarctic veteran from an Antarctic-experienced family background; he had been to Harrow School and concealed behind a relaxed, easy-going manner, immense determination and an extremely well-ordered mind. He did much to soften and warm Vivian Fuchs' cool, unemotional – at times apparently insensitive – approach to his fellow expedition members.

From the very start it was slow going. They were not making much better progress than had the reconnaissance. The vehicles regularly smashed into concealed crevasses or were forced to make long and painful diversions. By the 29th November, five days out from Shackleton Base, they had covered only forty miles. On that same day, Ed Hillary reached Depot 480 on the plateau; he was 480 miles into his journey, some 770 miles from the South Pole.

But now they were on the move, the morale of the Fuchs party was high. Lowe commented:

> I had always been critical of the lack of cohesion, of bad communications, of being kept in the dark about expedition plans, of the failure to give both men and vehicles at least a taste of rehearsal before the big journey began; and I tended also to be the channel through whom Bunny would receive the grievances of others in the party. As I followed the yellow tail of Bunny's Cat into the wilderness, I felt a little contrite and resolved to be more reasonable.

Other members of the team, the old polar hands, were less critical than George Lowe. Hal Lister, who shared a tent throughout the expedition with George, had already had a two-year stint on the Greenland ice cap. He was a glaciologist and accepted the discipline and structured command which prevails in polar circles. Indeed, he even found Bunny Fuchs to be positively easy-going compared with the Naval commander who had been in charge of his Greenland expedition. He had that polar mentality that accepts, even welcomes, the long monotonous grind of polar travel, the conservatism that rejects new foods, equipment or ways of doing things in favour of the well-tried ways of tradition. There were aspects of Fuchs' approach that even Lowe found he had to agree with. The question of tent-sharing was one. Rather than leave it to the individual, Fuchs posted on the notice board the list of the six tent pairings with a footnote stressing that they were final and that there would be no swapping during the journey. Lowe wrote:

> At first I thought this was a mistake but looking back I realise that Bunny was right. Over the long journey where the going was mostly a monotonous unchanging ice desert with occasional moments of fear and excitement, there had to be an attitude of hardness and an intelligent determination to quash the inevitable personal differences and be ever-aware that we simply must live cheerfully together. The philosophy took the general line, 'You volunteered, so get on with it.'

Above all, whatever reservations Lowe or others might have had about Fuchs' style of leadership, they could not help respecting both his determination and ability. Nobody ever challenged his commands. The morale of the traversing team remained high throughout.

It was a long-drawn-out marathon with its own built-in routine. There was, of course, no night and they could have travelled twenty-four hours a day, around the clock – as indeed Hillary did on quite a few occasions. Fuchs, on the other hand, settled into a steady routine, partly dictated by his own policy of staying out in front the whole time. He could only motor for as long as his own endurance would keep him going. On the whole they worked an eighteen-hour day, with six hours in each twenty-four given over to rest and sleep. At the end of a stint, Fuchs would signal the stop, the vehicles would draw up and the pyramid tents would be taken off the sledges. There was always something of a race to be the first party to erect one's tent and have a brew going. One man would have the outside berth and he would do all the outside jobs, while the one with the inside berth would disappear into the tent the moment it was erected, would accept and place the reindeer-skin mats, sleeping bags, food box and stove and would then get a brew on, trying to have it ready by the time the outside man had finished his chores of staking out the tent and preparing everything for the 'night' outside.

The evening meal was the traditional sledging ration of pemmican hooch, a huge slab of butter plastered over a biscuit and very sweet cocoa. It was monotonous, never varied but somehow in extreme cold the taste buds seem to be anaesthetised and you can eat almost anything. The key thing was that this sledging ration had sufficient calories to keep them going in the extreme cold. One of the reasons that Scott's party had died was that they were not taking enough calories each day and, as a result, slowly starved to death, losing the strength to withstand the cold and the gruelling labour of hauling their sledges. Hillary had shrugged aside the traditional Arctic ration and, in this perhaps, made a mistake. Fuchs told me:

> Hillary threw out all the sledging rations and put in a lot of tins of sausages and beans and other tinned foods. The Americans said to me when we arrived at the Pole, 'We're glad to see you're in such good shape. Hillary and his party were on their last legs when they got here.' That was their comment. It was the food they'd taken with them. They didn't have enough sustenance.

And then sleep – it was warm enough in the down sleeping bags, though through the journey the bags got progressively more damp from the condensation of sweat as it reached the outer layers which could be −30°C. The jangle of the alarm having woken them, the outside man would reach out, struggle to light the Primus stove and then shove on to it a panful of snow or ice collected the previous night. He would then have a few more precious minutes of warmth, lying dozing to the sound of the Primus. Once it was ready, a big mugful of tea and a biscuit overloaded with butter, perhaps some porridge, preceded the most painful moment of the day – getting out of the warmth of the pit for another gruelling day of travel. Everything was in an automated routine: outside man gets dressed and out first, then the inside man, who passes everything out of the tent, including the ground sheet. His final act is to drop his trousers and relieve himself in the precious shelter and comparative warmth of the now empty tent. Having done this he crawls out and the outside man takes his turn. It is very important to get one's bowels into the correct rhythm to avoid the agony of a frozen bum!

Once the gear was loaded onto the sledge, it was time to start up the vehicles. Every piece of metal was around −30°C, cold enough to give you a frost-burn if you touched it with a bare hand. The gasolene had been specially treated to expel all water or water vapour, since this would inevitably freeze, and little particles of ice would then block the jets of the carburettor. Even so, there could still be some icing. They used hot air guns, sometimes even played a blow torch over the cylinder block and fuel tubes to warm up the engine and get it going. An engine would roar into life, then another; the laggards might be given a tow start, or one of the engineers would come over to give the unfortunate driver the benefit of his expertise until, at last, all the engines were throbbing away.

Fuchs would give a wave from his Sno-cat, *Rock 'n Roll*, and away he'd go, his team obediently following. Sometimes it was easy going in smooth, firm snow and the vehicles could cream along at a steady four to five miles per hour, but more often the snow was deep with the tracks sinking and thrashing into a slough of snow or, even worse, the ground was heavily crevassed with huge chasms, some of them 300 metres deep and big enough to house St. Paul's Cathedral. It was the covered crevasses that were the problem. A dog team could have crossed many of them, unaware that they even existed, but a big Sno-cat could break through a snow bridge several metres thick. The only way to get through a badly crevassed area was to go

A Sno-cat straddles a crevasse, pontoons slewed at crazy angles. Some crevasses were deep enough to house St. Paul's Cathedral.

On the polar plateau.

out on foot and probe for the holes – slow, tiring work. Even so, it was possible to miss some. Snow would suddenly collapse under the front Sno-cat and it would lunge forwards and downwards, restrained only by the tow rope leading back to the heavily-laden sledge. Pontoons swung at crazy angles, the vehicle poised over the dark chasm. It could take anything from five to twenty hours using all five vehicles, either heaving or anchoring, to lift it out smoothly.

There were the occasional cocoa-breaks during the day, when drivers from different vehicles might come over and chat for a few minutes. Hal Lister and George Lowe held literary lunches in the Weasel cabin; lunch was a buttered biscuit, and their guests would take turns at discussing and describing the books they were each reading at the time.

The only change in the routine came when a day, or part of a day, was devoted to maintenance. This happened all too often, for the tracks had to be greased every few hundred miles. This was a hideous job, for the grease, congealed by the cold, resisted all pressure to pump it into the frozen nipples on the tracks. If you got any grease on your anorak, and it was almost inevitable that you did, the windproof quality of that particular patch was lost for ever; you had to lie in the snow, crawl under the vehicle, bend contorted to reach round awkward corners, all in the bitter cold. For someone like myself who is unmechanical, the very thought is appalling, and yet the crews became fond of their charges, attributing to them an almost human character as they coaxed and struggled with their foibles on the long drive across the Antarctic.

Fuchs, at last, reached South Ice – the depot and advanced base they had established the previous year – on the 21st December. Unemotional as ever, he quickly diffused any euphoria amongst his team with the admonishment, as they approached the little hut covered in snow; 'Well, there it is. We're going in now. And don't forget – no looting.'

And, as Fuchs addressed his little team, Hillary had actually set out on the last leg of his dash for the Pole. He had fulfilled all his duties in reaching and supervising the stocking by air of Depot 700. By this time the Weasel had come to a grinding halt, but the three farm tractors were still going strong. Even so, some members of Hillary's team were worried about their prospects. Now out of range of aerial support, they were wondering what would happen if their way was barred by soft snow or extensive crevasse systems. Bob Marsh and George Miller, the two dog men, wanted to explore the region around Depot 700, but to do this effectively they needed another depot put in by the tractors. Hillary suspected this was a ploy to deflect him from the Pole and felt that it would be just as easy to put in a depot from the air. They spent a day talking round the pros and cons, the one thing remaining fixed in Hillary's mind being the determination to make a push for the Pole, even if it meant taking just one tractor. He felt that he had fulfilled his duties as the leader of a big scientific expedition with the prime task of supporting Vivian Fuchs' crossing. Now he was the climber, sitting in the top camp, with the summit in sight. He talked the others round to his view and they resolved to go for the Pole.

They set out on the 20th December with the three tractors. That evening there was a message from his Committee, forbidding him to go beyond Depot 700. Since he was already beyond it, he chose to ignore the directive, sending a message to Fuchs that he was heading for the Pole, the first time that he had actually declared his intention.

They stormed on through soft snows and heavily crevassed regions, travelling twenty-four hours at a go, taking turns at the stressful job of making the route out in front, swapping the driving between the five men who were now divided between the three tractors. On Christmas Day they paused to listen to a special Christmas broadcast from New Zealand and to eat a Christmas dinner washed down by brandy. It was warm and cosy in the caboose. They were now about 250 miles from the Pole.

Fuchs and his party were still at South Ice, where the entire team managed to cram into the little hut, now buried in snow, for their Christmas dinner. The following day Fuchs sent a message to Hillary, asking him to put in another depot between Depot 700 and the Pole, and to abandon all attempts at going to the Pole. Hillary commented:

> I didn't have to do much figuring. We had just enough fuel to reach either the Pole or back to Depot 700. The only way we could establish a depot was to stop and sit where we were – and hope that Bunny would arrive when our food ran out. It would be a lot easier – and safer – to fly some more fuel into Depot 700. Or get a few drums deposited at the Pole by the Americans. I had the unkind suspicion that this was an excuse to stop us going on to the Pole without actually telling us not to.

Hillary ignored the edict and kept going. It was savagely cold; the snow was soft and their progress worryingly slow. He abandoned everything that was not absolutely essential, paring down their food and fuel to the bare minimum needed to reach the Pole, and still they pushed on. At last, on the 4th January, they sighted a tiny black dot in the distance – then another – and another; it was the line of marker flags leading them to the Pole, where the Americans had an International Geophysical Year base. He had reached his summit, with the minimum of reserves to spare. They were tired and hungry, had only twenty gallons of fuel left, but that did not matter for they had achieved their objective. There was no scientific or geographical purpose in their dash; it was an adventurous self-indulgence that any climber would find irresistible. Hillary wrote:

> What did we achieve by our Southern journey? We had located the crevasse areas and established the route and we had been the first vehicle party to travel overland to the South Pole – that was something, I suppose. But we had produced no scientific data about the ice, and little information about its properties. We showed that if you were enthusiastic enough and had good mechanics you could get a farm tractor to the South Pole – which doesn't sound much to risk your life for. The press had a field day on the pros and cons of our journey, but for me the decision had been reasonably straightforward. I would have despised myself if I hadn't continued – it was as simple as that – I just had to go on.

How different were Fuchs' motives. A great deal of invaluable scientific work was done both by Fuchs on his side of the continent and also by the large scientific contingent attached to Hillary's support party. But the journey itself was an adventure, similar in concept to sailing round the world or making the traverse of a mountain top. Fuchs claimed that his reasons for crossing the Antarctic were those of scientific curiosity but, by making it a single, dramatic push from one side to the other, there was undoubtedly a conflict between the needs of a comprehensive

The South Pole, a geographical point on the Antarctic plateau, but only halfway point for the expedition.

scientific programme and the exigencies of a tight schedule. It could be argued that more would have been achieved if the traverse had been spread over several years. As it was, they did manage to make a series of seismic soundings of the depth of the ice cap, but the other scientific work was inevitably of a fairly perfunctory nature. Hal Lister, the glaciologist, admitted rather ruefully that he had to fit his own programme, of examining snow and ice layers immediately below the surface, into periods when the expedition happened to pause for maintenance or some other purpose. I suspect that Fuchs, the scientist and Antarctic explorer, was after all not so very different from Ed Hillary in his motivation.

But Fuchs was still 380 miles from the Pole and the Antarctic autumn was approaching. At the Pole, Hillary was becoming more and more worried by Fuchs' slow progress. He was haunted by the appalling spectre of spending another winter in Antarctica. He had done his job, had achieved his goal, and wanted to go home to his family. Already he had been away for over a year, average by polar standards, but a long time to a mountaineer whose expeditions are unlikely to last for more than six months. Hillary's two mechanics, Murray Ellis and Jim Bates, stated categorically that it was getting too late in the season and that under no circumstances were they prepared to wait for Fuchs to arrive at the Pole. Hillary, therefore, sent Fuchs a message, suggesting that on reaching the South Pole, Fuchs should fly out for the winter, leaving his vehicles behind, and then return the following summer to complete the journey. This, of course, was completely unacceptable to Fuchs, who immediately replied, 'Appreciate your concern but there can be no question of abandoning journey at this stage. Innumerable reasons make it impracticable to remount the expedition after wintering outside Antarctica. Our vehicles can be and have been operated at −60 but I do not expect such temperatures in March.'

Fuchs called one of his rare expedition meetings and read out both Hillary's message and his own reply. In Lowe's words, 'There was no discussion of either the message or the decision – and we drove on. Nobody in the party had the slightest wish to postpone our crossing of the continent; on that score we were in full accord with our leader.'

It was unfortunate that a copy of Hillary's message was released to the press by his Committee in New Zealand. It had been meant as a helpful suggestion, but the press, who already had had a field day in creating a 'race for the Pole' between Fuchs and Hillary, with the big question of whether Hillary was disobeying orders, now had the sniff of another controversy in the doubts expressed about Fuchs' ability to complete the trip that year. Fuchs, as always, remained aloof. He had stated that he was going to finish the trip that year and, as far as he was concerned, that was enough. Hillary accepted Fuchs' decision and offered his services as guide once Fuchs reached the Pole. He did not wait there, however, but flew back to Scott Base for a few days' rest.

Fuchs pressed on, now making very much better progress, the going being over reasonably firm snow and free of crevasses. On the 19th January, the small convoy of vehicles, bedecked in flags and bunting, reached the Pole at last. In that moment of intense excitement, as the vehicles cruised up to the little collection of huts that marked the South Pole Base, and as Fuchs jumped out of the leading vehicle to be greeted by Ed Hillary and Admiral Dufek, Commander of the Americans in the Antarctic, George Lowe was still baffled, downright exasperated by the enigmatic Fuchs. 'Bunny Fuchs was like the profile of the continent itself – tough, flat, unchanging, dogged; and after three years in his company I could not say I knew him.'

In many ways, Fuchs' own appraisal of himself mirrors Lowe's observations. Fuchs told me in the summer of 1980:

Hillary and Fuchs, centre, with Admiral Dufek of the American polar station.

I don't allow things to unbalance me; I try to keep a steady course. Some people say this is very uninteresting. George, for instance, actually said to me, 'Come on. Why is it that you never seem to get enthusiastic about anything?' I said, 'You mean you want Caesar to exhort his troops?' And he said, 'Well, something like that.' I said, 'Well, if we get into a state of euphoria we're going to make mistakes just as much as we would if we get into a state of melancholia. As far as I'm concerned we just proceed and things come to pass. No need to get excited about it!'

And proceed they did. After a few days at the South Pole, sleeping in warm beds, eating gigantic meals in the American mess hall and working on the Sno-cats, they were ready to start once again.

The significance of the Pole was strange. Unlike the top of a mountain, it was merely a geographical point on the Antarctic plateau, barely half-way across in journey terms. The presence of a hutted camp, with many of the comforts of civilisation, made it all the more bizarre. And yet there was a feeling of having reached a top, certainly one that Hillary had felt and one that Fuchs' party could also share. Even though the journey from the Pole to Scott Base had some very difficult and heavy ground to cross, it had the qualities of the down-hill run on known ground, with the tracks of Hillary's vehicles marking the way. Hillary himself flew into Depot 700 to help guide them to the head of the Skelton Glacier and then down it. Even so, this was the most exhausting part of the journey. Racing against the Antarctic winter, they still stopped at regular intervals to make their seismic soundings of the ice cap. They were beginning to get run down and tired, all too ready to end their journey.

At last, on the 2nd March, the four Sno-cats, the only vehicles to complete the entire crossing, rolled into Scott Base. They had travelled 2,158 miles across the Antarctic continent. Vivian Fuchs had estimated that it would take them a hundred days. He had completed the journey in ninety-nine.

The last great polar journey

The two Poles provide parallels but also extreme contrasts, as opposite to each other as their seasons, when the perpetual darkness of mid-winter at one Pole is contrasted by the continuous glare of summer sun on the other. In common they have the cold, the wind, the snows and the ice, but that is all. The South Pole is set on an ice cap 2861 metres thick, in the heart of a huge continent. The North Pole is in the midst of an ice-clad ocean, a gigantic jig-saw of shifting ice floes, whose geography is in constant flux, dictated by the surge of seas beneath and around the ice. Floes are split, then subdivided again and again; great floes are swept together, one climbing on to another, a microcosm of the action of the drift of the Earth's tectonic plates. Pressure ridges of ice blocks are hurled up as the floes crash and grind together. From the air the line of a pressure ridge seems little more than a few ripples, but to a man standing on the bucking ice it has all the threat and violence of a severe earthquake.

The interior of Antarctica is the most sterile, empty desert in the world. There is no life, no vegetation, not even lichen, just snow, ice and barren rock. There is, however, life in the Arctic, nurtured by the black seas beneath the ice. Fish provide food for the seals, and polar bears stalking the seals have been spotted wandering in the remotest parts of the Arctic Ocean, far from solid land. But this animal life cycle is insufficient to sustain man. As in the Antarctic, he must carry his food and fuel with him as he combats the fierce cold, the glare of the long summer and the dark of winter. In the Antarctic there are the dangers of hidden crevasses, while in the Arctic there is the ever shifting sea, the threat of your shelter being split in two, of falling into the icy waters, or being engulfed in the gigantic grinder of a shifting pressure ridge.

The heroic age of exploration at both Poles was around the end of the nineteenth century and the beginning of the twentieth, but whilst the Antarctic has a theme of conventional heroism, of good team-work and good chaps where, even in disaster, they died with a stiff upper lip leaving the right kind of message, in the Arctic there has always been a strain of the contentious that goes back to the earliest efforts to find the fabled North-West Passage. There are tales of mutiny, of cannibalism, of disintegration. In the story of the first men to reach the North Pole there is an ugly dispute that has not been fully resolved even today.

In many ways, Robert Edwin Peary was of the same mould as Captain Scott or Ernest Shackleton. An officer in the Civil Engineer Corps of the U.S. Navy, he devoted a large part of his adult life to Arctic exploration in Northern Greenland and then to his efforts to reach the North Pole. A gruff, outspoken man, he was weak in both tact and diplomacy, but was almost obsessively thorough and very determined. His attempt in 1909 was carefully planned, using a combination of Eskimo experience of the Arctic and the modern technology of the time. His specially-designed ship, *Roosevelt*, sailed as far north as possible into the ice before the arrival of winter. Early the following spring he set out using a series of trail-breaking parties to force the way for him to a point just 153 miles from the Pole. Then, with his Negro manservant, Henson, and two Eskimoes, he cut loose to push through to the Pole in the space of five days' hard sledging. It was only on his way back home he learned that Frederick A. Cook, who had been his doctor on his first polar expedition, had claimed to have reached the Pole a full year before.

Cook's story was certainly remarkable. He claimed to have set out from the north point of Axel Heiberg Island, 520 miles from the Pole, with four Eskimoes. Two of them returned after a few days, leaving the threesome to make their push for the Pole. Cook claimed to have reached it on the 21st April 1908, but there were many discrepancies in his claim. How could he have carried all the food that the three of them, plus the dogs, would need for the length of time he claimed they took to get there and back? He had lost all the paper-work of his navigational readings, having left his instruments on his way out with a member of Peary's party. Cook claimed that they vanished, while Whitney, the man who had accepted Cook's belongings, denied there had ever been any written records and claimed he had only been given instruments. Two factions quickly formed, each bent on discrediting the other. The problem is that there is no way anyone can prove he has been to the Pole. It is not like a mountain, where, except in the worst weather, photographs can give positive evidence that the climber has reached the top. It all comes down to credibility. In the end Cook's story was dismissed, not just on the evidence or lack of it, but also in the light of earlier claims he had made to have climbed Mount McKinley for the first time – a claim which was also discredited. Peary was given official recognition and his name appears in all atlases today, though even in his case the proof was not conclusive. His average progress rate while breaking trail with support parties had never exceeded twelve miles a day and yet, once he pushed forward with Henson and his two Eskimo companions, he claimed to have averaged twenty-five miles a day, both on the way to the Pole and all the way back to *Roosevelt*. This was remarkable if compared with the progress of others; Nansen, one of the greatest Arctic travellers, had only once managed to travel twenty-five miles in a day on polar pack ice.

Wally Herbert who conceived the idea of a complete crossing of the Arctic Ocean, via the North Pole.

It is just possible that the North Pole was still untouched until it was invaded by modern technology, when man could reach it not only from the air but also by nuclear submarine and USS *Nautilus* cruised beneath it on the 3rd August 1958, only a few months after Fuchs had completed his crossing of Antarctica. But no-one had reached the North Pole across the surface since Peary made his bid in 1909 and the greatest journey of all – a complete crossing of the Arctic Ocean – was still untried.

It was this concept that captured the imagination of Wally Herbert. A luxuriant beard and a quiet intensity of manner, eyes wrinkled from gazing into the wind and glare of the snows on the British Antarctic Survey give him the stamp of a polar explorer. Born in 1934, he was the son of an Army officer who had risen up from the ranks.

By the age of fourteen he was dreaming of being an explorer, but there seemed little chance of realising this ambition. His father, with whom he had a strained relationship, partly no doubt because of his long absences, wanted him to go into the Army. But Wally felt uncomfortable with what he had already seen of life in the officers' mess. He told me: 'I was given a kind of grooming in officer's behaviour; I would have to play billiards with the captains and talk politely with the CO, dress for dinner and all that sort of thing. It was a deadly, deadly way of spending your holidays as a teenage lad.'

And yet the Army seemed to open up the only road to any kind of adventure, and so he signed on for twenty-two years at the age of seventeen, going into the Engineers to train as a surveyor which he hoped would take him into unexplored lands. Diffident, unsure of himself, he failed to get a commission and, within weeks, bitterly regretted joining the Army. He spent most of the next three years fretting over whether they would let him out at the end of this initial period. Fortunately they did; once again, he showed an adventurous streak, hitch-hiking home from Egypt around the Middle Eastern countries and back to England, where he started looking for a job. He seemed a long way from a life of exploration and adventure in a job at a surveyors' office on the South Coast.

He made few friends; quiet, introverted and very lonely, he seemed trapped in a humdrum life with very little future. As so often happens, it was a coincidence that led him to the life to which he was most suited. Wally told me:

> I was sitting in a bus; my raincoat was soaking wet and there were drips coming off everything, steaming in this horrible smelly bus. The bus lurched and a newspaper fell off the luggage rack smack into my lap. It was open at the public appointments page and two of the things I noticed straight away were one advert for a surveyor in Kenya and another one for team members for an expedition to the Antarctic.

He had found the answer to his discontent. On reaching work he didn't dare answer the advertisements during working hours, so slipped into the lavatory, sat on the loo with the top down and wrote off for further details. Interviews followed and he was offered both jobs.

> I had to make a choice, Kenya or the Antarctic. I'd always dreamed of going to Kenya and had never really thought much about the Antarctic at all, but at this point, without really thinking it out, I immediately chose the Antarctic. There was some magic in the word 'expedition' which touched the romantic in me. I could easily have gone to Kenya and have spent the rest of my life in the hotter parts of the world.

At twenty, Wally Herbert joined the Falkland Islands Dependencies Survey, at Hope Bay, Antarctica, and found a contentment he had never known before:

> . . . a monastic life without religious exercise. There, we were a world of men in harmony

with our environment – twelve men around a bunkhouse fire, or two men in a drumming tent, or one man in the solitude of summer-warmed hills. We saw a paradise in snowscapes and heard music in the wind, for we were young and on our long exploratory journeys we felt, with the pride of youth, that we were making history.

At the end of his two-and-a-half-year stint, Wally hitch-hiked through South America and the United States before returning home to England. A trip to Spitsbergen, another stint in the Antarctic, this time with a New Zealand expedition operating out of Scott Base, and he had achieved the experience and, perhaps, the spur that led him to undertake his journey across the Arctic. In Antarctica he had conceived an exciting plan of exploring a range of mountains last visited on Scott's expedition and then, at the end of the season, making his own dash to the South Pole to mark the fiftieth anniversary of Scott's ill-fated journey. It meant a tremendous amount to Wally Herbert, but the authorities turned it down. He had too great a respect for authority to ignore the veto, as his name had allowed Hillary to do in 1958. As a consolation, he made his way with his dog teams down the Axel Heiberg Glacier, the route taken by Amundsen in his historic journey to the Pole in 1910. But Herbert's memory of the Antarctic was forever tarnished by his disappointment.

> I didn't ever ever want to go to the South Pole from that moment on or to ever go back to the Antarctic – I'd worked it completely out of my system because I knew that next year they'd be coming in with aeroplanes to photograph the area and to put their surveyors on our bloody mountain peaks and on our survey cairns. They'd make better maps than we'd made ourselves. It seemed like the end of this whole phase of my life – I must go and do something new.

Back in England, living at his parents' home, he was existing off the small advance on a book about his Antarctic experience and the proceeds of a few lectures. It was at this stage that he started to think of the Arctic and that last great polar journey, the crossing of the Arctic Ocean. Wally has a strong sense of history and is intensely patriotic.

> It was absolutely *imperative* that it was a British expedition that did it because of the four-hundred-year tradition and heritage and all the blood, sweat and scurvy and folklore that was built into this.
> But at the time it didn't occur to me that it should be me because I hadn't enough experience. I was still too young and I hadn't had an expedition on my own. I'd led expeditions in the field, but I'd never actually organised them or raised the money for them.

The idea was there, but also the self-doubt. I felt very much the same before I led my first expedition to the South Face of Annapurna. In Wally's case the transition from vague dreams to a dogged determination to get his concept off the ground came through a growing realisation of how feasible the scheme was, given the right mixture of dedication and support. The ice floes of the Arctic Ocean are in constant movement, driven by the ocean currents. Explorers of the past had tried to utilise this movement; Nansen, in *Fram*, allowed himself to be trapped in the ice off the coast of Siberia, hoping to drift over or close to the Pole. In the event, he did not get close enough to make a successful dash over the ice to his objective. But now much more was known about the pattern of drift. The Russians had been establishing scientific stations on the ice and were drifting slowly across towards North Greenland. Since the drift was in a circular direction, swinging round and over the Pole, Wally saw that it would be possible to go in with a small party using dog teams for fast, light progress when conditions were suitable, but always going on the line of drift, so that even when sitting out the summer period when there were too many open leads of water, or the winter when it was too cold and dark, they would still be sweeping, however slowly, in the right direction. He liked the idea of dog teams, had little sympathy with the encroaching technology of the noisy Snowmobile that he had seen used more and more in the Antarctic. His preference for dogs was both romantic and practical. Quite apart from being a traditional mode of transport, completely in keeping with the spirit of adventure, there was less to go wrong with a dog and, if it should die, at least its fellow-dogs could eat it. A broken-down Skidoo or Snowmobile, if you could not repair it, was just a pile of useless scrap metal.

Even so, Wally realised that he could not be completely independent. There was no way his party could carry enough food for the sixteen months it would take dogs and men to cross the Arctic Ocean on its longest axis from Point Barrow to Spitsbergen. This meant he would have to depend on supplies from the air, which also meant that he would need good radio communications with the outside world. All this was going to cost a lot of money, and the co-operation of government bodies, not just in Britain but in the United States and Canada as well. It was a formidable challenge for a thirty-two-year-old, who was not well-known, had no connections with the establishment or media, and no real qualifications except for some sound experience in the Antarctic. But in spite of his doubts and frequent rebuffs Wally Herbert doggedly pursued his vision.

In 1964 he took the first draft of his plan to Sir Vivian Fuchs who was both interested and encouraging. Wally then managed to get a small grant from the Royal Geographical Society and went off to the States to research his project. He even flew his proposed route in a DC8 but, on his return to England, now heavily in debt, the Royal Geographical Society rejected his 20,000-word submission on the grounds that there was too much adventure and insufficient scientific weight to the scheme.

But Wally struggled on, writing hundreds of letters to everyone who had ever had anything to do with the Arctic. His determination paid off and, slowly, he gathered a body of influential people to support his plans in a Committee of Management, bristling with illustrious names, from Sir Vivian Fuchs to the Sergeant Surgeon to the Queen. With this kind of support, Wally was now able to get the approval of the Royal Geographical Society. It was important to him not merely for the launching of his expedition, but also on a personal level, as a seal of acceptance by the exploratory and scientific establishment of which Wally desperately wanted to be part. This extract from his book *Across the Top of the World* is revealing:

> . . . by the time I left I was almost certain I had, at last, the approval of the Society – an approval confirmed later by the pleasant expressions and, in some cases, even the smiles of the members of the Committee as they walked in threes and fours through the halls to the gentlemen's cloakroom (where I had hung about for almost half an hour, knowing that I would, if I waited long enough, meet them as they came in to collect their bowler hats).

Wally was now able to go forward at full bore with his plans, but it was still very much a one-man venture. He had chosen his team – all of them old hands from the Antarctic – Roger Tufft, a school teacher living in the Lake District, Allan Gill, whose life has been devoted to the empty spaces of the Antarctic and Arctic, and Fritz Koerner, a glaciologist who was working at an American university. From my own experience of climbing expeditions, I have always found that a level of involvement by all members of the team has helped in both increasing commitment to the venture and in building a sense of unity before setting out. It was perhaps unfortunate that as Wally's team were all so scattered, it was impractical for any of them to help in the actual organisation. This led to even greater pressure on Wally, while the others remained almost uninvolved until they actually joined the expedition,

Allan Gill, the toughest and most experienced member of the expedition was also its emotional anchor man.

though it seems unlikely that Wally would have delegated much responsibility, even given the chance. Allan Gill commented, 'I think Wally has to do the whole lot; he has to do it his way and I would never even suggest taking on a share because I just don't think it would work.' Roger Tufft, who was particularly interested in the design of the sledges and practical details of the training expedition, regretted that he was not consulted and been more involved.

It was now October 1966; Wally was still a long way from getting the £54,000 he thought he was going to need, but he had just enough to carry out the training expedition that he felt was an essential prelude to the main venture. Fritz Koerner was tied up with his job in America, but Allan Gill and Roger Tufft were free to go. They planned to spend the winter near the Eskimo settlement of Qanaq, in North-West Greenland, so that they could try out the little prefabricated hut Wally had ordered for wintering on the main expedition. In the early spring they set out on a long sledge journey across Ellesmere Island and then up the Nansen Sound to the tip of Axel Heiberg Island, the place that Cook had claimed to have set out from on his bid for the Pole. They had to prove themselves and their gear capable of a long sledge journey over the broken pack ice of the sounds between the islands to convince potential sponsors that their plans for the polar crossing had at least a chance of success. So Wally was determined, at all costs, to complete the journey.

The project also provided a test in their own relationships. Roger Tufft was the same age as Wally, had joined the Falkland Islands Dependencies Survey at the same time; they had sledged together and had got on well, but that was ten years before. Since then they had seen little of each other. After leaving the Antarctic Roger Tufft had gone with Bill Tilman on two of his long and adventurous sea voyages; he had also been exploring in Lapland and Spitsbergen and manhauling sledges across the Greenland Ice Cap. Welsh by birth, a school teacher with an excellent mind, he was used to taking the initiative and it was, perhaps, inevitable that he and Wally would clash. Allan Gill, on the other hand, was much more easy-going than Roger. Polar regions were his life, with the short periods he spent in civilisation a slightly uncomfortable interlude. Quiet, very modest, lean almost to the degree of emaciation, Allan Gill, then aged thirty-six, was the oldest member of the team. He had learnt as much as possible about polar regions, turning himself into a first-class scientific assistant who could cope with almost any aspect of polar life or research. He did not have the same conflict of loyalties that Roger had between a life and career in civilisation and the expedition they were about to undertake. For Allan, if he were not on the polar crossing, would have joined some other Arctic expedition and, in fact, had already turned down an invitation to lead a very attractive American scientific expedition.

Their journey stretched them and their equipment to the limit. The lightweight sledges disintegrated under the loads and they had to obtain the heavier Eskimo variety. Having thought themselves proficient dog drivers from their experience in the Antarctic, they now found that they were little better than novices when compared with the Eskimoes. They ran out of food, reached the last stages of exhaustion, were well behind their schedule and yet Wally still clung doggedly to his original plan, knowing how vital it was to gaining his sponsors' confidence.

Altogether, they travelled 1,200 miles and were only 143 miles short of Resolute Bay, their eventual destination, when Wally realised that they could afford no more time. In only six months' he wanted to set out from Point Barrow on their great journey. He therefore radioed for a 'plane to fly in to pick them up.

It was on the 19th June, while they waited for the 'plane, that Roger Tufft told Wally he had decided to pull out of the expedition. Roger felt that there was insufficient time to get the main trip organised; their gear had proved inadequate and the radio had not been sufficiently powerful but, most important of all, Roger and Wally had found their personalities no longer seemed compatible. There had been a level of stress throughout their journey, with Roger frequently disagreeing with Wally's decisions.

Wally flew out first with some of the gear and it was six days before the 'plane was able to fly back to pick up Allan Gill and Roger Tufft – six days of agony for Wally for he could not help wondering whether Allan, also, might decide to defect. Wally wrote:

> I knew, and I guess he knew too, that if he joined Roger and backed out, the trans-Arctic expedition would fold up; for it would be impossible for me to convince my Committee, sponsors and many supporters that the plan was still viable and that I, as the leader, was still competent, if two of my chosen companions, after a nine-month trial in the Arctic, had lost confidence in my leadership and in the feasibility of the plan.

There would be no time for private discussion, for Allan Gill had to fly straight on from Resolute Bay to join a summer scientific camp on Devon Island. As he climbed into the aircraft, he said to Wally, 'I'll see you in London in September.' It was an expression of support and loyalty that Wally would never forget.

The Committee were undoubtedly shaken by Roger Tufft's resignation, insisting that Wally telegram Gill and Koerner to obtain their assurance that they were still part of the expedition. Fritz Koerner who had not been on the training expedition had a difficult decision to make. A close friend of Roger Tufft, he had great respect for his judgement. In addition, Fritz's wife, Anna, was due to have their first baby around the time they were going to set out from Point Barrow. He was also concerned about the scientific content of the expedition. He was attracted by the adventurous concept of the crossing of the Arctic Ocean, but only if he was also going to be able to complete some sound glaciological research on the way. Nevertheless, setting aside his doubts, he cabled his acceptance.

But Wally still had to find a replacement for Roger Tufft. His Committee of Management favoured a doctor and, accordingly, made enquiries through the Royal Army Medical Corps for a suitable candidate. This was how Ken Hedges came into the expedition. At thirty-one, he was medical officer for the crack Special Air Service Regiment. He had no polar experience, but did have an impressive set of adventurous credentials as a military parachutist and frogman.

While working for the necessary qualifications to get into the Royal Military Academy, Sandhurst, he had had a serious motor bike accident. He was very lucky to survive at all and was in hospital for nine months. He made an almost complete recovery but had lost some mobility in his limbs and this was sufficient to stop him getting through the Army medical tests. The trauma of the accident with the accompanying physical pain, enforced immobility and fears for the future proved an important turning point in his life. He had had a happy childhood with a close-knit family background in which a Christian belief had played an important part; the accident had strengthened this belief, directing it into a positive evangelistic conviction which was to form the main stream of his life. With a strong sense of gratitude for the medical skill that had saved him, he resolved to devote his life to medicine and thought initially in terms of studying to be a male nurse. It was his father who gave him the necessary encouragement and financial backing to get the 'A' levels needed to gain a place at medical college, become a doctor and eventually join the Royal Army Medical Corps.

Wally had never seen the need to have a doctor on the expedition. Of the

The 1967 training journey

Ken Hedges, a late replacement from the Royal Army Medical Corps.

applicants, he favoured a seasoned Antarctic man, who was also a geophysicist, called Geoff Renner. With the same background as the other three, he knew and understood polar life and travel. But Wally was overruled partly, I suspect, because he did not put over his own views strongly enough, always having been in awe of the polar establishment on his Committee. He told me:

> It was easier for Fuchs. He was very much older than I at the time he did his trans-Antarctic crossing, and had a certain authority and charisma through having been the Director of the British Antarctic Survey. He could say, 'Right, now look here gentlemen we'll do it this way', and they would listen and go along with it. But I couldn't do that. Possibly it was my training from Dad; I had a kind of awe and respect for age, prestige, position and title. I felt that I had to call them Sir. One or two of them called me Wally occasionally, but it sometimes seemed to stick in their throats. They were absolutely charming and very helpful, but there was this very strange sort of relationship I had with them.

So Wally went along with the Committee's preference for Ken Hedges who, but for his complete lack of polar experience, seemed a tough and pleasant personality. They first met in a London pub. Wally remembers how he spent the entire interview trying to describe to Ken just what polar travel and living was like and, as a result, he hardly asked Ken anything at all, discovering very little about his background and interests.

There was little enough time to balance out the question of team composition anyway. With so many things to do and Wally scurrying between his parents' home in Warwickshire and his office in London, it was still very much a one-man-band. Ken Hedges and Allan Gill were due to fly out by RAF Hercules transport 'plane with the bulk of the gear, first to Thule to collect the dogs, and then on to Point Barrow at the end of December. Wally was going to fly out direct to meet them there in early January 1968. Anna Koerner's baby was due towards the end of January and Fritz was determined to be with her at the birth and make sure everything was all right before leaving her for sixteen months. This didn't suit the Committee and Fritz and Anna were brought over to London to discuss the problem. Fritz remembers the incident vividly.

> The Committee said: 'You must leave on the dot.' We went on to discuss this and the discussion got down to the birth being induced. I can remember the exact words Old Smiler (that's what we called Sir Miles Clifford) said: 'I think it's a good idea. You don't mind having the child induced, do you, Anna?' Anna was just looking at them, amazed, and they were all sitting there, puffing on their pipes.

Wally flew out of England on the 10th January and joined his party at Point Barrow a few days later. Point Barrow is like so many Arctic stations, a collection of huts and hangars jutting out of the empty, snow-covered tundra. Their 70,000 pounds of supplies, sledges, tents, food for men and dogs, were stored in a big warehouse. Ken Hedges had certainly been plunged in at the deep end, having already driven a dog team seventy miles in the pitch dark and cold of mid-winter from Qanaq to the US Air Force Base at Thule. It was the first time he had ever handled dogs or been exposed to such extreme cold. The next weeks were spent in frantic preparation. Dog harnesses were adjusted and restitched by the Eskimo women, sledges and tents were checked, radios tested. The supplies which were going to be air-dropped by the Canadian Air Force had to be sorted out. They made short journeys over the ice to try out the gear and train the dog teams and all the time, out there to the north, was the vast stretch of ice covering the Arctic Ocean – implacable, huge, menacing. They were not yet a complete team, but Fritz Koerner's daughter arrived, by natural birth, on the 31st January; Fritz was at Point Barrow by the 8th February and, at last, they were ready to set out.

Fritz Koerner.
His baby daughter arrived just in time for him to join the expedition at Point Barrow.

The overall plan was to put in as much sledging progress across the polar pack ice before the summer melt made travel impossible. Then for two months they would camp on a suitably substantial floe which would itself continue creeping on towards the Pole in the circular polar drift. In the autumn they would sledge on again until the four months of winter darkness obliged them to set up camp once more; then with the spring would come the last frantic dash for Spitsbergen before the ice broke up beneath them.

The first and perhaps most difficult problem of the entire journey was to find a way of crossing the eighty-mile belt of fractured young ice between the Point Barrow coast and the relative solidity of the polar pack ice. This was a region of shifting currents, where the great ice floes were ground together against the immovable land mass, an area of piled up, ever moving pressure ridges, of changing leads of open water. Day after day Wally flew over it in a Cessna 180, but what he saw was never encouraging. There was no sign of the ice compressing to form the vital bridge they needed and, as the days slipped by, the tension increased. Back in London the media printed stories of gloom and doom, while the worries of the Committee could almost be felt over the radio waves.

The crossing of the Arctic

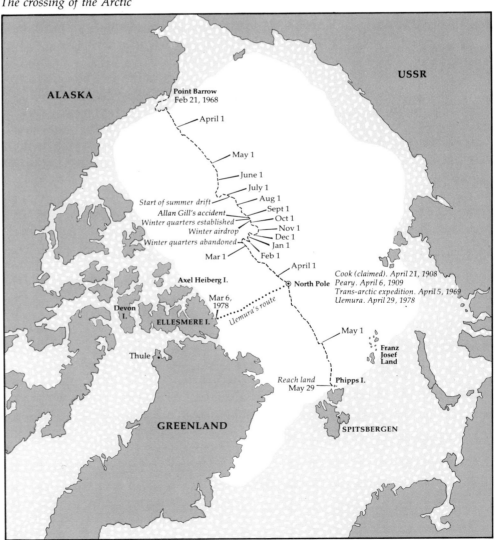

At last, on the 22nd February, the ice bridge to the polar pack seemed at least feasible, and the four set out with their dog teams and sledges, along the coastline and then out onto the piled rubble of ice that marked the edge of the Arctic Ocean. For the next eighteen months they would be travelling across the constantly shifting ice, which would rarely be more than two metres thick and which could split beneath them at any moment. The dash for the relatively stable pack ice foundered into a laborious crawl almost immediately, their way barred by the first pressure ridge, a six-metre high wall of ice blocks. They scrambled up to get a wider view. What they saw was discouraging.

As far as the eye could see there was chaos – no way seemed possible except the route by which we had come. It was like a city razed to the ground by a blitz or an act of God, an alabaster city so smashed that no landmarks remained. It was a desolate scene, purified by a covering of snow that had been packed down by the wind; dazzling bright yet horrifying.

The only way to get through was to cut down the walls of ice, using the debris to

331

build ramps for the sledges to be heaved or pushed across and down into the rut beyond. It was −41°C, but their clothes were soon damp with sweat, a dampness that would turn to bitter chill as soon as they stopped their exertion. And then, once they had forced the first ridge, there was another, another and yet another. There was mush ice, which was just particles jumbled together, barely fused by the pressure of the floes on either side, only a few inches thick, a quaking bog with thousands of metres of black, sub-zero waters beneath. They skeetered across these sections, the dogs scrambling, yapping frantically, the men shuffling, striding, fearful of the easily-imagined horrors of immersion in the waters below. There was little rest at night with the constant groaning of the ice and the fear of it splitting beneath the tents. And there was the even greater fear of disgrace and ridicule. What if they couldn't break through to the pack ice beyond? They would have to return to face the waiting media, the sceptics who had said they had no chance anyway. They were all frightened, but the fear of failure and of ridicule was even greater than that of death. It was the same feeling that Heyerdahl had had as *Kon-Tiki* limped painfully from the coast of Peru, or John Ridgway and Chay Blyth rowing against the wind and current off Cape Cod.

Doggedly they fought their way from floe to floe, edging northwards whenever possible, though they were also at the mercy of the winds and currents which were sweeping the ice they were crossing steadily towards open waters. After sixteen days of struggle, they were only seventeen miles from Point Barrow. At this stage they were travelling light, carrying only a few days' food and relying on being resupplied by the Cessna, whose pilot also tried to advise them on the terrain lying ahead. For most of the time his information was discouraging. They were now 400 miles behind schedule. This was serious, since they needed to be in the right place by the height of summer to find a suitably large ice floe on which to drift through the summer months towards the Pole. If they were forced to stop short of their planned destination, they would be in the wrong region of drift and could be swept away to one side of the Pole. Wally, therefore, resolved to keep sledging well into the summer, even though this would mean more problems with open leads between the ice floes. He had anticipated this and had designed the sledges so that they could be turned into boats for crossing short stretches of open water.

Crossing the polar ice; each man was responsible for his own dog team.

By the 20th March they had at last broken through the coastal fracture zone and were on the permanent polar pack ice. There were still pressure ridges to cross, open leads to negotiate, but their progress was now very much faster. They were making sixteen or seventeen miles in a day. But they were now increasingly confronted with another problem. There were seams within the fragile unity of the group, the beginnings of a division into three and one, and Ken Hedges was becoming the odd man out. Wally wrote:

> Ken's problems were social; physically he was in good shape, professionally he was admired and encouraged by his regiment for joining the expedition, but it was inevitable that the difference in training and temperament would set him apart from the three of us.
> Ken was a good officer, a Christian and a gentleman. We were three seasoned polar men. The many years we had lived in isolated polar camps had left their mark on us; we would no doubt be regarded by a genteel society as rough, crude, self-reliant and irreligious. We were obsessed by and in love with the polar setting and the hard physical challenge of polar exploration. We were old friends; Allan and I had made a tough journey together the previous year; Allan and Fritz had made others; the three of us had gone through the same basic polar training at the same Antarctic base – Hope Bay. There was a close bond between us, a mutual trust and respect; we spoke the same language. Only a man with precisely the same background would have fitted instantly into such a society; it was therefore no surprise to us that Ken had felt alien at the start of the journey; but it had been worrying us for some time that he did not appear to be slipping naturally into our way of life.

In any enclosed community little idiosyncrasies can become a savage irritant, and the way a person scratches his nose, stresses certain syllables or gulps his tea can become a quite irrational focus to externalise much deeper and more serious differences. The most obvious difference between Ken and the others was more than a mere mannerism. It was his religious belief, but this seems to have focussed all the other differences of experience and background into something that was easily definable, and indeed mentioned to me by each of the others. Ken was a devout Baptist, the other three either atheist or agnostic. They found Ken difficult to live with. Little things would grate, like the way he would often go off to pray or meditate on top of a nearby pressure ridge – 'humbling' the others called it, because of the characteristic stance he adopted, or the meek yet impenetrable front which they felt he put up between them in all arguments. It was a rift which was only to get wider as the months passed, driving Ken ever further in on himself. Wally writes: 'Ken, by his own admission, was unhappy in our society because he felt we were not "bringing him in", and there was little we could do to improve the situation, for as far as we were concerned we had tried to interest him in our way of life and evidently failed.'

Their daily routine did nothing to alleviate Ken's feeling of isolation. For a start, they each had their own dog team and through the day travelled separately, often hundreds of metres apart. The only time they came together was at an obstacle and, even here, Ken must have been forced anew to face the difference between himself and the others, as the three polar experts pooled their knowledge and experience to manoeuvre a sledge over a pressure ridge or across an open lead. It was inevitable that Ken remained an onlooker, however willing he may have been to take an active part.

When I went to see him, he did not want to talk about the differences that occurred between himself and the other three; he did observe, however:

> We didn't meet as a team until a week before we set out and so there was no fellowship in that team. There was amongst the other three because they had all sledged together, but as a team, in which twenty-five per cent was new, meaning myself, there was not that sense of fellowship. I didn't have this sense of friendship, facing the fifty-fifty chance of dying, which is how I rated our chances. I was carried along by several conceptions; one was of

acquitting myself as honourably as circumstances permitted, coming from the SAS and being a commissioned officer; also, there was this vague sense of British history, particularly in its polar sense. There was an absolute dedication and I put my life on the line on this one. I would endeavour to commit myself with honour, come what may, and just hope that I wouldn't have to pay the full price. There was a sense of resignation about it all.

It was also very frightening; Wally Herbert described it for me:

We were all shit scared in our own desperate sort of ways to come through this period and each of the four men had their own way of handling this situation. We'd been in the Antarctic and Arctic in many dangerous situations; we'd experienced the dark before, but to Ken it was new, and he was cold, he was uncomfortable; he was afraid as we all were, but for him it was new and so presumably for him it was very much more frightening.

And there was also the dog team. This was what Ken found the most difficult. Much of polar living and travel is simple, basic survival, of getting used to putting up a tent in a blizzard, of struggling with a Primus stove, of plodding over mile upon mile of featureless ice, but managing a dog team is a real skill and one that needs years of experience to master fully. The other three had all driven dog teams in the Antarctic and the previous year Wally and Allan had gained further experience, but Ken had to learn from scratch. Essentially a kind man, he found it difficult to discipline his team in the way to which they were accustomed. He told me:

I wasn't driving my dogs; I was walking out in front of them, whistling to the silly creatures to follow me, which they did. I remember Fritz saying to me, 'Come on, Ken, you know you can't walk across the Arctic like this. You'll have to learn sooner or later to drive from behind rather than lead from the front.' Eventually I did, though I don't rate myself a masterful sledge driver by any manner of means.

As spring crept into summer, with its eternal, glaring daylight, the going became harder, with more and more open leads to find their way through. Everything was wet with snow – a watery quagmire, the ice increasingly mushy, their sleeping bags perpetually damp, their rucksacks soaked through, the tents a soggy mess. There was the growing worry of whether they could find a sufficiently large and solid floe on which to drift through the summer into the following autumn when, once again, they would be able to resume their progress. They had sledged 1,180 miles over the polar pack ice – further from land than any other polar traveller; at the same time they had managed to carry out some scientific work. Each day Fritz had contrived to measure the floe thickness and snow density. They had seen the tracks of the Arctic fox and polar bear, but they had actually seen only twelve seals, four gulls, a little auk, a flight of duck and two long-tailed jaegers in the five months they had spent in this icy wilderness. Some Arctic explorers had theorised that you could survive by hunting in the Arctic Ocean, but Wally's team would have gone very hungry on what they had observed and certainly could not have fed the dogs!

This was becoming a disturbingly relevant topic, for the little radio – their only link with the outside world – had developed a fault. Without it they would be unable to guide in the supply aircraft, and it was unlikely that they could be found without an exact fix on their location. After two days' nerve-wracking struggle they found the fault, a broken wire coming in from the power source. A day later they had a glimpse of the sun through the clouds, made a fix and were able to radio their position.

They had now reached their destination for the summer, a large and solid-looking floe that seemed as if it would survive both the long summer melt and any battering the seas might give it. On the 12th July a Canadian Air Force Hercules brought their supplies for the summer – food, fuel, replacement clothing, tentage and scientific

Negotiating a shear-zone in the polar pack ice.

Managing a dog team is a skill requiring years of practice. Wally Herbert, Allan Gill and Fritz Koerner had had experience in the Antarctic. Ken Hedges had to learn from scratch.

Fritz Koerner contrived to carry out scientific measurements each day, even through the depths of the Arctic winter.

instruments for Fritz Koerner's research programme. For a few weeks, until the ice hardened up once again, they could relax, relying on the constant drift of the current to carry them towards the Pole. Although relatively warm, with the temperature just above freezing, it was misty, miserable, very humid and they saw the sun through a screen of drizzle. There was always some tension. Would the floe survive through the summer? It had already split once, only a hundred metres from the little village of tents the Press had named Meltville. On another day, one of the very few fine, cloudless days they had, their floe was invaded by a polar bear and its two cubs. Alerted by the yapping and snarling of the dogs, they had no choice but to kill the bears before the dogs were killed or scattered. Ken Hedges had grabbed a rifle, but it jammed and it was Wally who shot the bear and cubs. They were all shocked by the incident but Ken particularly so, both because of the failure of his rifle and also by the necessity for killing these magnificent, beautiful yet deadly animals.

They were still behind schedule and Wally wanted to start out again as early as possible to try to make some more progress across the floes before the arrival of winter. When they set out on the 4th September, the temperature had dropped to below freezing – but only just. The surface of the slushy snow covering the ice was frozen into a thin crust which broke at almost every step and they sank through to their knees into the icy, soggy mush. At the cost of constant, exhausting effort they were making only two miles or so a day. Everything was wet and their way was forever barred by open leads between the floes. Inevitably, tempers were short and the stress within the group came closer and closer to the surface. After Fritz had had a blazing row with Ken over tactics, he and Wally talked over the problem:

Once again, we found ourselves talking about the relationship between Ken and the rest of the party – which was clearly strained. The incompatibility did not manifest itself in dramatic outbursts but in a deep and nagging disapproval of each other's ideas and ideals. It was like a marriage that had failed in spite of efforts on both sides to make a go of it. The big question, not unlike the married couple's, was whether to put an end to the relationship before the winter set in [Ken could be sent out on a light aircraft which would attempt to land about September 25th to bring in some delicate scientific instruments], or whether out of respect for the institution of 'the polar expedition' (as with couples who respect the institution of matrimony), we should stick it out to the end. Both Allan and Fritz felt Ken should be sent out. To Ken, a devout man, forgiveness and reconciliation were not only basic principles of his faith but a solution he considered dignified and honourable. While I agreed with Allan and Fritz, I felt bound as leader of the expedition to give Ken the opportunity to see the expedition through to the end for his own sake and for the sake of those whom, in a sense, he represented.

At least three of them could, on occasion, talk it out amongst themselves, fortify themselves with a sense of unity, but it must have been much more difficult for Ken who inevitably felt totally isolated and must have sensed that the others were talking behind his back.

But the struggle went on; their way was now barred by a strip of mush ice about sixty metres wide at its narrowest point. It was a jumble of everything from three-metre blocks to a porridge-like mush, held together only by the pressure of the two big floes on either side. The nightmare thought was of being caught in the middle of the strip when the pressure from the two floes was released. Should they drift apart only a few feet, the larger blocks would capsize and plunge, the mush would dissipate and dogs, sledges and men would be struggling in the heaving, tumbling sea. Wally and Fritz had gone ahead to find a way over the strip, but it was too wide, too chaotic. Discouraged, they returned to be confronted by an even greater crisis.

Allan was sitting, huddled in the snow beside his sledge, his face contorted in agony. The previous day he had pulled a muscle in his back, but this was something which was obviously very much worse. He was unable to move and in extreme pain. Quickly, they erected a tent and somehow manoeuvred him into it. Ken diagnosed that Allan had either badly slipped a disc or torn a muscle and gave him a morphine injection. Whichever it was, it was essential to get him evacuated as soon as possible, but before that could be done they had to find somewhere safer to camp. They were on a very small floe that was already beginning to break up. Fritz and Wally went back to search for the floe on which they had spent the summer and had left only a few days before. It was only a few miles away and when they returned Ken reported that Allan's condition had not improved. Wally sent out the first news of the accident, stating: 'If no miraculous recovery within next few days, will have to ask ARL to fly him out in the Cessna that brings the geophysical equipment. Need with the utmost urgency a replacement ex-Falkland Islands Dependency or ex-British Antarctic Survey geophysicist. Renner first choice.'

After a few days' rest, Allan Gill was fit enough to be moved and they carried him, carefully strapped onto a sledge, back to the big floe on which they had spent the summer. But in these few days, as so often happens after any catastrophe, they were beginning to reassess the situation. Allan was feeling a little bit better. They were not going to be able to move now until after the winter. He could not come to much harm resting in their winter quarters and, if he did recover, he would be able to complete the journey with them after all. Wally and Fritz even concocted some other schemes. They had been trying to hand over their winter quarters, complete, to another research organisation, so that their scientific work could be carried on through the following summer. Should Allan be unfit to travel, he could stay on at the winter hut to run the scientific programme with Ken Hedges to look after him. This would free Wally and Fritz for their dash to Spitsbergen. Plans floated back and forth in their tiny microcosm but they were also linked to the big, outside world, were dependent on it for supplies and the winter hut, and unfortunately had already involved their Committee, 6,000 miles away in London, in the decision-making.

Wally now told Ken Hedges that they had decided that Allan would stay for the winter; there was no need for him to be lifted out straight away, but Ken thought differently, pointing out that Allan needed proper hospital treatment if he were not to risk suffering for years from a weak back. He could even be crippled for life. Ken was not moved by Allan's plea that he was prepared to take the risk and stated that if Wally ignored his advice he would have no other choice but to resign from the expedition, though he would remain with Allan to care for him as long as he was on the ice.

It was a stalemate. It was also another crisis both for the expedition and for Ken. This was the first occasion when his own expertise had been needed, and the other three had rejected it. One can sympathise with and understand both stances. As so often happens, there was no clearly right course to take, but it certainly accentuated the split within the expedition still further. If Ken had felt isolated before, it was very much worse now. Ken gave Wally his medical report on Allan, addressed to the Commandant of the Royal Army Medical Corps, and asked him to send it out. The following day Wally sent out his own assessment of the situation to the Committee, recommending that Allan Gill should be allowed to stay through the winter and be evacuated the following spring, should this still be necessary. A few days went by and then the fatal message arrived: 'While recognising Allan's great wish to winter, we regretfully decided that on medical grounds and to enable earliest possible start next spring, he must, repeat must, be evacuated in Phipps' 'plane. A three-man party is regarded as the minimum acceptable risk, therefore Wally, Ken and Fritz to winter and complete journey.'

Wally was furious. In effect, the Committee, sitting in a cosy London office all those thousands of miles away, were taking over the command of the expedition and making operational decisions over his head. Confronted by the two conflicting opinions on the fitness of a member of the team, the Committee had to act as arbiter and had no real choice but to back the medical opinion, inevitably supported by the Commandant of the RAMC, against the opinion of the expedition leader. Wally described the impact their judgement made on him:

> Ken was with me at the time the message came through. I read it out with difficulty for the words stuck in my throat . . . Ken went back ahead of me to the tent where Allan and Fritz were having a brew; I walked around for a while trying to get a grip on what I suppose was a mixture of anger and the deepest personal sympathy for my old sledging companion . . . I crawled through the tent and squatted on a box at the foot of Ken's bed. Allan and Fritz looked up expectantly.
> 'You've shot your bolt, mate. They want you out.'

It is not surprising that Wally exploded that night over the radio to Squadron-Leader Freddie Church, their communications link man at Point Barrow. They used to chat for half an hour each day on a seldom-used frequency, and Wally had come to treat it as a direct, private conversation which must have been an important thera-peutic release for him. Now, speaking about the Committee's decision, Wally said into the microphone, 'They don't know what the bloody hell they are talking about.' It was the exasperated outburst that any of us might have made to a close friend, knowing that it would go no further. But Peter Dunn, the *Sunday Times* correspon-dent who was covering the story, had made quite sure that he, also, was in the little radio shack that day. Freddie Church had had no chance to warn Wally of this and Peter Dunn heard the entire outburst. Freddie tried to persuade Peter Dunn that this was confidential, that it could destroy Wally's career if his remarks were publicised, but Dunn, the newsman, was adamant. Someone else could have been listening in to the conversation and to protect himself with his own paper he had to send the story out. He did so, with an embargo that it should not be published without his clearance. The cable arrived in London on the Monday, when the staff of Sunday papers take a rest day. But the duty sub-editor, recognising it was hot news, passed it on to *The Times* – but left out Peter Dunn's embargo. The newsdesk of *The Times* immediately saw it as a headline scoop and had it set up for the following day's paper. It was only just before going to print that editor, William Rees-Mogg, felt he should warn Wally's Committee what he was doing. He 'phoned Sir Miles Clifford first, but he was out of the country. He then 'phoned Sir Vivian Fuchs, the deputy Chairman. Fuchs was appalled that this had been leaked to the press and even threatened *The Times* with an injunction, but Rees-Mogg responded, quoting their right to publish anything they wanted about the expedition – and did so. Up to this moment the rest of the media had taken comparatively little interest in the expedition but now, with a big juicy scandal, they seized upon the story, besieging Fuchs and the other members of the Committee for an explanation. Caught off-balance, anxious to justify their actions, the Committee muttered about Wally Herbert suffering from 'winteritis' – a condition of isolation and stress that can cloud judgement and become a danger to all concerned.

But the expedition had to go on. They were now due to have an air drop of the

A Canadian Airforce plane makes a low pass overhead after an airdrop of winter supplies.

prefabricated hut and all their supplies for the winter. This came in on time. But Wally was determined to keep Allan with them if he possibly could and luckily for him the smooth, new ice around them was undoubtedly on the thin side for a light 'plane to land. Very soon it would be too dark. So ice and weather conditions collaborated to prevent the 'plane landing and, in the meantime, Allan Gill was showing positive signs of recovery, hobbling around the camp and doing his best to help in the day-to-day work wherever he could. Their autumn progress had been negligible. In the eight days they had been moving they had covered only six and a half miles. They were now 240 miles short of their scheduled wintering place, but even so they set to and started to prepare themselves for the winter, assembling the little hut, building primitive furniture and preparing the various scientific programmes they planned to pursue – while the floe on which they were living would, they hoped, drift steadily closer to the North Pole.

They were faced with six months of immobility, much of the time in total darkness, squeezed into a tiny hut whose floor space was four and a half metres square. Each man had his own little area. Ken built a nook of shelves around his bed, with a blanket to give himself some privacy; he was to disappear behind it, into his own little world, for days on end, coming out only to relieve his bodily functions. Wally built a packing-case desk on which he could work on his reports and the book he would have to produce at the end of the expedition, while Fritz had an area devoted to his scientific work. Allan opted for sleeping throughout the winter outside in one of the tents, where it was bitterly cold, but at least he could get away from the tension of that tiny hut.

There was external stress as well. On the 20th November, when they were plunged in perpetual darkness, the floe cracked only seventy-five metres from the hut, between them and some of the supply dumps they had laid out scattered over the floe. They could hear the creaking and groaning of the ice, interspersed with staccato cracks, as the floes jostled and ground against each other in the black of the night. Picking their way across their floe by the light of hurricane lanterns, they saw that what had been a substantial island was now reduced to one half a mile long and only 250 metres wide. Wally and Fritz set out with dog teams and found a more substantial home for the rest of the winter about two miles away. The next few days were spent in relaying their twenty-seven tons of food, fuel, other supplies and, finally, the prefabricated hut to the site of their new home; all of this in the dark, in temperatures of around −35°C.

And then back to the routine of scientific work for ten hours a day – of cooking and washing up, of reading and sleeping, all in the unchanging dark and cold. Added to the stress of their uneven relationship was the worry of whether they would be able to complete their journey; they were so far behind their schedule, so far from the North Pole, let alone Spitsbergen. Allan Gill exercised quietly, slowly building up his mobility, strengthening his back. He was determined to finish the course if he possibly could. Ken Hedges, isolated and now in a profound depression created by a near-insufferable situation, was still equally determined to complete the expedition.

At this stage Fritz Koerner was probably the least unhappy member, for he was totally involved in a massive scientific programme, too extensive for one man to carry out. He was working flat out throughout the winter, going out in all weathers to check his instruments, exercising at the same time both himself and his dog team, working for hours over his figures and snatching the minimum of sleep.

They had relied on drifting steadily towards the Pole, but their star shots showed that their progress was more of an erratic zigzag. Yet through the winter they did

Wally Herbert in his corner of the expedition's cramped winter quarters made daily contact with Squadron-Leader Freddie Church at Point Barrow.

slowly drift closer to their goal. And, as the winter slipped by, they started preparing for their journey the following spring. Wally built a snow house out of blocks in which each one of them worked on his own new sledge which had been dropped in with all the other supplies, strengthening the framework, sewing harnesses and making sure that everything was ready for their dash to Spitsbergen.

There were still plans to fly Allan Gill out in the early spring and Geoff Renner had been brought to Point Barrow to replace him. Wally was quietly determined, however, to hang on to Allan if he possibly could. He wanted to set out from his winter quarters on the 25th February, still in the dark and cold of winter, to give them the maximum time to make the journey all the way to Spitsbergen. They were almost ready to go, the sledges part-packed on the 24th, when the seas decided for them. Suddenly the ice around them began to erupt in a terrifying icequake, splitting and breaking all around the hut. It was time to get out – fast. They finished packing, scrambled over opening leads to rescue dogs and loads and, still in the dark in temperatures of around −43°C, set out on the last, and by far the longest, leg of their journey. They were carrying not only the food and supplies they were going to need in the next months but also a huge load of scientific instruments and specimens, the fruits of Fritz Koerner's work from the previous summer and all that winter.

The journey to the Pole was even more fierce than the previous year. It was bitterly cold, with temperatures down to −50°C. Even in the depths of winter the ice was no less active, heaving into rippling pressure ridges, breaking up into leads of black waters – even blacker than the sky above. They froze over in moments, but there was always the fear of the fresh ice breaking. They kept going for eight hours at a

A few miles from the Pole Wally Herbert had a close call with a polar bear when the bolt of his rifle jammed in the cold.

time; that was as much as they could manage in the bitter cold. Sometimes they only made a couple of miles, the broken ice was so bad. And it went on day after day, as they slowly clawed their way towards the Pole. They saw little of each other during the day. It was usually Fritz out in front, with Wally taking up the rear to give Ken, or anyone else, a helping hand. Allan Gill was usually just behind Fritz and would slip into the lead whenever he had a chance, though he was not meant to go out in front. Ken was nearly always in third position, infinitely methodical and careful in the way he packed his sledge, but travelling through the day in what seemed to Fritz a dream.

There were moments of great beauty as well as excitement and danger. Wally wrote: 'On 12th March we saw the sun for the first time since 6th October. It was a blood-red, beautiful sight after five months and seven days – a living, pulsating thing it seemed to be, slowly drifting on a sea stained red with the blood it released.'

A few days later Wally, bringing up the rear, realised that he was being followed by a polar bear. His rifle was not loaded and the few rounds of ammunition he always carried were in the pocket of an anorak stuffed into the front of the sledge, out of his reach. The bear was rapidly overtaking the sledge as Wally crawled along the top, screaming at the dogs to keep going, and dug out the anorak. By the time he had loaded his rifle the bear was only fifty metres away; he raised the rifle and pulled the trigger, but it had jammed in the cold. The bear was closing fast. In desperation, Wally slapped the bolt with the palm of his hand; the rifle fired, sending a shot up into the air, but it was enough to alarm the bear which ambled away behind some ice blocks. This was just a few miles from the Pole.

Allan was still due to be flown out once a 'plane could land near them; this was still a constant source of irritation within the party and Fritz, who was sharing a tent with Ken Hedges, had some blazing arguments on the subject. Not only was Wally trying to find every possible means of postponing a landing, but Fritz also had a feeling that Weldy Phipps, the pilot who was meant to fly in, was quietly conspiring to help Allan Gill remain with the crossing party by finding various excuses for not coming. And so, as the sun slowly crept up into the sky Allan who was by far the toughest and most attuned to this environment – in Wally's words 'the emotional anchor man of the party' – stayed on with the expedition.

On the 5th April Wally calculated that they had, at last, reached the Pole. It looked like any other bit of ice, anywhere in the Arctic Ocean, but this was it – the very top of the world. Immediately Wally sent a message to the Queen to announce their achievement. And then, a few moments later, Allan Gill, who had also been calculating the results, poked his head into the tent to announce that he thought they might be seven miles short. There followed an exhausting hide and seek game in slow motion, as they tried to find this elusive point. It took them another twenty hours of hard sledging before they finally satisfied themselves that they had truly reached it. Wally described the moment:

> It had been an elusive spot to find and fix – the North Pole, where two separate sets of meridians meet and all directions are south. Trying to set foot upon it had been like trying to step on the shadow of a bird that was hovering overhead, for the surface across which we were moving was itself a moving surface on a planet that was spinning about an axis beneath our feet. We were dog tired and hungry. Too tired to celebrate our arrival on the summit of this super-mountain around which the sun circles almost as though stuck in a groove.

The traditional photograph at the North Pole, 6th April 1969, after some frantic sledging to establish the elusive exact spot.

One cannot help wondering if Cook or Peary hadn't fudged their calculations when standing exhausted in this featureless, shifting expanse of sea-borne ice some

sixty years before. The Pole had, however, been reached overland the previous year, when Ralph Plaisted and his party drove their Skidoos from the region of Ellesmere Island, but then they had been flown back to the safety of land. That same summer of 1968, Roger Tufft, who had withdrawn from Wally's expedition, had joined up with Hugh and Myrtle Simpson, a husband and wife team who combined science with polar and mountain adventures. They had tried to reach the Pole on skis, hauling their sledges and carrying all their food with them to be independent of air drops. It was a simple, lightweight venture that had appealed to Roger. But the initial rough ice had been too difficult, their gear inadequate, and they had been forced to abandon their attempt.

Wally's team were undoubtedly on the Pole; they had spent twenty-four precious hours making sure. They put the camera on a tripod and took a delayed-action shot of themselves standing, statuesque in their furs, by a laden sledge and an unfurled Union Jack. The picture has a nostalgic, slightly sad quality about it. It could have been taken sixty years before; the furs, the sledge, the bearded frosted figures would have looked just the same.

Their journey was by no means over but at least they were now making some fast times, the four sledges stretched out over several miles, following in each other's tracks, heading ever southwards towards Spitsbergen. It became something of a mad gallop. Fritz Koerner remembers:

> You'd make a frantic dash in the morning to get off first because whoever was off first led. It was quite childish really. It was a mad rush to pack. Allan and I would just bundle everything into a couple of tarpaulins, chuck them onto the sledges and then go like hell to the other side of the first pressure ridge, where we would pack things a bit better and then tear off again, to make sure that we were first. Wally and Ken were much more methodical; Wally even had a special place for his ice axe, though I think Ken was the most efficient of all.
>
> Once out in front, you'd stay there all day. Allan wasn't meant to lead, because of his back, but every now and then he'd catch me up and he'd say, 'Look, Uncle Ben's out of the way, what if I lead for a bit?' We called Ken Uncle Ben – the very fact that we had a different name for him showed that he was away from us. And I'd say, 'Sure.' And away he'd go.
>
> Then Wally would come up at the end of the day and he'd quietly say, 'Allan led a bit, didn't he?' And I'd say, 'How the bloody hell did you know?' 'Oh, I noticed the tracks curling round the other set.'

They were all tired, underfed and stretched to the limit, both physically and mentally. It was a race with the summer melt, for they had to reach solid land before the southern edges of the pack ice began to break up and drift off into the Atlantic. There were plenty of crises to test them still further. The tent Allan and Fritz were sharing was burnt down one day, when they left the Primus stove unattended. The tent could be patched up, but Allan's sleeping bag was badly damaged and most of his spare clothes destroyed. Ken Hedges very nearly lost his sledge and dogs when he tried to cross a wide lead. The others came up only just in time to rescue them. There was the constant threat of marauding polar bears, who became more numerous the further south they went. But the ice was very much smoother than it had been on the approach to the Pole and they were making good, fast progress. There were signs of land, an old tree trunk sticking out of an ice floe, sea shells and moss on the surface of the ice, an increase in bird life.

Then, on the 23rd May, Wally saw some piled clouds on the distant horizon. They looked like the kind of clouds you would see above a mountain range. That evening he was able to pick out the exposed rocky peaks jutting up into the sky. They were very nearly at the end of their journey. But the ice floes were now beginning to break up, and there was a real risk of being swept out into the open sea before they could

actually make a landfall. The frigate, HMS *Endurance*, had sailed up towards Spitsbergen to meet them and could always rescue them by helicopter, but this just would
not have been the same. There now seemed little hope of reaching the shores of
Spitsbergen, but there were some small islands just to the north and they decided to
go for these.

No longer on the permanent pack ice, they were dodging from the haven of one
small floe to the next, at the mercy of currents and wind, heading for Phipps Island, a
little pile of barren rocks jutting out of the ice. To reach it they had to cross wide areas
of broken mush ice, manoeuvring from ice block to ice block. It was probably the
most dangerous moment of the entire journey. Wally described it:

'Our route back to the floe was cut off. The whole floating mass of ice rubble was
simmering like some vast cauldron of stew. We rushed from one sledge to another as
each in turn jammed in the pressure, or lurched as the ice which was supporting it
relaxed or heaved; at one point my sledge turned completely turtle and ran awkwardly over a six-foot drop from one block of ice to another.'

*Ken Hedges very nearly lost
sledge and dogs in a wide lead.*

The four sledges stretched out over several miles following in each other's tracks.

They spent a frightening, uncomfortable part of a night on a tiny floe. They had failed to reach Phipps Island and were being swept to the north, but there was an even smaller island in the path of their drift. On the 29th May they were close enough to make a dash across the broken mush ice to the island. Fritz stayed behind on the floe, to keep an eye on the camp, and Wally gestured Allan and Ken to make a dash for the land. Wally wrote: 'It was some moments before the full significance of what Allan and Ken had done got through to me and, when it did, it was through a small chunk of granite Ken pressed into my hand. "Brought you a small bit of the island," he said.'

346

They had completed their crossing of the Arctic Ocean, without doubt one of the greatest and most exacting journeys ever made. They had been very dependent upon air support, but it is unlikely that they could have attempted the journey without it. In many ways, the stresses within the team and how each man somehow came through makes the achievement even more impressive. In the short period that the four had to wait for the helicopter to pick them up, and take them back to that big, wide world, of receptions, press conferences and questions, Wally, as any leader would, desperately sought unity within the team, wanting the story of their achievement to have the weight and majesty it deserved as one of the great polar journeys of all time. There was a long and bitter argument over how much of their differences should be revealed but, finally, they all agreed to present a united front.

The helicopter from *Endurance* came sweeping in and hovered down on to their little ice floe. The captain of *Endurance* jumped out, shook hands with Wally and the rest of the team. The journey was over. The stress, depressions, despair and discomfort of the past fifteen months were now something of the past. In the wardroom of *Endurance* Ken was laughing and joking with the ship's officers, providing a fund of amusing stories from the past months, most of which for him had been a nightmare. Allan Gill was already thinking of his next trip out into the empty wastes of the Arctic, while Fritz was absorbed by the vast mass of work he had in front of him from his scientific observations during the journey.

And Wally – this journey represented six years of hard, grinding effort, of solitary work and responsibility, of endless obstacles, many of which had seemed insuperable at the time. He had overcome them all. He had been successful. But success is so very ephemeral and, for Wally, that success was tainted. Somehow, the achievement did not gain the recognition that he felt and I believe it most certainly did deserve.

In the early part of the century there was a huge, devouring interest in all things polar. The early polar explorers were international heroes whose names really were household words. In 1969, however, Wally Herbert's journey across the top of the earth gained scant attention. It was the time of the moon shots. Apollo XI had gone into orbit round the moon only a few days before Wally made his landfall; Neil Armstrong was the first man to set foot on the moon just a few weeks later. The media and the rest of the world, craning their necks into space and obsessed with fast-moving technology, hadn't time to follow the slow, laborious movement of four men with their dog teams, across the top of their own planet.

Solo to the Pole

Naomi Uemura loves wandering alone among the world's wild places, be they mountains or polar wastes.

Uemura was awaked by the dogs barking. Just four days out on the ice, in his solitary journey to the North Pole, he had spent sixteen hours the previous day, cutting through the ice of endless pressure ridges, levering ice blocks, heaving his heavily-laden sledge over roughly-built ice ramps. At the end of it all he had made only a mile of progress and now he was snuggled deep into his sleeping bag, only the tip of his nose showing through the tiny gap he had left for air. It certainly wasn't a dog fight, for the barking had a panic-stricken quality. As Uemura reached for the zip of his sleeping bag, the barking trailed away. He could hear a scampering in the snow – the dogs must have broken loose and scattered. And then, from outside the tent, came another sound – a heavy shuffling tread that transmitted tremors through the snow to his pillow. It could only be a polar bear! His rifle was beside him in the tent, but it was not loaded. He did not dare make a sound or even the slightest movement for fear of attracting the bear, as he listened to it tearing through the sacks of seal meat with its great claws, then chewing the frozen meat just a few feet away.

Uemura's first instinctive terror turned to a strange calm. As he thought of his wife, Kimi-chan, back home in Tokyo, the cold fear was replaced by that vast feeling of regret yet resignation which overcomes so many at the moment of expected death; at the same time, he was fighting – albeit passively – for his life, trying to still his breathing and slow down the racing pump of his heart. The sweat poured off him, making him itch all over, but he dared not scratch, couldn't shift a muscle if he were to survive. He just prayed that the polar bear would be satisfied with the sledge-load of seal meat, pemmican and whale blubber. But the bear was moving once again. It was coming closer. He could feel its weight against the tent, then heard the sound of ripping nylon as it tore through. The bear's nose nuzzled against his back. He'd had it! But still he lay silent, motionless, his breath held – though knowing he couldn't hold it for very much longer – when suddenly, unaccountably, the bear turned away. It had lost interest and its footsteps slowly receded into the distance.

Uemura took a huge lungful of air and then just lay there, panting and shaking in shocked relief. The tent was ripped open, the food scattered over the ice – most of it eaten or spoilt – but he was still alive, even though he had barely started his journey to the Pole. The mountains of Ellesmere Island still filled the southern horizon and the North Pole was 472 miles away. Gazing at the chaos about him, he couldn't help wondering whether to go on. The polar bear must be somewhere quite close and would, no doubt, come back again once it was hungry. He could hear the dogs yapping with glee in the distance. The threat of the bear now forgotten, they had gone off in pursuit of one of the females who happened to be on heat. Quickly, he thrust aside any thoughts of defeat, radioed for a replacement tent and provisions, loaded his rifle and set out in search of the dogs.

Naomi Uemura has been an adventurer in the broadest sense for his entire adult life. Born in south-west Japan in 1941, the youngest of seven children, he was brought up on a small farm, had shown no particular ability at school either academically or at conventional sports, but had managed to get into university to study agriculture. He became aware of the mountains for the first time while at university and was quickly captivated, not so much by technical rock climbing, but rather by the mountains themselves. He loved to wander amongst them, started to venture into them on his own and savoured the freedom of solitary climbing, where he was dependent upon no-one but himself. It was characteristic that, as soon as he had completed his university course, he set out on his own for the United States with only $110, aiming to work his way across to the European Alps. He reached Chamonix in the late summer of 1964 and pitched a tent by the Aiguille du Midi Téléphérique Station. He knew no-one, could speak hardly any English or French, and therefore had no choice but to climb on his own. His career very nearly ended then and there, when he fell into a crevasse whilst making a solitary attempt on Mont Blanc. Having fallen a couple of metres, he was saved when his rucksack jammed against a constriction in the ice walls.

That winter he managed to get a job with a ski patrol in a small resort, even though he was only an average skier. Then, the following year, he had his first trip to the Himalaya, to join his own university expedition to Cho Oyu II, a peak of 7646 metres. The next five years were crammed with adventure as he wandered the world, most of the time on his own with very little money, climbing Mont Blanc, Kilimanjaro, Mount Kenya, Aconcagua, the highest peak in South America, and Mount Sanford in Alaska. It was during this period that he descended the river Amazon on a raft.

Then, in 1969, Uemura was invited to join a Japanese expedition making a reconnaissance of the South-West Face of Everest. That autumn they reached a height of 8300 metres, just below the Rock Band, the barrier which guards the upper part of the Face. The following year the Japanese returned, but split their effort between the South-West Face and the South Col route. They wanted to be certain of putting the first Japanese on the summit of Everest. Assigned to the South Col team, Uemura reached the top, while the Face team were stopped by the Rock Band – partly, I suspect, because the main drive of the expedition was being directed at the easier alternative. That same year he flew to Alaska to make a solo ascent of Mount McKinley and became the first man to reach the highest points of five continents.

In 1971 Uemura joined an International expedition to Everest. This, also, had two objectives, the South-West Face and the West Ridge. They failed to attain either for a number of reasons, the main one being appalling weather conditions, but an accident in the early stages of the expedition and discord within the team also contributed. Nevertheless, this expedition achieved a great deal, reaching a height of 8380 metres on the face. Dougal Haston and Don Whillans were out in front on the face the whole time; this was one of the points of contention with some members of the team, but neither Uemura nor his climbing partner and compatriot, Ito, ever complained. Loyally, they supported Whillans and Haston throughout the climb, ferrying up supplies from the camp immediately beneath the top camp – a monotonous, exhausting task, particularly if there is no likelihood of having a turn out in front. I asked Uemura what he felt about this, and he simply replied: 'They never asked us. We did our best to support them. It was our duty.'

His experience on this expedition probably strengthened Uemura's preference for solitary ventures, when there could be none of the complications of team rivalry and dissension. It was at this time that he began to look away from the mountains towards the polar wastes. Uemura was not so much a technical climber as a traditional, all-round mountaineer. Most of his ascents had been on mountains by their easiest routes. Now, he wanted to stretch himself, to find new ground and, at the same time no doubt, maintain his reputation as one of Japan's most outstanding adventurers. It was becoming more and more difficult to do this in the mountains, however, since climbing – even on the highest peaks of the Himalaya – was going increasingly towards technically difficult ground on ice and rock. Uemura knew that there were plenty of Japanese climbers more proficient than he. Polar travel, however, seemed to offer all the ingredients he needed, and he began, literally, to dream of a crossing of the Antarctic continent. Then, from 1974 to 1976, he made an incredible 7500-mile journey across Northern Canada, from Greenland to Alaska, travelling on his own with a dog team through the winter and resting up through the summer.

But it was the North Pole that intrigued him and, most of all, the thought of going there alone. Having served a sound apprenticeship in the Arctic he had, at the same time, built up the patronage and support to undertake his ventures. This was provided by a large Japanese publishing house and television network which provided both the money and the administrative back-up. Like Wally Herbert, he was going to depend on air support for his dash to the Pole. This meant he could keep the loads on his sledge to a reasonable level and, of course, in an emergency could call in help. Not only did he have a radio to call his base at Resolute Bay, but also a small transponder that sent out a continuous signal to a satellite that orbited the earth round the axis of the two Poles. Each time it passed overhead, this gave his exact position to the support team.

Setting up camp on the ice.

It is easy to under-rate his achievement because of this level of technological support, but the fact remains that he was alone on the ice, trying to cross one of the most rugged and difficult obstacle courses in the world. In an emergency, if he lost his sledge in an open lead, was attacked by a polar bear, or if the ice opened up beneath him during the night, the transponder and aircraft backing would have been very little use.

He set out from Cape Columbia, on the north coast of Ellesmere Island, on the 6th March, 1978. It is 476 miles to the Pole, very much shorter in distance than the route chosen by Wally Herbert, but Uemura was on his own with only seventeen dogs for company. The way was hard going from the very start, with pressure ridges criss-crossing the route. On heavy ground Wally Herbert's team had worked together, manhandling each sledge in turn over the piled ice blocks, but Uemura had to do it alone, cutting them away with his axe, levering blocks out of the way with a crowbar and then heaving and pushing the sledge across each barrier with the help of his dogs. It was early season, bitterly cold, with the temperature going down to −44°C, and only a few hours' daylight each day. The sun, which threw out no heat, was an orange orb, low on the horizon. After three days' exhausting struggle he had made only a few miles progress from the low-lying coast, with hundreds of miles lying ahead. He had adopted both the Eskimo food and also their clothing of polar bear trousers, caribou parka and sealskin mukluks. He cooked as little as possible, for the condensation inside the tent quickly soaked, and then froze, his sleeping bag. In the mornings he ate a few biscuits washed down by sweetened tea, keeping his main meal for the evening when he ate caribou or seal meat with a few mouthfuls of whale blubber.

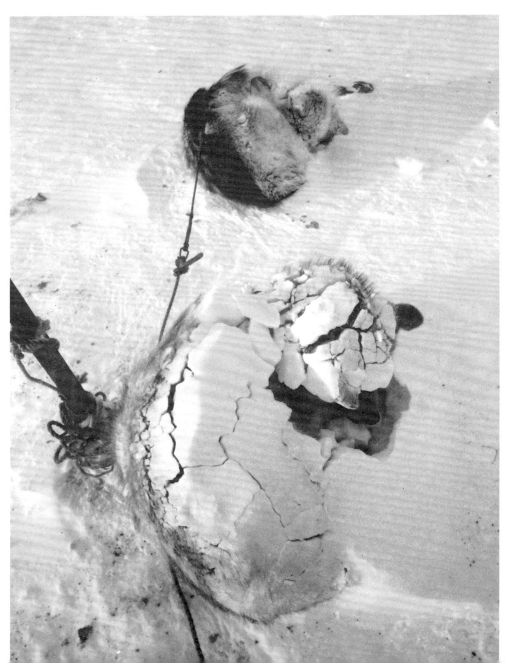

It was on the morning of the fourth day that he was attacked by the polar bear. Afterwards, having collected the dogs, he tethered them securely and huddled into the ruined tent to await the arrival of the emergency airlift. At the same time he also waited for the bear; it was sure to come back in search of more food. Although his rifle was now loaded there was still a high element of risk. In those temperatures it could easily freeze up or hang fire. He took the precaution of soaking the firing mechanism in kerosene. Once again, the dogs gave first warning of the bear's approach. Grabbing the rifle, Uemura crouched and waited by the tent as the bear emerged from the piled ice blocks near the camp and padded confidently towards what it hoped would be its next meal. Uemura waited until it was only fifty metres away before squeezing the trigger. The bear reared up onto its hind legs and then collapsed in the snow. It tried to drag itself back to the shelter of the ice blocks, but fell motionless after Uemura had pumped some more shots into its massive body. In spite of his narrow escape, he couldn't help feeling saddened at the death of this magnificent animal.

A few hours later the aircraft came roaring overhead and dropped fresh supplies and a replacement tent. He was able to renew the journey across the seemingly endless ice. He was still in the coastal strip, where the shifting floes are squeezed and smashed against the immovable bulk of Ellesmere Island. It was a nightmare obstacle course that had stopped several larger expeditions. But Uemura just kept on doggedly, hacking out a trail over the jumbled ice blocks, exhorting, driving, coaxing his dog team as they heaved the heavily loaded sledge over each obstacle. At this stage he was making only a couple of miles progress each day. The peaks of Ellesmere Island never seemed to get any further away.

Undoubtedly, the presence of the dogs lessened the loneliness of his journey. In looking after them he came to know each one in a way that he might never have done if he had had a human companion. He came to know all their traits – who was lazy, who were the hard workers, who were the trouble-makers. Inevitably, some of the dogs tired, were injured in fights or cut their paws on the sharp ice, when frostbite followed all too quickly. He allowed injured dogs out of their traces so that they could run alongside the sledge and then, instead of shooting them and feeding them to the others, as would have been done in the old days, he had them airlifted out whenever he could find a stretch of ice suitable for the 'plane to land. Altogether, he had five re-supply flights in which the 'plane landed beside him, and was able to replace his sledge with a lighter model in an effort to speed up his progress.

For all that, some kind of crisis was never far away. Uemura was nearly half-way to the Pole when he saw that one of the dogs was becoming noticeably pregnant. Soon he might have to take on the role of midwife. On the night of 9th April she went into labour, delivering the first pair just outside the tent. The other dogs pounced upon the newly born pups and devoured them before Uemura was able to reach them. He then took Shiro, the mother, inside the tent. Another four plopped out, three alive and one dead. He made a nest of caribou skin for the mewing pups and, the following morning, bundled them all up on top of the sledge. The next night another three were born, of which two survived the night. Another died of exposure before the next supply flight could take out the mother and four surviving pups.

Preoccupation with the dogs, and particularly with the new young lives in the empty wastes, reduced the sense of loneliness, but the physical stress never let up. Uemura was sleeping for only five or six hours at night, keeping going through the day for fifteen or sixteen hours at a time and, as the days lengthened, it got marginally warmer and the open leads between ice floes became more frequent. He had to wait for them to close or take long diversions to get round them, sometimes

The support plane meant Uemura could travel comparatively light and be resupplied en route. But in a life or death emergency on the ice, it would have been of little practical help.

Looking after his dogs, Uemura came to know all their traits of character and they in turn lessened the loneliness of his venture.

making desperate dashes from one small ice plate to the next, or even using the sledge as a bridge over a lead and then walking the dogs over before heaving it across to the other side. Always there was the danger of slipping into the black waters. There was no-one to pull him out and it would have been almost impossible to climb out onto the slippery ice, weighed down as he was with his polar clothing.

Even more frightening was when the ice around him began to break up, so that what had started out as a secure island became little more than a block that could tumble over at any moment, depositing him, dogs and sledge into the icy waters. An eddy of current caught the ice block and swept it against a larger one; Uemura and his dogs scrambled across the gap, pulling the sledge with them.

Throughout his journey there had been some element of competition, for another Japanese expedition was also making the attempt by a different route. Uemura would have liked to have been the first Japanese to reach the Pole, and had been forcing his route as much as possible to achieve his aim, but he now realised that the others would almost inevitably get there first and that he could not afford to force the pace any more. Being alone, there was less margin for error. He decided, therefore, to wait for the ice around him to freeze together into a single mass. It was now −20°C, almost warm by polar standards, and the water took a long time to freeze over. Frequently, he checked the new ice with a steel crowbar to determine whether it was strong enough to withstand the loaded sledge, but had to wait all day. The following morning, 21st April, it had frozen and he was able to set out once again, travelling more than twenty-five miles. On the 23rd he did even better, covering over thirty-seven miles on flat, open ice floes before the ice became broken once again into interminable pressure ridges and open leads.

In some ways he was not as isolated as Wally Herbert's party, who had had supply drops but did not actually meet anyone throughout the entire eighteen months of their journey. Uemura's fifty-four days presented a different kind of stress, the pressure of being alone on the ice, totally dependent on his own initiative in any emergency. He finally reached the Pole on the 29th April. There was no-one there and he spent a complete day taking a series of sightings with his sextant to ensure that he had, indeed, reached the right place. At the same time, his transponder was pumping out its signal to the Nimbus 6 satellite which passed directly above him every 108 minutes.

And then the support 'plane, carrying a load of journalists and a film team, came flying in to record the moment before taking Uemura back to Resolute. The following year he made another solitary journey that was, in some ways, even more impressive than his dash to the Pole. He was the first man to traverse the Greenland ice cap from north to south, 1400 miles over ice and snow as bleak and high and empty as the Antarctic continent.

Uemura still dreams of crossing Antarctica by himself and has certainly shown that, with adequate air support, he is capable of doing so. One day, given the necessary support and permission, no doubt he will do this as well.

Double Eagle

Seated on a ledge on a Lakeland crag, I have often gazed with envy at a peregrine falcon as it hovers and swoops past me, screeching its warning; high on a sea cliff, I have wondered at the streamlined speed and grace of gulls as they wheel, plunging and diving in ever-changing patterns. But the contrast between my own landlocked slowness and the freedom of a bird is at its greatest in the Himalaya. At 7900 metres I can do little more than plod, breathless, a few paces at a time. A Himalayan chough – squat, black and ugly with its great crow's bill – soars past effortlessly on the updraught of the wind. There is a beauty of motion that is both an expression of freedom and yet of perfect control – something that men have striven for throughout the ages. Many followed Icarus and Daedalus with man-made wings, in doomed efforts to emulate the flight of birds. But it was the invention of the balloon that gave man his first freedom from the bonds of gravity.

Hydrogen, at first called 'inflammable air' for obvious reasons, was discovered in 1766; its lifting properties were quickly noticed. The problem, however, was to find a way of containing the gas since it passed straight through the finest woven materials available at that time. And then another discovery was made. Joseph Montgolfier, a Frenchman and owner of a string of paper mills, observed that if you heated air it would rise and, if contained in some kind of envelope, could therefore raise a vessel above the ground. In addition, the heated air could be contained more easily than hydrogen.

He made this observation in 1782, built a small experimental hot air balloon that November, a bigger one which carried a sheep, a cock and a duck in September 1783 and then came the greatest step of all, man's first excursion into the air, more exciting and fundamental in some ways even than the first flight into space. On the 21st November 1783, Jean-François Pilâtre de Rozier and the Marquis d'Arlandes made man's first free ascent, without the constraint of a safety rope to anchor them to the ground. Using straw soaked in spirit to fire the small furnace suspended beneath the canopy, they were in the air for twenty-five minutes, travelled about 9,000 yards and were said to have reached an altitude of 3,000 feet, though most of their journey was at a much lower height.

While Montgolfier was working on his hot air balloon, another French scientist was trying to develop a hydrogen balloon. He was only just behind Montgolfier and, on the 1st December 1783, Jacques Charles and Aîné Robert made a successful flight, reaching a height of 1,800 feet. It was so successful that immediately after landing, Charles took off once again, this time by himself. With the lighter load, the balloon shot upwards almost like a rocket, reaching a height of 10,000 feet. He must have known all the wonder, apprehension and elation of Hillary on the summit of

Everest, of Armstrong on the moon, but his leap into the high air was even more revolutionary – the quality of the unknown at that time even greater. He commented: 'I passed in ten minutes from the temperature of spring to that of winter. The cold was keen and dry but not insupportable. I examined my sensations calmly. I could hear myself live, so to speak.'

The fabric of his balloon was a perfect sphere of rubberised silk, with an open neck at the bottom, so that gas could escape freely as it expanded, and a valve at the top to enable gas to be released once the balloonist wished to descend. He also carried ballast, which he could discard to give him greater lift. In principle, the balloons of today, both the hot air and gas variety, are identical to the originals, though the fuel to heat the air has changed from spirit-soaked straw to the more convenient and efficient bottled gas, and helium has replaced the dangerously inflammable hydrogen in gas balloons.

For over a hundred years the balloon reigned supreme. The English Channel was crossed, steam-driven propellers were introduced to change the balloon from a plaything of the winds into a ship of the air, but then, in 1903, the balloon was eclipsed by the invention of the aeroplane and powered flight. The balloon – even the powered airship – could never emulate a bird. The balloon was a flying bubble on the winds, the airship a cumbersome leviathan in the air. But the aeroplane quickly evolved from its lumbering, fragile beginnings into a machine that was as manoeuvrable as a bird, but very much faster. The most adventurous journeys by aeroplane took place during the period between the First and Second World Wars, the open cockpit days of Francis Chichester, with the minimum of instruments or navigational aids. In the post-war period innovative air adventure has moved into the realms of high technology.

The modern 'plane now bears very little relation to the bird in flight which was its original inspiration. It is the hang-glider pilot who has really come closest to the bird and, through this, perhaps knows the greatest elation. He uses the subtle shifts of his own bodyweight suspended in the air to control and steer his fragile craft. The experience of a hang-glider pilot could be compared to that of an aqualung swimmer, or even a technical rock climber. The experience is intense, a delicate tightrope walk with danger, where judgement and control must be perfect but the period of exposure is short-lived. The hang-glider sinks to the ground, the aqualung swimmer returns to the surface, the climber reaches the top of his crag. This is undoubtedly adventure, perhaps in its purest and most uncomplicated form, but it is beyond the ground rules that I have set myself, for these lack that element of endurance needed in an expedition or long voyage.

In this respect ballooning, the oldest, the least changed of all aeronautical activities, has a vast potential. A powered aircraft can cleave its way through the air, ignoring the winds and air currents; but the balloonist places himself in the hands of the wind. He becomes part of the air itself, his only controls his own ability to vent off gas to enable him to descend, or to throw away ballast to allow him to rise. He must understand the air and the way it can be heated by the sun or cooled by a bank of clouds; he must use the prevailing winds and find the right altitude where the winds might take him where he wants to go. There is always an intriguing, perhaps infuriating, often dangerous level of uncertainty. Will the winds change unexpectedly? And the air itself is still full of invisible mysteries, of powerful up-draughts that can lift the balloon with almost rocket force into dangerously rare altitudes or, even more frightening, huge down-draughts, invisible torrents of air that can hurl a balloon down towards the earth's surface with remorseless speed.

There is something fascinating and challenging in the concept of crossing a stretch of water. The English Channel was first crossed in 1785, the more turbulent and much wider Irish Sea was crossed in 1815. The next logical challenge was the Atlantic. Only sixteen years after the Wright brothers made the first powered aircraft flight in 1903, Alcock and Brown flew the Atlantic, but there was to be a gap of very nearly 200 years between the first manned balloon flight in France and the crossing of the Atlantic by balloon. It certainly wasn't for want of trying. There were fourteen serious attempts between 1873 and 1977. Five balloonists died, all of them in the 1970s, partly perhaps because of the growing intensity of competition. The most successful bid was made in 1977 by the American balloonist Ed Yost; a taciturn individualist, he made his attempt solo in his helium balloon, *Silver Fox*, establishing records for both duration and distance in manned flight but, even so, dropped into the sea 700 miles short of the coast of Europe. Fortunately, he had sighted a tramp steamer and was able to ditch the balloon alongside it.

It was an article in the *National Geographic Magazine* about this attempt that inspired Max Anderson, an American balloonist and very successful businessman, to take up the challenge. Maxie Anderson, at the age of forty-two, had reached that critical stage when one wonders if one has slipped past one's prime and realises that life and the duration of one's own physical powers are definitely finite. By any standards he had had a very successful life. The son of a self-made millionaire who had fought his way up in the rough world of oil and mining, Max had been sent to the Missouri Military Academy at the age of eight, after the divorce of his parents. He managed to get his pilot's licence at the age of fifteen by lying about his age and, even whilst still at college, started working for his father during the vacations – not merely as the apprentice learning from the bottom, but as his father's representative, trouble-shooting and clinching deals. At the age of twenty he negotiated a deal which gave his father and himself control of the richest uranium mine in the United States. Before he was thirty, he was President of his own company and a millionaire in his own right. A broken nose and blinded eye are tokens of a life lived and played hard. But he has a quiet voice and an old-world courtesy. At the same time, though, his success and his position are reflected in a tendency to deliver a soliloquy rather than to conduct a conversation. He is used to being listened to without interruption.

By 1977 Max Anderson certainly had everything that most people could want; an exciting and very successful business, a happy marriage that had lasted twenty-five years, four bright children, a large and handsome house, a ski condominium at Taos, New Mexico, aeroplanes, cars, a string of Arab horses, a yacht moored off the coast of California, and a hot air balloon, in which he had already picked up some satisfying firsts, including winning the first balloon race from the Bahamas to the United States in 1973. But still there was discontent, a need to stretch himself to the limit, a need perhaps also to command a wider respect and recognition than just that of the successful businessman and local sportsman.

He has always been hyperactive, finding difficulty in sleeping at night, and it was during one of his wakeful periods that he picked up the magazine telling of Ed Yost's attempt to balloon the Atlantic. Suddenly, he knew that he had found his goal; it answered so many of his needs and was a huge romantic challenge in a field in which he already had some experience and success. A childhood hero had been Charles Lindbergh, the first man to make a solo flight across the Atlantic – here was another truly exciting first, in a world where so many of the great journeys and adventures had already been completed. He resolved straight away to be the first man to cross the Atlantic by balloon because, as he put it, 'To me it's a way of entering history.'

Maxie Anderson has that combination, important to all successful adventurers – a romantic streak tempered by a coolly analytical mind. The decision to attempt the

Atlantic was made on emotional impulse, but every step after that was weighed carefully, was approached with the same precision with which he had built up his business empire.

He never contemplated doing it alone, feeling that the task was too big for one man and, perhaps more to the point, he has never been a loner. Although in some ways a self-contained man, he undoubtedly likes to share his experiences with others. One of his closest friends was Ben Abruzzo; they had known each other for about fifteen years, had skied together and had bought their first hot air balloon as a joint venture. Their personalities complemented each other; Anderson, Nordic, precise, controlled and cool; Abruzzo dark, short but powerfully built, fast talking and very fast moving. Also a millionaire, Abruzzo had fought his way up from comparatively poor beginnings in a Chicago suburb, had been made bankrupt once but bounced back and ended up making a fortune in property speculation. More of a risk-taker than Anderson, revelling in pushing himself to the limit on skis, hang-glider or light aircraft, he had had frequent smashes and was often hobbling around in a plaster cast. He, also, had a very happy and settled marriage. Although the two men were so different in appearance, background and temperament, their wives could almost be mistaken for sisters – both being of Scandinavian origin, good looking and blonde, and both called Pat. Each was happy to fulfil a loyal and very supportive role.

Ben Abruzzo immediately seized on Anderson's invitation and together they plunged into the practical planning of their venture. For a start, they had the personal wealth to finance their project and did not have the wearing, often distracting task of finding sponsors. The first step was to get a suitable balloon. Their own experience was in hot air ballooning, but the range of a hot air balloon is limited by the amount of fuel it can carry. A helium balloon was, therefore, an essential choice, and Ed Yost, whose solo attempt had first inspired Anderson, built it. At a cost of $50,000, it had to be specially made for the trip, and could only be used the one time. Also, they had to learn how to fly a helium balloon, which cost another $3,000 for a small balloon. Yost reckoned that with their experience of hot air ballooning a single practice session would be enough. Another $50,000 was spent on radio and navigational equipment, meteorological services, and a hundred and one other items.

It was a mere six months from Anderson's original conception of the scheme to the flight itself. During this time they built up a ground team to give them the vital meteorological advice they would need, for they had to time their start to catch one of the great high-pressure ridges of fair weather that roll, west to east, across the Atlantic. Then during the flight itself they would need instructions for adjusting their height – the only control they had over their direction – to capture the best winds to drive them to their eventual destination. It was rather like surfing, riding just in front of the crest of the wave represented by a frontal system. They had to stay as high as possible and be careful to stay on the crest, for once having dropped back into the system itself they would be within the storm, with its turbulent airs and conflicting winds. It was a strange combination of the super-scientific with its mission control and computer printouts, and the utmost simplicity of a vessel that has hardly changed since the first hydrogen balloon flights in 1783.

On the 9th September 1977 the balloon *Double Eagle*, the entire Anderson and Abruzzo families, ground crew, a large entourage of journalists and an inquisitive mob assembled in a gravel pit near Marshfield in Massachusetts. Like the departure of almost any expedition, it was frantic, at times chaotic, with a dozen last-minute preparations still being made. Ben and Max spent most of the time talking to journalists; it had been like this for the last three days. The children were filling the

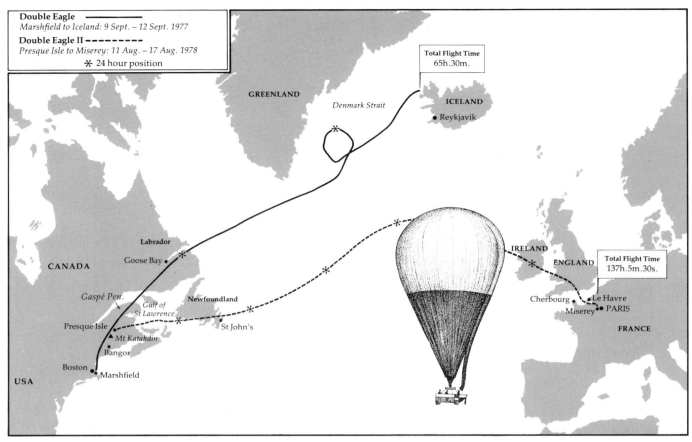

GREENLAND

Denmark Strait

Total Flight Time
65h.30m.

ICELAND

• Reykjavik

Labrador

Goose Bay •

CANADA

Gaspé Pen.

Gulf of St Lawrence

Newfoundland

Presque Isle •

▲ *Mt Katahdin*

• Bangor

Boston ••
• Marshfield

USA

St John's

IRELAND

ENGLAND

Total Flight Time
137h.5m.30s.

Cherbourg •
Miserey ••
Le Havre •
• PARIS

FRANCE

The flight of Double Eagle

ballast bags with sand; the two wives were loading the gondola with supplies, food, a small stove, portable toilet, ordinary, everyday camping items that once again emphasised the merging of simple adventure with the high technology of their wireless and navigational equipment. Each item had to be weighed and labelled, for everything in that gondola was potential ballast which would eventually be dumped to give them that extra little bit of lift, perhaps to enable them to make the last two or three miles across the sea to the shores of Europe, or the last mile to Paris which was their final, grand and romantic objective. The original birthplace of ballooning, Paris had also been the destination of Charles Lindbergh.

Already they were in a race, both against the elements and another competitor. Dewey Reinhard, another well-known American balloonist was also preparing to fly the Atlantic. Whilst Anderson and Abruzzo were planning a high-altitude crossing on the crest of a pressure ridge, Reinhard was going to the other extreme, staying close to the surface of the ocean so that he could scoop up sea water for use as ballast whenever he needed it, and drop a sea anchor if the winds ever started blowing him off his chosen course. A suitable weather system for Max and Ben's approach was already building up over Canada, but they had to get airborne at exactly the right moment to catch the strong southerly winds that would blow them up towards the coast of Labrador, where they could hope to catch the high-pressure ridge at just the moment to surf their way across the Atlantic. If they were too early or too late they could be caught in violent storms. If they missed it altogether, they might have to wait three weeks or more for another system and, of course, in that time their competitor – who was not dependent on a high-pressure ridge – could set out on his attempt. Bob Rice, the team's meteorologist and Rich Schwoebel, their technical director, had calculated that they needed to take off as soon as possible after sunset on the 9th to catch the high-pressure ridge.

It was all much too rushed. Ed Yost, the designer and manufacturer of the balloon, and the only man who could supervise its inflation, had been at work on another project in California. He was due back on a flight to Boston that afternoon, but in the general rush they had forgotten to arrange for someone to pick him up from the airport. As a result, it was late in the afternoon before he arrived. On his attempt at the Atlantic crossing Yost had spent days on the final check-out and count-down. Anderson and Abruzzo were doing it in a matter of hours.

As dusk fell the tension and confusion increased. In the harsh, television flood-lights the balloon, fully inflated, towered like a huge ice-cream cornet, black under-neath, and the perfect, silver hemisphere of its top gleaming brilliantly against the darkening sky. The gondola now had to be fastened to the straining balloon. Ed Yost called for the crimping tool that would lock it into position. It could not be found. It had been left behind at the warehouse where they had collected all their supplies, a good forty-five minutes away. A car was sent off to collect it, but now they were beginning to run out of time. The high-pressure ridge was racing across Canada at about sixty miles per hour.

Doc Wiley, Anderson's company pilot and head of the ground crew, was trying to brief Max on how to operate the wireless that had only just been mounted in the gondola. He had an uncomfortable feeling that Max was not really absorbing anything that he said. Ben Abruzzo was torn by his own private doubts, convinced that he would never see Pat and his family again. There was a last-minute agonising over the position of the high-pressure ridge. Had they missed that vital window? But the very momentum of the event, the excited, over-emotional crowd, the presence of the media and, most important of all, the personalities of the two men, made the launch that night inevitable.

At 8.16 p.m. Ed Yost cut the anchoring sandbags loose and, to the sound of 'The Star-Spangled Banner' played over the public address system, the balloon slowly, majestically rose out of the brilliant pool of light into the darkness beyond. The feelings that Max and Ben had were very similar to those of Heyerdahl or Ridgway and Blyth as they started out on their voyages – fear of the shame of a premature failure, of being swept back to their starting point, of being ditched almost im-mediately and having to face the disappointment and perhaps even ridicule of the crowd that had been waving and cheering their departure. The fear of ridicule completely submerged any fears Max might have had for his own safety:

'If we splashed like damn fools, I couldn't go home,' he told Ben.

Ben said nothing. He felt a stab of worry, part triggered by Maxie's remark, as they rose steadily into the darkness. By the time they had reached 2,000 feet, the initial excitement, tension and secret doubts had all vanished. The lights of Boston stretched, brilliant, below. The VHF radio, their link with the world, crackled with life, the ground controller telling Max their exact position as they swept at around twenty miles an hour in a north-easterly direction, at first along the coast but then east over the heavily forested, rugged State of Maine. Soon they were in dense cloud, unable to see even from one side of the gondola to the other. Max had snuggled down in his sleeping bag. A poor sleeper, he had trained himself before the trip to take cat-naps at almost any time, perhaps indicative of the tight self-discipline that he imposes on himself. Immediately, he dropped into a deep sleep, leaving Ben to plot their course from his own dead reckoning and the fixes given over the radio from flight controllers.

Ben was in charge of the ballast; he had the quick, precise mind that enabled him to keep a constant mental check of the exact state of *Double Eagle* at all times. The ballast was as important as the helium, for once they had nothing left to throw overboard, they could no longer hope to climb. The length of time they could spend aloft depended entirely on how economical they were both in venting off helium and throwing out ballast. They wanted to settle at an altitude of 2,000 feet. This meant throwing out just enough handfuls of sand – no more, no less – to bring the balloon's buoyancy into a state of exact equilibrium at that height.

Soon they were lost on the radar screens below, flying in mountainous country and, as Ben plotted their course, he realised that they were heading straight for Mount Katahdin, a rock spire of just over 1220 metres (4,000 feet). It was a disturbing situation. If he were to discharge ballast to allow them to fly over the peak, they could lose up to half a day in their endurance, particularly if they were caught in the down-draught that you almost always get on the lee side of a mountain range; the only way of escaping would be to jettison more precious ballast. Ben woke Max; they had never discussed the question of who was captain, or how they would make decisions; it just seemed good sense that they should consult each other over every major decision. In this way their relationship was the same as that of a pair of climbers on a mountain.

They consulted their own back-up team through the air controller at the Bangor airport tower. Bob Rice confirmed Max and Ben's opinion that the air currents would sweep round the peak, thus keeping them well away from its precipitous slopes. They decided, therefore, to maintain height and avoid losing any precious ballast. It must have been an eerie situation. They were still in dense cloud; it was pitch dark; there was no sound, no breath of wind, no hint that they were sweeping along at about twenty-five miles per hour, just the image in their minds of the sudden impact of hitting a steep rock face, the rupturing of their balloon, the appalling, tumbling fall.

Ben began yodelling at regular intervals into a brass yacht megaphone.

'Ben, what the hell are you doing?' asked Max.

'Yodelling. The sound bounces off the mountain. If my yodel comes back we can count the number of seconds it takes and find out how close we are to Mount Katahdin.'

Fortunately, the sound never did bounce back and they saw nothing of Mount Katahdin. The weather now cleared and the lights of villages twinkled from the dark forests, like mirror-images of the stars, shining brilliantly above them. Then, in the growing light of the dawn the two men felt full of optimism; they had faced and overcome their first crisis, were now approaching the Canadian border and were right on schedule to meet the ridge of high pressure that was fast approaching them from the west.

But not everything was going according to plan. In theory they should have reached an altitude of around 7,000 feet as the rays of the rising sun warmed up the black cone of the balloon and thus caused the helium to expand. The gas was venting as they expected, but the balloon was rising only very slowly. Max and Ben could not understand this. Then another emergency hit them. They were now over the Gaspé peninsula, at a height of around 3,600 feet above sea level – though they were only 1,700 feet above the forested mountains. Suddenly, the balloon began to drop; it was descending at a rate of 300 feet per minute. In five minutes they would hit the ground, but they resisted the temptation to throw out any ballast, hoping that the balloon would recover on its own. The rate of descent increased to 500 feet per minute and their two flags were standing straight up behind them; it was like being in a fast lift as they plummeted downwards. Now they could see separate trees; then each branch; in seconds they would be able to see the leaves and then it would be too late – they would be amongst them. Ben cut loose a bag of sand; Max cut another. Their descent slowed. Reassured, Ben and Max now threw sand out by the handful until, at last, little more than a hundred feet above the tree-tops, they reached a state of equilibrium before starting to rise. There was a tearing, splintering sound from below, a momentary pause, and then they leapt upwards, escaping from the gorge into which they had sunk. Glancing down, they could see that the homing beacon antenna had fouled the branch of a tree and had now parted a few feet from its end. They shot up to an altitude of 4,000 feet, but the descent had been more than costly on their nerves. They had also lost 120 pounds of ballast, a quantity they could ill afford so early in their voyage.

But that wasn't the end of it. In the next two hours they dropped on three more occasions, the last time reaching a descent rate of 700 feet per minute and stopping only eighty feet above the waves of the Gulf of St. Lawrence. Each time they delayed discarding ballast to the last minute. *Double Eagle* had been caught in a series of rotors, which are downward air currents caused by the steep terrain they had been passing over.

Now in stable air, they were flying across the Gulf of St. Lawrence at a height of around 1,700 feet; below was a floor of grey cloud. And then it started to rain. Living in New Mexico, which has a very low rainfall, they had never really thought much of the problems presented by rain. The gondola was completely open, for they had thought they would get some protection from the canopy of the balloon stretching over them. What happened was the very reverse; the smoothly overhanging surface of the balloon acted as a channel for the drops of rain to run down to the bottom of the cone and then to pour into the open gondola. They had a rain skirt made from sailcloth, but in the rush to get away, Ed Yost had not found time to tell them how to put it up. They now struggled to do so, but were soaked by the time they had got it in place. Max had taken the precaution of bringing a waterproof poncho and plenty of woollen clothing. Ben, on the other hand, had assumed that his goose down jacket and trousers would keep him dry and warm. They did not. The down clothing absorbed the rain as if it were blotting paper. The feathers became a congealed mess, losing all their insulating properties and Ben, soaked to the skin, was desperately cold. But he did not complain and Max, warm and dry in his poncho, did not notice.

Now they had time to take stock of their position. Quickly Ben calculated that, after only fourteen hours of flying, they had off-loaded 1,400 of their 3,400 pounds of ballast – and they had not even started to cross the Atlantic. They were now over Labrador; it was incredibly beautiful, but menacing, with rocky outcrops protruding from a carpet of dense, brilliant green forest, sprinkled with gleaming rivers and cataracts. They discussed the possibilities of aborting the flight. On the plus side, they were still heading in the right direction for their rendezvous with the high-pressure ridge and were making good speed over the ground. On the other hand, they were low in ballast and Ben was desperately wet and cold. The nature of the ground decided it. There was nowhere for them to land safely, and so they kept on flying into their second dusk.

It was Max's turn to sleep. Warm and dry, he dropped off immediately, leaving Ben to a solitary, shivering vigil. The balloon was at 5,000 feet, but even at this height he could hear the angry crash of the surf as they drifted over the coastline – over the Atlantic at last. Cold and desperately tired, Ben had not been able to eat or sleep in the last few hours; he envied Max, who had been able to do both with ease. Max took over at two in the morning. In contrast to Ben, he was able to enjoy the situation, not only because he still had dry clothes but also because of his basic temperament; he almost revelled in the wildness of the storm and the array of obstacles that confronted them.

That morning they made contact with the control centre through an American Air Force 'plane that had flown out to find them as part of a training exercise, and were told to attain an altitude of 10,000 feet, so that they could ride the crest of the wave that would take them over to Europe. They were rising steadily when Max noticed they were heading straight for a huge cumulus cloud. There was nothing they could do to avoid it; one moment they were in clear sky, the cloud a gigantic, boiling mushroom of white, and then they were inside it, white, opaque, a maelstrom of snow. Immediately they began to fall, soon descending at a rate of 600 feet a minute. Once again they delayed throwing out any ballast until the last possible moment; they showed no sign of stopping on their own volition, and finally pumped out just enough of the rain water they had been collecting to stop themselves at 2,000 feet. At least it was much warmer than it had been at 8,600 feet.

This was to be a crisis moment of the entire voyage. They were now 500 miles out into the Atlantic with 1,500 to go to reach the other side. Already, they had been swept further north than had been planned originally, but they were being carried in roughly the right direction, at a speed of around forty knots. This would enable them to reach the coast of Europe by the following day. A jet liner, flying far above the turbulent clouds, now came through to them on the radio; the skipper told them that their mission control advised them to stay at 2,500 feet. Ben could not understand it. In all their discussions before the flight, they had agreed that it was essential to stay high, at at least 10,000 feet, to gain the full advantage of the surf effect on the pressure ridge. Their catch phrase was 'Up is east, down is north' and, given their present position, 'north' meant being swept onto the high snow peaks of the Greenland ice cap.

After the flight, Ben remembered arguing that they should ignore the advice and gain height, while Max, although puzzled, felt that the back-up team had access to meteorological information which they, in the balloon, lacked, and favoured following instructions. Ben even thought, 'I can ballast off and take us up, but what if Max starts valving to bring us back down?' In the end he did nothing. Max remembered nothing of this argument, but whether it took place or not, they remained at 2,500 feet.

Back at the flight control centre, Bob Rice and Rich Schwoebel realised they had made a mistake almost as soon as they had transmitted the message. Their decision was based on the pattern of thunderstorms that they could see on the satellite pictures of the North Atlantic. Their responsibility was a frightening one, for their advice could drive the balloon either towards the inhospitable coast of Norway or, even worse, back on itself towards Greenland. They managed to get just one more message through to *Double Eagle*, urging the balloonists to gain height to between 8,000 and 10,000 feet. After this, *Double Eagle*'s radios, soaked by rain, finally died. Max and Ben were on their own. They could receive messages, but could not reply.

No longer sure where they were, bounced from one thunderstorm to the next, they had the most frightening fall they had yet experienced as the balloon dropped at a rate of over 1,300 feet per minute. They started to throw out everything – the bottles of oxygen, boxes of rations, bottled water – as they plummeted down towards the angry sea. At last, at 390 feet, their plunge slowed down and they reached a state of equilibrium. The white-capped waves seemed to be reaching up towards them, as if to pluck them from the sky. Suddenly, Max realised that the gleams of white were not only flecks of foam, but were also miniature icebergs and small ice floes. They emphasised the fierce inhospitality of the sea, and how limited would be their chances of survival if they did ditch in it.

Double Eagle now started to rise once again. Great sheets of ice were breaking away from the canopy of the balloon. It was this icing that had caused their near-fatal plunge. Both of them had thought they were about to die, had felt no panic, only a sadness at leaving their wives and children – a feeling very similar to my own when I was nearly drowned in the Blue Nile. Carefully, they adjusted the equilibrium of the balloon and then Max curled up in his sleeping bag and immediately dropped off to sleep, while Ben checked through the ballast that was left, calculating the exact amounts in his head. It was still raining; water was pouring down the underside of the balloon and sluicing into the gondola. Ben, now having been soaked for over twenty-four hours, was chilled and shivering, convinced he would die from exposure, if not drowning. It was at this point that he noticed the wind was carrying them back towards Greenland. Below them, the waves reached up towards them. Their distress beacon, picked up on the radio, bleeped piercingly, somehow emphasising their loneliness.

As the sun crept over the horizon, the gas in the balloon expanded and they rose effortlessly to 12,000 feet, the highest altitude of the voyage, and now they were being swept eastwards in the right direction. Max, once again on watch, felt rested and warm as he calculated their chances of making the coast of Norway in spite of everything that had happened. Ben, wet and chilled, suffering from the effects of hypothermia, lay huddled in a corner, unable to sleep, wracked with the cold. The radio came to life; they were being called by a US Navy 'plane that had picked them up on its radar. Remembering that they had a small walkie-talkie radio set, Max searched through the chaotic pile of wet equipment, found it and switched it on. It worked. At last they had direct contact. They were offered a rescue helicopter, which could fly from Iceland should they want to ditch. It was an agonising decision to have to take. Max tried to delay making it; they were being blown towards Iceland anyway – couldn't they decide then? But Ben had no doubts; he realised he would die of cold if they stayed aloft for very much longer. Finally, he told Max: 'Do what you want. I'm freezing to death. I won't make it either way. Go ahead and fly the sonofabitch.'

That settled it. Max had never realised how bad a state Ben was in, partly because Ben had never complained, partly perhaps because subconsciously he did not want to acknowledge the fact that Ben was not fit enough to complete the voyage. Almost at the moment he agreed to ask for a rescue helicopter, he was also suggesting to Ben that they might be able to rig a shelter in the corner of the gondola which they could heat, using a little gas stove. They could be over Norway in ten hours. Ben hardly took all this in; his mind kept coming back to the helicopter that was now flying out from Iceland, and to the problems of ditching the balloon into a sea with twenty-foot waves.

In the next few hours, as the helicopter flew towards them, Ben tried to get some sleep while Max went through the contents of the gondola, packing everything of value that could be used again into a duffel bag. There was undoubtedly a feeling of alienation between the two men at this point; Ben, desperately relieved that the decision to abort had been taken, glad for a chance of survival; Max, resentful that they had not flown to the limit, still half-hoping that they could change their minds and fly on to Norway. His collection of gear from the gondola was an affirmation of his determination to have another try.

With the rescue helicopter in sight, Ben valved off helium to bring it steadily down into the raging seas. Quick-witted and practical, he made a perfect landing, drop-

The first morning out.
Double Eagle II *was designed
to carry 160,000 cu. ft of helium,
59,000 more than its predecessor.
Larry Newman's hang-glider
is suspended below the gondola.
It was his ambition to glide
down to earth when the balloon
had crossed the Atlantic,
but as they approached the
Irish coast the hang-glider went
the way of the navigational
instruments and cine cameras
as ballast.*

ping the gondola into a trough between the huge waves, signalling Max to pull the lock pins at his end of the gondola when they were only a few feet above the water. The balloon, relieved of the gondola, shot up into the air, vanishing into the cloud base in a matter of seconds. The big helicopter roared in, dropped a line into the gondola and first Max, clinging to the duffel bag filled with instruments and radios, then Ben, were hauled up to warmth and safety. Within a few moments of boarding the helicopter, Max was thinking about another attempt; Ben, on landing in Iceland, told the press:

'It was an interesting trip, but one that I will never make again.'

They flew to London, where they met their wives and friends from the United States who were awaiting them there. Pat Abbruzzo could not believe it when told that Ben had said he'd had enough and, in fact, by the time he got to England Ben was already talking about another attempt as well. But he now had some serious medical problems – his left foot, which had been crushed in a yachting accident shortly before setting out, was severely frostbitten. Had they flown on towards the Norwegian coast, even had he not died from exposure, he would almost certainly have lost his toes and perhaps the entire foot. Treatment had been started only just in time, but he had to spend several days in hospital, and was on crutches for some weeks.

In the period immediately following the attempt, both Max and Ben were deeply depressed by the self-searching that failure nearly always brings. Max could not help regretting the decision to ditch, though he knew that at the time he had had no option. Ben agonised over the mistake of holding their height down to 2,000 feet, even though, soaked and cold as he was, it is unlikely that he could have survived a high-altitude flight across the North Atlantic. Max, obsessed with analysing what had gone wrong, and starting the preparations for another attempt, allowed his business to run itself. On the other hand, Ben soon became immersed with his own business, which was threatened with a take-over, and spared little real thought of trying again.

Adventure, particularly one in the public eye, has a momentum of its own. Given Max's enthusiasm and the fact that he very much wanted to make his second attempt with Ben, it was almost inevitable that Ben would once again be sucked into the vortex. Wherever he went, in business or amongst his friends, sooner or later the question came: 'When are you going to have another try?' Even his family assumed he would want to go again, and so he became committed; yet, right up to the moment they set out for their second attempt, he had doubts. He was convinced that the crew should be increased to three, giving strength in numbers and to reduce pilot fatigue. Max did not agree, feeling that the pair was sufficient but, because he wanted so much to have Ben with him on the flight, he let it ride until it was tacitly accepted that there would be three. Max did nothing about recruiting a third man, hoping that there would not be one. This meant that inevitably the new member of the crew was going to be Ben's nominee.

Larry Newman was a professional pilot whose passion in life was flying. At twenty-six, he was young enough to have been Ben Abruzzo's son, and a kind of father–son relationship had developed between the two men. In 1974, Larry, at that time out of work, had knocked on Ben's door to ask permission to fly his hang-glider off the top of Sandia Peak, the highest peak of the ski complex which Ben owned. Ben turned him down, and so Larry flew off the neighbouring Sandia Crest, landing with a fine effrontery in Ben's garden. Ben could not help admiring his nerve and a friendship started. Ben was almost everything that Larry admired, rich, dynamic, adventurous and successful in business, and in trying to emulate him he was soon

having some success himself with a hang-glider manufacturing company in premises rented from Ben. Then they went into partnership to buy a Lear jet. Brash, fast-talking, rather insecure, Larry was the very opposite of Max Anderson, but when Ben Abruzzo suggested him as a candidate for the voyage, Max agreed. Larry was to be brought in as a fully equal partner, putting up a third of the cost and sharing in responsibility and glory. But the introduction of a third member of the team brought its own strains – the danger of the odd man out and, almost inevitably, that odd man was Max Anderson. Larry owed his loyalty and affection to Ben, and felt little affinity for Max who, although scrupulously courteous, always seemed rather distant – very much the officer with the enlisted man. Ben was worried about his foot, which was still giving trouble, particularly if it got cold; he even contemplated backing out only a few weeks before departure.

They were also threatened again by competition; two British balloonists, Don Cameron and Christopher Davey, set out from St. John's, Newfoundland, in a very sophisticated balloon which had a helium envelope surrounded by a hot air balloon. The theory was that the hot air would control the temperature of the helium, thus providing controlled lift without wasting ballast. The British couple nearly succeeded, getting within 110 miles of the French coast before ditching in the sea. Their failure was caused by a combination of technical faults and the fatigue of the balloonists themselves. It seemed almost inevitable that anyone trying to balloon the Atlantic was doomed to failure on their first attempt.

Maxie Anderson drove both Ben Abruzzo and Larry Newman to extremes of boredom and irritation as he insisted on going over every single detail, every possible mistake they might have left uncorrected. By the time *Double Eagle II* was ready for her launch, on the 10th August 1976, every detail had been fined down. They had adequate waterproof and warm clothing, a heated shelter for the crew member who would be sleeping and weather-proofed communications equipment. The launch was much better organised and situated but, even so, there were last-minute panics. In the rush of final preparations they did not have time to check out the radios once they were mounted in the gondola; more serious, they discovered that the tanker carrying the helium had brought 13,000 cubic feet less than they had ordered. The high-pressure ridge was now very nearly upon them; Bob Rice told Max and Ben that it was travelling at quite a slow speed and that the crossing would take at least six days. Because of the mistake over the helium, they could not fill the balloon to capacity and therefore had lost a day's flight right at the beginning. This was their margin for error, but they decided to go just the same and, at 8.42 p.m. on the 11th August, the anchoring ballast was cut down from the gondola and the balloon started to rise.

Almost immediately it was caught in a down-draught which threatened to dash them back to the ground. Ben Abruzzo had to throw over some precious ballast and, at last, they gained height, rising to around 5,700 feet. Then something else went wrong. Larry, who had been appointed radio operator, turned on the radios to find that although he was receiving he could not send any messages since the radios were draining the batteries of too much power. Within the first few minutes of the voyage the entire venture appeared to be tinged with disaster.

But by morning Larry had managed to get the VHF radio to work. This meant they had short-range communication with any aircraft that happened to fly overhead, though the long-range radios, which should have given them direct contact with their control centre, still would not work. The following morning dawned fine; the balloon was coasting along under a warm sun. The three balloonists could get on with their own responsibilities, Max working quietly on the navigation, Ben patiently computing the exact quantity of ballast and Larry fiddling with the radios, taking pictures and talking almost non-stop. He is an extrovert who needs to communicate and, equally important, needs a response – a hyperactive person who finds difficulty in remaining passive. Max, rigidly self-controlled, simply ignored him, but Ben was finally driven to tell him: 'Larry, you're a goddamn babbling brook. Either talk less or say what you have to say in fewer words.'

Hanging below the gondola was Larry Newman's hang-glider. It was his ambition to use it to glide down to earth when the balloon had completed its voyage on the other side of the Atlantic. As they neared the eastern coast of Newfoundland, Max made a suggestion to Larry: 'If you've any second thoughts, Larry, you can fly down here or bail out and there'll be no hard feelings.'

Larry realised that Max meant what he said and seriously considered going down, but then he decided to stay. The omens had not improved. The balloon kept losing height for no apparent reason. Max could not rid himself of the conviction that there was a leak in the envelope, even though Ben had poked his head up into the open bottom of the balloon and seen no telltale pin-pricks of light. But the weather was fine, and although the balloon was travelling relatively slowly there were none of the crises of their first journey. Day slipped into night; Larry worked away at the radios and managed to master the special ham radio set they had brought with them as a back-up. He made contact with an English radio ham who, in turn, contacted someone in America who 'phoned the flight control centre. Larry was jubilant but soon felt deflated by the lack of enthusiasm shown by the two older men.

Day followed night, followed by day. They reached altitudes of up to 20,000 feet, started to use oxygen and settled into a regular routine. But back at the control centre, Rich Schwoebel and Bob Rice were wracked with doubt. Because of the failure of the high-frequency radio they did not have direct contact with the balloon. The problem was compounded by the failure of their satellite navigation system. A computer had broken down and the main NASA priority was being given to a Venus probe that had just been launched; as a result the transponder in the balloon was not being given the satellite fixes that it should have received. Their flight control neither knew the exact location of the balloon, nor were able to communicate with it. What they did know was that a large storm system was building up in the region where they thought the balloon was, and that it would be sucked into the system if it had not gained sufficient altitude. Finally, they managed to get through, using a ham radio station in Grand Rapids, Michigan, to tell the balloonists to maintain a height of 20,000 feet. Max Anderson and Ben Abruzzo had already decided to do just that; they were not going to let themselves get caught in any storms again.

They were worried by the amount of ballast they had already used. Max calculated that on their present course they would cross the Shetland Islands to the north of Scotland; he even rechecked Ben's ballast figures and reckoned they had barely enough ballast to get across the North Sea. It was at this point he suggested to Larry: 'How would you feel about flying your hang-glider down when we go over the Shetland Islands? That would give us a hell of a lift, losing your weight and the glider's. Ben and I could make it for sure then.'

Larry looked towards Ben for support, but Ben nodded. 'It's an idea,' he said.

Larry realised the risks involved, must have felt the rejection of the other two. He was just another bit of ballast! There was a very real danger of being swept out to sea by the winds, in which case his chances of survival would have been slight. Even so, he accepted the suggestion. But the following day their prospects began to improve as the winds shifted to a more easterly direction, blowing them towards Ireland. It looked as if they would make it after all. Now at a height of 23,000 feet, they were using oxygen and it was bitterly cold, but they were dry and had plenty of warm clothes. By this time, though, they were getting tired; tempers were beginning to fray. Ben had always considered the question of ballast to be his sphere of responsibility but the question was becoming so critical that Max wanted a part in the decision making. They were going to have to dump everything, radios, navigation equipment, spare food, oxygen. They even discussed the possibility of cutting the ends off the gondola to keep the balloon aloft. In a furious argument Ben, remembering his frozen foot the previous year, flatly refused to jettison the fuel for the heater, and the balloon swept steadily towards the coast of Ireland.

Nothing is ever certain in a balloon flight. It was the morning of their fifth day, with the Irish coast about 300 miles to the east, when suddenly the balloon started to drop. It was like the big down they had experienced on their first flight, but this was

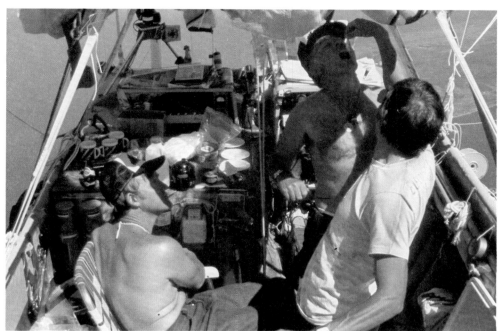

Over the Gulf of St. Lawrence, Larry Newman feeds Ben Abruzzo a sardine, as Maxie Anderson looks on.

At an altitude of 14,000 feet over Poole Harbour.

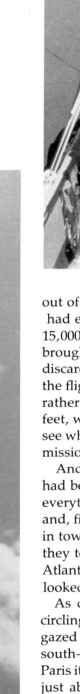

out of a clear, blank sky and bigger than anything they – or any other balloonist – had ever known. An invisible, silent avalanche of air carried them down for over 15,000 feet, towards a round blue hole in the low cloud covering the sea. The crisis brought Max and Ben together as they discussed the problem quietly; if they discarded too much ballast at this stage they would not have enough left to complete the flight. Larry became increasingly jittery and anxious, a state that was worsened rather than improved by the cool of the two older men. But at last, at a height of 4,500 feet, within sound of the waves below, the balloon came to a halt. They were able to see white-flecked crests as the balloon hung, poised. They were able to contact their mission control through the ham system, but did not learn much.

And then the balloon began to rise in the afternoon sun, going even higher than it had been before, to an altitude of 25,000 feet. As dusk approached, they stripped everything they could find to use as ballast, navigation instruments, cine cameras and, finally, Larry's hang-glider. The gondola was just an empty shell as they swept in towards the Irish coast. Soon they saw lights, then heard a distant sound which they took a few seconds to identify as that of dogs barking. They had crossed the Atlantic, but to do it in full they wanted to reach the mainland of Europe. It now looked as if they really could emulate Lindbergh's feat and reach Paris.

As dawn came over the Irish Sea their flight became a triumph, with aircraft circling them and the radio alive with a stream of messages. Thousands in Britain gazed up as the balloon, immensely graceful, drifted over the fields and towns of south-west England. And then the English Channel, the coast of France towards Paris itself, but the balloon's endurance was nearly exhausted. They had abandoned just about everything that could be discarded or chopped from the now-empty gondola. The balloon itself was sagging, so much helium had been vented. At only thirty-five minutes before dusk, *Double Eagle II* was approaching the village of Miserey and she was losing height fast; helicopters and light aircraft were buzzing around them; cars, nose to tail on the road below, were chasing them. There was a suitable field just ahead. Ben, now in charge, vented gas, dropped the trail ropes at just the right moment and they made a perfect landing.

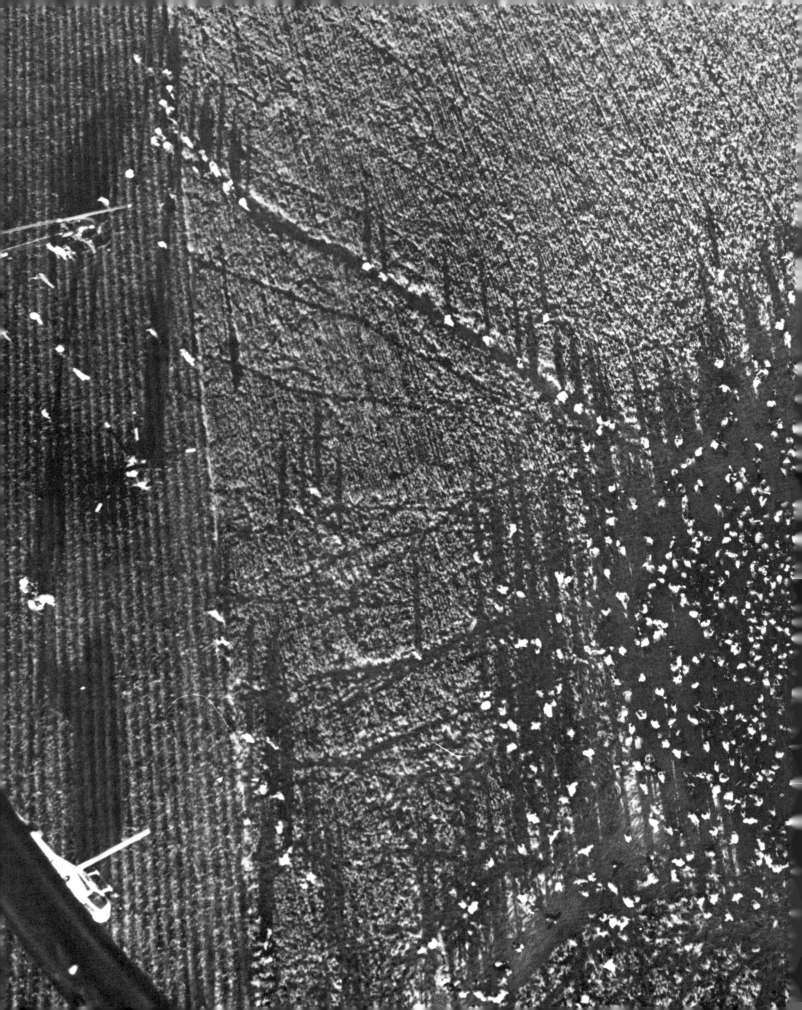

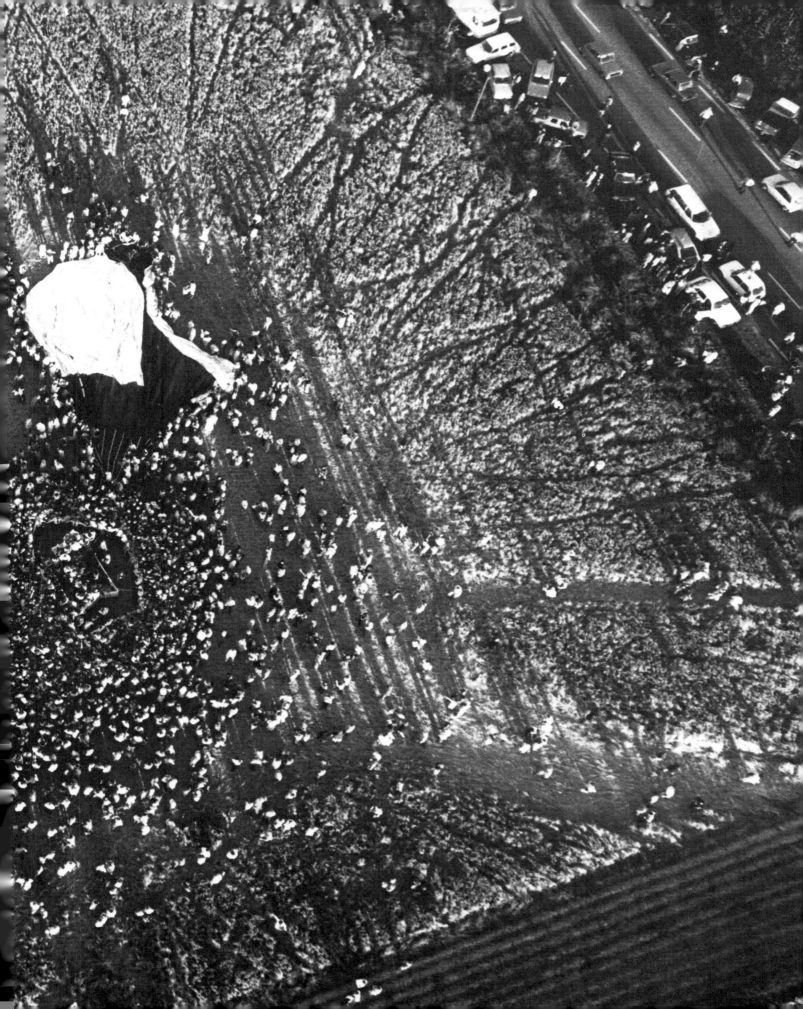

Overleaf]
Double Eagle II *came down in
a French barley field after a
flight of 137 hours, 5 minutes,
30 seconds from Presque Island,
Maine.*

The crowds poured forward, clambering into the gondola, swamping the three jubilant, but tired balloonists. The following weeks were similar to the aftermath of any great venture that had captured the imagination of the public – emotional reunions with their wives, endless press conferences, receptions, TV shows and public lectures, the presentation of awards, a visit to the White House. But with success came the stress that has divided and destroyed so many strong partnerships. As they came into land they had the same strong, emotional sense of unity that Ridgway and Blyth had experienced as they neared the coast of Ireland at the end of their long row, that Messner and Habeler had had, as they stood on the top of Everest, the first men to climb the mountain without oxygen. But with a return to earth came external pressures – the eternal questions of who had played the most important role.

There was no conscious effort by the media to elevate Anderson over Abruzzo, or Abruzzo over Anderson. Larry Newman never really had a look in, and didn't expect one. But the other two did. Even before the flight there had been an unspoken jockeying for position. Max Anderson felt that he was the real captain of the venture. After all, it was he who had conceived it, had pushed the second attempt through, even when Ben Abruzzo had nearly backed out. Max was the co-ordinator and, on the balloon itself, he was the navigator, the grand strategist. But Ben Abruzzo felt that he had been the man who really flew the balloon; lightning fast, practical, it was Ben who controlled the venting of helium, who held every single item of ballast in his mind, who brought the balloon in to land safely on both attempts. On the second venture Larry, owing his allegiance to Ben, commented, 'From the day we started

*Facing a heroes' welcome in Paris,
from the left Maxie, Ben and Larry.*

planning this flight, there was no question in my mind that the actual author, the real planner, and the real captain was Ben Abruzzo. I still believe it. From the moment we started the initial preparations until our landing, I always deferred to Ben's judgement. This was a little bit unfair to Maxie.'

It certainly was! But, most important of all, Ben was much more outgoing than Max; a fluent talker who enjoyed communication, he was good on TV chat shows. Max, on the other hand, tends to shy away from the media, had always resented the presence of the TV cameras – even on the balloon – and in interview is slightly slow and ponderous, tending to pontificate rather than tell a vivid story. Max felt that Ben was grabbing more than his fair share of the limelight and that he was claiming to be the true skipper of the balloon, a claim that Max came to resent bitterly. As Max saw it and, in fact, how Ben had once described it, Max was the Chairman of the Board and Ben was the President (or, in British terms, the Managing Director). In other words, Max decided on general policy and had the final say, while Ben looked after the day-to-day running of the business. This seems a very fair assessment of what actually took place and it is very sad that two men who had been such close friends and whose abilities had complemented each other so well, should have fallen out. They entered one balloon race together in 1979 but, when I talked to Max Anderson in early 1980, he said he would never fly with Ben Abruzzo again. Later on that year, Max notched up yet another first, crossing from the west to the east coast of the United States in a helium balloon. This time he flew with his son.

In January 1981 Maxie Anderson set out with a companion to balloon around the world non-stop. Starting from Luxor in Egypt, they reached India but were unable to attain sufficient height to clear the Himalaya. There are three other teams competing for what must be the ultimate ballooning adventure. One of these includes Ben Abruzzo.

First on the moon

'200 feet, 4½ down, 5½ down. 160, 6½ down.' Aldrin, the lunar module pilot, called out the rate of descent from the computer read-out. Neil Armstrong was controlling the descent as the strange, spiderlike space craft raced above the drab, matt surface of the moon, seeking a level spot on which to land. Boulders, their shapes carved out in sharp relief by the blackness of the shadows, jutted like tank traps from the flat surface. They had just skimmed across the dish of a crater.

'Sixty seconds,' called Capcom, the Lunar Mission Control in Houston, Texas, where a hundred technicians behind TV screens and banks of instruments had been monitoring and controlling each step of man's first flight to the moon. Now they were telling Armstrong and Aldrin that they had only sixty seconds of fuel left.

But Armstrong was still looking for a level patch of ground on which to place the module. Now in complete control, it was his skill, his coolness, his judgement that would bring man down to the surface of the moon. They were close enough to the surface for the rocket engines breaking their rate of descent to blow up a cloud of dust that swirled out like a great flower, part concealing the ground itself.

'Thirty seconds.' A note of urgency in the voice, but Armstrong was still skimming over the surface, looking for the right landing place. With only seconds to go, he saw it and adjusted the controls. With hardly more than a tremor, the lunar module landed on the moon, the probes in its four feet penetrating the coating of dust to solid ground beneath, as contact lights on the control panel gleamed.

Aldrin's voice, steady, computerlike: 'OK engine stop. ACA out of detente. Modes control both auto. Descent engine command override off. Engine arm off. 413 is in.'

'We copy you,' replied Capcom.

And then Armstrong, escaping briefly from jargon, flirted with the romance of the moment: 'Houston: Tranquility Base here. The Eagle has landed.'

500,000,000 people watched every moment of that landing on television. No venture has ever had such an audience, has ever made such an impact on the imagination. Perhaps the earthbound comparison the mind reaches for is Hillary and Tenzing's arrival on the summit of Everest. But how much, one then asks, does the first man on the moon really have in common with that achievement or, for that matter, what point of similarity is there between Armstrong and Aldrin landing on the moon and John Fairfax rowing the last miles of the Atlantic onto a Miami beach just a few hours before they stepped onto the moon?

The first impression is one of enormous differences – in the level of technology, the massive budget and need for national support and policy, in the personalities of the people involved. But in many ways some of these differences are more a question

The moon, photographed at a distance of 10,000 nautical miles, from the Apollo XI space craft.

of degree than anything else. In most of the adventures I have described, it is an individual who conceives a grand idea and then struggles to put it into effect. But doing this may involve clothing the idea in politico-patriotic garb to gain the necessary support, as was the case in the Commonwealth Antarctic expedition. The decision for man to go to the moon was also very much a patriotic and political grand idea. It could barely claim scientific necessity, since a significant number of the scientists involved in lunar space research favoured continuing with unmanned vehicles, as being simpler, cheaper and more practical. The Russians, however, had set the pace by putting a Sputnik into space and then the first man into orbit round the earth. Not only was this a ferocious blow to American pride, but it introduced an element of fear, some of it rational, much of it paranoid, ranging from an expectation of America being bombarded from space satellites, to the moon being taken over by the Russians. It was in this climate that John F. Kennedy authorised the lunar programme, in an endeavour that was to stretch both the scientific and economic resources of the greatest industrial country in the world.

Neil Armstrong is in many ways the archetype of what one imagines an astronaut to be – steady, conventional, phlegmatic, not over-imaginative, short-haired, neatly-suited, essentially an organisation man. But as I talked to him, I realised that we had much more in common than I had at first expected. I had trapped myself with my own preconceptions. Neil Armstrong loves flying as intensely as I love climbing. Born in 1930 at Wapakota, a small town in Ohio, he was fascinated with flight from an early age, as a teenager working at Wapakota's little airport to help pay for flying lessons and earning his pilot's licence before he was old enough to drive a car. He wanted to be a Naval pilot, won a Naval scholarship to university to study aeronautical science, and then became a Naval aviator in 1949, in time to serve in the Korean war, flying seventy-eight combat missions. Above all, Armstrong wanted to become a test pilot. To achieve this he left the Navy and returned to university before joining the National Aeronautics and Space Administration (NASA) to test fly, among other aircraft, the X15 rocket 'plane.

More rocket than 'plane, the X15 had to be carried into the upper air by conventional aircraft before being released to blast up to incredible heights. It was like riding a hugely powerful rocket that had just sufficient wings and tailplane to guide it and bring it back precariously to earth. In it, Neil Armstrong reached an altitude of 207,500 feet and a maximum speed five times the speed of sound. What he got out of it was very similar to what a brilliant technical climber experiences on a desperately steep and difficult wall of rock. In each case the risk is there, an inherent part of the challenge. The pilot is taking his craft to its extreme, trying to find the outer envelope of its performance; the closer he can get to it, the better he is doing his job and the greater his personal satisfaction. This is very much the same as the rock climber, posed on a thumb-nail-sized rugosity, reaching out for a minute hold at extreme arm extension, pushing his own body to the very limits of its physical agility and strength. It is not a question of daring do or die, it is almost the same as the test pilot, the body being the machine, manipulated by the intellect and coolness of its owner.

Opting for the astronaut programme was a natural step for Armstrong, but a little like a top climber applying to join a big expedition to Mount Everest. The individual has to sacrifice some of the immediate satisfaction of complete personal control to being part of a complex organisation, where Mission Control, like the expedition leader on Everest, inevitably has a major influence on what happens from moment to moment.

A mountaineering expedition can be slightly hierarchic, the NASA set-up was immensely so. But this was what the astronauts were used to. Most of them were

Neil Armstrong, commander of Apollo XI, training in the lunar module simulator at the Kennedy Space Centre.

378

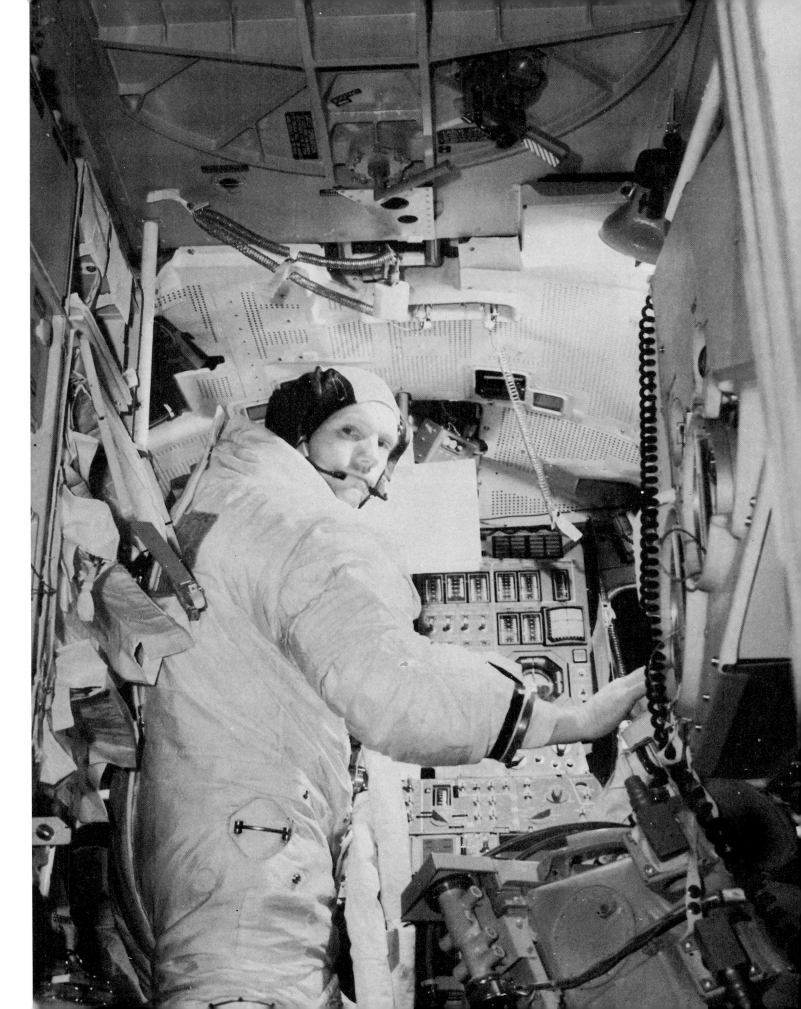

Michael Collins, command module pilot for Apollo XI.

Buzz Aldrin, lunar module pilot, photographed in Apollo XI by Neil Armstrong during the landing mission.

serving officers. When Neil Armstrong, one of the few civilians, applied to join the space programme in 1962, the first group of seven astronauts had already been selected. They were destined for the Mercury programme, America's response to Russia's successful launch of a man into space.

The Mercury capsule could take only one man, and the first astronauts were little more than passengers in a projectile that was blasted round the earth. Their only control was one to alter the angle of the capsule to prepare it for re-entry into the Earth's atmosphere. This was the first step. The next phase was more ambitious. The Gemini series had a bigger Titan rocket that could launch two men in a series designed to try out the various manoeuvring and docking functions which would enable the Apollo series, launched by a huge Saturn V rocket, to send three men all the way to the moon, and to enable two of them to land in their lunar module.

There were 300 applicants for the second group, all of them test pilots, for the eight positions available. Michael Collins was one, a career pilot who had chosen the Air Force, by his own admission, not so much from a burning ambition to fly, but because it offered the greatest opportunities. The selection tests were as thorough as any devised. The applicants had every bodily function tested, cold water poured in their ears, probes shoved up their backsides; they pounded treadmills, were spun in centrifuges; and then submitted to psychological tests, with ink blots, interviews and endless questionnaires, and technical sessions with the astronauts who were already in the programme.

Neil Armstrong was selected for this second group; Michael Collins was turned down but then in 1963 selected with the third group of astronauts. With him was Edwin (Buzz) Aldrin, academically the most highly-qualified of all the astronauts – already he had a doctorate in astronautics. Like Collins, he came from a military family, went to West Point and was commissioned into the Air Force. He served in Korea, but then chose a technological and academic road, rather than that of the test pilot. NASA, recognising the need for scientific and academic excellence as well as flying skill, no longer insisted on candidates being test pilots, although they still required a minimum of 1500 hours flying experience.

Buzz Aldrin had a single-minded intensity that made even his fellow astronauts slightly uncomfortable. He had specialised in the problems of rendezvous in space for his doctoral thesis, and followed it up within the Apollo programme. He could think of nothing else, talking about it obsessively to everyone he met, even complete laymen or the wives of his fellow astronauts. As a result he was given the nickname 'Dr. Rendezvous'.

There were now thirty astronauts, of which only two could be the first on the moon, with a third having the tantalising task of manning the command module in lonely orbit around the moon. The comparison with the siege-style ascent of a mountain suggests itself again. The astronauts are the lead climbers. Most have a turn out in front, but the order in which they go will have a profound influence on their chances of being in the right place at the right time to make a summit bid. There was intense, though muted and tightly-controlled competition, firstly just for a flight, but even more for the unique one to be first to land on the moon.

The Apollo programme was being rushed through at breakneck speed so the work was intense. There were classes in geology, meteorology, computing, rocket propulsion and other space-related sciences; there were courses in jungle and desert survival which sounded like a slightly bizarre touch of the Outward Bound. There were spells at public relations, when the astronauts took turns going before the press, attending innumerable conferences and other shindigs, often at the behest of the politicians who were approving this profligate spending of the tax-payers' money. But the most important, and certainly the most satisfying part of their work was their liaison with the scientists and technicians in specific areas of the project. Buzz Aldrin was associated with mission planning, which not only looked at overall planning, but also studied the problems of rendezvous in space, particularly the vital one, when the lunar module would have to take off from the moon and find the command module. Mike Collins was working on pressure suits and the problems encountered in the extra-vehicular activity (EVA). Neil Armstrong, being a member of the second group of astronauts, was directly involved in preparations for the Gemini programme and was also responsible for overall astronaut operations – he was one step up in the pecking order.

It was obviously very important, if not essential, to get a flight in the Gemini programme in order to be considered for the first attempt on the moon itself. All three of them did and, in their different ways, distinguished themselves. Of the three, Armstrong was the first to go into space in Gemini VIII, with David Scott, the first of the third group to get aloft. They were to attempt the first ever docking with another space vehicle, an unmanned rocket that had been sent up ahead of them. This was obviously of vital importance for the eventual return from the moon.

At first everything went smoothly; after four orbits of the earth, they caught up with the unmanned vehicle, an Agena, manoeuvred round her, and then Armstrong fired the guidance rockets which coaxed them into union. Their satisfaction was short-lived. Scott and Armstrong noticed that the linked space craft were not responding correctly to their controls. It could not have happened at a worse moment, for they were passing through the earth's shadow, so had no horizon as a reference and, at the same time, were out of communication with their ground control.

There was no question of their being helpless guinea pigs, acting on the orders of the technicians below. It was up to the two men in the space craft to make the split-second decisions to save themselves and their craft. It was a situation they had been in so many times before in high-performance aircraft; nevertheless, the sensors attached to their bodies recorded galloping pulse rates as they raced through the options before them, checking out what might have gone wrong. And as they switched off different systems in an attempt to identify and isolate the fault, they gyrated steadily faster. Finally, Armstrong decided to undock, hoping that the fault lay in the Agena. Scott punched the button and their space craft shot away, but instead of stabilising it went into a crazy, tumbling spin. The fault was in their own Gemini. The spin became so fast they had difficulty in raising their arms or turning their heads, vision was blurring; it was difficult to see the banks of dials and meters which extended round them in the crammed confines of the cockpit, some only a few inches from their faces. There was the danger of hitting the wrong button. They were in a race against losing consciousness and found the fault only just in time. One of the thruster rockets was stuck in the open position, causing the wild spin. Although back in control, they had now used up so much of their fuel that there could be no question of continuing the mission; they had to get down fast. They should have gone on for another three days and have landed in the Atlantic, but now they would be landing in the Pacific, just south of Japan. Neil Armstrong was cool enough to enjoy the view on the way down, telling me, 'One advantage was that we got a magnificent view of the Himalayas as we were in descent – we fired our retrofire rockets at night over Nigeria and as we came into daylight we were right over the Himalayas and falling at a very rapid rate. It seemed they were just coming up at us – it was clear right along the range.'

They were out of radio contact when they landed, but were quickly picked up by one of the recovery ships deployed round the world. The mission had been aborted prematurely and the comment of Walter Cunningham, one of Armstrong's fellow astronauts, in his book *The All American Boys*, shows the pressure and perhaps jealousy within this small group: 'Both performed well over the remainder of their careers, but at the same time their very progress ignored the fact that their peers – and many others at the space centre – felt they had botched their first mission.'

But Deke Slayton, one of the original seven astronauts from the first group, who had been grounded because of a slight heart murmur and was now Director of Flight Crew Operations, must have recognised Armstrong's precision and coolness under stress, for he would have had a major say in the final selection for the Apollo flights.

Collins and Aldrin also had successful flights in Gemini, both of them going outside the space craft to walk in that black, weightless vacuum of space, attached to the craft only by the thin umbilical cord of the safety harness. The patterned earth, though comparatively close, some 400 miles away, was still a separate planet, floating in the void. It must have been in many ways an experience both more extraordinary and exciting than walking on the moon.

Mike Collins was with John Young in Gemini X. They successfully found and docked with their Agena, but then they went in search of Agena III, the one used in Neil Armstrong's flight. It was now dead and passive, quietly orbiting the earth, but on its outer skin was attached a micrometeorite package and Collins was due to float over and pick it up. The thought of what he was about to do, to me the earthbound layman, is so immensely exciting, beautiful and at the same time frightening, that I long for a description that digs deep into his sensations. Is it like being on a big, blank rock wall, senses sharpened by fear, exhilarated by the feeling of space and one's own mastery of mind and muscle, when each movement is tensed, fluid, the focus of one's concentration? Or, is it more like being a deep-sea diver, cocooned in his special suit against the alien environment in which he is suspended?

But the astronaut is engulfed in so many technicalities that he cannot often afford the luxury of aesthetic wonder. Collins described his space walk in his book, *Carrying the Fire*:

> As I hang on to the open right hatch, I look up and slightly to my right at the Agena, which must be twenty feet away. I can't see the earth, only black starless sky behind the Agena, so I guess the earth must be somewhere behind me. I realise with a start that I have not been conscious of the earth one instant since I opened the hatch; I really don't give a damn where it is; all I care about is assembling the claptrap I require to get over to the Agena and retrieve that micrometeorite package.

Collins eased his way out of the small hatch of the space craft and gently pushed himself into space in the direction of the Agena, his umbilical cord trailing behind him. He collided gently with his objective, grasped the slippery lid of the docking cone with his hands, laboriously worked his way round it, shuffling along on hands impeded by the stiff pressurised gloves, to where he knew he would find the package. On his way round he dislodged part of the docking apparatus which sprang into the void, held by one attachment point. It looked like a sharp scythe, its wicked hook just waiting to entangle, perhaps cut his life-line. There was no up or down, just the infinite black void of space, the dead, shining, empty rocket and himself, clumsy, cumbersome in his space suit. There was the very real risk of being in the path of one of the rocket jets on the Gemini space craft. When his partner, John Young, adjusted the attitude of the craft its blazing heat could slice through the thin fabric of the space suit, destroying him in an explosion of fire and vanishing oxygen. He was, at last, at the packet:

Son-of-a-bitch, I am falling off! I have built up too much momentum and now the inertia of my torso and legs keeps me moving; first my right hand, and then my left, feel the Agena slither away, despite my desperate clutch. As I slowly cartwheel away from the Agena, I see absolutely nothing but black sky for several seconds and then Gemini hoves into view. John has apparently watched all this in silence, but now he croaks: 'Where are you Mike?'

'I'm up above. You don't want to sweat it. Only don't get any closer if you can help it. OK?'

'Yes.'

My motion is taking me away from the Agena, but it is tangential relative to the Gemini, which is not pleasant, because the laws of physics tell me that as I get closer it (as my radius decreases) my velocity will increase and I may splat up against it at a nasty rate of speed.

Collins fumbled for his squirt gun, which acted like a tiny rocket motor, but it was not in his holster; a jab near to panic, but it was attached to him by a hose; he pulled it in and used it to slow down his swing as he spun behind the Gemini. But he was now in the direct line of the thrusters and told Young not to fire them. Young, also was tensed for he had to keep position with the Agena and was worried about fouling it.

At last, Collins got back to the cockpit, took stock, got himself sorted out and then returned to the Agena for another try at recovering the package. This time he succeeded. The mission successful, Collins had undoubtedly scored up some good marks.

Buzz Aldrin was pilot on the last of the Gemini flights, Gemini XII, with Jim Lovell, as commander. The lift-off went smoothly, but once in space they discovered that their rendezvous radar, which should have homed them onto the Agena automatically, was not functioning. Chance had given Aldrin the opportunity of trying out his theories in practice. Using his specially prepared charts, taking readings with a sextant, he fed the data into the inboard computer and found the Agena with the minimum of delay. Aldrin had proved that the pilot could be master of his machines and computers. He went on to make the most successful space walk yet completed, carrying out a series of simple engineering tasks on the Agena, just to prove that a man could work out in space. He felt completely at home:

I have no particular fear of heights, but I was nevertheless surprised to see that a hundred and fifty miles above the surface of the earth there was no awareness of height at all. I was secure and comfortable, though encumbered, in the space suit. I felt enclosed and safe . . . the view was spectacular, the colours of the earth – a benign combination of blue, brown and green, with white and grey clouds formed above – the colours of life.

The flight was among the most successful of the Gemini series, particularly in terms of work outside the space craft, and it undoubtedly stood Aldrin in good stead.

By January, 1967, the Gemini series had ironed out many of the problems of rendezvous in space. Apollo was very nearly ready to reach out to the moon, but the tempo had, perhaps, been too frenetic. The Apollo space craft, with its 2,000,000 functioning components, inboard computers, miles of wiring, was the most complex craft ever built. There was no room for failure, and so every function had to be duplicated and, in some instances, re-duplicated. Everything had been tested and re-tested but, even so, it was almost impossible to ensure that every single component was perfect. In addition, the manufacture of the entire system had been shared around dozens of firms – there was no other way of doing it – but this also gave room for error.

It was on the 27th January, 1967. They were very nearly ready to launch the first manned Apollo space craft into orbit. It was a routine rehearsal, with the three crew

The Kennedy Space Centre monitors Apollo XI's countdown.

men, Gus Grissom, Ed White and Roger Chaffee going through the countdown inside their capsule for the first time. There was a muffled exclamation from the intercom, sounding like 'Hey!' or 'Fire!' Then another voice saying, 'We've got a bad fire. Let's get out. Open her up.' But the voice died into what sounded like a scream of pain and, before the support crew could do anything, the space craft burst open in an explosion of flames and smoke and fumes. The three astronauts must have been killed within seconds.

Inevitably, there were endless, recriminatory inquests over what had gone wrong and who was responsible. The fire had been caused by an electrical short circuit, probably because of some damaged insulation. It was the pure oxygen, pumped into the capsule under pressure, which turned it into a furnace. Undoubtedly, mistakes had been made but, viewing the American space programme as a whole, it is amazing that this was the only fatal accident, and even this was on the ground and not part of an actual launch. The fact, incidentally, that four astronauts died in aircraft accidents during this period, gives some perspective of the relative risk of day-to-day flying.

The accident caused a serious delay; a few heads rolled, but the Apollo programme was pushed on. The first manned flight of Apollo was made in October, 1968; they did not leave earth's orbit, but spent eleven days aloft, longer than the journey to the moon and back would take. The flight was so successful that after a lot of agonising it was decided to send the next flight, Apollo VIII, out of earth orbit and round the moon. This was the first time that the gigantic Saturn V rocket had been used. Standing 107 metres tall, it could develop seven and a half million pounds of thrust to heave the huge rocket off the ground and into orbit.

In some ways, Apollo VIII was the greatest adventure of all, for this was the first time man had left earth orbit, the first time – once the craft was the other side of the moon – that he had been out of sight of earth. To get there, the first two stages of the rocket were used to put him into orbit round the earth. Then, after two orbits, the third stage of the rocket was used to blast the space craft towards the moon. Its direction and speed had to be just right, so that the craft would be caught by the moon's gravity and start its orbit. They made ten lunar orbits, and as part of the public relations package, the crew delivered a Christmas message and read a Biblical lesson, televised live to the world.

There were two more Apollo flights, designed particularly to test out the lunar module, the fragile, spider-like craft which would take a crew down to the surface of the moon and back. By this time the crew and back-up had been selected for Apollo XI, the flight most likely to make the first moon landing. Neil Armstrong, perhaps because of his cool imperturbability, his exceptional skill as a pilot, and also, possibly, because of his easy personality, had got the plum position as commander of the mission. Buzz Aldrin was more abrasive and had brushed with the authorities on one or two occasions, but his sheer capability and his deep knowledge of the problems of rendezvous in space had given him an edge over all the competition. He was to be the lunar module pilot. Mike Collins was originally scheduled to fly with Apollo VIII, but had developed a bony growth on the vertebrae, pushing against the spinal cord. He had to have an operation, was inevitably taken off Apollo VIII and there seemed a good chance that this would be the end of his astronaut career. But Collins did not give up easily. Resisting the offer of a temporary desk job in Washington, he remained closely associated with the Apollo VIII flight, acting as liaison for the crew and working with Jim Lovell, who had taken his place. Then, when fully recovered, his seniority and Gemini experience ensured he got back into the crew rota in January 1968 to be the command module pilot on Apollo XI. He would at least be on the moon flight, though he would have to survive the frustration of remaining in orbit while the other two actually set foot on the moon.

Collins had known for some time that this would be his fate, ever since he had been allotted the role of command module pilot in the Apollo series. He commented in his book, *Carrying the Fire*:

> Slowly it sank in. No LM (lunar module) for me, no EVA (extra vehicle activity), no fancy flying, no need to practice in helicopters any more. Instead, I was the navigator, the guidance and control expert, the owner of the leaky plumbing – all the things I was least interested in doing. Years later I have answered a thousand times the question 'How did you and Armstrong and Aldrin decide who was going to stay in the command module, and who was going to walk on the moon?' I have answered it a hundred ways, none of them completely honest, but then it's so hard to say, 'Listen, lady, when they cancelled 014 (one of the proposed preliminary flights) I lost my chance,' even if that is ninety-nine per cent of it. From late 1966 on, I became a command module specialist, and though I changed crews, I never changed specialities again.

Collins accepted his role. Between Aldrin and Armstrong there was some friction.

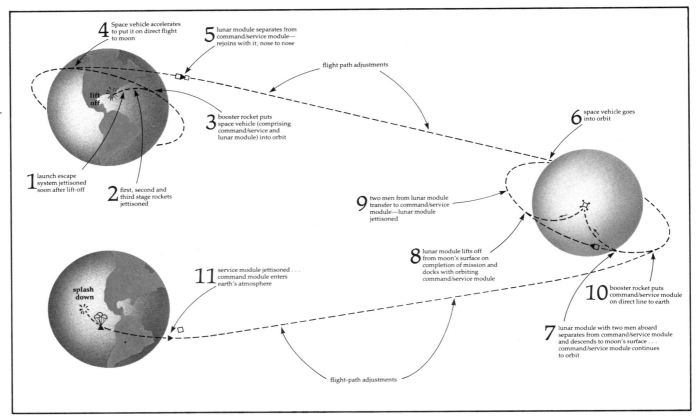

The flight of Apollo XI

It was over the question of who should get out of the lunar module and step onto the surface of the moon first. It was about as relevant and unimportant as whether Hillary or Tenzing stepped first onto the summit of Everest, having travelled all the way together, but inevitably it mattered to both the men involved. Aldrin commented:

> Throughout the short history of the space programme, beginning with Ed White's space walk and continuing on all subsequent flights, the commander of the flight remained in the space craft while his partner did the moving around. I had never given it much thought and had presumed that I would leave the LM and step onto the moon ahead of Neil.

Aldrin then heard, indirectly through general gossip, that Neil Armstrong was going to be the first to step on the moon:

> After I had mulled it over for a few days, I decided that the subject was potentially too explosive for even the subtlest manoeuvring, and that it would be best to be honest and direct about it. I went to Neil.
> Neil, who can be enigmatic if he wishes, was just that. Clearly, the matter was weighing on him as well, but I thought by now we knew and liked each other enough to discuss the matter candidly. Neil equivocated a minute or so, then with a coolness I had not known he possessed, he said that the decision was quite historical and he didn't want to rule out the possibility of going first.

But the decision was not to be that of either Armstrong or Aldrin; it was for the powers in NASA to decide, and what clinched it was probably the fact that the exit door from the lunar module was immediately behind where the commander was standing. It was to be Armstrong out first.

They were now working under considerable pressure, spending the month before blast off in the special crew quarters at Cape Canaveral, within walking distance of the rocket that was going to take them to the moon. Most of the time was spent in the simulators, endlessly going over every procedure, practising every conceivable eventuality or emergency. Aldrin and Armstrong had to work closely together and, on the whole, made a good team. There was only one altercation; they had been trying to land the lunar module simulator and Armstrong had let it crash – according to him, because he wanted to see whether the ground radar, controlled from Houston, could react quickly enough to take over before impact. Buzz was not happy, however, and that night in crew quarters he let off to Collins, who described what happened in his book:

> Buzz was in fine voice, and as the Scotch bottle emptied and his complaints became louder and more specific, Neil suddenly appeared in his pyjamas, tousle-haired and coldly indignant, and joined the fray. Politely, I excused myself and gratefully crept off to bed, not wishing to intrude in an intercrew clash of technique or personality.

Collins felt that the reason behind the outburst was probably the decision that Armstrong was to be first out of the capsule, but although, in Collins' words, 'Buzz's attitude took a noticeable turn in the direction of gloom and introspection shortly thereafter,' this did not affect his efficiency or the level of co-operation between the three men.

They were ready to go on the 16th July, 1969. A million people were encamped around the launch site to see the 107-metre Saturn V rocket take off. Millions more were watching on television. Collins wrote of those final moments:

> I am everlastingly thankful that I have flown once before, and that this period of waiting atop a rocket is nothing new. I am just as tense this time, but the tenseness comes mostly from an appreciation of the enormity of our undertaking rather than from the unfamiliarity of the situation. If the two effects, physical apprehension and the pressure of awesome responsibility, were added together, they might be too much to handle without making some ghastly mistake. As it is, I am far from certain that we will be able to fly this mission as planned. I think we will escape with our skins, or at least I will escape with mine, but I wouldn't give better than even odds on a successful landing and return. There are just too many things that can go wrong.

With nine seconds to go, the rocket motors were ignited, building up a crescendo of noise, sending great waves of red-gold fire tumbling down the trenches stretching out from the rocket base. As it rose slowly, sedately, like a phoenix from the flames, up past the gantry, and then with an imperceptible yet incredibly fast acceleration up into earth orbit, the astronauts were blind, the portholes of their cabin covered with shields attached to the emergency rocket on the nose of the command vehicle and designed to lift them out of trouble if anything were to go wrong with the firing procedure. But now they were plastered back on their couches, forced there by the G-force of their acceleration as the rocket, in a matter of minutes, built up a speed of 6,000 mph. As millions of pounds weight of fuel were consumed, the first, and then the second stages of the rocket were discarded – the most expensive banana skins of all time – and finally, 118.5 miles out, the third stage boosted them into orbit around the earth for just two orbits while they checked all their systems ready to leave planet earth. Another, final burst of the third stage took them to 24,200 mph – enough to take them out of earth's orbit and on towards the moon.

So far the astronauts had done very little other than check gauges and respond to commands from Mission Control, but now, Mike Collins had to complete a delicate

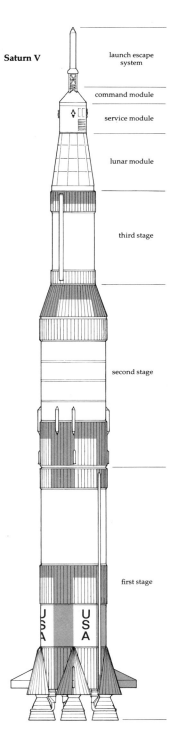

Saturn V

launch escape system

command module

service module

lunar module

third stage

second stage

first stage

USA USA

The Saturn rocket

operation where, should he make a mistake, the entire operation would certainly be ruined and they could lose their lives. The lunar module was stored on top of the third stage of the Saturn rocket, which was now expended – just another piece of space junk. Collins had to detach their own space craft, which consisted of the command module and the service module which carried the rocket engine and fuel that was to enable them to go into orbit round the moon and then propel them back to earth, and connect it with the lunar module, disengaging this from the third stage of the Saturn rocket. This was Mike Collins' show and consequently very important to him. The other two sat to one side, impotent spectators. He wrote: 'As we close, I can see the LM nestled in its container atop the Saturn like a mechanical tarantula crouched in its hole. Its one black eye peers malevolently at me; it is the drogue into which I must insert our probe.'

And then they were on their way to the moon. Up to this point they had worn their space suits, just in case Collins had collided with the Saturn rocket and had ruptured the skin of their pressurised cabin, but now they were able to wriggle out of their cumbersome shells, stow them under the couches and move around the tiny cabin more freely and settle down to weightless living. They had freeze-dried foods and powdered drinks in small plastic bags, which they had to fit closely over the nozzle of the hot water tap so that the liquid would not escape and then, once the food was reconstituted or the drink made, they had to squeeze it – rather like toothpaste – into their mouths. Bodily functions also called for concentration. To urinate, each had a neatly fitting condom connected by a tube to a valve on the side of the craft; this vented the urine away in a cloud of spectacular frozen amber crystals. To defecate, they had to fasten a plastic bag to their backsides with adhesive tape and then store the contents until their return to earth. If anyone made a mistake, they all had to live with it.

They were now in a state of eternal day and night – the sun, a glaring white orb, blazed relentlessly, while on the other side of the space craft the sky was an opaque black, the reflected glare of the sun, in the space craft, killing the glimmer of the stars. Collins wrote:

> I sense no motion on our part, other than the rotation required to distribute the sun's heat evenly, and the earth, like the minute hand on a watch, is not turning fast enough for the eye really to track its motion. But the effect is clear; we are hanging weightless in the void, while the earth turns slowly as it recedes above us or below us or to the side of us – I know not which. It is a totally different sensation than being in the race track of an earth orbit. I am conscious of distance this time, not speed, and distance away from home. It is a sobering, almost melancholy sight, this shrinking globe and for the first time in my life I think I know what outward bound means.

It was a three-day journey to the moon, a journey rather like midsummer above the Arctic Circle, when there is no night or day, just the circadian rhythm within each of the three astronauts to regulate their sleep and wakeful hours. At Houston's night-time they darkened the portholes of the space craft and strapped themselves in their couches. Collins describes it:

> It is a strange sensation to float in the total darkness, suspended by a cobweb's light touch, with no pressure points anywhere on my body. Instinctively, I feel I am lying on my back, not my stomach, but I am doing neither – all normal yardsticks have disappeared, and I am no more lying than I am standing or falling.

The earth was now a distant orb, much brighter than the moon is from earth, for the sea and clouds form a more reflective surface than the arid, atmosphere-less surface of the moon. But now the moon loomed huge and close. For Collins:

Apollo XI lifts off from the Kennedy Space Centre.

The moon I have known all my life, that two dimensional, small yellow disk in the sky, has gone away somewhere, to be replaced by the most awesome sphere I have ever seen. To begin with, it is huge, completely filling our window. Second, it is three dimensional. The belly of it bulges out towards us in a pronounced fashion that I almost feel I can reach out and touch it, while its surface obviously recedes towards its edges. It is between us and the sun, creating the most splendid lighting conditions imaginable. The sun casts a halo around it, shining on its rear surface and the sunlight which comes cascading around its rim serves mainly to make the moon itself seem mysterious and subtle by comparison emphasising the size and texture of its dimly lit and pockmarked surface.

Neil Armstrong, reticent, matter-of-fact, commented: 'It's a view worth the price of the trip.'

There was a lot to do. To get into lunar orbit they had to slow themselves down to exactly the right speed by blasting off with the engine of their module; they had to work out a whole series of eventualities before they went out of earth contact behind the moon. If anything went wrong they would have to take the right steps without help from Houston to get back to earth. They were now 200,000 miles from home. As they spun round the back of the moon, all three were tensed, closely watching the array of gauges and dials to see whether their pre-computed course was going to take them into the right orbit. The rocket engine blasted for exactly six minutes and then turned itself off. They were in orbit almost exactly sixty miles above the surface of the moon, racing over its bleak, pocked and cratered surface, picking out the landmarks which were going to be so important to them in just a few hours' time.

They spent the rest of the day spinning round the moon, preparing for their landing but also gazing in awe at a world so empty, so alien and strange that, through a porthole window, it was almost like a science fiction model created for a TV drama. It was too clear, too undisturbed; the craters, probably caused by the huge impact of meteors, unimpeded by atmosphere, are like the petrified, broken bubbles on a pan of boiling porridge. Another sleeping session before the crucial day. Collins recorded:

This day is about over, our fourth day out from earth, and I only want to rest now. Everything we have done so far amounts to zilch if we make a serious mistake, and we all know it, although Neil and Buzz seem less prone to admit our vulnerability than I do.

The following morning, by Houston time, the astronauts were wakened and plunged into preparations for the landing. Armstrong and Aldrin had to don their space suits, water-cooled to cope with the intense heat of the lunar surface, then crawl through the tunnel into the lunar module, seal the two craft and go through a complex series of checks before starting the most hazardous part of their mission. The lunar module had been taken for a long glide over the lunar surface on the previous Apollo flight, but it was the landing that would be critical. One serious mistake and they could crash into the surface or, perhaps even worse, be unable to take off again and have to wait for their oxygen to run out, dying in front of their TV camera with millions on earth their audience.

The interior of the lunar module, packed with miniature computers, communications equipment, dials, switches and circuit breakers, is even more constricted than that of the command vehicle. There are no seats, no couches, just a harness to hold the astronauts as they descend to the surface of the moon. From the outside it is unlike any craft that has ever flown, for it is the first designed for the vacuum of space alone – like some strange spider, with its four outstretched legs and squat, unwieldy body, covered in a tinsel of protective foil to guard its occupants from the heat of the sun's rays. Collins pressed the button to release the lunar module and it slid away from the space craft. Code names had already been given to the two vehicles. The module was Eagle, after the American Eagle and the symbol they had designed for their mission, and the command vehicle was Columbia, with derivations from Columbus and Columbiad, the rocket Jules Verne sent to the moon in the realms of fiction.

Back on earth, Mission Control at Houston was filled with everyone who could find an excuse to be there. Millions more were watching on television as Eagle glided down towards the surface of the moon. At this stage the computers were in control, those in Eagle backed up by the huge banks back in Houston. At just the right moment the rocket engine of Eagle switched itself on to start slowing down their descent; at 47,000 feet they were travelling at 3,000 mph, at 40,000 feet, with eighty miles to go to their proposed landing point, they had slowed down to 2,100 mph. And then an amber light started blinking. It was the computer programme alarm.

Quickly, Aldrin typed out the request to the computer to define the problem and received the reply that it was overloaded. More information than it could handle was being automatically poured in. There was nothing that Armstrong or Aldrin could do about it; this was a decision for Mission Control. But Houston reckoned they could afford to ignore the warning and gave the go-ahead. Again the warning light came on when they were only three thousand feet above the surface, just a few minutes from touch-down. Once again the call was to continue.

And then, as the Eagle skimmed down, still under the control of the computer, Armstrong had to take over. They were heading straight for a crater littered with boulders. In those final tense moments as Armstrong jockeyed the fragile vehicle down towards the surface of the moon, the ultimate mastery of the individual, the skilled, cool pilot, the adventurer was asserted. Man wasn't just a passenger to be taken down to the moon.

And yet after the initial excitement, the back-slapping both in the Eagle and back at Houston, and around countless TV sets all over the world, there was a certain anticlimax in man's first step onto the moon. Man in machine, reaching across space, skimming over the moon's surface to make the most hazardous, mysterious landing ever attempted, had been magnificent. This had been the adventure – in some ways man's greatest – but now he was there, his space ship parked on a level patch of lunar dirt, there was very little he could do. Cocooned in his pressure suit, scarcely able to bend either arms or legs because of the layers of protective plastic and nylon, Armstrong's movements were painfully cumbersome as he edged one step at a time down the ladder. He could barely look down, was unable to see where he was putting his feet. Visually, through the eye of the remote-controlled TV camera, he was a man in a diving suit climbing down a few steps onto a flat surface – it was almost less convincing than a science-fiction movie made on the cheap. For Armstrong, encumbered in this suit that brought his total body weight to well over 200 pounds and yet, because lunar gravity is a sixth that of earth, then reduced his effective weight to less than sixty pounds, it was all strange and surely frightening. Matter-of-factly, he said: 'I'm going to step off the LM now.'

Slowly, one foot was lowered, brushed the surface of the moon, pressed down upon it sinking little more than four millimetres into the smooth, grey dust as he transferred his full weight upon it.

'That's one small step for a man, one giant leap for mankind,' he said for the benefit of the viewing millions. His steps remained cautious and hesitant as he brought his other foot down and then ventured away from the security of the lunar module.

Overleaf]
The lunar module, Eagle, with astronauts Neil Armstrong and Buzz Aldrin aboard, viewed from the command and service module, Columbia.
The darker area of the moon's surface behind Eagle is Smyth's sea.
The earth rises above the lunar horizon.

Buzz Aldrin on the surface of the moon.

The perspective was unlike anything one could imagine on earth. The lack of atmosphere meant that there was no difference in clarity between a rock a few feet away and one on the far horizon; it was a world of extremes, of a black sky and brilliant white sun, of shadows as sharp as a cutting edge. Buzz Aldrin came out to join him. With the mind of an engineer, he sought to analyse his visual and tactile experience:

> I immediately looked down at my feet and became intrigued with the peculiar properties of the lunar dust. If one kicks sand on a beach, it scatters in numerous directions with some grains travelling further than others. On the moon the dust travels exactly and precisely as it goes in various directions, and every grain of it lands very nearly the same distance away.

Buzz Aldrin leaves the lunar module.

They were on the surface of the moon for about two and a half hours and in that time they performed very similar rituals to those of any other explorer or adventurer. They unfurled an American flag of nylon with a wire stiffener to stand proud on a windless world, posed beside it and even spoke to the President of the United States over their radios, mouthing the platitudes that inevitably are spoken on these occasions. They also carried out some scientific experiments, laying out various items of equipment and collecting rocks and dust samples from the surface of the moon before retreating to the shelter of the lunar module nearly four hours behind schedule.

It was now time for rest, seven hours of enforced inactivity, with Aldrin curled uncomfortably on the floor, Armstrong wedged above him, his buttocks on the housing of the rocket engine they hoped would take them to safety, his feet in a sling. They hardly slept; excitement, even euphoria combined perhaps with a sense of dread that now their supreme aim had been achieved they might not get back to enjoy it. It is the same on a mountain. Everything goes into getting to the top; you are prepared to take risks, hardly notice them but then, having achieved the peak, suddenly you become aware of your isolation, of your distance from safety, and after that first euphoria of just being there has died, you become super-cautious and conscious of risk, anxious to get down to level ground.

While Armstrong and Aldrin attempted to sleep, Collins was spinning some sixty miles up, in his lonely vigil round the moon. Altogether he made seven orbits, had more time, and perhaps more aptitude for reflection:

> I don't mean to deny a feeling of solitude. It is there, reinforced by the fact that radio contact with the earth abruptly cuts off at the instant I disppear behind the moon. I am alone now, truly alone, and absolutely isolated from any known life. I am it. If a count were taken, the score would be three billion plus two over on the other side of the moon, and one plus God only knows what on this side. I feel this powerfully – not as fear of loneliness – but as awareness, anticipation, satisfaction, confidence, almost exultation. I like the feeling. Outside my window I can see stars – and that is all. Where I know the moon to be, there is simply a black void: the moon's presence is defined solely by the absence of stars.
>
> To compare the sensation with something terrestrial, perhaps being alone in a skiff in the middle of the Pacific Ocean on a pitch black night would most nearly approximate my situation. In a skiff, one would see bright stars above and black sea below: I see the stars, minus the twinkling, of course, and absolutely nothing below. In each case, time and distance are extremely important factors. In terms of distance, I am much more remote, but in terms of time, lunar orbit is much closer to civilised conversation than is the mid-Pacific. Although I may be a quarter of a million miles away, I am cut off from human voices for only forty-eight minutes out of each two hours, while the man in the skiff – grazing the very surface of the planet – is not so privileged, or burdened. Of the two quantities, time and distance, time tends to be a much more personal one, so that I feel simultaneously closer to, and farther away from Houston than I would if I were on some remote spot on earth which would deny me conversation with other humans for months on end.

Mike Collins also had time to worry about the possible fate of Armstrong and Aldrin. In a way it was worse for him than it was for them, for he was the helpless spectator, while they were too involved, too busy to worry about their own fate. For the previous six months his nightmare had been that something might go wrong and that he could end up returning to earth on his own, to face the families of his friends and the questions of the entire world.

Now it was the final count-down; most critical of all, because there was no room for error, no back-up. The vital rocket engine on the lunar module was the only item of equipment not duplicated. The rocket ignited and Eagle lurched off its landing legs, yawed violently in a way that they had been warned to expect, but juddered

steadily upwards, away from the moon. This was the ultimate rendezvous, a complex series of mathematical problems that had obsessed Aldrin for the last two years. Eagle was aimed into a slightly lower orbit than that of Columbia, and would therefore travel faster. Coming up behind the command module, the lunar bug would catch up steadily and then, with a push from its thruster, could climb and make its union.

Mike Collins could pick up the exact angle of the approach with his sextant. At first it was just a blinking light in the viewpiece and then, as they came round from the back of the moon into the light of the sun, it became a visible bug, gliding golden and black over the crater fields below, steadily catching up with Columbia. Soon they were just fifty feet apart, and Collins turned the command module to face the lunar module to repeat the manoeuvre he had carried out when he pulled Eagle out from its nest at the top of the Saturn rocket. Once again he eased the probe into the drogue with hardly a judder but then, just as he completed the union, they had one last, adrenalin-pumping surprise; as if resenting its loss of freedom, Eagle suddenly turned into a bucking bronco. It yawed round to the right, spinning both craft out of alignment as Collins struggled with the controls to keep them steady. And then, just as suddenly, the docking latches slammed shut and the craft settled in its orbit.

The most difficult and risky part of their voyage was now over, but they were still a quarter of a million miles from home, still had to re-enter the earth's atmosphere at exactly the right angle and speed. If the angle were too steep, they could burn up – if too shallow, they would just bounce off it. But these were known problems that the computers back on earth and in the space craft could cope with.

They were on the way home to a carefully orchestrated heroes' welcome. They splashed down in the Pacific, within a mile of their projected target point, on the 24th July, after a voyage of over half a million miles lasting 195 hours 18 minutes. As the first men to touch the surface of the moon, they were put into quarantine, in a specially prepared sealed container on the aircraft-carrier *Hornet*. President Nixon flew out to talk to them through the sealed window and then, when finally released, they were faced with the full aftermath of being the first men on the moon, the visible tokens of a great American victory.

The moon had certainly changed the lives of all three astronauts, but how much was because of the actual experience of either standing on its surface, or spinning a lonely journey around it, I am not at all sure. I can remember, on the South-West Face of Everest in 1975, at an altitude of around 7925 metres, recording in my diary that I felt I would never ever be the same again. It was a statement born of an intense moment of emotion, created by the impact of the sight of serried ranges of snow peaks, combined with a sense of fulfilment at having carried one of the vital loads up to our top camp for Doug Scott and Dougal Haston to make the summit bid. At that moment I was the Collins of our venture, along with five others who had made that vital carry. Maybe Doug and Dougal experienced a similar wave of feeling on the summit. In a September dusk, with no hope of getting back to their top camp that night, they were very nearly as remote, and certainly in for a very much colder and more uncomfortable night than Armstrong and Aldrin. And yet these moments of intense feelings are, I suspect, essentially ephemeral. The deepest changes in the astronauts' characters – if there were any – would have been caused by the experience as a whole, by the slogging self-discipline required to master every aspect of flight to the moon.

The command module photographed in lunar orbit from the lunar module above the Sea of Fertility.

The biggest immediate change, and the one most difficult to handle, was their overnight fame. The three astronauts were now pawns of the public-relations machine. The United States was like any expedition sponsor, anxious to justify its investment – in this instance the biggest ever made for any adventure, several thousand times over. The astronauts spoke to Congress, went on a world tour of punishing dimensions and had honours piled upon them. Two of them, Armstrong and Collins, survived; the third did not. Two years after landing on the moon, Aldrin was in a mental hospital with a nervous breakdown, his marriage and career in a mess. His fellow astronauts were not particularly charitable, Collins commenting about Aldrin's personality, 'Heavy, man, heavy. Would make a champion chess player; always thinks several moves ahead. If you don't understand what Buzz is talking about today, you will tomorrow or the next day. Fame has not worn well on Buzz. I think he resents not being first more than he appreciated being second.'

Walter Cunningham, a fellow astronaut of the third intake, commented, 'In the opinion of his peers, Buzz was more concerned about having to get off stage than he was at being on.' He is one of the very few astronauts who seems to have failed to handle and exploit their experience.

Mike Collins had already decided to leave the astronaut programme before setting out for the moon. After a short spell in the State Department, he joined the Smithsonian Institution and is now its Under-Secretary and a Major-General, U.S. Air Force Reserves. Neil Armstrong also left NASA. A quiet, unassuming man, he became Professor of Aeronautical Engineering at the University of Cincinnati before moving on into private business. He is now chairman of an engineering group with an office in Lebanon, a small town in his home state of Ohio.

Looking at the lives of the astronauts as a whole, most of them have done extraordinarily well within the society that gave them their first chance. Almost all those who have left NASA are chairmen or vice-chairmen of large corporations, two are US Senators. In the marriage stakes their divorce rate is well below the national average.

Altogether, there were seven shots for the moon, of which six were successful. Apollo XIII came closest to disaster when an oxygen tank exploded when they were actually on their way to the moon. They had passed the point of no return, which meant they had to continue round the moon, to use its gravity to sling them back to earth. Using the lunar module, fastened to the nose of the command module as a kind of lifeboat with its self-contained oxygen system, they managed to get back – perhaps one of the most remarkable feats of the entire space programme.

It is no more easy to quantify the importance of man's landing on the moon in terms of money and intellectual effort than it is to justify the climbing of a mountain or the reaching of a Pole. And yet the landing on the moon – whatever the motives of science, politics, or romance – was indisputably one of the greatest adventures of all time.

Dead Man's Handshake

The only sound is the hiss of air, the 'phutt' of the demand valve closing and the gurgling bubbles of escaped breath, which seem to explode if the roof of the passage is close above. An air cylinder strikes a protruding rock and there is a hollow, reverberating-yet-muffled clang. The diver is in a tiny pool of light, filtered and distorted by the waters around him. His only point of reference is the bed of the passage. He is like the lunar module, skimming the surface of the moon, pebbles and rocks replacing craters, yet there is life in this strange world. A shoal of freshwater shrimps, transparent and colourless, stampede through the beam of light, but the diver is in an environment more alien, more threatening than the cold dark waters of the North Sea, as remote as the emptiness of space, for the waters he penetrates are contained by solid rock. He has swum through long corridors, wriggled through constrictions in a fog of mud, forever fearful of a cylinder jamming against a protruding rock, a hose being caught or torn, mindful his next breath might suck water not air. He does not know where the passage leads, does not know what might be beyond the limits of his beam of light. His only way back, along a maze of waterlogged passages, is the guide line he has laid behind him. Should his equipment fail or should he lose that line, a dark, lonely death will inevitably follow. He must keep cool in a situation which is a scenario for most people's nightmares.

Cave diving is at the extreme end of caving and it allows the cave explorer to venture where otherwise he would have had to admit defeat. The sport of caving has never had as wide a following as more visible and easy to publicise activities. It can boast no obvious Everests, for it can never be known for certain if one cave is indubitably the deepest or the longest in the world. There might always be another just waiting to be found. And yet this is also the fascination of caving, for on a planet that has had its surface thoroughly explored, whose every mountain peak is known and almost all the highest ones climbed by at least one route, and whose every ocean has been crossed, caving still gives vast scope for exploration, not just in distant parts, but beneath the gentle, rolling hills of the Yorkshire Dales, the Mendips and South Wales. Wherever there is limestone there are also caves, sinuous passages, gaping chasms, gigantic chambers, rivers, torrents and lakes, all formed by the slow, pervasive action of water on the calcium carbonate of limestone. Cavers use what artificial aids they can devise to help their exploration; they dig and even blast their way through blocked passages, but the amount of technology that can be used is strictly limited by the nature of the caves themselves. Everything has to be carried, shoved and pulled through narrow passages, down flue-like holes. This in itself defeats most modern technology. Man is still the most effective machine in the close confines of a cave.

In the early 'fifties cavers were intrigued by a system in the Yorkshire Dales between the villages of Dent and Ingleton. Skeletal outcrops of limestone, whitened by weathering, give a hint of what lies beneath; streams vanish into the hillside and then reappear lower down the slopes. One of these streams emerges in a pool at Keld Head in Kingsdale. A large team had drained the pool, hoping to penetrate the passage that led into it, but they were stopped after a few yards by flowing water filling the entire passage. Cave diving was still in its infancy. The Yorkshire cavers were prepared for short sections of waterlogged passage, which they free-dived, relying on coming up for air after only a few yards. It was a very frightening game, for if there was no air pocket, the diver then had to turn round, or if there was insufficient room, back out, and return to the surface before he ran out of breath.

Geoff Yeadon.

Oliver Statham.

Keld Head was left alone for nearly thirty years, its questions remained unanswered. The pattern of water inlets and caves explored around the high hill mass of Gragareth, extending over the three county boundaries of Cumbria, Lancashire and Yorkshire, showed that all these systems must somehow be linked underground with miles of passages, many of them waterlogged, but, equally, with many of them drained and empty, just waiting for the explorer to find them. A map of the caves already discovered was a little like an early map of Africa, with the spidery routes of European explorers slowly creeping forward into the dark unknown. Keld Head was of special interest to the cave diver for here there were clearly two caving systems, about a mile and a quarter apart, linked by flooded passages.

Geoff Yeadon was one of the cave divers who was to play a major part in linking them together. In appearance he has an uncanny resemblance to Mick Jagger, with the same large sensual mouth and slightly protruding jaw, framed by shoulder length hair. Born in 1950, just before the first effort was made to penetrate the mysteries of Keld Head, he was brought up in Skipton and went to the local grammar school, where he was fortunate enough to be introduced to caving at the age of eleven by one of the teachers, David Heap, an enthusiast who had started a caving club. In the early 'sixties the neoprene wet suit had not yet been developed and the caver made do with a pair of overalls and layers of woollen clothing underneath, that soon became soaked in a wet cave. But Geoff Yeadon never looked back. He took being saturated for hours on end completely for granted. He explored most of the difficult known caves in the Yorkshire area, helped discover a major caving system in Arctic Norway and in 1970 joined an expedition to the Gouffre Berger, which had only just lost its title as the deepest known cave in the world. Descending such a cave was like a Himalayan expedition in reverse, for it required thousands of feet of fixed rope and electron ladders, all of which had to be man-handled down narrow passages and deep shafts. It also meant camping on the way down, since it was too long a system to complete in one push. The main party had reached the second camp, in a huge chamber, and were all asleep, when another member of the team, Oliver Statham (known as 'Bear' because of his size and strength) came plummeting down the rope on his way to attempt the first complete descent and re-ascent in a day. In fact, Statham had come down prematurely, for they had not yet rigged the lower part of the cave. However, Geoff Yeadon decided to accompany him for the final push down, both on grounds of safety and to help carry the ropes. They managed to establish the record and, at the same time, started a partnership that was eventually to lead them from caving to one of the boldest cave dives that has ever been made.

Oliver Statham came from a very different background to Geoff Yeadon. Son of an ambassador, he had gone to Sedburgh School in North Yorkshire (now Cumbria) in the midst of superb caving country. He also had started caving whilst at school. Both of them had gone on to art college and had specialised in pottery. Geoff was now at the Bath Art College and Oliver was working in his own pottery in Skipton.

It was around this time that Keld Head came back into the picture. Oliver Statham had met a cave diver called Mike Wooding who had just undertaken one of the longest and boldest dives made so far in Britain. He had tried to penetrate Keld Head, diving over 300 metres into a labyrinth of water-filled passages. Somehow he had missed the main watercourse and had ended up in a cul-de-sac. Oliver Statham became intrigued by the challenge of cave diving and passed on his interest to Geoff Yeadon. Oliver's introduction was characteristic of his personality at that time. His first dive, without a full mask, flippers, or any form of training, was through a twenty-four-metre sump. It was a matter of putting an air bottle on his back, clenching the mouthpiece for the air line and valve between his teeth, and following the line through.

Geoff Yeadon was attracted by the idea but approached it slightly more cautiously and methodically, joining the Cave Diving Group to borrow equipment and going on regular training sessions, starting in the swimming baths of Bristol University. At the end of his period in college, Geoff came back north to do his teacher's training in Leeds. He and Oliver Statham were now able to cave dive together. They could afford to buy their own aqualung equipment and compressed air bottles and chose Boreham Cave in Upper Wharfedale for their first major exploration. Their initial

Boreham Cave in Upper Wharfedale. It was the exploration and mapping of cave systems that intrigued Geoff Yeadon as much as breaking records.

attempt was abortive and very nearly fatal. The first sump, which was forty-six metres long, had already been dived and they knew that it was quite straight-forward. Oliver, therefore, did not bother to fit his spare demand valve, but carried it packed away in an ammunition box. He dived first, followed by Geoff. They were very nearly through when Geoff saw Oliver's light coming back towards him. As he came up to Geoff, he made a few frantic gestures towards his valve to indicate that it wasn't working. One emergency procedure is to share a mouthpiece, taking alter-nate gulps of air from the same apparatus. This, however, needs very cool nerves and a high level of practice and understanding. Oliver, his lungs already bursting, couldn't afford to wait and swept past Geoff in a desperate bid for air, but on the way the tube leading to his mouthpiece caught round Geoff's cylinder, so that Oliver was now towing Geoff. Geoff quickly unhooked his tube from the valve to free himself and Oliver shot off like a torpedo. Geoff followed, hoping that if his friend did lose consciousness before getting back to the surface, he might just be able to tow him to safety and revive him. But Oliver made it and when Geoff followed to the surface, he was already lying on the side of the pool gulping in the air with great, agonised gasps. He had swum over thirty metres under water without the benefit of his air supply.

Nothing daunted, they returned to Boreham Cave a few weeks later. Another cave diver had started through the next sump in the early 'sixties. There were reports of a narrow squeeze, so tight that you had to take off your cylinder and push it through in front of you. This time Geoff set out, leaving Oliver sitting at the side of the underwater stream where it vanished into the rock. The role of support diver is more psychological than anything else, for there is very little he can do if anything goes wrong. It is not like being second man on a climb. If his partner does not come back within the prescribed time, he has to plunge into the water and follow the line to find out what has happened. It is just possible that the first diver could have run out of air or experienced a technical fault and has managed to find an air pocket in which to wait for help. But if there has been a serious delay, it is more likely that he has drowned.

The tension is always less for the leader. Geoff was now engrossed in finding his way through the first squeeze, as the walls converged around him. Getting himself and his bottles at the right angle, he was able to slide through the hole. This was the first time he had been underwater in an unexplored cave.

> I remember being incredibly excited by the size of this huge tunnel, the water all blue, stretching away from me, with no other lines going into it except the one I had in my hand on the line reel. I just finned off into the distance and the tunnel wound round. Occasionally there were lower bits to one side that I vaguely noticed, but I was so excited that everything was a bit of a daze. I didn't really take it all in. Eventually I popped up into an air space. It was tiny and I had to wriggle along sideways. I really wanted to go back then, but I had no excuse. There was plenty of line on the reel and I still had enough air. I was well within the thirds safety margin used by cave divers. That is, a third of your air to go in, a third to come out and a third for emergency. There was no reason to go back except in my head. My head kept telling me I wanted to go back, but I carried on.

He dived back into the water through another hole, came to another air space, slithered down a waterfall into yet another sump, this time twenty-four metres long, with another air space beyond that, and so it went on until at last, 165 metres from the start, he had run out of line and had an excuse to turn back. On the way in, the water had been beautifully clear, but he had disturbed the fine sediment on the bed, so that going back it was like being in a dense fog. His light bounced back on the myriad particles held suspended in the water and he could see little more than a few centimetres in front of his mask. It was a question of following the life line, since he

244 metres into Boreham Cave.

had no sense of direction or scale, but he now found that the roof above him was closing in, pressing him down onto the bed of the cave.

> I remember thinking it definitely wasn't this low. I had my head on one side, grinding over pebbles. I couldn't see a damn thing and, with my head on one side, occasionally I'd get a gulp of water which made me very aware that I was underwater and a long way from home. I had to keep stopping to calm down because my breathing rate kept going up and I knew that if I didn't calm down and slow my breathing rate down, I wasn't going to get out.

Geoff had made one mistake on the way in which could have cost him his life. He had omitted to anchor the line down on the outside of the corners he had turned and, as a result, it had been pulled tight round the bends in the narrowest part of the bedding plane. He had to keep hold of the line somehow, for, once lost, he would never have found his way back. But by dint of resting, wriggling and easing the line from the tightest edges of the passage, he finally managed to get back to where his partner was waiting by the side of the pool. This was the last time that Oliver Statham went cave diving for a period of six months. Even so, he needed the stimulus of risk in his life and sought it in the sky instead; he took up hang gliding.

Geoff Yeadon's first exploratory dive was considerably bolder than almost any that had been made in Britain at this time and he had learnt a great deal from the experience. He returned to Boreham Cave a few months later, anchored the line to keep it in the wider parts of the passage, and swam into the further recesses of the hole.

Straw stalactites first discovered by Geoff Yeadon in Boreham Cave.

404

It was like a cresta run, only underwater. It was a beautiful feeling, just flying through this tube without touching the roof or floor, banking over at the corners, with the line reel ticking out. There were beautiful curves, just like a snake with smooth silt banks on either side. I kept glancing behind me and could see this cloud of silt coming up after me. It was a good, safe passage with no nasty nicks in the corners – it was more like an arched tunnel. Then a peculiar phenomenon occurred in front. It was a layer, like a cloud of brown water approaching at roof level and I was in clear water underneath. Then this gradually came down until I was entirely in brown water, and then, unfortunately, the line ran out.

The only explanation seemed that there must have been an inlet, carrying running water, flowing over the still water through which he had been swimming.

Geoff Yeadon continued his exploration of Boreham Cave, stretching his own limits and developing the techniques that were later going to stand him in good stead in Keld Head. His club bought him a larger air bottle to give him greater range, and to combat the debilitating cold he wore three wet suits, as he embarked on progressively longer dives, finally making one of 762 metres down the outlet that he had sensed was there when he had encountered the ceiling of discoloured water. It was cave exploration at its best and it was this facet that intrigued Geoff as much as the element of making records. He was mapping the cave as he dived, noting compass bearings and distances on a small slate.

It was around this time that Oliver Statham began caving once more. He and Geoff got on well as friends, eventually working together in their pottery, and soon most of their cave diving energies were directed into solving the problems of Keld Head.

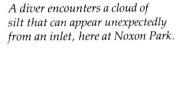

A diver encounters a cloud of silt that can appear unexpectedly from an inlet, here at Noxon Park.

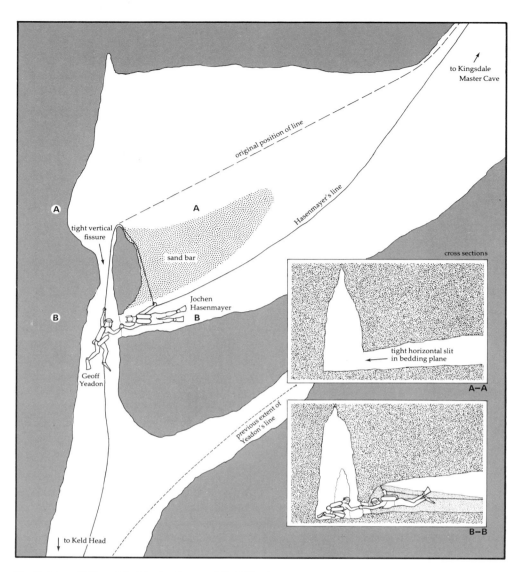

The linking of Kingsdale Master Cave and Keld Head

This was to become a long drawn out siege over a period of years rather than months. In their approach to it they now worked as one, developing techniques and equipment to cater for the sheer scale of a challenge which was at the extreme limit of cave diving expertise.

There was always the problem of funds, for they certainly couldn't afford to purchase the specialised equipment, but here the record nature of the dive became useful. Oliver Statham managed to persuade a diving manufacturer to supply them with specially modified dry suits on reduced terms. Dry suits work on a different principle from wet suits, for they seal the body in a cocoon of air which can be adjusted to allow for different levels of buoyancy by means of an inlet valve from the breathing system, and an escape valve to release excess air. They are not only warmer than wet suits but, perhaps more important, they insulate the diver from the water around him, making him feel that he has the security, however illusory, of being in a submarine. Using these suits, Statham and Yeadon made a series of forays into Keld Head, taking it in turns to run out the full contents of a reel before turning back to allow the other to follow it and then run out another length.

The downstream entrance of Keld Head was a labyrinth of waterlogged passages

Geoff Yeadon in Keld Head.

The sort of constriction cave divers have to negotiate, sometimes pushing their air bottles ahead of them, here at the Afon Hepste Resurgence, South Wales.

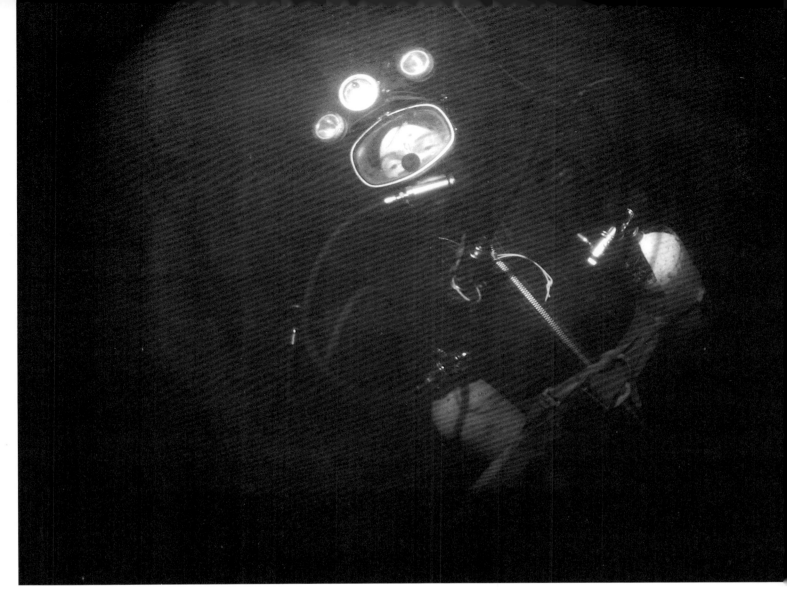

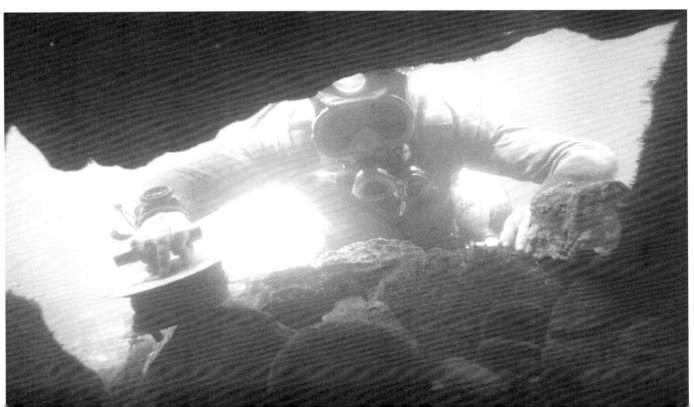

festooned with the guide lines of previous attempts. One of the first jobs was to clear these out of the way to avoid dangerous confusion. They got some help from fellow cave divers in doing this and it was during the clearing operation that the body of Alan Erith, a novice cave diver who had lost his life about four years earlier, was found. Geoff Yeadon and Oliver Statham helped in the recovery operation before returning to their own exploration. They had already run out 300 metres of line and were obviously in the main passage, which they hoped led to the Kingsdale Master Cave system, about a mile away. They were also gaining in confidence.

> We really became more like fish. We'd stop and rest on the bottom, sitting down on a rock, nattering to each other on our slates. We even had drinks of water because we found that after an hour or two of surveying and swimming you started getting a dry throat from the dryness of the air. You just took your mouthpiece out and had a drink.

And, weekend by weekend, they pushed the route out; to 450 metres, then 600 metres, 690. It was a slow, painstaking process. It took a week just to prepare for a dive, to check over all the equipment, clean it, grease it with a silicone spray, get all the bottles filled, and then check each valve again.

At this stage Oliver and Geoff began working from opposite ends of the system. Oliver had hurt his back, so concentrated on the Keld Head end which did not involve any caving prior to the dive, whilst Geoff started trying to find the way down from the Kingsdale Cave back towards Keld Head. There was a low sloping passage to the first sump, and he worked on this through the summer of 1976, always on his own, relying on casual help from cavers on their way down to help carry his gear to the first sump. This was in a chamber like a gigantic shower, with the water pattering down out of the dark above onto the pool into which he was going to dive. The pool led into a maze of winding, water-filled tunnels and blind alleys.

> I got to a five-way junction. It was completely bewildering. I just belayed the line to a rock and sat down (still submerged, of course) and looked at my compass and thought, 'Which one's Keld Head?' I picked what I thought was the right way and it dropped down a shaft which led into a big river tunnel. The flow increased and the place became enormously wide, but I wasn't quite sure where it was going. I just kept on a bearing, heading in roughly the right direction, until I ran out of line. The next trip it burst out into this incredible blackness with the floor dropping away downward and the roof shooting away up. The water was so clear I thought I might have wandered into another ox-bow but then it narrowed down so much that I would have had to take my cylinders off to squeeze through so I decided that this could not possibly be the way to Keld Head.

He had made, altogether, six dives from the Kingsdale Master Cave but still seemed nowhere nearer finding the connection with Keld Head. It had been lonely and, at times, frightening work and on one occasion he could very easily have lost his life. He was on his way back, finning quickly through the murky waters, and had just exhaled. When he inhaled, he received a mouthful of water instead of air. He could not see what was wrong because of the murk; it all had to be done by touch, with gloved fingers. He felt his mask and found that all he was left with was the disconnected rubber mouthpiece, the other bits having dropped off. He had to find the other valve, but this also had to be done by touch. The tubes were exactly the same thickness and on his first attempt he followed the wrong tube. His lungs were now bursting – it was like trying to hold your breath for thirty seconds after completing a hundred yards sprint. He was consciously slowing himself down, even though his body was beginning to take over in its desperate need for air, with muscular spasms in his lungs and involuntary twitching in his fingers that made it even harder to follow the tube down to the spare valve. At last he found it, brought it up to the mouthpiece, stuffed it in and pressed the button that would blow out the water flooding the system. He could breathe again. He lay on the bottom of the passage for some minutes to get his panting back under control before finning slowly back to the cave where he had started his dive. 'That was another lesson learnt. Never go that fast again. You've got to move slowly the whole time to keep your breathing rate down so that if anything does go wrong you can hold your breath for a long time.' Because of the difficult access to the start of the dive, Geoff could only wear a wet suit whilst diving from the Kingsdale Master Cave and carry a limited quantity of bottles. Eventually he felt he could go no further from that end. In February 1977 he made one more attempt from Keld Head, extending the line to 920 metres, which established yet another record for British diving and equalled the European record. They were also getting near to the link-up point from the Kingsdale Cave but, unfortunately, the limits reached by the two explorations were on different levels. The Keld Head passage seemed to be about eighteen metres below the last point that Geoff had reached from the Kingsdale end, and it could be difficult finding the connection between the two levels. In addition, they were now at the limit of the capacity of their bottles.

Meanwhile, Oliver had been writing to cave divers around the world to find out what they were doing. It was such a young activity that communication between different groups was still very poor. One of his correspondents was Jochen Hasenmayer, a very experienced German cave diver. He was intrigued by what he heard about Keld Head and offered to come over to help. Geoff was immediately impressed by Jochen, saying: 'We found that what we thought we'd been pioneering, he'd been doing nineteen years before.'

They were now ready for the big effort to join up with the Kingsdale Master Cave system. They decided to set out at three-quarter-hour intervals with Jochen Hasenmayer, who had larger capacity cylinders, going first, followed by Oliver Statham and then Geoff Yeadon. There had been a lot of rain and, consequently, the visibility was appalling. They could see little more than an arm's length ahead of them.

Jochen swam strongly to the end of the line and then set out, feeling his way along the bed of the cave. Geoff had gone into a cul-de-sac on his previous attempt, but Jochen sensed that there should be a route out to the left. He came upon a narrow fissure only forty-five centimetres wide. Jochen had his big cylinders mounted on his back and this made it particularly difficult and dangerous wriggling through narrow sections, since he was unable to see or even feel anything that might foul the back of the cylinders. Even so, he managed to worm his way through the gap to find that it widened out beyond, but the roof had dropped to a much lower level. He squeezed through, however, and continued running out the reel in a broader channel until it came to an end. Anchoring it in position, he started back, following the line. He had made the same mistake that Geoff Yeadon made on his first long exploratory dive in the Boreham Cave, for he had not anchored the line in places where the route went round corners. So, on his return, he found it had shifted into the side where it was much too shallow for him to squeeze through. Very quickly you lose all sense of direction. He was over 914 metres from the entrance in almost nil visibility. The more he searched and pushed and struggled, the more silt swirled up until he could barely see anything more than a few inches from his face.

Oliver Statham had set out three-quarters of an hour behind Jochen and followed the line to the constriction. He had one bottle mounted on his back and one on either side. This meant that his side dimensions were wider than Jochen's, so it was even more difficult, if not impossible, for the big man to wriggle through the narrow gap.

He was already very close to using up a third of his air supply and so, desperately worried, he started back down the line, to meet Geoff, who had set out another three-quarters of an hour behind Oliver.

Geoff Yeadon told me:

> I met Bear at about 2,750 feet, coming back. I immediately felt apprehensive because, of course, it should have been Jochen who came back first, and then Bear wrote this ghastly note on my slate: '3000, small with back and sides' – which meant the bottles mounted back and side – 'No Jochen. Trouble???!!!'
>   I replied on the slate: 'I will go and look and then turn back.'

Geoff swam on along the line until he reached the constriction. Peering into the gloom he was unable to see any sign of Jochen. He had the same problem as Oliver, for he also had one back-mounted and two side-mounted bottles. He decided to wait until a third of his air had been exhausted before returning. And so he waited in the

Cave divers communicate in a sump by writing on slates.

Oliver Statham's message about the overdue Jochen Hasenmayer, and Geoff Yeadon's reply: 'I will look and then turn back.'

cold, cloudy water, increasingly worried because Jochen had now been in the cave for more than an hour longer than he and so, even allowing for the greater capacity of his bottles, must be nearing the end of his reserves. There was also the terrible conflict of wanting to do something to help but being helpless to do it and having to face the prospect of abandoning a diving partner to his fate. He had very nearly exhausted his ration of air, and was steeling himself to return, when he felt the rope in his hand twitch. Jochen must be somewhere near. He tugged the rope, just to show Jochen that someone was close by and then somehow wriggled and jammed himself through the narrow gap so that he could at last see the dull, suffused glow of Jochen's head lights only five feet away. But between them a sandbank on the base of the passage pushed up to within a few centimetres of the roof. Jochen had not seen Geoff's light and was trying to get through at another point. There was no communication between them. Jochen was not even able to interpret the twitches on the line which he had felt. It could easily have meant that one of the others was stuck as well. And then Jochen's light vanished. He had obviously backed out and then pushed into another passage in his struggle to escape the trap.

There was nothing that Geoff could do, no way that he could catch Jochen's attention. He did not dare go any further through the squeeze, since it would have been almost impossible to retreat with his back and side-mounted cylinders and the guide line now hopelessly out of position. It was hard enough wriggling backwards to get out. Each time he jammed, it could have been for good. Keep calm, slow down the breathing, edge forward a little, wriggle again, very gently, and at last he was out of the squeeze. He looked at his gauges and saw that he was well into his second third of air, but the situation was now very different. Jochen was close at hand and desperately needed his help. The line twitched again. Geoff wriggled once more part way through the squeeze, could see Jochen's light, but Jochen was obviously not looking in his direction. Geoff retreated. His air was being consumed all too quickly, both because of the tension of the situation and because he was eighteen metres below the water surface level, which meant he was using air at three times the rate he would have consumed it just beneath the surface. And then Jochen's light appeared once more, but this time through a hole much too small for anyone to have squeezed through. He had at last seen Geoff's light and swum towards it until they were within touching distance. Geoff reached through and Jochen grasped his hand. Geoff told me:

> I could feel his fingers and his whole arm trembling as he squeezed my hand. I couldn't help wondering what the hell I'd do if he wouldn't let go, but I just tried to keep my hand absolutely still, to show him that I was perfectly all right and in the right place. I was willing him in my mind to go back and have another go at finding the right way out, but there was no way I could communicate that. He just squeezed and squeezed and I'd give a reassuring squeeze back and then, eventually, he let go, patted me on the hand and backed away. I interpreted this either that he was being a Captain Oates, going away and telling me to get out while I could, or that he was going to have another go. I was convinced at the time I was shaking a dead man's hand.

Geoff was now well into the second third of his air, but he waited by the squeeze, shining his light through it, hoping desperately that Jochen would now find the right way through, and this time he managed it, skirting the sandbank and, still clinging to the line, he manoeuvred himself through the awkward dog-leg leading back to safety. As he came through, Geoff cautiously held back in the roof of the passage. There were tales of divers in both Australia and Florida who had run out of air underwater and had attacked their companions in a desperate effort to take away their air bottles in a fight for survival.

I didn't know Jochen that well, so decided to keep my distance. I was holding the line so he'd be able to find me but I was in a position to see how nasty he was looking when he came out of the hole.

In fact Jochen's air just lasted out. One bottle was nearly empty and there was a little more left in the second. He would not show anyone just how little there was, perhaps to avoid alarming his wife who was waiting at the entrance. Jochen did not want to talk about what had gone through his mind when he was trapped on the other side of what has become known as the Dead Man's Handshake. He could only say that it was a nightmare. The fact that he survived at all was due to an extraordinary level of control and, within hours of getting out, they were already planning their return, discussing how they could make the passage safer by anchoring out the guide line, using bigger bottles and changing the way they carried them.

Geoff Yeadon set to work on his gear, making a set of harnesses that had four demand valves and four separate air supplies, all side-mounted. It was so heavy it made his back ache, even underwater. He had also evolved a new strategy to cope with the logistics of such a prolonged dive, planning to drop the two smaller bottles at 213 metres and 427 metres respectively, each of them with two-thirds of their capacity unused. This meant that he would have his reserves in place for the return and would only have to contend with the two large, side-mounted cylinders at the constriction by the Dead Man's Handshake. He went in on 16th April 1977, dropped his bottles as planned, and reached the constriction, which he was now able to negotiate more easily. Mooring the line with lead weights ensured that it would stay in place, guiding them all through the dog-leg at its widest and only feasible point. He went on to the end of Jochen's line and reeled out another thirty metres, but he was now creeping over the third safety factor and prudently returned. At 1036 metres it was another European record. They were getting very close to his furthest point of exploration in the Kingsdale Master Cave but they were still eighteen metres below, and so the junction was as elusive as ever. In addition, their cylinders were still not big enough to carry sufficient air to give them the reserves of safety they needed.

Another summer, autumn and winter went by. Geoff turned his attention once again to the Kingsdale Master Cave, doing another series of dives to try to find the vital link. On 11th June 1978, he organised himself a support team which enabled him to take in a dry suit, packed in a container, and big bottles for a long dive. This time he found the key, 732 metres into the labyrinth. He stumbled onto a passage he had not been down before and came across a hole in the floor. It was black and frightening, an abyss a long way from home.

On a practical level, a vertical shaft is potentially dangerous, for if it goes too deep, and the pressures become too great, there are problems with buoyancy and the danger of getting the bends on coming back up to the surface. There is also the psychological barrier that a hole presents. It is so easy to imagine it going down for ever into the depths of the earth. It's a plunge, perhaps, into our own black sub-conscious. For Geoff, having a dry suit made all the difference, for he could regulate the pressure inside it and, through this, control his rate of descent. He sank steadily, counting off his descent with the depth gauge strapped to his wrist. It bottomed out at nearly nineteen metres. He was almost level with the Keld Head Cave. The passage swept away in the right direction, wide and inviting. He swam down it for sixty-one metres and, although he could see no sign of their exploration from the lower end, nor of the reel he had left the previous year, he sensed that he must be very nearly there. But he had now reached the vital third capacity and was forced to return.

Their effort had now reached expedition proportions in terms of commitment, time and expense. They therefore began to look for sponsorship, gaining a Royal Geographical Society grant to help buy the big-capacity bottles they so desperately needed. In July that same year, Jochen Hasenmayer came over once again, bringing the bottles with him. They were ready to try again from Keld Head on 6th July. They changed their system yet again, taking in two massive 160 cubic foot bottles at either side and having a single ninety cubic foot bottle mounted on their backs, in such a way that they could easily remove it. This was the one they were going to dump on the way in. They also decided to do the dives one at a time, with Oliver going in first then, after his return, Geoff, followed by Jochen.

For Oliver it was the chance to make the vital link, but he didn't find the reel Geoff had left at his far point from the Kingsdale end. He had run out about sixty-one metres, so he should have met up with it; indeed, by their calculation, he should be well beyond it.

Puzzled, Geoff went in, following the route that had now become familiar, sliding carefully through the constriction and reaching the end of the line that Oliver had left: The moment is recorded by Geoff in Martin Farr's cave diving history, *The Darkness Beckons*:

> Nevertheless, as I came to the end of the line and started to press on into the unknown, I became tensely alert, head jerking from side to side like a night owl. Somehow I found that environment distinctly more alien than, say, that of the Moon. The loneliness gnawed at my nerves as I strained to see the Kingsdale line which I knew must be close at hand. Suddenly an orange line came into view. At first I didn't fully accept its existence but then I realised that I must have been swimming alongside it for some distance . . . The connection had been made, yet somehow the triumph was tinged with a certain sadness that we hadn't been able to do it together.

Oliver Statham had been so close, for Geoff's line from Kingsdale had been on the other side of the passage, a few feet away, obscured by the bad visibility.

The joining of Kingsdale and Keld Head was, undoubtedly, the climax to an exploration into the real unknown that is no longer possible on the surface of the earth. But it wasn't over, for a complete traverse had still to be made. Oliver Statham and Geoff Yeadon completed this on 16th January 1979. They had always worked as equals and never was this spirit more obvious than the moment when one of them had to take the lead on this record-breaking attempt. Unable to communicate, they both hung around just inside the entrance, neither wanting to go first. They made the through dive of 1830 metres (6,000 feet) in two and a half hours and came out together. It was a world record for a continuous through trip dive between two caves with no available air spaces to use as staging posts. It meant total commitment. There have been longer dives since abroad, but none in anything approaching such appalling conditions or cold, poor visibility and constricted passage ways.

There is also an immensely sad postscript to the end of this five-year saga of exploration, for in September 1979 Oliver Statham committed suicide. The huge stress of cave diving, the compelling need to be involved, which brought him back from his lay-off after his narrow escape in Boreham Cave, or maybe that escalator created by fame with the constantly repeated questions, 'What are you going to do next?', possibly, for him, they were too much. One cannot really know. But it was the end of a remarkably complementary partnership which had been essential to solving the problems of Keld Head.

Facets of adventure

Is there a common factor between the adventures described in this book and, through these adventures, the people who made them? In the basic motivation, spirit of adventure, call it what you will, I think there is, even though the adventures and the people who are attracted to them and moulded by them vary in a kaleidoscope of character and personality. At first glance there could hardly be two greater extremes than Reinhold Messner's solo ascent of Everest and the first landing on the moon. In the former the ambition was conceived and carried out by a single individual, answerable only to himself. He had stripped down technical aids to the minimum and was venturing alone to the threshold of where man can survive without an oxygen support system. Against this one sets the huge technological effort, elaborate selection procedures, organisation and discipline needed to put man on the moon.

Again, Reinhold Messner is an outspoken individualist, dreamer and philosopher, essentially a mountaineering artist, while Neil Armstrong is a man who has always worked within organisations, who is not adventurous in a physical sense, not even particularly interested in physical exercise. Messner's solo ascent of Everest can easily be seen as a direct extension of his imagination and drive; the moon landing was too vast an enterprise to be any single person's creation. Armstrong, the astronaut, was just one vital human component in that massive effort.

But taking the concepts behind the two expeditions, were they so very different? Putting man onto the moon had all the ingredients of adventure. It was a huge step into the unknown, with the challenge of risk, and a plunge into a natural beauty more strange than man has ever seen before. While the spirit of scientific curiosity was there in abundance, at times barely cloaking a competitive politico-patriotic compulsion to be there first.

Is this so very different from Messner wanting to be the first man to climb Everest alone without oxygen? He, too, was probing the unknown to new mental and physical thresholds. The professional test pilot, Neil Armstrong, talked to me of his flying in very similar language to that of the rock climber. The principles behind the two enterprises are surprisingly close, even though the means and the character are so very different.

And if we look into other ventures in my mosaic, the same pattern emerges; there are differences of proportion and shades of colour but the basic motivations seem to form a uniting theme. Every one of the ventures I have described represents a plunge into the unknown, to try to satisfy man's insatiable curiosity about himself and his own reactions to stress or danger, to find the boundaries of his physical capability or that of his craft. In each is some level of risk. Thor Heyerdahl or Vivian

Fuchs are not interested in risk for its own sake, considering themselves scientists rather than adventurers, but they were undoubtedly prepared to accept a very high level of risk to achieve their objectives. The same could also be said of the astronauts. The climber or cave diver, on the other hand, is much more directly stimulated by risk. He is not trying to do something dangerous dangerously, but rather is seeking out a situation of high risk and is gaining his stimulus, which can reach levels of euphoria, by being in complete command.

Tom Robbins, in his zany novel *Even Cowgirls Get the Blues*, caught it with:

> The principal difference between an adventurer and a suicide is that the adventurer leaves himself a margin of escape (the narrower the margin, the greater the adventure). A margin whose width and breadth may be determined by unknown factors, but whose successful navigation is determined by the measure of the adventurer's nerve and wits. It is always exhilarating to live by one's nerves or towards the summit of one's wits.

The margin of escape varies with the individual. In climbing it can be seen in the degree to which an individual is prepared to push himself solo. For my part, I am only prepared to climb well within my own capabilities when alone, but men like Bonatti or Messner are prepared to solo at the threshold of their climbing ability. Reinhold Messner and David Lewis use very similar language in describing their need to push themselves to the limit to 'find' themselves, though the ingredients of this experience at sea and on a mountain are very different. The solitary sailor needs greater reserves of self-sufficiency than the mountaineer, the period that he has to withstand loneliness being measured in hundreds of days. On Nanga Parbat or Everest Messner was alone for a few intense days. The moment-to-moment risk, and certainly the physical stress, was more continuous and unremitting than that of the solitary sailor, who matches it in concentrated moments of crisis, such as the horror, known to practically every round-the-world yachtsman, of being knocked down in the Southern Ocean. In David Lewis's case, when he completely turned turtle and was dismasted, the situation was even more extreme. But in each case the individual mastered the situation, eventually reached safety and through the experience delved deeper into his own self-discovery.

Geoffrey Moorhouse who used his desert journey to see 'how a human being copes with his most fundamental funk'.

It can also work the other way – the adventurer of the mind can turn to physical adventure as a testing bed. Writer Geoffrey Moorhouse had known danger in the course of his work as a journalist, but became fascinated by the concept of crossing the Sahara from west to east by camel, something that had never been done before. He wrote:

> The possibility of a giddy and unique success, however, was not enough by itself to set me on my way. One of my weaknesses is a deep need to justify my actions; I have always found it very difficult to do something simply for the fun – or the hell – of it. I did not need to look far for a justification of this journey. It was there in my instant recoil from the prospect of commitment, in the fearful sweat that sprang out of my palms. I would use this journey to examine the bases of my fear, to observe in the closest possible proximity how a human being copes with his most fundamental funk.

This is a very different attitude to that of the climber or sailor who feels attuned to his environment and is even stimulated by the concept of danger. Moorhouse's approach was also very different from that of Wilfred Thesiger, who had built his life around the desert and its people. For Moorhouse, desert life was a cruel trial. The clothes, the customs, the language, its very tempo, with the long-drawn-out ritual of conversation, all were alien, excruciatingly tiresome. He was eaten alive by lice (Thesiger had had the foresight to keep himself well stocked with DDT). He very nearly perished from thirst, illness and exhaustion. He fought a series of battles of personality with his guides, until at last he found one who became a real friend, a Tuareg called Ibrahim. In four months he covered 2000 miles of trackless desert, much of it on foot, leading the camels; he was very nearly half way to the Red Sea, but had had enough, writing:

> I was suddenly, furiously, abysmally certain that I could go no further than Tamanrasset. I had at last discovered beauty in the desert. It was around me now, the familiar beauty of mountains. But all I could feel was agony, suffering, pain, mindlessness, endlessness, futility.

Geoffrey Moorhouse did not return to the desert to complete the journey, for he had learnt enough, had plumbed the depths of his fears and had taken himself to his limit. For him there was none of the elation and pleasure, the feeling of oneness with his surroundings, that draws the addicted adventurer back again and again.

Robyn Davidson knew as little as Moorhouse about desert travel, survival or camels when she conceived the idea of crossing the Western Australian Desert. Brought up on a cattle station in Queensland, sent to boarding school in Brisbane, she went on to university to study biology and then music. She dipped into Japanese and philosophy, but finally, in a discontent with all things Brisbane, urban and Eastern Australian she hit on the idea of crossing the Western Australian Desert from Alice Springs to the Indian Ocean, using the camels whose ancestors had been brought into Australia in pioneering days and had since gone wild or were now used as a tourist attraction.

Robyn Davidson in the Western Australian Desert.

It was a romantic fantasy, but Robyn Davidson had the determination to push it through and went about it in a practical manner. Before setting out on her journey, she spent a year getting to know the desert, living in Alice Springs. She got a job for part of the time with a neurotic, unbelievably bad tempered camel expert who used the camels to give rides to tourists.

Her journey had nowhere the same risk level as those faced by Thesiger or Moorhouse, nor was it as arduous. The only people who hunted Robyn Davidson were journalists, anxious to get a story about the eccentric but extremely attractive 'camel lady'. Much of the journey was on jeep tracks. But there were stretches across the empty desert and it was this part that she found the most satisfying, being on her own in the immensity of the desert, her only companions her dog Diggity and her four camels. There were also moments of danger and fear; the camels all too often strayed, leaving her alone, miles from the nearest water hole, until she managed to track them down. There was also the threat of wild camels, particularly the bulls who could be dangerously aggressive. She had a rifle, but hated the thought of having to use it and, on one occasion, when four wild bull camels got uncomfortably close, the gun jammed:

> I threw a rock at one of the bulls. He burbled and disgorged his mouth bladder (a hideously repulsive pink, purple and green balloon, covered in slobber and smelling indescribably foul, that female camels perversely find attractive), shook his head at me and we played merry-go-rounds. I threw another rock and threatened him with my iron digging stick. He backed off and looked at me as if I was an idiot. It took half an afternoon of this cat and mouse game and many other crafty anti-camel manoeuvres to get rid of those animals. Much to my relief, they eventually got bored with terrorising me and stalked off into the glue-like mirage-riddled horizon. None of them actually attacked – well, I'd be dead if they had.

And because she had stayed in control both of the crisis and herself, she found the same elation that I, the climber, or Fairfax, the rower and shark-hunter, find in the risk games of our choice.

Being in control is really being attuned to everything around you, be it ocean, mountain, desert or the sinuous waterlogged passages of a cave. This was why Messner delayed his attempt on the Diamir Face of Nanga Parbat for several days. He did not feel attuned to the mountains. It is through the closeness of this bond with the environment that one's perception of beauty reaches a height the tourist carried to a mountain summit by cable car, or into the desert by charabanc can never know. Robyn Davidson found it in the Australian desert:

> Diggity and I explored. We found a cave in Pine Ridge which had Aboriginal paintings plastered all over it. Then we climbed up a narrow, treacherous rocky gap, the wind howling and whistling down at us. We pulled ourselves up to the flat top, where freakish rock strata ran in great buttresses and giant steps. The trees up there were gnarled into crippled shapes by the roar of the wind. Further along I could see a sandstorm being whipped up into a cloud of red, straight out of *Beau Geste*. Further west we discovered ancient desert palms called black boys. Rough black stumps shooting out fountains of green needles at the top, all huddled together by themselves, like an alien race left behind on a forgotten planet. There was a haunting hallucinatory quality about this place. I felt swelled by it, high as a kite. I was filled with an emotion I had not felt before – joy.

Doug Scott experienced similar feelings half-way up the vertical desert of El Capitan, in Yosemite. The Salathee Wall is 914 metres of steep granite, giving some of the finest and most committing rock climbing found anywhere in the world. He and his climbing partner, Peter Habeler, had already spent one night on the wall, hands were chafed and sore; they were fully committed, for retreat would have been extremely difficult, but Doug also was totally attuned to his surroundings:

> On Broad Ledge, a frog leapt on the scene. My surprise changed to wonder as I contemplated that little frog and its place on the vast monolith of El Cap. How many more were there, I wondered. Perhaps enough to fill a ten foot square box. Then he hopped away into the rock, so perfectly camouflaged that I couldn't spot him again. I felt really good up there because of that frog; he seemed to show that we were all in it together – not just the El Cap scene, but the whole business of being alive.
>
> I looked around with a new intensity and watched a drop of water trickle down the dusty granite, a clear crystal that flashed a brilliant light and was gone, to be burnt up by the sun that had momentarily given it life. I traced its wet path upwards to a crevice and considered its route down through the rock from the melting snow hundreds of feet above.
>
> I felt completely relaxed . . .

It is this sense of heightened awareness and perception of beauty, of being alive, of physical accomplishment, that raises adventure, despite its inevitable periods of grinding effort and agonising discomfort, from being an exercise in masochism to a much broader, richer experience.

There is, one must admit, an element of the self-imposed hair shirt present to a greater or lesser degree in every adventure. For my own part, I try to minimise it, finding a real satisfaction in rendering what might appear to be an appallingly uncomfortable situation into one that is tolerable. It is possible, for instance, to spend a night on a tiny ledge half-way up an Alpine face in the middle of winter in real comfort, because you have a warm sleeping bag and a small gas stove on which to brew mugs of sweet coffee through the night. On the other hand, if you are caught without a sleeping bag or any other form of bivouac gear at an altitude of 7300 metres, as Doug Scott and I were when we had climbed the Ogre in the Karakoram in 1977, you are then desperately cold and uncomfortable, but even at the time, you can tell yourself that the experience will only last a few hours. The seafarer needs much greater stoicism, since his discomfort level can continue for days on end. In retrospect discomfort and danger, however great, are either forgotten, or transmuted into treasured, or even humorous memories. How much do we savour an experience that went totally smoothly, without any particular incident, thrill of fear or twinge of discomfort?

Certainly adventure entails discomfort, but at the same time, once under way, it can offer a very comforting simplicity that is lacking in everyday life. There is a single all-consuming goal, which can, indeed must, be pursued without compromise. On an expedition or a voyage the rest of the world with all its power politics, threats of war or recession, or more personal problems of money, pressure of work, family obligations – all vanish in this tiny microcosm. Everything is black and white with very few grey areas; on an expedition or voyage there is even a fair amount of leisure to read or think, to talk or play cards. It is an expeditionary irony that, while away, the adventurer is all too often dreaming of getting home, even making heart-felt resolutions to slow down his expeditioning tempo for a while, but then within days, perhaps hours, of getting back home, he is planning the next venture. This need for strong contrasts becomes compulsive in the framework of the adventurer.

But there is that other all important factor, the ego, which rides in tandem with the inner urge of curiosity, taking the adventurer to his mental and physical limits, as well as to the furthest parts of the earth. The competitive urge is born from ego, from a desire to win and also from a desire for approval. In this respect almost all goal-orientated adventurers are extremely competitive, for they want to be first, not second, in achieving the unknown. Eric Shipton did not have a single-minded, driving ambition to reach the summit of Everest; he was constantly diverted by the intriguing mystery of unknown valleys, by the question of what lay on the other side

Bill Tilman put an ad. in
The Times: *'Hands wanted for long voyage in small boat; no pay, no prospects, not much pleasure.'*

of a mountain pass. Eventually he found profound satisfaction in exploring the empty windswept ice cap of South Patagonia and the mountains of Tierra del Fuego. He was essentially a mountain traveller and explorer, impatient of the narrow limits inevitably set by an expedition to climb a specific peak.

His climbing companion of pre-war years, Bill Tilman, shared the same philosophy. Tilman had established himself as one of the world's outstanding high-altitude mountaineers in 1936, when he climbed Nanda Devi (7816 metres), at the time the highest and by far the most technically difficult peak yet climbed in the Himalaya. But although Tilman, like Shipton, could not resist the challenge of Everest (he was invited to lead an expedition there in 1938) he, too, had always been a mountain wanderer, to whom the exploration of unknown areas was more important than the attainment of summits. After the war, now in his fifties, he turned away from high mountains and embarked on a series of adventurous sea voyages to the Southern Ocean and the Arctic, though he liked to have a mountaineering objective at the end of the voyage. He used an old pilot cutter, *Mischief*, with a variety of crews. His attitude was summed up by an advertisement he placed in the personal column of *The Times*: 'Hands wanted for long voyage in small boat; no pay, no prospects, not much pleasure.' To him, it was pure adventure. He sailed and adventured to the very end, having a Viking's funeral, when, aged seventy-nine, he joined the converted tug *En Avant* to sail to Smith Island off the Antarctic continent. The boat never reached its destination and was presumed to have foundered in the huge seas of the Southern Ocean.

Wilfred Thesiger is another adventurer untroubled by a competitive urge. It is his love of the desert, and nomadic people, that has ruled his life. Even his crossings of the Empty Quarter in Southern Arabia were almost incidental to his desire to understand and travel with the Bedu.

And then there is the compulsive traveller, who has no specific goal or plan, but simply loves the freedom of travel. One such is Christina Dodwell:

Christina Dodwell on the banks of Lake Rudolf in Kenya. She travelled in much the same way as other people stayed still.

I travelled in much the same way that other people stayed still – it was the way of life that suited me. As for purpose and goals in life, I didn't have any. Purpose sounded too single-minded for me, too restricted by fixed ideas; I preferred to be flexible. Also I rejected the concept of goals and ambitions; they implied success or failure. I wasn't interested in measuring myself against others or competing with them.

Christina Dodwell was born in Nigeria, spent her childhood there with interludes in English boarding schools and then seemed set for a conventional career which might well have ended in a conventional marriage; in Christina's words, 'I was home-loving, materialistic, possessive, insecure and very afraid of the dark.' She had a series of jobs around London, ranging from secretary of a fashion magazine's society column to manager of the Mayfair branch of a car hire company. The ending of a long-standing relationship and engagement undoubtedly gave her the initial jog to take off and see the world, but it all started quite conventionally with a plan for a trip around Africa, two men and two girls in a Land-Rover, brought together by a newspaper advertisement. The two men lost interest in the trip at Kano in Northern Nigeria, and insisted on selling the Land-Rover. The two girls could have easily cabled home for the air fare back to England, but they didn't. Instead they decided to continue their journey. They hitched for a while across Northern Nigeria, acquired a couple of horses, drew matches to decide where they should head for, and then, on reaching a tributary of the Zaire river, purchased a dug-out canoe and paddled down 900 miles of river to Brazzaville. They worked their way down to South Africa, where Christina's companion dropped out of the adventure game to get married, but Christina continued her wanderings through Zimbabwe at the height of the troubles and then on to Kenya, where, with another companion, she travelled with a horse and camel along the empty shores of Lake Rudolf and across the deserts of North Kenya.

In the course of her travels she was threatened on several occasions, sometimes with amorous advances, sometimes because she was a lone white, but by keeping cool, and taking a positive stance, she managed to talk her way out of each situation. In some ways her sex might have been a positive advantage, since a woman does not offer the same potential threat that a man might appear to, and is also much better at avoiding confrontation. She had the same sense of oneness with the land she was travelling through that a climber needs in the mountains, or the sailor at sea. She wrote:

> As I rode I became part of the world. I lived in it, I didn't just pass through it. Everything that happened and existed around me had direct effects, moulding my day, my mood and my whole being. Nothing was simply visual, it was all tangible. A mountain stream was not just a pretty sight – it was also water, the key to all living things. It came from deep inside the multi-million-year-old plateau. It was icy cold and made my skin tingle. It was refreshing and tasted sweet. Streams flowed, carrying the secrets of the forest and the songs of the hillsides. The rushing torrents expressed my longing for freedom. Their nature was ever changing; as they meandered so did I, and when they dawdled, I lingered.
>
> . . . A voice in my mind told me that I was doing what I had chosen to do. I realised that I had never been happier, that the life I had chosen was one which I loved wholeheartedly, that the security which I still craved was not something which could be given to me, it had to come from within myself. What I made of my life was my responsibility, though chance had much to do with it. Now I seemed to be steering upwards, riding high, riding free, scooping up life's ecstasy and terror in handfuls, throwing it in the air and catching it again.

Christina Dodwell continues the tradition of many renowned women travellers, of Gertrude Bell, Annie Taylor, Isabella Bird, Freya Stark and Ella Maillart. It is a facet of adventure in which women undoubtedly excel. Lack of physical strength is no hindrance to a traveller, while in qualities of mental and physical endurance women are certainly equal to men. It is in the activities which demand physical strength where women seem to be at a disadvantage.

Women have taken part in several expeditions to the Himalaya, both with men and in parties that have been entirely female. The summit of Everest has been reached by three women (and about a hundred men), two by the original South Col route and one from the north. In each case there was at least one man in the party. The Poles have been particularly forceful in the Himalaya in recent years, making, amongst many outstanding climbs, the first winter ascent of Everest. Polish women have also been successful, reaching several summits, including Everest, and climbing Gasherbrum II (8035 metres) in an all-female summit push.

In technical rock climbing women are at a lesser disadvantage since it is not so much strength as the power-weight ratio that is important. Several women rock climbers have led and soloed to a very high standard, only just below the most difficult climbs being completed at the time. The difference in performance is similar to that between men and women in competitive sports such as athletics or tennis.

In the realm of sailing, where strength is not at such a premium as in mountaineering, the achievement of women has come much closer to that of men. Clare Francis proved this in the 1976 Atlantic single-handed race, coming in seventh out of 125 entrants. New Zealander Naomi James did even better in 1977–8, when she sailed around the world single-handed in the fastest time that has yet been achieved, though she did have two stop-overs for repairs on the way round. She had been sailing for barely two years when she set out, but had the right mentors in her

Naomi James holds the record for the fastest single-handed circumnavigation.

husband, Rob, and his close friend, Chay Blyth, who gave her a great deal of support and lent her one of his boats.

She experienced all the vicissitudes that confront every sailor who ventures into the Southern Ocean. She was over half-way between New Zealand and Cape Horn when the stays supporting one side of the mast collapsed. This meant climbing the wildly gyrating mast and then struggling with what was left of the bracket to rig some kind of replacement. Storm followed storm, the stays collapsed again and the boat was knocked down by a huge wave. Her first reaction was to look out of the cabin to see if the mast was still standing; it was. After sorting out some of the shambles, she went out on deck to try to steer the boat in the hope of ensuring she would not be capsized a second time.

> I secured my safety harness to the compass binnacle and faced the waves so that I could see them coming. The vision scared me stiff. The waves were gigantic, a combination of twenty-foot swells with twenty- to thirty-foot waves on top. One crashed nearby and it didn't need any imagination to realize what would happen if one of these monsters fell on me.

She was back in England on the 8th June 1978 having taken 272 days for the round trip, an extraordinary achievement by any standards, and incredible for someone who had done so little sailing.

It is in long-distance flying, however, where the physical element is least important, that women have been most successful. Sheila Scott collected a clutch of world records for solo flights in light aircraft, through the 'sixties and early 'seventies. In circumnavigating the world in 1966 she made the longest solo flight, in consecutive stages, that had ever been made. In 1971 she also made a remarkable flight over the North Pole in her Piper Aztec Twin, *Mythre*, from the Nord in North Greenland to Point Barrow. In October to November 1980, Judith Chisholm flew round the world in a single-engined Cessna to make several fresh records. In her time to New Zealand she beat the forty-four-year-old record of eleven days forty-five minutes, made by Jean Batten, by six and a half days. She also broke Sheila Scott's record for round the world by eighteen days.

Flying light aircraft today is, of course, much easier than when Francis Chichester flew Gipsy Moth in the 1930s, or when Jean Batten flew her Percival Vega Gull. Today's planes are not only faster but much more reliable and filled with sophisticated navigational and communications equipment. Judith Chisholm even had a computer that gave her instant position from reference to a satellite. Even so her record-breaking flight demanded incredible stamina and pilot skill. To achieve the record she could not afford to stop for more rests than were absolutely essential. This meant flying non-stop for forty-two hours at a time. Before attempting their records Sheila Scott and Judith Chisholm also had to overcome the prejudice of a male dominated field, both in gaining professional acceptance and also in attracting sponsorship for their ventures.

The need to succeed, both for one's own personal satisfaction and in relation to others, is a strong basic motivation in every adventurer, but commercial considerations also put a premium on success. The venture has to be financed; it might be anything from the few hundred pounds required by Geoff Yeadon and Oliver Statham to pay for their diving equipment for the linking of the Kingsdale Master Cave with Keld Head, or the hundreds of millions required to place the first man on the moon. The larger the sum required, the greater the adventurer's commitment to the sponsor and the greater the publicity involved.

This leads to the question of justification of expedition costs in terms of resources

Judith Chisholm. Despite the benefits of modern technology, her record-breaking solo flight demanded considerable stamina and pilot skill.

and human life. In 1975 I had got permission from the Nepalese Government to attempt the South-West Face of Everest. Five expeditions had already tried and failed; it was obviously going to be expensive to launch the expedition. We were fortunate in getting the sponsorship of Barclays Bank, but when their support was announced they were badly shaken at being attacked from every quarter for wasting money on this gigantic, dangerous venture that appeared to have no chance of success. The climbing press fulminated: 'Is such a route really worth the expenditure of £100,000? . . . Involvement in such an extravagant project at this time of austerity lays the expedition and, indeed, the entire climbing world open to the charge of irresponsibility and frivolity.'

One can argue, with some justification, that adventures such as the attempt to climb the South-West Face of Everest provide an inspiration to people leading their everyday lives and that without this spark of adventure mankind would never have progressed as far as it has. These are ideas that are difficult to quantify and impossible to prove. The adventurer, however, has to justify his activity much more prosaically, since he has to find the money to pay for it. The amount he can raise is a reflection of the popular appeal of his enterprise and this is very directly reflected in the number of books sold after the conclusion of the venture.

There is always the risk of the sponsorship taking over the adventure, of changing its nature, perhaps even its aims. In trying to raise money an expedition can take on a film crew, only to find that, to make a successful film, the entire venture must revolve not round the problems of surmounting a natural obstacle, but the exigencies imposed by the filming. In addition, this media attention, there to create public interest and thereby satisfy a sponsor who is paying for the trip, can create problems of ego amongst the participants. It certainly seems that the high percentage of break ups between talented partnerships – Ridgway and Blyth, or more recently Messner and Habeler – is at least triggered by a feeling that one partner is getting more than his fair share of attention. With this question of attention and gratified ego comes also the question of making money. I am convinced that making money is a very low initial motive for almost any venturer, certainly of any mentioned in this book, but once there is money to be made at the end of a successful venture, resentment can all too easily arise if one party seems to be getting more than his fair share.

Some adventurers just pull out of the limelight altogether. Moitessier did this when he abandoned the Golden Globe Race and continued round the world for a second time, preferring to retire to Tahiti rather than sail back to Europe and almost certainly collect the £5,000 prize and all the plaudits for making the fastest non-stop single-handed voyage round the world. Crowhurst on the other hand became the victim of his own ego and the publicity machine that he had created, and committed suicide rather than face the inevitable exposure of his fraud.

Robyn Davidson was profoundly disturbed by the necessity of getting sponsorship from the *National Geographic Magazine*, which she needed to buy her camels. The intermittent presence of the magazine's photographer, even though she liked him as a person, was an intrusion in her own very private venture. Originally Robyn Davidson had intended her journey as an end in itself, without any thought of writing the story for the benefit of others. It was only a year later that she decided to write a book about it, initially to get the story right and correct the myth of the 'camel lady' created by the Australian press. And then, in the writing, she discovered her own ability to express herself, and the need, perhaps of almost every venturer, to describe for a wider audience what she had found. A venture, be it a climb, or a voyage or a journey, is a creative entity, but until it is in some way recorded, it is all too ephemeral, just a memory that quickly becomes blurred, even distorted by changing perspectives.

The lure of adventure is a concept that is easy to understand, since I suspect that most of us are attracted to it. With some it gets no further than day-dreaming fantasies or the vicarious thrill of following others in print or on television. But it is also the thrill of climbing a Lakeland hill on a misty day, not sure of where you are, perhaps a little apprehensive and then finding the summit. Everyone has their Everests. But what is the drive and motivation at the extreme end of adventure, that made David Lewis sail to Antarctica in his tiny boat, took Wally Herbert and his three companions across the Polar ice cap, drove Reinhold Messner to Nanga Parbat and then Everest on his own, or captivated Geoff Yeadon and Oliver Statham with the waterlogged labyrinth of Keld Head?

There is no easy explanation or formula. Looking at the backgrounds of the adventurers described in this book, they come from every social class; some have had childhoods that have been emotionally deprived, others have come from extremely happy, well-integrated families. Physically they come in every shape and size, though here there is something in common. The keen-eyed adventurer gazing into the distance is maybe a cliché, but it is also true. All the adventurers I met and interviewed had eyes that had a piercing, almost compulsive quality. The other feature they had in common was the nature of their hands – strong, capable hands, very often large in proportion to their size. Even Clare Francis, the most petite and feminine of all adventurers, has hands designed for handling ropes. But these are physical characteristics that one could expect to develop from the individual's chosen life style; it doesn't get anywhere closer to the question 'Why?'.

When I have asked them 'Why?' the reply all too often has been, 'Well, why do you climb?' And the answer? 'I love doing it.' I can then try to analyse why I love it and come up with the formula of the fascination of the unknown, the love of risk, physical enjoyment and the natural beauty of the mountains. But even this seems facile, even inadequate, to explain the extremes to which I and my fellow venturers are prepared to push ourselves in pursuits that have no direct material benefit to ourselves or mankind in general. Man's quest for adventure is not so much 'because it is there'; the answer lies concealed, mysterious, in the complexity of man.

A Chronology of Adventure since 1945

Oceans

The reasons that man decides to take to the oceans are as limitless as the ingenuity he employs in his choice of craft for the purpose. He may be seeking to prove some historical or navigational theory; or he may rather be seeking to prove something about himself. There are others who hope to make a particular crossing first, or faster than anyone has done before them – and others whose boats *are* their homes, and who have opted to live at sea rather than in conventional society.

Since the *Observer* newspaper organised its first single-handed trans-Atlantic race in 1960, there has been a remarkable increase of interest in ocean racing. Francis Chichester won that first event from four other contenders; it took him 40 days. Twenty years later the sixth *Observer* single-handed trans-Atlantic race attracted 90 competitors and was won by American, Phil Weld, with a crossing of less than 19 days. There is now a regular circuit of big events for the serious yachtsman's calendar.

1947
Thor Heyerdahl (Norway) and his crew drifted 4300 nautical miles across the Pacific on the balsa-wood raft, *Kon-Tiki*.

1951
Patrick Ellam and Colin Mudie sailed from Falmouth to Barbados, via Spain, in the 6 m *Sopranino*, then on to New York.

1952
French doctor, Alain Bombard, crossed the Atlantic on a rubber raft, *L'Heretique*, from Las Palmas to Barbados. On his 65-day crossing he lived off plankton and fish.

1952–3
Ann Davison (GB) became the first woman to make a solo Atlantic crossing in her small yacht, *Felicity Ann*. She sailed from Plymouth to Dominica, making several stops en route.

1954
William Willis, a sixty-one-year-old American, made a solo voyage on a 10 m balsa-log raft, *Seven Little Sisters*, across the Pacific, Callao, to Samoa. The 115-day voyage, an estimated 6400–6700 miles, was almost half as far again as *Kon-Tiki*'s.

1955
Dr. Hannes Lindemann (Germany) sailed and paddled across the Atlantic from Las Palmas to the Virgin Islands, then on to Haiti, in a gaff rigged dug-out canoe, *Liberia II*. The next year he paddled from Las Palmas to the Leeward Islands in 76 days in a folding Klepper canoe, *Liberia III*. (This was not the first time the Atlantic had been crossed by canoe. In 1928 another German, Franz Romer, went from Lisbon to the Virgin Islands.)

1960
The first *Observer* single-handed trans-Atlantic Race was won by Francis Chichester in 40 days.

1962
Kenichi Horie (Japan) made a solo Pacific crossing in his 5.83 m sloop, *Mermaid*, leaving Osaka on 12th May and reaching San Francisco on 12th August.

1964–5
John Riding (GB) crossed the Atlantic from Plymouth to Newport in his 3.57 m mini-yacht, *Sjo Ag* (Sea Egg), stopping at Vigo, the Azores and Bermuda en route.

1964–7
Dr. David Lewis, with his wife and two small daughters aboard for much of the voyage, completed a circumnavigation in his catamaran, *Rehu Moana* (designed by Colin Mudie). Priscilla Cairns joined the family after the difficult passage through the Magellan Strait. Between Tahiti and New Zealand Dr. Lewis tested methods of the old navigator-priests with surprising success.

1965
Robert Manry (US), in *Tinkerbelle* (only 4.1 m), sailed solo from Falmouth, Mass., to Falmouth, England, in 78 days.

1966

David Johnstone and John Hoare set out to row the Atlantic. They were lost at sea and their waterlogged boat, *Puffin*, was found in mid-Atlantic on 14th October.

The same year John Ridgway and Chay Blyth, set off from Cape Cod in an open dory, *English Rose III*, and successfully rowed the Atlantic in 92 days.

J. R. L. Anderson led the *Guardian* newspaper-sponsored Vinland expedition, sailing 4000 miles to America in a 13.4 m cutter, *Griffin*, recreating as far as possible the Norse colonising voyages of Leif Eriksson, via Iceland, Greenland, Labrador, Newfoundland to Martha's Vineyard, Mass.

1966–7

At the age of sixty-six, Francis Chichester completed a solo circumnavigation via the three Capes in *Gypsy Moth IV* (16.6 m). His sailing time, 226 days, cut the previous round-the-world record by almost half. In all he covered 28,500 miles, stopping only at Sydney.

1967–8

Another British single-handed sailor, Alec Rose, completed a round-the-world passage. In his boat, *Lively Lady* (10.9 m) he spent 318 days at sea (interlude in Australia).

1968–9

Taking part in the *Sunday Times* round-the-world race, Robin Knox-Johnston, made the first non-stop solo circumnavigation in his yacht, *Suhaili* (10.87 m). The 30,000 (approx) miles took him 313 days and won him the paper's Golden Globe trophy.

Bernard Moitessier (France), who seemed a likely winner in the same contest in *Joshua*, decided against making landfall at the end of his circumnavigation. He continued sailing, re-passing the Cape of Good Hope, to Tahiti. In all he travelled 37,455 miles, one and a half times around the world, making what was the longest non-stop solo voyage.

1969

John Fairfax set off from Las Palmas on 20th January to row the Atlantic single-handed. After 160 days he landed on a deserted island in the Bahamas, then continued again to land eventually on 19th July near Miami after 180 days.

1969–70

Thor Heyerdahl's two *Ra* expeditions sought to cross the Atlantic from Morocco to Barbados (3270 sea miles) in a papyrus-reed vessel. The first attempt in *Ra I* (13.7 m) covered 3000 miles before foundering in a storm. *Ra II*, some 3 m shorter, set off the following year with a crew of eight and successfully crossed the Atlantic in 57 days, proving another of Heyerdahl's theories: ancient Mediterranean people could have crossed the Atlantic before Columbus to bring their ideas to Mexico and Peru.

1970

Solo Atlantic row, east to west, by Sidney Genders (GB), aged fifty-one. In his 6.02 m craft, *Khaggavisana*, he rowed from Penzance to Miami, via Antigua, in 162 days, 18 hrs.

1970–1

Chay Blyth in all-steel monohull, *British Steel* (specially designed by Robert Clark), made the first single-handed round-the-world voyage *against* the prevailing winds. Hamble river west to Hamble river took 292 days.

1971

Nicolette Milnes-Walker became the first woman to make a solo non-stop Atlantic crossing.

1971–2

John Fairfax and Sylvia Cook rowed from San Francisco across the Pacific to Hayman Island, Australia in 362 days with stops.

1972–4

David Lewis sailed single-handed to Antarctica in *Ice-Bird* in 14 weeks, and back to Cape Town the following winter.

1972–80

Super Shrimp, captained by Shane Acton (GB) became at 5.58 m the smallest vessel to complete a circumnavigation.

1973–4

Kenichi Horie (Japan) in *Mermaid III* (8.8 m) made fastest westabout circumnavigation, Osaka to Osaka via Cape Horn in 275½ days.

Solo circumnavigation in trimaran, *Manureva* (ex *Pen Duick IV*), by Alain Colas (France). With his 167 days he captured the record for the fastest time, one day notching up 323 miles.

1974

Anders Svedlund (Sweden) made the first solo trans-Pacific row from Chile to Samoa in 118 days.

H. W. (Bill) Tilman, aged seventy-six, with a crew of four circumnavigated (West) Spitsbergen, calling at Bear Island en route. This was one of some twenty adventurous voyages made by Tilman between 1955 and 1977 when he and his crew failed to make landfall in the Falkland Islands after calling at Rio.

1975

The fastest time for a circumnavigation was achieved by *Great Britain II* (23.52 m) sailing with two crews under two skippers, Mike Gill and R. Mullender (change over in Sydney). Each half of the 26,380-mile round trip took 67 days.

1976

Tim Severin in a reproduction Celtic curragh, *Brendan*, a 10.9 m banana-shaped leather-covered vessel, sailed north from Co. Kerry in Ireland to Iona and the Faeroes, then west to Iceland and Greenland, before heading south-west to Labrador and Boston. Severin sought to prove the viability of the legendary voyage of sixth century Irish monk, St. Brendan, said to have reached North America seven centuries before Columbus.

Clare Francis achieved an Atlantic solo crossing by the northern route in 29 days, 1 hr, 52 mins.

1976–8
Krystyna Chojnowska-Liskiewicz (Poland) was the first woman to make a solo circumnavigation, west from Las Palmas via Panama in *Mazurek* (9.5 m).

1977
The Caribbean Kayak expedition 1977, comprising John Dowd, leader (NZ), Beatrice Dowd (Canada), Ken Beard and Stephen Benson (GB), completed the 2000-mile journey by canoe from Venezuela up the West Indies to Florida. The voyage involved two open-sea crossings of 80 miles each and others of 45 and 60 miles.

1977–8
Round the world Dartmouth to Dartmouth via Cape Horn was accomplished in 272 days by Naomi James (NZ). It was the fastest solo monohull circumnavigation.

1978
Thor Heyerdahl sailed from Iraq through the Persian Gulf to the Indian Ocean with ten companions in a reed boat, *Tigris*. Because of war in Ethiopia, Somalia and the Yemen, he was refused landing permission at the end of his journey and in protest burnt his boat in the Gulf of Aden off Djibouti.

1980
Gérard d'Aboville succeeded in making a solo crossing from Cape Cod to Brest in 73 days in his 5.5 m rowing boat, *Capitaine Cook*. This is the longest solo row.

Eric Tabarly, sailing from New York in his 16.7 m trimaran, *Paul Ricard*, reached the Lizard in 10 days 5¼ hrs, breaking a record for this passage set in 1905 by a three-masted schooner.

Deserts

The Golden Age of desert exploration predates the period under consideration in this book. In the years of the last century and the first half of this, journeys were made across most of the great deserts of the world. Sir Richard Burton had reached Medina in 1853 and later, Charles Doughty pressed further into the Arabian desert to Hail and Buraydah; Bertram Thomas and H. St. John Philby were the first Europeans to cross the Empty Quarter – Thomas from south to north, Philby from north-east to south-west. French and German explorers ventured into the Sahara: René Caillé reached Tombouctou in 1828, Heinrich Barth made a number of journeys in the years 1844–55, followed by Gerhard Rohlfs during the 1860s and '70s. L. M. Nesbitt was the first to cross the savage and lawless Danikil country in Eastern Abyssinia in 1928.

Between them, in the years between 1886 and 1904, Sir Francis Younghusband, Sven Hedin and Sir Aurel Stein covered thousands of miles of little-known Central Asia.

The empty bushland wastes of Australia were also criss-crossed by a host of pioneers during the last century: Charles Sturt, Ludwig Leichhardt, Robert Burke and William Wills, John McDouall Stuart, the Forrest brothers, Colonel Peter Warburton and Ernest Giles.

There were redoubtable lady-travellers too: Gertrude Bell, Rosita Forbes, Freya Stark – they all wrote eloquently of their journeys in Libya, Syria, Iraq, Persia, the Hadhramaut. But by 1945 much of the desert mystique, of North Africa and the Levant in particular, had evaporated. It was a mystique that had been nurtured by the writings of romantic travellers, the exploits of T. E. Lawrence, and even by a glut of sheikh movies. With the greater reliability of motorised vehicles (first Saharan motor traverse 1922 by André Citroën), desert crossings gradually became less chancy. Over the last two decades a host of package safari firms have sprung up which annually bring truck-loads of tourists into the Sahara, or send them overland through Turkey and Afghanistan to the East. Additionally, vast reserves of oil, natural gas and even fresh water have been discovered beneath many of these deserts. They are no longer the empty places they once were.

1945–50
Wilfred Thesiger made several traverses of the Rub' al Khali (the Empty Quarter of Arabia).

1967–8
C. Warren Bonython walked across the Simpson Desert in Central Australia in 32 days.

1972
Sahara crossing by wind-powered car – Christian Nau (France) left Zouerte in Mauritania and cruised to Dakar on the Senegal coast in his three-wheeled 'car', *Saint Louis*.

1972–3
Geoffrey Moorhouse travelled with a few native companions by camel from Chinguetti, Mauritania to Tamanrasset where illness forced him to abandon his trek. Three of his four camels had died during the course of his 2000-mile journey.

1973
Dennis Wickham walked east to west across Australia with three camels and a dog. The 4025 miles took him eight months.

1974–5
An eccentric British clergyman, Geoffrey Howard, crossed the Sahara pushing a Chinese wheelbarrow with a sail from Béni-Abbès in Algeria to Kano in Northern Nigeria.

1978
An Australian girl, Robyn Davidson, trekked alone with four camels and a dog from Alice Springs across the Western Australian Desert to the west coast at Hamelin Pool.

Rivers

White-water canoeing is one of many sporting activities that has become increasingly popular since the war. This has mainly led to competitive racing on graded courses, but also produced a number of adventure-canoeists seeking to navigate the wilder, remoter rivers of the world. An International Long River Canoeist Club was formed in 1975 for the dissemination of information on distance canoeing.

One significant technological advance in recent years has been the appearance of jet boats and hovercraft, which have enabled rough water to be navigated upstream against the current. Shallows, too, present no problems. Here, what began as a fun sport for the privileged few, has been put to practical local use. A joint Services expedition, led by Mike Cole, tested a River Rover hovercraft on the Kali Gandaki in Nepal as a potential ambulance. It proved admirably suited and now regular services operate on a few suitable rivers.

1949–50
French Orinoco-Amazon expedition – Alain Gheerbrant, Luis Saenz, Pierre Gaisseau, Jean Fichter first followed the course of the Orinoco upriver, then navigated Uania/Cuato/Uraricoera river section in native canoes with Parima Indians.

1950s
Michel Mermod, Swiss mountaineer/adventurer, made a 3105 mile journey by canoe in the American far north, ending in Central Alaska, after touching the coast of the Arctic Ocean.

1952
Sebastian Snow (GB) with various local companions, journeyed from the source to the mouth of the Marañon-Amazon river system from Chuquiten to Jecumbuuy on a balsa-log raft, from Bagua Chica to Iquitos on a further series of rafts, and then by steamer to the river mouth.

1953–6
Two American canoeists paddled across South America in aluminium boats from the river Plate to the Orinoco, following the Tapajoz and Juruena rivers, some 6000 miles involving only a short portage between river systems.

1955
Herbert and Mary Rittlinger attempted to canoe the Blue Nile from the Shafartak bridge. The attempt was abandoned when Mrs. Rittlinger's canoe was bitten in half by crocodiles.

1962
A six-member Franco-Swiss expedition (Geneva Canoe Club), led by Dr. Amoudraz, paddled from Shafartak down the Blue Nile almost to the Sudanese border.

1964–5
Sebastian Snow and Robin Hanbury-Tenison set off in a 13-ft rubber dinghy with engine to attempt to navigate across South America. They followed the Orinoco, Negro and Casiquiare waters to Manaus where Snow had to pull out through sickness. Hanbury-Tenison continued alone to Buenos Aires. In 1965 Snow and M. Andrews made a 4500-mile trip from the Tapajoz-Juruena to the Plate system in native canoes.

1965
Arne Rubin (Sweden) canoed from Shafartak down the Blue Nile to Khartoum.

1968
The Great Abbai expedition, led by Captain John Blashford-Snell, successfully navigated the first 168 miles of the Blue Nile to the Shafartak bridge, avoiding only the worst cataracts, in four rubber dinghies.

Sir Edmund Hillary brought jet boats to Nepal. One was lost exploring a tributary of the river Arun, the other travelled 250 miles upriver on the Sun Kosi.

The Amazonas expedition, sponsored by the *Geographical Magazine*, in an SRN 6 hovercraft travelled from Manaus on the Amazon, via Rio Negro and the Casiquiare Canal to San Felix on the Orinoco. (Leader Graham Clarke).

1969
Trans-African expedition by hovercraft, sponsored by the *Geographical Magazine*, led by D. Smithers. Some 7000 miles in 70 days from St. Louis in Senegal to Matadi in Zaïre, following the rivers Senegal, Niger, Benue, Logone, Chari and Ubangi.

Sir Ranulph Twistleton-Wykeham Fiennes led an expedition up the White Nile by hovercraft, mouth to source.

Five British canoeists, led by Jeff Slater, set out to paddle 80 miles of the river Inn (Austria), sections of which were still reckoned to be impossible at that time. The journey took 5 days, during which eight canoes were lost. Dave Allen and Mike Jones were the only two to finish the course. (In 1973 Mike Jones returned with Mick Hopkinson to make the first descent of the Finster-Munster Shoot on the Austrian-Swiss border, a section not paddled in 1969.)

1971
Sir Ranulph Twistleton-Wykeham Fiennes led an expedition to 'the Headless Valley' in British Columbia, making a 1500 mile voyage up Nahanni river to Victoria Falls, then down to Fort Nelson. Some nine rivers and a hundred rapids were navigated, including Hell's Gate on the Fraser.

1972
Mike Jones led a small expedition to canoe down the Blue Nile from Lake Tana. He and Mick Hopkinson completed 220 miles of some of the most dangerous white water in the world.

1974
John and Julie Batchelor canoed the Zaïre river (formerly river Congo) from Moasampanga, near the source, to Banana on the Atlantic coast (2600 miles) in 128 days.

1974–5
The Zaïre river expedition, led by Major John Blashford-Snell was an ambitious project involving some 165 people at various stages, and having multi-scientific objectives. Inflatable boats were used with jet boats for reconnaissance and escort. All but seven rapids were run and the whole river negotiated by one or all of the craft, apart from the reedy, upper reaches and some 29 miles along the way.

1975
Christina Dodwell and Lesley Jamieson (now Johnson) paddled from Bangui to Brazzaville, more than a thousand miles, in a dugout canoe, on the Zaïre river.

1976
Mike Jones led a British canoe expedition to the Dudh Kosi in Nepal. From Everest Base Camp most sections were paddled down to where the river joins the Sun Kosi.

1977
Sir Edmund Hillary took a jet boat expedition from the Bay of Bengal 1500 miles up the Ganges to its Himalayan source.

Mike Jones' canoe expedition descended the Maipure Rapids, reputedly the world's biggest, on the Orinoco.

1978–79
Mike Higginson (Australia) led an eight-man team of canoeists on the Nile. They paddled from Nimule on the Ugandan border, hoping to reach the sea 3000 miles downriver. The first group were arrested by the military 27 miles from their destination, but a second party made it to the coast.

1980
300 miles of the Sun Kosi were navigated by the Australian Himalayan Canoe expedition, led by John Wilde. Using 22 kayaks in all, they went from Tatapaiu near the Tibetan border to the Sun Kosi barrage where Nepal meets India.

Mountains

The Second World War did not put a total stop to climbing and throughout the period some activity was possible. Indeed the formation of mountain training units by the Services introduced many new recruits to climbing, and intensively developed certain areas (eg the Cornish sea cliffs by the Commandos; Sonamarg in Kashmir by the RAF). The technological impetus as a result of the war also had its spin-off for mountaineers; the advent of nylon, for instance, revolutionised outdoor clothing and climbing ropes. After the war, too, there was a ready availability of ex-WD equipment for many years, of great assistance to impecunious climbers.

In the Alps, whilst standards had not advanced since the late 'thirties, new routes were still being made,

notably by such climbers as Giusto Gervasutti, Raymond Lambert, Lionel Terray, Louis Lachenal and Gaston Rébuffat etc.

1946
In North America climbers were quick to pick up where they had left off. Fred Beckey, in particular, maintained a steady stream of new routes, including KATE'S NEEDLE (3050 m) and DEVIL'S THUMB (2770 m) in Alaska's remote Coast Range with R. Craig and C. Schmidtke.

1947
In the Yosemite Valley, California, John Salathé and Anton Nelson made the first complete ascent of LOST ARROW CHIMNEY in five days. Salathé, an emigré Swiss blacksmith, developed a series of hard-steel pitons suitable for even the narrowest of granite cracks. This led to great surge in Yosemite big wall climbing.

Earl Denman, an eccentric Canadian, made a secret attempt on EVEREST. He climbed to just above the North Col (c.7150 m) with his Sherpas, Tenzing Norkay and Ang Dawa.

1949
Nepal, hitherto closed to outsiders, began allowing foreign expeditions to explore and climb.

1950
Chinese armies invaded Tibet. It was to remain closed to mountaineers for thirty years.

ANNAPURNA (8091 m) was climbed by a French expedition, led by Maurice Herzog. **First of the fourteen eight-thousanders to be climbed**.

H. W. (Bill) Tilman was also exploring in the Annapurna Himal. With a small party, including Jimmy Roberts and Dr. Charles Evans, he followed the Marsyandi Valley and unsuccessfully attempted ANNAPURNA IV (7525 m), as well as making reconnaissances of MANASLU and HIMALCHULI. Back in Kathmandu, Tilman joined Dr. Charles Houston, his father and two companions, for a trip to Sola Khumbu. They were the first European party to approach EVEREST from the south.

In the Andes, Dave Harrah and James Maxwell, with an American student expedition, climbed YERUPAJA (6632 m), a fierce peak in the Cordillera Huayhuash which had defeated several previous parties.

1951
Eric Shipton led a Reconnaissance expedition to the southern approaches of EVEREST (8848 m).

A French expedition, led by Roger Duplat, attempted a traverse of the two summits of NANDA DEVI (7816 m). In the summit region Duplat and G. Vignes were lost.

1952
During the winter of 1951–2 a French expedition climbed CERRO FITZROY (3375 m), a ferocious ice-coated granite

monolith in the Patagonian Andes. Reports of their climb were instrumental in attracting other climbers to this remote cluster of peaks bordering the Patagonian Ice-cap. The summit was reached by Lionel Terray and Guido Magnone. Both went on to have further successes that same year: Terray climbed HUANTSAN (6395 m) in the Andean Cordillera Blanca, Magnone was one of the team to make the first ascent of the West Face of the DRU, an Alpine face of 600 m plus which required eight days of siege tactics to achieve.

Swiss mountaineers mounted two expeditions to EVEREST. The spring assault, led by Dr. Wyss-Dunant, climbed the Geneva Spur to the South Col, from where Raymond Lambert and Tenzing Norkay reached a high point of 8595 m on the South-East Ridge. The autumn attempt failed to get beyond the South Col and suffered one fatality.

British mountaineers, led by Eric Shipton, went to CHO OYU (8153 m) by way of a trial of men and equipment for Everest the following year. The expedition failed at 6850 m.

At home the productive rock-climbing partnership of Joe Brown and Don Whillans had already yielded a number of fine new routes such as CEMETERY GATES. They were popularly known as the 'hard men' and were influential in bringing new impetus to British climbing. CENOTAPH CORNER was climbed by Joe Brown and Dave Belshaw.

1953

First ascent of Everest (8848 m) by a British expedition, led by John Hunt. The South Summit was reached by Dr. Charles Evans and Tom Bourdillon on 26th May and the main summit by Ed Hillary (NZ) and Sherpa Tenzing Norkay three days later. Oxygen apparatus was used.

Another eight-thousander was climbed a few weeks later when Hermann Buhl (Austria) struggled to the summit of NANGA PARBAT (8125 m). His forty-hour solo climb from Camp 5 (still four miles and nearly 1000 m below the summit) to the top and back astounded mountaineers the world over.

On K2, the world's second highest mountain (8611 m), Dr. Charles Houston's American expedition reached 7770 m when bad weather forced a retreat.

1954

K2 (8611 m) – first ascent by a large Italian expedition led by Professor A. Desio. The summit was reached 31st July by Lino Lacedelli and Achille Compagnoni.

Another eight-thousander, CHO OYU (8153 m), was climbed, by contrast, by a very small expedition organised by Herbert Tichy (Austria).

In Alaska, H. Harrer, F. Beckey and H. Maybohn made first ascents of HUNTER (4442 m) and DEBORAH (3822 m).

The very steep South Face of ACONCAGUA (6960 m), highest peak in the Americas, was climbed by a lightweight French expedition led by R. Ferlet. The first big difficult wall to be climbed at high altitude.

1955

KANGCHENJUNGA (8598 m), the world's third highest peak – first ascent by a nine-man British expedition, led by Dr. Charles Evans. George Band and Joe Brown climbed to within a few feet of the summit, 25th May, followed next day by Norman Hardie and H. R. A. Streather. The summit itself was untrodden in deference to the wishes of the Sikkimese people.

MAKALU (8481 m) received its first ascent in the same month. A French expedition, led by J. Franco, put three groups on summit on three consecutive days: J. Couzy and L. Terray; J. Franco, G. Magnone and Gyalzen Norbu; J. Bouvier, S. Coupe, P. Leroux and A. Vialette.

In the Alps, Walter Bonatti (Italy) made the first ascent of the South-West pillar of the PETIT DRU, a remarkable solo climb taking six days.

1956

LHOTSE (8511 m) – first ascent by Ernst Reiss and F. Luchsinger with a Swiss expedition which also made the second ascent of EVEREST, led by A. Eggler. Japanese climbers, led by Y. Maki, scaled MANASLU (8156 m).

In the Karakoram, four British climbers visited the striking pyramid of MUSTAGH TOWER (7237 m). Following the short, steep North-West Ridge, Joe Brown and Ian McNaught Davis climbed the West Summit and next day Tom Patey and Jon Hartog reached the main East Summit. A French expedition reached the top by the longer South-East Ridge five days later.

GASHERBRUM II (8035 m) was climbed by an Austrian expedition led by F. Moravec.

Collective climbing was preferred in Russia. V. Abalakov led a large party to the summit of POBEDA (7439 m), or Victory Peak, highest point in Tien Shan range. A Sino-Russian expedition climb MUZTAGH ATA (7546 m) in the Aghil range of Tibet.

1957

BROAD PEAK (8047 m) – first ascent by four-man Austrian team: Markus Schmuck (leader), Fritz Wintersteller, Kurt Diemberger and Hermann Buhl.

In South America PUMASILLO (6070 m) was climbed by a British student expedition, led by S. Clarke; and JIRISHANCA (6126 m), the Peruvian Matterhorn, by Austrians Toni Egger and S. Jungmaier; German climbers (leader G. Hauser) make the first complete ascent of ALPAMAYO.

The NOSE route on EL CAPITAN was completed over eighteen months by the persistence of Warren Harding and companions, using such unconventional aids as 'stove legs', 'Dolt cart', now folklore. The North-West Face of HALF DOME was climbed by Royal Robbins, V. Gallwas and M. Sherrick.

In the Alps, the East Face of the GRAND PILIER D'ANGLE was climbed by Walter Bonatti and T. Gobbi, and a route on the CIVETTA, PUNTA TISSI by W. Phillip and D. Flamm, considered the hardest free climb of its day in the Dolomites.

Scottish ice climbing was undergoing a period of development. ZERO GULLY on BEN NEVIS was climbed by Tom Patey, Hamish MacInnes and Graeme Nicol.

1958

Another eight-thousander, GASHERBRUM I (or HIDDEN PEAK 8068 m), was climbed by American mountaineers, P. Schoening and A. Kauffman (leaders: P. Schoening and N. Clinch). GASHERBRUM IV (7925 m) was climbed by Walter Bonatti and Carlo Mauri with an Italian expedition under Riccardo Cassin; RAKAPOSHI (7788 m) was climbed by British climbers, Mike Banks and Tom Patey with a British-Pakistani Forces expedition, led by Banks; and HARAMOSH (7406 m) by H. Roiss, S. Pauer, F. Mandl of an Austrian expedition.

In the Alps, where the absolute 'direttissima' was the ultimate ideal, four Germans – L. Brandler, D. Hasse, J. Lehne and S. Löw – climbed the North Face Direct of CIMA GRANDE.

1959

First ascent of CERRO TORRE (3128 m) in Patagonia – claimed by Cesare Maestri (Italy). He reported he reached the summit with Toni Egger (Austria), who was fatally injured during the descent. Maestri was incoherent when found. As years passed, people questioned whether the two could really have been to the top. The route seemed way ahead of its time and there was no photographic evidence. It remains one of mountaineering's great enigmas.

1960

DHAULAGIRI (8167 m), which had proved a most stubborn eight-thousander, was finally climbed by a Swiss expedition led by M. Eiselin. Eight men reached the summit.

The Chinese climbed EVEREST, the first ascent by the North Col route. The summit was reached by Wang Fu-Chou, Konbu and Cho Yin-Hua in darkness. Few details, no photographs.

Many seven-thousanders were climbed, including: ANNAPURNA II by the British Indian Services expedition, led by Jimmy Roberts (summit reached by Chris Bonington, Dick Grant and Ang Nyima); DISTAGIL SAR (7885 m); HIMALCHULI (7893 m), MASHERBRUM (7821 m); NOSHAQ (7492 m). A period of great activity throughout the Himalaya, Karakoram and Hindu Kush.

1961

NUPTSE (7879 m) in the Everest group was climbed by a British expedition led by Joe Walmsley. The summit was reached by Dennis Davis and Sherpa Tashi; then by Chris Bonington, Les Brown, Jim Swallow and Sherpa Pemba.

AMA DABLAM (6856 m), a shapely pyramid on the approach to Everest, was first climbed by an Anglo-American-NZ team. Mike Gill, B. Bishop, Mike Ward and W. Romanes reached the top.

Political tension closed Baltoro Karakoram to climbers until 1974.

On MOUNT McKINLEY (6194 m), Alaska, a mixed climb of over 3000 m was put up by Riccardo Cassin and party (Italy) in two weeks of siege climbing. (Nowadays the route is usually climbed Alpine-style and has been soloed.) In Yosemite, the SALATHÉ WALL on EL CAPITAN, a natural line described as the greatest rock-climbing route in the world, was climbed by Chuck Pratt, Tom Frost, Royal Robbins (US).

In the Alps, the coveted CENTRAL PILLAR OF FRÊNEY on MONT BLANC was finally climbed by Chris Bonington, Ian Clough, Don Whillans and Jan Djuglosz (Poland).

1962

A French expedition climbed JANNU (7710 m), fiercest of Kangchenjunga's satellites; the summit was reached by R. Desmaison, P. Keller, R. Paragot and Gyaltsen Mikchung.

Meanwhile on NANGA PARBAT (8125 m) a second route was climbed, this time on the Diamir Face, again by an expedition led by Dr. Karl Herrligkoffer. Toni Kinshofer, Siegi Löw and Anderl Mannhardt climbed to the summit via the Bazhin Gap; Löw died during the descent.

Winter ascents were becoming popular in the Alps. Matterhorn North Face received its first winter ascent by P. Etter and Hilti von Allmen, the Eigerwand having been climbed the previous winter by Toni Hiebeler, Toni Kinshofer, Anderl Mannhardt and W. Almberger.

1963

EVEREST – a powerful American expedition, led by Norman Dyhrenfurth, put six men on the summit and achieved the **first traverse** of the mountain.

American climbers were also making their mark in the Alps: John Harlin and Tom Frost made the first ascent of the HIDDEN PILLAR on the Frêney Face of MONT BLANC, and, with Garry Hemming and S. Fulton (GB), climbed AIGUILLE DU FOU.

EIGER North Face was soloed for the first time by Swiss guide, Michel Darbellay. Walter Bonatti climbed the GRAND PILIER D'ANGLE with C. Zapelli.

1964

Final eight-thousander climbed by Chinese – SHISHA PANGMA (or GOSAINTHAN, 8046 m).

NORTH AMERICA WALL on EL CAPITAN – first ascent by Yvon Chouinard, Tom Frost, Chuck Pratt and Royal Robbins.

1965

Mountains of Nepal closed to mountaineers until 1969.

In Norway the impressive North Face of TROLLRYGGEN (1742 m), the Troll Wall, was climbed by British climbers A. Howard, J. Amatt, B. Tweedale with five bivouacs.

In the Alps a direct West Face route was made on the DRU by John Harlin and Royal Robbins (US); Walter Bonatti soloed the MATTERHORN North Face in winter by a new direct route.

1966

EIGER DIRECT – a new North Face climb in winter. Siege tactics over thirty-eight days ultimately brought success to Anglo-American-German climbers, but only after John Harlin, one of the leaders, had been killed. Now known as Harlin Route.

The highest peak in Antarctica, VINSON MASSIF (5140 m), was first climbed by an American expedition, led by Nick Clinch.

1968

A long-cherished problem on the GRANDES JORASSES, the SHROUD, was finally climbed in winter by R. Desmaison and R. Flematty. A second, solo, ascent was made soon afterwards by P. Desailloud. The first solo ascent of the WALKER SPUR route was made by the young Italian climber, A. Gogna.

In Yosemite, Royal Robbins soloed the MUIR WALL on EL CAPITAN (ten days), and took part in the ascent of a new route on HALF DOME's North-West Face, TIS-SA-ACK (eight days, 110 bolts). Robbins has been instrumental in putting up all four routes that exist to date on this face.

1970

Chris Bonington led a British expedition to ANNAPURNA (8091 m) to climb the impressive South Face. The summit was reached by Dougal Haston and Don Whillans on 27th May and the era of Himalayan big wall climbing had begun.

The precipitous Rupal Flank of NANGA PARBAT (8125 m) was the ambitious objective of another expedition led by Dr. Karl Herrligkoffer. Reinhold and Günther Messner were first to the summit, followed next day by Felix Kuen and Peter Scholz. By descending the Diamir Face the Messners made the first complete traverse of the mountain. But Günther was killed by an avalanche at the foot of the face, Reinhold severely frost-bitten.

LHOTSE SHAR (8398 m), a subsidiary of Lhotse in the Everest group, was first climbed by a small Austrian party described as 'Old Timers'! (leader: S. Aeberli, summit reached by Sepp Mayerl and K. Walter.)

The WALL OF MORNING LIGHT on EL CAPITAN was climbed by W. Harding and D. Caldwell over a period of twenty-six-and-a-half days. 330 drilled anchor bolts were used.

On the EIGER, Japanese climbers established a new direct route on the North Face.

1971

Cesare Maestri returned to CERRO TORRE and, in a theatrical gesture to confound those critics who discounted his 1959 climb, bolted his way up the South-East Ridge, employing a pneumatic drill.

Polish mountaineers climbed the difficult Karakoram peak of KHINYANG CHHISH (7852 m).

French climbers, led by Robert Paragot, succeeded on the formidable West Ridge of MAKALU (8481 m) with Yannick Seigneur and Bernard Mellet reaching the summit; but an international attempt on the South-West Face of EVEREST brought only discord.

On MOUNT KENYA (5199 m) the main problems of the celebrated DIAMOND COULOIR were overcome by I. Howell and P. Snyder. (Two years later Snyder extended the climb through the Gate of the Mists to the summit with African climber P. Thumbi. Yvon Chouinard added a direct finish in 1975. The Diamond Couloir has become one of the world's most celebrated difficult ice climbs.)

1973

Two Japanese climbers reached the summit of EVEREST by the South Col route during the course of an unsuccessful attempt on the South-West Face. The first post-monsoon ascent.

1974

CHANGABANG (6864 m) – first ascent by Indian-British team led by Balwant Sandhu and Chris Bonington. Six climbers reached summit: Sandhu, Bonington, Martin Boysen, Dougal Haston, Doug Scott and Sherpa Tashi.

In the Alps, the partnership of Reinhold Messner and Peter Habeler produced swift ascents of the North Faces of the MATTERHORN and the EIGER.

1975

Two women climbed EVEREST. The first was Junko Tabei with the Japanese Ladies' expedition, led by E. Hisano. She reached the summit via the South Col/South-East Ridge on 16th May with Sherpa Ang Tsering. A very large Chinese expedition climbing the northern slopes had as its deputy leader a Tibetan named Phantog. She was one of nine to reach the summit.

A post-monsoon British expedition, led by Chris Bonington, finally met with success on the SOUTH-WEST FACE route on EVEREST, which had been attempted repeatedly since 1969. After discovery of a ramp, which solved the problem of the Rock Band, Doug Scott and Dougal Haston reached the summit 24th September. Peter Boardman and Pertemba reached it two days later.

DHAULAGIRI IV (7661 m), which had defeated several previous expeditions and claimed a number of lives, was finally climbed (twice) by Japanese climbers.

HIDDEN PEAK (8068 m) climbed by 2-man team of Reinhold Messner and Peter Habeler in Alpine style.

On nearby GASHERBRUM III (7952 m), at the time the world's highest unclimbed mountain, Polish mountaineers led by Wanda Rutkiewicz were busy. Mrs. Rutkiewicz reached the summit with Januscz and Alison Onyskiewicz and Krzysztof Zdzitowiecki. GASHERBRUM II was climbed by the same expedition by a new route.

Joe Tasker and Dick Renshaw (GB) made the first ascent of the South Face of DUNAGIRI (7066 m) in six days during October. The descent by the same route took a further five days.

YALUNG KANG, the West summit of KANGCHENJUNGA (ca. 8433 m) was climbed by an Austrian/German expedition led by S. Aeberli, all nine climbers reaching the summit.

1976

TRANGO'S NAMELESS TOWER was climbed by a British team – Joe Brown, M. Howells, Martin Boysen and Mo Anthoine made the summit.

On CHANGABANG (6864 m) Peter Boardman and Joe Tasker (GB) climbed the very tough West Face, which may be the hardest route yet accomplished in the Himalaya. Elsewhere in the Garhwal, Americans, L. Reichardt (climbing leader), and John Roskelley, climbed a new North Ridge route on NANDA

DEVI (7816 m). The expedition was co-led by H. Adams Carter and Willi Unsoeld. His daughter, Nanda Devi Unsoeld, died in Camp 3, prior to a second summit bid.

The South-West Ridge of NANGA PARBAT was climbed in lightweight style by four Austrians: H. Schell (leader), R. Schauer, H. Sturm and S. Gimpel.

1977

K2 – second ascent by a large Japanese team, following the original Abruzzi Ridge route.

A small British team climbed the OGRE (7285 m) during which Doug Scott and Chris Bonington made an epic retreat from the summit – Scott crawling with two broken legs, Bonington suffering broken ribs.

George Lowe and M. Kennedy (US) make a new route on the South Face of MOUNT FORAKER (5304 m), Alaska.

1977–78

Y. Ghirardini (France) soloed all three big Alpine North Faces in winter, the MATTERHORN, EIGER and GRANDES JORASSES.

1978

Having in the spring **climbed Everest without oxygen** with Peter Habeler, Reinhold Messner went on within weeks to launch a **successful solo bid on Nanga Parbat**.

On K2, a British expedition, led by Chris Bonington, abandoned an attempt on the West Ridge after the death of Nick Estcourt in an avalanche. Later, American climbers (leader J. Whittaker) were successful in putting two ropes on the summit by the North-East Ridge to 7700 m, then picking up the Abruzzi Ridge: L. Reichardt and J. Wickwire reached the top on 7th September; R. Ridgeway and John Roskelley followed the next day, having made the total ascent without oxygen.

KANGCHENJUNGA SOUTH (8490 m) – first ascent by Polish climbers, E. Chrobak and W. Wroz; KANGCHENJUNGA CENTRAL (8496 m) – climbed on the same Polish expedition by W. Branski, A. Heinrich and K. Olech.

The East Face of nearby JANNU (7710 m) was climbed Alpine-style by four British climbers: Rab Carrington, B. Hall, R. Baxter Jones and Al Rouse.

China began to readmit outside expeditions to mountains within China and Tibet, including EVEREST.

First ascent of CHANGABANG South Buttress by Anglo-Polish expedition of V. Kurtyka, Alex MacIntyre, J. Porter and K. Zureck. A technically difficult climb, undertaken Alpine-style.

1979

KANGCHENJUNGA (8598 m) – a four-man expedition put three on the summit after a semi-Alpine-style climb of a difficult new route: Peter Boardman, Doug Scott, Joe Tasker. No oxygen, no porters.

GUARI SANKAR (7150 m), twin-topped peak in Rolwaling Himal long on 'forbidden list', was eventually climbed in spring by American/Nepali team led by A. Read and Pertemba. In the autumn Peter Boardman climbed the South summit with Tim Leach, Guy Neithardt and Pemba Lama.

EVEREST. The long West Ridge from Lho La was climbed to the summit by Yugoslav expeditions (Americans had joined it at the West Shoulder in 1963). Five climbers went to the top, using oxygen higher up. Ang Phu was killed on the descent.

The North Face of nearby NUPTSE (7879 m) was climbed by Doug Scott, Georges Bettembourg, B. Hall and Al Rouse.

1980

The Nepalese authorities concede a new 'winter' climbing season. For first time a permit was granted and EVEREST ascended in winter (South Col route by a Polish expedition, leader A. Zawada). The Poles returned in the spring to make a new route on the South Pillar of EVEREST.

During the monsoon period Reinhold Messner **climbed Everest solo** from the north (Tibetan) side.

A major new Himalayan climb, the East Face of DHAULAGIRI (8167 m) was achieved by Alex MacIntyre, R. Ghilini, W. Kurtyka and L. Wilczyczynski in poor conditions during May. The summit itself was gained by the North-East Ridge.

The Poles

In 1945 there were already a number of military tracking stations spread across the Arctic, like the Thule Air Base in Greenland, and there was strong international pressure to explore and survey polar regions to assess their potential economic and strategic value.

In the *Antarctic* in 1946–7 *Operation Highjump*, a US exercise under the command of R. E. Byrd, involved 4000 men and 13 ships. A British scientific/exploration programme had been started in 1943 by the Admiralty (named in turn *Operation Tabarin, the Falkland Islands Dependencies Survey*, and now, *British Antarctic Survey*). The first direct flights from New Zealand were made in 1955 and the following year a plane actually landed at the South Pole. The first shipload of paying tourists arrived in 1968, and by 1971 there were forty-three occupied stations on the Continent.

At the time of the *International Geophysical Year* 1957–8, less than half of Antarctica was known, but before another decade had passed, there was scarcely an unmapped mile and pollution was already becoming a problem. In 1959 the *Antarctic Treaty* was signed, proclaiming the region south of 60°S a special conservation area for peaceful scientific research.

The story is similar in the *Arctic* where there has, if anything, been more and more haphazard development.

Despite changes, the polar regions still do offer

challenges to the adventurer, notably to a steady increase of small, mainly undergraduate, expeditions, visiting, in particular, Greenland, where they have made a very special contribution to the knowledge of coastal areas and to mountain climbing.

1947–8
American Graham Land expedition – leader Finn Ronne. Scientific purpose.

1948–57
French Arctic explorer, Paul Émile Victor, an anthropologist and ex-paratrooper, led a series of largely seismic/geological expeditions on the Greenland Ice Cap. And again in 1959–61.

1951–7
South Georgia Survey. Frequent trips by Duncan Carse remapped the island. On one lone visit his hut was blown down and he spent 116 days working from a makeshift shelter, waiting for the spring boat.

1952–4
British North Greenland expedition (Queen Louise Land) led by Cdr. C. Simpson.

1954–5
Five mountaineers visited virgin mountains of South Georgia: G. Sutton, R. Brown, H. Pretty, I. Brooker, E. Webb.

1955–6
Operation Deepfreeze, an American air expedition, landed a plane at the South Pole, unvisited since Scott in 1912.

1957–8
International Geophysical Year – **First surface crossing of Antarctica**, led by Sir Vivian Fuchs and supported by Sir Edmund Hillary, 2158 miles in 99 days.

1958–9
A Russian Antarctic journey covering 3700 miles passed through the South Pole, the South Magnetic Pole and the Pole of Relative Inaccessibility, the point on the Antarctic Continent furthest from the coast.

1958
The American atomic submarine *Nautilus* sailed *under* the North Pole, captained by W. R. Anderson.

1959
Antarctic Treaty – Twelve nations signed a treaty banning any military use of Antarctica, and agreeing to free exchange of scientific data. To operate for 30 years.

1962
Wally Herbert (GB) with a NZ expedition explored Queen Maud Range, Antarctica, sledging east from the head of the Beardmore Glacier, climbing and surveying.

1964–5
A Combined Services expedition to South Georgia, led by Lt. Cdr. M. Burley, retraced Shackleton's 1916 route.

1965
Greenland Ice Cap – a 440-mile crossing, east to west, Angmagssalik to Søndre Strømfjord, was made in 40 days by Hugh and Myrtle Simpson with Roger Tufft and Bill Wallace, using skis and sledges – no dogs.

1967
Sir Edmund Hillary led an Antarctic expedition, mapping and mountaineering. First ascent of Mount Herschel (3498 m).

1968
Ralph Plaisted (US) led a 42-day trek from Ellesmere Island to the North Pole with three Skidoos (motor scooters with skis). His team of twelve men were the first to arrive at the Pole over ice since Peary, 1909.

1968–9
Japanese eleven-man expedition led by Masami Murayama, reached the South Pole in Sno-cats on 19th December.

1968–9
Trans-Arctic expedition makes first surface crossing of the Arctic, Alaska to Spitsbergen, by dog sledge: Wally Herbert (leader), Allan Gill, Fritz Koerner and Ken Hedges. 476 days on the ice, 3620 miles, over-wintering on a frozen floe.

1970
A very large Italian expedition, led by G. Monzino, travelled to the North Pole with dog teams.

1971
Anglo-Danish trans-Greenland expedition led by Derek Fordham (GB) and J. Andersen (Denmark). Dogs were used only to the starting point, then the east to west crossing was the longest man-hauled sledge traverse over inland ice. (Fordham visited Greenland regularly from 1968 onwards and was responsible for many important exploratory journeys.)

1972–4
David Lewis sailed single-handed to Antarctica in his small yacht, *Ice Bird*, in 14 weeks, and the following winter back to Cape Town.

1974–6
Naomi Uemura (Japan) made a 7450 mile journey, Greenland to Alaska, solo with a dog team.

1977–8
A seven-man sailing/mountaineering expedition in their boat *En Avant*, led by S. Richardson and including H. W. Tilman, having Mt. Foster on Smith Island as its target, was not heard of again after landfall at Rio de Janeiro in November.

1977
British North Polar expedition (Wally Herbert and Allan Gill)

hope to circumnavigate Greenland by dog sledge and open boat, a journey of some 8000 miles. Ice conditions in the Nares Strait proved exceptionally severe and the venture which had been expected to be undertaken non-stop over 14 months, will now have to be completed in stages. By the spring of 1981, their fourth year, the two men had travelled only 1600 miles of coast by dog sledge and another 1000 in their Eskimo *umiak*, which they have now exchanged for two inflatable craft. They hope to finish their circumnavigation at Station Nord in North-East Greenland in May 1982.

1978
North Pole solo trek – Naomi Uemura covered 450 miles across the Arctic Sea in 57 days from Cape Columbia, Canada.

Another Japanese 10-man expedition from Nihon University led by Kaneshige Ikeda also sledged to the North Pole by a route slightly east of Uemura's. They got to the Pole two days ahead of Uemura.

1979
Seven Russian skiers reached the North Pole on foot and ski – leader D. Shparo. The 930-miles from Henrietta Island to the Pole took 77 days.

1979–81
British Transglobe expedition, led by Ranulph Fiennes. The Antarctic crossing was made in motorised vehicles in 75 days. The Arctic stage of the expedition to be undertaken 1981–2.

Ballooning

To ride the winds in a balloon basket is the oldest known method of air transport. The first manned flight was made in 1783 over Paris in a Montgolfier brothers' hot air balloon. A few days later the Charlière hydrogen-filled balloon also flew over Paris. Until propane burners were developed after the Second World War, which could heat air efficiently and quickly, it was the gas-filled balloons that were popular – initially these were inflated with hydrogen, but later the more expensive but infinitely safer helium began to be used also. For high altitude flights airtight gondolas with their own atmosphere replaced the traditional basket and in 1935 American balloonists reached a height of 72,394 ft.

1953
Ed Yost (US) began experimenting with polythene balloon envelopes and blow-torches, rekindling an interest in hot air balloons. By 1960 he had developed a hot air balloon capable of carrying a man.

1957
Capt. Joe Kittinger (US) ascended to 95,120 ft in a gas balloon.

1958–9
Arnold 'Bushy' Eiloart (the only man in Britain in possession of a valid balloon licence at that time) proposed a trans-Atlantic balloon attempt. In a gondola designed by marine-designer Colin Mudie, his balloon, *The Small World*, lifted off from the Canary Islands on 12th December. Aboard were Colin Mudie, his wife Rosemary, Bushy Eiloart and his son Tim. When the balloon came down after 94½ hrs and 1200 miles, Mudie navigated the gondola to the West Indies.

1962
Anthony Smith (GB) undertook five hydrogen balloon flights across Africa filming game in *Jambo*.

1966
British Balloon and Airship Club founded.

Tracy Barnes (US) made the first trans-continental USA hot air balloon voyage, flying for 200 hrs and in stages.

1967
First British crossing of the Alps – in a gas balloon by Gerry Turnbull and Tom Sage.

1972
First-ever hot air balloon crossing of Alps – by Don Cameron (GB) and Mark Yarry (US) in *Cumulo Nimbus*.

Two African 'safaris' – Anthony Smith returned to East Africa with Alan Root and Douglas Botting in hot air balloon *L'Engai*.

With two hot air balloons *Daffodil* and *Golden Eage*, Felix Pole, Don Cameron and Julian Nott visited the Sahara, testing balloons in 'thermic' conditions.

1973
Another trans-Atlantic attempt – Bobby Sparks in hot air/helium combination balloon *Yankee Zephyr*, took off 7th August and flew 23 hrs before coming down in storm.

1974
Altitude record. Julian Nott and Felix Pole took *Daffodil II* to 45,836 ft over Bhopal, India, on 25th January.

Maiden flight of the largest modern hot air balloon to date. *Gerard A. Heineken*, 500,000 cu. ft. This Cameron balloon was capable of carrying thirty-three passengers. It held the endurance record from 1975 of 18 hrs 56 mins.

1975
Bobby Sparks in *Atlantic Odyssey* made his second trans-Atlantic attempt on 21st August. After take off he discovered an unexpected stowaway, his ground crewman! Largely due to the extra weight, the balloon was forced down after 2 hrs 5 mins.

1976
Karl Thomas in *Spirit of 76* took off on 25th June from Lakehurst, New Jersey, for a trans-Atlantic attempt. He went 550 miles before ditching, and was rescued.

Ed Yost in *Silver Fox* came within 700 miles of Europe on his Atlantic bid, before a wind change brought him down.

1977
Maxie Anderson and Ben Abruzzo (US) travelled 2950 miles in *Double Eagle* on their 64-hr trans-Atlantic flight before ditching off Iceland in a storm.

1978
Philip Clarke flies 350.7 miles in Cameron hot air balloon *Sungas*, Bristol to Chalons-sur-Marne, a world distance record.

Trans-Atlantic attempt – Don Cameron and Major Christopher Davey in *Zanussi*, a hot air/helium balloon, took off from St. Johns, Newfoundland, on 26th July. They narrowly failed to make a complete crossing, coming down 110 miles off the Brittany coast. Their 1999 miles (96 hrs 24 mins) remain distance and endurance records, however, for a combination balloon.

First successful Atlantic crossing by balloon by Ben Abruzzo, Maxie Anderson and Larry Newman in *Double Eagle II*.

1979
First flight above the Himalaya in a hot air balloon by Hans Zoet (Holland).

Hot air altitude record taken by Chauncey M. Dunn (US) on 1st August with 53,198 ft in an unpressurised balloon.

1980
Maxie Anderson and his son Kris completed a non-stop trans-continental balloon flight across the USA in May. Their helium-filled ballon, *Kitty Hawk*, covered the 3314 miles from San Francisco to Matane in 99 hrs 54 mins.

An American team took a hot air balloon, *Joy of Sound*, to the Arctic and made a very short flight crossing the North Pole on 11th April (Pilot: Sid Conn).

On 16th June Bruce Comstock and Dave Schaffer (US) flew a 206,000 cu. ft balloon over Battle Creek, Michigan, for a new hot air duration record of 24 hrs 8 mins. In early December Comstock, this time with Jeff Van-Alstine as his co-pilot, flew the same balloon for a new distance mark of 493 miles.

Christopher Davey and Crispin Williams (GB) also made an attempt on the hot air distance record. In the world's biggest hot air balloon, *Crest Warrior* (the *Gerard A. Heineken*, renamed), they travelled 412 miles from North Ferriby in Yorkshire to Osann in the Moselle Valley, making the first hot air North Sea crossing west to east, if not a new distance record.

Julian Nott took a 375,000 cu. ft Cameron hot air ballon, *Innovation*, to a height of 56,100 ft over Last Chance, Colorado.

1981
The *Jules Verne*, a helium-filled balloon piloted by Maxie Anderson and Don Ida (US) left Luxor, Egypt, in an attempt to fly around the world. They covered 2800 miles before coming down in the village of Murchpur, 90 miles north-west of Delhi, after a 48 hr flight. With an apparent leak in their 400,000 cu. ft polyethylene balloon, they seemed unlikely to have been able to clear the Himalaya, which were directly ahead.

Space

Despite advances made in rocketry during the War, the concept of manned space craft still seemed pretty fantastic in 1945. As late as 1956, an Astronomer Royal was quoted as saying: 'All this talk about space travel is utter bilge.' Nevertheless Russia launched the first space satellites the following International Geophysical Year, *Sputnik II* orbiting the earth with a live dog aboard.

1961
Vostok I – the world's **first manned space ship** was launched 12th April. Pilot-space navigator: Flight Major Yuri Gagarin. The flight lasted 108 mins and successfully orbited earth.

May 1961 President Kennedy told Congress America should commit itself to landing man on the moon before the decade was out – and bringing him back safely.

Vostok II – piloted by Major Gherman Titov was launched 6th August. He completed 17 orbits, eating and sleeping in space.

1962
Mercury-Atlas VI, VII, VIII – Lt Col. John Glenn made three orbits in *Friendship VII* 20th February; Cdr M. Scott Carpenter, another three orbits, making important tests and scientific observations in *Aurora VII*, 24th May; and Cdr Walter Schirra six orbits in *Sigma VII*, 3rd October.

1963
Vostok V – a five-day flight, 14th/19th June with Lt Col. Valery Bykovsky. *Vostok VI* – launched 16th June with the first woman cosmonaut, Valentina Tereshkova. The two craft frequently came close together and were in radio contact.

1964
Ranger VII (unmanned) – relayed photos close to the moon surface.

1965
Voskhod II – launched 18th March with Col. Pavel Belyaev and Lt Col. Alexei Leonov on board. Leonov made the **first space walk** of ten mins.

Gemini III – launched 23rd March, piloted by Virgil Grissom with John Young. The first manned space craft to be manoeuvred out of one orbit into another.

Gemini IV – launched 3rd June with James McDivitt and Edward White. White went outside craft and propelled himself with aid of hand-held gas gun.

1966
Gemini X – launched 18th July with John Young and Michael Collins. They rendezvoused first with the concurrent Agena target to practise docking manoeuvres, then transferred orbit to match up with a four-month old Agena. Collins floated across to it to retrieve meteoroid collector – the first direct personal contact with another orbiting object.

Unmanned *Lunik IX* (USSR) and *Surveyor I* (US) both achieve soft landings on the moon.

1967–8
American *Surveyor* robot series lands on the moon, collects samples, and successfully takes off from the moon surface.

Apollo VIII Christmas round-the-moon-flight – Frank Borman, James Lovell and Bill Anders. The first manned mission to leave earth's influence and orbit the moon.

1969
Soyuz IV and *Soyuz V* – accomplished first docking between two manned craft 16th January. Two of *Soyuz V*'s crew of three, transferred to *Soyuz IV* to join its one-man crew, Col. Vladimir Shatalov.

In March two American craft, Spider and Gumdrop (*Apollo IX*), on earth orbital flight. James McDivitt and Rusty Schweickart transferred craft.

Apollo XI – launched 16th July with Neil Armstrong, Buzz Aldrin and Michael Collins. Touch down on the moon 20th July by *Eagle*, the lunar module. **Armstrong and Aldrin performed the first moon walk.**

Apollo XII – launched 14th November with Charles Conrad, Richard Gordon, Alan Bean. Lunar module *Intrepid* landed Conrad and Bean on the moon's Ocean of Storms, 19th November.

1970
Luna XVI – Russia's first automatic (unmanned) lunar craft launched 12th September and returned to earth with moon samples. Two months later Luna XVII landed a remote-controlled unmanned moon-rover on the moon's surface which continued its active research programme until 4th October 1971. Meanwhile the Zond series of unmanned circumlunar flights continued with *Zond VIII*.

1971
Apollo XIV – Alan Shepard, Stuart Roosa and Edgar Mitchell took off 31st January. Shepard and Mitchell in lunar module *Antares* landed in the Fra Mauro area.

Apollo XV – the beginning of a new phase with enlarged propellant tanks, improved battery power and life-support systems, permitting longer periods on the moon. David Scott, Alfred Worden, James Irwin launched 26th July. Scott and Irwin using a battery-powered buggy, were able to ride at 5 mph across the moon surface, thus covering wider areas.

Luna XVIII – completed 51 unmanned revolutions of the moon before crashing onto the moon surface. *Luna XIX* was launched into lunar orbit during October.

1972
Apollo XVI – with John Young, Thomas Mattingly and Charles Duke, took off 16th April. Young and Duke explored in the Cayley Plains/Descartes Mountains area of the moon, some 150 miles south-west of *Apollo XI*'s Tranquility Base, and left

an automated research station behind. Like *Apollo XV*, they also launched a scientific subsatellite into lunar orbit.

Some months earlier, *Luna XX* soft-landed on the moon and collected samples.

Apollo XVII – last of the moonshots, but the first night time manned launch, 33 mins into 7th December with Eugene Cernan, Dr. Harrison Schmitt and command module pilot Ronald Evans. Cernan, with geologist Schmitt, made three 7-hr EVAs in the Tauris-Littrau area, and returned with a record 250 lbs of lunar samples.

1973–4
Sylab I – an orbital workshop was carried into an initial 272-mile-high circular orbit by a *Saturn V* launch vehicle. Nine astronauts occupied it in three-man shifts of several weeks at a time. The first were Pete Conrad, Dr. Joseph Kerwin and Paul Weitz; followed by Alan Bean, Jack Lousma and Dr. Owen Garriott. The third crew, Gerald Carr, William Pogue and Dr. Edward Gibson, were making their first space flight. In a total of 84 days they photographed a comet in outer space, made the longest orbital space walk ever (7 hrs) and by clinical measurements revealed that under weightlessness the body increases in height by some one or two ins without the pull of gravity on the spine, accompanied by a certain redistribution of the organs.

1975
Apollo-Soyuz test project – a joint American-Russian venture. *Soyuz XIX* with Aleksey Leonov and Valery Kubasov aboard, docked with an *Apollo* craft (Thomas Stafford, Donald Deke, Vance Brand), and the astronauts were able to visit each other's craft.

1977
Russia launched the *Salyut VI* space station and orbital laboratory on 29th September.

1978
Soviet Intercosmos programme launched – an international programme of space research, involving France and India as well as other Comecon countries, and the linking of *Soyuz XXVII* and *Soyuz XXVI* with *Salyut VI*.

1980
Valery V. Ryumin broke the record for the longest time in space with 184 days, 20 hrs, 12 mins between 10th April and 11th October.

1981
After several years of preparation and a number of setbacks, the American Space Shuttle *Columbia* made its first successful flight on 12th-14th April.

It is hoped that eventually shuttle craft capable of making some 100 round trips each, could operate on a weekly basis, carrying such passengers as scientists, engineers and even astro-tourists.

Cave Diving

In his distant past, caves have been both man's refuge and his vision of Hell. Exploring caves for their own sake is an activity perhaps a couple of hundred years old. Archaeologists were amongst the first to venture underground, but by the turn of this century, caving as a sport was already becoming popular. Nowadays there are several hundred caving clubs in Britain and cave research groups for documenting scientific information.

Water has always posed problems for cave-explorers. Not only can underground water rise quickly and dangerously after rainfall, causing temporary flooding, but it can permanently block sections of passage even though there may be further dry sections beyond. It was not until the 1920s and '30s that cavers tried seriously to by-pass such water sumps or syphons with the aid of primitive diving equipment, and not until after the Second War that more suitable breathing apparatus became available and cave diving, as a specialised branch of caving, developed steadily.

1945–6
Graham Balcombe began experiments with closed-circuit oxygen apparatus and specialised diver's dress. Largely due to his and Jack Sheppard's efforts the Cave Diving Group was born in Britain.

1947
Deepest cave system explored at this time was the Trou du Glaz, France, where Pierre Chevalier and companions descended to a depth of 603 m.

1947–8
British cave divers made important new discoveries at Wookey Hole, Somerset (ninth underwater chamber and a large dry chamber). Exploration was also taking place in the Peak District where a 110 m through dive was accomplished (Peak Cavern, Swine Hole to the Resurgence).

1950–3
The Pierre St. Martin cave, Pyrenees, was discovered by G. Lépineux in 1950. Attempting a depth record in 1952 with N. Casteret, Marcel Loubens died when his harness broke as he was being lowered. The following year a record depth of 737 m was achieved by G. Lépineux, Casteret and team.

1955
British cave divers obtained an Aqualung compressed air set, pioneered in France in 1942, and tested it out in their native caves. But it was to be several years before it ousted traditional rebreathing apparatus.

1956
In the course of *Operation 1000 Metres*, cavers from the Grenoble Caving Club, led by Jean Lavigne, reached a sump at 1122 m in the Gouffre Berger (Isère, France).

Alfred Boegli and companions, working in the Hölloch cave system in Switzerland, extended the known passage to 37.8 miles. For several years the longest known cave in the world.

1958–61
British cave divers developed the Ogof Ffynnon Ddu system in South Wales, which was ultimately revealed as the longest and deepest British cave system so far discovered.

1963
Ken Pearce (GB) achieved a world depth record of 1133 m in the Gouffre Berger. The world record had been progressively broken in this cave in 1954, 1955, 1956. What Pearce succeeded in doing was to pass the 'terminal' sump with a dive of 61 m at a maximum depth of 12 m. This revealed a further section of dry passage and then another sump which was not negotiated on that occasion. Pearce passed this further sump in 1967 and in 1968, the Speleo Club de Seine descended to 1141 m.

1965
In Britain systematic exploration continued in the Ogof Ffynnon Ddu series. Divers C. George and J. Osbourne were the first to penetrate the Master System in the Swansea Valley. Later 26 miles of passages became known, perhaps the greatest cave discovery of all time in Britain.

1967
In the Neath Valley of South Wales, a new cave system (Little Neath River Cave) was discovered beyond a series of sumps in Bridge Cave.

In Mexico, Thomas Evans (US) led a team which descended a vertical cave (Golondrinas) for 333 m. It required descending (abseiling) and re-climbing free-hanging rope and was described as a turning point in cave exploration.

1968
During the Whitsun meet of the Bradford Pothole Club, a sump in Gaping Gill's Far End Passage was widened and passed to reveal 600 m of new passage. Subsequent digging and blasting revealed even more to this ever-popular system, where British caving first really began. The 110-m drop into Gaping Gill Hole is still the deepest known single shaft in Britain.

1970
Tony Waltham, led an expedition to Nepal to explore the limestone caves of Nilgiri/Annapurna and the Harpan River Cave near Pokhara.

A new cave endurance record of 463 days established by Yugoslav caver Milutin Veljkovic in the Samar Cavern, Sorljig Mountains.

In Britain, John Parker achieved dives of 146 m and 823 m to discover Chambers 20 and 22 at Wookey, as well as a new dry passage: Parker was also active at a new cave, Ogof Afon Hepste in the Upper Neath, South Wales. Meanwhile in Yorkshire Mike Wooding made a 51-min dive in Keld Head to reach a point 340 m from base.

1972

Roger Drucker (US), thanks to the discovery of a new corridor, was able to link the Flint Ridge and Mammoth Cave systems of Kentucky to give 1442 miles of development, the longest known cave system in the world.

1972–3

German cave diver Jochen Hasenmayer, reached 780 m in the Rinquelle Resurgence, Switzerland, in 1972 and the following year completed the sump after a four-hour 930 m dive.

1973

Florida cave divers (Smith, Holtzendorff, Exley and Turner) made a dive of 2155 m between the Orange Grove Sink Entrance to the Waterhole Entrance of the Peacock Springs system – this has proved to be the longest mapped underwater cave in North America with 5800 m so far surveyed.

1977–8

The Royal Geographical Society with the Sarawak Government took an expedition to explore and study the extraordinary caves of Mulu, one of which, Clearwater Cave, provided 16 miles of passage, the longest known cave outside of Europe and the USA.

1978

In Florida the Hole in the Wall Spring is explored for 1380 submerged metres by D. Sweet and S. Exley.

1978–9

Exploration in Britain's Keld Head cave culminated in a 2100 m through dive between two submerged caves by Geoff Yeadon and Oliver Statham (2½ hrs).

1979

Australian divers have explored 3140 m underwater in the Cocklebiddy Cave, West Australia.

1981

French divers P. Penez and F. Vergier reached a sump at the record depth of 1455 m in the Gouffre Jean Bernard.

Glossary

A

abeam at right-angles to the length of a vessel.

abseil method of descending a rock face by sliding down a rope.

arête a sharp rock or snow ridge.

B

belay a method of safeguarding a climbing partner from falling by paying out or taking in the rope and anchoring oneself.

bergschrund the gap or crevasse between the glacier proper and the upper snows of a face (q.v.).

bilge keel baby keels or projections on the outside of the hull running parallel to the central keel, which enable the boat to sit upright in shallow water.

bivouac to spend a night in the open on a mountain.

boom metal or wooden pole extending horizontally from the mast along the bottom of the mainsail.

broach when the wind blows the boat right over on one side, so much so that the rudder comes out of the water and the boat is uncontrollable.

bouldering climbing unroped on boulders or very small outcrops.

C

chang local Sherpa beer, brewed from fermented rice, maize or barley.

chimney a fissure in the rock or ice wide enough to climb up inside.

close hauled when a boat's sails are pulled in as tight as possible so that the wind strikes them at an acute angle.

col pass, or dip in a ridge, usually between two peaks.

cornice an overhanging mass of snow projecting over the edge of a ridge, formed by prevailing winds.

couloir an open gully.

crampons steel spiked frames which can be fitted to boots to give a grip on ice and firm snow slopes.

crevasse a crack in a glacier surface, which can be both wide and very deep, made by the movement of the glacier over the irregular shapes in its bed, or by bends in its course.

cwm a deep rounded hollow at the head or side of a valley, formed by glacial action.

D

drogue improvised contraption pulled along behind a boat to slow it down in heavy weather.

E

expansion bolt a bolt driven into a hole drilled in the rock which expands through internal pressure to create a friction grip.

F

face a steep aspect of a mountain between two ridges

fifi hook a metal hook attached to a thin cord, used in artificial climbing.

fixed ropes on prolonged climbs up steep ground the lead climber, having run out the full length of rope, ties it to an appropriate anchor, and subsequently all climbers move independently up and down the fixed rope, clipped on to it, using it either as a safety line or, on very steep ground, for direct progress. The rope is left in place for the duration of the climb.

foredeck area of deck in front of the mast.

G

gendarme a rock pinnacle obtruding from a ridge, often surrounded by snow.

genoa sail large triangular sail in front of mast which is so big that it overlaps the mainsail to some extent and gives the boat greater speed.

gunwale (pronounced gunnel) strip of wood or plastic running all the way round the outside of the boat at deck level to protect it from damage by other boats.

gybe when the mainsail boom crosses from one side of the boat to the other as the wind changes.

H

halyards ropes used to raise or lower sails.

J

jib sail triangular sail set forward of the mast.

jib boom wooden or metal pole extending out from the front end of a boat to the outer end of which is attached the forward end of the jib sail.

jumar clamps	devices which lock on a fixed rope (q.v.) to support a climber's weight when subjected to downward force, but which can be slid up the rope as a method of climbing it.
junk rig	boat with a four-sided sail which is stiffened with horizontal battens and pulled up a single mast like that of a Chinese boat.
jury mast	any temporary mast employed as a replacement after dismasting.

L

la	pass.
lead	area of open water between ice floes.
luffing	bringing the boat up into the wind so that the sails flutter and the boat moves more slowly.

M

mani wall	a drystone wall in Sherpa country, inscribed with Buddhist prayers in Tibetan script.
monohull	boat with one hull.
moraine	accumulation of stones and debris carried down by a glacier.
multihull	single boat made up of two or three hulls joined together.

P

pack ice	large area of floating ice in the polar sea.
pitch	section of climbing between two stances or belay points.
pitchpole	when a huge wave comes up behind causing the boat to turn a complete somersault.
piton	a metal peg hammered into a rock crack to support a belay (q.v.).
portage	carrying a boat round an unnavigable stretch or land obstacle to the next navigable reach of water.
pressure ridge	a wall thrown up by the pressure of ice floes grinding against each other.

R

reach	point of sail when wind is at right angles to the sail.
reef	reducing the area of sail exposed to the wind in heavy weather by rolling or tieing canvas up round the boom.
rotor	a descending whirlwind caused by air that has flowed over the crest of a mountain peak.

S

sea anchor	throwing out on the end of a line any old thing in such a way that it will hold the boat's nose into the waves in order to ride out a storm more easily.
self-steering	a wind vane device fitted to the rear of a boat which keeps it facing into the wind on a predetermined heading while the yachtsman works or sleeps.
sérac	pinnacle or tower of ice, invariably unstable and dangerous.
sheets	ropes for controlling the trim of the sails.
shroud plate	metal plate on the sides of a boat's hull to which are attached the stainless steel wires giving lateral support to the mast.
sirdar	head Sherpa on an expedition.
standing wave	an unbroken stationary wave in a river, caused by an underwater obstruction such as a boulder.
stays	stainless steel wire supports for the mast running fore and aft, to the front and back of the boat.
staysail	small triangular sail attached to the front stay.
stopper wave	a stationary wave which is breaking.
storm jib	smallest sail a boat possesses used in front of the mast in very heavy weather to provide basic stability.
sump	a cave passage completely filled with water, leaving no air space, also called a syphon.

T

thwarts	seat running across rowing boat on which oarsman usually sits.
traverse	to move horizontally or diagonally across a rock or snow slope. Also the ascent and descent of a mountain by different routes.
trimaran	a boat with three connected hulls.
tsampa	flour ground from barley and sometimes roasted, an important part of the Sherpa's diet.

V

valving	the process of releasing carefully calculated quantities of a balloon's gas in order to make the balloon descend.

Y

yards	horizontal spars two-thirds of the way up the mast which support the rigging.

A Select Bibliography

The author and publisher are grateful for permission to quote from the following books:

OCEANS

Thor Heyerdahl, *The Kon-Tiki Expedition*, Allen & Unwin, 1950.
  Fatu-Hiva, Allen & Unwin, 1974.
  Aku Aku, the Secret of Easter Island, Allen & Unwin, 1958.
  American Indians in the Pacific, Allen & Unwin, 1952.
  (with E. N. Ferdon) *Report of the Norwegian Archaeological Expedition
    to Easter Island and the East Pacific*, Allen & Unwin, 1962.
  The Ra Expeditions, Allen & Unwin, 1971.
Arnold Jacoby, *Señor Kon-Tiki*, Allen & Unwin, 1968.
John Ridgway and Chay Blyth, *A Fighting Chance*, Hamlyn, 1966
John Ridgway, *Journey to Ardmore*, Hodder & Stoughton, 1971.
Merton Naydler, *The Penance Way: the mystery of Puffin's Atlantic voyage*, Hutchinson, 1968.
John Fairfax, *Britannia: rowing alone across the Atlantic*, Kimber, 1971.
John Fairfax and Sylvia Cook, *Oars Across the Pacific*, Kimber, 1973.
Francis Chichester, *Alone Across the Atlantic*, Allen & Unwin, 1961.
  The Lonely Sea and the Sky, Hodder & Stoughton, 1964.
  Gipsy Moth Circles the World, Hodder & Stoughton, 1967.
Robin Knox-Johnston, *A World of my Own*, Cassell, 1969.
Nicholas Tomalin and Ron Hall, *The Strange Voyage of Donald Crowhurst*, Hodder & Stoughton, 1970.
Nigel Tetley, *Trimaran Solo*, Nautical Publishing Co., 1970.
Chay and Maureen Blyth, *Innocent Aboard*, Nautical Publishing Co., 1970.
Bernard Moitessier, *The Long Way*, Adlard Coles, 1974.
David Lewis, *Ice Bird*, Collins, 1975.

DESERTS

Wilfred Thesiger, *Arabian Sands*, Longman, 1959; Collins, 1980.
  Desert, Marsh and Mountain, Collins, 1980.

RIVERS

Richard Snailham, *Blue Nile Revealed*, Chatto & Windus, 1970.
Chris Bonington, *Next Horizon*, Gollancz, 1973.
John Blashford-Snell, *Where the Trails Run Out*, Hutchinson, 1974.
Mike Jones, Blue Nile expedition report, 1972.

MOUNTAINS

Maurice Herzog, *Annapurna*, Cape, 1952.
Lionel Terray, *Conquistadors of the Useless*, Gollancz, 1963.
Eric Shipton, *That Untravelled World*, Hodder & Stoughton, 1969.
John Hunt, *The Ascent of Everest*, Hodder & Stoughton, 1953.
  Life is Meeting, Hodder & Stoughton, 1978.
Edmund Hillary, *High Adventure*, Hodder & Stoughton, 1955
  Nothing Venture, Nothing Win, Hodder & Stoughton, 1975.
Wilfrid Noyce, *South Col*, Heinemann, 1954.
George Lowe, *Because It Is There*, Cassell, 1959.
Michael Ward, *In This Short Span*, Gollancz, 1972.
Tenzing Norkay (as told to James Ramsay Ullman), *Man of Everest*, Harrap, 1955.

Walt Unsworth, *Everest*, Allen Lane, 1981.
Herbert Tichy, *Cho Oyu*, Methuen, 1957.
Kurt Diemberger, *Summits and Secrets*, Allen & Unwin, 1971.
Walter Bonatti, *On the Heights*, Hart-Davis, 1964.
    Great Days, Gollancz, 1974.
Pierre Mazeaud, *Naked Before the Mountain*, Gollancz, 1974.
Hermann Buhl, *Nanga Parbat Pilgrimage*, Hodder & Stoughton, 1956.
Chris Bonington, *Annapurna, South Face*, Cassell, 1971.
Don Whillans, 'Annapurna, South Face', *Mountain*, issue 12, 1970.
Reinhold Messner, *The Big Walls*, Kaye and Ward, 1978.
    The Seventh Grade, Kaye and Ward, 1974.
    The Challenge, Kaye and Ward, 1977.
    Everest: expedition to the ultimate, Kaye and Ward, 1979.
    Solo Nanga Parbat, Kaye and Ward, 1980.
Felix Kuen, 'Der Sieg und die Tragödie' (Triumph and Tragedy), *Der Bergsteiger*, November 1970.

THE POLES

Vivian Fuchs and Edmund Hillary, *The Crossing of Antarctica*, Cassell, 1958.
Edmund Hillary, *No Latitude for Error*, Hodder & Stoughton, 1961.
    Nothing Venture, Nothing Win, Hodder & Stoughton, 1975.
George Lowe, *Because It Is There*, Cassell, 1959.
Noel Barber, *The White Desert*, Hodder & Stoughton, 1958.
Wally Herbert, *Across the Top of the World*, G. P. Putnam, New York, 1974.
    (The American edition was expanded from a shorter account published under the same title by Longman, 1969).
Naomi Uemura, 'First Solo Assault on the Pole', *National Geographic*.

AIR

Charles McCarry, *Double Eagle*, W. H. Allen, 1980.
Michael Collins, *Carrying the Fire*, W. H. Allen, 1975.
Edwin E. Aldrin, *Return to Earth*, Random House, New York, 1973.
Norman Mailer, *Of a Fire on the Moon*, Little, Brown, Boston, Mass., 1969.
Tom Wolf, *The Right Stuff*, Farrar, Strauss, Giroux, New York, 1979.
Walter Cunningham, *The All American Boys*, Macmillan, New York, 1977.
Hugo Young, Bryan Silcock and Peter Dunn, *Journey to Tranquility*, Cape, 1969.
First on the Moon: a voyage with Neil Armstrong, Michael Collins, Edwin E. Aldrin Jnr.,
    written with Gene Farmer and Dora Jane Hamblin, Michael Joseph, 1970.
William Joffe Numerof and Anthony J. Cipriano, *American Journeys into Space*, Wanderer Books, New York, 1979.

BENEATH THE EARTH

Martin Farr, *The Darkness Beckons: the history and development of cave diving*, Diadem.
'*Caving International* interview Geoff Yeadon on cave diving', *Caving International Magazine*, No. 5, October 1979.

FACETS OF ADVENTURE

Geoffrey Moorhouse, *The Fearful Void*, Hodder & Stoughton, 1974.
Robyn Davidson, *Tracks*, Cape, 1981.
Doug Scott, 'On the Profundity Trail', *Mountain,* issue 15, May 1971.
Christina Dodwell, *Travels With Fortune*, W. H. Allen, 1979.
Naomi James, *At One With the Sea*, Hutchinson, 1979.
Clare Francis, *Woman Alone*, Daily Express, 1978.
    Come Hell or High Water, Pelham, 1977.
    Come Wind or Weather, Pelham, 1978.
Sheila Scott, *I Must Fly*, Hodder & Stoughton, 1970.
J. R. L. Anderson, *The Ulysses Factor*, Hodder & Stoughton, 1970.
Ingrid Cranfield, *The Challengers*, Weidenfeld & Nicolson, 1976.
Wilfrid Noyce, *Springs of Adventure*, John Murray, 1958.

Picture Credits

The author and publisher are grateful to the following who supplied photographs on the pages listed.

Arlene Blum: 176
British Antarctic Survey: 304, 307, 316, 319, 321
British Nepalese Army Annapurna expedition 1970: 179
Bungei-shunju/Orion Press/Vision International: 348, 350–1, 352, 354
Niki Butler: 271, 273
Central Press Photos Ltd: 80
Francis Chichester Ltd: 73, 74, 75, 76, 77, 82
John Cleare: 213, 258, 280, 291
Colorific © Rick Smolan: 416
Sylvia Cook: 54, 56, 58, 61, 63, 64, 65, 66
Deutsches Institut für Auslandforschung/Fritz Aumann: 246
Leo Dickinson: 239
Kurt Diemberger: 249, 254, 257, 260
Christina Dodwell: 420
John Fairfax: 48, 60
Tom Frost: 274, 275
Peter Habeler: 288, 292
The Wally Herbert Collection: 323 (photo: Frank Hermann), 326, 328, 329, 331, 332, 334, 335, 336, 339, 341, 342, 343, 345, 346
Heyerdahl: 17, 18, 20, 21, 22, 23, 25, 29
Sir Edmund Hillary: 310, 311, 313, 316–17
Marcel Ichac/Federation Française Montaigne: 172, 175, 177, 181, 184, 185
Instituto di Fotografia Alpina/Vittorio Sella: 228
Molly Jones: 160
Dick Kent: 367, 370
Keystone Press Agency Ltd: 63

Robin Knox-Johnston: 86
David Lewis: 126 (photo: Dr. Dave Murrish), 127, 128, 133 (Photo: Patrick D. Smith)
London Express News and Features: 116, 415, 421, 422
Reinhold Messner: 284, 285, 293, 296, 297, 298, 299
NASA: frontispiece, 376, 379, 380, 384, 388, 392, 393, 394, 396
Popperfoto: 50, 54, 71
Gaston Rébuffat: 240
Rex Features: 374
John Ridgway: 40
Royal Geographical Society: 187, 191, 195, 197, 198, 200, 201, 203, 205, 206, 207, 208
Doug Scott: 188, 244, 250
Jason Spender: 417
Frank Spooner Pictures: 371, 372–3
Sir Norman Statham: 401, 403, 404, 405, 407, 410
Sunday Times: 78, 82, 86, 87, 88, 89, 90, 97, 101, 102, 104, 108, 110, 116, 120, 121, 122
Syndication International Ltd: 38, 42, 44, 49
Joe Tasker: 230
Wilfred Thesiger: 137, 139, 141, 142, 144, 146
Dr. Herbert Tichy: 214, 215, 216, 219, 222, 223, 224, 226, 227
The Tilman Collection: 419
H. Weyer: 247
Ken Wilson/Diadem Books: 284
Yorkshire Television: 400
Chris Bonington: 149, 152, 153, 154, 156, 157, 164–5, 234, 264, 268, 269, 270, 277

Index